Lecture Notes in Computer Science 12545

More information about this subseries at http://www.springer.com/series/7407

Violet Ka I Pun · Volker Stolz ·
Adenilso Simao (Eds.)

Theoretical Aspects of Computing – ICTAC 2020

17th International Colloquium
Macau, China, November 30 – December 4, 2020
Proceedings

 Springer

Organization

Program Committee Chairs

Violet Ka I Pun   Western Norway University of Applied Sciences and University of Oslo, Norway

Volker Stolz   Western Norway University of Applied Sciences, Norway

Adenilso Simao   University of São Paulo, Brazil

Steering Committee

Ana Cavalcanti   University of York, UK

Martin Leucker (Chair)   University of Lübeck, Germany

Zhiming Liu   Southwest University, China

Tobias Nipkow   Technische Universität München, Germany

Augusto Sampaio   Universidade Federal de Pernambuco, Brazil

Natarajan Shankar   SRI, USA

Tarmo Uustalu   Reykjavik University, Iceland, and Tallinn University of Technology, Estonia

Program Committee

Erika Ábrahám   RWTH Aachen University, Germany

Kamel Barkaoui   CNAM, France

Frédéric Blanqui   Inria, France

Simon Bliudze   Inria, France

Benedikt Bollig   LSV, ENS Cachan, CNRS, France

Eduardo Bonelli   Stevens Institute of Technology, USA

Ana Cavalcanti   University of York, UK

Antonio Cerone   Nazarbayev University, Kazakhstan

Yu-Fang Chen   National Taiwan University, Taiwan

Uli Fahrenberg   LIX, France

Bernd Fischer   Stellenbosch University, South Africa

Paola Giannini   Università del Piemonte Orientale, Italy

Edward Hermann Haeusler   Pontifícia Universidade Católica do Rio de Janeiro, Brazil

Thomas Troels Hildebrandt   University of Copenhagen, Denmark

Ross Horne   University of Luxembourg, Luxembourg

Reiner Hähnle   Technische Universität Darmstadt, Germany

Eun-Young Kang   University of Southern Denmark, Denmark

Jan Křetínský   Technische Universität München, Germany

Lars Michael Kristensen	Western Norway University of Applied Sciences, Norway
Martin Leucker	University of Lübeck, Germany
Michael Lienhardt	ONERA, France, and University of Turin, Italy
Dominique Méry	LORIA, France
Mohammad Rezad Mousavi	University of Leicester, UK
Maciej Piróg	Wroclaw University, Poland
Sanjiva Prasad	IIT Delhi, India
Violet Ka I Pun	Western Norway University of Applied Sciences and University of Oslo, Norway
Riadh Robbana	INSAT, Tunisia
Kristin Yvonne Rozier	Iowa State University, USA
Augusto Sampaio	Universidade Federal de Pernambuco, Brazil
César Sánchez	IMDEA Software Institute, Spain
Adenilso da Silva Simão	University of São Paulo, Brazil
Marjan Sirjani	Mälardalen University, Sweden, and Reykjavik University, Iceland
Volker Stolz	Western Norway University of Applied Sciences, Norway
Georg Struth	The University of Sheffield, UK
Jing Sun	The University of Auckland, New Zealand

Additional Reviewers

Pedro Antonino
Pablo Barenbaum
Imen Ben Hafaiedh
Domenico Bianculli
Jean-Paul Bodeveix
Olivier Bournez
Richard Bubel
Chenghao Cai
Cameron Calk
Georgiana Caltais
Zheng Cheng
Nacha Chondamrongkul
Horatiu Cirstea
Márcio Cornélio
Ali Dorri
Jérémy Dubut
Rohit Dureja
Mamoun Filali-Amine
Predrag Filipovikj
Marie Fortin
Reynaldo Gil-Pons

Kush Grover
Eduard Kamburjan
Benjamin Lucien Kaminski
Narges Khakpour
Tzu-Chi Lin
Mohammad Loni
Anastasia Mavridou
Tobias Meggendorfer
Hernan Melgratti
Andrzej Mizera
Stefanie Mohr
Fereidoun Moradi
David Naumann
Andrei Popescu
Laurence Rideau
José Miguel Rojas
Hamideh Sabouri
Martin Sachenbacher
Zdeněk Sawa
Torben Scheffel
Malte Schmitz

Maximilian Schwenger
Lilia Sfaxi
Neeraj Singh
Leopoldo Teixeira
Daniel Thoma
Vincent van Oostrom

Alicia Villanueva
Maximilian Weininger
Makarius Wenzel
Wojciech Widel
Di-De Yan
Semen Yurkov

Abstract of Invited Talks

Teaching Software Verification Using Snap!

Marieke Huisman (iD)

University of Twente, Enschede, The Netherlands
M.Huisman@utwente.nl

With the progress in deductive program verification research, new tools and techniques have become available to reason about non-trivial programs written in widely-used programming languages. However, deductive program verification remains an activity for experts, with ample experience in programming, specification, and verification. We would like to change this situation, by developing program verification techniques that are available to a larger audience. Therefore, in this presentation, we show how we developed program verification support for Snap!. Snap! is a visual programming language, aiming in particular at high school students. We support both static and dynamic verification of Snap! programs. Moreover, we also outline how program verification in Snap! could be introduced to high school students in a classroom situation.

Taming Delays in Cyber-Physical Systems

Naijun Zhan ⓘ

State Key Laboratory of Computer Science, Institute of Software Chinese
Academy of Sciences, Beijing, China
znj@ios.ac.cn

With the rapid development of feedback control, sensor techniques, and computer control, time delay has become an essential feature of cyber-physical systems (CPSs), underlying both the continuous evolution of physical plants and the discrete transition of computer programs, which may well annihilate the stability/safety certificate and control performance of CPSs. In the safety-critical context, automatic verification and synthesis methods addressing time-delay in CPSs should therefore abound. However, surprisingly, they do not, although time-delay has been extensively studied in the literature of mathematics and control theory from a qualitative perspective. In this talk, we will report our recent efforts to tackle these issues, including controller synthesis for time-delayed systems in the setting of discrete time, bounded and unbounded verification of delay differential equations, and discuss remaining challenges and future trends.

Contents

Keynote Paper

A Flight Rule Checker for the LADEE Lunar Spacecraft   3
   Elif Kurklu and Klaus Havelund

Regular Papers

Proof-Theoretic Conservative Extension of HOL
with Ad-hoc Overloading   23
   Arve Gengelbach and Tjark Weber

A Myhill-Nerode Theorem for Register Automata and Symbolic
Trace Languages   43
   Frits Vaandrager and Abhisek Midya

CiMPG+F: A Proof Generator and Fixer-Upper
for CafeOBJ Specifications   64
   Adrián Riesco and Kazuhiro Ogata

Statistical Analysis of Non-deterministic Fork-Join Processes   83
   Antoine Genitrini, Martin Pépin, and Frédéric Peschanski

On Two Characterizations of Feature Models   103
   Ferruccio Damiani, Michael Lienhardt, and Luca Paolini

The Complexity of Boolean State Separation   123
   Ronny Tredup and Evgeny Erofeev

Occupancy Number Restricted Boolean Petri Net Synthesis:
A Fixed-Parameter Algorithm   143
   Evgeny Erofeev and Ronny Tredup

Star-Freeness, First-Order Definability and Aperiodicity of Structured
Context-Free Languages   161
   Dino Mandrioli, Matteo Pradella, and Stefano Crespi Reghizzi

Formal Verification of Parallel Stream Compaction and Summed-Area
Table Algorithms   181
   Mohsen Safari and Marieke Huisman

Compositionality of Safe Communication in Systems of Team Automata   200
   Maurice H. ter Beek, Rolf Hennicker, and Jetty Kleijn

Analysis of Bayesian Networks via Prob-Solvable Loops............... 221
  Ezio Bartocci, Laura Kovács, and Miroslav Stankovič

Semantics of a Relational λ-Calculus.......................... 242
  Pablo Barenbaum, Federico Lochbaum, and Mariana Milicich

Implementing Hybrid Semantics: From Functional to Imperative.......... 262
  Sergey Goncharov, Renato Neves, and José Proença

Implementation Correctness for Replicated Data Types, Categorically 283
  *Fabio Gadducci, Hernán Melgratti, Christian Roldán,
  and Matteo Sammartino*

Tool Paper

Qsimulation V2.0: An Optimized Quantum Simulator 307
  Hua Wu, Yuxin Deng, Ming Xu, and Wenjie Du

Author Index 317

Keynote Paper

A Flight Rule Checker
for the LADEE Lunar Spacecraft

Elif Kurklu[1] and Klaus Havelund[2]($\boxtimes$)

[1] NASA Ames Research Center, KBR Wyle Services, Moffett Field, USA
[2] Jet Propulsion Laboratory, California Institute of Technology, Pasadena, USA
klaus.havelund@jpl.nasa.gov

Abstract. As part of the design of a space mission, an important part
is the design of so-called *flight rules*. Flight rules express constraints on
various parts and processes of the mission, that if followed, will reduce
the risk of failure. One such set of flight rules constrain the format of
command sequences regularly (e.g. daily) sent to the spacecraft to control its next near term behavior. We present a high-level view of the
automated flight rule checker FRC for checking command sequences sent
to NASA's LADEE Lunar mission spacecraft, used throughout its entire
mission. A command sequence is in this case essentially a program (a
sequence of commands) with no loops or conditionals, and it can therefore be verified with a trace analysis tool. FRC is implemented using
the TRACECONTRACT runtime verification tool, an internal Scala DSL
for checking event sequences against "formal specifications". The paper
illustrates this untraditional use of runtime verification in a real context, with strong demands on the expressiveness and flexibility of the
specification language, illustrating the advantages of an internal DSL.

1 Introduction

On September 7, 2013, NASA launched the LADEE (Lunar Atmosphere and
Dust Environment Explorer) spacecraft to explore the Moon's atmosphere,
specifically the occurrence of dust. The mission lasted seven months and ended
on April 18, 2014, where the spacecraft was intentionally instructed to crash into
the Moon. NASA Ames Research Center designed, built, and tested the spacecraft, and was responsible for its day-to-day operation. This included specifically
programming of *command sequences*, which were then uploaded to the spacecraft
on a daily basis. A command sequence is, as it says, a sequence of commands,
with no loops or conditionals. A command is an instruction to carry out a certain
task at a certain time. An obvious problem facing these day-to-day programmers
was whether the command sequences were well-formed.

The research by the second author was carried out at Jet Propulsion Laboratory,
California Institute of Technology, under a contract with the National Aeronautics and
Space Administration.

V. K. I. Pun et al. (Eds.): ICTAC 2020, LNCS 12545, pp. 3–20, 2020.
https://doi.org/10.1007/978-3-030-64276-1_1

Generally speaking, for each space mission, NASA designs *flight rules* that capture constraints that must be obeyed during the mission to reduce the risk of failures. One particular form of flight rules specifically concern the command sequences sent from ground to a spacecraft or planetary rover on a regular basis during the mission. We present in this paper the actual effort on building a flight rule checker, FRC, for programming (formalize) these flight rules in the SCALA programming language [25] using the TRACECONTRACT [3,27] API. TRACE-CONTRACT was originally developed in a research effort as an internal Domain-Specific Language (DSL) [14] in SCALA for runtime verification [6], supporting a notation allowing for a mixture of data parameterized state machines and temporal logic. An internal DSL is a DSL represented within the syntax of a general-purpose programming language, a stylized use of that language for a domain-specific purpose [14]. The programming language SCALA has convenient support for the definition of such internal DSLs. It is, however, fundamentally an API in the host language.

TRACECONTRACT is here used for the purpose of code analysis. The rationale for this use lies in the observation that a command sequence can be perceived as an event sequence. Using an internal DSL for such a task has the advantage that the full power of the underlying host programming language is available, which turns out to be critical in this case. This is in contrast to an external DSL, which is a small language with its own syntax, parsing, etc. Other advantages of internal DSLs compared to external DSLs include ease of development and adjustment, and use of existing tooling for the host programming language.

Missions traditionally write flight rule checkers in programming languages such as MATLAB or PYTHON. However, numerous impressive runtime verification systems have been developed over the last two decades. They all attempt to solve the difficult problem of simultaneously optimizing: Expressiveness of formalism, Elegance of properties, and Efficiency of monitoring (the three *E*s). Many external DSLs have been developed over time [7,8,11,13,15,21,22,24]. Most of these focus on specification elegance and efficiency. Our own external DSLs include [1,2,5,20]. Fewer internal DSLs have been developed [9,10,26]. In addition to TRACECONTRACT, we developed a rule-based internal SCALA DSL for log analysis [17]. TRACECONTRACT itself has evolved into a newer system, DAUT [12,16], which allows for better optimization wrt. efficiency. We might conclude by emphasizing that a language such as SCALA is generally well suited for modeling, as argued in [19].

Although the mission took place several years ago, we found that it was worth reporting on this effort since it represents an actual application of a runtime verification tool in a highly safety critical environment. Before the LADEE mission and before the development of FRC, an initial study of the problem was performed and documented in [4]. Due to restrictions on what can be published about a NASA mission, the presentation is generic, showing used *specification patterns*, without mentioning any mission data.

The rest of this paper is organized as follows. Section 2 outlines the problem statement, defining the concepts of commands, command sequences, and flight rules. Section 3 presents the TRACECONTRACT DSL, previously presented in [3]. Section 4 describes the overall high-level architecture of the flight rule checker FRC. Section 5 presents some of the patterns used for writing flight rules. Finally, Sect. 6 concludes the paper.

2   Command Sequences and Flight Rules

A command sequence to be uploaded to a spacecraft is typically generated by a software program referred to as a *command sequencer*. The input to the command sequencer is a high level plan, that describes a sequence of science or engineering activities to be achieved, which itself is produced either by humans or by another program, a *planner*. Command sequences are short, in the order 10s–100s commands. Figure 1 shows the generic format of such a command sequence. Each line represents a command, consisting of a calendar time (year, number of day in year, and a time stamp), the name of the command, and a list of parameters each of the form `name=value`.

```
2013-103-00:07:00 /Command₁ variable₁₁=value₁₁ ... variable₁ₙ₁=value₁ₙ₁
2013-103-00:07:10 /Command₂ variable₂₁=value₂₁ ... variable₂ₙ₂=value₂ₙ₂
2013-103-00:07:16 /Command₃ variable₃₁=value₃₁ ... variable₃ₙ₃=value₃ₙ₃
2013-103-00:07:17 /Command₄ variable₄₁=value₄₁ ... variable₄ₙ₄=value₄ₙ₄
2013-103-00:07:18 /Command₅ variable₅₁=value₅₁ ... variable₅ₙ₅=value₅ₙ₅
2013-103-00:07:20 /Command₆ variable₆₁=value₆₁ ... variable₆ₙ₆=value₆ₙ₆
```

. . .

Fig. 1. Format of a command sequence.

A command sequence must satisfy various flight rules. An example of such a rule pattern is the following. *A maximum of N commands can be issued per second.* That is, no more than N commands can be issued with the same time stamp. Another rule pattern is the following: *Component activation will be performed at least 1 s after application of power to the component, but no more than the upper limit for activation time.* In other words, at least one second must pass from a component has been powered on, but no more than some upper limit, till it is actually activated to perform its task.

As can be seen, a command sequence can be perceived as a sequence of events, each being a command consisting of a name, a time, and a mapping from parameter names to values. Such an event sequence can be verified against flight rules with the TRACECONTRACT tool introduced in the next Section.

3   TraceContract

This section introduces the TRACECONTRACT DSL through a complete running example and an overview of the implementation.

3.1   A Complete TraceContract Example

TRACECONTRACT is a SCALA API for writing trace monitors. We also refer to it as an internal (or embedded) DSL since it is a Domain-Specific Language for writing monitors in an existing host language, in this case SCALA. A trace is a sequence of events. We don't really care where the event stream comes from, whether it is emitted from a running system, or, as in this case, a sequence of commands (where a command is an event). The DSL supports a flavor of temporal logic combined with state machines, both parameterized with data to support verification of events that carry data. TRACECONTRACT can be used for monitoring event streams online (as they are generated) as well as offline (e.g. stored in files as in this case).

We shall illustrate TRACECONTRACT with a single complete executable example. Due to lack of space, the reader is referred to [3, 27] for a more complete exposition. Figure 2 shows a SCALA program using the TRACECONTRACT DSL. The line numbers below refer to this figure. It first defines the type of events we are monitoring (line 3), namely commands, a **case** class (allowing pattern matching against objects of the class). The program contains two monitors, DistinctTimes (lines 5–11) and ActivateTimely (lines 13–24), each extending the TRACECONTRACT Monitor class, parameterized with the event type.

The DistinctTimes monitor (lines 5–11) checks that commands are issued with strictly increasing stamps. It waits for any Cmd object to be submitted to it (line 7). The require function (line 6) takes as argument a partial function, enclosed in curly brackets (lines 6–10), and defined by **case** statements, in this case one, ready to fire when an event matches one of the case patterns, in which case the "transition" is taken. In this case, when a command arrives, matching the pattern Cmd(_,time1) (line 7), the monitor transitions to the inner anonymous *cold* state, where it waits for the next command to be submitted (line 8), which does not need to occur since it is a cold state (a final state). If a second command is submitted, however, it is asserted that the time stamp of the second command is bigger than that of the first. The require function works like the temporal logic always-operator ($\square$).

The ActivateTimely monitor (lines 13–24) checks that if a power command is observed then a subsequent activate command must be observed within 30 time units. The activate command must occur, which is modeled by a hot state (lines 21–23). For illustration purposes, we have defined this rule a bit more long-winded than needed by defining a function activateTimely(powerTime: Int) (lines 20–23), which when called (line 17) returns the hot state. This style illustrates how to write state machines using SCALA functions. As can be seen, states can be parameterized with data, and can be written in a way resembling temporal logic (lines 7–8) or state machines (lines 17 + 20–23), or even a mixture.

There are different kinds of states inspired by temporal logic operators [23], including the *cold* (line 7) and *hot* states (line 21) as we have seen. These states differ in (1) how they react to an event that does not match any transition (stay in the state, fail, or drop the state), (2) how they react to an event that matches a transition to another state (keep staying in the source state or leave it), and

```
1   import tracecontract._
2
3   case class Cmd(name: String, time: Int)
4
5   class DistinctTimes extends Monitor[Cmd] {
6     require {
7       case Cmd(_,time1) ⇒ state {
8         case Cmd(_,time2) ⇒ time2 > time1
9       }
10    }
11  }
12
13  class ActivateTimely extends Monitor[Cmd] {
14    val upperBound : Int = 30
15
16    require {
17      case Cmd("power", time) ⇒ activateTimely(time)
18    }
19
20    def activateTimely(powerTime: Int): Formula =
21      hot {
22        case Cmd("activate", time) ⇒ time − powerTime < upperBound
23      }
24  }
25
26  class Monitors extends Monitor[Cmd] {
27    monitor(new DistinctTimes, new ActivateTimely)
28  }
29
30  object Run {
31    def main(args: Array[String]) {
32      val monitors = new Monitors
33      val trace = List(Cmd("power",100), Cmd("transmit", 130), Cmd("activate", 150))
34      monitors.verify(trace)
35    }
36  }
```

Fig. 2. A complete TRACECONTRACT example.

(3) how they evaluate at the end of the trace (true or false). Beyond the hot state having the three attributes: (stay if no match, leave if match, false at end), there are the following states: state (stay, leave, true), strong (fail, leave, false), weak (fail, leave, true), drop (drop, leave, true), and always (stay, stay, true). A require(f) call (lines 6 and 16) creates and stores an always(f) state. Un-named (anonymous) states are allowed, as shown in the DistinctTimes monitor (lines 7–9), thereby relieving the user from naming intermediate states in a progression of transitions, as shown in the ActivateTimely monitor (lines 17 + 20–23). This gives a flavor of temporal logic. The target of a transition can be a conjunction of

states as well as a disjunction, corresponding to alternating automata (although this is not used in this work).

Since these monitors are classes, we can write SCALA code anywhere SCALA allows it, e.g. declaring constants, variables, methods, etc., and use these in the formulas. Note that although we in our example associate one property with each monitor, it is possible to define several properties in a monitor. It is also possible to combine monitors for purely organizational purposes, with no change in semantics. E.g. in our example, we define the monitor Monitors (lines 26–28), the only purpose of which is to group the two other monitors into one. In the main method (lines 31–35) we instantiate this parent monitor and feed it a trace of three commands. This event sequence in fact violates the ActivateTimely monitor, causing the following error message to be issued (slightly shortened), showing an error trace of relevant events:

```
Total number of reports: 1
Monitor Monitors.ActivateTimely property violations: 1

Monitor: Monitors.ActivateTimely Property violated
Violating event number 3: Cmd(activate,150)
Trace:
  1=Cmd(power,100)
  3=Cmd(activate,150)
```

3.2   The TraceContract Implementation

In this section we shall very briefly give an idea of how TRACECONTRACT is implemented[1], see [3,27] for more details. A monitor is parameterized with an event type Event, and monitors a collection of formulas over such events, each kind of formula sub-classing the class Formula:

```
class Monitor[Event] {
  var formulas: List[Formula] = List()
  ...
}

abstract class Formula {
  def apply(event: Event): Formula
  def reduce(): Formula = this
  def and(that: Formula): Formula = And(this, that).reduce()
  def or(that: Formula): Formula = Or(this, that).reduce()
  ...
}
```

---

[1] Note that we have made some simplifications for ease of presentation.

The **apply** function allows one to apply a formula f to an event e as follows: $f(e)$, resulting in a new formula. For each new event, each formula is evaluated by applying it to the event, to become a new formula. The function is defined as abstract and is overridden by the different subclasses of **Formula** corresponding to the various kinds of formulas. The **reduce** function, also specific for each kind of formula (by default being the identity), will simplify a formula by rewriting it according to the classical reduction axioms of propositional logic, e.g. $true \wedge f = f$.

In the monitors above, the function require(f) takes as argument a partial function f of type PartialFunction[Event,Formula], which represents a transition function, and creates and stores a formula object always(f) to be monitored, where always(f) is a formula of the class below.

```
type Block = PartialFunction[Event, Formula]

def require(block: Block) {
    formulas ++= List(always(block))
}

case class always(block: Block) extends Formula {
    override def apply(event: Event): Formula =
        if (block.isDefinedAt(event)) And(block(event),this) else this
}
```

Similarly for cold and hot states, we have the following definitions, which are identical (the difference between cold and hot states shows at the end of a trace, as explained below):

```
case class state(block: Block) extends Formula {
    override def apply(event: Event): Formula =
        if (block.isDefinedAt(event)) block(event) else this
}

case class hot(block: Block) extends Formula {
    override def apply(event: Event): Formula =
        if (block.isDefinedAt(event)) block(event) else this
}
```

Other states follow the same pattern, but vary in the definition of the apply function. We saw in Fig. 2 Boolean expressions, such as time2 > time1 occur as formulas on the right-hand side of **case** transitions. This is permitted by implicit functions (applied by the compiler) lifting these values to formulas. E.g., the functions below are applied by the compiler when a value of the argument type occurs in a place where the return type (Formula) is expected. Note that True and False are TRACECONTRACT Formula objects. The second implicit function allows code with side-effects, not returning a value (of type Unit), as the result of transitions.

```
implicit def convBoolean2Formula(cond: Boolean): Formula = if (cond) True else False
implicit def convUnitToFormula(unit: Unit): Formula = True
```

Finally, a monitor offers a method for verifying a single event, a method for ending verification (verifying that all active states are cold, e.g. no hot states), and a method for verifying an entire trace, which calls the previous two methods.

```
def verify(event: Event): Unit {...}

def end(): Unit {
  for (formula ← formulas) {
    if (!end(formula)) reportError(formula)
  }
}

def end(formula: Formula): Boolean = {
  formula match {
    case always(_) ⇒ true
    case state(_) ⇒ true
    case hot(_) ⇒ false
    ...
  }
}

def verify(trace: Trace): MonitorResult[Event] = {
  for (event ← trace) verify(event)
  end()
  getMonitorResult
}
```

TRACECONTRACT also offers Linear Temporal Logic (LTL) [23] operators, and rule-based operators for recording facts, useful for checking past time properties. These features were not used in FRC.

TRACECONTRACT was developed with expressiveness in focus rather than efficiency. However, for the small command sequences of up to 100s of commands, efficiency is not an issue. As previously mentioned, TRACECONTRACT evolved into a newer system, DAUT [12,16]. In [18] is described a performance evaluation of DAUT, processing a log of 218 million events. DAUT is here able to process between 100,000+ - 400,000+ events per second, depending on the property being verified.

4 Architecture of Flight Rule Checker

Figure 3 shows the architecture of the flight rule checker. It takes as input a command sequence, an initial state of the spacecraft (the expected current state), and an identification of which rules to verify. The catalog of rules programmed in TRACECONTRACT is provided as a SCALA library. It produces a verification report as result. Which rules to execute is selected by a mission operator in a flight rule editor, a GUI showing all LADEE flight rules, see Fig. 4. The initial state is also specified in the GUI. Descriptions of the flight rules are stored as an XML file, see Fig. 5, grouped into sub-systems. Each rule has an id, a descriptive title, and a class name indicating which is the corresponding TRACECONTRACT monitor.

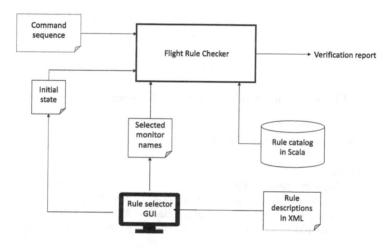

Fig. 3. The flight rule checker architecture.

Figure 6 shows the SCALA **case** class FRCCommand, instantiations of which will represent the commands found in the command sequence file (Fig. 1). The figure also shows the flight rule checker's verification function, which takes as arguments a list of names of monitor classes selected, representing the choices made in the GUI in Fig. 4; the location of the command sequence file; and other arguments. The function first locates and instantiates the SCALA monitor classes according to their names (using reflection), adding each instance as a sub-monitor to the ruleVerifier parent monitor. It then builds the command sequence, verifies the command sequence, and finally produces an error report based on the data stored in the ruleVerifier monitor.

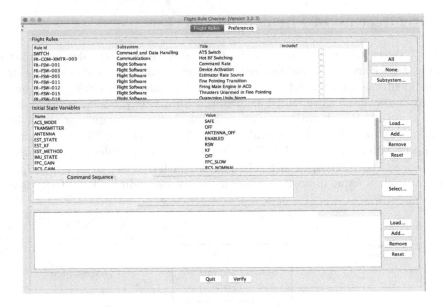

Fig. 4. The flight rule checker GUI for selecting rules.

```xml
<?xml version='1.0' encoding='UTF−8'?>
<frc>
  <rules>
    <subsystem name=" System₁" >
        <rule id=" ID₁" title=" Title₁" class=" Monitor₁" ></rule>
        <rule id=" ID₂" title=" Title₂" class=" Monitor₂" ></rule>
        <rule id=" ID₃" title=" Title₃" class=" Monitor₃" ></rule>
        ...
    </subsystem>

    <subsystem name=" System₂" >
        ...
    </subsystem>
    ...
  </rules>
</frc>
```

Fig. 5. Flight rule catalog in XML format, organized into sub systems.

```
case class FRCCommand(name: String, time: Calendar, params: Map[String, String]) {..}

object FRCService extends ... {
  def verify(rules: List[String], cmdSequence: File, ...): Report = {

    // build monitor containing a sub−monitor for each rule:
    val ruleVerifier = new Monitor[FRCCommand]
    rules.foreach(key ⇒ {
      val ruleInstance = FlightRuleCatalog.getRuleInstance(key)
      ruleVerifier.monitor(ruleInstance)
    })

    // create command sequence:
    val commands: List[FRCCommand] = ...

    // verify command sequence:
    ruleVerifier.verify(commands)

    // create and return report:
    generateReport(ruleVerifier)
  }
  ...
}
```

Fig. 6. The flight rule checker.

5   Flight Rules

A total of 37 flight rules were programmed, out of which 31 were actively used. We will here present the patterns of six of the most generic ones, illustrating different aspects. The rules concern the Flight Software (FSW) subsystem, specifically expressing constraints on how the commands should be sent, etc. Each rule is programmed as a class extending the TRACECONTRACT Monitor class.

5.1   Command Rate

Figure 7 shows the 'Command Rate' monitor. It verifies that no more than MAX = N commands are issued per second, that is: with the same time stamp, for some constant N. For each command, let's call it the *initiator command*, the monitor calls the function count, which itself returns a formula, and which recursively consumes commands until either a command with a bigger time stamp is observed (ok causes the monitor to end tracking this particular initiator command), or the limit of N is reached, in which case an error is issued. Note that the require function initiates this tracking for every observed command. A new counting state machine is created for each command, tracking commands with the same time stamp.

```
// The maximum rate of command issuance is N issued commands per second.

class CommandRate extends Monitor[FRCCommand] {
  val MAX = N

  require {
    case FRCCommand(_, time, _) ⇒ count(time)
  }

  def count(time: Calendar, nr: Int = 1): Formula =
    state {
      case FRCCommand(_, time2, _) ⇒ {
        if (time2 > time) ok else if (nr == MAX) error else count(time, nr + 1)
      }
    }
}
```

Fig. 7. Command Rate monitor.

5.2 Device Activation

Figure 8 shows the '*Device Activation*' monitor. It verifies that if a device is powered on at time t, it must be eventually activated within the time interval $[t + N_1, t + N_2]$ for two positive natural numbers $N_1 < N_2$, stored in the constants activateMin and activateMax. The monitor defines a map from device *power on* commands to their corresponding *activation* commands, which is used in the formula to match them up. There are K such map entries for some not small K. This mapping is manually created and cannot be calculated. The formula itself shows use of SCALA's conditioned **case** statements (a match requires the condition after **if** to hold), and the hot state to indicate that activation must eventually occur. The pattern 'activationCommand' (a variable name in single quotes) means: match the value of the variable activationCommand. The formula states that if we observe an FRCCommand("power", t_1, *params*) command, where *params*("state") = "on" and *params*("device") = d (*power device d on*) and deviceMap(d) = a (d's *activation command is a*), then we want to eventually see an FRCCommand($a,t_2,...$) such that $t_2 \in [t_1 + N_1, t_1 + N_2]$. An alternative would have been to define a monitor for each pair of *power on* and *activate* commands. Since there are K such pairs this would become heavy handed. This illustrates the advantage of an internal DSL, where maps are available as a data structure.

```
// Component activation will be performed at least N₁ seconds
// after application of power to the component, but no more than N₂ seconds.

class DeviceActivation extends Monitor[FRCCommand] {
  val activateMin = N₁
  val activateMax = N₂

  val deviceMap: Map[String, String] = Map(
    "device₁_pwr" → "name₁_activate",
    "device₂_pwr" → "name₂_activate",
    "device₃_pwr" → "name₃_activate",
    ...
    "device_K_pwr" → "name_K_activate"
  )

  require {
    case FRCCommand("power", powerOnTime, params)
      if deviceMap.keys.toList.contains(params.get("device").get) &&
        params.get("state").get.equals("on") ⇒
          val device = params.get("device").get
          val activationCommand = deviceMap.get(device).get
          hot {
            case FRCCommand('activationCommand', activateTime, _) ⇒
              val timeDiff = activateTime.toSeconds − powerOnTime.toSeconds
              timeDiff ≥ activateMin && timeDiff ≤ activateMax
          }
  }
}
```

Fig. 8. Device Activation monitor.

5.3 Time Granularity

Figure 9 shows the 'Time granularity' monitor. It verifies that the millisecond part of a flight command is 0. That is, the smallest time granularity allowed is seconds. This property shows a simple check on a command argument. It also shows the classification of a monitor as a warning rather than an error if violated.

```
// No stored command sequence shall include commands or command sequences whose
// successful execution depends on command time granularity of less than 1 second.

class TimeGranularity extends Monitor[FRCCommand](Severity.WARNING) {
  require {
    case FRCCommand(_, cmd_time, _) ⇒
      cmd_time.get(Calendar.MILLISECOND) == 0
  }
}
```

Fig. 9. Time granularity monitor.

```
// The y_value will not be changed while the x_mode is M.

class ValueChange extends Monitor[FRCCommand] {
  var xMode = Config.getVarValue("x_mode")
  var yValue = Config.getVarValue("y_value")

  val specialMode = M

  require {
    case FRCCommand("set_x_mode", _, params) ⇒
      xMode = params.get("mode").get
    case FRCCommand("set_y_value", _, params) ⇒ {
      val yValueNew = params.get("value").get
      if (xMode.equals(specialMode) && !yValueNew.equals(yValue) & ...) {
        error
      } else {
        yValue = yValueNew
      }
    }
  }
}
```

Fig. 10. Value Change monitor.

5.4   Value Change

Figure 10 shows the 'Value Change' monitor. It verifies that some value y will not change while the mode of some component x is M. The monitor is not temporal, but illustrates the use of class variables, xMode for holding the current mode of x, and yValue for holding the current value of y. "set_x_mode" commands change the x mode, and "set_y_value" commands change the value of y.

5.5   Unsafe Activation

Figure 11 shows the 'Unsafe Activation' property. It verifies that some feature y is not being activated, while some other feature x is being disabled (disabling has a duration). The first outer **case** treats the situation where first an x disabling command ("disable_x") is observed, followed by a y activating command ("activate_y"). In this case it is checked that the time of y activation does not occur within the duration of the x disabling. The second outer **case** treats the situation where we first observe a y activating command and subsequently an x disabling command. y activation will happen normally after x disabling, but if it happens at the same time it could occur before in the command sequence. This monitor shows this more complicated timing constraint.

```
// Feature y will not be activated while feature x is being disabled.

class UnsafeActivation extends Monitor[FRCCommand] {
  require {
    case FRCCommand("disable_x", disableStart, disableParams) ⇒
      state {
        case FRCCommand("activate_y", activateTime, _)
          if activateTime ≥ disableStart &&
            activateTime.toSeconds − disableStart.toSeconds ≤
            disableParams.get("duration").get.toInt ⇒
              error
      }
    case FRCCommand("activate_y", activateTime, _) ⇒
      state {
        case FRCCommand("dispable_x", disableStart, disableParams)
          if disableStart==activateTime ||
            (disableStart.toSeconds + disableParams.get("duration").get.toInt
            == activateTime.toSeconds) ⇒
              error
      }
  }
}
```

Fig. 11. Unsafe Activation monitor.

5.6 Mathematical Constraint

Figure 12 shows the '*Mathematical Constraint*' property. It verifies that for a selection of commands $command_1 \ldots command_k$, the constraint W is satisfied on a function F of parameter variables $x_1 \ldots x_n$. That is, it verifies that $W(F(x_1,\ldots,x_n))$ holds. The formula is not temporal and mainly shows validation of command arguments using a function for performing a non-trivial mathematical computation.

```
// Commands command₁ ... commandₖ must satisfy a non−trivial mathematical
// well−formedness constraint W on a function F of their arguments.

class MathematicalConstraint extends Monitor[FRCCommand] {
  def wellformed(command: FRCCommand): Boolean = {
    val v₁ = command.valueOf("x₁").get.toDouble
    ...
    val vₙ = command.valueOf("xₙ").get.toDouble
    val value =F(v₁,...,vₙ) // non−trivial mathematical computation
    return W(value)
  }

  require {
    case cmd @ FRCCommand("command₁", _, _) if (!wellformed(cmd)) ⇒ error
    ...
    case cmd @ FRCCommand("commandₖ", _, _) if (!wellformed(cmd)) ⇒ error
  }
}
```

Fig. 12. Mathematical Constraint monitor.

6 Conclusion

The manual translation of rules expressed in English to monitors in the TRACE-CONTRACT DSL was performed by the first author. The biggest challenges were finding out which command parameters corresponded to those mentioned in the flight rules expressed in natural language, and finding programming patterns in the DSL that would work. Coding errors in SCALA was not an issue. We have some testimony to the value of the developed framework, as the person who was responsible for command sequencing and verification back then wrote (in response to the question of how often FRC found errors in command sequences): "*I would actually say it was often, perhaps every other command sequencing cycle.*".

The effort has shown the use of a runtime verification tool, TRACECON-TRACT, for code analysis. The tool was largely not changed for the purpose, and hence provided all needed features. We attribute this in part to the fact that it was an internal DSL, as opposed to an external DSL. In addition it was reliable with no bugs reported. Many real-life log analysis problems in practice are performed with programming languages, and the reason is in part the attractiveness of Turing completeness. However, internal DSLs do have drawbacks, specifically the difficulty of analyzing "specifications" since they effectively are programs. It is always possible to design an external DSL for a particular problem, also for this application, which more easily can be subject to analysis. However, an external DSL may fit one problem but not another. An internal DSL can be more flexible.

References

1. Barringer, H., Goldberg, A., Havelund, K., Sen, K.: Rule-based runtime verification. In: Steffen, B., Levi, G. (eds.) VMCAI 2004. LNCS, vol. 2937, pp. 44–57. Springer, Heidelberg (2004). https://doi.org/10.1007/978-3-540-24622-0_5
2. Barringer, H., Groce, A., Havelund, K., Smith, M.: Formal analysis of log files. J. Aerospace Comput. Inf. Commun. **7**(11), 365–390 (2010)
3. Barringer, H., Havelund, K.: TraceContract: a Scala DSL for trace analysis. In: Butler, M., Schulte, W. (eds.) FM 2011. LNCS, vol. 6664, pp. 57–72. Springer, Heidelberg (2011). https://doi.org/10.1007/978-3-642-21437-0_7
4. Barringer, H., Havelund, K., Kurklu, E., Morris, R.: Checking flight rules with TraceContract: application of a Scala DSL for trace analysis. In: Scala Days 2011, Stanford University, California (2011)
5. Barringer, H., Rydeheard, D., Havelund, K.: Rule systems for run-time monitoring: from Eagle to RuleR. In: Sokolsky, O., Taşıran, S. (eds.) RV 2007. LNCS, vol. 4839, pp. 111–125. Springer, Heidelberg (2007). https://doi.org/10.1007/978-3-540-77395-5_10
6. Bartocci, E., Falcone, Y., Francalanza, A., Reger, G.: Introduction to runtime verification. In: Bartocci, E., Falcone, Y. (eds.) Lectures on Runtime Verification. LNCS, vol. 10457, pp. 1–33. Springer, Cham (2018). https://doi.org/10.1007/978-3-319-75632-5_1
7. Basin, D.A., Klaedtke, F., Marinovic, S., Zălinescu, E.: Monitoring of temporal first-order properties with aggregations. Formal Methods Syst. Des. **46**(3), 262–285 (2015)
8. Bauer, A., Küster, J.-C., Vegliach, G.: From propositional to first-order monitoring. In: Legay, A., Bensalem, S. (eds.) RV 2013. LNCS, vol. 8174, pp. 59–75. Springer, Heidelberg (2013). https://doi.org/10.1007/978-3-642-40787-1_4
9. Bodden, E.: MOPBox: a library approach to runtime verification. In: Khurshid, S., Sen, K. (eds.) RV 2011. LNCS, vol. 7186, pp. 365–369. Springer, Heidelberg (2012). https://doi.org/10.1007/978-3-642-29860-8_28
10. Colombo, C., Pace, G.J., Schneider, G.: LARVA – safer monitoring of real-time Java programs (tool paper). In: SEFM 2009, pp. 33–37. IEEE (2009)
11. D'Angelo, B., et al.: LOLA: runtime monitoring of synchronous systems. In: TIME 2005, pp. 166–174. IEEE (2005)
12. Daut on github. https://github.com/havelund/daut
13. Decker, N., Leucker, M., Thoma, D.: Monitoring modulo theories. Int. J. Software Tools Technol. Transfer **18**(2), 205–225 (2016)
14. Fowler, M., Parsons, R.: Domain-Specific Languages. Addison-Wesley, Reading (2010)
15. Hallé, S., Villemaire, R.: Runtime enforcement of web service message contracts with data. IEEE Trans. Serv. Comput. **5**(2), 192–206 (2012)
16. Havelund, K.: Data automata in Scala. In: TASE 2014, pp. 1–9. IEEE (2014)
17. Havelund, K.: Rule-based runtime verification revisited. Int. J. Software Tools Technol. Transfer **17**(2), 143–170 (2015)
18. Havelund, K., Holzmann, G.: A programming approach to event monitoring. In: Rozier, K. (ed.) Formal Methods for Aerospace Engineering, Progress in Computer Science and Applied Logic. Springer (2021). Draft version, in preparation, to appear
19. Havelund, K., Joshi, R.: Modeling with Scala. In: Margaria, T., Steffen, B. (eds.) ISoLA 2018. LNCS, vol. 11244, pp. 184–205. Springer, Cham (2018). https://doi.org/10.1007/978-3-030-03418-4_12

20. Havelund, K., Peled, D.: Runtime verification: from propositional to first-order temporal logic. In: Colombo, C., Leucker, M. (eds.) RV 2018. LNCS, vol. 11237, pp. 90–112. Springer, Cham (2018). https://doi.org/10.1007/978-3-030-03769-7_7

21. Kim, M., Kannan, S., Lee, I., Sokolsky, O.: Java-MaC: a run-time assurance tool for Java. In: RV 2001, ENTCS, vol. 55, no. 2. Elsevier (2001)

22. Meredith, P.O., Jin, D., Griffith, D., Chen, F., Roşu, G.: An overview of the MOP runtime verification framework. Int. J. Software Tools Technol. Transfer **14**, 249–289 (2011)

23. Pnueli, A.: The temporal logic of programs. In: SFCS 1977, pp. 46–57. IEEE Computer Society (1977)

24. Reger, G., Cruz, H.C., Rydeheard, D.: MarQ: monitoring at runtime with QEA. In: Baier, C., Tinelli, C. (eds.) TACAS 2015. LNCS, vol. 9035, pp. 596–610. Springer, Heidelberg (2015). https://doi.org/10.1007/978-3-662-46681-0_55

25. Scala. http://www.scala-lang.org

26. Stolz, V., Huch, F.: Runtime verification of concurrent Haskell programs. Electr. Notes Theor. Comput. Sci. **113**, 201–216 (2005)

27. TraceContract on github. https://github.com/havelund/tracecontract

Regular Papers

Proof-Theoretic Conservative Extension of HOL with Ad-hoc Overloading

Arve Gengelbach[✉][iD] and Tjark Weber[✉][iD]

Department of Information Technology, Uppsala University, Uppsala, Sweden
{arve.gengelbach,tjark.weber}@it.uu.se

Abstract. Logical frameworks are often equipped with an extensional mechanism to define new symbols. The definitional mechanism is expected to be conservative, i.e. it shall not introduce new theorems of the original language. The theorem proving framework Isabelle implements a variant of higher-order logic where constants may be ad-hoc overloaded, allowing a constant to have different definitions for non-overlapping types. In this paper we prove soundness and completeness for the logic of Isabelle/HOL with general (Henkin-style) semantics, and we prove model-theoretic and proof-theoretic conservativity for theories of definitions.

Keywords: Classical higher-order logic · Conservative theory extension · Proof-theoretic conservativity · Ad-hoc overloading · Isabelle

1 Introduction

With the help of theorem provers such as HOL4 [14] and Isabelle [13], users formalise mathematical reasoning to create machine-checkable proofs. For convenience and abstraction, these systems allow the user to define new types and constants. Definitions extend the theory that is underlying a formalisation with additional axioms, but they are expected to be *proof-theoretically conservative* (and Wenzel [16] adds further requirements). Informally, any formula that is derivable from the extended theory but expressible prior to the definition should be derivable also from the original theory. As a special case, extension by definitions shall preserve *consistency*; any extension by a definition shall not enable the derivation of a contradiction. Design flaws in definitional mechanisms have repeatedly led to inconsistencies in theorem provers [12, 16].

In this paper we establish proof-theoretic conservativity for higher-order logic (HOL) with ad-hoc overloading, meaning that constant symbols may have different definitions for non-overlapping types. Proof-theoretic conservativity is not obvious in this setting [12]: type and constant definitions may depend on one another, and type definitions cannot be unfolded in the same way as constant definitions. Moreover, type and constant symbols may be declared and used, e.g. to define other symbols, before a definition for them is given.

© Springer Nature Switzerland AG 2020
V. K. I. Pun et al. (Eds.): ICTAC 2020, LNCS 12545, pp. 23–42, 2020.
https://doi.org/10.1007/978-3-030-64276-1_2

In this setting the notion of proof-theoretic conservativity as informally described above does not hold. Consider a theory extension that defines a previously declared constant symbol: the equational axiom that is introduced by the definition is expressible, but in general not derivable prior to the definition. Therefore, we consider a notion of proof-theoretic conservativity that separates signature extensions (declarations) from theory extensions (definitions). We prove that any formula that is derivable from a definitional extension but *independent* of the newly defined symbol is also derivable prior to the extension.

Our results are particularly relevant to the foundations of Isabelle/HOL [13], which is an implementation of the logic and definitional mechanisms considered in this paper. As a practical consequence, proof-theoretic conservativity allows independence to be used as a syntactic criterion for deciding [8] whether a definition may be ignored when searching for the proof of a formula.

We establish proof-theoretic conservativity via several intermediate results that are of interest in their own right. Proof-theoretic conservativity has a semantic counterpart, *model-theoretic conservativity*. It is known [5,6] that HOL with ad-hoc overloading satisfies model-theoretic conservativity w.r.t. *lazy ground semantics*, that is a semantics that defines interpretations only for ground (i.e. type-variable free) symbols and for which semantic entailment is quantified over term variable valuations parametrised by ground type instantiation. In this paper, we generalise the model-theoretic conservativity result to a *general* (Henkin-style) [7] version of the lazy ground semantics. Subsequently, we prove the HOL deductive system sound and complete for general semantics. Soundness and completeness imply that provability and semantic validity coincide; thus we obtain proof-theoretic conservativity from model-theoretic conservativity.

Proof-theoretic conservativity of HOL with ad-hoc overloading has been studied before, notably by Kunčar and Popescu [9], who showed proof-theoretic conservativity of definitional theories relative to a fixed minimal theory, called *initial HOL*. Our result is stronger: we show proof-theoretic conservativity of definitional extensions relative to an arbitrary definitional theory. From this, we can immediately recover Kunčar and Popescu's result by noting that initial HOL is definitional; but our conservativity result also applies to formulae that do not belong to the language of initial HOL.

Contributions. We make the following contributions:

- We define a Henkin-style [7] generalisation of the lazy ground semantics [1] for HOL by relaxing the interpretation of function types to subsets of the set-theoretic function space (Sect. 4).
- We show model-theoretic conservativity for HOL with ad-hoc overloading w.r.t. general semantics (Sect. 5.1) by adapting an earlier proof of model-theoretic conservativity for lazy ground semantics [5,6].
- We prove soundness (Sect. 5.2) and completeness (Sect. 5.3) of the HOL deductive system for general semantics. The former is proved by induction over derivations, the latter by adapting ideas from Henkin's original completeness proof for the theory of types [7].

– From model-theoretic conservativity, soundness and completeness we derive a proof-theoretic conservativity result for HOL with ad-hoc overloading (Sect. 5.4). This result generalises the conservativity result of Kunčar and Popescu [9].

2   Related Work

We briefly review related work on meta-theoretical properties of higher-order logic for both standard and Henkin semantics, and discuss the different approaches to consistency and conservativity of HOL with ad-hoc overloading. Finally, we outline how our own work connects to these results.

Higher-Order Logic and Standard Semantics. HOL extends the *simple theory of types* introduced by Church [4] with rank-1 polymorphism. The logic is implemented, e.g. in HOL4 [14] and Isabelle/HOL [13], with slightly different definitional mechanisms. In Isabelle/HOL, ad-hoc overloading is a feature of the logic; in HOL4, it is supported through extensions of parsing and pretty-printing.

Pitts [15, § 15.4] introduces standard models for HOL (without ad-hoc overloading). These are set-theoretic models of theories whose signature contains the constants $\Rightarrow_{\mathsf{bool}\to\mathsf{bool}\to\mathsf{bool}}$, $\doteq_{\alpha\to\alpha\to\mathsf{bool}}$ and $\mathsf{some}_{(\alpha\to\mathsf{bool})\to\alpha}$ that are interpreted as logical implication, equality and Hilbert-choice, respectively. Types are inhabited, i.e. their interpretation is a non-empty set, and function types are interpreted by the corresponding set-theoretic function space.

This semantics and its properties in interplay with the deductive system are discussed in detail in the HOL4 documentation. For standard semantics HOL is sound [14, § 2.3.2] but incomplete, as by Gödel's incompleteness theorem there are unprovable sequents that hold in all standard models.

Henkin Semantics. Despite its incompleteness for standard semantics, HOL is complete for *Henkin semantics* [7], which relaxes the notion of a model and allows function types to be interpreted by proper subsets of the corresponding function space. For this semantics Andrews [2] proves completeness of a monomorphic logic $\mathcal{Q}_0$ whose built-in symbols are expressed in terms of equality. Andrews approaches the completeness proof as follows.

Each (syntactically) consistent theory is contained in a *maximal* consistent set of formulae, i.e. adding any other formula to the set would render it inconsistent. For maximal consistent theories one can construct a model by defining a term's interpretation as the equivalence class of provably equal terms. Hence, every consistent theory has a model (as there is a model of a maximal consistent superset of that theory). Completeness follows by contraposition.

Both Andrews and Henkin discuss completeness of variants of the simple theory of types. Their results transfer to HOL with Henkin-style semantics.

HOL with Ad-hoc Overloading. Wenzel [16] considers proof-theoretic conservativity "a minimum requirement for wellbehaved extension mechanisms." He introduces the stronger notion of *meta-safety*, which additionally requires that new constants are syntactically realisable, i.e. they can be replaced with a term in the language of the original theory while preserving provability.

Kunčar and Popescu [9] extend meta-safety to type definitions and show meta-safety of definitional theories over *initial HOL*, the theory of Booleans with Hilbert-choice and the axiom of infinity. Their result is achieved by unfolding constant definitions and removing type definitions via a relativisation predicate over the corresponding host type. It follows that any definitional theory is a proof-theoretically conservative extension of initial HOL, and (as a special case) that any definitional theory is consistent. This result regards definitional theories as monolithic extensions of initial HOL, despite the incremental nature of theory extension by iterated application of definitional mechanisms.

The same authors prove definitional theories consistent by a semantic argument [12], introducing a so-called *ground* semantics for HOL, where validity of formulae is quantified over ground type instantiations. Hence ground semantics only ever interprets type-variable free terms. Given a definitional theory, Kunčar and Popescu construct a model for ground semantics by recursion over a well-founded *dependency relation* that relates each definiendum (i.e. each left-hand side of a definition) to any symbol occurring in the definiens. Åman Pohjola and Gengelbach [1] mechanise this model construction in HOL4 and correct fixable mistakes, leading to a larger dependency relation and a term semantics that applies type substitutions *lazily*, i.e. at the latest possible moment when interpreting a term.

In earlier work [6], we show model-theoretic conservativity of HOL with ad-hoc overloading by refining Kunčar and Popescu's monolithic model construction (which builds a model from the ground up) to instead extend a given model of a definitional theory. Gengelbach et al. [5], again using lazy ground semantics, mechanise this result in HOL4.

Connection to Our Work. This paper combines some of the mentioned related work in new ways. First, we generalise lazy ground semantics in the sense of Henkin, relaxing the interpretation of function types. The deductive system of HOL is sound and complete with respect to general (Henkin-style) lazy ground semantics. For the proof of completeness, we adapt ideas from Henkin's and Andrews's completeness proofs to account for polymorphism. Second, re-using and extending our earlier proof of model-theoretic conservativity, we strengthen this result to general (Henkin-style) lazy ground semantics. Third, we combine soundness, completeness, and model-theoretic conservativity to obtain proof-theoretic conservativity of HOL with ad-hoc overloading relative to an arbitrary definitional theory, thereby generalising the conservativity result of Kunčar and Popescu.

3   Background

We introduce the language of polymorphic higher-order logic (HOL) (Sect. 3.1), definitional theories (Sect. 3.2), and the deductive system (Sect. 3.3). Parts of this section are adapted from our previous work [6, §2]. Our notation and terminology largely agree with other [1,5,12] related work.

3.1   The Language of Polymorphic HOL

The syntax of polymorphic HOL is that of the simply-typed lambda calculus, enriched with a first-order language of types. We fix two infinite sets TVar of *type variables*, ranged over by α, β, and Var of *term variables*, ranged over by x, y.

Signatures. A *signature* is a quadruple $(K, \text{arOf}, \text{Const}, \text{tpOf})$, where K and Const are two countably infinite, disjoint sets. The elements of K are *type constructors*, and those of Const are *constants*. Each type constructor has an associated *arity*, given by the function $\text{arOf} : K \to \mathbb{N}$. Each constant has an associated *type*, given by the function $\text{tpOf} : \text{Const} \to \text{Type}$, where the set Type, ranged over by σ, τ, is defined inductively as the smallest set such that

- TVar $\subseteq$ Type, and
- $(\sigma_1, \ldots, \sigma_n)k \in$ Type whenever $k \in K$, $\text{arOf}(k) = n$ and $\sigma_1, \ldots, \sigma_n \in$ Type.

For technical reasons (cf. Lemma 2), we assume that Const contains infinitely many constants a with $\text{tpOf}(\text{a}) \in$ TVar.

Built-in Types and Constants. For the remainder of this paper, we will assume a fixed signature. Moreover, we assume that K contains the following *built-in* type constructors: bool of arity 0, ind of arity 0, and $\to$ a right-associative type constructor of arity 2. A type is *built-in* if its type constructor is.

We also assume that Const contains the following *built-in* constants:
- $\Rightarrow$ of type bool $\to$ bool $\to$ bool,   - zero of type ind,
- $\doteq$ of type $\alpha \to \alpha \to$ bool,   - succ of type ind $\to$ ind.
- some of type $(\alpha \to$ bool$) \to \alpha$,

Instances. A *type substitution* is a function $\rho \colon$ TVar $\to$ Type that replaces type variables by types. We extend type substitutions homomorphically to all types, and denote the set of type substitutions by TSubst. For any $\rho \in$ TSubst and any type $\sigma \in$ Type, $\rho(\sigma)$ is a *(type) instance* of σ, written $\rho(\sigma) \leq \sigma$.

The set of *constant instances* CInst is a subset of the cartesian product Const$\times$ Type that contains exactly those tuples $(c, \sigma) \in$ CInst for which the type σ is a type instance of the type of c, namely $\sigma \leq \text{tpOf}(c)$. We use c_σ as shorthand notation for the tuple (c, σ). A constant instance is *built-in* if it is an instance of a built-in constant. For example, the constant instances $\doteq_{\text{bool}\to\text{bool}\to\text{bool}}$ and $\doteq_{\text{ind}\to\text{ind}\to\text{bool}}$ are built-in as both are instances of the built-in constant $\doteq$, which has the type $\text{tpOf}(\doteq) = \alpha \to \alpha \to$ bool.

Terms. The *terms* of our language are given by the following grammar, where x ranges over term variables, σ and τ are types, and c_σ ranges over constant instances:

$$t, t' \quad ::= \quad x_\sigma \quad | \quad c_\sigma \quad | \quad (t_{\sigma \to \tau}\, t'_\sigma)_\tau \quad | \quad (\lambda x_\sigma . t_\tau)_{\sigma \to \tau}$$

We may write t for t_σ when there is no risk of ambiguity. We require all terms to be *well-typed*, e.g. in $t\, t'$ the type of t' equals the argument type of t. Equality of terms is considered modulo α-equivalence. The set of all terms is denoted by Term.

A term is *closed* if it does not contain any free (term) variables. We extend tpOf to terms by defining $\mathrm{tpOf}(t_\sigma) := \sigma$. Terms of type bool are called *formulae*.

For $u \in \mathsf{Term} \cup \mathsf{Type}$, we write $\mathrm{TV}(u)$ for the set of type variables that occur syntactically in u. We can apply a type substitution ρ to a term t, written $\rho(t)$, by applying ρ to all type variables that occur in t.

Non-Built-Ins. To obtain the immediate non-built-in sub-types of a type, we define the following function $\cdot^\bullet$ on types:

$$\alpha^\bullet := \{\alpha\} \qquad \mathsf{bool}^\bullet := \emptyset \qquad \mathsf{ind}^\bullet := \emptyset \qquad (\sigma \to \tau)^\bullet := \sigma^\bullet \cup \tau^\bullet$$
$$((\sigma_1, \ldots, \sigma_n)\, k)^\bullet := \{(\sigma_1, \ldots, \sigma_n)\, k\} \text{ for } k \notin \{\mathsf{bool}, \to, \mathsf{ind}\}$$

For instance, if K contains a unary type constructor list, $(\alpha\ \mathsf{list} \to \mathsf{bool})^\bullet = \{\alpha\ \mathsf{list}\}$. We overload $\cdot^\bullet$ for terms, to collect non-built-in types of terms:

$$x_\sigma{}^\bullet := \sigma^\bullet \qquad c_\sigma{}^\bullet := \sigma^\bullet \qquad (s\, t)^\bullet := s^\bullet \cup t^\bullet \qquad (\lambda x.t)^\bullet := x^\bullet \cup t^\bullet$$

The *non-built-in types* of $M \subseteq \mathsf{Type}$ are those types for which $\cdot^\bullet$ is invariant, i.e. $M^\bullet := \{x \in M \mid x^\bullet = \{x\}\}$.

The operator $\cdot^\circ$ collects all non-built-in constant instances in a term:

$$x_\sigma{}^\circ := \emptyset \quad c_\sigma{}^\circ := \begin{cases} \emptyset & \text{if } c \text{ is built-in} \\ \{c_\sigma\} & \text{otherwise} \end{cases} \quad (s\, t)^\circ := s^\circ \cup t^\circ \quad (\lambda x.t)^\circ := t^\circ$$

Similar as defined for types, the *non-built-in constant instances* of $M \subseteq \mathsf{CInst}$ are those constant instances for which $\cdot^\circ$ is invariant, i.e. $M^\circ := \{x \in M \mid x^\circ = \{x\}\}$.

Ground Symbols. A type is *ground* if it contains no type variables. The set of ground types is denoted by GType. The type substitutions that map all type variables to ground types are written GTSubst. A constant instance $c_\sigma \in \mathsf{CInst}$ is *ground* if its type σ is ground, and the set of ground constant instances is GCInst.

3.2   Definitional Theories

Definitional theories are theories that consist of definitions $u \equiv t$, with the constant instance or type u that is being defined on the left-hand side, and the defining term t on the right-hand side. Constant instances are defined by a term, and types are defined by a predicate. In short we say *symbol* for a constant instance or a type. Definitions of symbols can be of two kinds:

- A *constant instance definition* is of the form $c_\sigma \equiv t_\sigma$ where $c_\sigma \in \mathsf{CInst}^\circ$, $t \in \mathsf{Term}$ contains no free term variables, $\mathrm{TV}(t) \subseteq \mathrm{TV}(\sigma)$, and $c \notin \{\mathsf{rep}, \mathsf{abs}\}$.
- A *type definition* is of the form $\tau \equiv t_{\sigma \to \mathsf{bool}}$ where $\tau = (\alpha_1, \ldots, \alpha_{\mathrm{arOf}(k)})k \in \mathsf{Type}^\bullet$, $\alpha_i \in \mathsf{TVar}$ (for $0 \le i \le \mathrm{arOf}(k)$) distinct, $t \in \mathsf{Term}$ contains no free term variables, and $\mathrm{TV}(t) \subseteq \mathrm{TV}(\sigma)$.

We now define the semantics of constant and type definitions. A constant instance definition equates the constant instance with the defining term. A type definition asserts the existence of a bijection $\mathsf{rep}_{\tau \to \sigma}$ (with inverse $\mathsf{abs}_{\sigma \to \tau}$) between the type τ and the subset of σ that is given by the predicate t, provided this subset is non-empty. As a technical detail, as opposed to existentially quantifying over rep and abs in the resulting axiom [12], we assume that these two constants are present in the signature (with type $\alpha \to \beta$), and reserve them as not definable.

- A constant instance definition $c_\sigma \equiv t$ stands for the formula $c_\sigma \doteq t$.
- A type definition $\tau \equiv t_{\sigma \to \mathsf{bool}}$ stands for the formula

$$(\exists x_\sigma.\, t\, x) \quad \Rightarrow \quad (\forall x_\sigma.\, t\, x \Rightarrow \mathsf{rep}_{\tau \to \sigma}\,(\mathsf{abs}_{\sigma \to \tau}\, x) \doteq x)$$
$$\wedge\, (\forall y_\tau.\, t\,(\mathsf{rep}\, y)) \wedge (\forall y_\tau.\, \mathsf{abs}\,(\mathsf{rep}\, y) \doteq y)$$

The signature needs to contain all logic symbols from these axioms (Sect. 3.3).

We impose two additional constraints [1, 12] that ensure consistency of theories of definitions: orthogonality of definitions, and termination of a certain relation.

Orthogonality. Two types σ and τ are *orthogonal*, written $\sigma \# \tau$, if they have no common instance, i.e. if for all $\rho, \rho' \in \mathsf{TSubst}\ \rho(\sigma) \neq \rho'(\tau)$. Orthogonality extends to constant instances, written $c_\sigma \# d_\tau$, if $c \neq d$ or $\sigma \# \tau$. Two definitions $u \equiv t$, $v \equiv s$ are orthogonal if they are either of different kinds or if $u \# v$.

Dependency Relation. Given a set of definitions D, the *dependency relation* for D, written $\leadsto_D$, is a binary relation on symbols. It tracks dependencies of defined symbols on their definiens, and is defined by $u \leadsto_D v$ (for $u, v \in \mathsf{CInst} \cup \mathsf{Type}$) if:

1. $u \equiv t \in D$ and $v \in t^\bullet \cup t^\circ$, or
2. u is a constant of type σ and $v \in \sigma^\bullet$, or
3. u is a type $(\alpha_1, \ldots, \alpha_{\mathrm{arOf}(k)})\, k$ and $v \in \{\alpha_1, \ldots, \alpha_{\mathrm{arOf}(k)}\}$.

We may simply write $\leadsto$ when D is clear from the context.

Type-Substitutive Closure. When R is a binary relation on $\mathsf{CInst} \cup \mathsf{Type}$, we write $R^{\downarrow}$ for the *type-substitutive closure* of R, defined as the smallest relation such that, for any $(s, t) \in R$ and any $\rho \in \mathsf{TSubst}$, $(\rho(s), \rho(t)) \in R^{\downarrow}$. Thus, the type-substitutive closure extends R to its image under arbitrary type substitutions.

Definitional Theories. A binary relation R is *terminating* (also converse well-founded or Noetherian) if there exists no infinite sequence $(a_i)_{i \in \mathbb{N}}$ such that $a_i \, R \, a_{i+1}$ for all $i \in \mathbb{N}$.

Finally, a theory D is *definitional* if it is a finite set of pairwise orthogonal definitions for which the relation $\rightsquigarrow_D^{\downarrow}$ is terminating. As a result of [1, 12], every definitional theory has a (lazy ground semantics) model.

3.3   The Deductive System

We follow Kunčar and Popescu [10, 11] in our description of the deductive system for HOL. The system is motivated by and abstracts from the implementation of higher-order logic in Isabelle.

We assume that the usual logical connectives and quantifiers are present in the signature, and define the set Ax of axioms to contain the formulae in Fig. 1. We note that the formulae on the left-hand side of the figure can be regarded as definitions of the logical connectives. For simplicity, we do not consider the axioms mem_Collect_eq and Collect_mem_eq in this paper, which introduce set-builder notation. The notation $t \not\doteq t'$ is shorthand for $\neg(t \doteq t')$. We let φ range over formulae.

Inference rules of the deductive system, given in Fig. 2, have the shape

$$\frac{T, \Gamma_1 \vdash \varphi_1 \quad \cdots \quad T, \Gamma_n \vdash \varphi_n}{T, \Gamma \vdash \varphi}$$

where T is the theory from which φ is derived by assuming the formulae in Γ [14]. Hereinafter, we deliberately omit empty assumption lists.

$\mathsf{True} \doteq ((\lambda x_{\mathsf{bool}}.\ x) \doteq (\lambda x_{\mathsf{bool}}.\ x))$	refl: $x_\alpha \doteq x$
$\forall \doteq (\lambda p_{\alpha \to \mathsf{bool}}.\ (p \doteq (\lambda x.\ \mathsf{True})))$	subst: $x_\alpha \doteq y \Rightarrow P\, x \Rightarrow P\, y$
$\exists \doteq (\lambda p_{\alpha \to \mathsf{bool}}.\ \forall\, (\lambda q.\ (\forall\, (\lambda x.\ p\, x \Rightarrow q)) \Rightarrow q))$	iff: $(p \Rightarrow q) \Rightarrow (q \Rightarrow p) \Rightarrow (p \doteq q)$
$\mathsf{False} \doteq (\forall\, (\lambda p_{\mathsf{bool}}.\ p_{\mathsf{bool}}))$	True_or_False: $(b \doteq \mathsf{True}) \vee (b \doteq \mathsf{False})$
$\neg \doteq (\lambda p.\ (p \Rightarrow \mathsf{False}))$	some_intro$_\alpha$: $p_{\alpha \to \mathsf{bool}}\, x \Rightarrow p\, (\mathsf{some}\, p)$
$\wedge \doteq (\lambda p\, q.\ \forall\, (\lambda r.\ (p \Rightarrow (q \Rightarrow r)) \Rightarrow r))$	suc_inj: $\mathsf{succ}\, x \doteq \mathsf{succ}\, y \Rightarrow x \doteq y$
$\vee \doteq (\lambda p\, q.\ \forall\, (\lambda r.\ (p \Rightarrow r) \Rightarrow (q \Rightarrow r) \Rightarrow r))$	suc_not_zero: $\mathsf{succ}\, x \not\doteq \mathsf{zero}$

Fig. 1. Axioms for Isabelle/HOL.

$$\frac{}{T,\emptyset \vdash \varphi} \; [\varphi \in \mathsf{Ax} \cup T] \; (\textsc{Fact})$$

$$\frac{}{T,\Gamma \vdash (\lambda x_\sigma . t) \, s \doteq t[s/x_\sigma]} \; (\textsc{Beta})$$

$$\frac{}{T,\{\varphi\} \vdash \varphi} \; (\textsc{Assum})$$

$$\frac{T,\Gamma_1 \vdash \varphi \Rightarrow \psi \quad T,\Gamma_2 \vdash \varphi}{T,\Gamma_1 \cup \Gamma_2 \vdash \psi} \; (\textsc{MP})$$

$$\frac{T,\Gamma \vdash f \, x_\sigma \doteq g \, x_\sigma}{T,\Gamma \vdash f \doteq g} \; [x_\sigma \notin \Gamma] \; (\textsc{Ext})$$

$$\frac{T,\Gamma \vdash \psi}{T,\Gamma \setminus \{\varphi\} \vdash \varphi \Rightarrow \psi} \; (\textsc{ImpI})$$

$$\frac{T,\Gamma \vdash \varphi}{T,\Gamma \vdash (\varphi[\overline{\sigma}/\overline{\alpha}])[\overline{t}/\overline{x_\tau}]} \; [\overline{\alpha}, \overline{x_\tau} \notin \Gamma, t_i : \tau_i] \; (\textsc{Inst})$$

Fig. 2. Inference rules for Isabelle/HOL.

4 General Semantics

In this section, we define a general (Henkin-style) semantics for HOL. Our semantics generalises the lazy ground semantics of [1], by incorporating ideas of Henkin [2,7]: in a general model, function types may be interpreted by a proper (non-empty) subset of the corresponding function space.

Built-in Closure. For a set of types $T \subseteq \mathsf{Type}$ let $\mathsf{Cl}(T)$ denote the *built-in closure* of T, defined as the smallest set such that: $T \subseteq \mathsf{Cl}(T)$, bool, ind $\in \mathsf{Cl}(T)$, and for any two types $\sigma, \tau \in \mathsf{Cl}(T)$ the function type $\sigma \to \tau$ is in $\mathsf{Cl}(T)$. Thus, $\mathsf{Cl}(T)$ contains those types that can be constructed from T by repeated application of built-in type constructors.

Fragments. A *(signature) fragment* F is a pair $F = (T, C)$ of types $T \subseteq \mathsf{GType}^\bullet$ and constant instances $C \subseteq \mathsf{GCInst}^\circ$, with the constraint that for each $c_\sigma \in C$: $\sigma \in \mathsf{Cl}(T)$. The types generated by the fragment are $\mathsf{Type}^F := \mathsf{Cl}(T)$, and its terms $\mathsf{Term}^F := \{t \in \mathsf{Term} \mid t^\bullet \subseteq \mathsf{Type}^F, t^\circ \subseteq C\}$ are those whose non-built-in symbols are from the fragment. Term^F is closed under taking sub-terms. We call the largest fragment $(\mathsf{GType}^\bullet, \mathsf{GCInst}^\circ)$ the *total fragment*.

Fragment Pre-interpretations. We fix the set of Booleans $\mathbb{B} := \{\mathsf{true}, \mathsf{false}\}$. For a fragment $F = (T, C)$ an *F-pre-interpretation* is a pair of families $\mathcal{I} = \left(([\sigma])_{\sigma \in \mathsf{Type}^F}, ([c_\sigma])_{c_\sigma \in C}\right)$ that for all symbols $\sigma, \tau \in \mathsf{Type}^F$ and $c_\sigma \in C$ satisfies[1]

$$[\sigma] \neq \emptyset, \qquad [\mathsf{bool}] = \mathbb{B}, \qquad [\mathsf{ind}] = \mathbb{N},{}^1 \qquad [c_\sigma] \in [\sigma], \text{ and} \qquad [\sigma \to \tau] \subseteq [\sigma] \to [\tau].$$

Valuations. A *valuation* for $\mathcal{I}$ is a function ξ_ρ parameterised by a ground type substitution $\rho \in \mathsf{GTSubst}$ that assigns meaning to all variables whose type is contained in the fragment, i.e. $\rho(\sigma) \in \mathsf{Type}^F$ implies $\xi_\rho(x_\sigma) \in [\rho(\sigma)]$ for all term variables $x_\sigma \in \mathsf{Var} \times \mathsf{Type}$.

---

[1] We use $[\mathsf{ind}] = \mathbb{N}$ for simplicity but could allow any infinite set. [1,12].

General Fragment Interpretations. For an F-pre-interpretation $\mathcal{I}$ and a valuation ξ_ρ, we define a partial function $[\![\cdot]\!]_{\xi_\rho}$ that extends $\mathcal{I}$ to terms t with $\rho(t) \in \mathsf{Term}^F$:

$$[\![x_\sigma]\!]_{\xi_\rho} := \xi_\rho(x_\sigma) \qquad\qquad [\![c_\sigma]\!]_{\xi_\rho} := [c_{\rho(\sigma)}] \text{ for } c \text{ non-built-in}$$

$$[\![s\,t]\!]_{\xi_\rho} := [\![s]\!]_{\xi_\rho}([\![t]\!]_{\xi_\rho}) \qquad [\![\lambda x_\sigma.t_\tau]\!]_{\xi_\rho} : [\rho(\sigma)] \to [\rho(\tau)], z \mapsto [\![t_\tau]\!]_{\xi_\rho(\!|x \mapsto z|\!)}$$

Here, function update $f(\!|x \mapsto z|\!)$ denotes the function that is equal to f except for the argument x, for which its value is z. The built-in constants have a fixed interpretation:

$[\![{\Rightarrow}_{\mathsf{bool}\to\mathsf{bool}\to\mathsf{bool}}]\!]_{\xi_\rho}$ is implication $\qquad [\![\mathsf{zero}_{\mathsf{ind}}]\!]_{\xi_\rho} := 0$

$[\![\dot{=}_{\sigma\to\sigma\to\mathsf{bool}}]\!]_{\xi_\rho}$ is equality on $[\rho(\sigma)]$ $\qquad [\![\mathsf{succ}_{\mathsf{ind}\to\mathsf{ind}}]\!]_{\xi_\rho}$ is the successor function

$[\![\mathsf{some}_{(\sigma\to\mathsf{bool})\to\sigma}]\!]_{\xi_\rho}$ is Hilbert-choice

In general, $[\![\cdot]\!]_{\xi_\rho}$ is partial because the interpretations of function types in $\mathcal{I}$ may not contain enough elements to interpret all terms. We say that $\mathcal{I}$ is a *general F-interpretation* if $[\![\cdot]\!]_{\xi_\rho}$ is total for every $\rho \in \mathsf{GTSubst}$ and every valuation ξ_ρ for $\mathcal{I}$, and $[\![t]\!]_{\xi_\rho} \in [\mathrm{tpOf}(\rho(t))]$ for all t with $\rho(t) \in \mathsf{Term}^F$.

General Models and Validity. A *general model* is a general $(\mathsf{GType}^\bullet, \mathsf{GCInst}^\circ)$-interpretation, i.e. a general interpretation for the total fragment. A general model is *standard* if $[\sigma \to \tau] = [\sigma] \to [\tau]$ for all $\sigma, \tau \in \mathsf{GType}$.

A formula φ is *valid* in a general model $\mathcal{M}$, written $\mathcal{M} \models \varphi$, if for all ground type substitutions $\rho \in \mathsf{GTSubst}$ and all valuations ξ_ρ it holds that $[\![\varphi]\!]_{\xi_\rho} = \mathsf{true}$. We write $\mathcal{M} \models E$ if all formulae within a set E are valid in a general model $\mathcal{M}$.

5   Results

In this section we derive model-theoretic conservativity, and prove soundness and completeness for the deductive system w.r.t. general semantics. We finish the section by transferring the semantic conservativity result to a syntactic one.

5.1   Model-Theoretic Conservativity

We discuss how symbols in a definitional theory extended by a symbol definition can be interpreted before and after the extension.

We write $\rightsquigarrow^{\downarrow*}$ for the reflexive-transitive type-substitutive closure of the dependency relation.

For a set of symbols U, we recall the *U-independent fragment* F_U [5,6]. In [6] F_U was introduced for singleton sets U (corresponding to the definition of a single symbol); this was generalised to arbitrary sets in [5].

Lemma 1. *Let D be a definitional theory, and let $U \subseteq \mathsf{Type}^\bullet \cup \mathsf{CInst}^\circ$. We write V_U for the pre-image of type instances of elements in U under the reflexive-transitive, type-substitutive closure of the dependency relation $\rightsquigarrow_D$, i.e.*

$$V_U := \left\{ v \in \mathsf{GType}^\bullet \cup \mathsf{GCInst}^\circ \mid \exists u \in U, \rho \in \mathsf{TSubst}.\ v \left(\rightsquigarrow_D^{\downarrow} \right)^* \rho(u) \right\}.$$

Then $F_U := (\mathsf{GType}^\bullet \setminus V_U, \mathsf{GCInst}^\circ \setminus V_U)$ is a fragment, called the U-independent fragment.

Model-theoretic conservativity as we prove it extends a model for possibly several definitional updates, keeping the interpretations for all symbols that are independent of the updates, i.e. all symbols that are in the independent fragment where U are the updated symbols.

In the proof a part of a general model $\mathcal{M}$ of a definitional theory D is expanded to a general model of a definitional extension D' by well-founded recursion over parts of the $\rightsquigarrow^{\downarrow}$ relation. The part of the general model that is extended corresponds to the fragment independent of the defined symbols from $D' \setminus D$. The earlier monolithic model construction [1,12] obtains a model from the ground up, by recursion over the entire $\rightsquigarrow^{\downarrow}$ relation. The incremental model construction in [5,6] considers standard models and extension by a single definition (although the latter can be generalised to any finite definitional extension).

We make use of a fragment of dependencies $E_{\rightsquigarrow_D}$, which is defined as all instances of elements in E and their dependencies.

$$E_{\rightsquigarrow_D} := \left\{ x \in \mathsf{GType}^\bullet \cup \mathsf{GCInst}^\circ \Big| \exists u \in E, \rho \in \mathsf{TSubst} : \rho(u) \rightsquigarrow_D^{\downarrow *} x \right\}$$

Indeed, this is a fragment: for any $c_\sigma \in E_{\rightsquigarrow_D}$ we have $\sigma \in \mathsf{Cl}(\mathsf{Type} \cap E_{\rightsquigarrow_D})$, which is simply by $c_\sigma \rightsquigarrow_D v$ for $v \in \sigma^\bullet$ because $\sigma \in \mathsf{Cl}(\sigma^\bullet)$.

Theorem 1 (Model-theoretic conservativity). *Let $\mathcal{M}$ be a general model of a definitional theory D, and let $D' \supseteq D$ be a definitional extension of D (by possibly several definitions). Let U be the symbols defined in $D' \setminus D$, i.e. $U = \{ u \mid \exists t.\, u \equiv t \in D' \setminus D \}$. There exists a general model $\mathcal{M}'$ of the extended theory D' with the following property: the models $\mathcal{M}$ and $\mathcal{M}'$ agree on the interpretation of all types and terms in $\mathsf{Type}^{F_U} \cup \mathsf{Term}^{F_U}$.*

Proof. Any dependency relation in this proof is w.r.t. D'. Let U be the set of symbols defined in $D' \setminus D$ and let V_U be defined as in Lemma 1. We define an interpretation for the total fragment $\mathsf{T} = (\mathsf{GType}^\bullet, \mathsf{GCInst}^\circ)$. For any ground symbol $w \in \mathsf{T} \setminus V_U$ we define $[w]$ as the interpretation of w within the model $\mathcal{M}$. For all elements in V_U we define an interpretation by well-founded recursion over $\rightsquigarrow^{\downarrow +}$, which is the transitive closure of the type substitutive dependency relation. From the definitional theory D' we get a terminating dependency relation $\rightsquigarrow^{\downarrow +}$ [1], and we can define an interpretation $[v]$ for any symbol $v \in V_U$, basing on $[w]$ for w such that $v \rightsquigarrow^{\downarrow +} w$, and their standard interpretation. Thus in each step we define the interpretation for v from the interpretation of symbols $E_{\rightsquigarrow}$ for $E = \{ w \mid v \rightsquigarrow^{\downarrow +} w \} \cup F_U$.

We say $v \in$ GSymb *matches* definition $(s \equiv r) \in D'$ if $v = \rho(s)$ is a type instance of s for $\rho \in$ GTSubst. Due to orthogonality of D', a matching definition is uniquely determined. If there is no match for v, as v is ground, it is orthogonal to any definition in D'.

Case 1. v matches $s \equiv r$ and $v = \rho(s)$. Because $v \rightsquigarrow^{\downarrow+} \rho(r)^{\bullet}$ and $v \rightsquigarrow^{\downarrow+} \rho(r)^{\circ}$ the closed term $\rho(r)$ has an interpretation $[\![r]\!]_{\xi_\rho}$ for an arbitrary ξ_ρ w.r.t. ρ.

Sub-case 1.1. s is a constant instance. We assign $[v] = [\![r]\!]_{\xi_\rho}$.

Sub-case 1.2. s is a (non-built-in) type with $\mathrm{tpOf}(r) = \sigma \to$ bool. We set $[v] = \{a \in [\rho(\sigma)] \,|\, [\![r]\!]_{\xi_\rho}(a) = \mathsf{true}\}$ if this set is non-empty and $[v] = \mathbf{1}$ alternatively.

Case 2. there is no matching definition for v in D'. We distinguish two sub-cases.

Sub-case 2.1. v is a non-built-in type. If $v = \tau \to \sigma$ we define $[v] = [\tau] \to [\sigma]$. Otherwise we define $[v] = \mathbf{1}$.

Sub-case 2.2. v is a constant instance and $v \rightsquigarrow^{\downarrow+} \mathrm{tpOf}(v)^{\bullet}$.

- $v = \mathsf{abs}_{\sigma \to \tau}$, or $v = \mathsf{rep}_{\tau \to \sigma}$ and there is a definition in $s \equiv r \in D'$ with a type substitution $\rho \in$ TSubst such that $\rho(s) = \sigma$ and $\rho(\mathrm{tpOf}(r)) = \tau \to$ bool. (Again, due to orthogonality there can only be one such matching definition.) In this case $[v]$ is undefined and it holds $[\sigma] \subseteq [\tau]$ as $\sigma \in V_u$.
  - $v = \mathsf{abs}_{\sigma \to \tau}$ then we define $[v]$ as the (identical) embedding $[\sigma] \subseteq [\tau]$ which exists in $[\sigma \to \tau]$, or
  - $v = \mathsf{rep}_{\tau \to \sigma}$ then we define $[v]$ as some embedding of $[\tau]$ to $[\sigma]$ such that $[v]\big|_{[\sigma]}$ is the identity
- $v = c_\sigma$ for some $c_\sigma \in$ GCInst$^{\circ}$ then we define $[v] = \mathsf{choice}([\sigma])$.

We get a model from the constructed pre-interpretation $[\cdot]$ of $\top$ by $[\![\cdot]\!]$ to arrive at an interpretation of terms from Term.

We prove that the recursively constructed total fragment interpretation is indeed a model for D'. For types $\tau \in$ Type$^{E\rightsquigarrow}$ the built-in constants equality $\doteq_{\tau \to \tau \to \mathsf{bool}}$ and Hilbert-choice $\mathsf{some}_{(\tau \to \mathsf{bool}) \to \tau}$ are both interpretable within any of their ground types either by induction hypothesis, or otherwise as both of the constants' types are the full function spaces.

Let $s \equiv r \in D'$, and let $\rho \in$ GTSubst be a ground type substitution for which we show $[s \equiv r]_{\xi_\rho} = \mathsf{true}$ for an arbitrary ξ_ρ (as $s \equiv r$ is a closed term). By orthogonality, $\rho(s)$ matches only the definition $s \equiv r$. If $\rho(s) \notin V_U$ then $\rho(s \equiv r) \in$ Term^{F_U}, and $s \equiv r \in D$, and for (even arbitrary) ρ and any ξ_ρ it holds, with the interpretation from $\mathcal{M}$ written as $\mathcal{M}(\cdot)$:

$$[s \equiv r]_{\xi_\rho} = \mathcal{M}(s \equiv r)_{\xi_\rho} = \mathsf{true}.$$

Otherwise if $\rho(s) \in V_U$ we distinguish by the kind of s. If s is a constant instance by the first case

$$[s \equiv r]_{\xi_\rho} = [s \doteq r]_{\xi_\rho} = [s]_{\xi_\rho} [\doteq]_{\xi_\rho} [r]_{\xi_\rho} = [r]_{\xi_\rho} [\doteq]_{\xi_\rho} [r]_{\xi_\rho} = \text{true}$$

for any ξ_ρ. If $s = \tau$ is a type instance and the predicate $[r_{\sigma \to \text{bool}}]_{\xi_\rho}$ is satisfied for some element of $[\rho(\sigma)]$, proving $[s \equiv r]_{\xi_\rho} = \text{true}$ means to prove that the properties for $\text{rep}_{\rho(\sigma \to \sigma)}$ and $\text{abs}_{\rho(\tau \to \sigma)}$ hold, because the first-order logic operators are behaving in a standard sense. For any $a \in [\rho(\sigma)]$ by definition we have $[r]_{\xi_\rho}(a)$ which is the first conjunct as $[\text{rep}_{\rho(\sigma \to \tau)}]([\rho(\sigma)]) = [\rho(\sigma)] \subseteq [\rho(\tau)]$. Similarly by sub-case 2.2 above, both

$$[\text{rep}_{\rho(\tau \to \sigma)}] \circ [\text{abs}_{\rho(\sigma \to \tau)}] \qquad \text{and} \qquad [\text{abs}_{\rho(\sigma \to \tau)}] \circ [\text{rep}_{\rho(\tau \to \sigma)}]$$

are identity on $[\rho(\tau)] \subseteq [\rho(\sigma)]$.

The axioms trivially hold, also by the definition of general model. $\square$

In the proof a model for general semantics can be extended, as terms from the fragment of all dependencies $E_{\leadsto_D}$ are interpretable and as function types within the recursion are interpreted by the full set-theoretic function space. For example, for a type τ whose interpretation is defined in the recursion, the type $\tau \to \text{bool}$ of predicates on τ is interpreted by the set of all functions $[\tau] \to \mathbb{B}$.

Corollary 1. *Any definitional theory has a general model.*

The proof is by induction on the size of the theory. The base case is the empty theory, which has a (standard) model. The induction step is by Theorem 1. (Of course, the corollary also follows directly from the stronger result that any definitional theory has a standard model [1,12].)

5.2   Soundness

The deductive system is sound w.r.t. general semantics: any formula that is derivable is valid in all general models.

Theorem 2 (Soundness for general semantics). *Let T be a set of formulae. If φ is a formula such that $T \vdash \varphi$, then for every general model $\mathcal{M}$ with $\mathcal{M} \models T$ it holds that $\mathcal{M} \models \varphi$.*

The proof is by induction over the derivation $T \vdash \varphi$ (which we omit here). Since any definitional theory has a general model, soundness implies that False is not derivable, i.e. any definitional theory is (syntactically) *consistent*.

5.3   Completeness

In this section we lay out the completeness proof of the deductive system with respect to general models. Completeness means for any formula which is valid in all models of a theory there is a proof from the theory. Our proof follows the argumentation of Henkin [2, 7]: we show that any consistent theory is contained in a consistent super-set that is *extensionally complete*. From these properties we construct a general model, which is also a model of the original theory. Completeness follows from the existence of a model for any consistent set in Theorem 4.

Negation-Complete. A theory T is *negation-complete* if for any closed formula φ, we can derive $T \vdash \varphi$ or $T \vdash \neg\varphi$.

Extensionally Complete. A theory T is *extensionally complete* if for any closed term t and t' there is an a such that $T \vdash (t\ a \doteq t'\ a) \Rightarrow (t \doteq t')$. The contrapositive $t \neq t' \Rightarrow t\ a \neq t'\ a$ means that a witnesses the inequality of t and t'.

Lemma 2 (Extension Lemma). *Any finite consistent set of formulae has a consistent, negation-complete and extensionally complete theory extension.*

Proof. For a finite theory T in the given countably infinite language we construct a theory extension T'' which satisfies the stated properties.

We well-order all closed formulae of the language of T and denote them by ψ^n for n a natural number. Let $\mathcal{C}$ denote the set of countably many constants Const whose type is a type variable minus all (finitely many) constants that syntactically appear within T. We define a sequence $(T_n)_{n \in \mathbb{N}_0}$ of theory extensions of T.

For a theory T_n and for two closed terms $t_{\sigma \to \tau}$ and t' of same type, let a be the constant instance of type σ whose name is smallest in $\mathcal{C}$ less all constant names from T_n. The finite number of symbols used in T_n is at most n plus the number of symbols appearing in T. We define $T_0 := T$, $T' := \bigcup_{n \in \mathbb{N}_0} T_n$ and

$$T_{n+1} := \begin{cases} T_n \cup \{\psi^n\} & \text{if the union is consistent} \\ T_n & \text{otherwise, if } \psi^n \text{ is no equality of two functions} \\ T_n \cup \{t\ a \neq t'\ a\} & \text{otherwise, for } \psi^n = (t \doteq t') \text{ and } a \text{ as described} \end{cases}$$

By induction any T_n is consistent: Assuming T_n is consistent, we prove its successor T_{n+1} consistent. For the first two sub-cases consistency is immediate. For the third sub-case, assume that a is chosen as remarked above and $T_n \cup \{t \doteq t'\}$ is inconsistent. Consequently, $T_n \vdash t \neq t'$. Suppose that also $T_n \cup \{t\ a \neq t'\ a\}$ is inconsistent, and thus we have $T_n \vdash t\ a \doteq t'\ a$. It is derivable that $t \doteq t'$ is equivalent to $t\ x \doteq t'\ x$. Instantiating the contrapositive at a, we get $T_n \vdash t\ a \neq t'\ a$ in contradiction to consistency of T_n.

We show that T' is negation-complete. Let φ be any closed formula. Then there is an n such that $\psi^n = \varphi$. If $T_{n+1} = T_n \cup \{\varphi\}$ then $T' \vdash \varphi$. Otherwise $T_n \cup \{\varphi\}$ is inconsistent and by law of excluded middle we derive $T' \vdash \neg\varphi$.

We prove that T' is extensionally complete. For two closed terms t and t' of same function type, if $T' \vdash t \doteq t'$ then by extensionality this holds at any x: $T' \vdash t\ x \doteq t'\ x$. Otherwise there is n such that $\psi^n = t \doteq t'$ and T_{n+1} is defined as $T_n \cup \{t\ a \neq t'\ a\}$ for some a. $\qquad\square$

We will use the previous Lemma 2 to obtain an extensionally complete extension of a definitional theory. This extension T' is not a definitional theory, but this is not problematic.

For a theory we want consistency to be equivalent to the existence of a general model. To construct a model of a consistent theory, we—different from Henkin and Andrews—also define interpretations for (non-built in) types. We show that the construction gives a model for our semantics.

Theorem 3 (Henkin's Theorem). *Every consistent set of closed formulae has a general model.*

Proof. Let T' be an extension according to Lemma 2 of a consistent set of formula. We define an interpretation $[t]_{t \in \mathsf{Term}}$ (initially only for closed ground terms) and $[\sigma]_{\sigma \in \mathsf{GType}}$ for the extension T'. The construction goes by induction on the types $\sigma \in \mathsf{GType}$ such that the two properties hold:

1. $[\sigma] = \{[t_\sigma] | t_\sigma$ closed (ground) term of type $\sigma\}$
2. for all closed (ground) terms s_σ, t_σ: $[t_\sigma] = [s_\sigma]$ iff $T' \vdash t_\sigma \doteq s_\sigma$

At several instances we use that ground types are closed under the sub-type relation. Closed terms of type σ, like $\mathsf{some}(\lambda x_\sigma.\mathsf{True})$, ensure that each type's interpretation $[\sigma]$ is non-empty if defined according to Item 1.

Booleans. For $[\mathsf{bool}] := \mathbb{B}$, Items 1 and 2 hold, when setting $[\varphi_{\mathsf{bool}}] := \mathsf{true}$ iff $T' \vdash \varphi_{\mathsf{bool}}$ and otherwise $[\varphi_{\mathsf{bool}}] := \mathsf{false}$ as by maximality of T' otherwise the formula $\neg\varphi_{\mathsf{bool}}$ is deducible from T'.

Natural Numbers. Define $[\mathsf{ind}] := \mathbb{N}$. Define for t_{ind} a closed term of type ind:

$$[t_{\mathsf{ind}}] := \{n \in \mathbb{N} | T' \vdash t_{\mathsf{ind}} \doteq \underbrace{\mathsf{succ}(\ldots(\mathsf{succ}(\mathsf{zero}))\ldots)}_{n \text{ times}}\}$$

We have $[\mathsf{ind}] = \{[t_{\mathsf{ind}}] | t_{\mathsf{ind}}$ a closed term$\}$, as reflexivity of $\doteq$ gives ($\subseteq$) and on the other hand the only possible constructors for the ind type are zero and succ. Clearly both properties hold.

Function Types. Let $\sigma, \tau \in \mathsf{GType}$, $[\sigma]$ and $[\tau]$ be defined. We define

$$[t_{\sigma \to \tau}] : [\sigma] \to [\tau], \quad [s_\sigma] \mapsto [t_{\sigma \to \tau} \, s_\sigma].$$

The term $[t_{\sigma \to \tau}][s_\sigma]$ is well-defined, as the choice of s_σ as the representative of the equivalence class $[s_\sigma]$ is irrelevant: let s'_σ be such that $[s_\sigma] = [s'_\sigma]$ holds and thus equivalently $T' \vdash s_\sigma \doteq s'_\sigma$, which implies $T' \vdash t_{\sigma \to \tau} \, s_\sigma \doteq t_{\sigma \to \tau} \, s'_\sigma$.

We define $[\sigma \to \tau] := \{[t_{\sigma \to \tau}] | t_{\sigma \to \tau}$ a closed term$\}$ satisfying Item 1 and proceed with the proof of Item 2. Let $t_{\sigma \to \tau}$, $t'_{\sigma \to \tau}$ and s_σ be closed terms. If $T' \vdash t_{\sigma \to \tau} \doteq t'_{\sigma \to \tau}$ then especially $t_{\sigma \to \tau} \, s_\sigma \doteq t'_{\sigma \to \tau} \, s_\sigma$ is provable in T'. By

$$[t_{\sigma \to \tau}][s_\sigma] = [t_{\sigma \to \tau} \, s_\sigma] = [t'_{\sigma \to \tau} \, s_\sigma] = [t'_{\sigma \to \tau}][s_\sigma],$$

the functions $[t_{\sigma\to\tau}]$ and $[t'_{\sigma\to\tau}]$ coincide at every value.

On the other hand assume the equality $[t_{\sigma\to\tau}] = [t'_{\sigma\to\tau}]$. As T' is extensionally complete there exists a closed term s_σ for the term $t_{\sigma\to\tau} \doteq t'_{\sigma\to\tau}$ such that

$$(t_{\sigma\to\tau}s_\sigma \doteq t'_{\sigma\to\tau}s_\sigma) \Rightarrow (t_{\sigma\to\tau} \doteq t'_{\sigma\to\tau})$$

holds in T'. By $[t_{\sigma\to\tau}\ s_\sigma] = [t_{\sigma\to\tau}][s_\sigma] = [t'_{\sigma\to\tau}][s_\sigma] = [t'_{\sigma\to\tau}\ s_\sigma]$, and induction hypothesis, we have that $t_{\sigma\to\tau}s_\sigma \doteq t'_{\sigma\to\tau}s_\sigma$ holds in T'. Ultimately it holds:

$$[t_{\sigma\to\tau}\ s_\sigma] = [t'_{\sigma\to\tau}\ s_\sigma] \qquad \text{iff} \qquad T' \vdash t_{\sigma\to\tau}\ s_\sigma \doteq t'_{\sigma\to\tau}\ s_\sigma.$$

Non-built-in types. All other types $\sigma \in \mathsf{GType}$ are either instances of a definition or are undefined. In any case we define the interpretation as the equivalence class for all closed (ground) terms t_σ, which satisfies Items 1 and 2.

$$[t_\sigma] = \{s_\sigma | T' \vdash t_\sigma \doteq s_\sigma \text{ for closed } s_\sigma\}$$
$$[\sigma] = \{[t_\sigma] | t_\sigma \text{ closed (ground) term of type } \sigma\}$$

If $T' \vdash \exists x_\sigma.\ t\ x_\sigma$ then we can derive from T' that

$$(\forall x_\sigma.\ t\ x \Rightarrow \mathsf{rep}_{\tau\to\sigma}\,(\mathsf{abs}_{\sigma\to\tau}\ x) \doteq x) \wedge \forall y_\tau.\ t\ (\mathsf{rep}\ y) \wedge \mathsf{abs}\,(\mathsf{rep}\ y) \doteq y$$

As the properties of quantifiers, equality and logical connectives proof-theoretically correspond to those of the meta logic, we get al.l the desired properties for the interpretations of rep and abs.

General Model. Now all ground closed terms are interpretable w.r.t. $[\cdot]$. For this to become a model we define a function $[\cdot]_{\xi_\rho}$ that will become the interpretation function for this model, to also interpret terms w.r.t. a ground type substitution ρ and a term variable assignment ξ_ρ.

We write y^{ξ_ρ} for t such that $[t] = \xi_\rho(y)$ and extend interpretation to non-ground formulae by defining $[t']_{\xi_\rho} = [\rho(t'[x^{\xi_\rho}/x]_{x\in\mathrm{FV}(t)})]_{\xi_\rho}$ for any ground type substitution ρ and any ξ_ρ such that $\xi_\rho(x_\sigma) \in [\rho(\sigma)]$ for any term variable x_σ. By induction we see that this gives an interpretation with the desired properties:

- $[x_\sigma]_{\xi_\rho} = [\rho(x^{\xi_\rho})] = [x_\sigma{}^{\xi_\rho}] = \xi_\rho(x_\sigma) \in [\rho(\sigma)]$
- $[c_\sigma]_{\xi_\rho} = [c_{\rho(\sigma)}]$
- Syntactic juggling gives $[s\,t]_{\xi_\rho} = \left[\rho\left((s\,t)\,[y^{\xi_\rho}/y]_{y\in\mathrm{FV}(s\,t)}\right)\right]$

$$= \left[\rho\left(s\,[y^{\xi_\rho}/y]_{y\in\mathrm{FV}(s)}\right)\right]\left[\rho\left(t\,[y^{\xi_\rho}/y]_{y\in\mathrm{FV}(t)}\right)\right] = [s]_{\xi_\rho}\,[t]_{\xi_\rho}.$$

- By Beta rule for any closed term a of type σ we have $T' \vdash (\lambda x_\sigma.\ t'_\tau)\ a \doteq t'_\tau[a/x_\sigma]$ for any t'_τ. Followed by type instantiation and meta-level rewriting (note that ρ is ground) we have that $T' \vdash \rho((\lambda x_\sigma.\ t'_\tau)\ a) \doteq \rho(t'_\tau[\rho(a)/x_\sigma])$. Let $[s]$ be an arbitrary element of $[\rho(\sigma)]$, then the above holds for $\rho(a) = s$

and for $t'_\tau = t_\tau \left[y^{\xi_\rho}/y\right]_{y\in\mathrm{FV}(\lambda x_\sigma.\, t_\tau)}$. And thus (without loss of generality rewriting variable names) we have

$$
[\lambda x_\sigma.\, t_\tau]_{\xi_\rho}[s] = \left[\rho\left((\lambda x_\sigma.\, t_\tau)\left[y^{\xi_\rho}/y\right]_{y\in\mathrm{FV}(\lambda x_\sigma.\, t_\tau)}\right)\right][s]
$$

$$
= \left[\rho\left((\lambda x_\sigma.\, t_\tau)\left[y^{\xi_\rho}/y\right]_{y\in\mathrm{FV}(\lambda x_\sigma.\, t_\tau)}\, s\right)\right]
$$

$$
= \left[\rho\left(t_\tau \left[y^{\xi_\rho(\!|x_\sigma\mapsto[s]|\!)}/y\right]_{y\in\mathrm{FV}(t_\tau)}\right)\right] = [t_\tau]_{\xi_\rho(\!|x_\sigma\mapsto[s]|\!)}.
$$

For the built-in constant $\mathsf{some}_{(\sigma\to\mathsf{bool})\to\sigma}$ we require that $[\mathsf{some}_{(\sigma\to\mathsf{bool})\to\sigma}]$ is Hilbert-choice. For any $[p_{\sigma\to\mathsf{bool}}]$ and any $[x] \in [\sigma]$ that satisfies $[p]$, we show $[p\,(\mathsf{some}\,p)]$ holds. By $[p][x] = [p\,x] = \mathsf{true}$ we get $T' \vdash p\,x$ equivalently. From the axiom we prove $T' \vdash p\,(\mathsf{some}\,p) \doteq \mathsf{True}$, thus $[p\,(\mathsf{some}\,p)]$ holds.

Also for any ground type τ, equality $\doteq_{\tau\to\tau\to\mathsf{bool}}$ should be interpreted as equality on $[\tau]$. Immediately by construction, we have for any $[s], [t] \in [\tau]$ that

$$
[s] = [t] \quad\text{iff}\quad T' \vdash s \doteq t \quad\text{iff}\quad [s][\doteq][t] = [s \doteq t] = \mathsf{true}.
$$

As any ground type is non-empty, there are no empty types overall. Hence, as the axioms hold and as there is a valuation function this gives a general model. The constructed model is a general model of T' and any of its subsets. □

The semantics $[\![t]\!]_{\xi_\rho}$ of a term t is defined to apply type substitutions *lazily*, i.e. at the latest possible moment when interpreting a term (and never to term variables). Applying type substitutions eagerly would erroneously force equal valuation of distinct variables, e.g. x_α and x_bool under a type substitution ρ with $\rho(\alpha) = \mathsf{bool}$ [1].

However in the proof we see a different characterisation of the term semantics, namely as $[\![t]\!]_{\xi_\rho} = [\![\rho(t[y^{\xi_\rho}/y]_{y\in\mathrm{FV}(t)})]\!]_{\xi_\rho}$, which eagerly applies ρ to t, but only after replacing each free variable $y \in \mathrm{FV}(t)$. Therein y is replaced by a closed term y^{ξ_ρ} that has the same interpretation. The resulting term $\rho(t[y^{\xi_\rho}/y]_{y\in\mathrm{FV}(t)})$ is closed, hence a capture of term variables does not occur. This characterisation requires for any type σ and valuation ξ_ρ that the function $[\![\cdot]\!]_{\xi_\rho} : \mathsf{Term}_\sigma \to [\rho(\sigma)]$ is surjective, which is not given in Åman Pohjola and Gengelbach [1].

Completeness follows by Theorem 3 and a generic argument.

Theorem 4 (Completeness for general semantics). *Let T be a set of formulae. If φ is a formula that is valid in every general model $\mathcal{M}$ with $\mathcal{M} \models T$, then $T \vdash \varphi$.*

Proof. Let ψ be a universal closure of φ, then also ψ is valid in every general model of T. Suppose that $T' := T \cup \{\neg\psi\}$ is consistent, then by Theorem 3 let $\mathcal{M}$ be a general model of T'. We have $\mathcal{M} \models \neg\psi$ but also $\mathcal{M} \models T$, hence $\mathcal{M} \models \psi$. This is a contradiction. Consequently $T \cup \{\neg\psi\}$ is inconsistent, i.e. $T \cup \{\neg\psi\} \vdash \mathsf{False}$, thus $T \vdash \psi$. Eliminating the universal closure, we obtain $T \vdash \varphi$. □

As noted by a reviewer, completeness w.r.t. general lazy ground semantics can also be proved more directly from completeness of the monomorphic calculus. We briefly sketch the idea (but we have not worked out the technical details). If a (polymorphic) theory T is consistent, the theory of all ground instances of formulas in T is consistent. By completeness this theory has a (general) model. This model is also a model of T w.r.t. ground semantics.

5.4 Proof-Theoretic Conservativity

Having proven the deductive system with general semantics sound and complete, we derive proof-theoretic conservativity from model-theoretic conservativity in this section.

Lemma 3. *If a deductive system is sound and complete then model-theoretic conservativity implies proof-theoretic conservativity.*

Proof. Consider a theory extension $D' \supseteq D$. Assume $D' \vdash \varphi$ (with suitable assumptions on φ). We need to show $D \vdash \varphi$. Due to completeness it is sufficient to prove that φ holds in all models of D. By model-theoretic conservativity, for any model $\mathcal{M}$ of D there is a model $\mathcal{M}'$ of D' such that $\mathcal{M}'$ agrees with $\mathcal{M}$ on the interpretation of φ. Since $D' \vdash \varphi$, soundness implies that $\mathcal{M}'$ is a model of φ, hence $\mathcal{M}$ is a model of φ. □

We recall the main model-theoretic conservativity theorem [6, Theorem 3.3]. For U a set of symbol, the *U-independent fragment* F_U [5,6] defines the ground symbols which are not in the pre-image of type instances of U under the reflexive-transitive, type-substitutive closure of the dependency relation. The terms Term^{F_U} are all terms whose ground instances can be interpreted within F_U and accordingly are Type^{F_U} all the types that occur in the terms Term^{F_U} (see also Theorem 1).

Lemma 3 shows how the constraint in our model-theoretic notion of conservativity translates to a syntactic constraint:

Theorem 5 (Proof-theoretic conservativity). *Let D be a definitional theory and $D' \supseteq D$ be a definitional theory extension of D (by possibly several definitions), and let U be the set of symbols defined in $D' \setminus D$.*
If $\varphi_{\mathsf{bool}} \in \mathsf{Term}^{F_U}$ and $D' \vdash \varphi$ then $D \vdash \varphi$.

Proof. For a definitional theory extension $D' \supseteq D$, $\varphi_{\mathsf{bool}} \in \mathsf{Term}^{F_U}$ and $D' \vdash \varphi$, it is sufficient to prove that φ holds in all models of D, due to completeness (Theorem 4). Let $\mathcal{M}$ be a model of D. From model-theoretic conservativity (Theorem 1), we obtain a model extension $\mathcal{M}'$ for D' such that $\mathcal{M}$ and $\mathcal{M}'$ agree on the interpretation of all types and terms in $\mathsf{Type}^{F_U} \cup \mathsf{Term}^{F_U}$. Consequently, we have $\mathcal{M} \models \varphi$ iff $\mathcal{M}' \models \varphi$. Soundness implies that $\mathcal{M}' \models \varphi$, hence also $\mathcal{M} \models \varphi$. □

6 Conclusion

We introduced general models as a generalisation of standard models, and proved soundness and completeness (by using ideas by Henkin [2,7]) for HOL with ad-hoc overloading. We extended our earlier model-theoretic conservativity result [5] to general models, and applied these results to show proof-theoretic conservativity for HOL with ad-hoc overloading: for a definitional theory extension $D' \supseteq D$, any formula φ that is derivable in D' and that does not (explicitly or implicitly) depend on symbols defined in $D' \setminus D$ is already derivable in D.

The established notion of proof-theoretic conservativity should be extensible to hold for related settings, for example with further axioms [14], with Arthan's constant specification [3], and with explicit signature extensions like in [1]. Using our results and unfolding definitions with ideas from [11] may allow a *relative* meta-safety result, i.e. unfolding the symbols defined in a definitional extension relative to an arbitrary definitional base theory.

Acknowledgements. We thank Andrei Popescu, Georg Struth and the anonymous reviewers for their valuable feedback on earlier versions of this paper.

References

1. Åman Pohjola, J., Gengelbach, A.: A mechanised semantics for HOL with ad-hoc overloading. In: Albert, E., Kovács, L. (eds.) LPAR23. LPAR-23: 23rd International Conference on Logic for Programming, Artificial Intelligence and Reasoning. EPiC Series in Computing, vol. 73, pp. 498–515. EasyChair (2020). https://doi.org/10.29007/413d, https://easychair.org/publications/paper/9Hcd
2. Andrews, P.B.: An Introduction to Mathematical Logic and Type Theory: To Truth through Proof. Applied logic series, No. 27, 2nd edn.. Kluwer Academic Publishers, Dordrecht; Boston (2002)
3. Arthan, R.: HOL constant definition done right. In: Klein, G., Gamboa, R. (eds.) ITP 2014. LNCS, vol. 8558, pp. 531–536. Springer, Cham (2014). https://doi.org/10.1007/978-3-319-08970-6_34
4. Church, A.: A formulation of the simple theory of types. J. Symbol. Logic 5(02), 56–68 (1940). https://doi.org/10.2307/2266170, http://www.journals.cambridge.org/abstract_S0022481200108187
5. Gengelbach, A., Åman Pohjola, J., Weber, T.: Mechanisation of Model-theoretic Conservative Extension for HOL with Ad-hoc Overloading (2020, Under submission)
6. Gengelbach, A., Weber, T.: Model-theoretic conservative extension of definitional theories. In: Proceedings of 12th Workshop on Logical and Semantic Frameworks with Applications (LSFA 2017), pp. 4–16. Brasília, Brasil, September 2017. https://doi.org/10.1016/j.entcs.2018.10.009
7. Henkin, L.: Completeness in the theory of types. J. Symbol. Logic 15(2), 81–91 (1950). https://doi.org/10.2307/2266967
8. Kuncar, O.: Correctness of Isabelle's cyclicity checker: implementability of overloading in proof assistants. In: Leroy, X., Tiu, A. (eds.) Proceedings of the 2015 Conference on Certified Programs and Proofs, CPP 2015, Mumbai, India, January 15–17, 2015, pp. 85–94. ACM (2015). https://doi.org/10.1145/2676724.2693175, https://doi.org/10.1145/2676724.2693175

9. Kunčar, O., Popescu, A.: Safety and conservativity of definitions in HOL and Isabelle/HOL. Proc. ACM Program. Lang. 2(POPL), 24:1–24:26 (2017). https://doi.org/10.1145/3158112

10. Kunčar, O.: Types, Abstraction and Parametric Polymorphism in Higher-Order Logic. Ph.D. thesis, Technische Universität München (2016). http://www21.in.tum.de/~kuncar/documents/kuncar-phdthesis.pdf

11. Kunčar, O., Popescu, A.: Comprehending Isabelle/HOL's consistency. In: Yang, H. (ed.) ESOP 2017. LNCS, vol. 10201, pp. 724–749. Springer, Heidelberg (2017). https://doi.org/10.1007/978-3-662-54434-1_27

12. Kunčar, O., Popescu, A.: A consistent foundation for Isabelle/HOL. J. Autom. Reasoning **62**(4), 531–555 (2018). https://doi.org/10.1007/s10817-018-9454-8

13. Nipkow, T., Wenzel, M., Paulson, L.C. (eds.): Isabelle/HOL - A Proof Assistant for Higher-Order Logic. LNCS, vol. 2283. Springer, Heidelberg (2002). https://doi.org/10.1007/3-540-45949-9

14. Norrish, M., Slind, K., et al.: The HOL System LOGIC, August 2019. http://sourceforge.net/projects/hol/files/hol/kananaskis-13/kananaskis-13-logic.pdf/download

15. Pitts, A.: The HOL logic. In: Introduction to HOL: A Theorem Proving Environment for Higher Order Logic, pp. 191–232. Cambridge University Press, Cambridge; New York (1993)

16. Wenzel, M.: Type classes and overloading in higher-order logic. In: Gunter, E.L., Felty, A. (eds.) TPHOLs 1997. LNCS, vol. 1275, pp. 307–322. Springer, Heidelberg (1997). https://doi.org/10.1007/BFb0028402

A Myhill-Nerode Theorem for Register Automata and Symbolic Trace Languages

Frits Vaandrager[(✉)] and Abhisek Midya

Institute for Computing and Information Sciences, Radboud University,
Nijmegen, The Netherlands
{F.Vaandrager,A.Midya}@cs.ru.nl

Abstract. We propose a new symbolic trace semantics for register automata (extended finite state machines) which records both the sequence of input symbols that occur during a run as well as the constraints on input parameters that are imposed by this run. Our main result is a generalization of the classical Myhill-Nerode theorem to this symbolic setting. Our generalization requires the use of three relations to capture the additional structure of register automata. Location equivalence $\equiv_l$ captures that symbolic traces end in the same location, transition equivalence $\equiv_t$ captures that they share the same final transition, and a partial equivalence relation $\equiv_r$ captures that symbolic values v and v' are stored in the same register after symbolic traces w and w', respectively. A symbolic language is defined to be regular if relations $\equiv_l$, $\equiv_t$ and $\equiv_r$ exist that satisfy certain conditions, in particular, they all have finite index. We show that the symbolic language associated to a register automaton is regular, and we construct, for each regular symbolic language, a register automaton that accepts this language. Our result provides a foundation for grey-box learning algorithms in settings where the constraints on data parameters can be extracted from code using e.g. tools for symbolic/concolic execution or tainting. We believe that moving to a grey-box setting is essential to overcome the scalability problems of state-of-the-art black-box learning algorithms.

1 Introduction

Model learning (a.k.a. active automata learning) is a black-box technique which constructs state machine models of software and hardware components from information obtained by providing inputs and observing the resulting outputs. Model learning has been successfully used in numerous applications, for instance for generating conformance test suites of software components [20], finding mistakes in implementations of security-critical protocols [13–15], learning interfaces of classes in software libraries [23], and checking that a legacy component and a refactored implementation have the same behavior [35]. We refer to [26, 38] for surveys and further references.

Supported by NWO TOP project 612.001.852 Grey-box learning of Interfaces for Refactoring Legacy Software (GIRLS).

V. K. I. Pun et al. (Eds.): ICTAC 2020, LNCS 12545, pp. 43–63, 2020.
https://doi.org/10.1007/978-3-030-64276-1_3

Myhill-Nerode theorems [21,32] are of pivotal importance for model learning algorithms. Angluin's classical L^* algorithm [3] for active learning of regular languages, as well as improvements such as [27,34,36], use an observation table to approximate the Nerode congruence. Maler and Steiger [30] established a Myhill-Nerode theorem for ω-languages that serves as a basis for a learning algorithm described in [4]. The SL^* algorithm for active learning of register automata of Cassel et al. [11] is directly based on a generalization of the classical Myhill-Nerode theorem to a setting of data languages and register automata (extended finite state machines). Francez and Kaminski [16], Benedikt et al. [5] and Bojańczyk et al. [6] all present Myhill-Nerode theorems for data languages.

Despite the convincing applications of black-box model learning, it is fair to say that existing algorithms do not scale very well. In order to learn models of realistic applications in which inputs and outputs carry data parameters, state-of-the-art techniques either rely on manually constructed mappers that abstract the data parameters of inputs and outputs into a finite alphabet [2], or otherwise infer guards and assignments from black-box observations of test outputs [1,11]. The latter can be costly, especially for models where the control flow depends on data parameters in the input. Thus, for instance, the RALib tool [9], an implementation of the SL^* algorithm, needed more than two hundred thousand input/reset events to learn register automata with just 6 to 8 locations for TCP client implementations of Linux, FreeBSD and Windows [14]. Existing black-box model learning algorithms also face severe restrictions on the operations and predicates on data that are supported (typically, only equality/inequality predicates and constants).

A natural way to address these limitations is to augment learning algorithms with white-box information extraction methods, which are able to obtain information about the system under learning at lower cost than black-box techniques [25]. Constraints on data parameters can be extracted from the code using e.g. tools for symbolic execution [8], concolic execution [19], or tainting [22]. Several researchers have successfully explored this idea, see for instance [7,12,18,24]. Recently, we showed how constraints on data parameters can be extracted from Python programs using tainting, and used to boost the performance of RALib with almost two orders of magnitude. We were also able to learn models of systems that are completely out of reach of black-box techniques, such as "combination locks", systems that only exhibit certain behaviors after a very specific sequence of inputs [17]. Nevertheless, all these approaches are rather ad hoc, and what is missing is Myhill-Nerode theorem for this enriched settings that may serve as a foundation for grey-box model learning algorithms for a general class of register automata. In this article, we present such a theorem.

More specifically, we propose a new symbolic trace semantics for register automata which records both the sequence of input symbols that occur during a run as well as the constraints on input parameters that are imposed by this run. Our main result is a Myhill-Nerode theorem for symbolic trace languages. Whereas the original Myhill-Nerode theorem refers to a single equivalence relation $\equiv$ on words, and constructs a DFA in which states are equivalence classes of $\equiv$, our generalization requires the use of three relations to capture the additional structure of register automata. Location equivalence $\equiv_l$ captures that symbolic traces end in the same location, transition equivalence $\equiv_t$ captures that they share the same final transition, and a partial equivalence relation $\equiv_r$ captures that symbolic values v and v' are stored in the same register after symbolic traces w and w', respectively. A symbolic language is defined to be regular if relations $\equiv_l$, $\equiv_t$ and $\equiv_r$ exist that satisfy certain conditions, in particular, they all have finite index. Whereas in the classical case of regular languages the Nerode equivalence $=$ is uniquely determined, different relations $\equiv_l$, $\equiv_t$ and $\equiv_r$ may exist that satisfy the conditions for regularity for symbolic languages. We show that the symbolic language associated to a register automaton is regular, and we construct, for each regular symbolic language, a register automaton that accepts this language. In this automaton, the locations are equivalence classes of $\equiv_l$, the transitions are equivalence classes of $\equiv_t$, and the registers are equivalence classes of $\equiv_r$. In this way, we obtain a natural generalization of the classical Myhill-Nerode theorem for symbolic languages and register automata. Unlike Cassel et al. [11], we need no restrictions on the allowed data predicates to prove our result, which drastically increases the range of potential applications. Our result paves the way for efficient grey-box learning algorithms in settings where the constraints on data parameters can be extracted from the code.

Due to the page limit, proofs have been omitted from this article, except for outlines of the proofs of main Theorems 2 and 3. All proofs can be found in the report version on arXiv [39].

2   Preliminaries

In this section, we fix some basic vocabulary for (partial) functions, languages, and logical formulas.

2.1   Functions

We write $f : X \rightharpoonup Y$ to denote that f is a partial function from set X to set Y. For $x \in X$, we write $f(x) \downarrow$ if there exists a $y \in Y$ such that $f(x) = y$, i.e., the result is defined, and $f(x) \uparrow$ if the result is undefined. We write $domain(f) = \{x \in X \mid f(x) \downarrow\}$ and $range(f) = \{f(x) \in Y \mid x \in domain(f)\}$. We often identify a partial function f with the set of pairs $\{(x, y) \in X \times Y \mid f(x) = y\}$. As usual, we write $f : X \rightarrow Y$ to denote that f is a total function from X to Y, that is, $f : X \rightharpoonup Y$ and $domain(f) = X$.

2.2   Languages

Let Σ be a set of *symbols*. A *word* $u = a_1 \ldots a_n$ over Σ is a finite sequence of symbols from Σ. The *length* of a word u, denoted $|u|$ is the number of symbols occurring in it. The empty word is denoted ϵ. We denote by Σ^* the set of all words over Σ, and by Σ^+ the set of all nonempty words over Σ (i.e. $\Sigma^* = \Sigma^+ \cup \{\epsilon\}$).

Given two words u and w, we denote by $u \cdot w$ the concatenation of u and w. When the context allows it, $u \cdot w$ shall be simply written uw. We say that u is a *prefix* of w iff there exists a word u' such that $u \cdot u' = w$. Similarly, u is a *suffix* of w iff there exists a word u' such that $u' \cdot u = w$. A *language* L over Σ is any set of words over Σ, so therefore a subset of Σ^*. We say that L is prefix closed if, for each $w \in L$ and each prefix u of w, $u \in L$ as well.

2.3 Guards

We postulate a countably infinite set $V = \{v_1, v_2, \ldots\}$ of *variables*. In addition, there is also a variable $p \notin V$ that will play a special role as formal parameter of input symbols; we write $V^+ = V \cup \{p\}$. Our framework is parametrized by a set R of relation symbols. Elements of R are assigned finite *arities*. A *guard* is a Boolean combination of relation symbols from R over variables. Formally, the set of *guards* is inductively defined as follows:

- If $r \in R$ is an n-ary relation symbol and $x_1, \ldots, x_n$ are variables from V^+, then $r(x_1, \ldots, x_n)$ is a guard.
- If g is a guard then $\neg g$ is a guard.
- If g_1 and g_2 are guards then $g_1 \wedge g_2$ is a guard.

We use standard abbreviations from propositional logic such as $\top$ and $g_1 \vee g_2$. We write $Var(g)$ for the set of variables that occur in a guard g. We say that g is a guard *over* set of variables X if $Var(g) \subseteq X$. We write $\mathcal{G}(X)$ for the set of guards over X, and use symbol $\equiv$ to denote syntactic equality of guards.

We postulate a structure $\mathcal{R}$ consisting of a set $\mathcal{D}$ of *data values* and a distinguished n-ary relation $r^{\mathcal{R}} \subseteq \mathcal{D}^n$ for each n-ary relation symbol $r \in R$. In a trivial example of a structure $\mathcal{R}$, R consists of the binary symbol '=', $\mathcal{D}$ the set of natural numbers, and $=^{\mathcal{R}}$ is the equality predicate on numbers. An n-ary operation $f : \mathcal{D}^n \to \mathcal{D}$ can be modelled in our framework as an $n+1$-ary predicate. We may for instance extend structure $\mathcal{R}$ with a ternary predicate symbol $+$, where $(d_1, d_2, d_3) \in +^{\mathcal{R}}$ iff the sum of d_1 and d_2 equals d_3. Constants like 0 and 1 can be added to $\mathcal{R}$ as unary predicates.

A *valuation* is a partial function $\xi : V^+ \rightharpoonup \mathcal{D}$ that assigns data values to variables. If $Var(g) \subseteq domain(\xi)$, then $\xi \models g$ is defined inductively by:

- $\xi \models r(x_1, \ldots, x_n)$ iff $(\xi(x_1), \ldots, \xi(x_n)) \in r^{\mathcal{R}}$
- $\xi \models \neg g$ iff not $\xi \models g$
- $\xi \models g_1 \wedge g_2$ iff $\xi \models g_1$ and $\xi \models g_2$

If $\xi \models g$ then we say valuation ξ *satisfies* guard g. We call g is *satisfiable*, and write $Sat(g)$, if there exists a valuation ξ such that $\xi \models g$. Guard g is a *tautology* if $\xi \models g$ for all valuations ξ with $Var(g) \subseteq domain(\xi)$.

A *variable renaming* is a partial function $\sigma : V^+ \rightharpoonup V^+$. If g is a guard with $Var(g) \subseteq domain(\sigma)$ then $g[\sigma]$ is the guard obtained by replacing each occurrence of a variable x in g by variable $\sigma(x)$. The following lemma is easily proved by induction.

Lemma 1. $\xi \circ \sigma \models g$ *iff* $\xi \models g[\sigma]$.

3   Register Automata

In this section, we introduce register automata and show how they may be used as recognizers for both data languages and symbolic languages.

3.1   Definition and Trace Semantics

A register automaton comprises a set of locations with transitions between them, and a set of registers which can store data values that are received as inputs. Transitions contain guards over the registers and the current input, and may assign new values to registers.

Definition 1. *A* register automaton *is a tuple* $\mathcal{A} = (\Sigma, Q, q_0, F, V, \Gamma)$, *where*

- Σ *is a finite set of* input symbols,
- Q *is a finite set of* locations, *with* $q_0 \in Q$ *the* initial location, *and* $F \subseteq Q$ *a set of* accepting locations,
- $V \subset \mathcal{V}$ *is a finite set of* registers, *and*
- Γ *is a finite set of* transitions, *each of form* $\langle q, \alpha, g, \varrho, q' \rangle$ *where*
  - $q, q' \in Q$ *are the* source *and* target *locations, respectively; we require that* $q' \in F \Rightarrow q \in F$,
  - $\alpha \in \Sigma$ *is an* input symbol,
  - $g \in \mathcal{G}(V \cup \{p\})$ *is a* guard, *and*
  - $\varrho : V \rightharpoonup V \cup \{p\}$ *is an* assignment; *we require that* ϱ *is injective.*

Register automata are required to be completely specified *in the sense that for each location* $q \in Q$ *and each input symbol* $\alpha \in \Sigma$, *the disjunction of the guards on the* α-transitions *with source* q *is a tautology. Register automata are also required to be* deterministic *in the sense that for each location* $q \in Q$ *and input symbol* $\alpha \in \Sigma$, *the conjunction of the guards of any pair of distinct* α-transitions *with source* q *is not satisfiable. We write* $q \xrightarrow{\alpha, g, \varrho} q'$ *if* $\langle q, \alpha, g, \varrho, q' \rangle \in \Gamma$.

Example 1. Figure 1 shows a register automaton $\mathcal{A} = (\Sigma, Q, q_0, F, V, \Gamma)$ with a single input symbol a and four locations q_0, q_1, q_2 and q_3, with q_0, q_1, q_2 accepting and q_3 non-accepting. The initial location q_0 is marked by an arrow "start" and accepting locations are indicated by a double circle. There is just a single register x. Set Γ contains six transitions, which are indicated in the diagram. All transitions are labeled with input symbol a, a guard over formal parameter p and the registers, and an assignment. Guards represent conditions on data values. For example, the guard on the transition from q_1 to q_2, expresses that the data value of action a must be smaller than the data value currently stored in register x. We write $x := p$ to denote the assignment that stores the data parameter p in register x, that is, the function ϱ satisfying $\varrho(x) = p$. Trivial guards ($\top$) and assignments (empty domain) are omitted. Note that location q_3 is actually a sink location, i.e., there is no way to get into an accepting state from q_3. Thus the register automaton satisfies the condition that for each transition either the source location is accepting or the target location is not accepting.

When drawing register automata, we often only depict the accepting locations, and leave a non-accepting sink location and the transitions leading to it implicit. Note that in locations q_1 and q_2, which have more than one outgoing transition, the disjunction of the guards of these transitions is equivalent to true, whereas the conjunction is equivalent to false.

The semantics of a register automaton is defined in terms of the set of *data words* that it accepts.

Definition 2. *Let Σ be a finite alphabet. A* data symbol *over Σ is a pair $\alpha(d)$ with $\alpha \in \Sigma$ and $d \in \mathcal{D}$. A* data word *over Σ is a finite sequence of data symbols, i.e., a word over $\Sigma \times \mathcal{D}$. A* data language *over Σ is a set of data words over Σ.*

We associate a data language to each register automata as follows.

Definition 3. *Let $\mathcal{A} = (\Sigma, Q, q_0, F, V, \Gamma)$ be a register automaton. A* configuration *of $\mathcal{A}$ is a pair (q, ξ), where $q \in Q$ and $\xi : V \rightharpoonup \mathcal{D}$. A* run *of $\mathcal{A}$ over a data word $w = \alpha_1(d_1) \cdots \alpha_n(d_n)$ is a sequence*

$$\gamma = (q_0, \xi_0) \xrightarrow{\alpha_1(d_1)} (q_1, \xi_1) \quad \cdots \quad (q_{n-1}, \xi_{n-1}) \xrightarrow{\alpha_n(d_n)} (q_n, \xi_n),$$

where, for $0 \leq i \leq n$, (q_i, ξ_i) is a configuration of $\mathcal{A}$, $domain(\xi_0) = \emptyset$, and for $0 < i \leq n$, Γ contains a transition $q_{i-1} \xrightarrow{\alpha_i, g_i, \varrho_i} q_i$ such that

- $\iota_i \models g_i$, *where $\iota_i = \xi_{i-1} \cup \{(p, d_i)\}$, and*
- $\xi_i = \iota_i \circ \varrho_i$.

We say that run γ is accepting *if $q_n \in F$ and* rejecting *if $q_n \notin F$. We call w the* trace *of γ, notation $trace(\gamma) = w$. Data word w is* accepted *(rejected) if $\mathcal{A}$ has an accepting (rejecting) run over w. The* data language *of $\mathcal{A}$, notation $L(\mathcal{A})$, is the set of all data words that are accepted by $\mathcal{A}$. Two register automata over the same alphabet Σ are* trace equivalent *if they accept the same data language.*

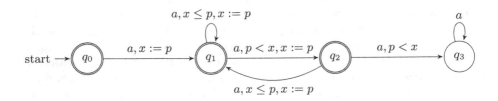

Fig. 1. Register automaton.

Example 2. Consider the register automaton of Fig. 1. This automaton accepts the data word $a(1)\ a(4)\ a(0)\ a(7)$ since the following sequence of steps is a run (here ξ_0 is the trivial function with empty domain):

$$(q_0, \xi_0) \xrightarrow{a(1)} (q_1, x \mapsto 1) \xrightarrow{a(4)} (q_1, x \mapsto 4) \xrightarrow{a(0)} (q_2, x \mapsto 0) \xrightarrow{a(7)} (q_1, x \mapsto 7).$$

Note that the final location q_1 of this run is accepting. Upon receiving the first input $a(1)$, the automaton jumps to q_1 and stores data value 1 in the register x. Since 4 is bigger than 1, the automaton takes the self loop upon receiving the second input $a(4)$ and stores 4. Since 0 is less than 4, it moves to q_2 upon receipt of the third input $a(0)$ and updates x to 0. Finally, the automaton gets back to q_1 as 7 is bigger than 0.

Suppose that in the register automaton of Fig. 1 we replace the guard on the transition from q_0 to q_1 by $x \leq p$. Since initial valuation ξ_0 does not assign a value to x, this means that it is not defined whether ξ_0 satisfies guard $x \leq p$. Automata in which such "runtime errors" do not occur are called *well-formed*.

Definition 4. *Let $\mathcal{A}$ be a register automaton. We say that a configuration (q, ξ) of $\mathcal{A}$ is reachable if there is a run of $\mathcal{A}$ that ends with (q, ξ). We call $\mathcal{A}$ well-formed if, for each reachable configuration (q, ξ), ξ assigns a value to all variables from V that occur in guards of outgoing transitions of q, that is,*

$$(q, \xi) \text{ reachable} \wedge q \xrightarrow{\alpha, g\varrho} q' \Rightarrow Var(g) \subseteq domain(\xi) \cup \{p\}.$$

As soon as the set of data values and the collection of predicates becomes non-trivial, well-formedness of register automata becomes undecidable. However, it is easy to come up with a sufficient condition for well-formedness, based on a syntactic analysis of $\mathcal{A}$, which covers the cases that occur in practice. In the remainder of article, we will restrict our attention to well-formed register automata. In particular, the register automata that are constructed from regular symbolic trace languages in our Myhill-Nerode theorem will be well-formed.

Relation with Automata of Cassel et al. Our definition of a register automaton is different from the one used in the SL^* algorithm of Cassel et al. [11] and its implementation in RALib [9]. It is instructive to compare the two definitions.

1. In order to establish a Myhill-Nerode theorem, [11] requires that structure $\mathcal{R}$, which is a parameter of the SL^* algorithm, is *weakly extendible*. This technical restriction excludes many data types that are commonly used in practice. For instance, the set of integers with constants 0 and 1, an addition operator $+$, and a less-than predicate $<$ is not weakly extendable. For readers familiar with [11]: a structure (called theory in [11]) is weakly extendable if for all natural numbers k and data words u, there exists a u' with $u' \approx_{\mathcal{R}} u$ which is k-extendable. Intuitively, $u' \approx_{\mathcal{R}} u$ if data words u' and u have the same sequences of actions and cannot be distinguished by the relations in $\mathcal{R}$. Let $u = \alpha(0)\alpha(1)\alpha(2)\alpha(4)\alpha(8)\alpha(16)\alpha(11)$. Then there exists just one u' different

from u with $u' \approx_{\mathcal{R}} u$, namely $u' = \alpha(0)\alpha(1)\alpha(2)\alpha(4)\alpha(8)\alpha(16)\alpha(13)$. Now both u and u' are not even 1-extendable: if we extend u with $\alpha(3)$, we cannot find a matching extension $\alpha(d')$ of u' such that $u\alpha(3) \approx_{\mathcal{R}} u'\alpha(d')$, and if we extend u' with $\alpha(5)$ we cannot find a matching extension $\alpha(d)$ of u such that $u\alpha(d) \approx_{\mathcal{R}} u'\alpha(5)$. In the terminology of model theory [33], a structure is k-extendable if the Duplicator can win certain k-move Ehrenfeucht-Fraïssé games. For structures $\mathcal{R}$ that are homogeneous, one can always win these games, for all k. Thus, homogeneous structures are weakly extendible. An even stronger requirement, which is imposed in work of [31] on nominal automata, is that $\mathcal{R}$ is ω-categorical. In our approach, no restrictions on $\mathcal{R}$ are needed.

2. Unlike [11], we do not associate a fixed set of variables to each location. Our definition is slightly more general, which simplifies some technicalities.

3. However, we require assignments to be injective, a restriction that is not imposed by [11]. But note that the register automata that are actually constructed by SL^* are *right-invariant* [10]. In a right-invariant register automaton, two values can only be tested for equality if one of them is the current input symbol. Right-invariance, as defined in [10], implies that assignments are injective. As illustrated by the example of Fig. 2, our register automata are exponentially more succinct than the right-invariant register automata constructed by SL^*. As pointed out in [10], right-invariant register automata in turn are more succinct than the automata of [5,16].

4. Our definition assumes that, for any transition from q to q', $q' \in F \Rightarrow q \in F$. Due to this assumption, which is not required in [11], the data language accepted by a register automaton is prefix closed. We need this property for technical reasons, but for models of reactive systems it is actually quite natural. RALib [9] also assumes that data languages are prefix closed.

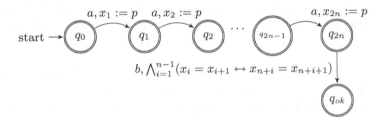

Fig. 2. For each $n > 0$, $\mathcal{A}_n$ is a register automaton that first accepts $2n$ input symbols a, storing all the data values that it receives, and then accepts input symbol b when two consecutive values in the first half of the input are equal iff the corresponding consecutive values in the second half of the input are equal. The number of locations and transitions of $\mathcal{A}_n$ grows linearly with n. There exist right-invariant register automata $\mathcal{B}_n$ that accept the same data languages, but their size grows exponentially with n.

Since register automata are deterministic, there exists a one-to-one correspondence between the accepted data words and the accepting runs. From every accepting run γ of a register automaton $\mathcal{A}$ we can trivially extract a data word $trace(\gamma)$ by forgetting all information except the data symbols. Conversely, for each data word w that is accepted by $\mathcal{A}$, there exists a corresponding accepting run γ, which is uniquely determined by the data word since from each configuration (q, ξ) and data symbol $\alpha(d)$, exactly one transition will be enabled.

Lemma 2. *Suppose γ and γ' are runs of a register automaton $\mathcal{A}$ such that $trace(\gamma) = trace(\gamma')$. Then $\gamma = \gamma'$.*

3.2 Symbolic Semantics

We will now introduce an alternative trace semantics for register automata, which records both the sequence of input symbols that occur during a run as well as the constraints on input parameters that are imposed by this run. We will explore some basic properties of this semantics, and show that the equivalence induced by symbolic traces is finer than data equivalence.

A symbolic language consists of words in which input symbols and guards alternate.

Definition 5. *Let Σ be a finite alphabet. A symbolic word over Σ is a finite alternating sequence $w = \alpha_1 G_1 \cdots \alpha_n G_n$ of input symbols from Σ and guards. A symbolic language over Σ is a set of symbolic words over Σ.*

A symbolic run is just a run, except that the valuations do not return concrete data values, but markers (variables) that record the exact place in the run where the input occurred. We use variable v_i as a marker for the i-th input value. Using these symbolic valuations (variable renamings, actually) it is straightforward to compute the constraints on the input parameters from the guards occurring in the run.

Definition 6. *Let $\mathcal{A} = (\Sigma, Q, q_0, F, V, \Gamma)$ be a register automaton. A symbolic run of $\mathcal{A}$ is a sequence*

$$\delta \;=\; (q_0, \zeta_0) \xrightarrow{\alpha_1, g_1, \varrho_1} (q_1, \zeta_1) \;\cdots\; \xrightarrow{\alpha_n, g_n, \varrho_n} (q_n, \zeta_n),$$

where ζ_0 is the trivial variable renaming with empty domain and, for $0 < i \leq n$,

- *$q_{i-1} \xrightarrow{\alpha_i, g_i, \varrho_i} q_i$ is a transition in Γ,*
- *ζ_i is a variable renaming with $domain(\zeta_i) \subseteq V$, and*
- *$\zeta_i = \iota_i \circ \varrho_i$, where $\iota_i = \zeta_{i-1} \cup \{(p, v_i)\}$.*

We also require that $G_1 \wedge \cdots \wedge G_n$ is satisfiable, where $G_i \equiv g_i[\iota_i]$, for $0 < i \leq n$.

We say that symbolic run δ is accepting if $q_n \in F$ and rejecting if $q_n \notin F$. The symbolic trace of δ is the symbolic word $strace(\delta) = \alpha_1 G_1 \cdots \alpha_n G_n$. Symbolic word w is accepted (rejected) if $\mathcal{A}$ has an accepting (rejecting) symbolic run δ with $strace(\delta) = w$. The symbolic language of $\mathcal{A}$, notation $L_s(\mathcal{A})$, is the set of all symbolic words accepted by $\mathcal{A}$. Two register automata over the same alphabet Σ are symbolic trace equivalent if they accept the same symbolic language.

Example 3. Consider the register automaton of Fig. 1. The following sequence constitutes a symbolic run:

$$(q_0, \zeta_0) \xrightarrow{a, \top, x := p} (q_1, x \mapsto v_1) \xrightarrow{a, x \leq p, x := p} (q_1, x \mapsto v_2)$$

$$\xrightarrow{a, p < x, x := p} (q_2, x \mapsto v_3) \xrightarrow{a, x \leq p, x := p} (q_1, x \mapsto v_4).$$

Since

$$\iota_1 = \{(p, v_1)\}$$
$$\iota_2 = \{(x, v_1), (p, v_2)\}$$
$$\iota_3 = \{(x, v_2), (p, v_3)\}$$
$$\iota_4 = \{(x, v_3), (p, v_4)\}$$

and the final location q_1 of this symbolic run is accepting, the register automaton accepts the symbolic word $w = a \top a v_1 \leq v_2 a v_3 < v_2 a v_3 \leq v_4$. Note that the guard of w is satisfiable, for instance by valuation ξ with $\xi(v_1) = 1$, $\xi(v_2) = 4$, $\xi(v_3) = 0$ and $\xi(v_4) = 7$.

The two technical lemmas below state some basic properties about variable renamings in a symbolic run. The proofs are straightforward, by induction.

Lemma 3. *Let δ be a symbolic run of $\mathcal{A}$, as in Definition 6. Then $range(\zeta_i) \subseteq \{v_1, \ldots, v_i\}$, for $i \in \{0, \ldots, n\}$, and $range(\iota_i) \subseteq \{v_1, \ldots, v_i\}$, for $i \in \{1, \ldots, n\}$.*

As a consequence of our assumption that assignments in a register automaton are injective, all the variable renamings in a symbolic run are injective as well.

Lemma 4. *Let δ be a symbolic run of $\mathcal{A}$, as in Definition 6. Then, for each $i \in \{0, \ldots, n\}$, ζ_i is injective, and for each $i \in \{1, \ldots, n\}$, ι_i is injective.*

All symbolic words accepted by a register automaton satisfy some basic sanity properties: guards may only refer to the markers for values received thus far, and the conjunction of all the guards is satisfiable. We call symbolic words that satisfy these properties *feasible*. Note that if a symbolic word is feasible, any prefix is feasible as well.

Definition 7 (Feasible). *Let $w = \alpha_1 G_1 \cdots \alpha_n G_n$ be a symbolic word. We write $length(w) = n$ and $guard(w) = G_1 \wedge \cdots \wedge G_n$. Word w is feasible if $guard(w)$ is satisfiable and $Var(G_i) \subseteq \{v_1, \ldots, v_i\}$, for each $i \in \{1, \ldots, n\}$. A symbolic language is feasible if it is prefix closed and consists of feasible symbolic words.*

Lemma 5. *$L_s(\mathcal{A})$ is feasible.*

Since register automata are deterministic, each symbolic trace of $\mathcal{A}$ corresponds to a unique symbolic run of $\mathcal{A}$.

Lemma 6. *Suppose δ and δ' are symbolic runs of a register automaton $\mathcal{A}$ such that $strace(\delta) = strace(\delta')$. Then $\delta = \delta'$.*

Definition 8. *Let $\mathcal{A}$ be a register automaton and $w \in L_s(\mathcal{A})$. Then we write $symb(w)$ for the unique symbolic run δ of $\mathcal{A}$ with $strace(\delta) = w$.*

There exists a one-to-one correspondence between runs of $\mathcal{A}$ and pairs consisting of a symbolic run of $\mathcal{A}$ and a satisfying assignments for the guards from its symbolic trace.

Lemma 7. *Let δ be a symbolic run of $\mathcal{A}$, as in Definition 6, and $\xi : \{v_1, \ldots, v_n\} \to \mathcal{D}$ a valuation such that $\xi \models G_1 \wedge \cdots \wedge G_n$. Let $run_{\mathcal{A}}(\delta, \xi)$ be the sequence obtained from δ by (a) replacing each input α_i by data symbol $\alpha_i(\xi(v_i))$ (for $0 < i \leq n$), (b) removing guards g_i and assignments ϱ_i, and (c) replacing valuations ζ_i by $\xi_i = \xi \circ \zeta_i$ (for $0 \leq i \leq n$). Then $run_{\mathcal{A}}(\delta, \xi)$ is a run of $\mathcal{A}$.*

Lemma 8. *Let γ be a run of register automaton $\mathcal{A}$. Then there exist a valuation ξ and symbolic run δ such that $run_{\mathcal{A}}(\delta, \xi) = \gamma$.*

Using the above lemmas, we can prove that whenever two register automata accept the same symbolic language, they also accept the same data language.

Theorem 1. *Suppose $\mathcal{A}$ and $\mathcal{B}$ are register automata with $L_s(\mathcal{A}) = L_s(\mathcal{B})$. Then $L(\mathcal{A}) = L(\mathcal{B})$.*

Example 4. The converse of Theorem 1 does not hold. Figure 3 gives a trivial example of two register automata with the same data language but a different symbolic language.

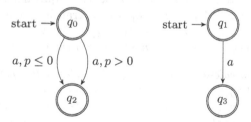

Fig. 3. Trace equivalent but not symbolic trace equivalent.

Lemma 7 allows us to rephrase the well-formedness condition of register automata in terms of symbolic runs.

Corollary 1. *Register automaton $\mathcal{A}$ is well-formed iff, for each symbolic run δ that ends with (q, ζ), $q \xrightarrow{\alpha, g\varrho} q' \Rightarrow Var(g) \subseteq domain(\zeta) \cup \{p\}$.*

4   Nerode Equivalence

The Myhill-Nerode equivalence [21,32] deems two words w and w' of a language L equivalent if there does not exist a suffix u that distinguishes them, that is, only one of the words $w \cdot u$ and $w' \cdot u$ is in L. The Myhill-Nerode theorem states that L is regular if and only if this equivalence relation has a finite index, and moreover that the number of states in the smallest deterministic finite automaton (DFA) recognizing L is equal to the number of equivalence classes. In this section, we present a Myhill-Nerode theorem for symbolic languages and register automata. We need three relations $\equiv_l$, $\equiv_t$ and $\equiv_r$ on symbolic words to capture the structure of register automata. Intuitively, two symbolic words w and w' are *location equivalent*, notation $w \equiv_l w'$, if they lead to the same location, *transition equivalent*, notation $w \equiv_t w'$, if they share the same final transition, and marker v of w, and marker v' of w' are *register equivalent*, notation $(w, v) \equiv_r (w', v')$, when they are stored in the same register after occurrence of words w and w'. Whereas $\equiv_l$ and $\equiv_t$ are equivalence relations, $\equiv_t$ is a partial equivalence relation (PER), that is, a relation that is symmetric and transitive. Relation $\equiv_r$ is not necessarily reflexive, as $(w, v) \equiv_r (w, v)$ only holds when marker v is stored after symbolic trace w. Since a register automaton has finitely many locations, finitely many transitions, and finitely many registers, the equivalences $\equiv_l$ and $\equiv_t$, and the equivalence induced by $\equiv_r$, are all required to have finite index.

Definition 9. *A feasible symbolic language L over Σ is regular iff there exist three relations:*

- *an equivalence relation $\equiv_l$ on L, called* location equivalence,
- *an equivalence relation $\equiv_t$ on $L \setminus \{\epsilon\}$, called* transition equivalence, *and*
- *a partial equivalence relation $\equiv_r$ on $\{(w, v_i) \in L \times \mathcal{V} \mid i \leq length(w)\}$, called* register equivalence. *We say that w stores v if $(w, v) \equiv_r (w, v)$.*

We require that equivalences $\equiv_l$ and $\equiv_t$, as well as the equivalence relation obtained by restricting $\equiv_t$ to $\{(w, v) \in L \times \mathcal{V} \mid w$ stores $v\}$ have finite index. We also require that relations $\equiv_l$, $\equiv_t$ and $\equiv_r$ satisfy the conditions of Table 1, for $w, w', u, u' \in L$, $length(w) = m$, $length(w') = n$, $\alpha, \alpha' \in \Sigma$, G, G' guards, $v, v' \in \mathcal{V}$, and $\sigma : \mathcal{V} \rightharpoonup \mathcal{V}$. Condition 1 implies that, given w, w' and v, there is at most one v' s.t. $(w, v) \equiv_r (w', v')$. Therefore, we may define $matching(w, w')$ as the variable renaming σ satisfying:

$$\sigma(v) = \begin{cases} v' & \text{if } (w, v) \equiv_r (w', v') \\ v_{n+1} & \text{if } v = v_{m+1} \\ \text{undefined otherwise} \end{cases}$$

Intuitively, the first condition captures that a register can store at most a single value at a time. When $w\alpha G$ and $w'\alpha'G'$ share the same final transition, then in particular w and w' share the same final location (Condition 2), input symbols α and α' are equal (Condition 3), G' is just a renaming of G (Condition 4), and $w\alpha G$ and $w'\alpha'G'$ share the same final location (Condition 5) and final

Table 1. Conditions for regularity of symbolic languages.

$$(w, v) \equiv_r (w, v') \Rightarrow v = v' \tag{1}$$

$$w\alpha G \equiv_t w'\alpha'G' \Rightarrow w \equiv_l w' \tag{2}$$

$$w\alpha G \equiv_t w'\alpha'G' \Rightarrow \alpha = \alpha' \tag{3}$$

$$w\alpha G \equiv_t w'\alpha G' \wedge \sigma = matching(w, w') \Rightarrow G[\sigma] \equiv G' \tag{4}$$

$$w \equiv_t w' \Rightarrow w \equiv_l w' \tag{5}$$

$$w \equiv_t w' \wedge w \text{ stores } v_m \Rightarrow (w, v_m) \equiv_r (w', v_n) \tag{6}$$

$$u \equiv_t u' \wedge u = w\alpha G \wedge u' = w'\alpha G' \wedge (w, v) \equiv_r (w', v') \wedge u \text{ stores } v$$
$$\Rightarrow (u, v) \equiv_r (u', v') \tag{7}$$

$$u \equiv_t u' \wedge u = w\alpha G \wedge u' = w'\alpha G' \wedge (u, v) \equiv_r (u', v') \wedge v \neq v_{m+1}$$
$$\Rightarrow (w, v) \equiv_r (w', v') \tag{8}$$

$$w \equiv_l w' \wedge w\alpha G \in L \wedge v \in Var(G) \setminus \{v_{m+1}\} \Rightarrow \exists v' : (w, v) \equiv_r (w', v') \tag{9}$$

$$w \equiv_l w' \wedge w\alpha G \in L \wedge \sigma = matching(w, w')$$
$$\wedge Sat(guard(w') \wedge G[\sigma]) \Rightarrow w'\alpha G[\sigma] \in L \tag{10}$$

$$w \equiv_l w' \wedge w\alpha G \in L \wedge w'\alpha G' \in L \wedge \sigma = matching(w, w')$$
$$\wedge Sat(G[\sigma] \wedge G') \Rightarrow w\alpha G \equiv_t w'\alpha G' \tag{11}$$

assignment (Conditions 6, 7 and 8). Condition 6 says that the parameters of the final input end up in the same register when they are stored. Condition 7 says that when two values are stored in the same register, they will stay in the same register for the rest of their life (this condition can be viewed as a right invariance condition for registers). Conversely, if two values are stored in the same register after a transition, and they do not correspond to the final input, they were already stored in the same register before the transition (Condition 8). Condition 9 captures the well-formedness assumption for register automata. As a consequence of Condition 9, $G[\sigma]$ is defined in Conditions 4, 10 and 11, since $Var(G) \subseteq domain(\sigma)$. Condition 10 is the equivalent for symbolic languages of the well-known right invariance condition for regular languages. For symbolic languages a right invariance condition

$$w \equiv_l w' \wedge w\alpha G \in L \wedge \sigma = matching(w, w') \Rightarrow w'\alpha G[\sigma] \in L$$

would be too strong: even though w and w' lead to the same location, the values stored in the registers may be different, and therefore they will not necessarily enable the same transitions. However, when in addition $guard(w') \wedge G[\sigma]$ is satisfiable, we may conclude that $w''\alpha G[\sigma] \in L$. Condition 11, finally, asserts that L only allows deterministic behavior.

The simple lemma below asserts that, due to the determinism imposed by Condition 11, the converse of Conditions 2, 3 and 4 also holds. This means that

$\equiv_t$ can be expressed in terms of $\equiv_l$ and $\equiv_r$, that is, once we have fixed $\equiv_l$ and $\equiv_r$, relation $\equiv_t$ is fully determined.

Lemma 9. *Suppose symbolic language L over Σ is regular, and equivalences $\equiv_l$, $\equiv_t$ and $\equiv_r$ satisfy the conditions of Definition 9. Then*

$$w \equiv_l w' \wedge w\alpha G \in L \wedge w'\alpha G' \in L \wedge \sigma = matching(w, w') \wedge G' \equiv G[\sigma]$$
$$\Rightarrow w\alpha G \equiv_t w'\alpha G'.$$

We can now state our "symbolic" version of the celebrated result of Myhill & Nerode. The symbolic language of any register automaton is regular (Theorem 2), and any regular symbolic language can be obtained as the symbolic language of some register automaton (Theorem 3).

Theorem 2. *Suppose $\mathcal{A}$ is a register automaton. Then $L_s(\mathcal{A})$ is regular.*

Proof. (outline) Let $L = L_s(\mathcal{A})$. Then, by Lemma 5, L is feasible. Define equivalences $\equiv_l$, $\equiv_t$ and $\equiv_r$ as follows:

- For $w, w' \in L$, $w \equiv_l w'$ iff $symb(w)$ and $symb(w')$ share the same final location.
- For $w, w' \in L \setminus \{\epsilon\}$, $w \equiv_t w'$ iff $symb(w)$ and $symb(w')$ share the same final transition.
- For $w, w' \in L$ and $v, v' \in \mathcal{V}$, $(w, v) \equiv_r (w', v')$ iff there is a register $x \in V$ such that the final valuations ζ of $symb(w)$ stores v in x, and the final valuation ζ' of $symb(w')$ stores v' in x, that is, $\zeta(x) = v$ and $\zeta'(x) = v'$.
  (Note that, by Lemma 3, $range(\zeta) \subseteq \{v_1, \ldots, v_m\}$, for $m = length(w)$, and $range(\zeta') \subseteq \{v_1, \ldots, v_n\}$, for $n = length(w')$.)

Then $\equiv_l$ has finite index since $\mathcal{A}$ has a finite number of locations, $\equiv_t$ has finite index since $\mathcal{A}$ has a finite number of transitions, and the equivalence induced by $\equiv_r$ has finite index since $\mathcal{A}$ has a finite number of registers. We refer to the full version of this paper for a proof that, with this definition of $\equiv_l$, $\equiv_t$ and $\equiv_r$, all 11 conditions of Table 1 hold.

The following example shows that in general there is no coarsest location equivalence that satisfies all conditions of Table 1. So whereas for regular languages a unique Nerode congruence exists, this is not always true for symbolic languages.

Example 5. Consider the symbolic language L that consists of the following three symbolic words and their prefixes:

$$
\begin{aligned}
w &= & a\ v_1 > 0\ a\ v_1 > 0\ b\ \top \\
u &= & a\ v_1 = 0\ a\ v_1 = 0\ b\ \top \\
z &= & a\ v_1 < 0\ c\ v_1 + v_2 = 0\ a\ v_2 > 0\ c\ \top
\end{aligned}
$$

Symbolic language L is accepted by both automata displayed in Fig. 4. Thus, by Theorem 2, L is regular. Let w_i, u_i and z_i denote the prefixes of w, u and

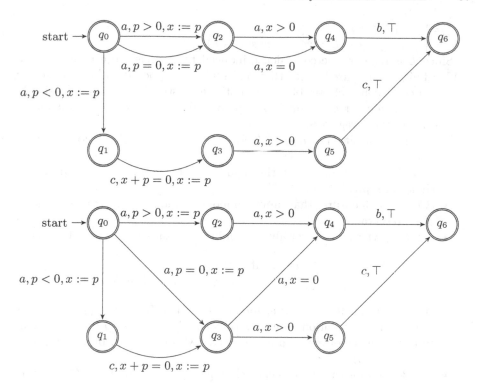

Fig. 4. There is no unique, coarsest location equivalence.

z, respectively, of length i. Then, according to the location equivalence induced by the first automaton, $w_1 \equiv_l u_1$, and according to the location equivalence induced by the second automaton, $u_1 \equiv_l z_2$. Therefore, if a coarsest location equivalence relation would exist, $w_1 \equiv_l z_2$ should hold. Then, by Condition 9, $(w_1, v_1) \equiv_r (z_2, v_2)$. Thus, by Lemma 9, $w_2 \equiv_t z_3$, and therefore, by Condition 5, $w_2 \equiv_l z_3$. But now Condition 10 implies $a\, v_1 > 0\, a\, v_1 > 0\, c\, \top \in L$, which is a contradiction.

Theorem 3. *Suppose L is a regular symbolic language over Σ. Then there exists a register automaton $\mathcal{A}$ such that $L = L_s(\mathcal{A})$.*

Proof. (Outline) Since any register automaton without accepting locations accepts the empty symbolic language, we may assume without loss of generality that L is nonempty. Let $\equiv_l, \equiv_t, \equiv_r$ be relations satisfying the properties stated in Definition 9. We define register automaton $\mathcal{A} = (\Sigma, Q, q_0, F, V, \Gamma)$ as follows:

- $Q = \{[w]_l \mid w \in L\} \cup \{q_{sink}\}$, where q_{sink} is a special *sink location*.
  (Since L is regular, $\equiv_l$ has finite index, and so Q is finite, as required.)
- $q_0 = [\epsilon]_l$.
  (Since L is regular, it is feasible, and thus prefix closed. Therefore, since we assume that L is nonempty, $\epsilon \in L$.)

- $F = \{[w]_l \mid w \in L\}$.
- $V = \{[(w, v)]_r \mid w \in L \land v \in \mathcal{V} \land w \text{ stores } v\}$.

  (Since L is regular, the equivalence induced by $\equiv_r$ has finite index, and so V is finite, as required. Note that registers are supposed to be elements of $\mathcal{V}$, and equivalence classes of $\equiv_r$ are not. Thus, strictly speaking, we should associate a unique register of $\mathcal{V}$ to each equivalence class of $\equiv_r$, and define V in terms of those registers.)

- Γ contains a transition $\langle q, \alpha, g, \varrho, q' \rangle$ for each equivalence class $[w\alpha G]_t$, where

  - $q = [w]_l$

    (Condition 2 ensures that the definition of q is independent from the choice of representative $w\alpha G$.)

  - (Condition 3 ensures that input symbol α is independent from the choice of representative $w\alpha G$.)

  - $g \equiv G[\tau]$ where τ is a variable renaming that satisfies, for $v \in Var(G)$,

    $$\tau(v) = \begin{cases} [(w, v)]_r & \text{if } w \text{ stores } v \\ p & \text{if } v = v_{m+1} \land m = length(w) \end{cases}$$

    (By Condition 9, w stores v, for any $v \in Var(G) \setminus \{v_{m+1}\}$, so $G[\tau]$ is well-defined. Condition 4 ensures that the definition of g is independent from the choice of representative $w\alpha G$.) Also note that, by Condition 1, τ is injective.)

  - ϱ is defined for each equivalence class $[(w'\alpha G', v')]_r$ with $w'\alpha G' \equiv_t w\alpha G$ and $w'\alpha G'$ stores v'. Let $n = length(w')$. Then

    $$\varrho([(w'\alpha G', v')]_r) = \begin{cases} [(w', v')]_r & \text{if } w' \text{ stores } v' \\ p & \text{if } v' = v_{n+1} \end{cases}$$

    (By Condition 8, either $v' = v_{n+1}$ or w' stores v', so $\varrho([(w'\alpha G', v')]_r)$ is well-defined. Also by Condition 8, the definition of ϱ does not depend on the choice of representative $w'\alpha G'$. By Conditions 6 and 7, assignment ϱ is injective.)

  - $q' = [w\alpha G]_l$

    (Condition 5 ensures that the definition of q' is independent from the choice of representative $w\alpha G$.)

In order to ensure that $\mathcal{A}$ is completely specified, we add transitions to the sink location q_{sink}. More specifically, if $q \in Q$ is a location with outgoing α-transitions with guards $g_1, \ldots, g_m$, then we add a transition $\langle q, \alpha, \neg(g_1 \lor \cdots \lor g_m), \varrho_0, q_{sink} \rangle$ to Γ, for ϱ_0 the trivial assignment with empty domain. Finally, we add, for each $\alpha \in \Sigma$, a self loop $\langle q_{sink}, \alpha, \top, \varrho_0, q_{sink} \rangle$ to Γ. Since L is regular, $\equiv_t$ has finite index and therefore Γ is finite, as required.

We claim that $\mathcal{A}$ is deterministic and prove this by contradiction. Suppose $\langle q, \alpha, g', \varrho', q' \rangle$ and $\langle q, \alpha, g'', \varrho'', q'' \rangle$ are two distinct α-transitions in Γ with $g' \land g''$ satisfiable. Then there exists a valuation ξ such that $\xi \models g' \land g''$. Note that $q \neq q_{sink}$, $q' \neq q_{sink}$ and $q'' \neq q_{sink}$. Let the two transitions correspond to (distinct) equivalence classes $[w'\alpha G']_t$ and $[w''\alpha G'']_t$, respectively.

Then $g' = G'[\tau']$ and $g'' = G''[\tau'']$, with τ' and τ'' defined as above. Now observe that $G'[\tau'] \equiv G'[\sigma][\tau'']$, for $\sigma = matching(w', w'')$. Using Lemma 4, we derive

$$\xi \models g' \wedge g'' \Leftrightarrow \xi \models G'[\sigma][\tau''] \wedge G''[\tau''] \Leftrightarrow \xi \models (G'[\sigma] \wedge G'')[\tau''] \Leftrightarrow \xi \circ \tau'' \models G'[\sigma] \wedge G''.$$

Thus $G'[\sigma] \wedge G''$ is satisfiable and we may apply Condition 11 to conclude $w'\alpha G' \equiv_t w''\alpha G''$. Contradiction.

So using the assumption that L is regular, we established that $\mathcal{A}$ is a register automaton. Note that for this we essentially use that equivalences $\equiv_l$, $\equiv_t$ and $\equiv_r$ have finite index, as well as all the conditions, except Condition 10. We claim $L = L_s(\mathcal{A})$.

5 Concluding Remarks

We have shown that register automata can be defined in a natural way *directly* from a regular symbolic language, with locations materializing as equivalence classes of a relation $\equiv_l$, transitions as equivalence classes of a relation $\equiv_t$, and registers as equivalences classes of a relation $\equiv_r$.

It is instructive to compare our definition of regularity for symbolic languages with Nerode's original definition for non-symbolic languages. Nerode defined his equivalence for all words $u, v \in \Sigma^*$ (not just those in L!) as follows:

$$u \equiv_l v \Leftrightarrow (\forall w \in \Sigma^* : uw \in L \Leftrightarrow vw \in L).$$

For any language $L \subseteq \Sigma^*$, the equivalence relation $\equiv_l$ is uniquely determined and can be used (assuming it has finite index) to define a unique minimal finite automaton that accepts L. As shown by Example 5, the equivalence $\equiv_l$ and its corresponding register automaton are not uniquely defined in a setting of symbolic languages. For such a setting, it makes sense to consider a symbolic variant of what Kozen [29] calls *Myhill-Nerode relations*. These are relations that satisfy the following three conditions, for $u, v \in \Sigma^*$ and $\alpha \in \Sigma$,

$$u \equiv_l v \implies (u \in L \Leftrightarrow v \in L) \tag{12}$$

$$u \equiv_l v \implies u\alpha \equiv_l v\alpha \tag{13}$$

$$\equiv_l \text{ has finite index} \tag{14}$$

Note that Conditions 12 and 13 are consequences of Nerode's definition. Condition 13 is the well-known right invariance property, which is sound for non-symbolic languages, since finite automata are completely specified and every state has an outgoing α-transition for every α. A corresponding condition

$$u \equiv_l v \implies u\alpha G \equiv_l v\alpha G$$

for symbolic languages would not be sound, however, since locations in a register automaton do not have outgoing transitions for every possible symbol α and every possible guard G. We see basically two routes to fix this problem. The first route is to turn $\equiv_l$ into a partial equivalence relation that is only defined for symbolic words that correspond to runs of the register automaton. Right invariance can then be stated as

$$w \equiv_l w' \wedge w\alpha G \equiv_l w\alpha G \wedge \sigma = matching(w, w') \wedge w'\alpha G[\sigma] \equiv_l w'\alpha G[\sigma]$$
$$\Rightarrow w\alpha G \equiv_l w'\alpha G[\sigma]. \tag{15}$$

The second route is to define $\equiv_l$ as an equivalence on L and restrict attention to prefix closed symbolic languages. This allows us to drop Condition 12 and leads to the version of right invariance that we stated as Condition 10. Since prefix closure is a natural restriction that holds for all the application scenarios we can think of, and since equivalences are conceptually simpler than PERs, we decided to explore the second route in this article. However, we conjecture that the restriction to prefix closedness is not essential, and Myhill-Nerode characterization for symbolic trace languages without this restriction can be obtained using Condition 15.

An obvious research challenge is to develop a learning algorithm for symbolic languages based on our Myhill-Nerode theorem. Since for symbolic languages there is no unique, coarsest Nerode congruence that can be approximated, as in Angluin's algorithm [3], this is a nontrivial task. We hope that for register automata with a small number of registers, an active algorithm can be obtained by encoding symbolic traces and register automata as logical formulas, and using SMT solvers to generate hypothesis models, as in [37].

As soon as a learning algorithm for symbolic traces has been implemented, it will be possible to connect the implementation with the setup of [17], which extracts symbolic traces from Python programs using an existing tainting library for Python. We can then compare its performance with the grey-box version of the RALib tool [17] on a number of benchmarks, which include data structures from Python's standard library. An area where learning algorithms for symbolic traces potentially can have major impact is the inference of behavior interfaces of legacy control software. As pointed out in [28], such interfaces allow components to be developed, analyzed, deployed and maintained in isolation. This is achieved using enabling techniques, among which are model checking (to prove interface compliance), observers (to check interface compliance), armoring (to separate error handling from component logic) and test generation (to increase test coverage). Recently, automata learning has been applied to 218 control software components of ASML's TWINSCAN lithography machines [40]. Using black-box learning algorithms in combination with information from log files, 118 components could be learned in an hour or less. The techniques failed to successfully infer the interface protocols of the remaining 100 components. It would be interesting to explore whether grey-box learning algorithm can help to learn models for these and even more complex control software components.

References

1. Aarts, F., Heidarian, F., Kuppens, H., Olsen, P., Vaandrager, F.: Automata learning through counterexample guided abstraction refinement. In: Giannakopoulou, D., Méry, D. (eds.) FM 2012. LNCS, vol. 7436, pp. 10–27. Springer, Heidelberg (2012). https://doi.org/10.1007/978-3-642-32759-9_4
2. Aarts, F., Jonsson, B., Uijen, J., Vaandrager, F.: Generating models of infinite-state communication protocols using regular inference with abstraction. Formal Methods Syst. Des. 46(1), 1–41 (2014). https://doi.org/10.1007/s10703-014-0216-x
3. Angluin, D.: Learning regular sets from queries and counterexamples. Inf. Comput. 75(2), 87–106 (1987)
4. Angluin, D., Fisman, D.: Learning regular omega languages. Theor. Comput. Sci. 650, 57–72 (2016)
5. Benedikt, M., Ley, C., Puppis, G.: What you must remember when processing data words. In: Proceedings International Workshop on Foundations of Data Management, CEUR Workshop Proceedings 619. CEUR-WS.org (2010)
6. Bojanczyk, M., Klin, B., Lasota, S.: Automata with group actions. In: Proceedings LICS 2011, pp. 355–364. IEEE Computer Society (2011)
7. Botinčan, M., Babić, D.: Sigma*: symbolic learning of input-output specifications. In: Proceedings POPL 2013, New York, NY, USA, pp. 443–456. ACM (2013)
8. Cadar, C., Sen, K.: Symbolic execution for software testing: three decades later. Commun. ACM 56(2), 82–90 (2013)
9. Cassel, S., Howar, F., Jonsson, B.: RALib: a LearnLib extension for inferring EFSMs. In: Proceedings DIFTS 15, Austin, Texas (2015)
10. Cassel, S., Howar, F., Jonsson, B., Merten, M., Steffen, B.: A succinct canonical register automaton model. J. Log. Algebr. Meth. Program. 84(1), 54–66 (2015)
11. Cassel, S., Howar, F., Jonsson, B., Steffen, B.: Active learning for extended finite state machines. Formal Aspects Comput. 28(2), 233–263 (2016). https://doi.org/10.1007/s00165-016-0355-5
12. Cho, C., Babić, D., Poosankam, P., Chen, K., Wu, E., Song, D.: Mace: model-inference-assisted concolic exploration for protocol and vulnerability discovery. In: Proceedings SEC 2011, Berkeley, CA, USA, p. 10. USENIX Association (2011)
13. Fiterău-Broştean, P., Janssen, R., Vaandrager, F.: Combining model learning and model checking to analyze TCP implementations. In: Chaudhuri, S., Farzan, A. (eds.) CAV 2016. LNCS, vol. 9780, pp. 454–471. Springer, Cham (2016). https://doi.org/10.1007/978-3-319-41540-6_25
14. Fiterău-Broştean, P., Howar, F.: Learning-based testing the sliding window behavior of TCP implementations. In: Petrucci, L., Seceleanu, C., Cavalcanti, A. (eds.) FMICS/AVoCS -2017. LNCS, vol. 10471, pp. 185–200. Springer, Cham (2017). https://doi.org/10.1007/978-3-319-67113-0_12
15. Fiterău-Broştean, P., Lenaerts, T., Poll, E., de Ruiter, J., Vaandrager, F., Verleg, P.: Model learning and model checking of SSH implementations. In: Proceedings SPIN 2017, New York, NY, USA, pp. 142–151. ACM (2017)
16. Francez, N., Kaminski, M.: An algebraic characterization of deterministic regular languages over infinite alphabets. Theor. Comput. Sci. 306(1–3), 155–175 (2003)
17. Garhewal, B., Vaandrager, F., Howar, F., Schrijvers, T., Lenaerts, T., Smits, R.: Grey-box learning of register automata. In: Proceedings ICTAC 2020. Full version available as CoRR arXiv:2009.09975, September 2020, to appear
18. Giannakopoulou, D., Rakamarić, Z., Raman, V.: Symbolic learning of component interfaces. In: Miné, A., Schmidt, D. (eds.) SAS 2012. LNCS, vol. 7460, pp. 248–264. Springer, Heidelberg (2012). https://doi.org/10.1007/978-3-642-33125-1_18

19. Godefroid, P., Klarlund, N., Sen, K.: Dart: directed automated random testing. SIGPLAN Not. **40**(6), 213–223 (2005)
20. Hagerer, A., Margaria, T., Niese, O., Steffen, B., Brune, G., Ide, H.: Efficient regression testing of CTI-systems: testing a complex call-center solution. Ann. Rev. Commun. Int. Eng. Consortium (IEC) **55**, 1033–1040 (2001)
21. Hopcroft, J.E., Ullman, J.D.: Introduction to Automata Theory, Languages and Computation. Addison-Wesley, Reading (1979)
22. Höschele, M., Zeller, A.: Mining input grammars from dynamic taints. In: Proceeding ASE 2016, pp. 720–725. ACM (2016)
23. Howar, F., Isberner, M., Steffen, B., Bauer, O., Jonsson, B.: Inferring semantic interfaces of data structures. In: Margaria, T., Steffen, B. (eds.) ISoLA 2012. LNCS, vol. 7609, pp. 554–571. Springer, Heidelberg (2012). https://doi.org/10.1007/978-3-642-34026-0_41
24. Howar, F., Giannakopoulou, D., Rakamarić, Z.: Hybrid learning: interface generation through static, dynamic, and symbolic analysis. In: Proceedings ISSTA 2013, New York, NY, USA, pp. 268–279. ACM (2013)
25. Howar, F., Jonsson, B., Vaandrager, F.: Combining black-box and white-box techniques for learning register automata. In: Steffen, B., Woeginger, G. (eds.) Computing and Software Science. LNCS, vol. 10000, pp. 563–588. Springer, Cham (2019). https://doi.org/10.1007/978-3-319-91908-9_26
26. Howar, F., Steffen, B.: Active automata learning in practice. In: Bennaceur, A., Hähnle, R., Meinke, K. (eds.) Machine Learning for Dynamic Software Analysis: Potentials and Limits. LNCS, vol. 11026, pp. 123–148. Springer, Cham (2018). https://doi.org/10.1007/978-3-319-96562-8_5
27. Isberner, M., Howar, F., Steffen, B.: The TTT algorithm: a redundancy-free approach to active automata learning. In: Bonakdarpour, B., Smolka, S.A. (eds.) RV 2014. LNCS, vol. 8734, pp. 307–322. Springer, Cham (2014). https://doi.org/10.1007/978-3-319-11164-3_26
28. Jasper, M., et al.: RERS 2019: combining synthesis with real-world models. In: Beyer, D., Huisman, M., Kordon, F., Steffen, B. (eds.) TACAS 2019. LNCS, vol. 11429, pp. 101–115. Springer, Cham (2019). https://doi.org/10.1007/978-3-030-17502-3_7
29. Kozen, D.: Automata and Computability. Undergraduate Texts in Computer Science. Springer, Heidelberg (1997). https://doi.org/10.1007/978-1-4612-1844-9
30. Maler, O., Staiger, L.: On syntactic congruences for omega-languages. Theor. Comput. Sci. **183**(1), 93–112 (1997)
31. Moerman, J., Sammartino, M., Silva, A., Klin, B., Szynwelski, M.: Learning nominal automata. In: Proceedings POPL 2017, pp. 613–625. ACM (2017)
32. Nerode, A.: Linear automaton transformations. Proc. Am. Math. Soc. **9**(4), 541–544 (1958)
33. Poizat, B.: A Course in Model Theory - An Introduction to Contempary Mathematical Logic. Springer-Verlag, New York (2000). https://doi.org/10.1007/978-1-4419-8622-1
34. Rivest, R.L., Schapire, R.E.: Inference of finite automata using homing sequences. Inf. Comput. **103**(2), 299–347 (1993)
35. Schuts, M., Hooman, J., Vaandrager, F.: Refactoring of legacy software using model learning and equivalence checking: an industrial experience report. In: Ábrahám, E., Huisman, M. (eds.) IFM 2016. LNCS, vol. 9681, pp. 311–325. Springer, Cham (2016). https://doi.org/10.1007/978-3-319-33693-0_20

36. Shahbaz, M., Groz, R.: Inferring mealy machines. In: Cavalcanti, A., Dams, D.R. (eds.) FM 2009. LNCS, vol. 5850, pp. 207–222. Springer, Heidelberg (2009). https://doi.org/10.1007/978-3-642-05089-3_14

37. Smetsers, R., Fiterău-Broştean, P., Vaandrager, F.: Model learning as a satisfiability modulo theories problem. In: Klein, S.T., Martín-Vide, C., Shapira, D. (eds.) LATA 2018. LNCS, vol. 10792, pp. 182–194. Springer, Cham (2018). https://doi.org/10.1007/978-3-319-77313-1_14

38. Vaandrager, F.W.: Model learning. Commun. ACM **60**(2), 86–95 (2017)

39. Vaandrager, F.W., Midya, A.: A Myhill-Nerode theorem for register automata and symbolic trace languages. CoRR arXiv:2007.03540, July 2020

40. Yang, N., et al.: Improving model inference in industry by combining active and passive learning. In: Proceedings SANER 2019, pp. 253–263. IEEE (2019)

CiMPG+F: A Proof Generator and Fixer-Upper for CafeOBJ Specifications

Adrián Riesco[1(✉)] and Kazuhiro Ogata[2,3(✉)]

[1] Facultad de Informática, Universidad Complutense de Madrid, Madrid, Spain
ariesco@fdi.ucm.es
[2] School of Information Science, JAIST, Nomi, Japan
ogata@jaist.ac.jp
[3] Research Center for Theoretical Computer Science, JAIST, Nomi, Japan

Abstract. CafeOBJ is a language for writing formal specifications of software and hardware systems. It implements equational logic by rewriting and has been used to verify properties of systems using both proof scores and theorem proving. In this paper, we present CiMPG+F, an extension of the CafeInMaude interpreter that, for a large class of CafeOBJ specifications, (i) generates complete proofs from scratch and (ii) fixes incomplete proof scores. CiMPG+F allowed us to prove from scratch the correctness of different protocols, giving us confidence in the approach.

Keywords: CafeOBJ · Theorem Proving · Automatic Proof Inference

1 Introduction

As systems become more and more complex, the verification techniques required to prove that they fulfill some given properties must also evolve to deal with them. Theorem proving is a key methodology for verifying critical properties, such as soundness and completeness, of systems. In contrast to other techniques like model checking [4], theorem proving provides complete confidence in the proven results, but requires in general more effort from the user. Theorem provers usually present a trade-off between flexibility and automation: more flexibility implies less automation and vice versa.

CafeOBJ [6] is a language for writing formal specifications for a wide variety of software and hardware systems, and verifying properties of them. CafeOBJ implements equational logic by rewriting and can be used as a powerful platform for specifying and proving properties of systems. We choose CafeOBJ as specification language because it provides several features to ease the definition

Research partially supported by the Japanese project KAKEN 19H04082, the Spanish projects TIN2015-67522-C3-3-R, PID2019-108528RB-C22, and the Comunidad de Madrid as part of the program S2018/TCS-4339 (BLOQUES-CM) co-funded by EIE Funds of the European Union.

V. K. I. Pun et al. (Eds.): ICTAC 2020, LNCS 12545, pp. 64–82, 2020.
https://doi.org/10.1007/978-3-030-64276-1_4

of systems. These features include a flexible mix-fix syntax, powerful and clear typing system with ordered sorts, parameterized modules and views for instantiating the parameters, module expressions, operators for defining terms (which may include equational axioms, like being associative or having a unit element), and equations for defining the (possibly conditional) equalities between terms, among others. In particular, reasoning modulo equational axioms allows for very natural specifications but also requires proof systems to deal with them in specific ways.

In this paper we focus on CafeInMaude [16], an interpreter of CafeOBJ implemented in Maude [5] that supports both standard theorem proving [15] and proof scores [7] as techniques for verifying properties. CafeInMaude is implemented using Maude's metalevel, which allows users to manipulate Maude modules and terms as usual data. In this way, we have implemented meta-heuristics to help users with their proofs.

The CafeInMaude Proof Assistant (CiMPA) uses structural induction on constructors, implements the theorem of constants [8] and case splitting by equations and terms (with special commands to deal with associative sequences), and uses rewriting as execution mechanism. On the other hand, proof scores are proof outlines that use the same syntax as CafeOBJ, hence providing great flexibility to the user; in particular, new terms can be defined (i.e. to generate the appropriate inductive cases), new case splittings can be added by means of equations, and proofs are carried by using the **red** command, which *reduces* the goal in the enriched module by using all the equations as left-to-right rewrite rules. This proof methodology is very flexible and allows users to prove results using the same features available to specify the system, instead of restricting users to a specific set of proof commands. However, CafeInMaude does not check proof scores in any way, so only standard theorem proving ensures that the given properties really hold. Regarding the trade-off between flexibility and automation discussed above, proof scores are more flexible but less reliable than CiMPA proofs.

In [15], the authors showed that this gap between both tools can be partially closed, at least for those properties that can be proved by using the commands available in CiMPA. Each module in a proof score can be understood as a leaf in a proof tree and presented to the CafeInMaude Proof Generator, CiMPG, which generates a CiMPA proof from a correct proof score, hence guaranteeing the soundness of the proof score. In this paper we present the CafeInMaude Proof Generator & Fixer-upper (CiMPG+F), an extension of CiMPG that:

- Infers proofs from scratch for a wide range of systems. CiMPG+F requires the user to introduce the properties to be proven and the induction variable, and the system tries to find a CiMPA proof that proves the given properties.
- Combines this generation mechanism with proof scores in two ways: (i) if a CiMPA proof is required from an incomplete proof score, CiMPG+F tries to fix it by using the given information to prune the search space; and (ii) when a proof cannot be generated from scratch, the user can provide a (partial) proof score guiding the process; in this way, CiMPG+F is in charge of the mechanical work and leaves the user the creative tasks.

– If the proof fails, the tool shows all the case splittings that it tried, including those goals that were proven and those that failed. This information may guide the user towards the most appropriate case splittings.

The rest of the paper is organized as follows: Sect. 2 presents the basics of CafeOBJ and proof scores and summarizes the main features of the previous version of the tool. Section 3 describes our algorithm for inferring new proofs, while Sect. 4 presents how this mechanism is combined with partial information from proof scores. Section 5 discusses some related work and Sect. 6 presents the benchmarks we have used to test the tool. Finally, Sect. 7 concludes and outlines some lines of future work. The tool and several case studies are available at https://github.com/ariesco/CafeInMaude.

2   Preliminaries

CafeOBJ [6] implements order-sorted equational logic by rewriting. It supports the definition of datatypes by means of sorts and subsort relations, constructors for these datatypes, and functions whose behavior is specified by means of equations. We present as our running example a simplified cloud synchronization protocol as an observational transition system. In this protocol we have a cloud computer and an arbitrary number of PCs, and they try to keep a value synchronized, so new values appearing in the PCs must be uploaded to the cloud and, similarly, PCs must retrieve new values from the cloud. We represent values as natural numbers and consider that larger values are newer to simplify the presentation. In this setting the cloud computer is represented by:

– Its status (`statusc`), which takes the values `idlec` and `busy` (a PC is connected).
– Its current value (`valc`).

Given these ideas, we start our CafeOBJ specification by defining the appropriate datatypes for statuses and values. The module `LABELC` defines the sort `LabelC`, with constructors `idlec` and `busy` (both with the attribute `constr`, standing for *constructor*). It also defines an equation for the built-in function `_=_`; this function is defined for every sort but, by default, it only states that it holds (that is, it returns `true`) for syntactically equal terms, so it does not define the cases when it is reduced to `false`. In this case we indicate that `idlec` is different from `busy`:

```
mod! LABELC {   [LabelC]
  ops idlec busy : -> LabelC {constr}
  eq (idlec = busy) = false . }
```

where the keyword `mod!` indicates the module has tight semantics [2]. Similarly, the module `VALUE` requires the existence of a sort `Value` for values, which has a minimum value `mv` and implements a `_<=_` function that verifies that any value is equal to itself and is larger than `mv`, with `V` of sort `Value`. Note that this module is defined with mod*, indicating it has loose semantics [2].[1] We choose this semantics because, in contrast with to LABELC, different types of values could be used without affecting the behavior of the system:

```
mod* VALUE {   [Value]
  op mv : -> Value {constr}
  op _<=_ : Value Value -> Bool .
  eq (V <= V) = true .
  eq (mv <= V) = true .}
```

In turn, the PCs are represented by:

- Its status (statusp), which takes values idlep, gotval (the PC has fetc.hed the value from the cloud), and updated (the PC has updated either its value or the cloud's value).
- Its current value (valp).
- A temporal value retrieved from the cloud. This value is used to avoid over-writing newer values.

We would specify a module LABELP, similar to LABELC above, for the possible statuses of the PCs. Then, the module CLIENT below requires the existence of a sort Client, which stands for PC identifiers:

```
mod* CLIENT { [Client] }
```

The module CLOUD imports the modules above and defines the sort Sys for the system. The values of the system are obtained via *observers*, that return the status and the value of the cloud (statusc and valc, respectively) and the status, the value, and the temporary value (statusp, valp, and tmp, respectively):

```
mod* CLOUD { pr(LABELP) pr(LABELC) pr(CLIENT) pr(VALUE)
  [Sys]
  op statusc : Sys -> LabelC
  op valc : Sys -> Value
  op statusp : Sys Client -> LabelP
  ops valp tmp : Sys Client -> Value
```

The system is built by means of transitions, whose behavior is shown by using equations for the observers above. These transitions must make sure that only one PC can be connected to the cloud at the same time and that the cloud keeps the newest value. The constructor init stands for the initial state, where all elements are idle and we are not interested in the remaining values:

```
  op init : -> Sys {constr}
  eq statusc(init) = idlec .
  eq statusp(init,I) = idlep .
```

---

[1] Modules with tight semantics have a single model (the initial model), which is unique up to isomorphism. On the other hand, modules with loose semantics indicate that many different implementations (models) for the sorts and operators in the specification satisfy the given axioms.

Next we define the transition `getVal`, that takes as arguments a system and the identifier of the client that is retrieving the value from the cloud. This transition can only be applied if both the cloud computer and the current computer are idle. Hence, we first indicate that, if these conditions do not hold, then the transition is skipped:

```
op getval : Sys Client -> Sys  {constr}
ceq getval(S,I) = S if not(statusp(S,I) = idlep and statusc(S) = idlec) .
```

If the conditions hold then the status of the cloud is busy and the PC goes to gotVal:

```
ceq statusc(getval(S,I)) = busy
  if statusp(S,I) = idlep and statusc(S) = idlec .
ceq statusp(getval(S,I),J) = (if I = J then gotval else statusp(S,J) fi)
  if statusp(S,I) = idlep and statusc(S) = idlec .
```

Similarly, if the conditions hold the temporary value of the computer must be the one of the cloud:

```
ceq tmp(getval(S,I),J) = (if I = J then valc(S) else tmp(S,J) fi)
  if statusp(S,I) = idlep and statusc(S) = idlec .
```

Because this transition retrieves the value from the cloud and stores it in as temporary value, the current values does not change:

```
eq valc(getval(S,I)) = valc(S) .
eq valp(getval(S,I),J) = valp(S,J) .
```

The remaining transitions are `gotoidle`, which indicates the PC has finished the connection and both the PC and the cloud go to idle, `modval`, which updates the value stored in the PC by creating a new value (using an auxiliary function `new(S, C)`, for S a system and C a PC identifier), and `update`, which updates the older value (either in the PC or in the cloud). All of them are defined following the ideas above and are available in the repository. Finally, we define seven properties that must hold in the system:

- If a PC is updated then it has the same value as the cloud PC (inv1).
- If a PC is in gotval, then its temporary value is the one in the cloud (inv2).
- If two PCs are connected to the cloud (the status is different to idlep in both cases) then they are the same PC (invariants inv3, inv4, and inv5).
- If a PC is not idle then the cloud cannot be idle at the same time (invariants inv6 and inv7).

```
ops inv1 inv2 inv6 inv7 : Sys Client -> Bool
ops inv3 inv4 inv5 : Sys Client Client -> Bool
eq inv1(S,I) = (statusp(S,I) = updated implies valp(S,I) = valc(S)) .
eq inv2(S,I) = (statusp(S,I) = gotval implies tmp(S,I) = valc(S)) .
eq inv3(S,I,J) = (statusp(S,I) = updated and
```

```
                       statusp(S,J) = gotval implies I = J) .
  eq inv4(S,I,J) = (statusp(S,I) = gotval and
                       statusp(S,J) = gotval implies I = J) .
  eq inv5(S,I,J) = (statusp(S,I) = updated and
                       statusp(S,J) = updated implies I = J) .
  eq inv6(S,I) = not(statusp(S,I) = updated and statusc(S) = idlec) .
  eq inv7(S,I) = not(statusp(S,I) = gotval and statusc(S) = idlec) . }
```

We can prove these properties using both proof scores and CiMPA, as partially shown in Fig. 1. On the left we present an open-close environment that imports the CLOUD module and discharges the subgoal inv1(getval(s,j),i) in the particular case that the three equations defined in the module hold. Note that all required constants are defined in the environment and that we use the induction hypothesis (shown first with the :nonexec attribute, which indicates that it cannot be directly used for reducing terms; the induction hypotheses for the remaining goals have been skipped for clarity) as the premise of an implication. Because the reduction command returns true when executed we know this particular case holds, but we need another three open-close environments for discharging this subgoal. Note that these environments follow cafeOBJ syntax and can be freely defined by the user; CafeOBJ supports the proof by executing the red command but it does not check that all cases have been discharged (i.e., that all environments have been defined). On the other hand, the code on the right introduces the goal (the remaining goals have been skipped for clarity), asks CiMPA to apply induction on S:Sys and applies the theorem of constants (:apply(tc)), which substitutes variables by fresh constants and generates seven subgoals, one for each property that we want to prove, the first subgoal being inv1(getval(S#Sys,C#Client),C@Client) (where fresh constants generated by induction contain # followed by the sort name and fresh constants generated by the theorem of constants use @ instead of #). Then, we ask CiMPA to apply case splitting on a given equation (note that it is equivalent to the first equation on the proof score), which would generate two subgoals (one where the equation holds and another one where it does not hold); we would introduce two more case splittings and use the implication command to reach the same case shown for the open-close environment on the left and then, that would be discharged with CiMPA red command; then we would continue with the subgoals generated by the case splittings. Note that in this case we use CiMPA syntax but the tool makes sure we prove all required cases. CiMPG+F aims to generate a CiMPA proof (like the one on the right) from an incomplete set of open-close environments (like the one on the left). In particular, CiMPG+F can generate proofs by providing a single environment indicating the goals and the variable used for induction.

```
open CLOUD .                    open CLOUD .
  op s : -> Sys .                 :goal{
  ops i j : -> Client .             eq [cloud :nonexec] :
  eq [inv1 :nonexec] :                  inv1(S:Sys,C:Client) = true .
      inv1(s,K:Client) = true .     ...}
  ...                             :ind on (S:Sys)
  eq statusp(s,j) = idlep .       :apply(si)
  eq statusc(s) = idlec .         :apply(tc)
  eq i = j .                      :def csb1 = :ctf {
  red inv1(s,i) implies             eq statusp(S#Sys,C#Client) = idlep .}
      inv1(getval(s,j),i) .       :apply(csb1)
close                             ...
```

Fig. 1. Proof fragments: proof score (left) and CiMPA proof (right)

Require: Module m, goal g, depth d, implication bound i, variables bound v.
Ensure: p contains the proof for g or $\emptyset$ if the proof is not found.

1: $p \leftarrow \emptyset$
2: **if** INDUCTIONREQUIRED(g) **then** $(g, m, p) \leftarrow$ APPLYINDUCTION(m, g)
3: **end if**
4: **return** GENPROOF(m, g, d, i, v, p)
5: **function** GENPROOF(m, g, d, i, v, p)
6:     **if** HASVARS(g) **or** MULTIPLEGOALS(g) **then** $(g, m, p) \leftarrow$ THOFCONS(m, g, p)
7:     **end if**
8:     $(found, p') \leftarrow$ DISCHARGE(m, g, i, v, p)
9:     **if** $\neg found$ & $(d > 0)$ **then**
10:         $cs \leftarrow$ GENERATE(m, g)
11:         **while** $cs \neq \emptyset$ **and** $\neg found$ **do**
12:             $c \leftarrow$ POP(cs)
13:             $(m', g', p') \leftarrow$ APPLY(m, p, c)
14:             $(found, p') \leftarrow$ GENPROOF($m', g', d - 1, i, v, p'$)
15:         **end while**
16:     **end if**
17:     **return** $(found, p')$
18: **end function**

Fig. 2. Main algorithm for CiMPG+F

3   Inferring New Proofs

In this section we briefly describe how to generate proofs for a given goal (either the initial goal or a subgoal), describing in detail the main functions of the algorithm. Then, we will illustrate these ideas with the Cloud protocol above.

3.1 Proof Generation

Figure 2 presents the main algorithm for CiMPG+F. Because the tool requires the user to introduce the goal and to identify the variable used for induction, the first step might be applying induction (Line 2); in this sense, the function INDUCTIONREQUIRED just checks whether there is a variable pointed out by the user for induction. If induction has been applied, the main function, GENPROOF (Lines 5–18), is called. This function requires, in addition to the goal, the module where the evaluation takes place, and the maximum depth, two extra parameters: how many implications can be used (in addition to the implication with the hypothesis corresponding to the goal we want to prove, which is always tried) and how many variables can be instantiated. The function first checks whether there are other variables that must be transformed into constants by using the theorem of constants (Line 6). This command is also used to split the goal into several subgoals when required. Once the goal contains no variables and consists of exactly one property, we start the backtracking algorithm. The base case is reached when the goal can be discharged by the DISCHARGE function (Line 8, see Section 3.2). Otherwise, if we have not reached the depth given as parameter, the GENERATE function (Line 10, see Section 3.3) returns a list of case splittings for continuing the process. The function APPLY (Line 13), in charge of applying the case splitting, was already implemented in CiMPA.

Note that, by interacting with the d, i, and v bounds the user can reduce/widen the search space for particular subgoals, hence finding proofs for more complex goals but making the process more expensive.

3.2 Discharging Goals

The function DISCHARGE in the previous section checks whether the current subgoal can be discharged (i.e. it is reduced to **true**) by using reductions and implications with the induction hypotheses. That is, the term to be reduced has the general form $\ldots \rightarrow hypothesis_j(h_1, \ldots, h_{n_j}) \rightarrow \ldots \rightarrow subgoal(t_1, \ldots, t_{n_s})$. We have a twofold combinatorial explosion when dealing with implications:

1. We need to try all possible sequences of hypotheses, varying both the number of hypotheses and their order.
2. Induction hypotheses may have free variables, which must be instantiated with either fresh constants or terms built with constructors.

Because the DISCHARGE function is used in all nodes, it should not be expensive. In order to control the issues above we use the values i (for the first issue) and v (for the second one) introduced in the previous section. Recommended values for d, i, and v are 5, 1, and 2,[2] respectively, although the values can be customized for each specific case, as discussed in Sect. 7.

In order to alleviate the second issue, we noticed that, when reducing terms with variables, we obtained some terms of the form $f(\ldots, v_i, \ldots) = f(\ldots, t_i, \ldots)$,

---

[2] These values are obtained empirically, refining possibly bigger values that might ensure the proof is found.

with v_i a variable and t_i a ground term. We used these terms to compute a "pre-instantiation" $\ldots, v_i \mapsto t_i, \ldots$ that greatly reduces the number of free variables and makes the function cost-effective for large specifications. Finally, take into account that if the number of free variables is greater than the parameter v the instantiation is not tried.

3.3   Finding Case Splittings

The case splittings that can be inferred by CiMPG+F are those that can be executed by CiMPG [15]: by equations (distinguishing whether the equation holds or not) and by terms (distinguishing the different values, built using only

Require: Module m and goal g.
Ensure: cs is a list of pairs $(c, type)$, being c a term and $type$ the type of case splitting.
1: **function** GENERATE(m, g)
2:     $cs \leftarrow []$ $noSubs \leftarrow \emptyset$
3:     $red \leftarrow$ REDUCE(m, g)
4:     $equals \leftarrow$ GETEQUALITIES(red)
5:     **for each** $hypothesis \in m$ **do**
6:         $red \leftarrow$ REDUCE$(m, hypothesis \rightarrow g)$
7:         $equals \leftarrow equals \cup$ GETEQUALITIES(red)
8:     **end for**
9:     **for each** $t = t' \in equals$ **do**   ▷ The following loop would be repeated for t'
10:         **for each** $\theta \mid \theta(l) = t \mid_{pos}$ & $eq\ l = r\ if c_1 = c'_1 \wedge \cdots \wedge c_n = c'_n \in m$ **do**
11:             $cond \leftarrow$ REDUCE$(m, \theta c_i = \theta c'_i)$ ▷ for i the first condition that fails
12:             $equals \leftarrow equals \cup$ GETEQUALITIES$(cond)$
13:         **end for**
14:         **if** not entered any of the previous loops **then** $noSubs \leftarrow noSubs \cup t = t'$
15:         **end if**
16:     **end for**
17:     **for each** $t = t' \in noSubs$ **do**   ▷ We assume $t > t'$
18:         **if** ONLYCTORS(t') **then** $cs \leftarrow cs +$ SUBTERMS(t)
19:         **else** $cs \leftarrow cs + (t = t', eq) +$ SUBTERMS$(t) +$ SUBTERMS(t')
20:         **end if**
21:     **end for**
22:     **return** cs
23: **end function**
24: **function** SUBTERMS(t)
25:     $cs \leftarrow []$
26:     **for each** subterm t' of t s.t. t' has a function symbol at the top **do**
27:         **if** ISASSOCSEQ(t') **then** $cs \leftarrow cs + (t, seq)$
28:         **else** $cs \leftarrow cs + (t, term)$
29:         **end if**
30:     **end for**
31:     **return** PRIORITIZE(cs)
32: **end function**

Fig. 3. GENERATE and SUBTERMS functions

constructors and fresh constants, that this term might take). In the second case CiMPG provides special cases for associative sequences of elements with identity, so it is possible to distinguish particular elements in different positions of the sequence.

As the number of terms that can be built in any given module is generally infinite, the number of case splittings that can be defined for a given proof are potentially infinite as well. CiMPG+F uses the current goal to focus on those case splittings that might lead to true. Figure 3(Lines 1–23) presents the structure of the GENERATE function. It first initializes in Line 2 cs (the list of case splittings) and $noSubs$ (the set of equalities with candidates for case splitting), reduces the current goal to its normal form (Line 3), and extracts the equalities in the thus obtained term (Line 4). It might be also the case that an implication with an induction hypothesis is required to obtain the appropriate case splitting, hence requiring beforehand to introduce a case splitting related to that hypothesis. For this reason, we extract in Lines 5–8 the equalities when using implication with each hypothesis (we assume repeated terms are not taken into account).

We traverse these equalities (Lines 9–16) looking for substitutions that make the left-hand side of an equation match the terms in the equality at any position (note that the figure only presents the loop for t, another one would be required for t'). If such a substitution is found we analyze why the equation was not applied (we know it was not applied because we have previously reduced the term); because it matches the left-hand side the only reason is that one of the conditions failed, so we pick the first one that failed and add it to set of equalities we are traversing. If no substitution is found it means the equality cannot be further reduced, so we keep it in $noSubs$.

In Lines 17–22 we traverse the equalities we could not apply equations to ($noSubs$). It is important to note that the specification must keep being terminating after adding the case splittings. For this reason, the loop assumes a total order $>$ over the terms, so given the terms t and t', with $t > t'$, then we use the equation $t = t'$ instead of $t' = t$. Note that, given the terms t, built only with constructors, and t, which includes at least a function symbol, we always have $t > t'$. This order is automatically created by CiMPG+F in each case.

Because we assume equalities are defined for constructors, for an equality $t = t'$ ($t > t'$) that was not reduced at least t contains a function symbol. If t' does not contain a function symbol then we only focus on the case splittings generated by t (because in this case the equation is included in the case splitting by terms) using the auxiliary function SUBTERMS, explained below; otherwise we extract case splittings from both t and t' and include the case splitting by equations of the whole equality.

Finally, the PRIORITIZE function implements two heuristics for ordering the case splittings that we found empirically useful: it first tries those case splittings directly obtained from the goal, instead of the ones obtained from the implications in Lines 5–8. It also prioritizes case splittings for associative sequences, because they are more detailed and usually more powerful than standard case splittings.

The auxiliary function SUBTERMS traverses all the subterms of a given term with a function symbol at the top and selects the most appropriate case splitting for it: if the sort of the term is built by means of an associative constructor with unit element, then the special for case splitting for associative sequences is used; otherwise, standard case splitting by terms is used.

3.4   Analyzing the Cloud Protocol

We present here how the proof for the Cloud protocol in Sect. 2 is generated; the parameters d, i, and v from Sect. 3.1 take the values 5, 1, and 2, respectively. The proof starts when the user introduces the open-close environments below. The one on the left, labeled as proofCLOUD, introduces the goals. It uses a variable S:Sys, which indicates that induction takes place on this argument, and fresh constants for the remaining parameters. Then, the environment on the right uses the command :infer to ask CiMPG+F to generate a proof for proofCLOUD:

```
open CLOUD .                          open CLOUD .
  :id(proofCLOUD)                       :infer(proofCLOUD)
                                      close
  ops i j : -> Client .

  red inv1(S:Sys, i) .
  red inv2(S:Sys, i) .
  red inv3(S:Sys, i, j) .
  red inv4(S:Sys, i, j) .
  red inv5(S:Sys, i, j) .
  red inv6(S:Sys, i) .
  red inv7(S:Sys, i) .
close
```

CiMPG+F starts by applying simultaneous induction, which generates five subgoals corresponding to the five constructors shown above (each of them containing the seven properties) following the alphabetical order of constructors, and the main body of the GENPROOF function (see Fig. 2) is started. It first applies the theorem of constants, which generates seven subgoals (one for each property) for the first constructor, getval. Hence, the first subgoal that needs to be proven is inv1(getval(S, C),i), for S and C fresh constants of sort Sys and Client, respectively. Note that CiMPG+F stores the definition of the fresh constants and the induction hypotheses using S (e.g.. inv1(S, I:Client), inv2(S, I:Client), inv3(S, I:Client, J:Client), etc.).

We would apply now the DISCHARGE function to the goal, which will not find any way to reduce it to true. As our bounds allow CiMPG+F to use one extra implication (besides the one with inv1 itself) it tries, for example, an implication with all the possible instantiations of inv3(S, I:Client, J:Client). This is allowed because we indicated that up to two free variables are allowed, so a possible instantiation would be inv3(S, C, C) and CiMPG+F would try inv3(S, C, C) implies inv1(S, i) implies inv1(getval(S,C), i).

Because the goal was not discharged we use the GENERATE function to obtain the possible case splittings. Figure 4 summarizes the generation process. For the sake of simplicity, we do not show the analysis for the terms generated by using implications with the hypotheses (Lines 5–8 in Fig. 3). We take the goal (top of the figure) and reduce it, obtaining the next term (note that it contains functions such as xor, obtained by applying the predefined equations for Boolean expressions). This term contains two equalities (one of them, updated = statusp(getval(S,C),i), appears twice), that are extracted in the next level, which shows the initial members of the *equals* variable.

For the term statusp(getval(S,C),i) we find an equation that could be applied but the first condition, statusp(S,C) = idlep, failed. We add this equality to *equals*, but we do not find any other substitution that allows us to instantiate an equation, so the *noSubs* set consists of both statusp(S,C) = idlep and valc(S) = valp(S,i).

Finally, we traverse these equalities to obtain *cs*. Because idlep is a constructor, for the first equality we just generate (statusp(S,C), term), indicating that it requires case splitting by constructors. On the other hand, for the second equality we have a case splitting for the whole term by true/false and case splittings by constructors for the left-hand and the right-hand sides. Note that in our example we have no sequences, so this case splitting cannot be found.

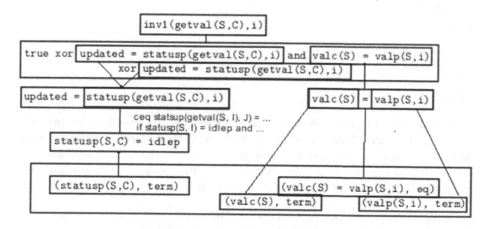

Fig. 4. Case splitting inference

As shown in Fig. 1, the first case splitting required for this proof is (statusp(S,C), term). If chosen by the backtracking algorithm, the next set of case splitting generated by the tool would be very similar to the one above, because the goal is reduced to the same term shown in Fig. 4. In this case the condition that fails is the second one, statusc(S) = idlec, which in turn generates the case splitting (statusc(S), term). Figure 1 also shows that this case splitting is required for the proof.

CiMPG+F would continue the proof with this strategy, finally finding a proof that requires 530 commands (the computation time is less than one second). In order to find this proof it needs to use some extra strategies not shown here, in particular using implications with the hypotheses as premises. Note that not even one of these commands can be inferred with the previous version of the tool without the user intervention.

3.5   Understanding Failures

In case a proof is not found, CiMPG+F shows the case splittings that were applied, the subgoals that could be discarded and the ones that failed because either (i) no more case splittings were available or (ii) the bound on the depth of the backtracking algorithm is reached. For each goal and subgoal it shows the case splitting that was tried and how it behaved; because several case splittings are in general possible for each goal it shows all of them, numbering them and using indentation for the sake of readability.

In our cloud example we can reduce the number of backtracking levels to 1 to see how this feature behaves, because it is not enough to prove the first goal. It starts the proof and first applies induction and the theorem of constants, just as we discussed in the previous sections:

```
open CLOUD .
 :goal{...}

 :ind on (S:Sys)
 :apply(si)

 :apply(tc)
```

Then, it tries to prove the first goal. It first tries to apply a case splitting by the equation valc(S#Sys) = valp(S#Sys,i@Client), which generates two subgoals. The fist one can be discharged (it just requires the term to be reduced), but the second one would require more case splittings, so it fails because the maximum depth for backtracking has been reached:

```
*** Goal 1, Try 1 -  inv1(getval(S#Sys,C#Client),i@Client) - Failure
:def csb1 = :ctf {eq valc(S#Sys) = valp(S#Sys,i@Client).}
:apply(csb1)

 *** Goal 1-1 Success by reduction
 :apply (rd)

*** Goal 1-2 cannot be discharged. Maximum depth reached.
```

It tries next a case splitting by the term statusc(S#Sys). Again the first subgoal can be discharged (in this case it requires to use an implication first) but again the second one reaches the maximum depth:

```
*** Goal 1, Try 2 -  inv1(getval(S#Sys,C#Client),i@Client) - Failure
:def csb1 = :ctf [statusc(S#Sys) .]
:apply(csb1)


*** Goal 1-1 Success by implication and reduction.
:imp [proofCLOUD] by {i:Client <- i@Client ;}
:apply (rd)


*** Goal 1-2 cannot be discharged. Maximum depth reached.
```

Once all possible case splittings have been tried CiMPG+F would move to the next goal (for `inv2`) and would show similar information. Using this information the user can decide if a particular case splitting is promising and use it to guide the proof, as described in the next section, or just provide a larger bound if he/she considers the current one was too small.

```
open CLOUD .
  op s : -> Sys .
  ops i j : -> Client .
  eq [inv1 :nonexec] :
       inv1(s,K:Client) = true .
  . . .
  eq statusp(s,j) = idlep .
  red inv1(getval(s,j),i) .
close
```

Fig. 5. Proof score for guiding the proof

4   Guiding CiMPG+F Using Proof Scores

As explained above, CiMPG+F uses backtracking to try to find a proof. However, for large specifications each step is computationally expensive because many case splittings are possible and many implications and instantiations can be used to check whether a subgoal has been proven, making the approach unfeasible. Moreover, because fully automated theorem provers cannot deal with large or complex specifications, user interaction is required to complete proofs for these systems. Finally, it might be the case that the user is stuck in a particular subgoal; because CiMPG+F prints all the branches it tried, it might help the user to focus on more promising case splittings.

In [15], we showed that each open-close environment in a proof score stands for a "branch" of the proof tree that can be reproduced by a CiMPA proof. Using this idea, it is possible to feed CiMPG+F with an incomplete proof score, which must contain the case splittings that will be used first. The CiMPG algorithm will reconstruct the proof to that point and then execute CiMPG+F to try to generate the rest of the proof.

Note, however, that a single equation might not determine the case splitting. For example, Fig. 5 presents a reduced version of the proof score in Fig. 1 for the inductive case `getval`. It suggests a case splitting using `eq statusp(s,j) = idlep`. Because `idlep` is a constructor we do not know whether it suggests a case-splitting true/false (with the complementary equation `eq (statusp(s,j) = idlep) = false`) or by constructors (with the complementary equations `eq pc2(s) = gotval` and `eq pc2(s) = updated`). In this case CiMPG+F would collect the equations from the remaining open-close environments related to this inductive case and analyze whether: (i) all the equations required to the splitting are present. In this case the case splitting is applied and the standard analysis used by CiMPG continues; (ii) if the splitting is not unambiguously identified, we need to try each of them and, if the proof fails, try again with the next possible splitting. If all proofs fail a new proof is tried following the algorithm in Sect. 3.

Assume now that part of the proof for the cloud protocol is too complex for generating it automatically, or we just know it requires some extra implications that will slow down the rest of the proof so we want to feed them to CiMPG+F directly, which may happen in our case for the inductive case `inv1(update(s,j),i)`. In that case we can introduce environments like:

```
open CLOUD .
  :id(proofCLOUD)

  op s : -> Sys .
  ops i j : -> Client .
  eq statusc(s) = busy .
  eq statusp(s,j) = gotval .
  eq i = j .
  eq tmp(s,j) <= valp(s,j) = false .
  red inv2(s,j) implies inv1(s,i) implies inv1(update(s,j),i) .
close
open CLOUD .
  :id(cloud)

  op s : -> Sys .
  ops i j : -> Client .
  eq (statusc(s) = busy) = false .
  red inv1(s,i) implies inv1(update(s,j),i) .
close
```

where we specify the case splittings and the implications required to partially prove the goal. Note that we have specified the case splittings partially, because for `statusp(s,j) = gotval` CiMPG+F does not know if it is case splitting by terms or by equations, but for `statusc(s) = busy` it can infer it is by equations (it finds the complementary equation in the second environment), for `i = j` it must be by equations, because `j` is not a constructor, and for `tmp(s,j) <= valp(s,j) = false` it only makes sense to have the complementary equation `tmp(s,j) <= valp(s,j) = true`, that is, we have case splitting by terms with `tmp(s,j) <= valp(s,j)`.

Regarding the implication, these environments state both the hypotheses and the instantiations required, so CiMPG+F does not need to try all possible cases.

5   Related Work

Theorem proving is a well established field, with several state-of-the-art theorem provers. Possibly two of the most used interactive theorem provers are Isabelle/HOL [14] and Coq [11]. These theorem provers implement powerful commands combining several heuristics for trying to automatically discharge goals. Regarding automatic theorem provers, although they are usually more limited than interactive ones, some of them, like Spass [17], even support (limited) inductive proofs. The advantages of CiMPG+F with respect to these provers are: (i) CafeOBJ is a high-level language for specifying systems, not for specifically proving theorems, which provides users with a much richer syntax, and (ii) while heuristics are general, CiMPG+F strategies are specific for each goal, making them appropriate for novel situations. Finally, note that the trace returned when a proof fails might help the user for the next try.

Table 1. Benchmarks for CiMPG+F

Name	Spec. size	Proof size	Time	Description
2p-mutex	58	23	<1 s	2 processes mutex
ABP	320	1370	~2.5 h	Alternating bit protocol
Cloud	127	530	<1 s	Simplified cloud synchronization protocol
NSLPK	188	342	617 s	Authentication protocol NSLPK
Qlock	124	88	<1 s	Variant of Dijkstra's binary semaphore
SCP	182	200	340 s	Simple Communication Protocol
TAS	73	88	<1 s	Spinlock - Mutual exclusion protocol

Automatic software repair [10] is a field of growing interest. For example, in model checking a logic-based machine learning technique (inductive logic programming) has been used to automatically repair models [1]. We propose the complementary approach, where the model is assumed correct and we try to "fix" the proof by closing gaps. Note that this fixing includes automatically generating new case splittings, which is beyond the standard automatic strategies integrated in other theorem provers, where a fixed set of previously generated lemmas is applied.

A similar approach to CiMPG+F was proposed in [13], whose authors present Crème, a tool checking invariants in CafeOBJ OTS specifications by trying case splitting. Crème's main advantage with respect to CiMPG+F is that Crème is able to generate a counterexample when the invariant does not hold. However, it presents a number of problems: it can only use case splitting for Boolean terms, greatly limiting the proofs it can tackle; it is not directed by the current goal and the module, hence generating a much bigger state space; and it is not directly implemented in Maude but in Common Lisp, which greatly reduces its efficiency. For these reasons Crème is restricted to particular examples, while CiMPG+F has been applied to many protocols implemented in CafeOBJ.

6 Benchmarks

We discuss in this section the benchmarks we have used to test CiMPG+F. We have used CiMPG+F to completely generate proofs for different protocols; the results are presented in Table 1 (times measured with a Mac Book Pro i5 2,4 GHz, 16 GB). In particular, we have:

- The 2p-mutex benchmark is a simple mutual exclusion protocol with exactly two processes, where we prove mutual exclusion between them (a single goal).
- The ABP benchmark, which will be explained in detail below, is a communication protocol between two agents that can be understood as a simplified version of TCP. In this protocol we consider that the channels are unreliable, in the sense the information might be repeated or lost. In our case we prove that all messages are delivered in the proper order.
- Cloud refers to the simplified cloud protocol discussed in the previous sections of this paper.
- The Needham-Schroeder-Lowe Public Key Protocol, NSLPK [12], is an improvement of the NSPK protocol that fixes a man-in-the-middle attack. In this case we prove that an intruder cannot reach the information. Although this protocol is simpler than ABP, the case splittings are non trivial and illustrate an interesting application of our tool.
- Qlock is a mutual exclusion protocol that introduces a queue to deal with the different processes. We check both mutual exclusion and that only the process on the top of the queue can go into the critical section.
- SCP is a simplified version of the ABP, which uses unreliable cells as communication channels between senders and receivers. In this case we need to prove the reliable communication property: if a receiver gets n packets, then they are the first n packets dispatched by the sender, and they have been received in the same order they were sent.
- TAS (Test & Set) is a mutual exclusion protocol that uses a shared lock to grant the access to the critical section. The proof ensures that at most one process enters the critical section.

All the proofs are equal to or simpler than the manual proofs already developed for these protocols by the authors and others, see [15] for details. In particular, in many cases the implication with the induction hypothesis was used in manual proofs but nor really required. All the benchmarks but ABP work with a single configuration each (definition of bounds for implications, free variables, and backtracking depth); ABP requires 5 configurations, one for 95 out of 99 subgoals and one for each one of the remaining subgoals. These different configurations are required because the number of implications or free variables is higher, so using these bounds for the whole proof would generate a much bigger search space. Moreover, in these cases the required depth is also smaller, which allows us to optimize them. It is worth noting that the values used for the configurations are the smallest possible; they have been obtained empirically by progressively reducing larger values.

It is worth briefly discussing the most complex benchmark, ABP. The ABP protocol [3] has been used for benchmarking many different formal verification approaches, as discussed in [9]; a completely automatic proof indicates that the tool has a fair maturity level and can be used in practice. In fact, all the approaches thus far required user interaction in some degree, so in this sense CiMPG+F improves previous results obtained in the context of rewriting systems. ABP requires complex case splittings on associative sequences so, besides its size, the proof obtained is complex and illustrates the power of CafeOBJ as specification language and CiMPG+F as theorem generator. Moreover, ABP makes intensive use of pre-instantiation of variables and requires a limitation in the number of implications (in this case 11 properties are proven, including lemmas) to work, because otherwise the state space grew too quickly. In fact, pre-instantiation makes the computation of each node more than 300 times faster in some cases (from more than 3 min to less than one second).

7   Concluding Remarks and Ongoing Work

In this paper we have presented CiMPG+F, a tool that tries to automatically prove properties of CafeOBJ specifications. These proofs can be based on known information or completely generated by using a bounded depth-first search directed by the current goal and system, which greatly reduces the state space. CiMPG+F optimizes some subtasks, like instantiation of free variables, and provides three parameters to customize the generated proofs. The performance of the tool has been tested with some benchmarks; the results show that it behaves well in general and can be successfully used with average protocols.

As future work, we are interested in informing the user whether a goal is not provable, which happens when we are able to reduce it to `false` and there are no contradictions in the module. Finally, although CiMPG+F works well in general, we have already discussed that we do not want to limit its application to the generation of complete proofs. For this reason, we think it is worth making CiMPG+F more interactive. It could show information in a graphical way about those branches that have been traversed without reaching a result and those branches that have not been traversed yet; in this way the user could understand which case-splittings are not working, pick some of the ones that have not been used and suggest new ones. We think that this interaction would ease the proofs of advanced protocols, which cannot be automatically generated in general and require too much time from users.

References

1. Alrajeh, D., Kramer, J., Russo, A., Uchitel, S.: Elaborating requirements using model checking and inductive learning. IEEE Trans. Software Eng. **39**(3), 361–383 (2013)
2. Astesiano, E., Kreowski, H.-J., Krieg-Brueckner, B. (eds.): Algebraic Foundations of Systems Specification, 1st edn. Springer, Heidelberg (1999). https://doi.org/10.1007/978-3-642-59851-7
3. Bartlett, K.A., Scantlebury, R.A., Wilkinson, P.T.: A note on reliable full-duplex transmission over half-duplex links. Commun. ACM **12**(5), 260–261 (1969)
4. Clarke, E.M., Grumberg, O., Peled, D.A.: Model Checking. MIT Press, Cambridge (1999)
5. Clavel, M., Durán, F., Eker, S., Lincoln, P., Martí-Oliet, N., Meseguer, J., Talcott, C.: All About Maude - A High-Performance Logical Framework. LNCS, vol. 4350. Springer, Heidelberg (2007). https://doi.org/10.1007/978-3-540-71999-1
6. Futatsugi, K., Diaconescu, R.: CafeOBJ Report. AMAST Series. World Scientific, Singapore (1998)
7. Futatsugi, K., Gâinâ, D., Ogata, K.: Principles of proof scores in CafeOBJ. Theoret. Comput. Sci. **464**, 90–112 (2012)
8. Găină, D., Lucanu, D., Ogata, K., Futatsugi, K.: On automation of OTS/CafeOBJ method. In: Iida, S., Meseguer, J., Ogata, K. (eds.) Specification, Algebra, and Software. LNCS, vol. 8373, pp. 578–602. Springer, Heidelberg (2014). https://doi.org/10.1007/978-3-642-54624-2_29
9. Gâinâ, D., Tutu, I., Riesco, A.: Specification and verification of invariant properties of transition systems. In: 25th Asia-Pacific Software Engineering Conference, APSEC 2018, pp. 99–108. IEEE (2018)
10. Gazzola, L., Micucci, D., Mariani, L.: Automatic software repair: a survey. IEEE Trans. Software Eng. **45**(1), 34–67 (2019)
11. Huet, G., Kahn, G., Paulin-Mohring, C.: The Coq proof assistant: a tutorial: version 7.2. Technical report 256, INRIA (2002)
12. Lowe, G.: An attack on the needham-schroeder public-key authentication protocol. Inf. Process. Lett. **56**(3), 131–133 (1995)
13. Nakano, M., Ogata, K., Nakamura, M., Futatsugi, K.: Creme: an automatic invariant prover of behavioral specifications. Int. J. Software Eng. Knowl. Eng. **17**(6), 783–804 (2007)
14. Nipkow, T., Wenzel, M., Paulson, L.C. (eds.): Isabelle/HOL. LNCS, vol. 2283. Springer, Heidelberg (2002). https://doi.org/10.1007/3-540-45949-9
15. Riesco, A., Ogata, K.: Prove it! Inferring formal proof scripts from CafeOBJ proof scores. ACM Trans. Software Eng. Methodol. **27**(2) (2018)
16. Riesco, A., Ogata, K., Futatsugi, K.: A maude environment for CafeOBJ. Formal Aspects Comput. **29**(2), 309–334 (2016). https://doi.org/10.1007/s00165-016-0398-7
17. Weidenbach, C., Dimova, D., Fietzke, A., Kumar, R., Suda, M., Wischnewski, P.: SPASS Version 3.5. In: Schmidt, R.A. (ed.) CADE 2009. LNCS (LNAI), vol. 5663, pp. 140–145. Springer, Heidelberg (2009). https://doi.org/10.1007/978-3-642-02959-2_10

Statistical Analysis of Non-deterministic Fork-Join Processes

Antoine Genitrini⍟, Martin Pépin$^{(\boxtimes)}$⍟, and Frédéric Peschanski⍟

Sorbonne Université, CNRS, LIP6, UMR7606, 75005 Paris, France
{antoine.genitrini,martin.pepin,frederic.peschanski}@lip6.fr

Abstract. We study the combinatorial structure of concurrent programs with non-deterministic choice and a fork-join style of coordination. As a first step we establish a link between these concurrent programs and a class of combinatorial structures. Based on this combinatorial interpretation, we develop and experiment algorithms aimed at the statistical exploration of the state-space of programs. The first algorithm is a uniform random sampler of bounded executions, providing a suitable default exploration strategy. The second algorithm is a random sampler of execution prefixes that allows to control the exploration with respect to the uniform distribution. The fundamental characteristic of these algorithms is that they work on the control graph of the programs and not directly on their state-space, thus providing a way to tackle the state explosion problem.

Keywords: Concurrency · Non-determinism · Fork-Join processes · Loops · Combinatorics · Uniform random generation

1 Introduction

Analyzing the state-space of concurrent programs is a notoriously difficult task, if only because of the infamous *state explosion* problem. Several techniques have been developed to "fight" this explosion: symbolic encoding of the state-space, partial order reductions, exploiting symmetries, etc. An alternative approach is to adopt a probabilistic point of view, for example by developing statistical analysis techniques such as [14]. The basic idea is to generate random executions from program descriptions, sacrificing exhaustiveness for the sake of tractability. However, there is an important difference between generating an *arbitrary* execution and generating a random execution according to a known (typically the uniform) distribution. Only the latter allows to estimate the coverage of the state-space of a given analysis.

As a preliminary, we have to find suitable combinatorial interpretations for the fundamental constructions of concurrent programs. In this paper, we study

---

This research was partially supported by the ANR MetACOnc project ANR-15-CE40-0014.

V. K. I. Pun et al. (Eds.): ICTAC 2020, LNCS 12545, pp. 83–102, 2020.
https://doi.org/10.1007/978-3-030-64276-1_5

a class of programs that uses a *fork-join* model of synchronization, together with loops and a choice construct for *non-determinism*. This is a simple formalism but it is non-trivial in terms of the concurrency features it provides. Most importantly, the underlying combinatorial interpretation is already quite involved. In previous work we studied the combinatorial interpretation of three fundamental aspects of concurrency: *parallelism* (as interleaving) interpreted as (strictly) increasing labelled structures [8], *non-determinism* as partial labelling [7] and *synchronization* as non-strict labelling [9]. In this paper, we integrate these various interpretations into a single unified combinatorial specification based on the *symbolic method* of [2]. The main interest of this specification of process behaviors is that we can then obtain, in a systematic way, the *generating function* for the possible executions of a given program. Because we only study finite objects, the executions are considered of bounded length. At the theoretical level, this is often a suitable starting point for the study of a quantitative problem in analytic combinatorics (cf. e.g. [8]). At a more practical level, the combinatorial specification is also a good source of algorithmic investigations, which is our main concern in the present paper.

The first problem we study is that of *counting* the number of executions (of bounded length) of the programs. This is the problem one has to tackle to precisely quantify the so-called state "explosion", and it is also an important building block of our algorithmic toolbox. Unfortunately, counting executions of concurrent programs is in fact hard in the general case. We show in [9] that even for simple programs only allowing *barrier synchronization*, counting executions is a $\sharp P$-complete problem[1]. Fork-join parallelism enables a good balance between tractability and expressivity by enforcing some structure in the state-space. A second problem is caused by non-determinism because for each non-deterministic choice we have to select a unique branch of execution. Moreover, choices can be nested so that the number of possibilities can grow exponentially. Relying on an efficient encoding of the state-space as generating functions, we manage to count executions without expanding the choices. Of course counting executions has no direct practical application, but it is an essential requirement for two complementary and more interesting analysis techniques. First, we develop an efficient algorithm to generate executions of a given process uniformly at random, for a given bounded execution length. Without prior knowledge of the state-space, the uniform distribution yields the best coverage, with the best diversity of outputs. The second algorithm generates random prefixes, which allows the user to introduce some *bias* in the statistical exploration strategy, e.g. towards regions of interest of the state-space, while still giving a good coverage and most importantly still giving control over the distribution. A fundamental characteristics of these algorithms is that they work on the syntactic representation of the program and do not require the explicit construction of the state-space, hence enabling the analysis of systems of a rather large size.

---

[1] A function f is in $\sharp P$ if there is a polynomial-time non-deterministic Turing machine M such that for any instance x, $f(x)$ is the number of executions of M that accept x as input [23].

The outline of the paper is as follows. In Sect. 2 we present the program class of non-deterministic fork-join programs, as well as its combinatorial interpretation. In Sect. 3 we present in details the two random sampling algorithms discussed above. Finally, Sect. 4 provides a preliminary experimental study of the algorithms[2].

Related Work. Our study combines viewpoints and techniques from concurrency theory and combinatorics. A similar line of work exists for the so-called "true concurrency" model (by opposition to the interleaving semantics that we use in our study) based on the trace monoid using *heaps combinatorics* (see [1,18]). To our knowledge these only address the parallelism issue and not non-determinism *per se*. In [3], the authors cover the problem of the uniform random generation of words in a class of synchronised automata. This approach is able to cover a slightly more expressive set of programs but this comes at the cost of the construction of a product (synchronizing) automaton of exponential size in the worst case. Another approach, investigated in the context of Monte-Carlo model-checking, is based on the combinatorics of *lassos*, which relates to the verification of some temporal-logic properties over potentially *infinite* executions. In [15], the authors of this method highlight the importance of uniformity. Later [21] gives a uniform random sampler of *lassos*, however relying on the costly explicit construction of the whole state-space, hence unpractical for even small processes. Finally [10] studies the random generation of executions in a model similar to the one we cover by extending the framework of Boltzmann sampling. Although Boltzmann samplers are usually fast, they turn out to be impractical in this context because of the heavy symbolic computations imposed by the interplay between parallelism and synchronisation.

If compared to [7], which discusses non-determinism without synchronization, we adopt in the present paper a more direct and simpler encoding of non-deterministic choices, which significantly improves both the theoretical and practical developments. The algorithms presented in the paper are in consequence much more efficient in practice, while covering a more expressive language.

2 Non-deterministic Fork-Join Programs with Loops

We introduce in this section a simple class of concurrent programs featuring a fork-join programming style with non-deterministic choices and loops. The interest is twofold. First it showcases non-determinism in interaction with a non-trivial programming model, which gives insights about its quantitative and algorithmic aspects. Second the language supports a simple model of iteration, for which we give a combinatorial interpretation. In terms of expressivity, this is an important step forward compared to our previous work (see [5,7,8] for instance). Throughout the paper we will refer to this class as the class of *non-deterministic fork-join programs*.

---

[2] An implementation of our algorithms and all the scripts used for the experiments can be found on the companion repository at https://gitlab.com/ParComb/libnfj.

2.1 Syntax

Definition 1 (Non-deterministic fork-join programs). *Given a set of symbols $\mathcal{A}$ representing the "atomic actions" of the language, the class of non-deterministic fork-join programs (over this set $\mathcal{A}$), denoted NFJ, is defined as follows:*

$$
\begin{array}{lll}
P, Q & ::= P \parallel Q & \textit{(parallel composition (or fork))} \\
     & \mid P; Q & \textit{(sequential composition (or join))} \\
     & \mid P + Q & \textit{(non-deterministic choice)} \\
     & \mid P^\star & \textit{(loop)} \\
     & \mid a \in \mathcal{A} & \textit{(atomic action)} \\
     & \mid 0 & \textit{(empty program, noop).}
\end{array}
$$

Informally, the first two constructions form the fork-join "core" of the language: $P \parallel Q$ expresses the fact that P is run in parallel with Q and $P; Q$ means that P must terminate before Q starts. In $a; (b \parallel (c; d)); e$, the program starts by firing a, then it *forks* two processes b and $c; d$ which run in parallel and when they terminate e is run, which is called a "join". The third construction $P + Q$ expresses a *choice*: either P or Q is executed but not both. This can model an "internal" choice of the system such as a random event, a system failure etc., or an "external" choice, that is a choice depending on a user input[3]. Finally, the construction $P^\star$ expresses loops that can have any (finite) number of iterations. For instance $(a; (b \parallel c))^\star$ can be unrolled at runtime to 0 (zero iteration), $a; (b \parallel c)$ (one iterations), $a; (b \parallel c); a; (b \parallel c)$ (two iterations), etc.

It is important to mention now that the nature of the atomic actions will remain abstract in the present work, we treat them as black boxes and will consider that the different occurrences of an action across a term are distinct. These are sometimes referred to as *events* in the literature. Our focus is set on the order in which these actions can be fired and scheduled by the different operators of the language. In all our examples we use a different lowercase roman letters as a unique identifiers to help distinguishing between each action.

This simple model is expressive enough to write simple programs in the fork-join style. Moreover, the four combinators present in the grammar above can be modelled and well-understood using the tools from analytic combinatorics, which is at the core of our random sampling procedures in Sect. 3.

2.2 Semantics

We give NFJ an operational semantics in the style of [17]. We define a "reduction" relation $P \xrightarrow{a} P'$ between two programs and an atomic action, it reads "program P reduces to P' by firing action a". The idea behind the rules is explained just below.

---

[3] Since we do not interpret the action symbols, no distinction is possible in the provided semantics between a choice being triggered internally or externally.

$$\frac{P \overset{a}{\to} P'}{P \parallel Q \overset{a}{\to} P' \parallel Q} \; (Lpar) \qquad \frac{Q \overset{a}{\to} Q'}{P \parallel Q \overset{a}{\to} P \parallel Q'} \; (Rpar) \qquad \frac{P \overset{a}{\to} P'}{P;Q \overset{a}{\to} P';Q} \; (Lseq)$$

$$\frac{\text{nullable}(P) \quad Q \overset{a}{\to} Q'}{P;Q \overset{a}{\to} Q'} \; (Rseq) \qquad \frac{P \overset{a}{\to} P'}{P+Q \overset{a}{\to} P'} \; (Lchoice) \qquad \frac{Q \overset{a}{\to} Q'}{P+Q \overset{a}{\to} Q'} \; (Rchoice)$$

$$\frac{}{a \overset{a}{\to} 0} \; (act) \qquad \frac{P \overset{a}{\to} P'}{P^\star \overset{a}{\to} P';P^\star} \; (loop)$$

The nullable predicate, defined just below, tells whether a program can terminate without firing any action.

$$\text{nullable}(P \parallel Q) = \text{nullable}(P) \wedge \text{nullable}(Q) \qquad\qquad \text{nullable}(0) = \top$$
$$\text{nullable}(P;Q) = \text{nullable}(P) \wedge \text{nullable}(Q) \qquad\qquad \text{nullable}(a) = \bot$$
$$\text{nullable}(P + Q) = \text{nullable}(P) \vee \text{nullable}(Q) \qquad\qquad \text{nullable}(P^\star) = \top$$

The rules for the parallel composition (*Lpar* and *Rpar*) express the interleaving semantics of the language: if an action can be fired in any of P or Q, then it can be fired in $P \parallel Q$ and the term is rewritten. By iterating these two rules, we can obtain any interleaving of an execution of P and an execution of Q. Sequential composition is more asymmetric. The *Lseq* rule is similar to *Lpar* but *Rseq* captures the synchronisation: an execution can be fired on the right-hand-side only if the left-hand-side is ready to terminate (expressed by nullable(P)), in which case it is erased. The choice rules *Lchoice* and *Rchoice* allow actions to be fired from both sides but once we have made the choice of the branch, it is made definitive by erasing the other branch. Finally the loop $P^\star$ can be unrolled any number of times, which is expressed by giving $P^\star$ the same semantics as $0 + (P; P^\star)$. The fact that nullable $P^\star$ holds expresses that the loop can be unrolled zero times, and thus behave as the 0 program.

We call "execution step" a *proof-tree* built from the above rules (and not simply its conclusion) and we define an execution as a sequence of such steps leading to a nullable term.

Definition 2 (Execution). *An execution of an NFJ program P_0 is a sequence of steps of the form $P_0 \overset{a_1}{\Rightarrow} P_1 \overset{a_2}{\Rightarrow} P_2 \ldots \overset{a_n}{\Rightarrow} P_n$, such that* nullable($P_n$) *holds, and where for all i, $P_{i-1} \overset{a_i}{\Rightarrow} P_i$ is a proof-tree ending on the conclusion $P_{i-1} \overset{a_i}{\to} P_i$.*
We refer to the set of all possible executions of a program as its state-space.

Remark 1 (on equality). We purposely based our notion of execution on the proof-trees rather than simply on the relation $P \overset{a}{\to} P'$ to capture the choices hidden inside these steps. For instance there are two distinct executions depicted by $a^{\star\star} \overset{a}{\Rightarrow} (0; a^\star; a^{\star\star}) \overset{a}{\Rightarrow} (0; a^\star; a^{\star\star})$. One corresponds to the case where the outer loop is only unrolled once (i.e. the (*loop*) rule is applied once) but the inner loop twice. The other corresponds to the case where the outer loop is unrolled twice and the two occurrences of the inner loop once. The reason behind this choice is that we focus on the control-flow of programs here rather than the actual content of the atomic actions.

We will take the following program as a running example for the rest of the paper: $P_0 = ((a + (b \parallel c))^\star \parallel (d + 0))^\star ; (e + (f \parallel g))$. This program has one length-1 execution, with the following proof tree:

$$
\cfrac{\text{nullable}(((a + (b \parallel c))^\star \parallel (d+0))^\star)\quad \cfrac{\cfrac{}{e \xrightarrow{e} 0}\ (act)}{e + (f \parallel g) \xrightarrow{e} 0}\ (Lchoice)}{P_0 \xrightarrow{e} 0}\ (Rseq)
$$

There are also four length-2 executions, as follows[4]:

- $P_0 \xrightarrow{f} (0 \parallel g) \xrightarrow{g} 0 \parallel 0$
- $P_0 \xrightarrow{g} (f \parallel 0) \xrightarrow{f} 0 \parallel 0$
- $P_0 \xrightarrow{a} ((0;(a + (b \parallel c))^\star) \parallel (d+0)); ((a + (b \parallel c))^\star \parallel (d+0))^\star;(e + (f \parallel g)) \xrightarrow{e} 0$
- $P_0 \xrightarrow{d} ((a + (b \parallel c))^\star \parallel 0); ((a + (b \parallel c))^\star \parallel (d+0))^\star;(e + (f \parallel g)) \xrightarrow{e} 0.$

2.3   Combinatorial Interpretation

We now give an interpretation of the executions of an NFJ program as combinatorial objects, which will open us the toolbox of analytic combinatorics for the rest of the paper. We model the set of the executions of a program as a *combinatorial class* using the formalism from [12], which we recall here. A combinatorial class is a potentially infinite set of objects where each object has been given a (finite) size and in which there is only a finite number of objects of each size. In our case, the combinatorial class of interest is the set of finite executions of a given program and the size of an execution is its length i.e. its number of reduction steps.

The combinatorial class $S(P)$ modelling the executions of P is inductively defined in Table 1. The explanations for the combinatorial constructions are given bellow.

The empty program 0 and the atomic action a have only one execution, of length 0 and 1 respectively. This is modelled combinatorially by the neutral class $\mathcal{E}$: the class containing only one element of size 0, and the atom class $\mathcal{Z}$: the class with only one element of size 1.

---

[4] In general, the notation $P \xrightarrow{a} P'$ is ambiguous since there may be several different proof-trees with the same conclusion $P \xrightarrow{a} P'$. An example of this is given in Remark 1. For the sake of simplicity and in order to keep the notations light, in the examples given here, each step $P \xrightarrow{a} P'$ identifies only one possible proof-tree.

Table 1. Recursive rules for the computation of the generating function of executions of an NFJ program.

Construction	Specification
P	$S(P)$
0	$\mathcal{E}$
a	$\mathcal{Z}$
$P \parallel Q$	$S(P) \star S(Q)$
$P; Q$	$S(P) \times S(Q)$
$P + Q$ when nullable(P) $\wedge$ nullable(Q)	$S(P) + (S(Q) \setminus \mathcal{E})$
$P + Q$ otherwise	$S(P) + S(Q)$
P^* when nullable(P)	$\text{SEQ}(S(P) \setminus \mathcal{E})$
P^* otherwise	$\text{SEQ}(S(P))$

The first interesting case is the parallel composition: the executions of $P \parallel Q$ are made of any interleaving of one execution of P and one execution of Q. For instance if $P = a + (b; c)$ and $Q = d^*$, then P admits for instance an execution firing b and then c (denoted by bc for short) and Q admits an execution firing two ds (denoted by dd for short). Then all the 6 possible interleavings of these executions are executions of $P \parallel Q$: $bcdd$, $bdcd$, $bddc$, $dbcd$, $dbdc$ and $ddbc$ (again, we only denote the executions by their firing sequences for conciseness). The labelled product[5] of combinatorics expresses exactly this and is denoted using the $\star$ symbol. The executions of $P; Q$ are given by an execution of P followed by an execution of Q. So for instance, using the same example programs P and Q as above, $bcdd$ is an execution of $(P; Q)$ but not $dbcd$. So they can be seen as a pair of an execution of P and an execution of Q which is naturally modelled using the Cartesian product. The set of executions of $P + Q$ is the union of the executions of P and Q. Moreover this union is "almost" disjoint in the sense that the only execution that these programs may have in common is the empty execution, hence the two cases in the definition. Combinatorially, the fact that nullable(P) holds corresponds to the fact that the class of its executions contains one object of size 0: the empty execution. It is in fact important that we can express this in terms of *disjoint* unions because they fit in the framework of analytic combinatorics whereas arbitrary unions are more difficult to handle[6].

Finally, the executions of P^* are sequences of executions of P or, equivalently, sequences of *non-empty* executions of P. This second formulation leads to a non-ambiguous specification as the unique class $\mathcal{P}'$ satisfying $\mathcal{P}' = \mathcal{E} + \mathcal{P}_+ \times \mathcal{P}'$,

---

[5] The word "labelled" is not particularly relevant in our setup. It refers to the fact that another way to represent the interleaving of two executions is to put an integer label on each step of both execution carrying the position of each step in the interleaving.

[6] Grammar descriptions involving non-disjoint unions are referred to as "ambiguous" and lack most of the benefits, if not all, of the symbolic method, essentially because some objects may be counted multiple times when applying the method.

where $\mathcal{P}_+$ denotes the non-empty executions of P. This implicitly defined class $\mathcal{P}'$ is denoted $\mathrm{SEQ}(\mathcal{P}_+)$ and is called the *sequence* of $\mathcal{P}_+$. Once again we must distinguish whether nullable(P) holds or not in the definition of $\mathcal{P}_+$ to avoid ambiguities and thus double-counting.

The S function described above maps each program to a combinatorial specification of its executions. As an example, for our example program we have $S(P_0) = \mathrm{SEQ}(\mathrm{SEQ}(\mathcal{Z} + (\mathcal{Z} \star \mathcal{Z})) \star (\mathcal{Z} + \mathcal{E}) \setminus \mathcal{E}) \times (\mathcal{Z} + (\mathcal{Z} \star \mathcal{Z}))$. Such a specification is often the starting point of the study of a problem in analytic combinatorics, because it has many outcomes, and one of the most important of them is that it gives a systematic way to compute the generating function of the combinatorial class. We recall that the generating function of a class $\mathcal{C}$ is the formal power series given by $C(z) = \sum_{n \geqslant 0} c_n z^n$ where c_n is the number of elements of size n in $\mathcal{C}$.

The generating function of the executions of a program, i.e. of the class $S(P)$, constitutes a summary of the counting information of its state space. Moreover, this encoding as a power series gives a convenient formalism to compute the number of executions of length n, for bounded n. The *symbolic method* from [12] gives an automatic translation from the specification of a class to its generating function, which we recall in Table 2.

Table 2. The rules of the symbolic method for computing a generating function from a combinatorial specification. In the case of the labelled product $\mathcal{A} \star \mathcal{B}$, the corresponding operation on the series is called the *coloured product* $\odot$ and is defined in [6] by $A(z) \odot B(z) = \sum_{n \geqslant 0} \sum_{k=0}^{n} \binom{n}{k} a_k b_{n-k} z^n$.

Specification $\mathcal{A}$	Gen. Function $A(z)$
$\mathcal{E}$	1
$\mathcal{Z}$	z
$\mathcal{A} \setminus \mathcal{B}$ (only when $\mathcal{B} \subset \mathcal{A}$)	$A(z) - B(z)$
$\mathcal{A} + \mathcal{B}$	$A(z) + B(z)$
$\mathcal{A} \star \mathcal{B}$	$A(z) \odot B(z)$
$\mathcal{A} \times \mathcal{B}$	$A(z) \cdot B(z)$
$\mathrm{SEQ}(\mathcal{A})$	$(1 - A(z))^{-1}$

We now illustrate the power of the analytic combinatorics tools, by showing how a few manipulations on polynomials can lead to interesting algorithmic applications and precise quantitative results. Further resource on this topic can be found in the book [12]. We study the generating function ϕ of the example program P_0 given above, which we recall here for convenience: $P_0 = [(a + (b \parallel c))^* \parallel (d + 0)]^* ; [e + (f \parallel g)]$. Let $\phi(z) = \sum_{n \geqslant 0} p_n z^n$ denote the expansion in power series of the generating function of $S(P_0)$ and recall that the n-th coefficient p_n is the number of executions of P_0 of length n. By applying the rules from Table 2 to $S(P_0)$ we obtain that:

$$\phi(z) = \left[(1 - z - 2z^2)^{-1} \odot (z+1)\right]^{-1} \cdot [z + 2z^2]$$

$$= \frac{(2z+1)(2z-1)^2(z+1)^2 z}{1 - 4z - 4z^2 + 6z^3 + 8z^4}$$

The second line of the above formula is obtained by applying the calculus rule[7] $z \odot A(z) = z \frac{d(zA(z))}{dz}$. From this formula we derive two applications. First, from the denominator of this rational expression we deduce that for all $n > 6$ we have $p_n - 4p_{n-1} - 4p_{n-2} + 6p_{n-3} + 8p_{n-4} = 0$. The obtained recurrence formula can be used to compute the number of executions of length n of P_0 in linear time. On the analytic side, ϕ being a rational function, we can do a *partial fraction decomposition* to obtain ϕ as a sum of four terms of the form $C_i(1 - z\rho_i^{-1})$ (plus a polynomial). Each of these terms expands as $\sum_{n \geqslant 0} C_i \rho_i^{-n} z^n$, hence the number of executions of P_0 of length n satisfies $p_n = C \cdot \rho^{-n} \cdot (1 + o(1))$ for some constants C and ρ and with an exponentially small error term hidden in the $o(1)$. In this case we have $\rho \approx 0.221987$, $C \approx 0.146871$ and the error term is of the order of 0.327950^n. Table 3 compares the values of p_n and of the proposed approximation for a few values of n. One can see that already for small values of n, the relative error of this approximation is rather low.

Table 3. Value of p_n, of its approximation $C \cdot \rho^{-n}$ and of the relative error $|p_n - C \cdot \rho^{-n}|/p_n$ for small values of n.

n	6	7	8	9	10	11	12
p_n	1226	5528	24904	112196	505424	2276832	10256616
approx	1227	5529	24907	112199	505429	2276839	10256626
rel. err.	0.000816	0.000181	0.00012	2.67e-05	9.89e-06	3.07e-06	9.75e-07

20	30	50
1739330569856	5985551205783341568	708839958242125966666294027026432
1739330570089	5985551205783353055	708839958242125966666294055205537
1.34e-10	1.92e-15	3.98e-25

3 Statistical Analysis Algorithms

In this section, we study the problem of exploring the state-space of a given process through random generation. We describe first a uniform random sampler of executions of given length, and second a uniform random sampler of execution prefixes. Our approach relies on the counting information contained in the generating functions, as defined previously.

---

[7] This is the only "non-standard" computation rule we use in this example. All the rest is usual polynomial manipulations. General rules for computing $A(z) \odot B(z)$ are beyond the scope of this article.

3.1 Preprocessing: The Generating Function of Executions

As explained in the previous section, the symbolic method gives a systematic way of computing the generating function of the class of the executions of a program P from its specification $S(P)$ using the rules from Table 2. A straightforward application of this method leads to Algorithm 1 for computing the first terms of the series.

Algorithm 1. Computation of the generating function of the executions of an NFJ program up to degree n

---

Input: An NFJ program P and a positive integer n.
Output: The first $n + 1$ terms of the generating function of P
  function GFUN(P, n)
   if $P = 0$ **then return** 1
   else if $P = a$ **then return** z
   else if $P = Q \parallel R$ **then return** GFUN (Q, n) ⊚ GFUN (R, n) mod z^{n+1}
   else if $P = Q; R$ **then return** GFUN (Q, n) · GFUN (R, n) mod z^{n+1}
   else if $P = Q + R$ **then**
    $q(z) \leftarrow$ GFUN $(Q, n),$ $r(z) \leftarrow$ GFUN (R, n)
    if $q(0) = r(0) = 1$ **then return** $q(z) + r(z) - 1$ **else return** $q(z) + r(z)$
   else if $P = Q^{\star}$ **then**
    $q(z) \leftarrow$ GFUN (Q, n)
    return $(1 - (q(z) - q(0)))^{-1}$ mod z^{n+1}

The coloured product ⊚ used in the parallel composition case can be implemented using the formula $A(z) \circledcirc B(z) = \mathrm{Lap}(\mathrm{Bor}(A) \cdot \mathrm{Bor}(B))$ where Bor and Lap are respectively the combinatorial Borel and Laplace transforms (see [6] for insights on the coloured product). This approach has the advantage of benefiting from the efficient polynomial multiplication algorithms from the literature at the cost of three linear transformations. To be implemented efficiently, the coefficients of the result of the Borel transform should share $n!$ as a common denominator so that it is only stored once and we keep working with integer coefficients. The computation of $(1 - A(z))^{-1}$ can be carried out efficiently using Newton iteration (see [22] for instance). The idea is to iterate the formula $S_{i+1}(z) \leftarrow S_i(z) + S_i(z) \cdot (A(s) \cdot S_i(z) - (S_i(z) - 1))$, starting from $S_0(z) = 1$. It has been shown that only $\lceil \log_2(n + 1) \rceil$ iterations are necessary for the coefficients of $S_i(z)$ to be equal to those of $(1 - A(z))^{-1}$ up to degree n. Moreover the total cost of this procedure in terms of integer multiplication is of the same order of magnitude as that of the multiplication of two polynomials of degree n.

Theorem 1. *Let P be an NFJ program and let $|P|$ denote its syntactic size (i.e. the number of constructors $\parallel$, $+$, $;$, $\star$ and atomic actions) in its definition). Algorithm 1 can be implemented to compute the first n coefficients of the generating function of the executions of P in $O(|P|M(n))$ operations on big integers where $M(n)$ is the complexity of the multiplication of two polynomials of degree n.*

Moreover, these coefficients are bounded by $n!$ *and hence have at most* $n \log_2(n)$ *bits.*

Proof. The proof of Theorem 1 follows from the above discussion: each constructor incurs one polynomial operation among addition, multiplication, coloured product and inversion and all of them can be carried out in $O(M(n))$.

To give a rough idea of the performance that can be achieved by Algorithm 1: we computed the generating function of P_0 up to degree $n = 10000$—and thus its number of executions of length k for all $k \leqslant 10000$—in less that 4s on a standard PC. A detailed benchmark of Algorithm 1 is given in Sect. 4.1.

3.2 Random Sampling of Executions

Another consequence of having a combinatorial specification of the state-space at our disposal is that we can apply well-known random sampling methods from the combinatorics toolbox. Our random sampling procedure for program executions is based on the so-called "recursive-method" from [13]. It operates in a similar fashion to the symbolic method, that is by induction on the specification by combining the random samplers of the sub-structures with simple rules depending on the grammar construction. For the sake of clarity we represent executions as sequences of atomic actions. This encoding does not contain all the information that defines an execution, typically it does not reflect in which iteration of a loop an atomic action is fired for instance. However it makes the presentation clearer and the algorithm can be easily adapted to a more faithful encoding. Our uniform random sampler of executions is described in Algorithm 2 and the detailed explanations about the different constructions are given below.

Choice. The simplest rule of the recursive method is that of the disjoint union used at line 4 of Algorithm 2. If q_n and r_n denote the number of length-n executions of Q and R, then a uniform random length-n execution of $P = Q + R$ is a uniform length-n execution of Q with probability $q_n/(q_n + r_n)$ and a uniform length-n execution of R otherwise. One way to draw the Bernoulli variable is to draw a uniform random big integer x in $[0; q_n + r_n[$ and to return **true** if and only if $x < q_n$. As an example, consider the programs $Q = (a + (b \parallel c))$ and $R = d^\star$. We count that Q has two executions of length two: bc and cb and R has only one: dd. Hence, to sample a length-2 execution in $(Q + R)$, one must perform a recursive call on Q with probability $2/3$ and on R with probability $1/3$.

Parallel Composition. The other rules build on top of the disjoint union case. For instance, the set of length-n executions of $P = Q \parallel R$ can be seen as $\mathcal{Q}_0 \star \mathcal{R}_n + \mathcal{Q}_1 \star \mathcal{R}_{n-1} + \cdots + \mathcal{Q}_n \star \mathcal{R}_0$ where $\mathcal{Q}_k$ (resp. $\mathcal{R}_k$) denotes the set of length-k executions of Q (resp. R). By generalising the previous rule to disjoint unions of $(n + 1)$ terms, and using the fact that the number of elements of $\mathcal{Q}_k \star \mathcal{R}_{n-k}$ is $q_k r_{n-k} \binom{n}{k}$, one can select in which one of these terms to sample by drawing a random variable which is k with probability $q_k r_{n-k} \binom{n}{k}/p_n$. Then it remains to sample

---

Algorithm 2. Uniform random sampler of executions of given length

Input: A program P and an integer n such that P has length n executions.
Output: A list of atomic actions representing an execution
1: **function** UNIFEXEC(P, n)
2:     **if** $n = 0$ **then return** the empty execution
3:     **else if** $P = a$ **then return** a
4:     **else if** $P = Q + R$ **then**
5:         **if** BERNOULLI $\left(\frac{q_n}{q_n + r_n}\right)$ **then return** UNIFEXEC (Q, n)
6:         **else return** UNIFEXEC (R, n)
7:     **else if** $P = Q \parallel R$ **then**
8:         draw $k \in [\![0; n]\!]$ with probability $\binom{n}{k} q_k r_{n-k} / p_n$
9:         **return** SHUFFLE (UNIFEXEC (Q, k), UNIFEXEC $(R, n - k)$)
10:     **else if** $P = Q; R$ **then**
11:         draw $k \in [\![0; n]\!]$ with probability $q_k r_{n-k} / p_n$
12:         **return** CONCAT (UNIFEXEC (Q, k), UNIFEXEC $(R, n - k)$)
13:     **else if** $P = Q^\star$ **then**
14:         draw $k \in [\![1; n]\!]$ with probability $q_k p_{n-k} / p_n$
15:         **return** CONCAT (UNIFEXEC (Q, k), UNIFEXEC $(P, n - k)$)

The lower case letters p_n, q_k, r_{n-k} etc. indicate the number of executions of length n, k, $n - k$ of programs P, Q and R.

---

a uniform element of $\mathcal{Q}_k$, a uniform element of $\mathcal{R}_{n-k}$ and a uniform shuffling of their labellings among the $\binom{n}{k}$ possibilities. This is described at line 7 of Algorithm 2. We do not detail the implementation of the shuffling function here, an optimal algorithm in terms of random bits consumption, can be found in [5]. As an example, consider the same programs as above: $Q = (a + (b \parallel c))$ and $R = d^\star$. The number of length-3 executions of $(Q \parallel R)$ is $1 \cdot 1 \cdot \binom{3}{1} + 2 \cdot 1 \cdot \binom{3}{1} = 9$ using the decomposition $Q_1 \star R_2 + Q_2 \star R_1$. Say $k = 1$ is selected (with probability $1/3$), then the recursive calls to $(Q, 1)$ and $(R, 2)$ necessarily return a and dd and the SHUFFLE procedure must choose a shuffling uniformly between add, dad and dda.

Sequential Composition. The case of the sequential composition is similar (see line 10 of Algorithm 2). We use the same kind of decomposition, using the Cartesian product $\times$ in place of the labelled product $\star$. This has the consequence of removing the binomial coefficient in the formula for the generation of the k random variable. Once k is selected, we generate an execution of Q_k, an execution of R_{n-k} and we concatenate the two.

Loop. Finally, the case of the loop is a slight adaptation of the case of the sequential composition using the fact that the executions of $Q^\star$ are the executions of $(0 + Q; Q^\star)$. However, care must be taken to avoid issues related to double-counting. More specifically, when sampling an execution of $(Q; Q^\star)$ we must not choose an execution of length 0 for the left-hand-side Q. This is related to the same reason we had to specify the executions of $Q^\star$ as all the sequences of *non-empty* executions of Q. This is presented at line 13 of Algorithm 2, note that $k > 0$. As an example, for sampling a length-3 execution in $(a + (b; c))^*$, one may select $k = 1$ with probability $2/3$, which yields abc or aaa depending on the recursive call to $(Q^*, 2)$ or $k = 2$, with probability $1/3$, which yields bca.

Generation of Random Variables. We did not give details on how to generate the random variable k for the parallel, sequential and loop case. Molinero showed in [19,20] that good performance can be achieved by using the so-called boustrophedonic order. For instance, in the case of the sequential composition $P = (Q; R)$, the idea is to generate a random integer x in the interval $[0; p_n[$ and to find the minimum number ℓ such that the sum of ℓ terms $q_0 r_n + q_n r_0 + q_1 r_{n-1} + q_{n-1} r_1 + q_2 r_{n-2} + \cdots$ (taken in this particular order) is greater than x. Then k is such that the last term of this sum is $q_k r_{n-k}$.

Theorem 2. *Using the boustrophedonic order, the complexity of the random generation of an execution of length n in P in terms of arithmetic operations on big integers is $O(n \cdot \min(\ln(n), h(P)))$ where $h(P)$ refers to the height of P i.e. its maximum number of nested operators.*

Contrary to the classical context of random generation in the context of analytic combinatorics (like in [13,19,20]), the grammar enumerating the executions is not a constant but rather a parameter of the problem. Hence its size cannot be considered constant and the complexity analysis needs to be carefully crafted to take this variable into account.

Proof. The $O(n \ln(n))$ bound follows from Theorem 11 of [20]. We obtain the other bound by refining the result of Theorem 12 from the same source. The combinatorial classes we are considering are built from the $*, \times, +$ and $\text{SEQ}(\cdot)$ operators without recursion, they hence fall under the scope of *iterative classes* for which Molinero proved a linear complexity in n. However the proof given in [20] does not give an explicit bound for the multiplicative constants, which actually depends on the size of the grammar and which we cannot consider constant in our context. Let $C(P, n)$ denote the cost of $\text{UNIFEXEC}(P, n)$ in terms of arithmetic operations on big integers. We show that $C(P, n) \leqslant \alpha n h(P)$ by induction for some constant α to be specified later.

– The base cases have a constant cost.
– The case of the choice only incurs a constant number c of arithmetic operations in addition to the cost of the recursive calls. Hence $C(Q + R, n)$ is bounded by $c + \alpha \max(C(Q, n), C(R, n)) \leqslant c + \alpha n \max(h(Q), h(R)) = c + \alpha n(h(Q+R) - 1)$ by induction. Thus, if $\alpha \geqslant c$, then $C(Q+R, n) \leqslant \alpha n h(Q+R)$.
– The parallel composition case incurs a number of arithmetic operations of the form $c' \min(k, n - k)$ where k is the random variable generated using the boustrophedonic order technique. Hence $C(Q \parallel R, n)$ is bounded by $c' \min(k, n-k) + C(Q, k) + C(R, n-k)$ and by induction by $c' \min(k, n - k) + \alpha k h(Q) + \alpha(n - k)h(R) \leqslant \alpha n h(Q \parallel R) + c' \min(k, n - k) - \alpha n$. The last term on the right is bounded by 0 if $\alpha \geqslant c'$.

- Sequential composition is treated using the same argument as for parallel composition.
- Finally, the loop must be handled by reasoning "globally" on the total number of unrollings. Say the loop $Q^\star$ is unrolled r times. Then its cost $C(Q^\star, n)$ is bounded by $\sum_{i=1}^{r} c' \min(k_i, k_{i+1} + \cdots + k_r) + \sum_{i=1}^{r+1} C(Q, k_i)$. The first sum is bounded by $c'n$ and the second is bounded by induction by $\sum_{i=1}^{r+1} \alpha k_i h(Q)$ which simplified to $\alpha n h(Q)$. Hence, reusing the bound $\alpha \geqslant c'$ and the fact that $h(Q^\star) = 1 + h(Q)$, we get $C(Q^\star, n) \leqslant \alpha n h(Q^\star)$ which terminates the proof.

3.3　Execution Prefixes

The uniform sampler of executions described above provides one way of exploring the state space of a program, but it does not offer much flexibility. In this subsection we develop, as a complementary tool, a uniform random sampler of execution *prefixes* of given length. Note that this is different from using the previous algorithm until a length threshold n because this would not yield *uniform* prefixes. An execution prefix is a sequence of evaluation steps as in Definition 2 but unlike an execution, its resulting program P_n does not necessarily satisfy nullable(P_n). We see this algorithm as an elementary building block for statistical exploration of the state-space, enabling a variety of different exploration strategies, possibly biased towards some areas of interest in the state-space of the program but in a *controlled* manner.

The idea here is to apply our previous algorithm to a new program pref(P) defined inductively using Table 4. Note that pref(P) (as well as its specification) can be implemented in linear space by using pointers to refer to the substructures of P.

Table 4. In the second column: the pref() transformation, mapping a program P to a program whose executions are in correspondence with the prefixes of executions of P. In the third column: the combinatorial specification of the prefixes of P.

Program P	Prefix program pref(P)	Specification of the prefixes $\langle P \rangle$
0	0	$\mathcal{E}$
a	$0 + a$	$\mathcal{E} + \mathcal{Z}$
$P \parallel Q$	$(\mathrm{pref}(P) \parallel \mathrm{pref}(Q))$	$\langle P \rangle \star \langle Q \rangle$
$P; Q$	$\mathrm{pref}(P) + (P; \mathrm{pref}(Q))$	$\langle P \rangle + S(P) \times (\langle Q \rangle \setminus \mathcal{E})$
$P + Q$	$\mathrm{pref}(P) + \mathrm{pref}(Q)$	$\langle P \rangle + (\langle Q \rangle \setminus \mathcal{E})$
$P^\star$	$P^\star; \mathrm{pref}(P)$	$\mathcal{E} + S(P^\star) \times (\langle P \rangle \setminus \mathcal{E})$

Proposition 1. *Let P be an NFJ program. The executions of the pref(P) are in one-to-one correspondence with the prefixes of executions of P.*

Proof. The way execution prefixes are defined, the transformation is direct. We only discuss the cases where a $\mathcal{E}$ must be removed. In the case of the sequential composition, a prefix of execution of $P; Q$ is either a prefix of P or a *complete* execution of P followed by a *non-empty* prefix of Q. It is important to only consider non-empty prefixes in order to avoid counting the complete executions of P twice. In the case of the choice $P + Q$, we always subtract $\mathcal{E}$ from $\langle Q \rangle$ to avoid double-counting the empty prefix because all programs have it. Finally the case of the loop is a generalisation of the sequence: a prefix of P^* is made of any number of non-empty complete executions of P followed by a non-empty prefix of P.

As an example, using the notations $P_0 = P_1; (e + (f \parallel g))$, where $P_1 = (P_2 \parallel (d + 0))^*$ and $P_2 = (a + (b \parallel c))^*$, the specification of the prefixes of example program P_0 is given by:

$$\langle P_0 \rangle = \langle P_1 \rangle + S(P_1) \times ((\mathcal{E} + \mathcal{Z} + (\mathcal{E} + \mathcal{Z}) \star (\mathcal{E} + \mathcal{Z}) \setminus \mathcal{E}) \setminus \mathcal{E})$$
$$\langle P_1 \rangle = \mathcal{E} + S(P_1) \times (\langle P_2 \rangle \star (\mathcal{E} + \mathcal{Z} + \mathcal{E} \setminus \mathcal{E}) \setminus \mathcal{E})$$
$$\langle P_2 \rangle = \mathcal{E} + S(P_2) \times ((\mathcal{E} + \mathcal{Z} + (\mathcal{E} + \mathcal{Z}) \star (\mathcal{E} + \mathcal{Z}) \setminus \mathcal{E}) \setminus \mathcal{E})$$

where $S(P_1)$ and $S(P_2)$ are not given but can be obtained as sub-terms of the specification $S(P_0)$ of the executions of P_0 given earlier.

Theorem 3. *To sample uniformly a prefix of length n in P we sample uniformly a full execution in $\mathrm{pref}(P)$. This has the same complexity as sampling an execution of n up to a multiplicative constant.*

The latter theorem is a consequence of Proposition 1. The complexity bound is obtained by showing that the height of $\mathrm{pref}(P)$ is at most twice the height of P. Another possibility of equal complexity would be to express directly the specification of the prefixes of P without actually constructing the intermediate program. This specification is denoted $\langle P \rangle$ and is given in the third column of Table 4.

4   Experimental Study

In order to assess experimentally the efficiency of our method, in this section we put into use the algorithms presented in the paper and demonstrate that they can handle systems with a significantly large state space. We generated a few NFJ programs at random using a Boltzmann random generator. In its basic form, the Boltzmann sampler would generate a high number of loops and a large number of sub-terms of the form $P + 0$ in the programs which we believe is not realistic so we tuned it using [4] so that the number of both types of nodes represent only 10% of the size of the program in expectation. We rely on the FLINT library (Fast Library for number theory [16]) to carry all the computations on polynomials except for the coloured product and the inversion, which we implemented ourselves in order to achieve the complexity exhibited in the previous section. The former was not provided natively by the library and the latter was feasible using FLINT's primitives but slow compared to the dedicated algorithm based on Newton iteration.

Note that besides the choice of the algorithms, we did not optimize our code for efficiency nor ran extensive tests on a big dataset, hence the numbers we give should be taken as a rough estimate of the performance of our algorithms. For the sake of reproducibility, the source code of our experiments is available on the companion repository[8].

4.1 Preprocessing Phase

First, Table 5 gives the runtime of the preprocessing phase (Algorithm 1) that computes the generating functions of all the sub-terms of a program up to a given degree n. We measured this for programs of different sizes and for different values of n. Every measure was performed 7 times and we reported the median of these 7 values. The time reported is the CPU time as measured by C's clock function. The state-space column indicates the number of executions of length at most n obtained by evaluating the polynomial with $z = 1$. The figure on the right displays more data and focuses on the relation between the runtime of the preprocessing (on the y axis, in seconds) and the size of the state-space (the x axis is the $\log_2$ of the number of executions). Each line corresponds to a program

Table 5. On the left: runtime of the counting algorithm and size of the state-space (executions of length at most n) for programs of different sizes. On the right: plot of this runtime as a function of the $\log_2$ of the size of the state-space.

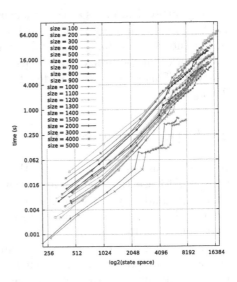

$\lvert P \rvert$	n	# exec°	runtime
100	500	$1.740825 \cdot 2^{1119}$	0.010s
100	1000	$1.073991 \cdot 2^{2235}$	0.037s
100	3000	$1.385924 \cdot 2^{6691}$	0.605s
500	500	$1.058776 \cdot 2^{1927}$	0.076s
500	1000	$1.081276 \cdot 2^{3832}$	0.462s
500	3000	$1.341591 \cdot 2^{11423}$	6.428s
1000	500	$1.473353 \cdot 2^{2330}$	0.159s
1000	1000	$1.044525 \cdot 2^{4712}$	0.874s
1000	3000	$1.092147 \cdot 2^{14181}$	13.488s
2000	100	$1.981851 \cdot 2^{410}$	0.012s
2000	200	$1.800651 \cdot 2^{926}$	0.049s
2000	500	$1.768618 \cdot 2^{2380}$	0.330s
2000	1000	$1.215440 \cdot 2^{4746}$	1.870s
5000	500	$1.607519 \cdot 2^{2923}$	0.897s
5000	1000	$1.469086 \cdot 2^{6016}$	5.434s
5000	3000	$1.226718 \cdot 2^{18116}$	75.649s

---

[8] All the benchmarks were run on a standard laptop with an Intel Core i7-8665U and 32G of RAM running Ubuntu 19.10 with kernel version 5.3.0–46-generic. We used FLINT version 2.5.2 and GMP version 6.1.2.

and each point corresponds to a different value of n for this program. Using a log-scale on both axis, this figure gives experimental "evidence" of a polynomial relation between the two. Besides the shape of the curves, the take-away here is that the preprocessing phase can be carried out for systems with a state-space of size $\approx 2^{18000}$ in a time of the order of one minute.

4.2   Random Generation

We then measure the runtime of the random generator of executions and execution prefixes for the same programs. Every measure was performed 100 times and for each one we report the median of these values as well as the interquartile range (IQR)[9], which gives an idea of the dispersion of the measures. We use these metrics rather than the mean and the variance to reduce the importance of extreme values and give a precise idea of what runtime the user should expect when running our sampler. A summary of the results is available in Table 6. Interestingly, the number of executions and the numbers of execution prefixes are rather close. We have clues about the reasons behind this phenomenon which relate to the analytical properties of the generating functions of executions and prefixes. We will investigate this in the future but this is way beyond the scope of this article. As the numbers show, both random sampling procedures take a

Table 6. Median and interquartile range (IQR) of the runtime of the executions and prefixes samplers for various program sizes and object lengths.

$|P|$	n	# exec°	UnifExec	IQR	# prefixes	UnifPrefix	IQR
100	500	$1.370 \cdot 2^{1119}$	0.129 ms	4 µs	$1.841 \cdot 2^{1128}$	0.147 ms	3 µs
100	1000	$1.690 \cdot 2^{2234}$	0.276 ms	10 µs	$1.124 \cdot 2^{2244}$	0.307 ms	18 µs
100	3000	$1.090 \cdot 2^{6691}$	1.076 ms	43 µs	$1.439 \cdot 2^{6700}$	1.371 ms	359 µs
500	500	$1.969 \cdot 2^{1926}$	0.218 ms	5 µs	$1.022 \cdot 2^{1997}$	0.281 ms	12 µs
500	1000	$1.004 \cdot 2^{3832}$	0.563 ms	21 µs	$1.404 \cdot 2^{3901}$	0.688 ms	33 µs
500	3000	$1.245 \cdot 2^{11423}$	3.718 ms	203 µs	$1.466 \cdot 2^{11492}$	4.005 ms	274 µs
1000	500	$1.420 \cdot 2^{2330}$	0.301 ms	10 µs	$1.556 \cdot 2^{2411}$	0.352 ms	19 µs
1000	1000	$1.005 \cdot 2^{4712}$	0.777 ms	28 µs	$1.293 \cdot 2^{4790}$	0.871 ms	46 µs
1000	3000	$1.051 \cdot 2^{14181}$	4.829 ms	481 µs	$1.127 \cdot 2^{14259}$	5.307 ms	569 µs
2000	500	$1.704 \cdot 2^{2380}$	0.308 ms	14 µs	$1.839 \cdot 2^{2484}$	0.416 ms	10 µs
2000	1000	$1.169 \cdot 2^{4746}$	1.021 ms	51 µs	$1.482 \cdot 2^{4856}$	1.225 ms	86 µs
2000	3000	$1.634 \cdot 2^{14120}$	7.291 ms	1.2 ms	$1.921 \cdot 2^{14256}$	7.245 ms	238 µs
5000	500	$1.589 \cdot 2^{2923}$	0.309 ms	7 µs	$1.933 \cdot 2^{3168}$	0.348 ms	14 µs
5000	1000	$1.448 \cdot 2^{6016}$	0.898 ms	43 µs	$1.340 \cdot 2^{6231}$	1.027 ms	41 µs
5000	3000	$1.208 \cdot 2^{18116}$	18.526 ms	1.5 ms	$1.034 \cdot 2^{18324}$	21.478 ms	1.2 ms

---

[9] The interquartile range of a set of measures is the difference between the third and the first quartiles. Compared with the value of the median, it gives a rough estimate of the dispersion of the measures.

few milliseconds, even for rather large state-spaces. Here, the two state-space columns refer respectively to the number of executions and the number of prefixes of length *exactly* n. This is the cardinal of the set in which we sample a *uniform* element.

4.3 Prefix Covering

This subsection presents an experimentation that highlights the importance of the uniform distribution for the purpose of state-space exploration. The setup is the following: consider a given NFJ program and randomly sample prefixes of given length n of this program using two different algorithms:

- our random sampler which is *globally* uniform among all prefixes of length n;
- a "naive" sampler that repeatedly generates one execution step uniformly among the legal steps, until we get a length n prefix. This strategy is called *locally uniform* or *isotropic*.

The question is: in average, how many random prefixes must be generated in order to discover a given proportion of the possible prefixes? This question actually falls under the scope of the Coupon Collector Problem, which is treated in depth in [11]. Table 7 gives numerical answers for both exploration strategies for a random NFJ program of size 25 and for a target coverage of 20% of the possible prefixes.

Table 7. Expected number of prefixes to be sampled to discover 20% of the prefixes of a random program of size 25 with either the isotropic or the uniform method.

Prefix length	1	2	3	4	5
# prefixes	11	18	30	60	128
Isotropic	2.1	4.45	11.17	35.09	$1.28 \cdot 10^{14}$
Uniform	2.1	3.18	6.57	13.26	27.69
Gain	0%	40%	70%	165%	$4.61 \cdot 10^{14}\%$

Expectedly the uniform strategy is faster but what is interesting to see is that the speedup compared to the isotropic method grows extremely fast. The more the state-space grows, the more the uniform approach is unavoidable.

Unfortunately, the formula given in [11] for the isotropic case involves the costly computation of power-sets which makes it impractical to give values for larger programs and prefix length. However, these small-size results already establish a clear difference between the two methods. It would be interesting to have theoretical bounds to quantify this explosion or to investigate more efficient ways to compute these values but this falls out of the scope of this article.

References

1. Abbes, S., Mairesse, J.: Uniform generation in trace monoids. In: 40th International Symposium MFCS, pp. 63–75 (2015)
2. Arora, S., Barak, B.: Computational Complexity - A Modern Approach. Cambridge University Press, New York (2009)
3. Basset, N., Mairesse, J., Soria, M.: Uniform sampling for networks of automata. In: 28th International Conference CONCUR (2017)
4. Bendkowski, M., Bodini, O., Dovgal, S.: Polynomial tuning of multiparametric combinatorial samplers, pp. 92–106 (2018)
5. Bodini, O., Dien, M., Genitrini, A., Peschanski, F.: Entropic uniform sampling of linear extensions in series-parallel posets. In: Weil, P. (ed.) CSR 2017. LNCS, vol. 10304, pp. 71–84. Springer, Cham (2017). https://doi.org/10.1007/978-3-319-58747-9_9
6. Bodini, O., Dien, M., Genitrini, A., Peschanski, F.: The ordered and colored products in analytic combinatorics: application to the quantitative study of synchronizations in concurrent processes. In: 14th SIAM Meeting ANALCO, pp. 16–30 (2017)
7. Bodini, O., Genitrini, A., Peschanski, F.: The combinatorics of non-determinism. IARCS Annu. Conf. FSTTCS **24**, 425–436 (2013)
8. Bodini, O., Genitrini, A., Peschanski, F.: A quantitative study of pure parallel processes. Electron. J. Comb. **23**(1), P1.11, 39 pages (2016)
9. Bodini, O., Dien, M., Genitrini, A., Peschanski, F.: The combinatorics of barrier synchronization. In: Donatelli, S., Haar, S. (eds.) PETRI NETS 2019. LNCS, vol. 11522, pp. 386–405. Springer, Cham (2019). https://doi.org/10.1007/978-3-030-21571-2_21
10. Darrasse, A., Panagiotou, K., Roussel, O., Soria, M.: Boltzmann generation for regular languages with shuffle. In: GASCOM 2010 - Conference on random generation of combinatorial structures. Montréal, Canada (September 2010)
11. Flajolet, P., Gardy, D., Thimonier, L.: Birthday paradox, coupon collectors, caching algorithms and self-organizing search. D. A. Math. **39**(3), 207–229 (1992)
12. Flajolet, P., Sedgewick, R.: Analytic Combinatorics. Cambridge University Press, New York (2009)
13. Flajolet, P., Zimmermann, P., Cutsem, B.V.: A calculus for the random generation of combinatorial structures (1993)
14. Gaudel, M., Denise, A., Gouraud, S., Lassaigne, R., Oudinet, J., Peyronnet, S.: Coverage-biased random exploration of models. Electr. Notes Theor. Comput. Sci. **220**(1), 3–14 (2008)
15. Grosu, R., Smolka, S.A.: Monte carlo model checking. In: Halbwachs, N., Zuck, L.D. (eds.) TACAS 2005. LNCS, vol. 3440, pp. 271–286. Springer, Heidelberg (2005). https://doi.org/10.1007/978-3-540-31980-1_18
16. Hart, W., Johansson, F., Pancratz, S.: FLINT: Fast Library for Number Theory (2013), version 2.5.2, http://flintlib.org
17. Koomen, C.J.: Calculus of communicating systems. In: The Design of Communicating Systems. The Springer International Series in Engineering and Computer Science (VLSI, Computer Architecture and Digital Signal Processing), vol 147. Springer, Boston (1991) https://doi.org/10.1007/978-1-4615-4020-5_2
18. Krob, D., Mairesse, J., Michos, I.: On the average parallelism in trace monoids. In: Alt, H., Ferreira, A. (eds.) STACS 2002. LNCS, vol. 2285, pp. 477–488. Springer, Heidelberg (2002). https://doi.org/10.1007/3-540-45841-7_39

19. Martínez, C., Molinero, X.: An experimental study of unranking algorithms. In: Ribeiro, C.C., Martins, S.L. (eds.) WEA 2004. LNCS, vol. 3059, pp. 326–340. Springer, Heidelberg (2004). https://doi.org/10.1007/978-3-540-24838-5_25
20. Molinero, X.: Ordered generation of classes of combinatorial structures. Ph.D. thesis, Universitat Politècnica de Catalunya (October 2005)
21. Oudinet, J., Denise, A., Gaudel, M.-C., Lassaigne, R., Peyronnet, S.: Uniform monte-carlo model checking. In: Giannakopoulou, D., Orejas, F. (eds.) FASE 2011. LNCS, vol. 6603, pp. 127–140. Springer, Heidelberg (2011). https://doi.org/10.1007/978-3-642-19811-3_10
22. Pivoteau, C., Salvy, B., Soria, M.: Algorithms for combinatorial structures: well-founded systems and newton iterations. J. Comb. Theory Ser. A **119**, 1711–1773 (2012)
23. Valiant, L.G.: The complexity of computing the permanent. Theor. Comput. Sci. **8**, 189–201 (1979)

On Two Characterizations of Feature Models

Ferruccio Damiani[1](✉) [ID], Michael Lienhardt[2](✉), and Luca Paolini[1] [ID]

[1] University of Turin, Turin, Italy
{ferruccio.damiani,luca.paolini}@unito.it
[2] ONERA, Palaiseau, France
michael.lienhardt@onera.fr

Abstract. Software-intensive systems can have thousands of interdependent configuration options across different subsystems. Feature models allow designers to organize the configuration space by describing configuration options using interdependent features: a feature is a name representing some functionality and each software variant is identified by a set of features. Different representations of feature models have been proposed in the literature. In this paper we focus on the propositional representation (which works well in practice) and the extensional representation (which has been recently shown well suited for theoretical investigations). We provide an algebraic and a propositional characterization of feature model operations and relations, and we formalize the connection between the two characterizations as monomorphisms from lattices of propositional feature models to lattices of extensional features models. This formalization sheds new light on the correspondence between the extensional and the propositional representations of feature models. It aims to foster the development of a formal framework for supporting practical exploitation of future theoretical developments on feature models and software product lines.

1 Introduction

Software-intensive systems can have thousands of interdependent configuration options across different subsystems. In the resulting configuration space, different software variants can be obtained by selecting among these configuration options and accordingly assembling the underlying subsystems. The interdependencies between options are dictated by corresponding interdependencies between the underlying subsysems [7].

Feature models [8] allow developers to organize the configuration space and facilitate the construction of software variants by describing configuration options using interdependent *features* [23]: a feature is a name representing some functionality, a set of features is called a *configuration*, and each configuration that fulfills the interdependencies expressed by the feature model, called a *product*, identifies a software variant. Software-intensive systems can comprise thousands of features and several subsystems [11,12,24,33]. The design, development

© Springer Nature Switzerland AG 2020
V. K. I. Pun et al. (Eds.): ICTAC 2020, LNCS 12545, pp. 103–122, 2020.
https://doi.org/10.1007/978-3-030-64276-1_6

and maintenance of feature models with thousands of features can be simplified by representing large feature models as sets of smaller interdependent feature models [11,29] that we call *fragments*. To this aim, several representations of feature models have been proposed in the literature (see, e.g., Batory [8] and Sect. 2.2 of Apel *et al.* [7]) and many approaches for composing feature models from fragments have been investigated [3,6,13,28,32].

In this paper we focus on the propositional representation (which works well in practice [10,27,34]) and the extensional representation (which has been recently shown well suited for theoretical investigations [25,31]). We investigate the correspondence between the formulation for these two representations of feature model operators and relations. The starting point of this investigation is a novel partial order between feature models, that we call the feature model *fragment relation*. It is induced by a notion of feature model composition that has been used to model industrial-size configuration spaces [25,31], such as the configuration space of the Gentoo source-based Linux distribution [20], that consists of many configurable packages (the March 1st 2019 version of the Gentoo distribution comprises 671617 features spread across 36197 feature models). We exploit this partial order to provide an algebraic characterization of feature model operations and relations. Then, we provide a propositional characterizations of them and formalize the connection between the two characterizations as monomorphisms from lattices of propositional feature models to lattices of extensional features models.

The remainder of this paper is organized as follows. In Sect. 2 we recollect the necessary background and introduce the feature model fragment relation. In Sect. 3 we present the algebraic characterization of feature model operations and relations, and in Sect. 4 we present the propositional characterization of the operations and relations together with a formal account of the connection between the two characterizations. We discuss related work in Sect. 5, and conclude the paper in Sect. 6 by outlining planned future work.

2   Background and Concept

We first recall the propositional and the extensional representations of feature models (in Sect. 2.1) together with the feature model composition operation (in Sect. 2.2), then we formalize the notion of feature model fragment in terms of a novel partial order relation on feature models (in Sect. 2.3).

2.1   Feature Model Representations

In this paper, we focus on the propositional and on the extensional representations of feature models (see, e.g., Batory [8] and Sect. 2.3 of Apel *et al.* [7] for a discussion about other representations).

Definition 1 (Feature model, propositional representation). *A propositional feature model Φ is a pair $(\mathcal{F}, \phi)$ where $\mathcal{F}$ is a set of features and ϕ is a propositional formula whose variables x are elements of $\mathcal{F}$:*

$$\phi = x \;\mid\; \phi \wedge \phi \;\mid\; \phi \vee \phi \;\mid\; \phi \rightarrow \phi \;\mid\; \neg\phi \;\mid\; \mathsf{false} \;\mid\; \mathsf{true}$$

Its products are the set of features $p \subseteq \mathcal{F}$ such that ϕ is satisfied by assigning value true *to the variables x in p and* false *to the variables in $\mathcal{F} \setminus p$.*

Example 1 (A propositional representation of the glibc feature model). Gentoo packages can be configured by selecting features (called *use flags* in Gentoo), which may trigger dependencies or conflicts between packages. Version 2.29 of the *glibc* library, that contains the core functionalities of most Linux systems, is provided by the package sys-libs/glibc-2.29-r2 (abbreviated to glibc in the sequel). This package has many dependencies, including (as expressed in Gentoo's notation):

doc? (sys−apps/texinfo)
    vanilla?(!sys−libs/timezone−data)

This dependency expresses that glibc requires the texinfo documentation generator (provided by any version of the sys-apps/texinfo package) whenever the feature doc is selected and if the feature vanilla is selected, then glibc conflicts with any version of the time zone database (as stated with the !sys-libs/timezone-data constraint). These *dependencies* can be expressed by a feature model $(\mathcal{F}_{\mathsf{glibc}}, \phi_{\mathsf{glibc}})$ where

$$\mathcal{F}_{\mathsf{glibc}} = \{\mathsf{glibc, texinfo, tzdata, glibc{:}doc, glibc{:}v}\}$$

$$\phi_{\mathsf{glibc}} = \mathsf{glibc} \wedge (\mathsf{glibc{:}doc} \rightarrow \mathsf{texinfo}) \wedge (\mathsf{glibc{:}v} \rightarrow (\neg\mathsf{tzdata}))$$

Here, the feature glibc represents the glibc package; texinfo represents any sys-apps/texinfo package; tzdata represents any version of the sys-libs/timezone-data package; and glibc:doc (resp. glibc:v) represents the glibc's doc (resp. vanilla) use flag.

The propositional representation of feature models works well in practice [10, 27, 34]. Recently, Schröter *et al.* [31] pointed out that using an extensional representation of feature models simplifies the presentation of feature model concepts.

Definition 2 (Feature model, extensional representation). *An extensional feature model $\mathcal{M}$ is a pair $(\mathcal{F}, \mathcal{P})$ where $\mathcal{F}$ is a set of features and $\mathcal{P} \subseteq 2^{\mathcal{F}}$ a set of products.*

Example 2 (An extensional representation of the glibc feature model). Let 2^{S} denote the powerset of S. The feature model of Example 1 can be given an extensional representation $\mathcal{M}_{\mathsf{glibc}} = (\mathcal{F}_{\mathsf{glibc}}, \mathcal{P}_{\mathsf{glibc}})$ where $\mathcal{F}_{\mathsf{glibc}}$ is the same as in Example 1 and

$$\mathcal{P}_{\mathsf{glibc}} = \{\{\mathsf{glibc}\}, \{\mathsf{glibc, texinfo}\}, \{\mathsf{glibc, tzdata}\}, \{\mathsf{glibc, texinfo, tzdata}\}\} \cup$$
$$\{\{\mathsf{glibc, glibc{:}doc, texinfo}\}, \{\mathsf{glibc, glibc{:}doc, texinfo, tz\text{-}data}\}\} \cup$$
$$\{\{\mathsf{glibc, glibc{:}v}\}, \{\mathsf{glibc, glibc{:}v, texinfo}\}\} \cup$$
$$\{\{\mathsf{glibc, glibc{:}doc, glibc{:}v, texinfo}\}\}$$

In the description of $\mathcal{P}_{\text{glibc}}$, the first line contains products with glibc but none of its use flags are selected, so texinfo and tz-data can be freely installed; the second line contains products with the use flag doc selected in glibc, so a package of sys-apps/texinfo is always required; the third line contains products with the use flag vanilla selected in glibc, so no package of sys-libs/timezone-data is allowed; finally, the fourth line contains products with both glibc's use flags selected, so sys-apps/texinfo is mandatory and sys-libs/timezone-data forbidden.

The following definition introduces the extensional representation of the empty feature model and of the void feature models.

Definition 3 (Empty feature model and void feature models). *The empty feature model, denoted $\mathcal{M}_{\emptyset} = (\emptyset, \{\emptyset\})$, has no features and has just the empty product $\emptyset$. A void feature model is a feature model that has no products, i.e., of the form $(\mathcal{F}, \emptyset)$ for some set of features $\mathcal{F}$.*

2.2 Feature Model Composition

Complex software systems, like the Gentoo source-based Linux distribution [20], often consist of many interdependent configurable packages [24–26]. The configuration options of each package can be represented by a feature model. Therefore, configuring two packages in such a way that they can be installed together corresponds to finding a product in the composition of their associated feature models. As pointed out by Lienhardt *et al.* [25], in the propositional representation of feature models this composition corresponds to logical conjunction: the composition of two feature models $(\mathcal{F}_1, \phi_1)$ and $(\mathcal{F}_2, \phi_2)$ is the feature model $(\mathcal{F}_1 \cup \mathcal{F}_2, \phi_1 \wedge \phi_2)$. Lienhardt *et al.* [25] also claimed that in the extensional representation of feature models this composition corresponds to the binary operator $\bullet$ of Schröter *et al.* [31], which combines the products sets in way similar to the join operator from relational algebra [14].

Definition 4 (Feature model composition). *The composition of two feature models $\mathcal{M}_1 = (\mathcal{F}_1, \mathcal{P}_1)$ and $\mathcal{M}_2 = (\mathcal{F}_2, \mathcal{P}_2)$, denoted $\mathcal{M}_1 \bullet \mathcal{M}_2$, is the feature model $(\mathcal{F}_1 \cup \mathcal{F}_2, \{p \cup q \mid p \in \mathcal{P}_1, q \in \mathcal{P}_2, p \cap \mathcal{F}_2 = q \cap \mathcal{F}_1\})$.*

As proved in [16,17], the composition operator $\bullet$ is associative and commutative, with $\mathcal{M}_{\emptyset}$ as identity element (i.e., $\mathcal{M} \bullet \mathcal{M}_{\emptyset} = \mathcal{M}$). Note that $(\mathcal{F}_1, \mathcal{P}_1) \bullet (\mathcal{F}_2, \emptyset) = (\mathcal{F}_1 \cup \mathcal{F}_2, \emptyset)$.

Example 3 (Composing glibc and gnome-shell feature models). Let us consider another important package of the Gentoo distribution: *gnome-shell*, a core component of the Gnome Desktop environment. Version 3.30.2 of *gnome-shell* is provided by the package gnome-base/gnome-shell-3.30.2-r2 (abbreviated to g-shell in the sequel), and its dependencies include the following statement:

```
networkmanager?( sys—libs/timezone—data )
```

This dependency expresses that g-shell requires any version of the time zone database when the feature networkmanager (abbreviated to g-shell:nm in the sequel) is selected.

The *propositional representation* of this dependency can be captured by the feature model $(\mathcal{F}_{\text{g-shell}}, \phi_{\text{g-shell}})$, where

$$\mathcal{F}_{\text{g-shell}} = \{\text{g-shell, tzdata, g-shell:nm}\} \quad \phi_{\text{g-shell}} = \text{g-shell} \wedge (\text{g-shell:nm} \to \text{tzdata})$$

The corresponding *extensional representation* of this feature model is $\mathcal{M}_{\text{g-shell}} = (\mathcal{F}_{\text{g-shell}}, \mathcal{P}_{\text{g-shell}})$, where:

$$\mathcal{P}_{\text{g-shell}} = \{\{\text{g-shell}\}, \{\text{g-shell, tzdata}\}\} \cup \{\{\text{g-shell, tzdata, g-shell:nm}\}\}$$

Here, the first line contains products with g-shell but none of its use flags are selected: tzdata can be freely selected; and the second line is the product where g-shell:nm is also selected and tzdata becomes mandatory.

The *propositional representation* of the composition is the feature model $(\mathcal{F}_{\text{full}}, \phi_{\text{full}})$, where

$$\mathcal{F}_{\text{full}} = \mathcal{F}_{\text{glibc}} \cup \mathcal{F}_{\text{g-shell}} = \{\text{glibc, texinfo, tzdata, g-shell, glibc:doc, glibc:v, g-shell:nm}\}$$
$$\phi_{\text{full}} = \phi_{\text{glibc}} \wedge \phi_{\text{g-shell}} = (\text{glibc} \wedge ((\text{glibc:doc} \to \text{texinfo}) \wedge (\text{glibc:v} \to (\neg\text{tz-data}))))$$
$$\wedge\, (\text{g-shell} \wedge (\text{g-shell:nm} \to \text{tzdata}))$$

The *extensional representation* of the composition is the feature model $\mathcal{M}_{\text{full}} = \mathcal{M}_{\text{glibc}} \bullet \mathcal{M}_{\text{g-shell}} = (\mathcal{F}_{\text{full}}, \mathcal{P}_{\text{full}})$ where

$$\mathcal{P}_{\text{full}} = \{\{\text{glibc, g-shell}\} \cup p \mid p \in 2^{\{\text{texinfo, tzdata}\}}\} \cup$$
$$\{\{\text{glibc, glibc:doc, texinfo, g-shell}\} \cup p \mid p \in 2^{\{\text{tzdata}\}}\} \cup$$
$$\{\{\text{glibc, glibc:v, g-shell}\} \cup p \mid p \in 2^{\{\text{texinfo}\}}\} \cup$$
$$\{\{\text{glibc, g-shell, g-shell:nm, tzdata}\} \cup p \mid p \in 2^{\{\text{texinfo}\}}\} \cup$$
$$\{\{\text{glibc, glibc:doc, glibc:v, texinfo, g-shell}\}\} \cup$$
$$\{\{\text{glibc, glibc:doc, texinfo, g-shell, g-shell:nm, tzdata}\}\}$$

Here, the first line contains the products where both glibc and g-shell are installed, but without use flags selected, so all optional package can be freely selected; the second line contains the products with the glibc's use flag doc selected, so sys-apps/texinfo becomes mandatory; the third line contains the products with the glibc's use flag vanilla selected, so sys-libs/timezone-data is forbidden; the fourth line contains the products with the g-shell's use flag net-workmanager, so sys-libs/timezone-data is mandatory; the fifth line contains the product with glibc's both flags selected and the sixth line contains the product with glibc's use flag doc and g-shell's use flag networkmanager are selected.

2.3   The Feature Model Fragment Relation

The notion of feature model composition induces the definition of the notion of feature model fragment as a binary relation between feature models.

Definition 5 (Feature model fragment relation). *A feature model $\mathcal{M}_0$ is a fragment of a feature model $\mathcal{M}$, denoted as $\mathcal{M}_0 \leq \mathcal{M}_1$, whenever there exists a feature model $\mathcal{M}'$ such that $\mathcal{M}_0 \bullet \mathcal{M}' = \mathcal{M}_1$.*

For instance, we have (by definition) that $\mathcal{M}_{\text{g-shell}} \leq (\mathcal{M}_{\text{g-shell}} \bullet \mathcal{M}_{\text{glibc}})$. It is worth observing that, as illustrated by the following example, some combination of features that are allowed in the members of the composition might be no longer available in the result of the composition.

Example 4 (Composing glibc and libical feature models). Consider for instance the version 3.0.8 of the library libical in Gentoo. Its feature model contains the following constraint (as expressed in Gentoo notation):

berkdb? (sys−libs/db) sys−libs/timezone−data

This dependency expresses that libical requires the db library whenever the feature berkdb is selected and requires the package sys-libs/timezone-data to be installed. These *dependencies* can be extensionally expressed by a feature model $\mathcal{M}_{\text{libical}} = (\mathcal{F}_{\text{libical}}, \mathcal{P}_{\text{libical}})$ where

$$\mathcal{F}_{\text{libical}} = \{\text{libical, berkdb, sys-libs/db, tzdata}\}$$

$$\mathcal{P}_{\text{libical}} = \{\{\text{libical, tzdata}\}, \{\text{libical, tzdata, berkdb, sys-libs/db}\}\}$$

Composing the feature model of glibc and libical gives the feature model $\mathcal{M}_c = (\mathcal{F}_c, \mathcal{P}_c)$ where $\mathcal{F}_c = \mathcal{F}_{\text{glibc}} \cup \mathcal{F}_{\text{libical}}$ and:

$$\mathcal{P}_c = \{\{\text{glibc, libical, tzdata}\} \cup p \mid p \in 2^{\{\text{texinfo, sys-libs/db}\}}\} \cup$$

$$\{\{\text{glibc, glibc:doc, texinfo, libical, tzdata}\} \cup p \mid p \in 2^{\{\text{sys-libs/db}\}}\} \cup$$

$$\{\{\text{glibc, libical, berkdb, sys-libs/db, tzdata}\} \cup p \mid p \in 2^{\{\text{texinfo}\}}\} \cup$$

$$\{\{\text{glibc, glibc:doc, texinfo, libical, berkdb, sys-libs/db, tzdata}\}\}$$

Here, the first line contains the products where both glibc and libical are installed, but without use flags selected, so only the annex package timezone-data is mandatory; the second line contains the products with the glibc's use flag doc selected, so sys-apps/texinfo becomes mandatory; the third line contains the products with the libical's use flag berkdb, so sys-libs/db becomes mandatory; finally, the fourth line contains the product with all optional features of both glibc and libical selected.

It is easy to see from the constraint, and also from the extensional representation, that combining glibc and libical makes the feature glibc:v dead (i.e., not selectable): when composed, the feature models interact and not all combinations of products are available. Feature incompatibilities such as this are a normal occurrence in many product lines (such as the linux kernel) but have two negative properties: first, it means that some features that are stated to be optional (i.e., can be freely selected or not by the user) actually are not optional in some cases, depending on some other packages being selected or not; second, it means that some packages cannot be installed at the same time because of their dependencies: consider for instance a package that requires the feature glibc:v being selected, that package is not compatible with libical.

3   Algebraic Characterization of Feature Models

In Sect. 3.1, we recall some relevant algebraic notions. In Sect. 3.2, we show that the feature model fragment relation induces a lattice of feature models where the join operation is feature model composition. Then, in Sect. 3.3, we show that the feature model fragment relation generalizes the feature model interface relation [31] and we provide some more algebraic properties.

3.1   A Recollection of Algebraic Notions

In this section we briefly recall the notions of lattice, bounded lattice and Boolean algebra (see, e.g., Davey and Priestley [18] for a detailed presentation). An *ordered lattice* is a partially ordered set $(P, \sqsubseteq)$ such that, for every $x, y \in P$, both the least upper bound (lub) of $\{x, y\}$, denoted $\sup\{x, y\} = \min\{a \mid x, y \leq a\}$, and the greatest lower bound (glb) of $\{x, y\}$, denoted $\inf\{x, y\} = \max\{a \mid a \leq x, y\}$, are always defined.

An *algebraic lattice* is an algebraic structure $(L, \sqcup, \sqcap)$ where L is non-empty set equipped with two binary operations $\sqcup$ (called *join*) and $\sqcap$ (called *meet*) which satisfy the following.

- Associative laws: $x \sqcup (y \sqcup z) = (x \sqcup y) \sqcup z$, $x \sqcap (y \sqcap z) = (x \sqcap y) \sqcap z$.
- Commutative laws: $x \sqcup y = y \sqcup x$, $x \sqcap y = y \sqcap x$.
- Absorption laws: $x \sqcup (x \sqcap y) = x$, $x \sqcap (x \sqcup y) = x$.
- Idempotency laws: $x \sqcup x = x$, $x \sqcup x = x$.

As known, the two notions of lattice are equivalent (Theorem 2.9 and 2.10 of [18]). In particular, given an ordered lattice $(P, \sqsubseteq)$ with the operations $x \sqcup y = \sup\{x, y\}$ and $x \sqcap y = \inf\{x, y\}$, the following three statements are equivalent (Theorem 2.8 of [18]):

$$x \sqsubseteq y, \qquad x \sqcup y = y, \qquad x \sqcap y = x.$$

A *bounded lattice* is a lattice that contains two elements $\bot$ (the lattice's *bottom*) and $\top$ (the lattice's *top*) which satisfy the following law: $\bot \sqsubseteq x \sqsubseteq \top$. Let L be a bounded lattice, $y \in L$ is a *complement* of $x \in L$ if $x \sqcap y = \bot$ and $x \sqcup y = \top$. If x has a unique complement, we denote this complement by $\bar{x}$.

A *distributive lattice* is a lattice which satisfies the following distributive law: $x \sqcap (y \sqcup z) = (x \sqcap y) \sqcup (x \sqcap z)$. In a bounded distributive lattice the complement (whenever it exists) is unique (see [18, Section 4.13]).

A *Boolean lattice* (a.k.a. *Boolean algebra*) L is a bounded distributive lattice such that each $x \in L$ has a (necessarily unique) complement $\bar{x} \in L$.

3.2   Lattices of Feature Models

Although (to the best of our knowledge) only finite feature models are relevant in practice, in our theoretical development (in order to enable a better understanding of the relation between the extensional and the propositional representations) we consider also feature models with infinitely many features and products. The following definition introduces a notation for three different sets of extensional feature models (see Definition 2) over a given set of features.

Definition 6 (Sets of extensional feature models over a set of features). *Let X be a set of features. We denote:*

- $\mathfrak{E}(X)$ *the set of the extensional feature models $(\mathcal{F},\mathcal{P})$ such that $\mathcal{F} \subseteq X$;*
- $\mathfrak{E}_{\text{fin}}(X)$ *the subset of the finite elements of $\mathfrak{E}(X)$, i.e., $(\mathcal{F},\mathcal{P})$ such that $\mathcal{F} \subseteq_{\text{fin}} X$; and*
- $\mathfrak{E}_{\text{eql}}(X)$ *the subset of elements of $\mathfrak{E}(X)$ that have exactly the features X, i.e., $(\mathcal{F},\mathcal{P})$ such that $\mathcal{F} = X$.*

Note that, if X has infinitely many elements then $\mathfrak{E}_{\text{fin}}(X)$ has infinitely many elements too. Instead, if X is finite then $\mathfrak{E}(X)$ and $\mathfrak{E}_{\text{fin}}(X)$ coincide and have a finite number of elements.

In order to simplify the presentation, $\mathcal{P}|_Y$ is used to denote $\{p \cap Y \mid p \in \mathcal{P}\}$ where $\mathcal{P}$ is a set of products and Y is a set of features.

Lemma 1 (Two criteria for the feature model fragment relation). *Given a set X, for all $\mathcal{M}_1 = (\mathcal{F}_1,\mathcal{P}_1)$ and $\mathcal{M}_2 = (\mathcal{F}_2,\mathcal{P}_2)$ in $\mathfrak{E}(X)$, the following statements are equivalent:*

i) $\mathcal{M}_1 \leq \mathcal{M}_2$
ii) $\mathcal{M}_1 \bullet \mathcal{M}_2 = \mathcal{M}_2$
iii) $\mathcal{F}_1 \subseteq \mathcal{F}_2$ *and* $\mathcal{P}_1 \supseteq \mathcal{P}_2|_{\mathcal{F}_1}$

Proof i) $\Rightarrow$ *ii).* It is straightforward to check that $\mathcal{M} \bullet \mathcal{M} = \mathcal{M}$, for all $\mathcal{M}$. Then, by definition of $\leq$ (Definition 5) there is $\mathcal{M}' \in \mathfrak{E}(X)$ such that $\mathcal{M}_2 = \mathcal{M}_1 \bullet \mathcal{M}'$. Thus,

$$\mathcal{M}_1 \bullet \mathcal{M}_2 = \mathcal{M}_1 \bullet (\mathcal{M}_1 \bullet \mathcal{M}') = (\mathcal{M}_1 \bullet \mathcal{M}_1) \bullet \mathcal{M}' = \mathcal{M}_1 \bullet \mathcal{M}' = \mathcal{M}_2.$$

ii) $\Rightarrow$ *iii).* By definition of $\bullet$ (Definition 4), it is clear from the hypothesis that $\mathcal{F}_1 \subseteq \mathcal{F}_2$. Moreover, $\mathcal{P}_2 = \{p \cup q \mid p \in \mathcal{P}_1, q \in \mathcal{P}_2, p \cap \mathcal{F}_2 = q \cap \mathcal{F}_1\}$ immediately implies that $\mathcal{P}_2 = \{q \mid p \in \mathcal{P}_1, q \in \mathcal{P}_2, p = q \cap \mathcal{F}_1\}$, which in turn implies $\mathcal{P}_2|_{\mathcal{F}_1} \subseteq \mathcal{P}_1$.

iii) $\Rightarrow$ *i).* By using the hypothesis, we have $(\mathcal{F}_1 \cup \mathcal{F}_2, \{p \cup q \mid p \in \mathcal{P}_1, q \in \mathcal{P}_2, p \cap \mathcal{F}_2 = q \cap \mathcal{F}_1\}) = (\mathcal{F}_2, \mathcal{P}_2)$, i.e. $\mathcal{M}_1 \bullet \mathcal{M}_2 = \mathcal{M}_2$. This implies, by definition of $\leq$, that $\mathcal{M}_1 \leq \mathcal{M}_2$. $\quad\square$

Lemma 2 (The operator $\bullet$ on $\mathfrak{E}_{\text{eql}}(X)$). *Given two feature models $\mathcal{M}_1 = (X,\mathcal{P}_1)$ and $\mathcal{M}_2 = (X,\mathcal{P}_2)$ in $\mathfrak{E}_{\text{eql}}(X)$, we have that: $\mathcal{M}_1 \bullet \mathcal{M}_2 = (X,\mathcal{P}_1 \cap \mathcal{P}_2)$.*

Proof According to the definition of $\bullet$ we have:
$\mathcal{M}_1 \bullet \mathcal{M}_2 = (X, \{p_1 \cup p_2 \mid p_1 \in \mathcal{P}_1, p_2 \in \mathcal{P}_2, p_1 = p_2\}) = (X, \mathcal{P}_1 \cap \mathcal{P}_2). \quad\square$

Theorem 1 (Lattices of feature models over a set of features). *Given a set X and two feature models $\mathcal{M}_1 = (\mathcal{F}_1,\mathcal{P}_1), \mathcal{M}_2 = (\mathcal{F}_2,\mathcal{P}_2) \in \mathfrak{E}(X)$, we define:*
$\mathcal{M}_1 \star \mathcal{M}_2 = (\mathcal{F}_1 \cap \mathcal{F}_2, \mathcal{P}_1|_{\mathcal{F}_2} \cup \mathcal{P}_2|_{\mathcal{F}_1})$, *and* $\overline{\mathcal{M}_1} = (\mathcal{F}_1, 2^{\mathcal{F}_1} \setminus \mathcal{P}_1)$. *Then:*

1. $(\mathfrak{E}(X), \leq)$ *is a bounded lattice with join* •, *meet* ⋆, *bottom* $\mathcal{M}_\emptyset = (\emptyset, \{\emptyset\})$ *and top* $(X, \emptyset)$.
2. *If* X *is an infinite set then* $\mathfrak{E}_{\mathrm{fin}}(X)$ *is a sublattice of* $\mathfrak{E}(X)$ *with the same bottom and no top.*
3. $\mathfrak{E}_{\mathrm{eql}}(X)$ *is a sublattice of* $\mathfrak{E}(X)$ *and it is a Boolean lattice with bottom* $(X, 2^X)$, *same top of* $\mathfrak{E}(X)$, *and complement* ⁻.

Proof. Let first prove that $\leq$ is a partial order. Let $\mathcal{M}_1 \leq \mathcal{M}_2 \leq \mathcal{M}_3$.

- Reflexivity. In $\mathfrak{E}(X)$ and $\mathfrak{E}_{\mathrm{fin}}(X)$ holds, because $\mathcal{M}_1 \bullet \mathcal{M}_\emptyset = \mathcal{M}_1$. In $\mathfrak{E}_{\mathrm{eql}}(X)$ holds, because $\mathcal{M}_1 \bullet (X, 2^X) = \mathcal{M}_1$. Clearly, $\mathcal{M}_\emptyset$ belongs to $\mathfrak{E}_{\mathrm{eql}}(X)$ only when $X = \emptyset$ (in this case, $(X, 2^X)$ is $\mathcal{M}_\emptyset$).
- Antisymmetry. Suppose additionally $\mathcal{M}_2 \leq \mathcal{M}_1$, so by hypothesis there are $\mathcal{M}, \mathcal{M}'$ such that $\mathcal{M}_2 = \mathcal{M}_1 \bullet \mathcal{M}'$ and $\mathcal{M}_1 = \mathcal{M}_2 \bullet \mathcal{M}$. Clearly,

$$\mathcal{M}_1 = \mathcal{M}_2 \bullet \mathcal{M} = \mathcal{M}_1 \bullet \mathcal{M}' \bullet \mathcal{M}' \bullet \mathcal{M} = \mathcal{M}_1 \bullet \mathcal{M}' \bullet \mathcal{M}' \bullet \mathcal{M}$$
$$= \mathcal{M}_2 \bullet \mathcal{M}' \bullet \mathcal{M} = \mathcal{M}_2 \bullet \mathcal{M} \bullet \mathcal{M}' = \mathcal{M}_1 \bullet \mathcal{M}' = \mathcal{M}_2.$$

  The proof is the same for $\mathfrak{E}(X)$, $\mathfrak{E}_{\mathrm{fin}}(X)$, $\mathfrak{E}_{\mathrm{eql}}(X)$.
- Transitivity. Let $\mathcal{M}, \mathcal{M}'$ such that $\mathcal{M}_3 = \mathcal{M}_2 \bullet \mathcal{M}$ and $\mathcal{M}_2 = \mathcal{M}_1 \bullet \mathcal{M}'$. Clearly, $\mathcal{M}_3 = \mathcal{M}_2 \bullet \mathcal{M} = (\mathcal{M}_1 \bullet \mathcal{M}') \bullet \mathcal{M} = \mathcal{M}_1 \bullet (\mathcal{M}' \bullet \mathcal{M})$ which ensures that $\mathcal{M}_1 \leq \mathcal{M}_3$. The proof is the same for $\mathfrak{E}(X)$, $\mathfrak{E}_{\mathrm{fin}}(X)$, $\mathfrak{E}_{\mathrm{eql}}(X)$.

Part 1: $(\mathfrak{E}(X), \leq)$ is a lattice with $\mathcal{M}_\emptyset$ as bottom and $(X, \emptyset)$ as top. Let $\uparrow \mathcal{M}$ be the set of upper bounds of $\mathcal{M}$ w.r.t. $\leq$, viz. $\{\mathcal{M}' \mid \mathcal{M} \leq \mathcal{M}'\}$; and, let $\downarrow \mathcal{M}$ be the set of lower bounds of $\mathcal{M}$ w.r.t. $\leq$, viz. $\{\mathcal{M}' \mid \mathcal{M}' \leq \mathcal{M}\}$.

- If $i = 1, 2$ then $\mathcal{M}_i \leq \mathcal{M}_1 \bullet \mathcal{M}_2$ by definition of $\leq$, thus $\mathcal{M}_1 \bullet \mathcal{M}_2 \in (\uparrow \mathcal{M}_1) \cap (\uparrow \mathcal{M}_2)$. Moreover, for all common upper bounds $\mathcal{M} \in (\uparrow \mathcal{M}_1) \cap (\uparrow \mathcal{M}_2)$, we have (cf. Lemma 1)

$$\mathcal{M} = \mathcal{M}_1 \bullet \mathcal{M} = \mathcal{M}_1 \bullet (\mathcal{M}_2 \bullet \mathcal{M}) = (\mathcal{M}_1 \bullet \mathcal{M}_2) \bullet \mathcal{M}$$

  And so we have that $\mathcal{M}_1 \bullet \mathcal{M}_2$ is the join $\mathcal{M}_1 \sqcup \mathcal{M}_2$.
- Let $\mathcal{M} = (\mathcal{F}, \mathcal{P}) = (\mathcal{F}_1 \cap \mathcal{F}_2, \mathcal{P}_1|_{\mathcal{F}_2} \cup \mathcal{P}_2|_{\mathcal{F}_1})$. We have $\{p \cap \mathcal{F} \mid p \in \mathcal{P}_i\} \subseteq \mathcal{P}$ and $\mathcal{F} \subseteq \mathcal{F}_i$ for $i \in \{1, 2\}$: we thus have $\mathcal{M} \in (\downarrow \mathcal{M}_1) \cap (\downarrow \mathcal{M}_2)$. Moreover, for all $(\mathcal{F}', \mathcal{P}') \in (\downarrow \mathcal{M}_1) \cap (\downarrow \mathcal{M}_2)$, it is easy to see that $\mathcal{F}' \subseteq \mathcal{F}_1 \cap \mathcal{F}_2 \subseteq \mathcal{F}$ and $\mathcal{P}|_{\mathcal{F}'} \subseteq \mathcal{P}'$ by Lemma 1. And so, again by Lemma 1, $\mathcal{M}$ is the meet.
- For all $\mathcal{M} \in \mathfrak{E}(X)$, we have $\mathcal{M} \bullet \mathcal{M}_\emptyset = \mathcal{M}$ which implies by definition that $\mathcal{M}_\emptyset \leq \mathcal{M}$. Similarily, it is easy to see that for all $\mathcal{M} \in \mathfrak{E}(X)$, we have $\mathcal{M} \bullet (X, \emptyset) = (X, \emptyset)$ which implies by definition that $\mathcal{M} \leq (X, \emptyset)$.

Part 2: $\mathfrak{E}_{\mathrm{fin}}(X)$, is a sublattice of $\mathfrak{E}(X)$ with the same bottom and no top. It is clear that for every $\mathcal{M}_1 \in \mathfrak{E}_{\mathrm{fin}}(X)$ and $\mathcal{M}_2 \in \mathfrak{E}(X)$ such that $\mathcal{M}_2 \leq \mathcal{M}_1$, we have that $\mathcal{M}_2 \in \mathfrak{E}_{\mathrm{fin}}(X)$. It follows that $\mathfrak{E}_{\mathrm{fin}}(X)$ is a sublattice of $\mathfrak{E}(X)$ with $\mathcal{M}_\emptyset$ as bottom. Moreover, if follows from the definition of • that if $\mathfrak{E}_{\mathrm{fin}}(X)$ with X infinite would have a top $(\mathcal{F}, \mathcal{P})$, we would have $S \subseteq \mathcal{F}$ for all $S \subseteq_{\mathrm{fin}} X$. This means that $\mathcal{F}$ should be equal to X, which is not possible.

Part 3: $\mathfrak{E}_{eql}(X)$ is a bounded sublattice of $\mathfrak{E}(X)$ and a Boolean lattice, with the same top and $(X, 2^X)$ as bottom. It is clear that for every $\mathcal{M}_1, \mathcal{M}_2 \in \mathfrak{E}_{eql}(X)$ we have that $\mathcal{M}_1 \bullet \mathcal{M}_2 \in \mathfrak{E}_{eql}(X)$ and $\mathcal{M}_1 \star \mathcal{M}_2 \in \mathfrak{E}_{eql}(X)$. It follows that $\mathfrak{E}_{fin}(X)$ is a sublattice of $\mathfrak{E}(X)$ with $(X, \emptyset)$ as top. Moreover, it is easy to see that $(X, 2^X) \in \mathfrak{E}_{eql}(X)$ and that for all $\mathcal{M}_1 \in \mathfrak{E}_{eql}(X)$, we have $(X, 2^X) \bullet \mathcal{M} = \mathcal{M}$. Let now prove the distributive law. Let us consider $\mathcal{M}_1 = (X, \mathcal{P}_1)$, $\mathcal{M}_2 = (X, \mathcal{P}_2)$, $\mathcal{M}_3 = (X, \mathcal{P}_3) \in \mathfrak{E}_{eql}(X)$, we have:

$$\mathcal{M}_1 \sqcap (\mathcal{M}_2 \sqcup \mathcal{M}_3) = (X, \mathcal{P}_1 \cup (\mathcal{P}_2 \cap \mathcal{P}_3))$$
$$= (X, (\mathcal{P}_1 \cup \mathcal{P}_2) \cap (\mathcal{P}_1 \cup \mathcal{P}_3)) = (\mathcal{M}_1 \sqcap \mathcal{M}_2) \sqcup (\mathcal{M}_1 \sqcap \mathcal{M}_3)$$

Finally, it is easy to see that $\mathcal{M}_1 \sqcap \overline{\mathcal{M}_1} = (X, 2^X)$ and $\mathcal{M}_1 \sqcup \overline{\mathcal{M}_1} = (X, \emptyset)$. $\square$

3.3   On Fragments and Interfaces

Feature model slices were defined by Acher et al. [4] as a unary operator Π_Y that restricts a feature model to the set Y of features.

Definition 7 (Feature model slice operator). *Let $\mathcal{M} = (\mathcal{F}, \mathcal{P})$ be a feature model. The slice operator Π_Y on feature models, where Y is a set of features, is defined by: $\Pi_Y(\mathcal{M}) = (\mathcal{F} \cap Y, \mathcal{P}|_Y)$.*

More recently, Schröter et al. [31] introduced the following notion of feature model interface.

Definition 8 (Feature model interface relation). *A feature model $\mathcal{M}_1 = (\mathcal{F}_1, \mathcal{P}_1)$ is an interface of feature model $\mathcal{M}_2 = (\mathcal{F}_2, \mathcal{P}_2)$, denoted as $\mathcal{M}_1 \preceq \mathcal{M}_2$, whenever both $\mathcal{F}_1 \subseteq \mathcal{F}_2$ and $\mathcal{P}_1 = \mathcal{P}_2|_{\mathcal{F}_1}$ hold.*

Remark 1 (On feature model interfaces and slices). As pointed out in [31], feature model slices and interfaces are closely related. Namely: $\mathcal{M}_1 \preceq \mathcal{M}_2$ holds if and only if there exists a set of features Y such that $\mathcal{M}_1 = \Pi_Y(\mathcal{M}_2)$.

Example 5 (A slice of the glibc feature model). Applying the operator $\Pi_{\{glibc, glibc:v\}}$ to the feature model $\mathcal{M}_{glibc}$ of Example 2 yields the feature model

$$\mathcal{F} = \{glibc, glibc:v\} \qquad \mathcal{P} = \{\emptyset, \{glibc\}, \{glibc, glibc:v\}\},$$

which (according to Remark 1) is an interface for $\mathcal{M}_{glibc}$.

The following theorem points out the relationship between the feature model interface relation (designed to abstract away a set of features from a feature model) and the feature model fragment relation (designed to support feature model decomposition).

Theorem 2 (Interfaces are fragments). *If $\mathcal{M}_1 \preceq \mathcal{M}_2$ then $\mathcal{M}_1 \leq \mathcal{M}_2$.*

Proof. Immediate by Definition 8 and Lemma 1. $\square$

We conclude this section by providing some algebraic properties that relate the slice operator and the interface an fragment relations.

Lemma 3 (Monotonocity properties of the feature model slice operator). *For all $\mathcal{F}, \mathcal{F}_1, \mathcal{F}_2 \subseteq X$ and $\mathcal{M}, \mathcal{M}_1, \mathcal{M}_2 \in \mathfrak{E}(X)$*

1. *If $\mathcal{F}_1 \subseteq \mathcal{F}_2$ then $\Pi_{\mathcal{F}_1}(\mathcal{M}) \preceq \Pi_{\mathcal{F}_2}(\mathcal{M})$.*
2. *If $\mathcal{F}_1 \subseteq \mathcal{F}_2$ then $\Pi_{\mathcal{F}_1}(\mathcal{M}) \leq \Pi_{\mathcal{F}_2}(\mathcal{M})$.*
3. *If $\mathcal{M}_1 \preceq \mathcal{M}_2$ then $\Pi_{\mathcal{F}}(\mathcal{M}_1) \preceq \Pi_{\mathcal{F}}(\mathcal{M}_2)$.*
4. *If $\mathcal{M}_1 \leq \mathcal{M}_2$ then $\Pi_{\mathcal{F}}(\mathcal{M}_1) \leq \Pi_{\mathcal{F}}(\mathcal{M}_2)$.*

Proof 1. Clearly $\Pi_{\mathcal{F}_1}(\mathcal{M}) \bullet \Pi_{\mathcal{F}_2}(\mathcal{M}) = \Pi_{\mathcal{F}_2}(\mathcal{M})$. Thus the proof follows by Definition 8.

2. Immediate by Lemma 3.1 and Theorem 2.
3. By Definition 8, we have that $\mathcal{F}_1 \subseteq \mathcal{F}_2$ and $\mathcal{P}_1 = \mathcal{P}_2 \mid_{\mathcal{F}_1}$. Consequently, for all $\mathcal{F} \subseteq X$, we have $(\mathcal{F}_1 \cap \mathcal{F}) \subseteq (\mathcal{F}_2 \cap \mathcal{F})$ and $\mathcal{P}_1 \mid_{\mathcal{F}} = \mathcal{P}_2 \mid_{\mathcal{F}_1} \mid_{\mathcal{F}}$. Still, $\Pi_{\mathcal{F}}(\mathcal{M}_1) \preceq \Pi_{\mathcal{F}}(\mathcal{M}_2)$ by Definition 8.
4. By Lemma 1, we have that $\mathcal{F}_1 \subseteq \mathcal{F}_2$ and $\mathcal{P}_1 \supseteq \mathcal{P}_2 \mid_{\mathcal{F}_1}$. Consequently, for all $\mathcal{F} \subseteq X$, we have $(\mathcal{F}_1 \cap \mathcal{F}) \subseteq (\mathcal{F}_2 \cap \mathcal{F})$ and $\mathcal{P}_1 \mid_{\mathcal{F}} \supseteq \mathcal{P}_2 \mid_{\mathcal{F}_1} \mid_{\mathcal{F}}$. Still, $\Pi_{\mathcal{F}}(\mathcal{M}_1) \leq \Pi_{\mathcal{F}}(\mathcal{M}_2)$ by Lemma 1.

We remark that Lemma 3.3 and Theorem 2 do not imply Lemma 3.4.

Theorem 3 (Algebraic properties of the feature model slice operator). *For all $\mathcal{M}_1, \mathcal{M}_2, \mathcal{M}_3 \in \mathfrak{E}(X)$ and $\mathcal{F}_4, \mathcal{F}_5 \subseteq X$, we have*

$\leq$-Monotonicity. *If $\mathcal{M}_1 \leq \mathcal{M}_2$ and $\mathcal{F}_4 \subseteq \mathcal{F}_5$, then $\Pi_{\mathcal{F}_4}(\mathcal{M}_1) \leq \Pi_{\mathcal{F}_5}(\mathcal{M}_2)$.*
$\preceq$-Monotonicity. *If $\mathcal{M}_1 \preceq \mathcal{M}_2$ and $\mathcal{F}_4 \subseteq \mathcal{F}_5$, then $\Pi_{\mathcal{F}_4}(\mathcal{M}_1) \preceq \Pi_{\mathcal{F}_5}(\mathcal{M}_2)$.*
Commutativity. $\Pi_{\mathcal{F}_4}(\Pi_{\mathcal{F}_5}(\mathcal{M}_3)) = \Pi_{\mathcal{F}_5}(\Pi_{\mathcal{F}_4}(\mathcal{M}_3))$.

Proof.   **$\leq$-Monotonicity.** Straightforward by Lemma 3.2 and Lemma 3.4.
$\preceq$-Monotonicity. Straightforward by Lemma 3.1 and Lemma 3.3.
Commutativity. In accordance with Definition 8, it is sufficient to observe that $\Pi_{\mathcal{F}_4}(\Pi_{\mathcal{F}_5}(\mathcal{M}_3)) = \Pi_{\mathcal{F}_4 \cup \mathcal{F}_5}(\mathcal{M}_3) = \Pi_{\mathcal{F}_5}(\Pi_{\mathcal{F}_4}(\mathcal{M}))$ holds.   ◻

4   Propositional Characterization of Feature Models Operations and Relations

In Sect. 4.1 we introduce a mapping that associates each propositional feature model to its corresponding extensional representation (cf. Sect. 2.1). Then, in Sect. 4.2, we provide a propositional characterization for the fragment relation ($\leq$), for the composition ($\bullet$) and the meet ($\star$) operations; for the the bottom of the Boolean lattice $\mathfrak{E}_{eql}(X)$ (the feature model $\mathcal{M}_X = (X, 2^X)$), for the bottom of the bounded lattice $\mathfrak{E}(X)$ (the feature model $\mathcal{M}_\emptyset = (\emptyset, \{\emptyset\})$) and for the top of bounded the lattice $\mathfrak{E}(X)$) (the feature model $\mathcal{M}^X = (X, \emptyset)$); and for the complement operation ($\bar{}$). Finally, in Sect. 4.3, we provide a propositional characterization for the slice operator (Π_Y) and for the interface relation ($\preceq$).

4.1 Relating Extensional and Propositional Feature Models

As stated at the beginning of Sect. 3.2, in our theoretical development we consider also feature models with infinitely many features and products, where each product may have infinitely many features. The following definition introduces a notion for three different sets of propositional feature models (see Definition 1) over a set of features (cf. Definition 6).

Definition 9 (Sets of propositional feature models over a set of features). *Let X be a set of features. We denote:*

- $\mathfrak{P}(X)$ *the set of the propositional feature models $(\mathcal{F}, \phi)$ such that $\mathcal{F} \subseteq X$;*
- $\mathfrak{P}_{\mathrm{fin}}(X)$ *the subset of the finite elements of $\mathfrak{P}(X)$, i.e., $(\mathcal{F}, \phi)$ such that $\mathcal{F} \subseteq_{\mathrm{fin}} X$; and*
- $\mathfrak{P}_{\mathrm{eql}}(X)$ *the subset of elements of $\mathfrak{P}(X)$ that have exactly the features X, i.e., $(\mathcal{F}, \phi)$ such that $\mathcal{F} = X$.*

We denote by $\mathrm{ftrs}(\phi)$ the (finite) set of features occurring in a propositional formula ϕ, and as usual we say that ϕ is *ground* whenever $\mathrm{ftrs}(\phi)$ is empty. We recall that an *interpretation* (a.k.a. truth assignment or valuation) $\mathcal{I}$ is a function which maps propositional logic variables to true or false [7,9]. As usual, $\mathrm{dom}(\mathcal{I})$ denotes the domain of an interpretation $\mathcal{I}$ and we write $\mathcal{I} \models \phi$ to mean that the propositional formula ϕ is true under the interpretation $\mathcal{I}$ (i.e., $\mathrm{ftrs}(\phi) \subseteq \mathrm{dom}(\mathcal{I})$ and the ground formula obtained from ϕ by replacing each feature x occurring in ϕ by $\mathcal{I}(x)$ evaluates to true). We write $\models \phi$ to mean that ϕ is valid (i.e., it evaluates to true under all the interpretations $\mathcal{I}$ such that $\mathrm{ftrs}(\phi) \subseteq \mathrm{dom}(\mathcal{I})$). We write $\phi_1 \models \phi_2$ to mean that ϕ_2 is a logical consequence of ϕ_1 (i.e., for all interpretations $\mathcal{I}$ with $\mathrm{ftrs}(\phi_1) \cup \mathrm{ftrs}(\phi_2) \subseteq \mathrm{dom}(\mathcal{I})$, if $\mathcal{I} \models \phi_1$ then $\mathcal{I} \models \phi_2$), and we write $\phi_1 \equiv \phi_2$ to mean that ϕ_1 and ϕ_2 are logically equivalent (i.e., they are satisfied by exactly the same interpretations with domain including $\mathrm{ftrs}(\phi_1) \cup \mathrm{ftrs}(\phi_2)$). We recall that: (i) $\mathcal{I}_1$ is *included* in $\mathcal{I}_2$, denoted $\mathcal{I}_1 \subseteq \mathcal{I}_2$, whenever $\mathrm{dom}(\mathcal{I}_1) \subseteq \mathrm{dom}(\mathcal{I}_2)$ and $\mathcal{I}_1(x) = \mathcal{I}_2(x)$, for all $x \in \mathrm{dom}(\mathcal{I}_1)$; (ii) $\mathcal{I}_1$ and $\mathcal{I}_2$ are *compatible* whenever $\mathcal{I}_1(x) = \mathcal{I}_2(x)$, for all $x \in \mathrm{dom}(\mathcal{I}_1) \cap \mathrm{dom}(\mathcal{I}_2)$; and (iii) if $\mathcal{I}_1 \models \phi$ then its *restriction* $\mathcal{I}_0$ to $\mathrm{ftrs}(\phi)$ is such that $\mathcal{I}_0 \models \phi$ and, for all interpretations $\mathcal{I}_2$ such that $\mathcal{I}_0 \subseteq \mathcal{I}_2$, it holds that $\mathcal{I}_2 \models \phi$.

The following definition gives a name to the interpretations that represent the products of the feature models with a given set of features.

Definition 10 (Interpretation representing a product). *Let $(\mathcal{F}, \mathcal{P})$ be an extensional feature model and $p \in \mathcal{P}$. The interpretation that represents the product p, denoted by $\mathcal{I}_p^{\mathcal{F}}$, is the interpretation with domain $\mathcal{F}$ such that: $\mathcal{I}_p^{\mathcal{F}}(x) =$ true if $x \in p$; and $\mathcal{I}_p^{\mathcal{F}}(x) =$ false if $x \in \mathcal{F} \setminus p$.*

The following definition gives a name to the mapping that associates each propositional feature model to its corresponding extensional representation.

Definition 11 (The ext mapping). *Let $(\mathcal{F}, \phi) \in \mathfrak{P}(X)$. We denote by $\mathit{ext}((\mathcal{F}, \phi))$ (or $\mathit{ext}(\mathcal{F}, \phi)$, for short) the extensional feature model $(\mathcal{F}, \mathcal{P}) \in \mathfrak{E}(X)$ such that $\mathcal{P} = \{p \mid p \subseteq \mathcal{F} \text{ and } \mathcal{I}_p^{\mathcal{F}} \models \phi\}$. In particular, ext maps $\mathfrak{P}_{\mathrm{fin}}(X)$ to $\mathfrak{E}_{\mathrm{fin}}(X)$, and maps $\mathfrak{P}_{\mathrm{eql}}(X)$ to $\mathfrak{E}_{\mathrm{eql}}(X)$.*

We denote by $\equiv$ the equivalence relation over feature models defined by: $(\mathcal{F}_1, \phi_1) \equiv (\mathcal{F}_2, \phi_2)$ if and only if both $\mathcal{F}_1 = \mathcal{F}_2$ and $\phi_1 \equiv \phi_2$. We write $[\mathfrak{P}(X)]$, $[\mathfrak{P}_{\mathrm{fin}}(X)]$ and $[\mathfrak{P}_{\mathrm{eql}}(X)]$ as short for the quotient sets $\mathfrak{P}(X)/{\equiv}$, $\mathfrak{P}_{\mathrm{fin}}(X)/{\equiv}$ and $\mathfrak{P}_{\mathrm{eql}}(X)/{\equiv}$, respectively.

Note that, if X has infinitely many elements and $(\mathcal{F}, \phi) \in \mathfrak{P}(X)$, then $\mathcal{F}$ may contain infinite many features, while the propositional formula ϕ is syntactically finite (cf. Definition 1). Moreover, $\mathfrak{P}_{\mathrm{fin}}(X)$ has infinitely many elements (even when X is finite). It is also worth observing that, if X is finite, then $\mathfrak{P}(X)$ and $\mathfrak{P}_{\mathrm{fin}}(X)$ coincide and the quotient set $[\mathfrak{P}_{\mathrm{fin}}(X)]$ is finite. Moreover, for all $\Phi_1, \Phi_2 \in \mathfrak{P}(X)$, we have that: $\mathtt{ext}(\Phi_1) = \mathtt{ext}(\Phi_2)$ if and only if $\Phi_1 \equiv \Phi_2$.

All the finite feature models have a propositional representation, i.e., if $(\mathcal{F}, \mathcal{P}) \in \mathfrak{E}_{\mathrm{fin}}(X)$, then there exists $(\mathcal{F}, \phi) \in \mathfrak{P}_{\mathrm{fin}}(X)$ such that $\mathtt{ext}(\mathcal{F}, \phi) = (\mathcal{F}, \mathcal{P})$. Take, for instance, the formula in disjunctive normal form $\phi = \bigvee_{p \in \mathcal{P}} \left((\wedge_{f \in p} f) \wedge (\wedge_{f \in \mathcal{F} \setminus p} \neg f) \right)$. Given $[\Phi] \in [\mathfrak{P}(X)]$, we define (with an abuse of notation) $\mathtt{ext}([\Phi]) = \mathtt{ext}(\Phi)$. Then, we have that $\mathtt{ext}$ is an injection from $[\mathfrak{P}(X)]$ to $\mathfrak{E}(X)$, an injection from $[\mathfrak{P}_{\mathrm{eql}}(X)]$ to $\mathfrak{E}_{\mathrm{eql}}(X)$, and a bijection from $[\mathfrak{P}_{\mathrm{fin}}(X)]$ to $\mathfrak{E}_{\mathrm{fin}}(X)$.

As shown by the following example, if X has infinitely many elements, then there are feature models in $\mathfrak{E}(X) \setminus \mathfrak{E}_{\mathrm{fin}}(X)$ that have no propositional representation.

Example 6 (Extensional feature models without a propositional representation). Consider the natural numbers as features. Then the extensional feature models $(\mathbb{N}, \{\{3\}\})$, $(\mathbb{N}, \{\{n \mid n \text{ is even}\}\})$ (which has a single product with infinitely many features) and $(\mathbb{N}, \{\{n\} \mid n \text{ is even}\})$ (which has infinitely many products with one feature each) have no propositional representation.

Remark 2 (On $\mathfrak{P}_{\mathrm{fin}}(X)$ and $\mathfrak{P}(X)$). It is worth observing that, since $\mathtt{ext}(\mathcal{F}, \phi) = \mathtt{ext}(\mathrm{ftrs}(\phi), \phi) \bullet (\mathcal{F} \setminus \mathrm{ftrs}(\phi), 2^{\mathcal{F} \setminus \mathrm{ftrs}(\phi)})$ and the set $\mathrm{ftrs}(\phi)$ is finite, then any infinite propositional feature model (i.e., in $\mathfrak{P}(X) \setminus \mathfrak{P}_{\mathrm{fin}}(X)$ with X infinite) is decomposable into a finite one (i.e., in $\mathfrak{P}_{\mathrm{fin}}(X)$) and a "free" one (i.e., one where all the features are optional). Therefore, if X has infinitely many elements, then there are *infinitely* many elements of $\mathfrak{E}(X) \setminus \mathfrak{E}_{\mathrm{fin}}(X)$ that do not have a propositional representation.

4.2 Propositional Characterization of the Lattices of Feature Models

The following theorem states that the feature model fragment relation $\leq$ corresponds to (the converse of) logical consequence.

Theorem 4 (Propositional characterization of the relation $\leq$). *Given $\Phi_1 = (\mathcal{F}_1, \phi_1)$ and $\Phi_2 = (\mathcal{F}_2, \phi_2)$ in $\mathfrak{P}(X)$, we write $\Phi_1 \leq \Phi_2$ to mean that both $\mathcal{F}_1 \subseteq \mathcal{F}_2$ and $\phi_2 \models \phi_1$ hold. Then: $\mathtt{ext}(\Phi_1) \leq \mathtt{ext}(\Phi_2)$ holds if and only $\Phi_1 \leq \Phi_2$ holds.*

Proof. We have: $(\mathcal{F}_1, \mathcal{P}_1) = \text{ext}(\Phi_1) \leq \text{ext}(\Phi_2) = (\mathcal{F}_2, \mathcal{P}_2)$

       iff $\mathcal{F}_1 \subseteq \mathcal{F}_2$ and $\mathcal{P}_1 \supseteq \mathcal{P}_2|_{\mathcal{F}_1}$ (by Lemma 1)

       iff $\mathcal{F}_1 \subseteq \mathcal{F}_2$ and $\{p_1 \mid \mathcal{I}_{p_1}^{\mathcal{F}_1} \models \phi_1\} \supseteq \{p_2 \cap \mathcal{F}_1 \mid \mathcal{I}_{p_2}^{\mathcal{F}_2} \models \phi_2\}$

       iff $\mathcal{F}_1 \subseteq \mathcal{F}_2$ and, for all $p \in \mathcal{P}_2$, $\mathcal{I}_p^{\mathcal{F}_2} \models \phi_2$ implies $\mathcal{I}_p^{\mathcal{F}_2} \models \phi_1$

       iff $\mathcal{F}_1 \subseteq \mathcal{F}_2$ and $\phi_2 \models \phi_1$

       iff $\Phi_1 \leq \Phi_2$.   □

The following theorem shows that the feature model composition operator • corresponds to propositional conjunction (cf. Sect. 2.2).

Theorem 5 (Propositional characterization of the operator •). *Given* $\Phi_1 = (\mathcal{F}_1, \phi_1)$ *and* $\Phi_2 = (\mathcal{F}_2, \phi_2)$ *in* $\mathfrak{P}(X)$, *we define:* $\Phi_1 \bullet \Phi_2 = (\mathcal{F}_1 \cup \mathcal{F}_2, \phi_1 \wedge \phi_2)$. *Then:* $\text{ext}(\Phi_1) \bullet \text{ext}(\Phi_2) = \text{ext}(\Phi_1 \bullet \Phi_2)$.

Proof. Let $\text{ext}(\mathcal{F}_i, \phi_i) = (\mathcal{F}_i, \mathcal{P}_i)$, for $i = 1, 2$.

$\text{ext}(\Phi_1) \bullet \text{ext}(\Phi_2) = (\mathcal{F}_3, \mathcal{P}_3)$

iff $\mathcal{F}_3 = \mathcal{F}_1 \cup \mathcal{F}_2$ and iff $\mathcal{P}_3 = \{p_1 \cup p_2 \mid \mathcal{I}_{p_1}^{\mathcal{F}_1} \models \phi_1, \mathcal{I}_{p_2}^{\mathcal{F}_2} \models \phi_1, p_1 \cap \mathcal{F}_2 = p_2 \cap \mathcal{F}_1\}$

iff $\mathcal{F}_3 = \mathcal{F}_1 \cup \mathcal{F}_2$ and $\mathcal{P}_3 = \{p \mid p_1 \cup p_2 \subseteq p$ and $\mathcal{I}_p^X \models \phi_1, \mathcal{I}_p^X \models \phi_2\}$

iff $\mathcal{F}_3 = \mathcal{F}_1 \cup \mathcal{F}_2$ and $\mathcal{P}_3 = \{p \mid \mathcal{I}_p^{\mathcal{F}_3} \models \phi_1 \wedge \phi_2\}$

iff $(\mathcal{F}_3, \mathcal{P}_3) = \text{ext}(\Phi_1 \bullet \Phi_2)$.   □

In order to provide a propositional characterization of the meet operator $\star$ (introduced in Theorem 1), we introduce an auxiliary notation expressing a propositional encoding of the existentially quantified formula $\exists x_1 \cdots \exists x_n.\phi$, where ϕ is a propositional formula. Given $Y = \{x_1, ..., x_n\}$, we define:

$$(\bigvee_Y \phi) = \begin{cases} \phi & \text{if } Y = \emptyset, \\ (\bigvee_{Y-\{x\}} (\phi[x := \text{true}]) \vee (\phi[x := \text{false}])) & \text{otherwise.} \end{cases}$$

Theorem 6 (Propositional characterization of the operator $\star$). *Given* $\Phi_1 = (\mathcal{F}_1, \phi_1)$ *and* $\Phi_2 = (\mathcal{F}_2, \phi_2)$ *in* $\mathfrak{P}(X)$, *we define:*

$$\Phi_1 \star \Phi_2 = \left(\mathcal{F}_1 \cap \mathcal{F}_2, (\bigvee_{\text{ftrs}(\phi_1) \backslash \mathcal{F}_2} \phi_1) \vee (\bigvee_{\text{ftrs}(\phi_2) \backslash \mathcal{F}_1} \phi_2)\right).$$

Then: $\text{ext}(\Phi_1) \star \text{ext}(\Phi_2) = \text{ext}(\Phi_1 \star \Phi_2)$.

Proof. Let $\text{ext}(\mathcal{F}_i, \phi_i) = (\mathcal{F}_i, \mathcal{P}_i)$ for $i = 1, 2$.

Since $\text{ext}(\mathcal{F}_1, \phi_1) \star \text{ext}(\mathcal{F}_2, \phi_2) = (\mathcal{F}_1 \cap \mathcal{F}_2, \mathcal{P}_1|_{\mathcal{F}_2} \cup \mathcal{P}_2|_{\mathcal{F}_1})$, we have that:

$\text{ext}(\Phi_1) \star \text{ext}(\Phi_2) = (\mathcal{F}_3, \mathcal{P}_3)$

iff $\mathcal{F}_3 = \mathcal{F}_1 \cap \mathcal{F}_2$ and $\mathcal{P}_3 = \{p_1 \cap \mathcal{F}_2 \mid \mathcal{I}_{p_1}^{\mathcal{F}_1} \models \phi_1\} \cup \{p_2 \cap \mathcal{F}_1 \mid \mathcal{I}_{p_2}^{\mathcal{F}_2} \models \phi_2\}$

iff $\mathcal{F}_3 = \mathcal{F}_1 \cap \mathcal{F}_2$ and $\mathcal{P}_3 = \{p_1 \cap \mathcal{F}_3 \mid \mathcal{I}_{p_1}^{\mathcal{F}_1} \models \phi_1\} \cup \{p_2 \cap \mathcal{F}_3 \mid \mathcal{I}_{p_2}^{\mathcal{F}_2} \models \phi_2\}$

iff $\mathcal{F}_3 = \mathcal{F}_1 \cap \mathcal{F}_2$ and $\mathcal{P}_3 = \mathcal{P}_1|_{\mathcal{F}_3} \cup \mathcal{P}_2|_{\mathcal{F}_3}$

iff $\mathcal{F}_3 = \mathcal{F}_1 \cap \mathcal{F}_2$ and, $p \in \mathcal{P}_3$ implies

either $\exists p_1$ s.t. $p = p_1 \cap \mathcal{F}_3$ and $\mathcal{I}_{p_1}^{\mathcal{F}_1} \models \phi_1$ or $\exists p_2$ s.t. $p = p_2 \cap \mathcal{F}_3$ and $\mathcal{I}_{p_2}^{\mathcal{F}_2} \models \phi_2$

iff $\mathcal{F}_3 = \mathcal{F}_1 \cap \mathcal{F}_2$ and, $p \in \mathcal{P}_3$ implies

either $\mathcal{I}_p^{\mathcal{F}_3} \models (\bigvee_{\text{ftrs}(\phi_1) \backslash \mathcal{F}_2} \phi_1)$ or $\mathcal{I}_p^{\mathcal{F}_3} \models (\bigvee_{\text{ftrs}(\phi_2) \backslash \mathcal{F}_1} \phi_2)$

iff $\mathcal{F}_3 = \mathcal{F}_1 \cap \mathcal{F}_2$ and, $p \in \mathcal{P}_3$ implies $\mathcal{I}_p^{\mathcal{F}_3} \models (\bigvee_{\text{ftrs}(\phi_1) \backslash \mathcal{F}_2} \phi_1) \vee (\bigvee_{\text{ftrs}(\phi_2) \backslash \mathcal{F}_1} \phi_2)$

iff $(\mathcal{F}_3, \mathcal{P}_3) = \text{ext}(\Phi_1 \star \Phi_2)$.   □

The following theorem states that the feature models of the form $\mathcal{M}_\mathcal{F} = (\mathcal{F}, 2^\mathcal{F})$ and $\mathcal{M}^\mathcal{F} = (\mathcal{F}, \emptyset)$ correspond to true and false, respectively—recall that (see Theorem 1) $\mathcal{M}_\emptyset$ is the bottom of the lattices $(\mathfrak{E}(X), \leq)$ and $(\mathfrak{E}_{\text{fin}}(X), \leq)$, while $\mathcal{M}_X$ is the bottom of the Boolean lattice $(\mathfrak{E}_{\text{eql}}(X), \leq)$, and $\mathcal{M}^X$ is the top of the lattice $(\mathfrak{E}(X), \leq)$ and of the Boolean lattice $(\mathfrak{E}_{\text{eql}}(X), \leq)$ and, if X is finite, of the lattice $(\mathfrak{E}_{\text{fin}}(X), \leq)$.

Theorem 7 (Propositional characterization of the feature models $\mathcal{M}_\mathcal{F}$ and $\mathcal{M}^\mathcal{F}$). *Let* $(\mathcal{F}, \phi) \in \mathfrak{P}(X)$.

1. $ext(\mathcal{F}, \phi) = \mathcal{M}_\mathcal{F} = (\mathcal{F}, 2^\mathcal{F})$ *if and only if* $\phi \equiv$ true.
2. $ext(\mathcal{F}, \phi) = \mathcal{M}^\mathcal{F} = (\mathcal{F}, \emptyset)$ *if and only if* $\phi \equiv$ false.

Proof 1. Immediate, because true is satisfied by all interpretations. *2.* Immediate, because no interpretation satisfies false. □

The following theorem shows that the feature model complement operator ⁻ (introduced in Theorem 1) corresponds to logical negation.

Theorem 8 (Propositional characterization of the operator ⁻). *Given* $\Phi = (\mathcal{F}, \phi)$ *in* $\mathfrak{P}(X)$, *we define:* $\overline{\Phi} = (\mathcal{F}, \neg\phi)$. *Then* $\overline{ext(\Phi)} = ext(\overline{\Phi})$.

Proof. Straightforward. □

Lemma 4 below provides a representation of logical disjunction in terms of a novel feature model operator, that we denote by $+$. Then, Lemma 5 sheds some light on the Boolean lattice $\mathfrak{E}_{\text{eql}}(X)$, by showing that on $\mathfrak{E}_{\text{eql}}(X)$ the meet operator $\star$ and the operator $+$ coincide.

Lemma 4 (The operator $+$ and its propositional characterization). *Given two sets of sets Y and Z, we define:* $Y \uplus Z = \{y \cup z \mid y \in Y, z \in Z\}$. *Given two feature models $\mathcal{M}_1 = (\mathcal{F}_1, \mathcal{P}_1)$ and $\mathcal{M}_2 = (\mathcal{F}_2, \mathcal{P}_2)$ in $\mathfrak{E}(X)$, we define:* $\mathcal{M}_1 + \mathcal{M}_2 = (\mathcal{F}_1 \cup \mathcal{F}_2, (\mathcal{P}_1 \uplus 2^{(\mathcal{F}_2 \backslash \mathcal{F}_1)}) \cup (\mathcal{P}_2 \uplus 2^{(\mathcal{F}_1 \backslash \mathcal{F}_2)}))$. *Given $\Phi_1 = (\mathcal{F}_1, \phi_1)$ and $\Phi_2 = (\mathcal{F}_2, \phi_2)$ in $\mathfrak{P}(X)$, we define:* $\Phi_1 + \Phi_2 = (\mathcal{F}_1 \cup \mathcal{F}_2, \phi_1 \vee \phi_2)$. *Then:* $ext(\Phi_1) + ext(\Phi_2) = ext(\Phi_1 + \Phi_2)$.

Proof. Let $\text{ext}(\mathcal{F}_i, \phi_i) = (\mathcal{F}_i, \mathcal{P}_i)$ for $i = 1, 2$. We have that
$\text{ext}(\Phi_1) + \text{ext}(\Phi_2) = (\mathcal{F}_3, \mathcal{P}_3)$
iff $\mathcal{P}_3 = \mathcal{F}_1 \cup \mathcal{F}_2$ and $\mathcal{P}_3 = \{p_1 \uplus 2^{(\mathcal{F}_2 \backslash \mathcal{F}_1)}) \mid \mathcal{I}_{p_1}^{\mathcal{F}_1} \models \phi_1\} \cup \{p_2 \uplus 2^{(\mathcal{F}_1 \backslash \mathcal{F}_2)} \mid \mathcal{I}_{p_2}^{\mathcal{F}_2} \models \phi_2\}$
iff $\mathcal{P}_3 = \mathcal{F}_1 \cup \mathcal{F}_2$ and, $p \in \mathcal{P}_3$ implies
     either $p \in \{p_1 \uplus 2^{(\mathcal{F}_2 \backslash \mathcal{F}_1)}) \mid \mathcal{I}_{p_1}^{\mathcal{F}_1} \models \phi_1\}$ or $p \in \{p_2 \uplus 2^{(\mathcal{F}_1 \backslash \mathcal{F}_2)} \mid \mathcal{I}_{p_2}^{\mathcal{F}_2} \models \phi_2\}$
iff $\mathcal{P}_3 = \mathcal{F}_1 \cup \mathcal{F}_2$ and, $p \in \mathcal{P}_3$ implies either $\mathcal{I}_p^{\mathcal{F}_3} \models \phi_1$ or $\mathcal{I}_p^{\mathcal{F}_3} \models \phi_2$
iff $\mathcal{P}_3 = \mathcal{F}_1 \cup \mathcal{F}_2$ and, $p \in \mathcal{P}_3$ implies $\mathcal{I}_{p \cap \mathcal{F}_1}^{\mathcal{F}_3} \models \phi_1 \vee \phi_2$
iff $(\mathcal{F}_3, \mathcal{P}_3) = \text{ext}(\Phi_1 + \Phi_2)$. □

Lemma 5 (The operators $\star$ and $+$ on $\mathfrak{E}_{\text{eql}}(X)$). *Given two feature models $\mathcal{M}_1 = (X, \mathcal{P}_1)$ and $\mathcal{M}_2 = (X, \mathcal{P}_2)$ in $\mathfrak{E}_{\text{eql}}(X)$, we have that:* $\mathcal{M}_1 \star \mathcal{M}_2 = \mathcal{M}_1 + \mathcal{M}_2 = (X, \mathcal{P}_1 \cup \mathcal{P}_2)$.

Proof. Straightforward from the definitions of $\star$ and $+$. □

Given $[\Phi_1]$, $[\Phi_2] \in [\mathfrak{P}(X)]$, we define (with an abuse of notation): $[\Phi_1] \leq [\Phi_2]$ as $\Phi_1 \leq \Phi_2$, $[\Phi_1] \bullet [\Phi_2] = [\Phi_1 \bullet \Phi_2]$, $[\Phi_1] \star [\Phi_2] = [\Phi_1 \star \Phi_2]$, $[\Phi_1] + [\Phi_2] = [\Phi_1 + \Phi_2]$, and $\overline{[\Phi_1]} = [\overline{\Phi_1}]$. Recall that a *homomorphism* is a structure-preserving map between two algebraic structures of the same type (e.g.., between two lattices), a *monomorphism* is an injective homomorphism, and an *isomorphism* is a bijective homomorphism.

Theorem 9 (ext is a lattice monomorphism). *Given a set X of features:*

1. $([\mathfrak{P}(X)], \leq)$ *is a bounded lattice with join $\bullet$, meet $\star$, bottom $[(\emptyset, \mathsf{true})]$ and top $[(X, \mathsf{false})]$. Moreover, ext is a bounded lattice monomorphism from $([\mathfrak{P}(X)], \leq)$ to $(\mathfrak{E}(X), \leq)$.*
2. *If X has infinitely many elements, then $[\mathfrak{P}_{\mathrm{fin}}(X)]$ is a sublattice of $[\mathfrak{P}(X)]$ with the same bottom and no top. Moreover, ext is a lattice isomorphism from $[\mathfrak{P}_{\mathrm{fin}}(X)]$ to $\mathfrak{E}_{\mathrm{fin}}(X)$.*
3. $[\mathfrak{P}_{\mathrm{eql}}(X)]$ *is a sublattice of $[\mathfrak{P}(X)]$ and it is a Boolean lattice with bottom $[(X, \mathsf{true})]$, same top of $[\mathfrak{P}(X)]$, complement $^-$, and where the meet behaves like $+$. Moreover, ext is a Boolean lattice monomorphism from $[\mathfrak{P}_{\mathrm{eql}}(X)]$ to $\mathfrak{E}_{\mathrm{eql}}(X)$ and it is an isomorphism whenever X is finite.*

Proof. Straightforward from Theorems 1, 4–8 and Lemmas 2, 4 and 5.   □

4.3   Propositional Characterization of Slices and Interfaces

The following theorem provides a propositional characterization of the slice operator.

Theorem 10 (Propositional characterization of the operator Π_Y).
Let $\Phi = (\mathcal{F}, \phi)$ be in $\mathfrak{P}(X)$. We define: $\Pi_Y(\Phi) = (Y \cap \mathcal{F}, (\bigvee_{\mathrm{ftrs}(\phi) \setminus Y} \phi))$. Then:

$$\Pi_Y(\mathsf{ext}(\Phi)) = \mathsf{ext}(\Pi_Y(\Phi)).$$

Proof. We have: $\Pi_Y(\mathsf{ext}(\Phi)) = (\mathcal{F}_0, \mathcal{P}_0)$

iff $\mathcal{F}_0 = \mathcal{F} \cap Y$ and $\mathcal{P}_0 = \{p \mid \mathcal{I}_p^{\mathcal{F}} \models \phi\}|_Y$

iff $\mathcal{F}_0 = \mathcal{F} \cap Y$ and $\mathcal{P}_0 = \{p \cap Y \mid \mathcal{I}_p^{\mathcal{F}} \models \phi\}$

iff $\mathcal{F}_0 = \mathcal{F} \cap Y$ and $\mathcal{P}_0 = \{p \cap Y \mid \mathcal{I}_p^{\mathcal{F} \cap Y} \models \phi\}$

iff $\mathcal{F}_0 = \mathcal{F} \cap Y$ and, $p_0 \in \mathcal{P}_0$ implies $\mathcal{I}_{p_0}^{\mathcal{F} \cap Y} \models (\bigvee_{\mathrm{ftrs}(\phi) \setminus Y} \phi)$

iff $(\mathcal{F}_0, \mathcal{P}_0) = \mathsf{ext}(\Pi_Y(\Phi))$.   □

The following corollary provides a propositional characterization of the interface relation $\mathcal{M}_1 \preceq \mathcal{M}_2$ which is the same as the interpretation of the slice operator $\mathcal{M}_1 = \Pi_Y(\mathcal{M}_2)$ when Y are the features of $\mathcal{M}_1$ (cf. Theorem 10 and Remark 1).

Corollary 1 (Propositional characterization of the relation $\preceq$). *Given $\Phi_1 = (\mathcal{F}_1, \phi_1)$ and $\Phi_2 = (\mathcal{F}_2, \phi_2)$ in $\mathfrak{P}(X)$, we write $\Phi_1 \preceq \Phi_2$ to mean that both $\mathcal{F}_1 \subseteq \mathcal{F}_2$ and $\phi_1 \equiv (\bigvee_{\mathrm{ftrs}(\phi_2) \setminus \mathcal{F}_1} \phi_2)$ hold. Then: $\mathsf{ext}(\Phi_1) \preceq \mathsf{ext}(\Phi_2)$ holds if and only $\Phi_1 \preceq \Phi_2$ holds.*

Proof. We have:

$(\mathcal{F}_1, \mathcal{P}_1) = \mathsf{ext}(\Phi_1) \preceq \mathsf{ext}(\Phi_2) = (\mathcal{F}_2, \mathcal{P}_2)$

iff $\mathcal{F}_1 \subseteq \mathcal{F}_2$ and $\mathcal{P}_1 = \mathcal{P}_2|_{\mathcal{F}_1}$ (by Definition 8)

iff $\mathcal{F}_1 \subseteq \mathcal{F}_2$ and $\{p_1 \mid \mathcal{I}_{p_1}^{\mathcal{F}_1} \models \phi_1\} = \{p_2 \cap \mathcal{F}_1 \mid \mathcal{I}_{p_2}^{\mathcal{F}_2} \models \phi_2\}$

iff $\mathcal{F}_1 \subseteq \mathcal{F}_2$ and, for all $p \in \mathcal{P}_2$, both $\phi_2 \models \phi_1$ and $\phi_1 \models (\bigvee_{\mathrm{ftrs}(\phi_2) \setminus \mathcal{F}_1} \phi_2)$

iff $\mathcal{F}_1 \subseteq \mathcal{F}_2$ and $\phi_1 \equiv (\bigvee_{\mathrm{ftrs}(\phi_2) \setminus \mathcal{F}_1} \phi_2)$

iff $\Phi_1 \preceq \Phi_2$.   □

5 Related Work

Although the propositional representation of feature models is well known in the literature (see, e.g., Sect. 2.3 of Apel *et al.* [7]), we are not aware of any work that (as done in the present paper) provides a formal account of the correspondence between the algebraic and the propositional characterizations of feature model operators and relations, and encompasses the general case of feature models with infinitely many features. The investigation presented in this paper started from the feature model composition operator • and the induced fragment partial order relation ≤. In the following we briefly discuss relevant related work on feature model composition operators and on feature model relations.

Feature-model composition operators are often investigated in connection with multi software product lines, which are sets of interdependent product lines [22]. Eichelberger and Schmid [19] present an overview of textual-modeling languages which support variability-model composition (like FAMILIAR [5], VELVET [29], TVL [13], VSL [1]) and discuss their support for composition, modularity, and evolution. Acher *et al.* [6] consider different feature-model composition operators together with possible implementations and discuss advantages and drawbacks.

The feature-model fragment relation introduced in this paper generalizes the feature-model interface relation introduced by Schröter *et al.* [31], which (see Remark 1) is closely related to the feature model slice operator introduced by Acher *et al.* [4]. The work of Acher *et al.* [4] focuses on feature model decomposition. In subsequent work [2], Acher *et al.* use the slice operator in combination with a merge operator to address evolutionary changes for extracted variability models, focusing on detecting differences between feature-model versions during evolution. Analyzing fragmented feature models usually requires to compose the fragments in order to apply existing techniques [21,34]. Schröter *et al.* [31] proposed feature model interfaces to support evolution of large feature models composed by several feature models fragments. Namely, they propose to analyze a fragmented feature model where some fragments have been replaced by carefully chosen feature model interface to obtain results that hold for the original feature model and for all its evolution where the evolved version of the fragments replaced by the interfaces are still compatible with the interfaces. More recently, Lienhardt *et al.* [25] strengthen feature model interfaces to support efficient automated product discovery in fragmented feature models.

6   Conclusion and Future Work

The formalization presented in this paper sheds new light on the correspondence between the algebraic and propositional characterizations of feature model operations and relations. It aims to foster the development of a formal framework for supporting practical exploitation of future theoretical developments on feature models and software product lines. For instance, recent works [25,31] which introduced novel feature model relations by relying on the extensional representation for theory and on the propositional representation for experiments, do not show the propositional representation of the relations.

In future work we would like to extend this picture by considering other feature model representations [7,8], operators [6] and relations [25]. Moreover, we would like to investigate whether there are classes of infinite feature models without a propositional representation (see Remark 2) that have practical relevance—such feature models might admit convenient representations (e.g., by first order logic). We are also planning to extend out formalization to encompass cardinality-based feature models, which can also enable infinitely many products, without necessarily requiring infinitely many features [15]. Moreover, we want to investigate more in detail the feature model fragment relation and how it can be used to decompose large feature models in manageable parts. Recently [17], we have introduced the notion of software product signature in order to express dependencies between different product lines, and we have lifted to software product lines the notions of feature model composition and interface. In future work we would like to lift to software product lines other feature model operations and relations and to provide a formal account of the connection between different software product line implementation approaches [7,30,34]. This formalization would enable formal reasoning on multi software product lines comprising software product lines implemented according to different approaches.

Acknowledgments. We thank the anonymous reviewers for their useful comments.

References

1. Abele, A., Papadopoulos, Y., Servat, D., Törngren, M., Weber, M.: The CVM framework - a prototype tool for compositional variability management. In: Proceedings of 4th International Workshop on Variability Modelling of Software-Intensive Systems. ICB-Research Report, vol. 37, pp. 101–105. Universität Duisburg-Essen (2010)
2. Acher, M., Cleve, A., Collet, P., Merle, P., Duchien, L., Lahire, P.: Extraction and evolution of architectural variability models in plugin-based systems. Softw. Syst. Model. **13**(4), 1367–1394 (2014). https://doi.org/10.1007/s10270-013-0364-2
3. Acher, M., Collet, P., Lahire, P., France, R.: Comparing approaches to implement feature model composition. In: Kühne, T., Selic, B., Gervais, M.-P., Terrier, F. (eds.) ECMFA 2010. LNCS, vol. 6138, pp. 3–19. Springer, Heidelberg (2010). https://doi.org/10.1007/978-3-642-13595-8_3

4. Acher, M., Collet, P., Lahire, P., France, R.B.: Slicing feature models. In: 26th IEEE/ACM International Conference on Automated Software Engineering (ASE), 2011, pp. 424–427 (2011). https://doi.org/10.1109/ASE.2011.6100089
5. Acher, M., Collet, P., Lahire, P., France, R.B.: Familiar: a domain-specific language for large scale management of feature models. Sci. Comput. Program. **78**(6), 657–681 (2013). https://doi.org/10.1016/j.scico.2012.12.004
6. Acher, M., Combemale, B., Collet, P., Barais, O., Lahire, P., France, R.B.: Composing your compositions of variability models. In: Moreira, A., Schätz, B., Gray, J., Vallecillo, A., Clarke, P. (eds.) MODELS 2013. LNCS, vol. 8107, pp. 352–369. Springer, Heidelberg (2013). https://doi.org/10.1007/978-3-642-41533-3_22
7. Apel, S., Batory, D.S., Kästner, C., Saake, G.: Feature-Oriented Software Product Lines: Concepts and Implementation. Springer, Heidelberg (2013). https://doi.org/10.1007/978-3-642-37521-7
8. Batory, D.: Feature models, grammars, and propositional formulas. In: Obbink, H., Pohl, K. (eds.) SPLC 2005. LNCS, vol. 3714, pp. 7–20. Springer, Heidelberg (2005). https://doi.org/10.1007/11554844_3
9. Ben-Ari, M.: Mathematical Logic for Computer Science, 3rd edn. Springer, Heidelberg (2012). https://doi.org/10.1007/978-1-4471-4129-7
10. Benavides, D., Segura, S., Ruiz-Cortés, A.: Automated analysis of feature models 20 years later: a literature review. Inf. Syst. **35**(6), 615–636 (2010). https://doi.org/10.1016/j.is.2010.01.001
11. Berger, T., et al.: A survey of variability modeling in industrial practice. In: Proceedings of 7th International Workshop on Variability Modelling of Software-Intensive Systems, pp. 7:1–7:8. ACM Press (2013)
12. Berger, T., She, S., Lotufo, R., Wąsowski, A., Czarnecki, K.: Variability modeling in the real: a perspective from the operating systems domain. In: Proceedings of 25th International Conference on Automated Software Engineering (ASE 2010), pp. 73–82. ACM Press (2010). https://doi.org/10.1145/1858996.1859010
13. Classen, A., Boucher, Q., Heymans, P.: A text-based approach to feature modelling: syntax and semantics of TVL. Sci. Comput. Program. **76**(12), 1130–1143 (2011). https://doi.org/10.1016/j.scico.2010.10.005
14. Codd, E.F.: A relational model of data for large shared data banks. Commun. ACM **13**(6), 377–387 (1970). https://doi.org/10.1145/362384.362685
15. Czarnecki, K., Helsen, S., Eisenecker, U.: Formalizing cardinality-based feature models and their specialization. Softw. Process: Improv. Pract. **10**(1), 7–29 (2005). https://doi.org/10.1002/spip.213
16. Damiani, F., Lienhardt, M., Paolini, L.: A formal model for multi SPLs. In: Dastani, M., Sirjani, M. (eds.) FSEN 2017. LNCS, vol. 10522, pp. 67–83. Springer, Cham (2017). https://doi.org/10.1007/978-3-319-68972-2_5
17. Damiani, F., Lienhardt, M., Paolini, L.: A formal model for multi software product lines. Sci. Comput. Program. **172**, 203–231 (2019). https://doi.org/10.1016/j.scico.2018.11.005
18. Davey, B.A., Priestley, H.A.: Introduction to Lattices and Order, 2nd edn. Cambridge University Press, Cambridge (2002). https://doi.org/10.1017/CBO9780511809088
19. Eichelberger, H., Schmid, K.: A systematic analysis of textual variability modeling languages. In: Proceedings of 17th International Software Product Line Conference (SPLC 2013), pp. 12–21. ACM Press (2013). https://doi.org/10.1145/2491627.2491652
20. Foundation, G.: Gentoo Linux (2019). https://gentoo.org. Accessed 20 Aug 2019

21. Galindo, J.A., Benavides, D., Trinidad, P., Gutiérrez-Fernández, A.M., Ruiz-Cortés, A.: Automated analysis of feature models: Quo vadis? Computing 101(5), 387–433 (2019). https://doi.org/10.1007/s00607-018-0646-1

22. Holl, G., Grünbacher, P., Rabiser, R.: A systematic review and an expert survey on capabilities supporting multi product lines. Inf. Softw. Technol. 54(8), 828–852 (2012). https://doi.org/10.1016/j.infsof.2012.02.002

23. Kang, K.C., Cohen, S.G., Hess, J.A., Novak, W.E., Peterson, A.S.: Feature-oriented domain analysis (FODA) feasibility study. Tech. rep. CMU/SEI-90-TR-21, Carnegie Mellon Software Engineering Institute (1990)

24. Lienhardt, M., Damiani, F., Donetti, S., Paolini, L.: Multi software product lines in the wild. In: Proceedings of 12th International Workshop on Variability Modelling of Software-Intensive Systems, VAMOS 2018, pp. 89–96. ACM (2018). https://doi.org/10.1145/3168365.3170425

25. Lienhardt, M., Damiani, F., Johnsen, E.B., Mauro, J.: Lazy product discovery in huge configuration spaces. In: Proceedings of the 42th International Conference on Software Engineering, ICSE 2020. ACM (2020). https://doi.org/10.1145/3377811.3380372

26. Lotufo, R., She, S., Berger, T., Czarnecki, K., Wąsowski, A.: Evolution of the Linux kernel variability model. In: Bosch, J., Lee, J. (eds.) SPLC 2010. LNCS, vol. 6287, pp. 136–150. Springer, Heidelberg (2010). https://doi.org/10.1007/978-3-642-15579-6_10

27. Mendonca, M., Wasowski, A., Czarnecki, K.: SAT-based analysis of feature models is easy. In: Muthig, D., McGregor, J.D. (eds.) Proceedings of the 13th International Software Product Line Conference. ACM International Conference Proceeding Series, vol. 446, pp. 231–240. ACM (2009). https://doi.org/10.5555/1753235.1753267

28. Rosenmüller, M., Siegmund, N., Kästner, C., Rahman, S.S.U.: Modeling dependent software product lines. In: Proceeding Workshop on Modularization, Composition and Generative Techniques for Product Line Engineering, pp. 13–18 (2008)

29. Rosenmüller, M., Siegmund, N., Thüm, T., Saake, G.: Multi-dimensional variability modeling. In: Proceedings of the 5th International Workshop on Variability Modelling of Software-Intensive Systems, pp. 11–20. ACM Press (2011). https://doi.org/10.1145/1944892.1944894

30. Schaefer, I., et al.: Software diversity: state of the art and perspectives. Int. J. Softw. Tools Technol. Transf. 14(5), 477–495 (2012). https://doi.org/10.1007/s10009-012-0253-y

31. Schröter, R., Krieter, S., Thüm, T., Benduhn, F., Saake, G.: Feature-model interfaces: the highway to compositional analyses of highly-configurable systems. In: Proceedings of the 38th International Conference on Software Engineering, ICSE 2016, pp. 667–678. ACM (2016). https://doi.org/10.1145/2884781.2884823

32. Schröter, R., Thüm, T., Siegmund, N., Saake, G.: Automated analysis of dependent feature models. In: Proceedings of 7th International Workshop on Variability Modelling of Software-Intensive Systems, pp. 9:1–9:5. ACM Press (2013). https://doi.org/10.1145/2430502.2430515

33. Tartler, R., Lohmann, D., Sincero, J., Schröder-Preikschat, W.: Feature consistency in compile-time-configurable system software: facing the Linux 10,000 feature problem. In: Proceedings of 6th European Conference on Computer systems (EuroSys 2011), pp. 47–60. ACM Press (2011). https://doi.org/10.1145/1966445.1966451

34. Thüm, T., Apel, S., Kästner, C., Schaefer, I., Saake, G.: A classification and survey of analysis strategies for software product lines. ACM Comput. Surv. 47(1), 6:1–6:45 (2014). https://doi.org/10.1145/2580950

The Complexity of Boolean State Separation

Ronny Tredup[1](✉) and Evgeny Erofeev[2]

[1] Institut für Informatik, Theoretische Informatik, Universität Rostock,
Albert-Einstein-Straße 22, 18059 Rostock, Germany
`ronny.tredup@uni-rostock.de`
[2] Department of Computing Science, Carl von Ossietzky Universität Oldenburg,
26111 Oldenburg, Germany
`evgeny.erofeev@informatik.uni-oldenburg.de`

Abstract. For a Boolean type of nets τ, a transition system A is synthesizeable into a τ-net N if and only if distinct states of A correspond to distinct markings of N, and N prevents a transition firing if there is no related transition in A. The former property is called τ-state separation property (τ-SSP) while the latter – τ-event/state separation property (τ-ESSP). A is embeddable into the reachability graph of a τ-net N if and only if A has the τ-SSP. This paper presents a complete characterization of the computational complexity of τ-SSP for all Boolean Petri net types.

Keywords: Boolean Petri nets · Boolean state separation · Complexity characterization

1 Introduction

Providing a powerful mechanism for the modeling of conflicts, dependencies and parallelism, Petri nets are widely used for studying and simulating concurrent and distributed systems. In system analysis, one aims to check behavioral properties of system models, and many of these properties are decidable [7] for Petri nets and their reachability graphs, which represent systems' behaviors. The task of system synthesis is opposite: a (formal) specification of the system's behavior is given, and the goal is then to decide whether this behavior can be implemented by a Petri net. In case of a positive decision, such a net should be constructed.

Boolean Petri nets form a simple yet rich and powerful family of Petri nets [3,4,8,10,12,13,16], applied in asynchronous circuits design [25,27], concurrent constraint programs [9] and analysis of biological systems models [6]. In Boolean nets, each place contains at most one token, for any reachable marking. Hence, a place can be interpreted as a Boolean condition that is *true* if marked

E. Erofeev—Supported by DFG through grant Be 1267/16-1 `ASYST`.

and *false* otherwise. A place p and a transition t of such a net are related by one of the Boolean *interactions* that define in which way p and t influence each other. The interaction inp (out) defines that p must be *true* (*false*) before and *false* (*true*) after t's firing; free (used) implies that t's firing proves that p is *false* (*true*); nop means that p and t do not affect each other at all; res (set) implies that p may initially be both *false* or *true* but after t's firing it is *false* (*true*); swap means that t inverts p's current Boolean value. Boolean Petri nets are classified by the sets of interactions that can be applied. A set τ of Boolean interactions is called a *type of net*, and a net N is of type τ (a τ-*net*) if it applies at most the interactions of τ. For a type τ, the τ-*synthesis* problem consists in deciding whether a specification given in the form of a labeled transition system (TS) is isomorphic to the reachability graph of some τ-net N, and in constructing N if it exists. The complexity of τ-synthesis has been studied in different settings [17,20,23], and varies substantially from polynomial [16] to NP-complete [2].

In order to perform synthesis, that is, to implement the behavior specified by the given TS with a τ-net, two general problems have to be resolved: The τ-net has to distinguish the global states of the TS, and the τ-net has to prevent actions at states where they are not permitted by the TS. In the literature [3], the former requirement is usually referred to as τ-*state separation property* (τ-SSP), while the latter $- \tau$-*event/state separation property* (τ-ESSP). Both τ-SSP and τ-ESSP define decision problems that ask whether a given TS fulfills the respective property. The present work focuses exclusively on the computational complexity of τ-SSP. The interest to state separation is motivated in several ways. First, many synthesis approaches are very sensitive to the size of the input's state space. This raises the question if some initial, so-called *pre-synthesis* procedures [5,26] can be employed as a quick-fail mechanism, i.e., techniques with a small computational overhead that would gain some helpful information for the main synthesis, or reject the input if exact (up to isomorphism) synthesis is not possible. Since τ-synthesis allows a positive decision if and only if τ-SSP and τ-ESSP do [3], an efficient decision procedure for τ-SSP could serve as a quick-fail pre-process check. Second, if exact synthesis is not possible for the given TS, one may want to have a simulating model, i.e., a τ-net that over-approximates [14,15] the specified behavior with some possible supplement. Formally, the TS then has to be injectively embeddable into the reachability graph of a τ-net. It is well known from the literature [3] that a TS can be embedded into the reachability graph of a τ-net if and only if it has the τ-SSP. Finally, in comparison to τ-ESSP, so far the complexity of τ-SSP is known to be as hard [1,16,23,24] or actually less hard [18,19]. On the contrary, in this paper, for some types of nets, deciding the τ-SSP is proven harder (NP-complete) than deciding the τ-ESSP (polynomial), e.g., for $\tau = \{\text{nop}, \text{res}, \text{set}\}$. From the contribution perspective, the τ-SSP has been previously considered only in the broader context of τ-synthesis, and only for selected types [16,19,22,23]. In this paper, we completely characterize the complexity of τ-SSP for all 256 Boolean types of nets and discover 150 new hard types, cf. §1–§3, §6, §9 of Fig. 1, and 4 new tractable types, cf. Fig. 1 §10, and comprise the known results for the other 102 types as well, cf. Fig. 1 §4, §5, §7, §8. In particular, our characterization categorizes Boolean types with regard to their behavioral capabilities, resulting from the Boolean interactions involved. This reveals the internal organization of the entire class of Boolean nets, suggesting a general approach for reasoning about its subclasses.

This paper is organized as follows. In Sect. 2, all the necessary notions and definitions will be given. Section 3 presents NP-completeness results for the types with nop-interaction. τ-SSP for types without nop is investigated in Sect. 4. Concluding remarks are given in Sect. 5. Due to space restrictions, one proof is omitted but can be found in [21].

§	Type of net τ	Complexity	Quantity
1	$\{\mathsf{nop, res, set, swap}\} \cup \omega$ with $\omega \subseteq \{\mathsf{inp, out, used, free}\}$	NP-complete	16
2	$\{\mathsf{nop, res, swap}\} \cup \omega$ with $\omega \subseteq \{\mathsf{inp, out, used, free}\}$, $\{\mathsf{nop, set, swap}\} \cup \omega$ with $\omega \subseteq \{\mathsf{inp, out, used, free}\}$	NP-complete	32
3	$\{\mathsf{nop, res, set}\} \cup \omega$ with $\omega \subseteq \{\mathsf{inp, out, used, free}\}$, $\{\mathsf{nop, out, res}\} \cup \omega$ with $\omega \subseteq \{\mathsf{inp, used, free}\}$, $\{\mathsf{nop, inp, set}\} \cup \omega$ with $\omega \subseteq \{\mathsf{out, used, free}\}$	NP-complete	32
4	$\{\mathsf{nop, res}\} \cup \omega$ with $\omega \subseteq \{\mathsf{inp, used, free}\}$, $\{\mathsf{nop, set}\} \cup \omega$ with $\omega \subseteq \{\mathsf{out, used, free}\}$	polynomial	16
5	$\{\mathsf{nop, inp, out}\}$ and $\{\mathsf{nop, inp, out, used}\}$	NP-complete	2
6	$\{\mathsf{nop, inp, out, free}\}$ and $\{\mathsf{nop, inp, out, used, free}\}$, $\{\mathsf{nop, inp}\} \cup \omega$ and $\{\mathsf{nop, out}\} \cup \omega$ with $\omega \subseteq \{\mathsf{used, free}\}$	NP-complete	10
7	$\{\mathsf{nop, swap}\} \cup \omega$ with $\omega \subseteq \{\mathsf{inp, out, used, free}\}$, $\{\mathsf{nop}\} \cup \omega$ with $\omega \subseteq \{\mathsf{used, free}\}$	polynomial	20
8	$\omega \subseteq \{\mathsf{inp, out, res, set, used, free}\}$	polynomial	64
9	$\{\mathsf{swap}\} \cup \omega$ with $\omega \subseteq \{\mathsf{inp, out, res, set, used, free}\}$ and $\omega \cap \{\mathsf{res, set, used, free}\} \neq \emptyset$	NP-complete	60
10	$\{\mathsf{swap}\} \cup \omega$ with $\omega \subseteq \{\mathsf{inp, out}\}$	polynomial	4

Fig. 1. Overview of the computational complexity of τ-SSP for Boolean types of nets τ. The gray area highlights the new results that this paper provides.

2   Preliminaries

In this section, we introduce necessary notions and definitions, supported by illustrations and examples, and some basic results that are used throughout the paper.

Transition Systems. A (finite, deterministic) *transition system* (TS, for short) $A = (S, E, \delta)$ is a directed labeled graph with the set of nodes S (called *states*), the set of labels E (called *events*) and partial *transition function* $\delta : S \times E \longrightarrow S$. If $\delta(s, e)$ is defined, we say that e *occurs* at state s, denoted by $s \xrightarrow{e}$. By $s \xrightarrow{e} s' \in A$, we denote $\delta(s, e) = s'$. This notation extends to paths, i.e., $q_0 \xrightarrow{e_1} \dots \xrightarrow{e_n} q_n \in$

A denotes $q_{i-1}\xrightarrow{e_i}q_i \in A$ for all $i \in \{1,\ldots,n\}$. A TS A is *loop-free*, if $s\xrightarrow{e}s' \in A$ implies $s \neq s'$. A loop-free TS A is *bi-directed* if $s'\xrightarrow{e}s \in A$ implies $s\xrightarrow{e}s' \in A$. We say $s_0\xleftarrow{e_1}\ldots\xleftarrow{e_n}s_n \in A$ is a simple bi-directed path if $s_i \neq s_j$ for all $i \neq j$ with $i,j \in \{0,\ldots,n\}$. An *initialized* TS $A = (S,E,\delta,\iota)$ is a TS with a distinct *initial* state $\iota \in S$, where every state $s \in S$ is *reachable* from ι by a directed labeled path.

Boolean Types of Nets [3]**.** The following notion of Boolean types of nets allows to capture *all* Boolean Petri nets in a *uniform* way. A *Boolean type of net* $\tau = (\{0,1\}, E_\tau, \delta_\tau)$ is a TS such that E_τ is a subset of the *Boolean interactions*: $E_\tau \subseteq I = \{\mathsf{nop}, \mathsf{inp}, \mathsf{out}, \mathsf{res}, \mathsf{set}, \mathsf{swap}, \mathsf{used}, \mathsf{free}\}$. Each interaction $i \in I$ is a binary partial function $i : \{0,1\} \to \{0,1\}$ as defined in Fig. 2. For all $x \in \{0,1\}$ and all $i \in E_\tau$, the transition function of τ is defined by $\delta_\tau(x,i) = i(x)$. Notice

x	$\mathsf{nop}(x)$	$\mathsf{inp}(x)$	$\mathsf{out}(x)$	$\mathsf{res}(x)$	$\mathsf{set}(x)$	$\mathsf{swap}(x)$	$\mathsf{used}(x)$	$\mathsf{free}(x)$
0	0		1	0	1	1		0
1	1	0		0	1	0	1	

Fig. 2. All interactions i of I. If a cell is empty, then i is undefined on the respective x.

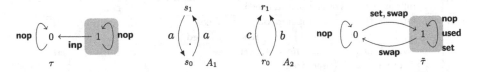

Fig. 3. Left: $\tau = \{\mathsf{nop}, \mathsf{inp}\}$. Right: $\tilde{\tau} = \{\mathsf{nop}, \mathsf{set}, \mathsf{swap}, \mathsf{used}\}$. The red colored area emphasizes the inside. The only SSP atom of A_1 is (s_0, s_1). It is $\tilde{\tau}$-solvable by $R_1 = (sup_1, sig_1)$ with $sup_1(s_0) = 0$, $sup_1(s_1) = 1$, $sig_1(a) = \mathsf{swap}$. Thus, A_1 has the $\tilde{\tau}$-separative set $\mathcal{R} = \{R_1\}$. The SSP atom (s_0, s_1) is not τ-solvable. The only SSP atom (r_0, r_1) in A_2 can be solved by $\tilde{\tau}$-region $R_2 = (sup_2, sig_2)$ with $sup_2(r_0) = 0$, $sup_2(r_1) = 1$, $sig_2(b) = \mathsf{set}$, $sig_2(c) = \mathsf{swap}$. Thus, A_2 has the $\tilde{\tau}$-SSP. The same atom can also be solved by τ-region $R_3 = (sup_3, sig_3)$ with $sup_3(r_0) = 1$, $sup_3(r_1) = 0$, $sig_3(b) = sig_3(c) = \mathsf{inp}$. Hence, A_2 has the τ-SSP, as well. (Color figure online)

$$s_0 \xrightarrow{a} s_1 \xrightarrow{b} s_2 \xrightarrow{c} s_3 \qquad \boxed{1} \xrightarrow{\mathsf{used}} \boxed{1} \xrightarrow{\mathsf{swap}} \boxed{0} \xrightarrow{\mathsf{set}} \boxed{1} \qquad \boxed{1} \xrightarrow{\mathsf{nop}} \boxed{1} \xrightarrow{\mathsf{swap}} \boxed{0} \xrightarrow{\mathsf{set}} \boxed{1}$$
$$A_3 \qquad\qquad\qquad A_3^R \qquad\qquad\qquad A_3^{R'}$$

Fig. 4. Left: TS A_3, a simple directed path. If $\tilde{\tau}$ is defined as in Fig. 3, then $sup(\iota) = 1$, $sig(a) = \mathsf{used}$, $sig(b) = \mathsf{swap}$ and $sig(c) = \mathsf{set}$ implicitly defines the $\tilde{\tau}$-region $R = (sup, sig)$ of A_3 as follows: $sup(s_1) = \delta_{\tilde{\tau}}(1, \mathsf{used}) = 1$, $sup(s_2) = \delta_{\tilde{\tau}}(1, \mathsf{swap}) = 0$ and $sup(s_3) = \delta_{\tilde{\tau}}(0, \mathsf{set}) = 1$. Middle: The image A_3^R of A_3 (under R). One easily verifies that $\delta_{A_3}(s, e) = s'$ implies $\delta_{\tilde{\tau}}(sup(s), sig(e)) = sup(s')$, cf. Fig. 3. In particular, R is sound. For event b, the edge defined by $\delta_{A_3}(s_1, b) = s_2$ is mapped into $\delta_{\tilde{\tau}}(1, \mathsf{swap}) = 0$ under R, i.e., b makes a state change on the path; similar for $sig(c) = \mathsf{set}$. R is not normalized, since $sup(s_0) = sup(s_1)$, but $sig(a) = \mathsf{used} \neq \mathsf{nop}$. Right: The image $A_3^{R'}$ of A_3 under the normalized $\tilde{\tau}$-region R' that is similar to R but replaces used by nop.

that a type τ is completely determined by E_τ. Hence we often identify τ with E_τ, cf. Fig. 1. Moreover, since I captures all meaningful Boolean interactions [23, p. 617] and τ is defined by $E_\tau \subseteq I$, there are 256 Boolean types of nets at all. For a Boolean type of net τ, we say that its state 1 is *inside* and 0 is *outside*. An interaction $i \in E_\tau$ *exits* if $1\xrightarrow{i}0$, *enters* if $0\xrightarrow{i}1$, *saves 1* if $1\xrightarrow{i}1$ and *saves 0* if $0\xrightarrow{i}0$. Accordingly, we group interactions together by $\mathsf{exit} = \{\mathsf{inp}, \mathsf{res}, \mathsf{swap}\}$, $\mathsf{enter} = \{\mathsf{out}, \mathsf{set}, \mathsf{swap}\}$, $\mathsf{save}_1 = \{\mathsf{nop}, \mathsf{set}, \mathsf{used}\}$, $\mathsf{save}_0 = \{\mathsf{nop}, \mathsf{res}, \mathsf{free}\}$ and $\mathsf{save} = \mathsf{save}_1 \cup \mathsf{save}_0$.

For a net of type τ (τ-net), the interactions of τ determine relations between *places* and *transitions* of the net. For instance, if a place p and a transition t are related via inp, then p has to be marked (*true*) to allow t to fire, and becomes unmarked (*false*) after the firing (cf. Fig. 2). Since we are only concerned with state separation, we omit the formal definition of τ-nets and rather refer to, e.g., [3] for a comprehensive introduction to the topic.

τ-**Regions.** The following notion of τ-regions is the key concept for state separation. A τ-region $R = (sup, sig)$ of TS $A = (S, E, \delta, \iota)$ consists of the mappings *support* $sup : S \to \{0, 1\}$ and *signature* $sig : E \to E_\tau$, such that for every edge $s\xrightarrow{e}s'$ of A, the edge $sup(s)\xrightarrow{sig(e)}sup(s')$ belongs to the type τ; we also say sup *allows* (sig and thus the region) R. If $P = q_0\xrightarrow{e_1}\dots\xrightarrow{e_n}q_n$ is a path in A, then $P^R = sup(q_0)\xrightarrow{sig(e_1)}\dots\xrightarrow{sig(e_n)}sup(q_n)$ is a path in τ. We say P^R is the *image* of P (under R). For region R and path P, event e_i with $1 \le i \le n$ is called *state changing* on the path P^R, if $sup(q_{i-1}) \ne sup(q_i)$ for $q_{i-1}\xrightarrow{e_i}q_i$ in P. Notice that R is *implicitly* defined by $sup(\iota)$ and sig: Since A is reachable, for every state $s \in S$, there is a path $\iota\xrightarrow{e_1}\dots\xrightarrow{e_n}s_n$ such that $s = s_n$. Thus, since τ is deterministic, we inductively obtain $sup(s_{i+1})$ by $sup(s_i)\xrightarrow{sig(e_{i+1})}sup(s_{i+1})$ for all $i \in \{0, \dots, n-1\}$ and $s_0 = \iota$. Hence, we can compute sup and thus R purely from $sup(\iota)$ and sig, cf. Fig. 4. If $\mathsf{nop} \in \tau$, then a τ-region $R = (sup, sig)$ of a TS A is called *normalized* if $sig(e) = \mathsf{nop}$ for as many events e as sup allows: for all $e \in E$, $sig(e) \notin \{\mathsf{used}, \mathsf{free}\}$ and if $sig(e) \in \mathsf{exit} \cup \mathsf{enter}$ then there is $s\xrightarrow{e}s' \in A$ such that $sup(s) \ne sup(s')$.

τ-**State Separation Property.** A pair (s, s') of distinct states of A defines a *state separation atom* (SSP atom). A τ-region $R = (sup, sig)$ *solves* (s, s') if $sup(s) \ne sup(s')$. If R exists, then (s, s') is called τ-*solvable*. If $s \in S_A$ and, for all $s' \in S_A \setminus \{s\}$, the atom (s, s') is τ-solvable, then s is called τ-solvable. A TS has the τ-*state separation property* (τ-SSP) if all of its SSP atoms are τ-solvable. A set $\mathcal{R}$ of τ-regions of A is called τ-*separative* if for each SSP atom of A there is a τ-region R in $\mathcal{R}$ that solves it. By the next lemma, if $\mathsf{nop} \in \tau$, then A has the τ-SSP if and only if it has a τ-separative set of normalized τ-regions:

Lemma 1. *Let A be a TS and τ be a nop-equipped Boolean type of nets. There is a τ-separative set $\mathcal{R}$ of A if and only if there is a τ-separative set of normalized τ-regions of A.*

Proof. The *if*-direction is trivial. *Only-if*: Let $R = (sup, sig)$ be a non-normalized τ-region, i.e., there is $e \in E_A$ such that $s \xrightarrow{e} s' \in A$ implies $sup(s) = sup(s')$. Since τ is nop-equipped, $sup(s) \xrightarrow{\mathsf{nop}} sup(s') \in \tau$ for all $s \xrightarrow{e} s' \in A$. Thus, a τ-region $R' = (sup, sig')$ can be constructed from R, where sig' is equal to sig except for $sig'(e) = \mathsf{nop}$. Since E_A is finite, a normalized region can be obtained from R by inductive application of this procedure.   □

By the following lemma, τ-SSP and $\tilde{\tau}$-SSP are equivalent if τ and $\tilde{\tau}$ are isomorphic:

Lemma 2 (Without proof). *If τ and $\tilde{\tau}$ are isomorphic types of nets then a TS A has the τ-SSP if and only if A has the $\tilde{\tau}$-SSP.*

In this paper, we consider the τ-SSP also as decision problem that asks whether a given TS A has the τ-SSP. The decision problem τ-SSP is in NP: By definition, A has at most $|S|^2$ SSP atoms. Hence, a Turing-machine can (non-deterministically) guess a τ-separative set $\mathcal{R}$ such that $|\mathcal{R}| \leq |S|^2$ and (deterministically) check in polynomial time its validity if it exists.

In what follows, some of our NP-completeness results base on polynomial-time reductions of the following decision problem, which is known to be NP-complete [11]:

Cubic Monotone 1-in-3 3Sat. (CM 1-IN-3 3SAT) The input is a Boolean formula $\varphi = \{\zeta_0, \ldots, \zeta_{m-1}\}$ of negation-free three-clauses $\zeta_i = \{X_{i_0}, X_{i_1}, X_{i_2}\}$, where $i \in \{0, \ldots, m-1\}$, with set of variables $X = \bigcup_{i=0}^{m-1} \zeta_i$; every variable $v \in X$ occurs in exactly three clauses, implying $|X| = m$. The question to decide is whether there is a (one-in-three model) $M \subseteq X$ satisfying $|M \cap \zeta_i| = 1$ for all $i \in \{0, \ldots, m-1\}$.

Example 1 (CM 1-IN-3 3SAT). The instance $\varphi = \{\zeta_0, \ldots, \zeta_5\}$ of CM 1-IN-3 3SAT with set of variables $X = \{X_0, \ldots, X_5\}$ and clauses $\zeta_0 = \{X_0, X_1, X_2\}$, $\zeta_1 = \{X_0, X_2, X_3\}$, $\zeta_2 = \{X_0, X_1, X_3\}$, $\zeta_3 = \{X_2, X_4, X_5\}$, $\zeta_4 = \{X_1, X_4, X_5\}$ and $\zeta_5 = \{X_3, X_4, X_5\}$ has the one-in-three model $M = \{X_0, X_4\}$.

3   Deciding the State Separation Property for nop-equipped Types

In this section, we investigate the computational complexity of nop-equipped Boolean types of nets. For technical reasons, we separately consider the types that include neither res nor set (§5–§7 in Fig. 1) and the ones that have at least one of them (§1–§4 in Fig. 1).

First of all, the fact that τ-SSP is polynomial for the types of §7 in Fig. 1 is implied by the results of [16] [23, p. 619]. Moreover, for the types of Fig. 1 §5 the NP-completeness of τ-SSP has been shown in [24] ($\tau = \{\mathsf{nop}, \mathsf{inp}, \mathsf{out}\}$), and in [19] ($\tau = \{\mathsf{nop}, \mathsf{inp}, \mathsf{out}, \mathsf{used}\}$, there referred to as 1-bounded P/T-nets). Thus, in order to complete the complexity characterization for the nop-equipped types that neither contain res nor set, it only remains to ascertain the complexity of τ-SSP for the types Fig. 1 §6. The following Subsect. 3.1 proves that τ-SSP is NP-complete for these types.

Then, we proceed with the types of §1–§4 in Fig. 1. The fact that τ-SSP is polynomial for the types of §4 follows from [23, p. 619]. The NP-completeness of τ-SSP for the remaining types (§1–§3) will be demonstrated in Subsect. 3.2.

3.1 Complexity of τ-SSP for nop-equipped Types Without res and set

The following theorem summarizes the complexity for the types of §5–§7 in Fig. 1.

Theorem 1. *Let τ be a nop-equipped Boolean type of nets such that $\tau \cap \{res, set\} = \emptyset$. The τ-SSP is NP-complete if $\tau \cap \{inp, out\} \neq \emptyset$ and swap $\notin \tau$, otherwise it is polynomial.*

As just discussed in Sect. 3, to complete the proof of Theorem 1 it remains to characterize the complexity of τ-SSP for the types of Fig. 1 §6. Since τ-SSP is NP-complete if $\tau = \{nop, inp, out\}$ [24], by Lemma 1, the τ-SSP is also NP-complete if $\tau = \{nop, inp, out, free\}$ and $\tau = \{nop, inp, out, free, used\}$.

Thus, in what follows, we restrict ourselves to the types $\tau = \{nop, inp\} \cup \omega$ and $\tau = \{nop, out\} \cup \omega$, where $\omega \subseteq \{used, free\}$, and argue that their τ-SSP are NP-complete. To do so, we let $\tau = \{nop, inp\}$ and show the hardness of τ-SSP by a reduction of CM 1-IN-3 3SAT. By Lemma 1, this also implies the hardness of $\tau \cup \omega$-SSP, where $\omega \subseteq \{used, free\}$. Furthermore, by Lemma 2, the latter shows the NP-completeness of τ-SSP if $\tau = \{nop, out\} \cup \omega$ and $\omega \subseteq \{used, free\}$. The following paragraph introduces the intuition of our reduction approach.

The Roadmap of Reduction. Let $\tau = \{nop, inp\}$ and $\varphi = \{\zeta_0, \ldots, \zeta_{m-1}\}$ be an input of CM 1-IN-3 3SAT with variables $X = \{X_0, \ldots, X_{m-1}\}$ and clauses $\zeta_i = \{X_{i_0}, X_{i_1}, X_{i_2}\}$ for all $i \in \{0, \ldots, m-1\}$. To show the NP-completeness of τ-SSP, we reduce a given input φ to a TS A_φ (i.e., an input of τ-SSP) as follows: For every clause $\zeta_i = \{X_{i_0}, X_{i_1}, X_{i_2}\}$, the TS A_φ has a directed labeled path P_i that represents ζ_i by using its variables as events:

$$P_i = \quad t_{i,0} \xrightarrow{X_{i_0}} t_{i,1} \xrightarrow{X_{i_1}} t_{i,2} \xrightarrow{X_{i_2}} t_{i,3}$$

We ensure by construction that A_φ has an SSP atom α such that if $R = (sup, sig)$ is a τ-region solving α, then $sup(t_{i,0}) = 1$ and $sup(t_{i,3}) = 0$ for all $i \in \{0, \ldots, m-1\}$. Thus, for all $i \in \{0, \ldots, m-1\}$, the path P_i^R is a path from 1 to 0 in τ. First, this obviously implies that there is an event $e \in \{X_{i_0}, X_{i_1}, X_{i_2}\}$ such that $sig(e) = inp$. Second, it is easy to see that there is no path in τ on which inp occurs twice, cf. Fig. 3. The following figure sketches all possibilities of P_i^R, i.e., $sig(X_{i_0}) = inp$ and $sig(X_{i_1}) = sig(X_{i_2}) = nop$, $sig(X_{i_1}) = inp$ and

$sig(X_{i_0}) = sig(X_{i_2}) = $ nop, and $sig(X_{i_2}) = $ inp and $sig(X_{i_0}) = sig(X_{i_1}) = $ nop, respectively:

$$1 \xrightarrow{\text{inp}} 0 \xrightarrow{\text{nop}} 0 \xrightarrow{\text{nop}} 0 \qquad 1 \xrightarrow{\text{nop}} 1 \xrightarrow{\text{inp}} 0 \xrightarrow{\text{nop}} 0 \qquad 1 \xrightarrow{\text{nop}} 1 \xrightarrow{\text{nop}} 1 \xrightarrow{\text{inp}} 0$$

Hence, the event e is unique. Since this is simultaneously true for all paths $P_0, \ldots, P_{m-1}$, the set $M = \{e \in X \mid sig(e) = \text{inp}\}$ selects exactly one variable per clause and thus defines a one-in-three model of φ. Altogether, this approach shows that if A_φ has the τ-SSP, which implies that α is τ-solvable, then φ has a one-in-three model.

Conversely, our construction ensures that if φ has a one-in-three model, then α and the other separation atoms of A_φ are τ-solvable, that is, A_φ has the τ-SSP.

The Reduction of A_φ for $\tau = \{\text{nop}, \text{inp}\}$. In the following, we introduce the announced TS A_φ, cf. Fig. 5. The initial state of A_φ is $t_{0,0}$. First of all, the TS A_φ has the following path P that provides the announced SSP atom $\alpha = (t_{m,0}, t_{m+1,0})$:

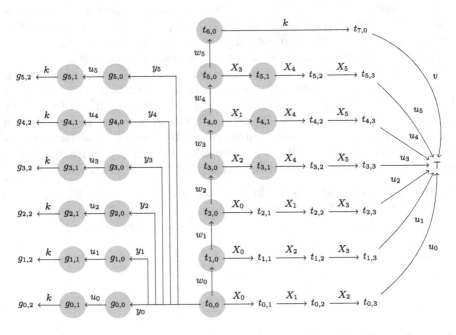

Fig. 5. The TS A_φ originating from the input φ of Example 1, which has the one-in-three model $M = \{X_0, X_4\}$. The colored area sketches the region R_M of Lemma 4 that solves $\alpha = (t_{6,0}, t_{7,0})$. (Color figure online)

$$t_{0,0} \xrightarrow{w_0} \cdots \xrightarrow{w_{i-1}} t_{i,0} \xrightarrow{w_i} \cdots \xrightarrow{w_{m-2}} t_{m-1,0} \xrightarrow{w_{m-1}} t_{m,0} \xrightarrow{k} t_{m+1,0} \xrightarrow{v} \top$$

Moreover, for every $i \in \{0, \ldots, m-1\}$, the TS A_φ has the following path T_i that uses the variables of $\zeta_i = \{X_{i_0}, X_{i_1}, X_{i_2}\}$ as events and provides the sub-path $P_i = t_{i,0} \xrightarrow{X_{i_0}} \ldots \xrightarrow{X_{i_2}} t_{i,3}$:

$$t_{i,0} \xrightarrow{\quad X_{i_0} \quad} t_{i,1} \xrightarrow{\quad X_{i_1} \quad} t_{i,2} \xrightarrow{\quad X_{i_2} \quad} t_{i,3} \xrightarrow{\quad u_i \quad} \top$$

Finally, the TS A_φ has, for all $i \in \{0, \ldots, m-1\}$, the following path G_i:

$$t_{0,0} \xrightarrow{\quad y_i \quad} g_{i,0} \xrightarrow{\quad u_i \quad} g_{i,1} \xrightarrow{\quad k \quad} g_{i,2}$$

Notice that the paths P and $T_0, \ldots, T_{m-1}$ have the same "final"-state $\bot$. Obviously, the size of A_φ is polynomial in the size of φ. The following Lemma 3 and Lemma 4 prove the validity of our reduction and thus complete the proof of Theorem 1.

Lemma 3. *Let $\tau = \{\mathsf{nop}, \mathsf{inp}\}$. If A_φ has the τ-SSP, then φ has a one-in-three model.*

Proof. Let $R = (sup, sig)$ be a τ-region that solves α, that is, $sup(t_{m,0}) \neq sup(t_{m+1,0})$. By $t_{m,0} \xrightarrow{k} t_{m+1,0}$ and $\tau = \{\mathsf{nop}, \mathsf{inp}\}$, this implies $sig(k) = \mathsf{inp}$, $sup(t_{m,0}) = 1$ and $sup(t_{m+1,0}) = 0$. If $s_0 \xrightarrow{e_0} \ldots \xrightarrow{e_i} s_i \xrightarrow{k} s_{i+1} \xrightarrow{e_{i+2}} \ldots \xrightarrow{e_n} s_n$ is a path in A_φ, then, by $sig(k) = \mathsf{inp}$, we get $sup(s_j) = 1$ for all $j \in \{0, \ldots, i\}$, $sup(s_j) = 0$ for all $j \in \{i+1, \ldots, n\}$ and $sig(e_j) = \mathsf{nop}$ for all $j \in \{1, \ldots, i, i+2, \ldots, n\}$. This implies $sup(\top) = 0$, $sig(v) = \mathsf{nop}$ as well as $sig(u_i) = \mathsf{nop}$ and $sup(t_{i,0}) = 1$ for all $i \in \{0, \ldots, m-1\}$. Furthermore, by $sup(\top) = 0$ and $sig(u_i) = \mathsf{nop}$, we get $sup(t_{i,3}) = 0$ for all $i \in \{0, \ldots, m-1\}$. Hence, for all $i \in \{0, \ldots, m-1\}$, the image P_i^R of P_i is a path from 1 to 0 in τ. Hence, as just discussed above, $M = \{e \in X \mid sig(e) = \mathsf{inp}\}$ selects exactly one variable per clause and defines a one-in-three model of φ. $\qquad\square$

Lemma 4. *Let $\tau = \{\mathsf{nop}, \mathsf{inp}\}$. If φ has a one-in-three model, then A_φ has the τ-SSP.*

Proof. Let M be a one-in-three model of φ.

The following region $R_1 = (sup, sig)$ solves (s, s') for all $s \in \bigcup_{i=0}^{m-1} S(P_i)$ and all $s' \in \bigcup_{i=0}^{m-1} S(G_i)$, where $s' \neq t_{0,0}$: $sup(t_{0,0}) = 1$; for all $e \in E_{A_\varphi}$, if $e \in \{y_0, \ldots, y_{m-1}\}$, then $sig(e) = \mathsf{inp}$, otherwise $sig(e) = \mathsf{nop}$.

Let $i \in \{0, \ldots, m-1\}$ be arbitrary but fixed. The following region $R_i^T = (sup, sig)$ solves (s, s') for all $s \in \{t_{i,0}, \ldots, t_{i,3}\}$ and all $s' \in \bigcup_{j=i+1}^{m-1} S(T_j) \cup \{t_{m,0}, t_{m+1,0}\}$: $sup(t_{0,0}) = 1$; for all $e \in E_{A_\varphi}$, if $e \in \{w_i\} \cup \{u_0, \ldots, u_i\} \cup \{y_{i+1}, \ldots, y_{m-1}\}$, then $sig(e) = \mathsf{inp}$, otherwise $sig(e) = \mathsf{nop}$.

The following region $R_2 = (sup, sig)$ solves $(t_{m+1}, \top)$ and $(g_{i,0}, g_{i,1})$ and $(g_{i,0}, g_{i,2})$ for all $i \in \{0, \ldots, m-1\}$: $sup(t_{0,0}) = 1$; for all $e \in E_{A_\varphi}$, if $e \in \{v\} \cup \{u_0, \ldots, u_{m-1}\}$, then $sig(e) = \mathsf{inp}$, otherwise $sig(e) = \mathsf{nop}$.

The following region $R_M = (sup, sig)$ uses the one-in-three model M of φ and solves α as well as $(g_{i,1}, g_{i,2})$ for all $i \in \{0, \ldots, m-1\}$: $sup(t_{0,0}) = 1$; for all $e \in E_{A_\varphi}$, if $e \in \{k\} \cup M$, then $sig(e) = \mathsf{inp}$, otherwise $sig(e) = \mathsf{nop}$. Note Fig. 5 for an example of R_M.

Let $i \in \{0, \ldots, m-2\}$ be arbitrary but fixed. The following region $R_i^G = (sup, sig)$ solves (s, s') for all $s \in \{g_{i,0}, g_{i,1}, g_{i,2}\}$ and all $s' \in \bigcup_{j=i+1}^{m-1} S(G_j)$, where $s' \neq t_{0,0}$: $sup(t_{0,0}) = 1$; for all $e \in E_{A_\varphi}$, if $e \in \{y_{i+1}, \ldots, y_{m-1}\}$, then $sig(e) = \text{inp}$, otherwise $sig(e) = \text{nop}$.

By the arbitrariness of i for R_i^T and R_i^G, it remains to show that $t_{i,0}, \ldots, t_{i,3}$ are pairwise separable for all $i \in \{0, \ldots, m-1\}$. Let $i \in \{0, \ldots, m-1\}$ be arbitrary but fixed. We present only a region $R_{i_0}^X = (sup, sig)$ that solves $(t_{i,0}, s)$ for all $s \in \{t_{i,1}, t_{i,2}, t_{i,3}\}$. It is then easy to see that the remaining atoms are similarly solvable. Let $j \neq \ell \in \{0, \ldots, m-1\} \setminus \{i\}$ select the other two clauses of φ that contain X_{i_0}, that is, $X_{i_0} \in \zeta_j \cap \zeta_\ell$. $R_{i_0}^X = (sup, sig)$ is defined as follows: $sup(t_{0,0}) = 1$; for all $e \in E_{A_\varphi}$, if $e \in \{X_{i_0}\} \cup \{v\} \cup \{u_0, \ldots, u_{m-1}\} \setminus \{u_i, u_j, u_\ell\}$, then $sig(e) = \text{inp}$, otherwise $sig(e) = \text{nop}$.

Similarly, one gets regions where X_{i_1} or X_{i_2} has inp-signature. These regions solve the remaining atoms of $S(T_i) \setminus \{\top\}$. Since i was arbitrary, this completes the proof. Please note that the technical report [21] that corresponds to this paper provides graphical representations and examples for the just presented regions.   □

3.2   Complexity of τ-SSP for nop-equipped Types with res or set

The next theorem states that τ-SSP is NP-complete for the nop-equipped types that have not yet been considered, cf Fig. 1 §1–§3. Moreover, it summarizes the complexity of τ-SSP for all types of Fig. 1 §1–§4:

Theorem 2. *Let τ and $\tilde{\tau}$ be Boolean type of nets and $\{\text{nop}, \text{res}\} \subseteq \tau$ and $\{\text{nop}, \text{set}\} \subseteq \tilde{\tau}$.*

1. *The τ-SSP is NP-complete if $\tau \cap \text{enter} \neq \emptyset$, otherwise it is polynomial.*
2. *The $\tilde{\tau}$-SSP is NP-complete if $\tilde{\tau} \cap \text{exit} \neq \emptyset$, otherwise it is polynomial.*

In this section we complete the proof of Theorem 2 as follows. Firstly, we let $\tau_0 = \{\text{nop}, \text{inp}, \text{out}\}$ and, by a reduction of τ_0-SSP, we show that the τ-SSP is NP-complete if $\tau = \{\text{nop}, \text{out}, \text{res}\} \cup \omega$ and $\omega \subseteq \{\text{inp}, \text{used}, \text{free}\}$ or if $\{\text{nop}, \text{res}, \text{set}\} \subseteq \tau$. By Lemma 2, the former also implies the NP-completeness of τ-SSP if $\tau = \{\text{nop}, \text{inp}, \text{set}\} \cup \omega$ and $\omega \subseteq \{\text{out}, \text{used}, \text{free}\}$. Altogether, this proves the claim for all the types listed in §1 and §3 of Fig. 1.

Secondly, we let $\tau_1 = \{\text{nop}, \text{inp}\}$ and reduce τ_1-SSP to τ-SSP, where $\tau = \{\text{nop}, \text{res}, \text{swap}\} \cup \omega$ and $\omega \subseteq \{\text{inp}, \text{used}, \text{free}\}$. Again by Lemma 2, this also implies the NP-completeness of τ-SSP if $\tau = \{\text{nop}, \text{set}, \text{swap}\} \cup \omega$ and $\omega \subseteq \{\text{out}, \text{used}, \text{free}\}$. Hence, this proves the claim for all the types listed in §2 of Fig. 1 and thus completes the proof of Theorem 2.

For the announced reductions, we use the following extensions of a TS A, cf. Fig. 6. Let $A = (S_A, E_A, \delta_A, \iota_A)$ be a loop-free TS, and let $\overline{E_A} = \{\overline{e} \mid e \in E_A\}$ be the set containing for every event $e \in E_A$ the unambiguous and fresh event $\overline{e}$ that is *associated with* e. The *backward-extension* $B = (S_A, E_A \cup \overline{E_A}, \delta_B, \iota_A)$ of A extends A by $\overline{E_A}$ and additional backward edges: for all $e \in E_A$ and all

$s, s' \in S_A$, if $\delta_A(s, e) = s'$, then $\delta_B(s, e) = s'$ and $\delta_B(s', \overline{e}) = s$. The *oneway loop-extension* $C = (S_A, E_A \cup \overline{E_A}, \delta_C, \iota_A)$ of a TS A extends B by some additional loops: for all $x \in E_A \cup \overline{E_A}$ and all $s \in S_A$, we define $\delta_C(s, e) = \delta_B(s, e)$ and, for all $e \in E_A$ and all $s, s' \in S_A$, if $\delta_A(s, e) = s'$, then $\delta_C(s', e) = s'$. Finally, the *loop-extension* $D = (S_A, E_A \cup \overline{E_A}, \delta_D, \iota_A)$ of A is an extension of C, where for all $x \in E_A \cup \overline{E_A}$ and all $s \in S_A$, we define $\delta_D(s, x) = \delta_C(s, x)$ and, for all $e \in E_A$ and all $s, s' \in S_A$, if $\delta_A(s, e) = s'$, then $\delta_D(s, \overline{e}) = s$.

Depending on the considered type τ, we let $\tilde{\tau} = \tau_0$ or $\tilde{\tau} = \tau_1$ and reduce a loop-free TS $A = (S_A, E_A, \delta_A, \iota_A)$ either to its backward-, oneway loop- or loop-extension and show that $sup : S_A \rightarrow \{0, 1\}$ allows a $\tilde{\tau}$-region of A if and only if it allows a τ-region of the extension:

Lemma 5. *Let* $\tau_0 = \{nop, inp, out\}$, $\tau_1 = \{nop, inp\}$, A *a loop-free TS,* $sup : S_A \rightarrow \{0, 1\}$ *and* B, C *and* D *the backward-, oneway loop- and loop-extension of* A, *respectively.*

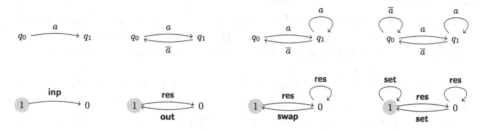

Fig. 6. Top, left to right: A TS A consisting of a single edge; backward-extension B of A; oneway loop-extension C of A; loop-extension D of A. Bottom, left to right: images of A and its extensions B, C, D under regions corresponding to the types of Lemma 5 solving (q_0, q_1): a $\{nop, inp\}$- ($\{nop, inp, out\}$-) region of A; a $\{nop, res, out\}$-region of B; a $\{nop, res, swap\}$-region of C; a $\{nop, res, set\}$-region of D.

1. *If* $\tau = \{nop, out, res\} \cup \omega$ *and* $\omega \subseteq \{inp, used, free\}$, *then* sup *allows a* τ_0-*region* $R = (sup, sig)$ *of* A *if and only if it allows a normalized* τ-*region* $R' = (sup, sig')$ *of* B.
2. *If* $\tau \supseteq \{nop, res, set\}$, *then* sup *allows a* τ_0-*region* $R = (sup, sig)$ *of* A *if and only if it allows a normalized* τ-*region* $R' = (sup, sig')$ *of* D.
3. *If* $\tau = \{nop, res, swap\} \cup \omega$ *and* $\omega \subseteq \{inp, used, free\}$, *then* sup *allows a* τ_1-*region* $R = (sup, sig)$ *of* A *if and only if it allows a normalized* τ-*region* $R' = (sup, sig')$ *of* C.

Proof. (1): *Only-if*: Let $R = (sup, sig)$ be a τ_0-region of A. Recall that $sig(e) = $ nop, $sig(e) = $ inp, $sig(e) = $ out imply $sup(s) = sup(t)$, $sup(s) = 1$ and $sup(t) = 0$, $sup(s) = 0$ and $sup(t) = 1$ for all edges $s \xrightarrow{e} t$ of A, respectively. Thus, it is easy to see that R induces a normalized τ-region $R' = (sup, sig')$ of B as follows, cf. Fig. 6: For all $e \in E_A$ and its associated event $\overline{e} \in \overline{E_A}$, if $sig(e) = $ nop, then

$sig'(e) = sig'(\bar{e}) = $ nop; if $sig(e) = $ inp, then $sig'(e) = $ res and $sig'(\bar{e}) = $ out; if $sig(e) = $ out, then $sig'(e) = $ out and $sig'(\bar{e}) = $ res.

If: Let $R' = (sup, sig')$ be a normalized τ-region of B, and let $e \in E_A$ and $s\xrightarrow{\ e\ }t \in B$ and $s'\xrightarrow{\ e\ }t' \in B$ be arbitrary but fixed. First of all, we argue that if $sup(s) \neq sup(t)$, then $sup(s) = sup(s')$ and $sup(t) = sup(t')$: By definition of B, we have that $t\xrightarrow{\ \bar{e}\ }s$ and $t'\xrightarrow{\ \bar{e}\ }s'$ are present. If $sup(s) = 1$ and $sup(t) = 0$, then $s\xrightarrow{\ e\ }t$ and $t\xrightarrow{\ \bar{e}\ }s$ imply $sig'(e) \in \{$inp, res$\}$ and $sig'(\bar{e}) = $ out. By $\xrightarrow{\ e\ }t'$ and $\xrightarrow{\ \bar{e}\ }s'$, this immediately implies $sup(s') = 1$ and $sup(t') = 0$. Similarly, if $sup(s) = 0$ and $sup(t) = 1$, then $sig'(e) = $ out and $sig'(\bar{e}) \in \{$inp, res$\}$, which implies $sup(s') = 0$ and $sup(t') = 1$. Consequently, since $s'\xrightarrow{\ e\ }t'$ was arbitrary, the claim follows. Note that this implies in return that if $sup(s) = sup(t)$, then $sup(s') = sup(t')$. Since both edges were arbitrary, it is easy to see that the following τ_0-region $R = (sup, sig)$ of A is well defined: for all $e \in E_A$, if there is $s\xrightarrow{\ e\ }t \in B$ such that $sup(s) \neq sup(t)$, then $sig(e) = $ inp if $sup(s) = 1$ and $sup(t) = 0$, else $sig(e) = $ out; otherwise, $sig(e) = $ nop.

(2): *Only-if:* Recall that $0\xrightarrow{\ \text{res}\ }0$ and $1\xrightarrow{\ \text{set}\ }1$ are present in τ. Consequently, if $R = (sup, sig)$ is a τ_0-region of A, then the region $R' = (sup, sig')$, similarly defined to the one for the Only-if-direction of (1), but replacing out by set, is a τ-region of D, cf. Fig. 6.

If: If $R' = (sup, sig')$ is a normalized τ-region of D, then it holds $sig'(e) \in \{$nop, res, set$\}$ for all $e \in E_D$. This is due to the fact that if $s\xrightarrow{\ x\ }s' \in D$, then $s'\xrightarrow{\ x\ }s' \in D$ for all $x \in E_D$ and all $s, t \in S_D$. Thus, $R = (sup, sig)$ is obtained from R' by the same arguments as the ones presented for the If-direction of (1).

(3): *Only-if:* Let $R = (sup, sig)$ be a τ_1-region of A. Recall that $sig(e) = $ nop and $sig(e) = $ inp imply $sup(s) = sup(t)$ and $sup(s) = 1, sup(t) = 0$ for all edges $s\xrightarrow{\ e\ }t$ of A, respectively. Moreover, $1\xrightarrow{\ \text{res}\ }0$, $0\xrightarrow{\ \text{res}\ }0$ and $0\xrightarrow{\ \text{swap}\ }1$ are present in τ. Thus, we get a normalized τ-region $R' = (sup, sig')$ of C as follows, cf. Fig. 6: For all $e \in E_A$ and its associated event $\bar{e} \in \bar{E}_A$, if $sig(e) = $ nop, then $sig'(e) = sig'(\bar{e}) = $ nop; if $sig(e) = $ inp, then $sig'(e) = $ res and $sig'(\bar{e}) = $ swap.

If: Let $R' = (sup, sig')$ be a normalized τ-region of C, and let $e \in E_A$ and $s\xrightarrow{\ e\ }t \in C$ and $s'\xrightarrow{\ e\ }t' \in C$ be arbitrary but fixed. We argue that $sup(s) \neq sup(t)$ implies $sup(s) = sup(s') = 1$ and $sup(t) = sup(t') = 0$: By definition of C and $s\xrightarrow{\ e\ }t \in C$, we get $t\xrightarrow{\ e\ }t \in C$. Thus, $sig'(e) \in \{$nop, res$\}$. Thus, if $sup(s) \neq sup(t)$, then $sig'(e) = $ res, which implies $sup(s) = 1$ and $sup(t) = 0$. Moreover, by $t\xrightarrow{\ \bar{e}\ }s \in C$, this also implies $sig'(\bar{e}) = $ swap. Finally, by $sig'(e) = $ res, $\xrightarrow{\ e\ }t'$, $sig'(\bar{e}) = $ swap and $t'\xrightarrow{\ \bar{e}\ }s'$, we get $sup(t') = 0$ and $sup(s') = 1$. Consequently, the following definition of sig yields a well-defined τ_1-region $R = (sup, sig)$ of A: for all $e \in E_A$, if $sig'(e) = $ res, then $sig(e) = $ inp, otherwise $sig(e) = $ nop. □

Notice that the TS A_φ of Sect. 3.1 is loop-free. Furthermore, in [24], it has been shown that $\{$nop, inp, out$\}$-SSP is NP-complete even if A is a simple directed path. Moreover, the introduced extensions of A are constructible in polynomial time. Thus, by Lemma 1 and Lemma 2, the following corollary, which is easily implied by Lemma 5, completes the proof of Theorem 2.

Corollary 1 (Without Proof). *Let $\tau_0 = \{nop, inp, out\}$ and $\tau_1 = \{nop, inp\}$, and let A be a loop-free TS and B, C and D its backward-, oneway loop- and loop-extension, respectively.*

1. *If $\tau = \{nop, out, res\} \cup \omega$ and $\omega \subseteq \{inp, used, free\}$, then A has the τ_0-SSP if and only if B has the τ-SSP.*
2. *If $\tau \supseteq \{nop, res, set\}$, then A has the τ_0-SSP if and only if D has the τ-SSP.*
3. *If $\tau = \{nop, res, swap\} \cup \omega$ and $\omega \subseteq \{inp, used, free\}$, then A has the τ_1-SSP if and only if C has the τ-SSP.*

4   Deciding the State Separation Property for **nop**-free Types

The following theorem summarizes the complexity of τ-SSP for nop-free Boolean types:

Theorem 3. *Let τ be a nop-free type of nets and A a TS.*

1. *If $swap \notin \tau$ or $swap \in \tau$ and $\tau \cap \mathfrak{save} = \emptyset$, then deciding if A has the τ-SSP is polynomial.*
2. *If $swap \in \tau$ and $\tau \cap \mathfrak{save} \neq \emptyset$, then deciding if A has the τ-SSP is NP-complete.*

The tractability of τ-SSP for nop-free types that are also swap-free has been shown in the broader context of τ-synthesis in [22]. Thus, restricted to Theorem 3.1, it remains to argue that τ-SSP is polynomial if $\tau = \{swap\} \cup \omega$ and $\omega \subseteq \{inp, out\}$. The following lemma states that separable inputs of τ-SSP are trivial for these types and thus proves its tractability:

Lemma 6. *Let $\tau = \{swap\} \cup \omega$, where $\omega \subseteq \{inp, out\}$, and $A = (S, E, \delta, \iota)$ be a TS. If A has the τ-SSP, then it has at most two states.*

Proof. If there is $s \overset{e}{\longrightarrow} s \in A$, then A has no τ-regions. Hence, if such A has more than one state, then it does not have the τ-SSP.

Let's consider the case when A is loop-free, that is, $s \overset{e}{\longrightarrow} s' \in A$ implies $s \neq s'$. First of all, note that there is at most one outgoing edge $\iota \overset{e}{\longrightarrow} s$ at ι, since if $\iota \overset{e}{\longrightarrow} s$, $\iota \overset{e'}{\longrightarrow} s'$ and $s \neq s'$, then s and s' are not separable. This can be seen as follows: If $R = (sup, sig)$ is a τ-region that solves (s, s'), then $sup(s) = 0$ and $sup(s') = 1$ or $sup(s) = 1$ and $sup(s') = 0$. If $sup(s) = 0$ and $sup(s') = 1$, then $sup(\iota) = 0$ contradicts $sig(e) \in \tau$, and $sup(\iota) = 1$ contradicts $sig(e') \in \tau$. Similarly, $sup(s) = 1$ and $sup(s') = 0$ yields a contradiction. Thus, a separating region R does not exist, which proves the claim. Secondly, if $\iota \overset{e}{\longrightarrow} s \overset{e'}{\longrightarrow} s'' \in A$, then $\iota = s''$, since otherwise, ι and s'' are not separable. This can be seen as follows: If $R = (sup, sig)$ is a τ-region that solves (ι, s''), then $sup(\iota) = 0$ and

$sup(s'') = 1$ or $sup(\iota) = 1$ and $sup(s'') = 0$. If $sup(\iota) = 0$ and $sup(s'') = 1$, then $sup(s') = 0$ contradicts $sig(e) \in \tau$, and $sup(s') = 1$ contradicts $sig(e') \in \tau$. Similarly, $sup(\iota) = 1$ and $sup(s'') = 0$ yields a contradiction. This implies again that a separating region does not exist, which proves the claim and, moreover, proves the lemma.   □

To complete the proof of Theorem 3, it remains to prove the NP-completeness of τ-SSP for the types listed in §9 of Fig. 1, which are exactly covered by Theorem Theorem 3.2. Thus, in the remainder of this section, if not stated explicitly otherwise, we let τ be a nop-free type such that swap $\in \tau$ and $\tau \cap$ save $\neq \emptyset$. Moreover, we reduce CM 1-IN-3 3SAT to τ-SSP again.

Basic Ideas of the Reduction. Similar to our previous approach we build a TS A_φ that has for every clause $\zeta_i = \{X_{i_0}, X_{i_1}, X_{i_2}\}$, where $i \in \{0, \ldots, m-1\}$, a (bi-directed) path $P_i = \ldots \xleftarrow{X_{i_0}} \ldots \xleftarrow{X_{i_1}} \ldots \xleftarrow{X_{i_2}} \ldots$ on which the elements of ζ_i occur as events. Together, the corresponding paths $P_0, \ldots, P_{m-1}$ are meant to represent φ. However, the current types are more diverse than $\{\text{nop}, \text{inp}\}$, since they also allow swap and other interactions. Simultaneously, they are more restricted than $\{\text{nop}, \text{inp}\}$, since they lack of nop. One of the main obstacles that occur is that if $s \xrightarrow{e} s' \in A_\varphi$, then the current types basically allow $sup(s) = 1$ and $sup(s') = 0$ as well as $sup(s) = 0$ and $sup(s') = 1$ for a τ-region $R = (sup, sig)$ that solves (s, s'). It turns out that this requires a second representation of φ. To do so, we use a copy φ' that originates from φ by simply renaming its variables. That is, φ' originates from φ by replacing every variable $v \in X$ of φ by a unique and fresh variable v'.

Example 2 (Renaming of φ). The instance $\varphi' = \{\zeta'_0, \ldots, \zeta'_5\}$ that originates from φ of Example 1 is defined by $X' = \{X'_0, \ldots, X'_5\}$ and $\zeta'_0 = \{X'_0, X'_1, X'_2\}$, $\zeta'_1 = \{X'_0, X'_2, X'_3\}$, $\zeta'_2 = \{X'_0, X'_1, X'_3\}$, $\zeta'_3 = \{X'_2, X'_4, X'_5\}$, $\zeta'_4 = \{X'_1, X'_4, X'_5\}$ and $\zeta'_5 = \{X'_3, X'_4, X'_5\}$.

It is immediately clear that φ is one-in-three satisfiable if and only if φ' is one-in-three satisfiable. The TS A_φ additionally has for every clause $\zeta'_i = \{X'_{i_0}, X'_{i_1}, X'_{i_2}\}$, where $i \in \{0, \ldots, m-1\}$, of φ' also a (bi-directed) path $P'_i = \ldots \xleftarrow{X'_{i_0}} \ldots \xleftarrow{X'_{i_1}} \ldots \xleftarrow{X'_{i_2}} \ldots$ on which the elements of ζ'_i occur as events. Moreover, by the construction, the TS A_φ has a SSP atom $\alpha = (s, s')$ such that if a τ-region solves α, then either the signatures of the variable events X of φ define a one-in-three model of φ or the signatures of the variable events X' of φ' define a one-in-three model of φ'. Obviously, both cases imply the one-in-three satisfiability of φ.

Conversely, the construction ensures, if φ has a one-in-three model then A_φ has the τ-SSP.

Similar to our approach for Theorem 1, the TS A_φ is a composition of several gadgets. The next Lemma 7 introduces some basic properties of τ-regions in bi-directed TS for nop-free types that we use to prove the functionailty of A_φ's gadgets. After that, Lemma 8 introduces TS that are the (isomorphic) prototypes of the gadgets of A_φ and additionally proves the essential parts of their intended functionality.

Lemma 7. *Let τ be a nop-free Boolean type of nets and A a bi-directed TS; let $s \xrightarrow{e} s'$ be an edge of A, $P_0 = s_0 \overset{e_1}{\longleftrightarrow} \ldots \overset{e_m}{\longleftrightarrow} s_m$ and $P_1 = q_0 \overset{e_1}{\longleftrightarrow} \ldots \overset{e_m}{\longleftrightarrow} q_m$ be two simple paths of A that both apply the same sequence $e_1 \ldots e_m$ of events, and $R = (sup, sig)$ be a τ-region of A.*

1. *If $sig(e) \in$ save, then $sup(s) = sup(s') = sup(q) = sup(q')$ for every edge $q \xrightarrow{e} q' \in A$.*
2. *If $sup(s_m) \neq sup(q_m)$, then $sig(e_i) =$ swap for all $i \in \{1, \ldots, m\}$.*
3. *If $sup(s_0) = sup(s_m)$, then $|\{e \in \{e_1, \ldots, e_m\} \mid sig(e) =$ swap$\}|$ is even.*

Proof. (1): A is bi-directed and $\xrightarrow{i} p \in \tau$ and $\xrightarrow{i} p' \in \tau$ imply $p = p'$ for all $i \in$ save.

(2): By definition of τ, if $sup(s_m) \neq sup(q_m)$, then, by $\xrightarrow{e_m} s_m$ and $\xrightarrow{e_m} q_m$, we get $sig(e_m) =$ swap. Clearly, by $sup(s_m) \neq sup(q_m)$, this implies $sup(s_{m-1}) \neq sup(q_{m-1})$. Thus, the claim follows easily by induction on m.

(3): Since $sup(s_0) = sup(s_m)$, the image P_0^R of P_0 is a path of τ that starts and terminates at the same state. Consequently, the number of changes between 0 and 1 on P_0^R is even. Since A is bi-directed, $sup(s) \neq sup(s')$ if and only if $sig(e) =$ swap for all $s \xrightarrow{e} s' \in P_0$. Thus, the number of events of P_0 with a swap-signature must be even. Hence, the claim. □

Lemma 8 (Basic Components of A_φ). *Let τ be a nop-free Boolean type and A a bi-directed TS with the following paths G, F, T and Q, and let $R = (sup, sig)$ be a τ-region of A:*

$$G = \quad g_0 \overset{v}{\longleftrightarrow} g_1 \overset{w}{\longleftrightarrow} g_2 \overset{k_0}{\longleftrightarrow} g_3 \overset{k_1}{\longleftrightarrow} g_4 \qquad\qquad F = \quad f_0 \overset{v}{\longleftrightarrow} f_1 \overset{w}{\longleftrightarrow} f_2 \overset{k_1}{\longleftrightarrow} f_3 \overset{k_0}{\longleftrightarrow} f_4$$

$$T = t_0 \overset{k_0}{\longleftrightarrow} t_1 \overset{v_0}{\longleftrightarrow} t_2 \overset{v_1}{\longleftrightarrow} t_3 \overset{X_0}{\longleftrightarrow} t_4 \overset{v_2}{\longleftrightarrow} t_5 \overset{X_1}{\longleftrightarrow} t_6 \overset{v_3}{\longleftrightarrow} t_7 \overset{X_2}{\longleftrightarrow} t_8 \overset{v_4}{\longleftrightarrow} t_9$$

$$Q = q_0 \overset{X_0}{\longleftrightarrow} q_1 \overset{v_6}{\longleftrightarrow} q_2 \overset{X_2}{\longleftrightarrow} q_3 \qquad\qquad\qquad\qquad \downarrow v_5$$

$$t_{11} \overset{}{\longleftrightarrow} t_{10}$$
$$k_0$$

1. *If R solves $\alpha = (g_2, g_4)$, then either $sig(k_0) \in$ save and $sig(k_1) =$ swap or $sig(k_0) =$ swap and $sig(k_1) \in$ save;*
2. *If $sig(k_0) \in$ save and $sig(k_1) =$ swap or $sig(k_0) =$ swap and $sig(k_1) \in$ save, then $sig(v) = sig(w) =$ swap;*
3. *If $sig(k_0) \in$ save and $sig(v_i) =$ swap for all $i \in \{0, \ldots, 6\}$, then there is exactly one $X \in \{X_0, X_1, X_2\}$ such that $sig(X) \neq$ swap.*

Proof. Since A is bi-directed, we have $sig(e) \notin \{$inp, out$\}$ for all $e \in E_A$.

(1): R solves α, thus $sup(g_2) \neq sup(g_4)$. If $sig(k_0) \neq$ swap $\neq sig(k_1)$ or $sig(k_0) = sig(k_1) =$ swap, then $sup(g_2) = sup(g_4)$, a contradiction. Hence the claim, cf. Fig. 7.

(2): If $sig(k_0) \in \mathfrak{save}$ and $sig(k_1) = \mathsf{swap}$, then we have $sup(g_2) = sup(f_3) \neq sup(f_2)$, cf. Fig. 7. By symmetry, the latter is also true if $sig(k_0) = \mathsf{swap}$ and $sig(k_1) \in \mathfrak{save}$. Hence, the claim follows from Lemma 7.2.

(3): Since $sig(k_0) \in \mathfrak{save}$, we get $sup(t_1) = sup(t_{10})$. By Lemma 7.3, this implies that $|\{e \in E(T) \mid sig(e) = \mathsf{swap}\}|$ is even. Moreover, since $sig(v_0) = \ldots sig(v_5) = \mathsf{swap}$, this implies $|\{e \in \{X_0, X_1, X_2\} \mid sig(e) = \mathsf{swap}\}| \in \{0, 2\}$. If $|\{e \in \{X_0, X_1, X_2\} \mid sig(e) = \mathsf{swap}\}| = 0$ then, we get $sup(t_3) = sup(t_4) \neq sup(t_5) = sup(t_6) \neq sup(t_7) = sup(t_8)$ by Lemma 7.1. This particularly implies $sup(t_4) = sup(t_7)$ and, again by Lemma 7.1, also $sup(t_4) = sup(q_1) = sup(q_2)$ and contradicts $sig(v_6) = \mathsf{swap}$, cf. Fig. 8. Thus, we have $|\{e \in \{X_0, X_1, X_2\} \mid sig(e) = \mathsf{swap}\}| = 2$, which proves the claim, cf. Fig. 7.   □

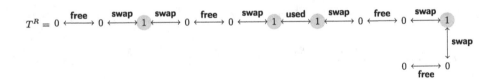

Fig. 7. Illustrations for Lemma 8. The images G^R, F^R, T^R and Q^R, where $R = (sup, sig)$ is a $\{\mathsf{swap}, \mathsf{free}\}$-region that solves (g_2, g_4) and satisfies $sig(k_0) = sig(X_0) = \mathsf{free}$ and $sig(k_1) = sig(v) = sig(w) = sig(X_1) = sig(X_2) = sig(v_i) = \mathsf{swap}$ for all $i \in \{0, \ldots, 6\}$.

$T^R = 0 \xleftrightarrow{\text{free}} 0 \xleftrightarrow{\text{swap}} 1 \xleftrightarrow{\text{swap}} 0 \xleftrightarrow{\text{free}} 0 \xleftrightarrow{\text{swap}} 1 \xleftrightarrow{\text{used}} 1 \xleftrightarrow{\text{swap}} 0 \xleftrightarrow{\text{free}} 0 \xleftrightarrow{\text{swap}} 1$
$\downarrow$ swap
$0 \xleftrightarrow{\text{free}} 0$

Fig. 8. Illustration for Lemma 8. A $\{\mathsf{swap}, \mathsf{used}, \mathsf{free}\}$-region $R = (sup, sig)$, restricted to T, where $sig(k_0) = sig(X_0) = sig(X_2) = \mathsf{free}$, $sig(X_1) = \mathsf{used}$ and $sig(v_i) = \mathsf{swap}$ for all $i \in \{0, \ldots, 5\}$ and, hence, $|\{e \in \{X_0, X_1, X_2\} \mid sig(e) = \mathsf{swap}\}| = 0$. R is not extendable to a region of a TS that has T and Q such that $sig(v_6) = \mathsf{swap}$, since $sig(v_6) = \mathsf{swap}$ would contradict $sup(q_0) = \cdots = sup(q_3) = 0$, which would be required by $sig(X_0) = sig(X_2) = \mathsf{free}$.

Let φ be an instance of CM 1-IN-3 3SAT with the set of variables $X = \{X_0, \ldots, X_{m-1}\}$ and φ' its renamed copy with event set $X' = \{X'_0, \ldots, X'_{m-1}\}$. In the following, we introduce the construction of A_φ.

Firstly, for every $i \in \{0, \ldots, 7m - 1\}$, the TS A_i has the following gadgets G_i, F_i, G'_i and F'_i with starting states $g_{i,0}$, $f_{i,0}$, $g'_{i,0}$ and $f'_{i,0}$, respectively, providing the atom $\alpha = (g_{0,2}, g_{0,4})$:

$$G_i = g_{i,0} \xleftrightarrow{v_i} g_{i,1} \xleftrightarrow{w_i} g_{i,2} \xleftrightarrow{k_0} g_{i,3} \xleftrightarrow{k_1} g_{i,4} \qquad F_i = f_{i,0} \xleftrightarrow{v_i} f_{i,1} \xleftrightarrow{w_i} f_{i,2} \xleftrightarrow{k_1} f_{i,3} \xleftrightarrow{k_0} f_{i,4}$$

$$G'_i = g'_{i,0} \xleftrightarrow{v'_i} g'_{i,1} \xleftrightarrow{w'_i} g'_{i,2} \xleftrightarrow{k_1} g'_{i,3} \xleftrightarrow{k_0} g'_{i,4} \qquad F'_i = f'_{i,0} \xleftrightarrow{v'_i} f'_{i,1} \xleftrightarrow{w'_i} f'_{i,2} \xleftrightarrow{k_0} f'_{i,3} \xleftrightarrow{k_1} f'_{i,4}$$

Secondly, for every $i \in \{0, \dots, m-1\}$, the TS A_φ has the following gadgets $T_{i,0}, T_{i,1}$ and $T'_{i,0}, T'_{i,1}$ that use the elements of $\zeta_i = \{X_{i_0}, X_{i_1}, X_{i_2}\}$ and $\zeta'_i = \{X'_{i_0}, X'_{i_1}, X'_{i_2}\}$ as events, respectively; their starting states are $t_{i,0,0}, t_{i,1,0}, t'_{i,0,0}$ and $t'_{i,1,0}$:

$$T_{i,0} = t_{i,0,0} \xleftrightarrow{k_0} t_{i,0,1} \xleftrightarrow{v_{7i}} t_{i,0,2} \xleftrightarrow{v_{7i+1}} t_{i,0,3} \xleftrightarrow{X_{i_0}} t_{i,0,4} \xleftrightarrow{v_{7i+2}} t_{i,0,5} \xleftrightarrow{X_{i_1}} t_{i,0,6} \xleftrightarrow{v_{7i+3}} t_{i,0,7}$$

$$X_{i_2} \downarrow$$

$$T_{i,1} = t_{i,1,0} \xleftrightarrow{X_{i_0}} t_{i,1,1} \xleftrightarrow{v_{7i+6}} t_{i,1,2} \xleftrightarrow{X_{i_2}} t_{i,1,3} \qquad t_{i,0,11} \xleftrightarrow{k_0} t_{i,0,10} \xleftrightarrow{v_{7i+5}} t_{i,0,9} \xleftrightarrow{v_{7i+4}} t_{i,0,8}$$

$$T'_{i,0} = t'_{i,0,0} \xleftrightarrow{k_1} t'_{i,0,1} \xleftrightarrow{v'_{7i}} t'_{i,0,2} \xleftrightarrow{v'_{7i+1}} t'_{i,0,3} \xleftrightarrow{X'_{i_0}} t'_{i,0,4} \xleftrightarrow{v'_{7i+2}} t'_{i,0,5} \xleftrightarrow{X'_{i_1}} t'_{i,0,6} \xleftrightarrow{v'_{7i+3}} t'_{i,0,7}$$

$$X'_{i_2} \downarrow$$

$$T'_{i,1} = t'_{i,1,0} \xleftrightarrow{X'_{i_0}} t'_{i,1,1} \xleftrightarrow{v'_{7i+6}} t'_{i,1,2} \xleftrightarrow{X'_{i_2}} t'_{i,1,3} \qquad t'_{i,0,11} \xleftrightarrow{k_1} t'_{i,0,10} \xleftrightarrow{v'_{7i+5}} t'_{i,0,9} \xleftrightarrow{v'_{7i+4}} t'_{i,0,8}$$

Finally, the gadgets are connected via their starting states to finally build A_φ as follows:

$$\begin{array}{ccccccccccccc}
T'_{m-1,1} & & T'_{m-1,0} & \cdots & T'_{0,1} & T'_{0,0} & & G'_0 & F'_0 & \cdots & G'_{7m-1} & & F'_{7m-1} \\
\uparrow\ominus'_{2m-1} & & \uparrow\ominus'_{2m-2} & & \uparrow\ominus'_1 & \uparrow\ominus'_0 & & \ominus'_0\downarrow & \ominus'_1\downarrow & & \ominus'_{14m-2}\uparrow & & \ominus'_{14m-1}\uparrow \\
\bot_{2m-1} & \xleftrightarrow{\oplus_{2m-1}} & \bot_{2m-2} & \cdots & \bot_1 & \xleftrightarrow{\oplus_1}\bot_0\xleftrightarrow{\oplus_0} & \iota & \xleftrightarrow{\otimes_0}T_0 & \xleftrightarrow{\otimes_1}T_1 & \cdots & T_{14m-2} & \xleftrightarrow{\otimes_{14m-1}} & T_{14m-1} \\
\uparrow\ominus_{2m-1} & & \uparrow\ominus_{2m-2} & & \uparrow\ominus_1 & \uparrow\ominus_0 & & \ominus_0\downarrow & \ominus_1\downarrow & & \ominus_{14m-2}\uparrow & & \ominus_{14m-1}\uparrow \\
T_{m-1,1} & & T_{m-1,0} & \cdots & T_{0,1} & T_{0,0} & & G_0 & F_0 & \cdots & G_{7m-1} & & F_{7m-1}
\end{array}$$

The following Lemma 9 and Lemma 10 prove the validity of our polynomial-time reduction and, hence, complete the proof of Theorem 3.

Lemma 9. *If A_φ has the τ-SSP, then φ is one-in-three satisfiable.*

Proof. Let G, F, T and Q be the paths defined in Lemma 8. First of all, we observe that $G \cong G_{7i+j} \cong G'_{7i+j}$ and $F \cong F_{7i+j} \cong F'_{7i+j}$ and $T \cong T_{i,0} \cong T'_{i,0}$ and $Q \cong T_{i,1} \cong T'_{i,1}$ for all $i \in \{0, \dots, m-1\}$ and $j \in \{0, \dots, 6\}$. Let $R = (sup, sig)$ be a τ-region that solves $\alpha = (g_{0,2}, g_{0,4})$ (which exists, since A_φ has the τ-SSP) and let $i \in \{0, \dots, m-1\}$ be arbitrary but fixed. By Lemma 8.1, we have either $sig(k_0) \in \mathfrak{save}$ and $sig(k_1) = \mathsf{swap}$ or $sig(k_0) = \mathsf{swap}$ and $sig(k_1) \in \mathfrak{save}$. This implies $sig(u_{7i}) = \cdots = sig(u_{7i+6}) = sig(u'_{7i}) = \cdots = sig(u'_{7i+6}) = \mathsf{swap}$ by Lemma 8.2. If $sig(k_0) \in \mathfrak{save}$ and $sig(k_1) = \mathsf{swap}$, then by Lemma 8.3, this implies that there is exactly one event $e \in \{X_{i_0}, X_{i_1}, X_{i_2}\}$ such that $sig(e) \neq \mathsf{swap}$. Consequently, since i was arbitrary, if $sig(k_0) \in \mathfrak{save}$ and $sig(k_1) = \mathsf{swap}$, then $M = \{e \in X \mid sig(e) \neq \mathsf{swap}\}$ selects exactly one variable of every clause ζ_i for all $i \in \{0, \ldots, m-1\}$. Thus, M is a one in three-model of φ. Otherwise, if $sig(k_0) = \mathsf{swap}$ and $sig(k_1) \in \mathfrak{save}$, then we similarly obtain that $M' = \{e \in X' \mid sig(e) \neq \mathsf{swap}\}$ defines a one-in-three-model of φ', which also implies the one-in-three satisfiability of φ. $\square$

Lemma 10. *If φ is one-in-three satisfiable, then A_φ has the τ-SSP.*

Due to space restrictions, the proof of Lemma 10 is omitted but can be found in the technical report that corresponds to this paper [21].

5   Conclusion

In this paper, we present the overall characterization of the computational complexity of the problem τ-SSP for all 256 Boolean types of nets τ. Our presentation includes 154 new complexity results (Fig. 1: §1–§3, §6, §9, §10) and 102 known results (Fig. 1: §4 [23], §5 [19,24], §7 [16,23], §8 [22]) and classifies them in the overall context of boolean state separation. Besides the new 150 hardness - and 4 tractability-results, this classification is one of the main contributions of this paper. First of all, it becomes apparent that the distinction between nop-free and nop-equipped types is meaningful: Within the class of nop-free types, τ-SSP turns out to be NP-complete if and only if $\mathsf{swap} \in \tau$ and $\tau \cap \mathfrak{save} \neq \emptyset$. Within the class of nop-equipped types, a differentiation between types τ that satisfy $\tau \cap \{\mathsf{res}, \mathsf{set}\} = \emptyset$ and the ones with $\tau \cap \{\mathsf{res}, \mathsf{set}\} \neq \emptyset$ is useful: τ-SSP for the former ones is NP-complete if and only if $\tau \cap \{\mathsf{inp}, \mathsf{out}\} \neq \emptyset$ and $\mathsf{swap} \notin \tau$. In particular, $\{\mathsf{swap}\} \cup \tau$-SSP becomes polynomial for all these types. On the other hand, for the latter ones, which include $i \in \{\mathsf{res}, \mathsf{set}\}$ such that $i \in \tau$, τ-SSP is NP-complete as long as there is also an interaction in τ that opposes i, that is, $\tau \cap \mathfrak{exit} \neq \emptyset$ if $i = \mathsf{set}$ and $\tau \cap \mathfrak{enter} \neq \emptyset$ if $i = \mathsf{res}$.

Moreover, our proofs discover that, up to isomorphism, there are essentially four hard kernels that indicate the NP-completeness of τ-SSP, namely $\{\mathsf{nop}, \mathsf{inp}\}$ and $\{\mathsf{nop}, \mathsf{inp}, \mathsf{out}\}$ for the nop-equipped types and $\{\mathsf{swap}, \mathsf{free}\}$ and $\{\mathsf{swap}, \mathsf{free}, \mathsf{used}\}$ for the nop-free types. That means, for a nop-equipped type τ, the hardness of τ-SSP can either be shown by a reduction of $\{\mathsf{nop}, \mathsf{inp}\}$-SSP or $\{\mathsf{nop}, \mathsf{inp}, \mathsf{out}\}$-SSP (or their isomorphic types), which is basically done in the proof of Lemma 5, or τ-SSP is polynomial otherwise. Similarly, one finds out that for the nop-free types τ in question, the hardness of τ-SSP can be shown by a reduction of $\{\mathsf{swap}, \mathsf{free}\}$-SSP or $\{\mathsf{swap}, \mathsf{free}, \mathsf{used}\}$-SSP. Due to the space limitation, a reduction that covers *all* hard nop-free types on one blow is given instead of explicit proof.

For future work, it remains to completely characterize the computational complexity of deciding if a TS A is isomorphic to the reachability graph of a Boolean Petri net, instead of only being embeddable by an injective simulation map.

References

1. Badouel, E., Bernardinello, L., Darondeau, P.: Polynomial algorithms for the synthesis of bounded nets. In: Mosses, P.D., Nielsen, M., Schwartzbach, M.I. (eds.) CAAP 1995. LNCS, vol. 915, pp. 364–378. Springer, Heidelberg (1995). https://doi.org/10.1007/3-540-59293-8_207
2. Badouel, E., Bernardinello, L., Darondeau, P.: The synthesis problem for elementary net systems is NP-complete. Theor. Comput. Sci. **186**(1–2), 107–134 (1997). https://doi.org/10.1016/S0304-3975(96)00219-8
3. Badouel, E., Bernardinello, L., Darondeau, P.: Petri Net Synthesis. TTCSAES. Springer, Heidelberg (2015). https://doi.org/10.1007/978-3-662-47967-4
4. Badouel, E., Darondeau, P.: Trace nets and process automata. Acta Inf. **32**(7), 647–679 (1995). https://doi.org/10.1007/BF01186645
5. Best, E., Devillers, R.R.: Pre-synthesis of Petri nets based on prime cycles and distance paths. Sci. Comput. Program. **157**, 41–55 (2018). https://doi.org/10.1016/j.scico.2017.07.005
6. Chatain, T., Haar, S., Kolčák, J., Paulevé, L., Thakkar, A.: Concurrency in Boolean networks. Nat. Comput. **19**(1), 91–109 (2020). https://doi.org/10.1007/s11047-019-09748-4
7. Esparza, J., Nielsen, M.: Decidability issues for Petri nets - a survey. Bull. EATCS **52**, 244–262 (1994)
8. Kleijn, J., Koutny, M., Pietkiewicz-Koutny, M., Rozenberg, G.: Step semantics of Boolean nets. Acta Inf. **50**(1), 15–39 (2013). https://doi.org/10.1007/s00236-012-0170-2
9. Montanari, U., Rossi, F.: Contextual occurrence nets and concurrent constraint programming. In: Schneider, H.J., Ehrig, H. (eds.) Graph Transformations in Computer Science. LNCS, vol. 776, pp. 280–295. Springer, Heidelberg (1994). https://doi.org/10.1007/3-540-57787-4_18
10. Montanari, U., Rossi, F.: Contextual nets. Acta Inf. **32**(6), 545–596 (1995). https://doi.org/10.1007/BF01178907
11. Moore, C., Robson, J.M.: Hard tiling problems with simple tiles. Discret. Comput. Geom. **26**(4), 573–590 (2001). https://doi.org/10.1007/s00454-001-0047-6
12. Pietkiewicz-Koutny, M.: transition systems of elementary net systems with inhibitor arcs. In: Azéma, P., Balbo, G. (eds.) ICATPN 1997. LNCS, vol. 1248, pp. 310–327. Springer, Heidelberg (1997). https://doi.org/10.1007/3-540-63139-9_43
13. Rozenberg, G., Engelfriet, J.: Elementary net systems. In: Reisig, W., Rozenberg, G. (eds.) ACPN 1996. LNCS, vol. 1491, pp. 12–121. Springer, Heidelberg (1998). https://doi.org/10.1007/3-540-65306-6_14
14. Schlachter, U.: Over-approximative Petri net synthesis for restricted subclasses of nets. In: Klein, S.T., Martín-Vide, C., Shapira, D. (eds.) LATA 2018. LNCS, vol. 10792, pp. 296–307. Springer, Cham (2018). https://doi.org/10.1007/978-3-319-77313-1_23
15. Schlachter, U., Wimmel, H.: Optimal label splitting for embedding an LTS into an arbitrary Petri net reachability graph is NP-complete. CoRR abs/2002.04841 (2020). https://arxiv.org/abs/2002.04841
16. Schmitt, V.: Flip-flop nets. In: Puech, C., Reischuk, R. (eds.) STACS 1996. LNCS, vol. 1046, pp. 515–528. Springer, Heidelberg (1996). https://doi.org/10.1007/3-540-60922-9_42

17. Tredup, R.: The complexity of synthesizing nop-equipped Boolean nets from g-bounded inputs (technical report) (2019)
18. Tredup, R.: Fixed parameter tractability and polynomial time results for the synthesis of b-bounded Petri nets. In: Donatelli, S., Haar, S. (eds.) PETRI NETS 2019. LNCS, vol. 11522, pp. 148–168. Springer, Cham (2019). https://doi.org/10.1007/978-3-030-21571-2_10
19. Tredup, R.: Hardness results for the synthesis of b-bounded Petri nets. In: Donatelli, S., Haar, S. (eds.) PETRI NETS 2019. LNCS, vol. 11522, pp. 127–147. Springer, Cham (2019). https://doi.org/10.1007/978-3-030-21571-2_9
20. Tredup, R.: Parameterized complexity of synthesizing b-bounded (m, n)-T-systems. In: Chatzigeorgiou, A., et al. (eds.) SOFSEM 2020. LNCS, vol. 12011, pp. 223–235. Springer, Cham (2020). https://doi.org/10.1007/978-3-030-38919-2_19
21. Tredup, R., Erofeev, E.: The complexity of Boolean state separation (technical report) (2020). submitted to arxive.org
22. Tredup, R., Erofeev, E.: On the complexity of synthesis of nop-free Boolean Petri nets. In: van der Aalst, W.M.P., Bergenthum, R., Carmona, J. (eds.) Proceedings of the International Workshop on Algorithms & Theories for the Analysis of Event Data 2020 Satellite event of the 41st International Conference on Application and Theory of Petri Nets and Concurrency Petri Nets 2020, Virtual Workshop, June 24, 2020. CEUR Workshop Proceedings, vol. 2625, pp. 66–84. CEUR-WS.org (2020). http://ceur-ws.org/Vol-2625/paper-05.pdf
23. Tredup, R., Rosenke, C.: The complexity of synthesis for 43 boolean petri net types. In: Gopal, T.V., Watada, J. (eds.) TAMC 2019. LNCS, vol. 11436, pp. 615–634. Springer, Cham (2019). https://doi.org/10.1007/978-3-030-14812-6_38
24. Tredup, R., Rosenke, C., Wolf, K.: Elementary net synthesis remains NP-complete even for extremely simple inputs. In: Khomenko, V., Roux, O.H. (eds.) PETRI NETS 2018. LNCS, vol. 10877, pp. 40–59. Springer, Cham (2018). https://doi.org/10.1007/978-3-319-91268-4_3
25. Vogler, W., Semenov, A., Yakovlev, A.: Unfolding and finite prefix for nets with read arcs. In: Sangiorgi, D., de Simone, R. (eds.) CONCUR 1998. LNCS, vol. 1466, pp. 501–516. Springer, Heidelberg (1998). https://doi.org/10.1007/BFb0055644
26. Wimmel, H.: Presynthesis of bounded choice-free or fork-attribution nets. Inf. Comput. **271**, 104482 (2020)
27. Yakovlev, A., Koelmans, A., Semenov, A.L., Kinniment, D.J.: Modelling, analysis and synthesis of asynchronous control circuits using Petri nets. Integration **21**(3), 143–170 (1996). https://doi.org/10.1016/S0167-9260(96)00010-7

Occupancy Number Restricted Boolean Petri Net Synthesis: A Fixed-Parameter Algorithm

Evgeny Erofeev[1] and Ronny Tredup[2(✉)]

[1] Department of Computing Science, Carl von Ossietzky Universität Oldenburg,
26111 Oldenburg, Germany
evgeny.erofeev@informatik.uni-oldenburg.de
[2] Institut für Informatik, Theoretische Informatik, Universität Rostock,
Albert-Einstein-Straße 22, 18059 Rostock, Germany
ronny.tredup@uni-rostock.de

Abstract. Let τ be a Boolean type of net. For a given transition system A and a natural number ρ, the problem *occupancy ρ-restricted τ-synthesis* (ORτS) is the task to decide whether there is a Boolean Petri net N of type τ whose reachability graph is isomorphic to A and, moreover, every place of N contains a token in at most ρ reachable markings. In case of a positive decision, N should be constructed. In this paper, we argue that ORτS is fixed-parameter tractable when parameterized by ρ.

Keywords: Synthesis · Parameterized complexity · Boolean Petri net · Fixed-parameter tractability · Transition system

1 Introduction

Petri nets are a classical formalism which is widely used for modeling of parallel processes and distributed systems. Their concepts of transitions as atomic actions of the modeled system, and places as conditions for these actions allow to capture the relations of causal dependency, conflict and concurrency between system agents on a fine-grained level. This raises the interest to the possibility to synthesise a Petri net model for a system: Provided a specification of the desired behavior of the system, one has to construct a Petri net model implementing the specification. The problem of Petri net synthesis has been extensively studied in the literature [3], and finds its applications in various domains [1,10]. The variety of obtained results demonstrates that the computational complexity of this problem significantly depends on the restrictions which are either implied by the input specification [14,22,28], or imposed on the target system model [6,23,27], or both [13], and ranges from quadratic polynomial [12] via NP-complete [30,32] and up to undecidable [21]. Various formalisms can be used as an input for synthesis: formal languages [16], system event logs [8] or transition systems [7]. The present paper focuses on the latter case, and assumes the specification to be

© Springer Nature Switzerland AG 2020
V. K. I. Pun et al. (Eds.): ICTAC 2020, LNCS 12545, pp. 143–160, 2020.
https://doi.org/10.1007/978-3-030-64276-1_8

given as a labeled transition system. The goal of synthesis is then to construct a Petri net whose reachability graph is isomorphic to the specification. As a target model class we consider Boolean Petri nets, where each place contains at most one token, for any reachable marking, i.e., a place can encode at most two local states of the modeled system. According to this definition, a place p is interpreted as a Boolean condition which is *true* if p is marked and *false* otherwise.

In a Boolean Petri net, a place p and a transition t are related by one of the Boolean *interactions*: *no operation* (nop), *input* (inp), *output* (out), *unconditionally set to true* (set), *unconditionally reset to false* (res), *inverting* (swap), *test if true* (used), and *test if false* (free). These interactions define in which way p and t influence each other: The interaction inp (out) defines that p must be *true* (*false*) before and *false* (*true*) after t's firing; free (used) implies that t's firing proves that p is *false* (*true*); nop means that p and t do not affect each other at all; res (set) implies that p may initially be both *false* or *true* but after t's firing it is *false* (*true*); swap means that t inverts p's current Boolean value.

Boolean Petri nets are classified by the sets of interactions between places and transitions that can be applied. A set τ of Boolean interactions is called a *type of net*. A net N is of type τ (a τ-net) if it applies at most the interactions of τ. A number of different types of nets have been selectively studied in the literature, e.g., contextual nets ($\tau = \{\text{nop}, \text{inp}, \text{out}, \text{used}, \text{free}\}$) [5,18], inhibitor nets ($\tau = \{\text{nop}, \text{inp}, \text{out}, \text{free}\}$) [19], trace nets ($\tau = \{\text{nop}, \text{inp}, \text{out}, \text{set}, \text{res}, \text{used}, \text{free}\}$) [4], flip-flop nets ($\tau = \{\text{nop}, \text{inp}, \text{out}, \text{swap}\}$) [24], with their applications in asynchronous circuits design [33], concurrent constraint programs [17], analyzing of biological systems models [9]. For a type τ, the τ-*synthesis* problem consists in deciding whether a given transition system is isomorphic to the reachability graph of some τ-net N, and in constructing N if it exists. The complexity of τ-synthesis varies substantially for different types of nets. Thus, while τ-synthesis for elementary net systems ($\tau = \{\text{nop}, \text{inp}, \text{out}\}$) was shown to be NP-complete [2], the same problem for flip-flop nets is polynomial [24].

Since the notion of a type of net allows to define the plethora of Boolean nets uniformly, the present paper continues the systematic approach to study the complexity of τ-synthesis [31] and its parameterized settings [26,28]. Precisely, the paper addresses the computational complexity of the parameterized problem *Occupancy ρ-restricted τ-synthesis* (ORτS): The parameter ρ restricts the number of reachable markings at which a place can be marked. The problem of occupancy arises in the applications in different contexts. In the analysis of fault tolerant systems [15], for each activity its fault rate can be modeled as a function of the number of times the activity is performed. By modeling the system with random Boolean nets [25], the expected value of occupancy rate can be used to estimate the fault rate of the components. Besides, occupancy rate is of interest in simulations with Petri nets [20], where it provides important information on the system reliability. From the theoretical perspective, if τ-synthesis is NP-complete, then ORτS is also NP-complete. On the other hand, in this paper, we show that in terms of parameterized complexity theory, the natural parameterization of ORτS is fixed-parameter-tractable for the types which allow places and transitions to be independent, i.e., the types that include the interaction nop. This means that the problem can be solved efficiently for small values of the parameter. In ORτS, the parameter sets a behavioral limitation on the target net, unlike the parameterized settings of τ-synthesis studied previously [29] where the limitations were of a structural nature.

The paper is organized as follows. After introducing of the necessary definitions in Sect. 2, we present the results on fixed-parameter tractability of ORτS for nop-equipped types in Sect. 3, together with the corresponding algorithm. Section 4 suggests an outlook of the further research directions.

2   Preliminaries

Transition Systems. A (deterministic) *transition system* (TS, for short) $A = (S, E, \delta)$ is a directed labeled graph with the set of nodes S (called *states*), the set of labels E (called *events*) and the partial *transition function* $\delta : S \times E \longrightarrow S$. If $\delta(s, e)$ is defined, we say that event e *occurs* at state s, denoted by $s \xrightarrow{e}$. For $\delta(s, e) = s'$ (denoted $s \xrightarrow{e} s'$), we call s a *source* and s' a *sink* of e, respectively. An *initialized* TS $A = (S, E, \delta, \iota)$ is a TS with a distinct *initial* state $\iota \in S$ where every state $s \in S$ is *reachable* from ι by a directed labeled path.

Boolean Types of Nets [3]. The following notion of Boolean types of nets allows to capture *all* Boolean Petri nets in a *uniform* way. A *Boolean type of net* $\tau = (\{0, 1\}, E_\tau, \delta_\tau)$ is a TS such that E_τ is a subset of the *Boolean interactions*: $E_\tau \subseteq I = \{\text{nop, inp, out, set, res, swap, used, free}\}$. Each interaction $i \in I$ is a binary partial function $i : \{0, 1\} \to \{0, 1\}$ as defined in Fig. 1. For all $x \in \{0, 1\}$ and all $i \in E_\tau$, the transition function of τ is defined by $\delta_\tau(x, i) = i(x)$. Since a type τ is completely determined by E_τ, we often identify τ with E_τ.

x	$\text{nop}(x)$	$\text{inp}(x)$	$\text{out}(x)$	$\text{set}(x)$	$\text{res}(x)$	$\text{swap}(x)$	$\text{used}(x)$	$\text{free}(x)$
0	0		1	1	0	1		0
1	1	0		1	0	0	1	

Fig. 1. All interactions i of I. If a cell is empty, then i is undefined on the respective x.

Fig. 2. The type $\tau = \{\text{nop, inp, swap}\}$ and a τ-net N and its reachability graph A_N.

τ-**Nets.** Let $\tau \subseteq I$. A Boolean Petri net $N = (P, T, f, M_0)$ of type τ (a τ-*net*) is given by finite disjoint sets P of *places* and T of *transitions*, a (total) *flow function* $f : P \times T \to \tau$, and an *initial marking* $M_0 : P \longrightarrow \{0, 1\}$. A transition $t \in T$ can *fire* in a marking $M : P \longrightarrow \{0, 1\}$ if $\delta_\tau(M(p), f(p, t))$ is defined for all $p \in P$. By firing, t produces the marking $M' : P \longrightarrow \{0, 1\}$ where $M'(p) = \delta_\tau(M(p), f(p, t))$ for all $p \in P$, denoted by $M \xrightarrow{t} M'$. The behavior of τ-net N is captured by a (initialized) transition system A_N, called the *reachability graph* of N. A_N has M_0 as its initial state, and the states set $RS(N)$ of A_N consists of all markings that can be reached from M_0 by sequences of transition firings. A τ-net N is called *occupancy ρ-restricted* (or simply ρ-*restricted*) if for each place p, there are at most ρ reachable markings M of N such that $M(p) = 1$.

Example 1. Figure 2 shows the type $\tau = \{\mathsf{nop}, \mathsf{inp}, \mathsf{swap}\}$ and the τ-net $N = (\{R_1, R_2\}, \{a, a'\}, f, M_0)$ with places R_1, R_2, flow-function $f(R_1, a) = f(R_2, a') = \mathsf{inp}$, $f(R_1, a') = \mathsf{nop}$, $f(R_2, a) = \mathsf{swap}$ and initial marking M_0 defined by $(M_0(R_1), M_0(R_2)) = (1, 0)$. Since $1 \xrightarrow{\mathsf{inp}} 0 \in \tau$ and $0 \xrightarrow{\mathsf{swap}} 1 \in \tau$, the transition a can fire in M_0, which leads to the marking $M = (M(R_1), M(R_2)) = (0, 1)$. After that, a' can fire, which results in the marking $M' = (M'(R_1), M'(R_2)) = (0, 0)$. The reachability graph A_N of N is depicted on the right hand side of Fig. 2.

Let $\tau \subseteq I$ The problem of τ-synthesis is formulated as follows:

τ-**Synthesis.**

Input: transition system A.
Decide: whether there is a Boolean τ-net N such that A_N is isomorphic to A.

If an input A of τ-synthesis allows a positive decision, we want to construct a corresponding τ-net N. TS represents the behavior of a modeled system by means of *global states* (states of TS) and transitions between them (events). Dealing with a Petri net, we operate with *local states* (places) and their changings (transitions), while the global states of a net are markings, i.e., combinations of local states. Since A and A_N must be isomorphic, N's transitions correspond to the events of A. The connection between global states in TS and local states in the sought net is given by the notion of *regions of TS* that mimic places.

τ-**Regions.** A τ-region $R = (sup, sig)$ of TS $A = (S, E, \delta, \iota)$ consists of the *support* $sup : S \to \{0, 1\}$ and the *signature* $sig : E \to E_\tau$ where every edge $s \xrightarrow{e} s'$ of A leads to an edge $sup(s) \xrightarrow{sig(e)} sup(s')$ of type τ. For the sake of succinctness, for a region (sup, sig) we will often identify sup with its 1-image, i.e., the set $\{s \in S \mid sup(s) = 1\}$. For $S' \subseteq S$, a τ-region (sup, sig) is called S'-*minimal* if $S' \subseteq sup$ and $|sup| \leq |sup'|$, for any region (sup', sig') with $S' \subseteq sup'$. A τ-region (sup, sig) *respects the occupancy parameter* ρ, if $|sup| \leq \rho$; we will call such regions ρ-*restricted*. A region (sup, sig) models a place p and the associated part of the flow function f. In particular, $f(p, e) = sig(e)$ and $M(p) = sup(s)$, for marking $M \in RS(N)$ that corresponds to $s \in S$. Every set $\mathcal{R}$ of τ-regions of A

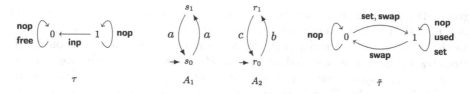

Fig. 3. The type $\tau = \{\mathsf{nop}, \mathsf{inp}, \mathsf{free}\}$, the TSs A_1 and A_2 and the type $\tilde{\tau} = \{\mathsf{nop}, \mathsf{swap},$ used, set$\}$.

Fig. 4. The $\tilde{\tau}$-net N (left), where $\tilde{\tau}$ is defined according to Fig. 3 and $N = N_{A_1}^{\mathcal{R}}$ according to Example 2, and its reachability graph A_N (right).

defines the *synthesized* τ-*net* $N_A^{\mathcal{R}} = (\mathcal{R}, E, f, M_0)$ with $f((sup, sig), e) = sig(e)$ and $M_0((sup, sig)) = sup(\iota)$ for all $(sup, sig) \in \mathcal{R}, e \in E$.

State and Event Separation. To ensure that the input behavior is captured by the synthesized net, we have to distinguish global states, and prevent the firings of transitions when their corresponding events are not present in TS. This is stated as so called *separation atoms*. A pair (s, s') of distinct states of A defines a *states separation atom* (SSP atom). A τ-region $R = (sup, sig)$ *solves* (s, s') if $sup(s) \neq sup(s')$. If every SSP atom of A is τ-solvable then A has the τ-*states separation property* (τ-SSP, for short). A pair (e, s) of event $e \in E$ and state $s \in S$ at which e does not occur, that is $\neg s \xrightarrow{e}$, defines an *event/state separation atom* (ESSP atom). A τ-region $R = (sup, sig)$ *solves* (e, s) if $sig(e)$ is not defined on $sup(s)$ in τ, that is, $\neg sup(s) \xrightarrow{sig(e)}$. If every ESSP atom of A is τ-solvable then A has the τ-*event/state separation property* (τ-ESSP, for short). A set $\mathcal{R}$ of τ-regions of A is called τ-*admissible* if for each SSP and ESSP atom, there is a τ-region R in $\mathcal{R}$ that solves it. We say that A is τ-solvable if it has a τ-admissible set. The next lemma establishes the connection between the existence of τ-admissible sets of A and the existence of a τ-net N that solves A:

Lemma 1 [3]. *A TS A is isomorphic to the reachability graph of a τ-net N if and only if there is a τ-admissible set $\mathcal{R}$ of A such that $N = N_A^{\mathcal{R}}$.*

Example 2. Let τ, $\tilde{\tau}$, A_1 and A_2 be defined as in Fig. 3. The TS A_1 has no ESSP atoms. Hence, it has the τ-ESSP and $\tilde{\tau}$-ESSP. The only SSP atom of A_1 is (s_0, s_1). It is $\tilde{\tau}$-solvable by $R_1 = (sup_1, sig_1)$ with $sup_1(s_0) = 0$, $sup_1(s_1) = 1$, $sig_1(a) = $ swap. Thus, A_1 has the $\tilde{\tau}$-admissible set $\mathcal{R} = \{R_1\}$, and the $\tilde{\tau}$-net $N_{A_1}^{\mathcal{R}} = (\{R_1\}, \{a\}, f, M_0)$ with $M_0(R_1) = sup_1(s_0) = 0$ and $f(R_1, a) = sig_1(a) = $ swap is 1-restricted and solves A_1. Figure 4 depicts $N = N_{A_1}^{\mathcal{R}}$ and its reachability graph A_N. The isomorphism φ between A_1 and A_N is given by $\varphi(s_0) = (0)$ and $\varphi(s_1) = (1)$. The SSP atom (s_0, s_1) is not τ-solvable, thus, neither is A_1. TS A_2 has ESSP atoms (b, r_1) and (c, r_0), which are both $\tilde{\tau}$-unsolvable. The only SSP atom (r_0, r_1) in A_2 can be solved by $\tilde{\tau}$-region $R_2 = (sup_2, sig_2)$ with $sup_2(r_0) = 0$, $sup_2(r_1) = 1$, $sig_2(b) = \mathsf{set}$, $sig_2(c) = \mathsf{swap}$. Thus, A_2 has the $\tilde{\tau}$-SSP, but not the $\tilde{\tau}$-ESSP. None of the (E)SSP atoms of A_2 can be solved by any τ-region.

By Lemma 1, every τ-admissible set $\mathcal{R}$ implies that $N_A^{\mathcal{R}}$ τ-solves A. In this paper, we investigate the complexity of synthezising a solving ρ-restricted τ-net N for a given transition system. By Lemma 1, there exists such a net N if and only if there is a ρ-restricted τ-admissible set $\mathcal{R}$, that is, every region $R = (sup, sig)$ of $\mathcal{R}$ is ρ-restricted. This finally leads to the following parameterized problem that is the main subject of the paper:

Occupancy Restricted τ-Synthesis (ORτS)

Input: transition system A, natural number ρ.
Parameter: ρ
Decide: whether there exists a ρ-restricted τ-admissible set $\mathcal{R}$ of Λ.

In particular, we shall prove that ORτS is *fixed parameter tractable* if $\mathsf{nop} \in \tau$.

Fixed-Parameter Tractability. A parameterized decision problem (X, κ), where κ is a parameter, is called *fixed-parameter tractable* if it can be solved in running time $f(\kappa) \cdot |X|^{\mathcal{O}(1)}$ for some computable function f. The interest to the FPT class is motivated by the fact that some of parameterized NP-hard problems can be solved by algorithms which are exponential only in the size of the parameter and polynomial in the size of the input. Hence, for fixed parameter values, these problems can be solved efficiently. We refer to [11] for detailed explanations and formal definitions on parameterized complexity.

3   Fixed-Parameter Tractability of τ-Synthesis with nop

In this section, we argue that (ORτS) parameterized by ρ is fixed-parameter tractable for the Boolean types that include the interaction nop. This is achieved by suggesting a synthesis algorithm, which constructs a τ-solving region for each separation atom, if one exists. For a given separation atom, the algorithm assumes the minimally necessary information about possible τ-region solving the atom, and iteratively updates this knowledge until a valid region is defined completely and consistently. The polynomiality of the algorithm in the size of the input transition system and its exponentiality in the value of the parameter ρ yields the result.

When seeking for a τ-region $R = (sup, sig)$ which solves an SSP atom (s, s'), the initial assumption about R can be $sup(s) = 0 \land sup(s') = 1$ or $sup(s) = 1 \land sup(s') = 0$. In this case, we start constructing R using either $S = \{s'\}$ or $S = \{s\}$ as a starting support, respectively. For a given ESSP atom (e, q), a region $R = (sup, sig)$ solving it has to define $sig(e)$ as one of the interactions inp, out, used, free (because all the other interactions are defined for any support value of the source state). The following initial assumptions about R can be used then:

- $sig(e) = \text{inp}$, $sup(q) = 0$: minimal initial support $S = \{s \in S_A \mid s \xrightarrow{e} \}$,
- $sig(e) = \text{out}$, $sup(q) = 1$: minimal initial support $S = \{q\} \cup \{s \in S_A \mid \xrightarrow{e} s\}$,
- $sig(e) = \text{used}$, $sup(q) = 0$: minimal initial support $S = \{s, s' \in S_A \mid s \xrightarrow{e} s'\}$,
- $sig(e) = \text{free}$, $sup(q) = 1$: minimal initial support $S = \{q\}$.

The initial assumption is not guaranteed to be a valid τ-support, and may need to be extended. In order to construct valid minimal regions starting from a given support-set, the notion of *conflict* (and *conflict-freeness*) will be used in what follows.

Transitions in Conflict. Let τ be a type of nets, A be a TS, $S \subseteq S_A$ be a set of states and $e \in E_A$ be an event. We say that edge $s \xrightarrow{e} s'$ of A is *in conflict with S* if there is no interaction $i \in \tau$ such that $S(s) \xrightarrow{i} S(s') \in \tau$. Moreover, we say that two distinct edges $s \xrightarrow{e} s'$ and $q \xrightarrow{e} q'$ are *in conflict with S* if there is no interaction $i \in \tau$ such that $S(s) \xrightarrow{i} S(s') \in \tau$ and $S(q) \xrightarrow{i} S(q') \in \tau$.

The next lemma essentially states that a subset $S \subseteq S_A$ of states of a TS A allows a τ-signature if and only if the transitions labeled with the same event are pairwise not in conflict with S.

Lemma 2. *Let A be a TS, τ be a type of nets and $S \subseteq S_A$ be a set of states of A. The set S allows a τ-region (S, sig) of A if and only if for each $e \in E_A$, one of the following conditions holds true:*

1. *e occurs uniquely in A, say at the edge $s \xrightarrow{e} s'$, and there is an interaction $i \in \tau$ such that $S(s) \xrightarrow{i} S(s') \in \tau$.*
2. *for any pair of distinct edges $s \xrightarrow{e} s'$ and $q \xrightarrow{e} q'$ of A, an interaction $i \in \tau$ exists such that $S(s) \xrightarrow{i} S(s') \in \tau$ and $S(q) \xrightarrow{i} S(q') \in \tau$.*

Proof. The *only-if* direction follows immediately, for $i = sig(e)$.
If: We have to show that for every $e \in E_A$, an interaction $i \in \tau$ exists such that $s \xrightarrow{e} s'$ implies $S(s) \xrightarrow{i} S(s') \in \tau$. Let $e \in E_A$ be an arbitrary event of A and define $X_e = \{(S(s), S(s')) \mid s \xrightarrow{e} s' \in A\}$. If $|X_e| = 1$, then the sought interaction exists by the condition, independent of which of items 1 or 2 is satisfied. Assume $|X_e| \geq 2$. Then condition 1 is excluded. If $\{(0,0),(0,1)\} \subseteq X_e$ or $\{(1,0),(1,1)\} \subseteq X_e$, then there is a pair of edges $s \xrightarrow{e} s'$ and $q \xrightarrow{e} q'$ for which there is no $i \in I$ such that $S(s) \xrightarrow{i} S(s')$ and $S(q) \xrightarrow{i} S(q')$ are satisfied (cf. Fig. 1). Since $\tau \subseteq I$, this contradicts the condition 2. Thus, in accordance to Fig. 5, we conclude

$$X_e \in T = \{\{(0,0),(1,0)\}, \{(0,1),(1,0)\}, \{(0,1),(1,1)\}\}$$

For all sets $X \in T$, there is exactly one $i \in I$ such that $x \xrightarrow{i} y \in \tau$ for all $(x, y) \in X$. Thus, i belongs to τ. Since e was arbitrary, for every $e \in E_A$, there is an interaction $i \in \tau$ such that $s \xrightarrow{e} s'$ implies $S(s) \xrightarrow{i} S(s') \in \tau$. $\qquad \square$

Set $S \subseteq S_A$ is called *conflict-free* if the condition of Lemma 2 is satisfied for every $e \in E_A$.

Having an initial assumption S about the support of the sought region, our goal is to extend S to a conflict-free set, if possible. This will be done by providing a recursive procedure SUP (Algorithm 1): For a given (E)SSP atom α of a TS A, the procedure SUP constructs a τ-support of size at most ρ, which allows a τ-region solving α, if there is one.

The input (A, S, ρ, τ) of SUP consists of a TS A, a set of states S, a natural number ρ and a type τ. Basically, SUP starts from the set S that is a subset of the support of some admissible region $R = (sup, sig)$ that solves α. For example, if $\alpha = (s, s')$ is an SSP atom to be solved by R, then either sup includes s (and excludes s') or it includes s' (and excludes s). In order to find a solving region, if one exists, we separately start SUP on $S = \{s\}$ and on $S = \{s'\}$. In every recursive call, SUP checks if the current value of S allows a fitting signature. To do so, the procedure looks for an event $e \in E_A$ and transitions $s \xrightarrow{e} s'$ and $q \xrightarrow{e} q'$ of A that are in conflict with S and τ, i.e., $sig(e)$ cannot be defined consistently. If no transitions are in conflict, then SUP terminates and returns $\{S\}$. Otherwise, S allows no signature and the conflict has to be resolved. For every recursive call, S contains only minimally necessary states. Hence, if conflicting transitions $s \xrightarrow{e} s'$ and $q \xrightarrow{e} q'$ are present, the only way to potentially get a τ-support that contains S is to add at least one of the states s, s', q, q' to S. Moreover, since $s \xrightarrow{e} s'$ and $q \xrightarrow{e} q'$ are in conflict, there is a state among s, s', q, q' that already belongs to S. Otherwise, $S(s) \xrightarrow{\mathsf{nop}} S(s') \in \tau$ and $S(q) \xrightarrow{\mathsf{nop}} S(q') \in \tau$ would be allowed. Thus, there are at most three states x, y, z of $\{s, s', q, q'\}$ that could possibly extend S. For every such state that does not belong to S, the procedure branches and calls SUP for the corresponding extension. That is, SUP recursively calls $\mathrm{SUP}(A, S \cup \{x\}, \rho, \tau), \mathrm{SUP}(A, S \cup \{y\}, \rho, \tau), \mathrm{SUP}(A, S \cup \{z\}, \rho, \tau)$ and returns the union of their outcomes: $\mathrm{SUP}(A, S \cup \{x\}, \rho, \tau) \cup \mathrm{SUP}(A, S \cup \{y\}, \rho, \tau) \cup \mathrm{SUP}(A, S \cup \{z\}, \rho, \tau)$. In particular, SUP has a ternary recursion-tree. Every extension of S is preceded by a check if this extension does not exceed ρ. This ensures that SUP terminates. Moreover, SUP adds only "necessary" states. Thus, if there is a fitting support sup of a solving region (sup, sig) (that contains at most ρ states), then sup is reached by at most one path of the recursion tree of SUP. That is, $sup \in \mathrm{SUP}$.

SUP has a ternary recursion tree of depth at most ρ. Hence, if there is a fitting region $R = (sup, sig)$ that solves an atom α, then the algorithm finds sup in time at most $\mathcal{O}^*(3^\rho)$[1].

---

[1] We use the $\mathcal{O}^*$-notation to suppress polynomial factors, that is, instead of $\mathcal{O}(f(\rho)|A|^c)$, where c is a constant, we write $\mathcal{O}^*(f(\rho))$.

Algorithm 1: SUP

Input: TS A with states S_A and events E_A. $S \subseteq S_A$. $\rho \in \mathbb{N}$. Type τ.
Result: Set $\mathfrak{S}$ of τ-supports of A such that $S \subseteq sup$ for all $sup \in \mathfrak{S}$.

1 **if** *some e occurs uniquely* **and** $\big[(s\xrightarrow{e}s', S(s) = 0,\ S(s') = 1,$

     $\{\mathsf{out}, \mathsf{set}, \mathsf{swap}\} \cap \tau = \emptyset)$ *or* $(s'\xrightarrow{e}s, S(s) = 0, S(s') = 1,$
     $\{\mathsf{inp}, \mathsf{res}, \mathsf{swap}\} \cap \tau = \emptyset)\big]$ **then**

2   **if** $|S| \geq \rho$ **then**   `// extending S exceeds ρ`

3 | **return** $\emptyset$;

4   **else**   `// i ∈ {nop, used}`

5 | $S_1 = S \cup \{s\}$;

6 | **return** $\text{SUP}(A, S_1, \rho, \tau)$;

7   **end**

8 **end**

9 **if** *there are $s\xrightarrow{e}s', q\xrightarrow{e}q' \in A$ that are in conflict with S* **then**

10   **if** $|S| \geq \rho$ **then**   `// extending S exceeds ρ`

11 | **return** $\emptyset$;

12   **end**

13   **if** $S(s) = S(s') = S(q) = 0,\ S(q') = 1$ **then** `// i ∈ {nop, out, set, swap, used}`

14 | $S_1 = S \cup \{s'\}$; $S_2 = S \cup \{q\}$; $S_3 = S \cup \{s\}$;

15 | **return** $\text{SUP}(A, S_1, \rho, \tau) \cup \text{SUP}(A, S_2, \rho, \tau) \cup \text{SUP}(A, S_3, \rho, \tau)$;

16   **end**

17   **if** $S(s) = 1, S(s') = 0, S(q) = 1, S(q') = 1$ **then**   `// i ∈ {nop, set, used}`

18 | $S_1 = S \cup \{s'\}$;

19 | **return** $\text{SUP}(A, S_1, \rho, \tau)$;

20   **end**

21   **if** $S(s) = 1, S(s') = 0, S(q) = 0, S(q') = 1$ **then**   `// i ∈ {nop, set, used}`

22 | $S_1 = S \cup \{s'\}$; $S_2 = S \cup \{q\}$;

23 | **return** $\text{SUP}(A, S_1, \rho, \tau) \cup \text{SUP}(A, S_2, \rho, \tau)$;

24   **end**

25   **if** $S(s) = 0, S(s') = 1, S(q) = 1, S(q') = 1$ **then**   `// i ∈ {nop, used}`

26 | $S_1 = S \cup \{s\}$;

27 | **return** $\text{SUP}(A, S_1, \rho, \tau)$;

28   **end**

29   **if** $S(s) = 0, S(s') = 1, S(q) = 0, S(q') = 1$ **then**   `// i ∈ {nop, used}`

30 | $S_1 = S \cup \{s\}$; $S_2 = S \cup \{q\}$;

31 | **return** $\text{SUP}(A, S_1, \rho, \tau) \cup \text{SUP}(A, S_2, \rho, \tau)$;

32   **end**

33   **if** $S(s) = 1, S(s') = S(q) = S(q') = 0$ **then** `// i ∈ {nop, inp, set, swap, used}`

34 | $S_1 = S \cup \{s'\}$; and $S_2 = S \cup \{q\}$; and $S_3 = S \cup \{q'\}$;

35 | **return** $\text{SUP}(A, S_1, \rho, \tau) \cup \text{SUP}(A, S_2, \rho, \tau) \cup \text{SUP}(A, S_3, \rho, \tau)$;

36   **end**

37   **if** $S(s) = 1, S(s') = 0, S(q) = 1, S(q') = 0$ **then**   `// i ∈ {nop, set used}`

38 | $S_1 = S \cup \{s'\}$; and $S_2 = S \cup \{q'\}$;

39 | **return** $\text{SUP}(A, S_1, \rho, \tau) \cup \text{SUP}(A, S_2, \rho, \tau)$;

40   **end**

41 **else**

42 | **return** $\{S\}$;

43 **end**

---

s	s'	q	q'
0	0	0	0
0	0	0	1
0	0	1	0
0	0	1	1

s	s'	q	q'
0	1	0	0
0	1	0	1
0	1	1	0
0	1	1	1

s	s'	q	q'
1	0	0	0
1	0	0	1
1	0	1	0
1	0	1	1

s	s'	q	q'
1	1	0	0
1	1	0	1
1	1	1	0
1	1	1	1

Fig. 5. The table shows how distinct states $s, s', q, q' \in S_A$ of a TS A can behave with respect to $S \subseteq S_A$. With a little abuse of notation, we abridge $S(x) = b$ by $x = b$ for all $x \in \{s, s', q, q'\}$ and $b \in \{0, 1\}$. There are five possibilities such that $|\{(S(s), S(s')), (S(q), S(q'))\}| \geq 2$ and $S(s) \neq S(s')$ or $S(q) \neq S(q')$, namely $\{(0,0), (0,1)\}, \{(0,0), (1,0)\}, \{(0,1), (1,0)\}, \{(0,1), (1,1)\}$ and $\{(1,0), (1,1)\}$.

The following lemma argues that SUP terminates and returns a set of valid τ-supports, which contains the supports of all S-minimal ρ-restricted regions, if there is any.

Lemma 3 (Termination, Correctness and Completeness). *Let τ be a Boolean type of nets, A be a TS with states S_A and events E_A, $S \subseteq S_A$ be a set of states, and $\rho \in \mathbb{N}$. For the input (A, S, ρ, τ),*

1. *SUP terminates and its running time is at most $\mathcal{O}^*(3^\rho)$;*
2. *SUP returns a set $\mathfrak{S}$ of τ-supports of A, and $S \subseteq \sup$ holds for all $\sup \in \mathfrak{S}$;*
3. *for any S-minimal ρ-restricted τ-region $(\sup, \mathrm{sig})$ of A, $\sup \in \mathfrak{S}$.*

Proof. 1. It is easy to see, that the recursive procedure SUP has a ternary recursion tree: Starting from a fixed recursive call, SUP generates at most three branches at a time. Every node of this tree is associated with its current input tuple (A, S, ρ, τ) and the corresponding output of SUP. Moreover, if P is an arbitrary but fixed path of this tree, starting at the root and terminating at a leaf, then P has at most length ρ: If neither the if-condition of line 1 nor the one of line 9 is satisfied, then SUP returns S (line 42) and, thus, terminates. In particular, by Lemma 2, S is a τ-support. Otherwise, the first if-condition or the second if-condition is satisfied, and SUP checks if $|S| \geq \rho$; if this check is positive then SUP returns $\emptyset$ and terminates, since otherwise the constructed support would not be ρ-restricted; if this check is negative then S is properly extended to S_1 or S_2 or S_3 (or several of them). That is, for all $i \in \{1, 2, 3\}$, if S_i exists then $|S_i| > |S|$ and SUP is recursively called on (A, S_i, ρ, τ). Since the bound ρ can not be exceeded, S is extended at most ρ times along P. Thus, after at most $\rho + 1$ calls (along P), SUP returns $\emptyset$ or $\{S'\}$ where S' comes from the input (A, S', ρ, τ) of the current call. In particular, P has at most length ρ.

Let us consider the running time of SUP: For an arbitrary but fixed call, the most computationally expensive part is to check whether there are edges which are in conflict with S. In the worst case, one has to check for all $e \in E_A$ and all $s \xrightarrow{e} s', q \xrightarrow{e} q' \in A$ if $s \xrightarrow{e} s'$ and $q \xrightarrow{e} q'$ are in conflict. Since A has at most $|E_A| \cdot |S_A|^2$ edges and $|S| \leq |S_A|$, this can be done in polynomial time in the size of A. Altogether, we have at most $3^{\rho+1}$ different calls of SUP, thus, the running time is $\mathcal{O}^*(3^\rho)$.

2. For the output set $\mathfrak{S}$ of $\textsc{Sup}(A, S, \rho, \tau)$, every $sup \in \mathfrak{S}$ is conflict-free with E_A. Hence, by Lemma 2, sup allows a valid τ-region of A. By the construction, every set $sup \in \mathrm{S}$ is an extension of S, hence $S \subseteq sup$.

3. Let (sup, sig) be an S-minimal τ-region of A that respects ρ. By the definition of S-minimality, $S \subseteq sup$. We shall prove by induction on $n = |sup \backslash S|$, that sup belongs to the output $\mathfrak{S}$ of $\textsc{Sup}$ on input (A, S, ρ, τ), for all S and the corresponding sup. If $n = 0$, i.e., $S = sup$, then S is conflict-free, and sup is returned in line 42 of the algorithm, hence we are done. Assume that the induction hypothesis is true for all S and sup with $|sup \backslash S| \leq k$, $k \in \mathbb{N}$. Consider the case $|sup \backslash S| = k + 1$. Without loss of generality, there exists $e \in E_A$ such that S is in conflict with some edge $r \stackrel{e}{\longrightarrow} r'$ (or a pair of edges $r \stackrel{e}{\longrightarrow} r'$ and $t \stackrel{e}{\longrightarrow} t'$). Since sup is conflict-free, for some $s \in \{r, r', t, t'\}$ we have $sup(s) \neq S(s)$. This means that $s \in sup \backslash S$, i.e., in the recursive tree of the run of $\textsc{Sup}$ on the input (A, S, ρ, τ), there is a branching point where an extension $S' = S \cup \{s\}$ has been constructed (in one of the lines 5, 14, 18, . . . , 38). Thus we have $S' \subseteq sup$. We will now prove that (sup, sig) is S'-minimal. Suppose this is not true, and there is an S'-minimal τ-region (sup', sig') such that $|sup'| < |sup|$. By the construction $S \subseteq S' \subseteq sup'$. This implies that (sup', sig') is a valid τ-region extending S, which contradicts the S-minimality of (sup, sig). Hence, (sup, sig) is S'-minimal. By the construction $|sup \backslash S'| = k$. Hence, by the induction hypothesis sup belongs to the output of $\textsc{Sup}(A, S', \rho, \tau)$. Since $\textsc{Sup}(A, S', \rho, \tau) \subseteq \textsc{Sup}(A, S, \rho, \tau)$, we get the claim. $\qquad\square$

The completeness of $\textsc{Sup}$ assumes that, when constructing a τ-region which solves some (E)SSP atom, it is sufficient to start from a minimally required assumption about the support of the sought region. Since the construction of $\textsc{Sup}$ implies possible extension(s) of the input set, we have to check the supports in the output, if the (E)SSP atom still can be solved. This can be done by the sets of "forbidden" states, i.e., the ones that should not be added. Precisely, if one seeks for a region $R = (sup, sig)$ that solves an ESSP atom $\alpha = (e, q)$, the following minimal initial assumptions S about R and the corresponding forbidding sets F can be utilized:

- $sig(e) = \mathsf{inp}$, $sup(q) = 0$: minimal initial support $S = \{s \in S_A \mid s \stackrel{e}{\longrightarrow}\}$, the states of $F = \{q\} \cup \{s \in S_a \mid \stackrel{e}{\longrightarrow} s\}$ should not be included.
- $sig(e) = \mathsf{out}$, $sup(q) = 1$: minimal initial support $S = \{q\} \cup \{s \in S_A \mid \stackrel{e}{\longrightarrow} s\}$, the states of $F = \{s \in S_A \mid s \stackrel{e}{\longrightarrow}\}$ should not be included.
- $sig(e) = \mathsf{used}$, $sup(q) = 0$: minimal initial support $S = \{s, s' \in S_A \mid s \stackrel{e}{\longrightarrow} s'\}$, the sates of $F = \{q\}$ should not be included.
- $sig(e) = \mathsf{free}$, $sup(q) = 1$: minimal initial support $S = \{q\}$, the states of $F = \{s, s' \in S_A \mid s \stackrel{e}{\longrightarrow} s'\}$ should not be included.

For an SSP atom (s, q), the minimal initial support can be either $S = \{s\}$ or $S = \{q\}$, and the set of states to be disjoint with the support is $F = \{q\}$ or $F = \{s\}$, respectively. By Lemma 3, if R is ρ-restricted S-minimal then $sup \in \textsc{Sup}(A, S, p, \tau)$ in all the cases above. The minimality of R ensures us that if there is a τ-region which solves α and respects the occupation parameter ρ, its support will be constructed by SUP.

If a τ-admissible support sup is given, the signature sig of a valid τ-region (sup, sig) can be reconstructed in time polynomial in the size of TS A. Indeed, by Lemma 2, for every event e of the TS, the set $X_e = \{(sup(s), sup(s')) \mid s \xrightarrow{e} s' \in A\}$ is one of the following seven alternatives

$$\{(0,0)\}, \{(0,1)\}, \{(1,1)\}, \{(1,0)\}, \{(0,0), (1,0)\}, \{(0,1), (1,0)\}, \{(0,1), (1,1)\}.$$

For each of these alternatives, there is a corresponding group of Boolean interactions which can implement them in the type of net τ, videlicet

$$\{\mathsf{nop}, \mathsf{res}, \mathsf{free}\}, \{\mathsf{out}, \mathsf{swap}, \mathsf{set}\}, \{\mathsf{nop}, \mathsf{set}, \mathsf{used}\}, \{\mathsf{inp}, \mathsf{swap}, \mathsf{res}\}, \{\mathsf{res}\}, \{\mathsf{swap}\}, \{\mathsf{set}\},$$

respectively. The particular choice of $sig(e)$ as one of the interactions in the corresponding set (if there are options) is not important, due to the fact that all the options are equally valid. This allows to assign some fixed order of choice within each of the sets of interactions.

For instance, if $\tau = \{\mathsf{inp}, \mathsf{out}, \mathsf{free}, \mathsf{used}\,\mathsf{nop}\}$, and e and sup are such that $X_e = \{(0,0)\}$, then $sig(e)$ has to be assign to one of $\{\mathsf{nop}, \mathsf{res}, \mathsf{free}\}$. Since both nop and free belong to τ, there is an alternative. But if the priority of the choice of one interaction over the other is present, e.g., nop has a priority over free, then the solution is "unique". Let us notice that such kind of prioritising does not prevent from finding of a solution if one exists. But the absence of choice allows to reconstruct a signature for the given support in time of $\mathcal{O}(|E_A| \cdot |S_A|^2)$.

Algorithm 2 describes the complete process of solving the ORτS problem. First, for each SSP atom (s, s'), the algorithm tries to find a ρ-restricted τ-region which solves the atom. In order to do this, in line 3 all $\{s\}$-minimal regions are constructed, and only the ones that distinguish s and s' are taken. In line 4, the same is done for the set of $\{s'\}$-minimal regions. If there is no ρ-restricted τ-region that solves (s, s'), the instance of ORτS is unsolvable, and the empty set of regions is returned in line 6. Otherwise, the found regions are included into the sought set $\mathcal{R}$ in line 8. If all the SSP atoms are solved, the algorithm deals with each ESSP atom (e, q) starting from line 10. All four possibilities to solve an ESSP atom with a region (sup, sig) are checked: in line 11, the case $sup(q) = 0$ and $sig(e) = \mathsf{inp}$ is described; in line 12, the case $sup(q) = 0$ and $sig(e) = \mathsf{used}$; in lines 13 and 14, the case $sup(q) = 1$ and $sig(e) = \mathsf{out}$ and the case $sup(q) = 1$ and $sig(e) = \mathsf{free}$ are handled, respectively. If none of the possibilities work, then there is no region solving the atom (e, q), and the empty set is returned in line 16, terminating the algorithm. Otherwise, the fitting regions are included in the sought set $\mathcal{R}$ (line 18). If all of the separation atoms are solved successfully, an admissible set of regions is returned in line 20.

Since there are only up to $|S_A|^2$ SSP atoms, and at most $|E_A||S_A|$ ESSP atoms, with a constant number of possibilities to solve each atom (2 for SSP and 4 for ESSP), we get a factor polynomial in size of A to the already known runtime $\mathcal{O}^*(3^\rho)$ of SUP. Hence, the overall runtime is $\mathcal{O}^*(3^\rho)$. Thus, the approach proves the following theorem that states the fixed-parameter tractability of ORτS.

Algorithm 2: ORτS

Input: Type τ. TS A with states S_A and events E_A. $S \subseteq S_A$. $p \in \mathbb{N}$.

Result: A τ-admissible set $\mathcal{R}$ of p-restricted regions of A.

1 $\mathcal{R} = \emptyset$;

2 **for** *every SSP* (s, s') *of A* **do**

3 $\quad R = \{S \in \text{Sup}(A, \{s\}, p, \tau) \mid S \cap \{s'\} = \emptyset\} \cup$ // $sup(s) = 1, sup(s') = 0$

4 $\quad \{S \in \text{Sup}(A, \{s'\}, p, \tau) \mid S \cap \{s\} = \emptyset\}$;   // $sup(s) = 0, sup(s') = 1$

5 $\quad$ **if** $R = \emptyset$ **then**

6 $\quad\quad$ | **return** $\emptyset$;

7 $\quad$ **end**

8 $\quad \mathcal{R} = \mathcal{R} \cup R$;

9 **end**

10 **for** *every ESSP* (e, q) *of A* **do**

11 $\quad R = \{S \in \text{Sup}(A, \{s \in S_A \mid s \xrightarrow{e}\}, p, \tau) \mid S \cap (\{q\} \cup \{s \in S_a \mid \xrightarrow{e} s\}) = \emptyset\} \cup$
      // $sup(q) = 0, sig(e) = \mathsf{inp}$

12 $\quad \{S \in \text{Sup}(A, \{s, s' \in S_A \mid s \xrightarrow{e} s'\}, p, \tau) \mid S \cap \{q\} = \emptyset\} \cup$
      // $sup(q) = 0, sig(e) = \mathsf{used}$

13 $\quad \{S \in \text{Sup}(A, \{q\} \cup \{s \in S_A \mid \xrightarrow{e} s\}, p, \tau) \mid S \cap \{s \in S_A \mid s \xrightarrow{e}\} = \emptyset\} \cup$
      // $sup(q) = 1, sig(e) = \mathsf{out}$

14 $\quad \{S \in \text{Sup}(A, \{q\}, p, \tau) \mid S \cap \{s, s' \in S_A \mid s \xrightarrow{e} s'\} = \emptyset\}$;
      // $sup(q) = 1, sig(e) = \mathsf{free}$

15 $\quad$ **if** $R = \emptyset$ **then**

16 $\quad\quad$ | **return** $\emptyset$;

17 $\quad$ **end**

18 $\quad \mathcal{R} = \mathcal{R} \cup R$;

19 **end**

20 **return** $\mathcal{R}$

Theorem 1. *The problem ORτS parameterized by ρ is fixed-parameter tractable.*

In the remainder of the section, we consider the application of the described synthesis algorithm.

Example 3 (Algorithm application). Consider TS A with the set of states $S_A = \{\iota, q, s\}$ and $E_A = \{a, b, c\}$ depicted on the left in Fig. 6. In order to synthesize a net solving A, one has to solve three SSP atoms: (ι, s), (ι, q), (q, s), and five ESSP atoms: (c, ι), (a, q), (a, s), (b, s), (c, s). We shall investigate three instances of ORτS for the TS A: for $p = 1$ and $\tau = \{\mathsf{nop}, \mathsf{set}, \mathsf{inp}\}$, for $p = 2$ and $\tau = \{\mathsf{nop}, \mathsf{set}, \mathsf{inp}\}$, for $p = 2$ and $\tau = \{\mathsf{nop}, \mathsf{set}, \mathsf{inp}, \mathsf{out}\}$; and apply Algorithm 2 (resp. Algorithm 1) in each of these cases.

Case ($\rho = 1, \tau = \{\mathsf{nop}, \mathsf{set}, \mathsf{inp}\}$): Initially the set of sought regions $\mathcal{R}$ is empty. We begin with the SSP atom (ι, s). According to lines 3–4 of Algorithm 2, for SSP atom we start Sup with $S = \{\iota\}$ and $S = \{s\}$. First, consider the former case, and run $\text{Sup}(A, \{\iota\}, 1, \tau)$. The if-condition in line 9 of Sup reports about

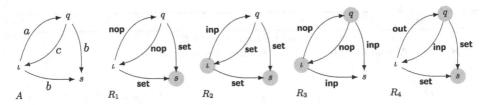

Fig. 6. A 2-restricted τ-solvable TS A (left) and (some) of its valid 2-restricted τ-regions, for $\tau = \{\mathsf{nop}, \mathsf{set}, \mathsf{inp}, \mathsf{out}\}$.

conflict in S for $\iota \xrightarrow{b} s$ and $q \xrightarrow{b} s$. In line 10, we check that $|S| \geq \rho = 1$, i.e., S cannot be extended, and the run $\mathrm{SUP}(A, \{\iota\}, 1, \tau)$ returns empty set of supports. For $S = \{s\}$, we run $\mathrm{SUP}(A, \{s\}, 1, \tau)$. The checks in line 1 and line 9 ensure that S is conflict-free, with the signatures $sig_1(a) = sig_1(c) = \mathsf{nop}$, $sig_1(b) = \mathsf{set}$. Hence, $\mathrm{SUP}(A, S, \rho, \tau)$ returns $S = \{s\}$ as a valid support of 1-restricted τ-region $R_1 = (\{s\}, sig_1)$ (see Fig. 6). Since $\{s\} \cap \{\iota\} = \emptyset$, we add this region to $\mathcal{R}$ in line 8 of Algorithm 2. Thus, the SSP atom (ι, s) is solved.

The atom (q, s) is similar to (ι, s) up to the swap of the roles of q and ι, hence also solvable.

We now consider the SSP atom (ι, q). The run of $\mathrm{SUP}(A, \{\iota\}, 1, \tau)$ terminates at line 11, returning the empty set of valid regions. For the run $\mathrm{SUP}(A, \{q\}, 1, \tau)$, the condition in line 9 is satisfied reporting a conflict for $\iota \xrightarrow{b} s$ and $q \xrightarrow{b} s$. The termination in line 11 follows with no valid region in output, as well. Thus, the atom (ι, q) has no 1-restricted τ-solving region. This implies that A is not 1-restricted τ-solvable.

Case $(\rho = 2, \tau = \{\mathsf{nop}, \mathsf{set}, \mathsf{inp}\})$: Since the parameter ρ is greater than in the previous case, we can reuse the regions solving atoms (ι, s) and (q, s) constructed above. Consider now (ι, q). Lines 3–4 of Algorithm 2 call SUP with the initial supports $\{\iota\}$ and $\{q\}$, respectively. The run of $\mathrm{SUP}(A, \{\iota\}, 2, \tau)$ reports a conflict in S for $\iota \xrightarrow{b} s$ and $q \xrightarrow{b} s$. Since $|S| < \rho = 2$, an extension of S is permitted, and we end up in line 31 which suggests recursive calls of SUP on $S \cup \{s\}$ and $S \cup \{q\}$. The support containing both ι and q is conflict-free. Hence, the set $\{\iota, q\}$ belongs to the output of $\mathrm{SUP}(A, \{\iota, q\}, 2, \tau)$. The run $\mathrm{SUP}(A, \{\iota, s\}, 2, \tau)$ finds no conflict and returns $\{\iota, s\}$ as a valid support of a 2-restricted region. In line 3 of Algorithm 2, we choose only supports that are disjoint with $\{q\}$, i.e., only $\{\iota, s\}$. A suitable signature is given by $sig_2(a) = \mathsf{inp}$, $sig_2(b) = sig_2(c) = \mathsf{set}$, yielding a necessary region $R_2 = (\{\iota, s\}, sig_2)$. Let us notice that the run of $\mathrm{SUP}(A, \{q\}, 2, \tau)$ returns a different valid region $R_2' = (\{q, s\}, sig_2')$ with $sig_2'(a) = sig_2'(b) = \mathsf{set}$ and $sig_2'(c) = \mathsf{inp}$. Thus, A has a τ-SSP property provided by 2-restricted regions.

We now have to deal with the ESSP atoms of A. Let us first consider (a, q). Among all the interactions in τ, only inp is of interest when solving ESSP atoms. Hence, we construct the minimal initial support $S = \{t \in S_A \mid t \xrightarrow{a}\} = \{\iota\}$. For the constructed S, we call $\mathrm{SUP}(A, S, 2, \tau)$ in line 11 of Algorithm 2. This call reports a conflict for $\iota \xrightarrow{b} s$ and $q \xrightarrow{b} s$ in line 9 of Algorithm 1. Since $|S| < 2$, we can extend S according to the line 33, i.e., $S \cup \{q\}$ and $S \cup \{s\}$. The former case returns $\{\iota, q\}$ as a conflict-free support. The recursive call $\text{SUP}(A, \{\iota, s\}, 2, \tau)$ finds no conflict and returns $\{\iota, s\}$ as a valid support. We then leave only supports which are disjoint with $\{q\}$ (line 11 of Algorithm 2), i.e., only $\{\iota, s\}$. For $sig'(b) = sig'(c) = \text{set}$, $sig'(a) = inp$, this implies a 2-restricted τ-region $R' = (\{\iota, s\}, sig')$, which coincides with R_2 constructed above.

The atom (c, ι) is similar to (a, q) up to roles swap between a and c, and between q and ι.

For the atom (b, s), we start with the initial support $S = \{t \in S_A \mid t \xrightarrow{b}\} = \{\iota, q\}$. The run $\text{SUP}(A, S, 2, \tau)$ ensures that there is no conflict in S, and $\{\iota, q\}$ is returned as a valid support. Since $\{\iota, q\} \cap \{s\} = \emptyset$, the support indeed solves the atom (b, s). With a suitable signature $sig_3(a) = sig_3(c) = \text{nop}$, $sig_3(b) = \text{inp}$, this yields a 2-restricted τ-region $R_3 = (\{\iota, q\}, sig_3)$.

For the atom (a, s), the initial support $S = \{t \in S_A \mid t \xrightarrow{a}\} = \{\iota\}$. The call $\text{SUP}(A, S, 2, \tau)$ has to resolve the conflict for the edges $\iota \xrightarrow{b} s$ and $q \xrightarrow{b} s$. This implies two recursive calls $\text{SUP}(A, \{\iota, q\}, 2, \tau)$ and $\text{SUP}(A, \{\iota, s\}, 2, \tau)$ in line 35 of Algorithm 1. Both these calls ensure conflict-freeness of their starting supports. But in line 11 of Algorithm 2, both are excluded. Hence, there is no possibility to solve atom (a, s) with a τ-region.

For the atom (c, s), the situation is analogous to the case of (a, s).

Case $(\rho = 2, \tau = \{\textbf{nop}, \textbf{set}, \textbf{inp}, \textbf{out}\})$: Since the parameter ρ is not less than in the cases above, and the set of interactions includes the ones used before, we can reuse the already constructed regions. Hence, it remains to consider the ESSP atoms (a, s) and (c, s). We begin with the former. Take the interaction out as the signature for a, and then construct the initial support $S = \{t \in S_A \mid \xrightarrow{a} t\} = \{q\}$ (line 13 in Algorithm 2). The run of $\text{SUP}(A, S, 2, \tau)$ finds a conflict for $\iota \xrightarrow{b} s$ and $q \xrightarrow{b} s$, and the line 34 suggests possible extentions of S: $S \cup \{\iota\}$ and $S \cup \{s\}$. For both extentions, the recursive runs of SUP ensure the conflict-freeness of $\{\iota, q\}$ and $\{q, s\}$. Since $\{\iota, q\}$ is non-disjoint with $\{\iota\}$, this support is not collected to $\mathcal{R}$. For $\{q, s\}$, with signature $sig_4(a) = \text{out}$, $sig_4(b) = \text{set}$, $sig_4(c) = \text{inp}$, we get a 2-restricted τ-region $R_4 = (\{q, s\}, sig_4)$ solving the atom (a, s).

The solution for atom (c, s) is similar to the case of (a, s).

Finally, we obtain 2-restricted τ-solvability of A, for $\tau = \{\text{nop}, \text{set}, \text{inp}, \text{out}\}$.

4   Conclusion

In this paper, we provided an algorithm which demonstrates the fixed-parameter tractability of the problem $\text{OR}\tau\text{S}$, for Boolean types of nets τ that contain the interaction nop and thus allow independence between places and transitions. The question for the complexity of $\text{OR}\tau\text{S}$ for the types without the interaction nop is still to be answered. From a different perspective, for the majority of

Boolean types, the original problem of τ-synthesis is known to be NP-complete. It is easy to see that if τ-synthesis is NP-complete, then occupancy number restricted τ-synthesis is NP-complete, too. However, if τ-synthesis is polynomial, then the tractability of ORτS is not necessarily implied. Hence, it remains an open question to investigate whether there exist Boolean types τ for which ORτS is intractable, while the original problem of τ-synthesis is polynomial.

References

1. van der Aalst, W.M.P.: Process Mining. Discovery, Conformance and Enhancement of Business Processes. Springer, Heidelberg (2011). https://doi.org/10.1007/978-3-642-19345-3
2. Badouel, E., Bernardinello, L., Darondeau, P.: The synthesis problem for elementary net systems is NP-complete. Theor. Comput. Sci. **186**(1–2), 107–134 (1997). https://doi.org/10.1016/S0304-3975(96)00219-8
3. Badouel, E., Bernardinello, L., Darondeau, P.: Petri Net Synthesis. TTCSAES. Springer, Heidelberg (2015). https://doi.org/10.1007/978-3-662-47967-4
4. Badouel, E., Darondeau, P.: Trace nets and process automata. Acta Inf. **32**(7), 647–679 (1995). https://doi.org/10.1007/BF01186645
5. Baldan, P., Bruni, A., Corradini, A., König, B., Rodríguez, C., Schwoon, S.: Efficient unfolding of contextual Petri nets. Theor. Comput. Sci. **449**, 2–22 (2012). https://doi.org/10.1016/j.tcs.2012.04.046. http://www.sciencedirect.com/science/article/pii/S0304397512004318, descriptional Complexity of Formal Systems (DCFS 2011)
6. Best, E., Devillers, R.: Characterisation of the state spaces of live and bounded marked graph Petri nets. In: Dediu, A.-H., Martín-Vide, C., Sierra-Rodríguez, J.-L., Truthe, B. (eds.) LATA 2014. LNCS, vol. 8370, pp. 161–172. Springer, Cham (2014). https://doi.org/10.1007/978-3-319-04921-2_13
7. Best, E., Hujsa, T., Wimmel, H.: Sufficient conditions for the marked graph realisability of labelled transition systems. Theor. Comput. Sci. **750**, 101–116 (2018). https://doi.org/10.1016/j.tcs.2017.10.006
8. Carmona, J., Cortadella, J., Kishinevsky, M.: A region-based algorithm for discovering Petri nets from event logs. In: Dumas, M., Reichert, M., Shan, M.-C. (eds.) BPM 2008. LNCS, vol. 5240, pp. 358–373. Springer, Heidelberg (2008). https://doi.org/10.1007/978-3-540-85758-7_26
9. Chatain, T., Haar, S., Kolčák, J., Paulevé, L., Thakkar, A.: Concurrency in Boolean networks. Nat. Comput. **19**(1), 91–109 (2020). https://doi.org/10.1007/s11047-019-09748-4
10. Cortadella, J., Kishinevsky, M., Kondratyev, A., Lavagno, L., Yakovlev, A.: Logic Synthesis of Asynchronous Controllers and Interfaces, vol. 8. Springer, Heidelberg (2002). https://doi.org/10.1007/978-3-642-55989-1
11. Cygan, M., et al.: Parameterized Algorithms. Springer, Cham (2015). https://doi.org/10.1007/978-3-319-21275-3
12. Devillers, R.R., Erofeev, E., Hujsa, T.: Synthesis of weighted marked graphs from circular labelled transition systems. In: van der Aalst, W.M.P., Bergenthum, R., Carmona, J. (eds.) ATAED@Petri Nets/ACSD 2019, Aachen, Germany, June 25, 2019. CEUR Workshop Proceedings, vol. 2371, pp. 6–22. CEUR-WS.org (2019). http://ceur-ws.org/Vol-2371/ATAED2019-6-22.pdf

13. Devillers, R., Erofeev, E., Hujsa, T.: Synthesis of weighted marked graphs from constrained labelled transition systems: a geometric approach. In: Koutny, M., Pomello, L., Kristensen, L.M. (eds.) Transactions on Petri Nets and Other Models of Concurrency XIV. LNCS, vol. 11790, pp. 172–191. Springer, Heidelberg (2019). https://doi.org/10.1007/978-3-662-60651-3_7
14. Erofeev, E.: Characterisation of a class of Petri net solvable transition systems. Ph.D. thesis, University of Oldenburg, Germany (2018)
15. Gannon, T., Shapiro, S.: An optimal approach to fault tolerant software systems design. IEEE Trans. Softw. Eng. **SE–4**, 390–409 (1978). https://doi.org/10.1109/TSE.1978.233859
16. Lorenz, R., Mauser, S., Juhas, G.: How to synthesize nets from languages - a survey, pp. 637–647 (January 2008). https://doi.org/10.1109/WSC.2007.4419657
17. Montanari, U., Rossi, F.: Contextual occurrence nets and concurrent constraint programming. In: Schneider, H.J., Ehrig, H. (eds.) Graph Transformations in Computer Science. LNCS, vol. 776, pp. 280–295. Springer, Heidelberg (1994). https://doi.org/10.1007/3-540-57787-4_18
18. Montanari, U., Rossi, F.: Contextual nets. Acta Inf. **32**(6), 545–596 (1995). https://doi.org/10.1007/BF01178907
19. Pietkiewicz-Koutny, M.: Transition systems of elementary net systems with inhibitor arcs. In: Azéma, P., Balbo, G. (eds.) ICATPN 1997. LNCS, vol. 1248, pp. 310–327. Springer, Heidelberg (1997). https://doi.org/10.1007/3-540-63139-9_43
20. Institute for Quality, Safety and Transportation: π-tool (2013). http://www.iqst.de
21. Schlachter, U.: Bounded Petri net synthesis from modal transition systems is undecidable. In: Desharnais, J., Jagadeesan, R. (eds.) 27th International Conference on Concurrency Theory, CONCUR 2016, August 23–26, 2016, Québec City, Canada. LIPIcs, vol. 59, pp. 15:1–15:14. Schloss Dagstuhl - Leibniz-Zentrum für Informatik (2016). https://doi.org/10.4230/LIPIcs.CONCUR.2016.15
22. Schlachter, U.: Petri net synthesis and modal specifications. Ph.D. thesis, University of Oldenburg, Germany (2018)
23. Schlachter, U., Wimmel, H.: k-bounded Petri net synthesis from modal transition systems. In: CONCUR. LIPIcs, vol. 85, pp. 6:1–6:15. Schloss Dagstuhl - Leibniz-Zentrum fuer Informatik (2017). https://doi.org/10.4230/LIPIcs.CONCUR.2017.6
24. Schmitt, V.: Flip-flop nets. In: Puech, C., Reischuk, R. (eds.) STACS 1996. LNCS, vol. 1046, pp. 515–528. Springer, Heidelberg (1996). https://doi.org/10.1007/3-540-60922-9_42
25. Shapiro, S.: A stochastic Petri net with applications to modelling occupancy times for concurrent task systems. Networks **9**(4), 375–379 (1979). https://doi.org/10.1002/net.3230090407
26. Tredup, R.: The complexity of synthesizing nop-equipped Boolean nets from g-bounded inputs (technical report) (2019)
27. Tredup, R.: Synthesis of structurally restricted b-bounded Petri nets: complexity results. In: Filiot, E., Jungers, R., Potapov, I. (eds.) RP 2019. LNCS, vol. 11674, pp. 202–217. Springer, Cham (2019). https://doi.org/10.1007/978-3-030-30806-3_16
28. Tredup, R.: Parameterized complexity of synthesizing b-bounded (m, n)-T-systems. In: Chatzigeorgiou, A., et al. (eds.) SOFSEM 2020. LNCS, vol. 12011, pp. 223–235. Springer, Cham (2020). https://doi.org/10.1007/978-3-030-38919-2_19

29. Tredup, R., Erofeev, E.: On the parameterized complexity of d-restricted Boolean net synthesis. In: Chen, J., Feng, Q., Xu, J. (eds.) Theory and Applications of Models of Computation. TAMC 2020. Lecture Notes in Computer Science, vol. 12337. Springer, Cham (2020). https://doi.org/10.1007/978-3-030-59267-7_20

30. Tredup, R., Rosenke, C.: Narrowing down the hardness barrier of synthesizing elementary net systems. In: CONCUR. LIPIcs, vol. 118, pp. 16:1–16:15. Schloss Dagstuhl - Leibniz-Zentrum fuer Informatik (2018). https://doi.org/10.4230/LIPIcs.CONCUR.2018.16

31. Tredup, R., Rosenke, C.: The complexity of synthesis for 43 boolean petri net types. In: Gopal, T.V., Watada, J. (eds.) TAMC 2019. LNCS, vol. 11436, pp. 615–634. Springer, Cham (2019). https://doi.org/10.1007/978-3-030-14812-6_38

32. Tredup, R., Rosenke, C., Wolf, K.: Elementary net synthesis remains NP-complete even for extremely simple inputs. In: Khomenko, V., Roux, O.H. (eds.) PETRI NETS 2018. LNCS, vol. 10877, pp. 40–59. Springer, Cham (2018). https://doi.org/10.1007/978-3-319-91268-4_3

33. Vogler, W., Semenov, A., Yakovlev, A.: Unfolding and finite prefix for nets with read arcs. In: Sangiorgi, D., de Simone, R. (eds.) CONCUR 1998. LNCS, vol. 1466, pp. 501–516. Springer, Heidelberg (1998). https://doi.org/10.1007/BFb0055644

Star-Freeness, First-Order Definability and Aperiodicity of Structured Context-Free Languages

Dino Mandrioli[1], Matteo Pradella[1,2(✉)], and Stefano Crespi Reghizzi[1,2]

[1] Dipartimento di Elettronica, Informazione e Bioingegneria (DEIB),
Politecnico di Milano, Piazza Leonardo Da Vinci 32, 20133 Milano, Italy
{dino.mandrioli,matteo.pradella,stefano.crespireghizzi}@polimi.it
[2] IEIIT, Consiglio Nazionale delle Ricerche, via Ponzio 34/5, 20133 Milano, Italy

Abstract. A classic result in formal language theory is the equivalence among aperiodic finite automata, star-free regular expressions, and first-order logic on words. Extending these results to structured subclasses of context-free languages, such as tree languages, did not work as smoothly: there are star-free tree languages that are counting. We argue that investigating the same properties within the family of operator precedence languages (OPLs) by going back to string languages rather than tree languages may lead to equivalences that perfectly match those on regular languages. We define operator precedence expressions; we show that they define exactly the class of OPLs and that, when restricted to the star-free subclass, coincide with first-order definable OPLs and are aperiodic.

Since operator precedence languages strictly include other classes of structured languages such as visibly pushdown languages, the same results given in this paper hold as trivial corollary for that family too.

Keywords: Operator precedence languages · First-order logic · Monadic second-order logic · Star-free languages · Aperiodic languages · Input-driven languages · Visibly-pushdown languages

1 Introduction

It is well known that regular languages are closed w.r.t. all basic operations and are characterized also in terms of classic monadic second-order (MSO) logic [8,17,36], but the same properties do not hold for general context-free (CF) languages with the exception of *structured CF languages*. With this term we mean those various families of languages whose typical tree structure is immediately visible in their sentences: two first equivalent examples are *parenthesis languages* [27] and *tree languages* [34]. More recently, *input-driven languages (IDLs)* [7], later renamed *visibly pushdown languages (VPLs)* [2], *height-deterministic languages* [29] have also been shown to share many important properties of regular languages. Tree-languages and VPLs, in particular, are closed w.r.t. Boolean

© Springer Nature Switzerland AG 2020
V. K. I. Pun et al. (Eds.): ICTAC 2020, LNCS 12545, pp. 161–180, 2020.
https://doi.org/10.1007/978-3-030-64276-1_9

operations, concatenation, Kleene *, and are characterized in terms of some MSO logic, although such operations and the adopted logic language are rather different in the two cases. For a more complete analysis of structured languages and how they extend various properties of regular languages, see [26].

In this paper we are interested in an important subfamily of regular languages and its extension to various types of (structured) CF languages, namely *noncounting (NC)* or *aperiodic* languages. Intuitively, aperiodicity is a property of a recognizing device which prevents from separating strings that differ from each other by the number of repetitions of some substring, e.g. odd versus even. It is well-known [28] that NC regular languages coincide with those expressible by means of *star-free* regular expressions or by the first-order (FO) fragment of MSO. FO definability has a strong impact on the success of model-checking, thanks to the first-order completeness of linear temporal logic [32].

Various attempts have been done to extend the notion of aperiodicity beyond regular languages, specifically to some kind of structured CF languages. In facts, linguists as well as language designers have observed over and over that modulo-counting features are not present or needed either in natural or in technical languages.

NC parenthesis languages have been first introduced in [10]; then an equivalent definition thereof has been given in [35]. That paper, however, showed that the same equivalences holding for regular languages do not extend to tree languages: e.g., there are counting star-free tree languages. Further investigations (e.g., [18,21,22,31]) obtained partial results on special subclasses of the involved families but the complete set of equivalences was lost.

In this paper we pursue a different approach to achieve the goal of restating the above equivalences in the larger context of structured CF languages. In essence, we go back to string languages as opposed to the approaches based on tree languages but we choose a family of languages where the tree structure is somewhat implicit in the string, namely *operator precedence languages (OPL)*. OPLs have been invented by Floyd to support efficient deterministic parsing [19]. We classify them as "structured but semivisible" languages since their structure is implicitly assigned by *precedence relations* between terminal characters which were inspired by the precedence rules between arithmetic operations: as an early intuition for readers who are not familiar with OPLs, the expression $a + b \cdot c$ "hides" the parenthetic structure $a + (b \cdot c)$ which is implied by the fact that multiplicative operations should be applied before the additive ones. Subsequent investigations characterized OPLs as the largest known family of structured CFLs that is closed under all fundamental language operations and can be defined through a natural extension of the classic MSO logic [26].

Our new results on the relations between aperiodicity, star-freeness, and FO-definability of OPLs are the following. We define *Operator precedence expressions (OPE)*, as a simple extension of regular expressions and show that they define exactly OPLs. We prove closure properties of NC OPLs and derive therefrom that the languages defined by star-free OPEs are NC. We show that star-free

OPEs and FO formulas define exactly the same subfamily of OPLs. We conjecture that all NC OPLs are FO-definable.

2   Background

For brevity, we just list our notations for the basic concepts we use from formal language and automata theory. The terminal alphabet is denoted by Σ, and the empty string is ε. We also take for granted the traditional logic and set theoretic abbreviations. For a string x, $|x|$ denotes its length. The character $\#$, not present in the terminal alphabet, is used as string *delimiter*, and we define the alphabet $\Sigma_\# = \Sigma \cup \{\#\}$.

Definition 1 (Regular expression and language). *A regular expression (RE) over an alphabet Σ is a well-formed formula made with the characters of Σ, $\emptyset$, ε, the Boolean operators $\cup, \neg, \cap$, the concatenation $\cdot$, the Kleene star * and plus $^+$ operators. When neither * nor $^+$ are used, the RE is called star-free (SF). An RE E defines a language over Σ, denoted by $L(E)$. REs define the language family of regular languages.*

A regular language L over Σ is called noncounting or aperiodic if there exists an integer $n \geq 1$ such that for all $x, y, z \in \Sigma^*$, $xy^n z \in L$ iff $xy^{n+m} z \in L$, $\forall m \geq 0$.

Proposition 2. *The family of aperiodic regular languages coincides with the family of languages defined by star-free REs.*

Definition 3 (Grammar and language). *A (CF) grammar is a tuple $G = (\Sigma, V_N, P, S)$ where Σ and V_N, with $\Sigma \cap V_N = \emptyset$, are resp. the terminal and the nonterminal alphabets, the total alphabet is $V = \Sigma \cup V_N$, $P \subseteq V_N \times V^*$ is the rule (or production) set, and $S \subseteq V_N$, $S \neq \emptyset$, is the axiom set. For a generic rule $B \to \alpha$, where B and α are resp. called the left/right hand sides (lhs/rhs) the following forms are relevant:*

> axiomatic: $B \in S$,   terminal: $\alpha \in \Sigma^+$,   empty: $\alpha = \varepsilon$,
> renaming: $\alpha \in V_N$,
> operator: $\alpha \notin V^* V_N V_N V^*$,
> parenthesized: $\alpha = (\!|\beta|\!)$, with $(\!|$, $|\!)$ new terminals.

G is called backward deterministic (or BD-grammar) if $(B \to \alpha, C \to \alpha \in P)$ implies $B = C$.
If all rules of G are in operator form, G is called an operator grammar or O-grammar.
$\tilde{G} = \left(\Sigma \cup \{(\!|, |\!)\}, V_N, \tilde{P}, S \right)$ is a parenthesis grammar (Par-grammar) if the rhs of every rule is parenthesized. $\tilde{G}$ is called the parenthesized version of G, if $\tilde{P}$ consists of all rules $B \to (\!|\beta|\!)$ such that $B \to \beta$ is in P. For brevity we take for granted the usual definition of derivation; the language defined by a grammar starting from a nonterminal A is $L_G(A) = \left\{ x \in \Sigma^* \mid A \xRightarrow[G]{*} x \right\}$. The subscript

G will be omitted whenever clear from the context. The string x is derivable *from A and we call x a sentence if A ∈ S. The union of $L_G(A)$ for all A ∈ S is the language L(G) defined by G. Two grammars defining the same language are* equivalent. *Two grammars such that their parenthesized versions are equivalent, are* structurally equivalent. *The language generated by a Par-grammar is called a* parenthesis language, *and its sentences are well-parenthesized strings.*

From now on we only consider w.l.o.g. [5, 20] BD-, unless otherwise stated, O-grammars without renaming rules, and without empty rules except, if the empty string is in the language, the axiomatic rule $B \to \varepsilon$ where B does not appear in the rhs of any rule.

Definition 4 (Backward deterministic reduced grammar [27,33]). *A* context *over an alphabet Σ is a string in $\Sigma^*\{-\}\Sigma^*$, where the character '−' $\notin \Sigma$ and is called a* blank. *We denote by $\alpha[x]$ the context α with its blank replaced by the string x. Two nonterminals B and C of a grammar G are termed* equivalent *if, for every context α, $\alpha[B]$ is derivable exactly in case $\alpha[C]$ is derivable (not necessarily from the same axiom). A nonterminal B is* useless *if there is no context α such that $\alpha[B]$ is derivable or B generates no terminal string. A terminal b is* useless *if it does not appear in any sentence of L(G). A grammar is* clean *if it has no useless nonterminals and terminals. A grammar is* reduced *if it is clean and no two nonterminals are equivalent. A BDR-grammar is both backward deterministic and reduced.*

From [27], every parenthesis language is generated by a unique, up to an isomorphism of its nonterminal alphabet, Par-grammar that is BDR.

2.1   Operator-Precedence Languages

Intuitively, operator precedence grammars (OPG) are based on three precedence relations, called *equal*, *yield* and *take*, included in $\Sigma_\# \times \Sigma_\#$. For a given O-grammar, a character a is *equal in precedence* to b iff some rhs contains as substring ab or a string aBb, where B is a nonterminal; in fact, when evaluating the relations between terminal characters for OPG, nonterminals are "transparent". A character a *yields precedence* to b iff a can occur immediately to the left of a syntax subtree whose leftmost *terminal* character is b. Symmetrically, a *takes precedence* over b iff a can occur as the rightmost *terminal* character of a subtree and b is the immediately following terminal character.

Definition 5 [19]. *Let $G = (\Sigma, V_N, P, S)$ be an O-grammar. Let a, b denote elements in Σ, A, B in V_N, C in V_N or ε, and α, β range over $(V_N \cup \Sigma)^*$. The left and right terminal sets of nonterminals are respectively:*

$$\mathcal{L}_G(A) = \left\{ a \mid \exists C : A \xRightarrow[G]{*} Ca\alpha \right\} \quad and \quad \mathcal{R}_G(A) = \left\{ a \mid \exists C : A \xRightarrow[G]{*} \alpha aC \right\}.$$

(The grammar name will be omitted unless necessary to prevent confusion.)

The *operator precedence relations (OPRs) are defined over $\Sigma_\# \times \Sigma_\#$ as follows:*

- *equal in precedence:* $a \doteq b \iff \exists A \to \alpha a C b \beta \in P, \# \doteq \#$
- *takes precedence:* $a \gtrdot b \iff \exists A \to \alpha B b \beta \in P, a \in \mathcal{R}(B); a \gtrdot \# \iff a \in \mathcal{R}(B), B \in S$
- *yields precedence:* $a \lessdot b \iff \exists A \to \alpha a B \beta \in P, b \in \mathcal{L}(B); \# \lessdot b \iff b \in \mathcal{L}(B), B \in S$.

The OPRs can be collected into a $|\Sigma_\#| \times |\Sigma_\#|$ array, called the operator precedence matrix *of the grammar,* $\text{OPM}(G)$: *for each (ordered) pair* $(a, b) \in \Sigma_\# \times \Sigma_\#$, $\text{OPM}_{a,b}(G)$ *contains the OPRs holding between* a *and* b.

Consider a square matrix: $M = \{M_{a,b} \subseteq \{\doteq, \lessdot, \gtrdot\} \mid a, b \in \Sigma_\#\}$. Such an OPM matrix, is called *conflict-free* iff $\forall a, b \in \Sigma_\#, 0 \le |M_{a,b}| \le 1$. A conflict-free matrix is called *total* or *complete* iff $\forall a, b \in \Sigma_\#, M_{a,b} \ne \emptyset$. A matrix is $\doteq$-*acyclic* if $\nexists a_i \in \Sigma$ such that $a_i \doteq \ldots \doteq a_i$.

In this we assume that an OPM is $\doteq$-acyclic. Such a hypothesis is stated for simplicity despite the fact that, rigorously speaking, it affects the expressive power of OPLs. It could be avoided if we adopted OPGs extended by the possibility of including regular expressions in production rhs [12,14], which however would require a much heavier notation.

We extend the set inclusion relations and the Boolean operations in the obvious cell by cell way, to any two matrices having the same terminal alphabet. Two matrices are *compatible* iff their union is conflict-free.

Definition 6 (Operator precedence grammar). *An O-grammar* G *is an* operator precedence *grammar (OPG) iff the matrix* $\text{OPM}(G)$ *is conflict-free, i.e., the three OPRs are pairwise disjoint. Then the language generated by* G *is an* operator precedence language (OPL). *An OPG is* $\doteq$-*acyclic if* $\text{OPM}(G)$ *is so.*

It is known that the OPL family is strictly included within the deterministic and reverse-deterministic CF family and strictly includes the VPL one [12].

Example 7. For the grammar GAE_1 (see Fig. 1, left), the left and right terminal sets of nonterminals E, T and F are, respectively: $\mathcal{L}(E) = \{+, *, e\}$, $\mathcal{L}(T) = \{*, e\}$, $\mathcal{L}(F) = \{e\}$, $\mathcal{R}(E) = \{+, *, e\}$, $\mathcal{R}(T) = \{*, e\}$, and $\mathcal{R}(F) = \{e\}$.

Figure 1 (center) displays the conflict-free OPM associated with the grammar GAE_1; for instance $\text{OPM}_{*,e} = \lessdot$ tells that $*$ yields precedence to e.

$$S = \{E, T, F\}$$
$$E \to E + T \mid T * F \mid e$$
$$T \to T * F \mid e$$
$$F \to e$$

	+	*	e	#
+	$\gtrdot$	$\lessdot$	$\lessdot$	$\gtrdot$
*	$\gtrdot$	$\gtrdot$	$\lessdot$	$\gtrdot$
e	$\gtrdot$	$\gtrdot$		$\gtrdot$
#	$\lessdot$	$\lessdot$	$\lessdot$	$\doteq$

$$\# \quad e \quad + \quad e \quad * \quad e \quad + \quad e \quad \#$$
$$0 \quad 1 \quad 2 \quad 3 \quad 4 \quad 5 \quad 6 \quad 7 \quad 8$$

Fig. 1. GAE_1 (left) and its OPM (center); the string $e + e * e + e$, with relation $\frown$ (right).

Unlike the arithmetic relations having similar typography, the OPRs do not enjoy any of the transitive, symmetric, reflexive properties.

A conflict-free matrix associates to every string at most one structure, i.e., a unique parenthesization. This aspect, paired with a way of deterministically choosing rules' rhs to be reduced, are the basis of Floyd's natural bottom-up deterministic parsing algorithm. E.g., the following BD version of GAE_1 (axioms and OPM are unchanged) drives the parsing of the string $e + e * e + e$ to the unique structure $(\!(\!(\!(e\!) + (\!(\!(e\!) * (\!(e\!)\!)\!)\!) + (\!(e\!)\!)$:

$$E \to E + T \mid E + F \mid T + T \mid F + F \mid F + T \mid T + F$$
$$T \to T * F \mid F * F \qquad F \to e.$$

Various formal properties of OPGs and languages are documented in the literature, chiefly in [12,13,26]. For convenience, we just recall and collect the ones that are relevant for this article in the next proposition.

Proposition 8. (Relevant properties of OPGs and OPLs).
Let M be a conflict-free OPM over $\Sigma_\# \times \Sigma_\#$.

1. *The class of OPGs and OPLs compatible with M are:*
   $\mathscr{C}_M = \{G \mid G \text{ is an OPG}, \text{OPM}(G) \subseteq M\}$, $\mathscr{L}_M = \{L(G) \mid G \in \mathscr{C}_M\}$.
2. *The class $\mathscr{C}_M$ contains a unique grammar, called the* maxgrammar *of M, denoted by $G_{max,M}$, such that for all grammars $G \in \mathscr{C}_M$, the inclusion holds $L(G) \subseteq L(G_{max,M})$. $L(G_{\max,M})$ is called* max-language. *If M is total, then $L(G_{\max,M}) = \Sigma^*$.*
3. *Let M be total. With a natural overloading, we define the function $M : \Sigma^* \to (\Sigma \cup \{(\!,)\!\})^*$ as $M(x) = y$, if $A \xRightarrow[G_{max,M}]{*} x, A \xRightarrow[\bar{G}_{max,M}]{*} y$ are*

   corresponding derivations.
   E.g. with M such that $a \lessdot a$, $a \doteq b$, $b \gtrdot b$, $M(aaaabbb) = (\!a(\!a(\!a(\!ab\!)b\!)b\!)\!)$.
4. *Let M be total.*
   - *$\mathscr{L}_M$ is closed under all set operations, therefore it is a Boolean algebra.*
   - *$\mathscr{L}_M$ is closed under concatenation and Kleene star.*

In summary, an OPM assigns a universal structure to strings in Σ^*, thus we call the pair (Σ, M) an *OP alphabet*. The following characterizations of OPLs, in terms of logic and expressions, are bound to the OP alphabet.

Logic Characterization. In [25] the traditional monadic second order logic (MSO) characterization of regular languages by Büchi, Elgot, and Trakhtenbrot [8,17,36] is extended to the case of OPL. To deal with the typical tree structure of CF languages the original MSO syntax is augmented with the predicate $\curvearrowright$, based on the OPL precedence relations: informally, $x \curvearrowright y$ holds between the rightmost and leftmost positions of the context encompassing a subtree, i.e., respectively, of the character that yields precedence to the subtree's leftmost leaf, and of the one over which the subtree's rightmost leaf takes precedence.

Unlike similar but simpler relations introduced, e.g., in [23] and [2], the $\curvearrowright$ relation is not one-to-one. For instance, Fig. 1 (right) displays the $\curvearrowright$ relation holding for the sentence $e + e * e + e$ generated by grammar GAE_1: we have $0 \curvearrowright 2$, $2 \curvearrowright 4$, $4 \curvearrowright 6$, $6 \curvearrowright 8$, $2 \curvearrowright 6$, $0 \curvearrowright 6$, and $0 \curvearrowright 8$. Such pairs correspond to contexts where a reduce operation is executed during the parsing of the string (they are listed according to their execution order).

Formally, we define a countable infinite set of first-order variables $\boldsymbol{x}, \boldsymbol{y}, \ldots$ and a countable infinite set of monadic second-order (set) variables $\boldsymbol{X}, \boldsymbol{Y}, \ldots$. We adopt the convention to denote first and second-order variables in boldface font.

Definition 9 (Monadic Second-order Logic over (Σ, M)). *Let $\mathcal{V}_1$ be a set of first-order variables, and $\mathcal{V}_2$ be a set of second-order (or set) variables. The $MSO_{\Sigma, M}$ (monadic second-order logic over (Σ, M)) is defined by the following syntax (symbols Σ, M will be omitted unless necessary to prevent confusion), where $c \in \Sigma_\#$, $\boldsymbol{x}, \boldsymbol{y} \in \mathcal{V}_1$, and $\boldsymbol{X} \in \mathcal{V}_2$:*

$$\varphi := c(\boldsymbol{x}) \mid \boldsymbol{x} \in \boldsymbol{X} \mid \boldsymbol{x} < \boldsymbol{y} \mid \boldsymbol{x} \curvearrowright \boldsymbol{y} \mid \neg\varphi \mid \varphi \vee \varphi \mid \exists \boldsymbol{x}.\varphi \mid \exists \boldsymbol{X}.\varphi.$$

A MSO formula is interpreted over a (Σ, M) string w, with respect to assignments $\nu_1 : \mathcal{V}_1 \rightarrow \{0, 1, \ldots |w| + 1\}$ and $\nu_2 : \mathcal{V}_2 \rightarrow \wp(\{0, 1, \ldots |w| + 1\})$, in this way:

- $\#w\#, M, \nu_1, \nu_2 \models c(\boldsymbol{x})$ *iff* $\#w\# = w_1 c w_2$ *and* $|w_1| = \nu_1(\boldsymbol{x})$.
- $\#w\#, M, \nu_1, \nu_2 \models \boldsymbol{x} \in \boldsymbol{X}$ *iff* $\nu_1(\boldsymbol{x}) \in \nu_2(\boldsymbol{X})$.
- $\#w\#, M, \nu_1, \nu_2 \models \boldsymbol{x} < \boldsymbol{y}$ *iff* $\nu_1(\boldsymbol{x}) < \nu_1(\boldsymbol{y})$.
- $\#w\#, M, \nu_1, \nu_2 \models \boldsymbol{x} \curvearrowright \boldsymbol{y}$ *iff* $\#w\# = w_1 a w_2 b w_3$, $|w_1| = \nu_1(\boldsymbol{x})$, $|w_1 a w_2| = \nu_1(\boldsymbol{y})$, *and* w_2 *is the frontier of a subtree of the syntax tree of w.*
- $\#w\#, M, \nu_1, \nu_2 \models \neg\varphi$ *iff* $\#w\#, M, \nu_1, \nu_2 \not\models \varphi$.
- $\#w\#, M, \nu_1, \nu_2 \models \varphi_1 \vee \varphi_2$ *iff* $\#w\#, M, \nu_1, \nu_2 \models \varphi_1$ *or* $\#w\#, M, \nu_1, \nu_2 \models \varphi_2$.
- $\#w\#, M, \nu_1, \nu_2 \models \exists \boldsymbol{x}.\varphi$ *iff* $\#w\#, M, \nu_1', \nu_2 \models \varphi$, *for some ν_1' with $\nu_1'(\boldsymbol{y}) = \nu_1(\boldsymbol{y})$ for all $\boldsymbol{y} \in \mathcal{V}_1 - \{\boldsymbol{x}\}$.*
- $\#w\#, M, \nu_1, \nu_2 \models \exists \boldsymbol{X}.\varphi$ *iff* $\#w\#, M, \nu_1, \nu_2' \models \varphi$, *for some ν_2' with $\nu_2'(\boldsymbol{Y}) = \nu_2(\boldsymbol{Y})$ for all $\boldsymbol{Y} \in \mathcal{V}_2 - \{\boldsymbol{X}\}$.*

To improve readability, we drop M, ν_1, ν_2 and the delimiters $\#$ from the notation whenever there is no risk of ambiguity; furthermore we use some standard abbreviations in formulas, e.g., $\wedge$, $\forall$, $\boldsymbol{x} + 1$, $\boldsymbol{x} - 1$, $\boldsymbol{x} = \boldsymbol{y}$, $\boldsymbol{x} \leq \boldsymbol{y}$.

A sentence is a formula without free variables. The language of all strings $w \in \Sigma^*$ such that $w \models \varphi$ is $L(\varphi) = \{w \in \Sigma^* \mid w \models \varphi\}$.

The above MSO logic describes exactly the OPL family [25]. We denote the restriction of the MSO logic to the first-order as FO. Whenever we deal with logic definition of languages we implicitly exclude from such languages the empty string, according with the traditional convention adopted in the literature (e.g., [28]); thus, when talking about MSO or FO definable languages we exclude empty rules from their grammars.

2.2 Parenthesis and OPLs and the Noncounting Property

We briefly recall the standard definition of the NC property for CF parenthesis languages [10] and its decidability, then we apply it to OPLs.

Definition 10 (NC parenthesis language and grammar [10]). *A parenthesis language L is NC (or aperiodic) iff $\exists n > 1$ such that, for all strings x, u, w, v, y in $(\Sigma \cup \{(\!|, |\!)\})^*$ where w and uwv are well parenthesized, $xu^n wv^n y \in L$ iff $xu^{n+m} wv^{n+m} y \in L$, $\forall m \geq 0$.*

A derivation of a Par-grammar is counting iff it has the form $B \overset{*}{\Longrightarrow} u^m B v^m$, with $m > 1$, and there is not a derivation $B \overset{*}{\Longrightarrow} uBv$. A Par-grammar is NC iff none of its derivations is counting.

The next proposition ensures the decidability of the NC property.

Theorem 11. *[NC language and grammar (Th. 1 of [10])] A parenthesis language is NC iff its BDR grammar has no counting derivation.*

Definition 12 (NC OPLs and grammars). *For a given OPL L with OPM M, L_p is the language of the parenthesized strings x_p uniquely associated to L's strings x by M. An OPL L is NC iff its corresponding parenthesized language L_p is NC.*

A derivation of a grammar G is counting iff the corresponding derivation of the associated Par-grammar G_p is counting.

Thus, an OPL is NC iff its BDR OPG (unique up to an isomorphim of nonterminal alphabets) has no counting derivations.

In the following, unless parentheses are explicitly needed, we refer to unparenthesized strings since their correspondence to parenthesized strings is one-to-one. It is also worth recalling [11] the following peculiar property of OPLs: such languages are NC or not independently on their OPM, in other words, although the NC property is defined for structured languages (parenthesis or tree languages [27, 34]), in the case of OPLs this property does not depend on the structure given to the sentences by the OPM.

It is important to stress, however, that, despite the above peculiarity of OPLs, aperiodicity remains a property that makes sense only with reference to the structured version of languages. Consider the following languages, with the same OPM consisting of $\{c \lessdot c, c \doteq a, c \doteq b, a \gtrdot b, b \gtrdot a\}$ besides the implicit relations w.r.t. #: $L_1 = \{c^{2n}(ab)^n \mid n \geq 1\}$, $L_2 = (ab)^+$. They are both clearly NC and so is their concatenation $L_1 \cdot L_2$, according to Definition 12, which in its parenthesized version is $\{(\!|^{2(m-n)}((\!|c)^{2n}(a\!|b\!|))^m \mid m > n \geq 1\}$, (see also Theorem 20); however, if we applied Definition 10 to $L_1 \cdot L_2$ without considering parentheses, we would obtain that, for every n, $c^{2n}(ab)^{2n} \in L_1 \cdot L_2$ but not so for $c^{2n+1}(ab)^{2n+1}$.

3   Expressions for OPLs

Operator Precedence Expressions (OPE) extend traditional REs in a similar way as in other cases such as, e.g., REs for tree-languages [35]. We show that OPEs define exactly the OPL family, so that, by joining this result with the previous characterizations of OPL in terms of MSO definability and recognizability by *Operator Precedence Automata (OPA)* [25], we have that *the class OPL can be defined equivalently as the class of languages generated by OPGs, or described through MSO formulas, or recognized by OPAs, or defined by OPEs.*

As well as for MSO logic and OPA, OPE's definition is based on an OP alphabet.

Definition 13 (OPE). *Given an OP alphabet* (Σ, M), *where* M *is complete, an OPE* E *and its language* $L_M(E) \subseteq \Sigma^*$ *are defined as follows. The meta-alphabet of OPE uses the same symbols as REs, together with the two symbols* '[', *and* ']'. *Let* E_1 *and* E_2 *be OPEs:*

1. $a \in \Sigma$ *is an OPE with* $L_M(a) = a$.
2. $\neg E_1$ *is an OPE with* $L_M(\neg E_1) = \Sigma^* - L_M(E_1)$.
3. $a[E_1]b$, *called the* fence operation, *i.e., we say* E_1 *in the fence* a, b, *is an OPE with*

   if $a, b \in \Sigma$: $L_M(a[E_1]b) = a \cdot \{x \in L_M(E_1) \mid M(a \cdot x \cdot b) = (\!| a \cdot M(x) \cdot b |\!)\} \cdot b$
   if $a = \#, b \in \Sigma$: $L_M(\#[E_1]b) = \{x \in L_M(E_1) \mid M(x \cdot b) = (\!| M(x) \cdot b |\!)\} \cdot b$
   if $a \in \Sigma, b = \#$: $L_M(a[E_1]\#) = a \cdot \{x \in L_M(E_1) \mid M(a \cdot x) = (\!| a \cdot M(x) |\!)\}$
   where E_1 *must not contain* $\#$.
4. $E_1 \cup E_2$ *is an OPE with* $L_M(E_1 \cup E_2) = L_M(E_1) \cup L_M(E_2)$.
5. $E_1 \cdot E_2$ *is an OPE with* $L_M(E_1 \cdot E_2) = L_M(E_1) \cdot L_M(E_2)$, *where* E_1 *does not contain* $a[E_3]\#$ *and* E_2 *does not contain* $\#[E_3]a$, *for some OPE* E_3, *and* $a \in \Sigma$.
6. E_1^* *is an OPE defined by* $E_1^* := \bigcup_{n=0}^{\infty} E_1^n$, *where* $E_1^0 := \{\varepsilon\}$, $E_1^1 = E_1$, $E_1^n := E_1^{n-1} \cdot E_1$; $E_1^+ := \bigcup_{n=1}^{\infty} E_1^n$.

Among the operations defining OPEs, concatenation has the maximum precedence; set-theoretic operations have the usual precedences, the fence operation is dealt with as a normal parenthesis pair. A star-free (SF) OPE is one that does not use $*$ *and* $+$.

The conditions on $\#$ are due to the peculiarities of OPLs closure w.r.t. concatenation (see also Theorem 20). In 5. the $\#$ is not permitted within, say, the left factor E_1 because delimiters are necessarily positioned at the two ends of a string.

Besides the usual abbreviations for set operations (e.g., $\cap$ and $-$), we also use the following derived operators: $a\Delta b := a[\Sigma^+]b$, and $a\nabla b := \neg(a\Delta b) \cap a \cdot \Sigma^+ \cdot b$. It is trivial to see that the identity $a[E]b = a\Delta b \cap a \cdot E \cdot b$ holds.

The fact that in Definition 13 matrix M is complete is w.l.o.g.: to state that for two terminals a and b, $M_{a,b} = \emptyset$ (i.e. that there should be a "hole" in the OPM for them), we can use the short notations: $\text{hole}(a, b) := \neg(\Sigma^*(ab \cup a\Delta b)\Sigma^*)$, $\text{hole}(\#, b) := \neg(\#\Delta b\Sigma^*)$, $\text{hole}(a, \#) := \neg(\Sigma^* a\Delta \#)$ and intersect them with the OPE.

The following examples illustrate the meaning of the fence operation, the expressiveness of OPLs w.r.t. less powerful classes of CF languages, and how OPEs naturally extend REs to the OPL family.

Example 14. Let Σ be $\{a, b\}$, $\{a < a, a \doteq b, b > b\} \subseteq M$. The OPE $a[a^*b^*]b$ defines the language $\{a^n b^n \mid n \geq 1\}$. In fact the fence operation imposes that any string $x \in a^*b^*$ embedded within the context a, b is well-parenthesized according to M.

The OPEs $a[a^*b^*]\#$ and $a^+a[a^*b^*]b \cup \{a^+\}$, instead, both define the language $\{a^n b^m \mid n > m \geq 0\}$ since the matrix M allows for, e.g., the string $aaabb$ parenthesized as $⟦a⟦a⟦ab⟧b⟧⟧$.

It is also easy to define Dyck languages with OPEs, as their parenthesis structure is naturally encoded by the OPM. Consider L_{Dyck} the Dyck language with two pairs of parentheses denoted by a, a' and b, b'. This language can be described simply through an incomplete OPM, reported in Fig. 2 (left). In other words it is $L_{\text{Dyck}} = L(G_{max,M})$ where M is the matrix of the figure. Given that, for technical simplicity, we use only complete OPMs, we must refer to the one in Fig. 2 (center), and state in the OPE that some OPRs are not wanted, such as a, b', where the open and closed parentheses are of the wrong kind, or $a, \#$, i.e. an open a must have a matching a'.

	a	a'	b	b'	#
a	<	≐		<	
a'	<	>	<	>	>
b	<			<	≐
b'	<	>	<	>	>
#	<			<	≐

	a	a'	b	b'	#
a	<	≐	<	>	>
a'	<	>	<	>	>
b	<	>	<	≐	>
b'	<	>	<	>	>
#	<	<	<	<	≐

	call	ret	int	#
call	<	≐		>
ret	>	>	>	>
int	>		>	>
#	<		<	≐

Fig. 2. The incomplete OPM defining L_{Dyck} (left), a possible completion M_{complete} (center), and the OPM M_{int} for the OPE describing an interrupt policy (right).

The following OPE defines L_{Dyck} by suitably restricting the "universe" $L(G_{max,M_{\text{complete}}})$:

$$\text{hole}(a, b') \cap \text{hole}(b, a') \cap \text{hole}(\#, a') \cap \text{hole}(\#, b') \cap \text{hole}(a, \#) \cap \text{hole}(b, \#).$$

Example 15. For a more application-oriented case, consider the classical LIFO policy managing procedure calls and returns but assume also that interrupts may occur: in such a case the stack of pending calls is emptied and computation is resumed from scratch.

This policy is already formalized by the incomplete OPM of Fig. 2 (right), with $\Sigma = \{call, ret, int\}$ with the obvious meaning of symbols. For example, the string *call call ret call call int* represents a run where only the second call returns, while the other ones are interrupted. On the contrary, *call call int ret* is forbidden, because a return is not allowed when the stack is empty. If we further want to say that there must be at least one terminating procedure, we can use the OPE: $\Sigma^* \cdot call \Delta ret \cdot \Sigma^*$.

Another example is the following, where we state that the run must contain at least one sub-run where no procedures are interrupted: $\Sigma^* \cdot \text{hole}(call, int) \cdot \Sigma^*$.

Notice that the language defined by the above OPE is not a VPL since VPLs only allow for unmatched returns and calls at the beginning or at the end of a string, respectively.

Theorem 16. *For every OPE E on an OPM M, there is an OPG G, compatible with M, such that $L_M(E) = L(G)$.*

Proof. By induction on E's structure. The operations $\cup, \neg, \cdot$, and * come from the closures of OPLs (Proposition 8). The only new case is $a[E]b$ which is given by the following grammar. The function $\eta : \Sigma_\# \to \Sigma$, such that $\eta(\#) = \varepsilon$, $\eta(a) = a$ otherwise, is used to take borders into account. If, by induction, G defines the same language as E, with axiom set S_E, then build the grammar G' from G by adding the following rules, where A and A' are new nonterminals of G' not in G, A is an axiom of G', and $B \in S_E$:

- $A \to \eta(a)B\eta(b)$, if $a \doteq b$ in M;
- $A \to \eta(a)A'$ and $A' \to B\eta(b)$, if $a \lessdot b$ in M;
- $A \to A'\eta(b)$ and $A' \to \eta(a)B$, if $a \gtrdot b$ in M.

The grammar for $a[E]b$ is then obtained by applying the construction for $L(G') \cap L(G_{max,M})$. This intersection is to check that $a \lessdot \mathcal{L}(B)$ and $\mathcal{R}(B) \gtrdot b$; if it is not the case, according to the semantics of $a[E]b$, the resulting language is empty.   □

Next, we show that OPEs can express any language that is definable through an MSO formula as defined in Sect. 2.1. Thanks to the fact that the same MSO logic can express exactly OPLs [25] and to Theorem 16 we obtain our first major result, i.e., the equivalence of MSO, OPG, OPA (see e.g., [26]), and OPE.

To construct an OPE from a given MSO formula we follow the traditional path adopted for regular languages (as explained, e.g., in [30]) and augment it to deal with the $\curvearrowright$ relation. For a MSO formula φ, let $x_1, x_2, \ldots, x_r$ be the set of first-order variables occurring in φ, and $X_1, X_2, \ldots, X_s$ be the set of second order variables. We use the new alphabet $B_{p,q} = \Sigma \times \{0,1\}^p \times \{0,1\}^q$, where $p \geq r$ and $q \geq s$. The main idea is that the $\{0,1\}^p$ part of the alphabet is used to encode the value of the first-order variables (e.g. for $p = r = 4$, $(1, 0, 1, 0)$ stands for both the positions x_1 and x_3), while the $\{0,1\}^q$ part of the alphabet is used for the second order variables. Hence, we are interested in the language $K_{p,q}$ formed by all strings where the components encoding the first-order variables contain exactly one occurrence of 1. We also use this definition $C_k := \{c \in B_{p,q} \mid$ the $(k+1)$-st component of $c = 1\}$.

Theorem 17. *For every MSO formula φ on an OP alphabet (Σ, M) there is an OPE E on M such that $L_M(E) = L(\varphi)$.*

Proof. By induction on φ's structure; the construction is standard for regular operations, the only difference is $x_i \curvearrowright x_j$. $B_{p,q}$ is used to encode interpretations of free variables. The set $K_{p,q}$ of strings where each component encoding a first-order variable is such that there exists only one 1, is given by: $K_{p,q} = \bigcap_{1 \leq i \leq p} (B_{p,q}^* C_i B_{p,q}^* - B_{p,q}^* C_i B_{p,q}^* C_i B_{p,q}^*)$. Disjunction and negation are naturally translated into $\cup$ and $\neg$; like in Büchi's theorem, for OPE $\exists \boldsymbol{x}_i \psi$ (resp. $\exists \boldsymbol{X}_j \psi$), first the expression E_ψ for ψ on an alphabet $B_{p,q}$ is built, then E for $\exists \boldsymbol{x}_i \psi$ is obtained from E_ψ by erasing the component i (resp. j) from $B_{p,q}$; $\boldsymbol{x}_i < \boldsymbol{x}_j$ is represented by $K_{p,q} \cap B_{p,q}^* C_i B_{p,q}^* C_j B_{p,q}^*$. Last, the OPE for $\boldsymbol{x}_i \curvearrowright \boldsymbol{x}_j$ is: $B_{p,q}^* C_i [B_{p,q}^+] C_j B_{p,q}^*$.   □

4   Closure Properties of Noncounting OPLs and Star-Free OPEs

Thanks to the fact that an OPM implicitly defines the structure of an OPL, i.e., its parenthesization, aperiodic OPLs inherit from the general class the same closure properties w.r.t. the basic algebraic operations. Such properties are proved in this section under the same assumption as in the general case (see Proposition 8), i.e., that *the involved languages have compatible OPMs*. As a major consequence we derive that star-free OPEs define aperiodic OPLs.

Theorem 18. *Counting and NC parenthesis languages are closed w.r.t. complement. Thus, for any OPM M, counting and NC OPLs in the family $\mathscr{L}_M$ (Proposition 8) are closed w.r.t. complement w.r.t. the max-language defined by M.*

Proof. We give the proof for counting languages which also implies the closure of NC ones.

By definition of counting parenthesis language and from Theorem 11, if L is counting there exist strings x, u, v, z, y and integers n, m with $n > 1, m > 1$ such that $xv^{n+r} zu^{n+r} y \in L$ for all $r = km > 0$, $k > 0$, but not for all $r > 0$. Thus, the complement of L contains infinitely many strings $xv^{n+i} zu^{n+i} y \in L$ but not all of them since for some i, $i = km$. Thus, for $\neg L$ too there is no n such that $xv^n zu^n y \in L$ iff $xv^{n+r} zu^{n+r} y \in L$ for all $r \geq 0$.   □

Theorem 19. *NC parenthesis languages and NC OPLs in the same family $\mathscr{L}_M$ are closed w.r.t. union and therefore w.r.t. intersection.*

Proof. Let L_1, L_2 be two NC parenthesis languages (resp. OPLs). Assume by contradiction that $L = L_1 \cup L_2$ is counting. Thus, there exist strings x, u, v, z, y such that for infinitely many m, $xv^m zu^m y \in L$ but for no n $xv^n zu^n y \in L$ iff $xv^{n+r} zu^{n+r} y \in L$ for all $r \geq 0$. Hence, the same property must hold for at least one of L_1 and L_2 which therefore would be counting.   □

Notice that, unlike the case of complement, counting languages are not closed w.r.t. union and intersection, whether they are regular or parenthesis or OPLs.

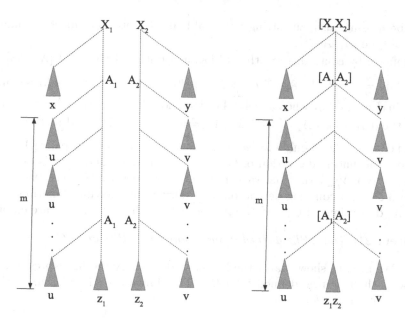

Fig. 3. An example of paired derivations combined by the concatenation construction. In this case the last character of u is in $\doteq$ relation with the first character of v.

Theorem 20. *NC OPLs are closed w.r.t. concatenation.*

Proof. Let $L_i = L(G_i)$, $i = 1, 2$, be NC OPLs with $G_i = (\Sigma, V_{Ni}, P_i, S_i)$ BDR OPGs. Let also $L_{pi} = L(G_{pi})$ be the parenthesized languages and grammars. We exploit the proof in [12] that OPLs with compatible OPM are closed w.r.t. concatenation. In general the parenthesized version L_p of $L = L_1 \cdot L_2$ is not the parenthesized concatenation of the parenthesized versions of L_1 and L_2, i.e., L_p may differ from $(\!| L'_{p1} \cdot L'_{p2} |\!)$, where $(\!| L'_{p1} |\!) = L_{p1}$ and $(\!| L'_{p2} |\!) = L_{p2}$, because the concatenation may cause the syntax trees of L_1 and L_2 to coalesce.

The construction given in [12] builds a grammar G whose nonterminal alphabet includes V_{N1}, V_{N2} and a set of pairs $[A_1, A_2]$ with $A_1 \in V_{N1}$, $A_2 \in V_{N2}$; the axioms of G are the pairs $[X_1, X_2]$ with $X_1 \in S_1$, $X_2 \in S_2$.[1] In essence (Lemmas 18 through 21 of [12]) G's derivations are such that $[X_1, X_2] \overset{*}{\underset{G}{\Rightarrow}} x[A_1, A_2]y$, $[A_1, A_2] \overset{*}{\underset{G}{\Rightarrow}} u$ implies $u = w \cdot z$ for some w, z and $X_1 \overset{*}{\underset{G_1}{\Rightarrow}} xA_1$, $A_1 \overset{*}{\underset{G_1}{\Rightarrow}} w$, $X_2 \overset{*}{\underset{G_2}{\Rightarrow}} A_2 y$, $A_2 \overset{*}{\underset{G_2}{\Rightarrow}} z$. Notice that some substrings of $x \cdot w$, resp. $z \cdot y$, may be derived from nonterminals belonging to V_{N1}, resp. V_{N2}, as the consequence of rules of type $[A_1, A_2] \rightarrow \alpha_1 [B_1, B_2] \beta_2$ with $\alpha_1 \in V_1^*$, $\beta_2 \in V_2^*$, where $[B_1, B_2]$

---

[1] This is a minor deviation from [12], where it was assumed that grammars have only one axiom.

could be missing; also, any string γ derivable in G contains at most one nonterminal of type $[A_1, A_2]$.[2]

Suppose, by contradiction, that G has a counting derivation[3] $[X_1, X_2] \underset{G}{\overset{*}{\Longrightarrow}}$
$x[A_1, A_2]y \underset{G}{\overset{*}{\Longrightarrow}} xu^m[A_1, A_2]v^m y \underset{G}{\overset{*}{\Longrightarrow}} xu^m z v^m y$ (one of u^m, v^m could be empty either in L or in L_p) whereas $[A_1, A_2]$ does not derive $u[A_1, A_2]v$: this would imply the derivations $A_1 \underset{G_1}{\overset{*}{\Longrightarrow}} u^m A_1$, $A_2 \underset{G_2}{\overset{*}{\Longrightarrow}} A_2 v^m$ which would be counting in G_1 and G_2 since they would involve the same nonterminals in the pairs $[A_i, A_j]$. If instead the counting derivation of G were derived from nonterminals belonging to V_{N1}, (resp. V_{N2}) that derivation would exist identical for G_1 (resp. G_2). Figure 3 shows a counting derivation of G derived by the concatenation of two counting derivations of G_1 and G_2; in this case neither u^m nor v^m are empty. $\square$

Theorem 21. *The OPLs defined through star-free OPEs are NC.*

Proof. We need to show that if the language defined by the SF expression E is NC, so is the language defined by $a[E]b$. This follows by the identity $a[E]b = a\Delta b \cap aEb = a[\Sigma^+]b \cap aEb$. $\square$

5   FO-Definable OPLs and SF OPEs

We now prove that SF OPE-definable languages coincide with FO-definable OPLs which are therefore NC as well; a result in sharp contrast with the negative results for NC tree-languages [35]. In Sect. 5.1 we show that NC linear OPLs are FO-definable too.

Lemma 22 (Flat Normal Form). *Any star-free OPE can be written in the following form, called* flat normal form: $\bigcup_i \bigcap_j t_{i,j}$, *where the elements* $t_{i,j}$ *have either the form* $L_{i,j} a_{i,j} \Delta b_{i,j} R_{i,j}$, *or* $L_{i,j} a_{i,j} \nabla b_{i,j} R_{i,j}$, *or* $H_{i,j}$, *for* $a_{i,j}, b_{i,j} \in \Sigma_\#$, *and* $L_{i,j}$, $R_{i,j}$, $H_{i,j}$ *star-free REs.*

Proof. The lemma is a consequence of the distributive and De Morgan properties, together with the following identities, where $\circ_1, \circ_2 \in \{\Delta, \nabla\}$, and L_k, $1 \le k \le 3$ are star-free REs:

$$a[E]b = a\Delta b \cap aEb$$

$$L_1 a_1 \circ_1 a_2 L_2 a_3 \circ_2 a_4 L_3 = (L_1 a_1 \circ_1 a_2 L_2 a_3 \Sigma^+ a_4 L_3) \cap (L_1 a_1 \Sigma^+ a_2 L_2 a_3 \circ_2 a_4 L_3)$$

$$\neg(L_1 a_1 \Delta a_2 L_2) = L_1 a_1 \nabla a_2 L_2 \cup \neg(L_1 a_1 \Sigma^+ a_2 L_2)$$

$$\neg(L_1 a_1 \nabla a_2 L_2) = L_1 a_1 \Delta a_2 L_2 \cup \neg(L_1 a_1 \Sigma^+ a_2 L_2)$$

---

[2] See Fig. 3.

[3] Note that the G produced by the construction is BD if so are G_1 and G_2, but it could be not necessarily BDR; however, if a BDR OPG has a counting derivation, any equivalent BD grammar has also a counting derivation.

The first two identities are immediate, while the last two are based on the idea that the only non-regular constraints of the left-hand negations are respectively $a_1 \triangledown a_2$ or $a_1 \triangle a_2$, that represent strings that are not in the set only because of their structure. □

Theorem 23. *For every FO formula φ on an OP alphabet (Σ, M) there is a star-free OPE E on M such that $L_M(E) = L(\varphi)$.*

Proof. Consider the formula φ, and its set of first-order variables: like in Sect. 3, $B_p = \Sigma \times \{0, 1\}^p$ (the q components are absent, φ being a first-order formula), and the set K_p of strings where each component encoding a variable is such that there exists only one 1.

First, K_p is star-free: $K_p = \bigcap_{1 \leq i \leq p} (B_p^* C_i B_p^* - B_p^* C_i B_p^* C_i B_p^*)$.

Disjunction and negation are naturally translated into $\cup$ and $\neg$; $\boldsymbol{x}_i < \boldsymbol{x}_j$ is covered by the star-free OPE $K_p \cap B_p^* C_i B_p^* C_j B_p^*$. The $\boldsymbol{x}_i \frown \boldsymbol{x}_j$ formula is like in the second order case, i.e. is translated into $B_p^* C_i [B_p^+] C_j B_p^*$, which is star-free.

For the existential quantification, the problem is that star-free (OP and regular) languages are not closed under projections. Like in the regular case, the idea is to leverage the encoding of the evaluation of first-order variables, because there is only one position in which the component is 1 (see K_p), to use the bijective renamings $\pi_0(a, v_1, v_2, ..., v_{p-1}, 0) = (a, v_1, v_2, ..., v_{p-1})$, and $\pi_1(a, v_1, v_2, ..., v_{p-1}, 1) = (a, v_1, v_2, ..., v_{p-1})$, where the last component is the one encoding the quantified variable. Notice that the bijective renaming does not change the Σ component of the symbol, thus maintaining all the OPRs.

Let E_φ be the star-free OPE on the alphabet B_p for the formula φ, with x a free variable in it. Let us assume w.l.o.g. that the evaluation of x is encoded by the last component of B_p; let $B = \Sigma \times \{0, 1\}^{p-1} \times \{0\}$, and $A = \Sigma \times \{0, 1\}^{p-1} \times \{1\}$.

The OPE for $\exists x \varphi$ is obtained from the OPE for φ through the bijective renaming π, and considering all the cases in which the symbol from A can occur.

First, let E' be an OPE in flat normal form, equivalent to E_φ (Lemma 22). The FO semantics is such that $L(\varphi) = L_M(E') = L_M(E') \cap B^* A B^*$.

By construction, E' is a union of intersections of elements $L_{i,j} a_{i,j} \triangle b_{i,j} R_{i,j}$, or $L_{i,j} a_{i,j} \triangledown b_{i,j} R_{i,j}$, or $H_{i,j}$, where $a_{i,j}, b_{i,j} \in \Sigma$, and $L_{i,j}, R_{i,j}, H_{i,j}$ are star-free regular languages.

In the intersection of E' and $B^* A B^*$, all the possible cases in which the symbol in A can occur in E''s terms must be considered: e.g. in $L_{i,j} a_{i,j} \triangle b_{i,j} R_{i,j}$ it could occur in the $L_{i,j}$ prefix, or in $a_{i,j} \triangle b_{i,j}$, or in $R_{i,j}$. More precisely, $L_{i,j} a_{i,j} \triangle b_{i,j} R_{i,j} \cap B^* A B^* = (L_{i,j} \cap B^* A B^*) a_{i,j} \triangle b_{i,j} R_{i,j} \cup L_{i,j} (a_{i,j} \triangle b_{i,j} \cap B^* A B^*) R_{i,j} \cup L_{i,j} a_{i,j} \triangle b_{i,j} (R_{i,j} \cap B^* A B^*)$ (the $\triangledown$ case is analogous, $H_{i,j}$ is immediate, being regular star-free).

The cases in which the symbol from A occurs in $L_{i,j}$ or $R_{i,j}$ are easy, because they are by construction regular star-free languages, hence we can use one of the standard regular approaches found in the literature (e.g. by using the *splitting lemma* in [16]). The only differences are in the factors $a_{i,j} \triangle b_{i,j}$, or $a_{i,j} \triangledown b_{i,j}$.

Let us consider the case $a_{i,j} \triangle b_{i,j} \cap B^* A B^*$. The cases $a_{i,j} \in A$ or $b_{i,j} \in A$ are like $(L_{i,j} \cap B^* A B^*)$ and $(R_{i,j} \cap B^* A B^*)$, respectively, because $L_{i,j} a_{i,j}$ and $b_{i,j} R_{i,j}$ are also regular star-free ($\triangledown$ is analogous).

The remaining cases are $a_{i,j}\Delta b_{i,j} \cap B^+AB^+$ and $a_{i,j}\nabla b_{i,j} \cap B^+AB^+$. By definition of Δ, $a_{i,j}\Delta b_{i,j} \cap B^+AB^+ = a_{i,j}[B^*AB^*]b_{i,j}$, and its bijective renaming is $\pi_0(a_{i,j})[\pi_0(B^*)\pi_1(A)\,\pi_0(B^*)]\pi_0(b_{i,j}) = a'_{i,j}[B^+_{p-1}]b'_{i,j}$, where $\pi_0(a_{i,j}) = a'_{i,j}$, and $\pi_0(b_{i,j}) = b'_{i,j}$, which is a star-free OPE. By definition of ∇, $a_{i,j}\nabla b_{i,j} \cap B^+AB^+ = \neg(a_{i,j}[B^+_p]b_{i,j}) \cap a_{i,j}B^+_p b_{i,j} \cap B^+AB^+ = \neg(a_{i,j}[B^+_p]b_{i,j}) \cap a_{i,j}B^*AB^*b_{i,j}$. Hence, its renaming is $\neg(\pi_0(a_{i,j})[\pi_0(B^+_p)\pi_1(B_p)\pi_0(B^*_p)]\,\pi_0(b_{i,j})) \cap \pi_0(a_{i,j}B^*)\pi_1(A)\pi_0(B^*\,b_{i,j}) = \neg(a'_{i,j}[B^+_{p-1}]b'_{i,j}) \cap a'_{i,j}B^+_{p-1}b'_{i,j}$, a star-free OPE. □

Theorem 24. *For every star-free OPE E on an OP alphabet (Σ, M), there is a FO formula φ on (Σ, M) such that $L_M(E) = L(\varphi)$.*

Proof. The proof is by induction on E's structure. Of course, singletons are easily first-order definable; for negation and union we use $\neg$ and $\vee$ as natural. Like in the case of star-free regular languages, concatenation is less immediate, and it is based on formula *relativization*. Consider two FO formulas φ and ψ, and assume w.l.o.g. that their variables are disjunct, and let x be a variable not used in either them. To construct a relativized variant of φ, called $\varphi_{<x}$, proceed from the outermost quantifier, going inward, and replace every subformula $\exists z\lambda$ with $\exists z((z < x) \wedge \lambda)$. Variants $\varphi_{\geq x}$ and $\varphi_{>x}$ are analogous. We also call $\varphi_{x,y}$ the relativization where quantifications $\exists z\lambda$ are replaced by $\exists z((x < z < y) \wedge \lambda)$. The language $L(\varphi) \cdot L(\psi)$ is defined by the following formulas: $\exists x(\varphi_{<x} \wedge \psi_{\geq x})$ if $\varepsilon \notin L(\psi)$; otherwise $\exists x(\varphi_{<x} \wedge \psi_{\geq x}) \vee \varphi$.

The last part we need to consider is the fence operation, i.e. $a[E]b$. Let φ be a FO formula such that $L(\varphi) = L_M(E)$, for a star-free OPE E. Let x and y be two variables unused in φ. Then the language $L(a[E]b)$ is the one defined by $\exists x\exists y(a(x) \wedge b(y) \wedge x \frown y \wedge \varphi_{x,y})$. □

5.1 Linear Noncounting OPLs Are First-Order Definable

Definition 25. *Let $G = (\Sigma, V_N, P, S)$ be a linear grammar, i.e., a grammar where all rule rhs $\in \Sigma^+ V_N \Sigma^* \cup \Sigma^* V_N \Sigma^+ \cup \Sigma^+$. The finite state stencil automaton associated to G is $\mathcal{A}^\Xi_G = (Q, \Xi, \delta, S, \{q_F\})$, where $Q = V_N \cup \{q_F\}$ are its states, $\Xi \subseteq (\Sigma^* \times \Sigma^*) \cup \Sigma^+$, its input alphabet, is the set of stencils of G,[4] and the transition relation $\delta \subseteq Q \times \Xi \times Q$ is defined as follows:*

$$\delta = \{A \xrightarrow{(x,y)} B \mid A \to xBy \in P\} \cup \{A \xrightarrow{z} q_F \mid A \to z \in P\}.$$

Lemma 26. *Let G be a linear OPG, with OPM M, and Ξ the set of stencils of G. $L(G)$ is NC iff $L(\mathcal{A}^\Xi_G)$ is a NC regular language.*

Proof. By construction, every derivation $A_0 \overset{*}{\Longrightarrow} x_1 A_1 y_1 \overset{*}{\Longrightarrow} x_1 x_2 A_2 y_2 y_1 \overset{*}{\Longrightarrow} x_1 x_2 \dots x_k A_k \, y_k y_{k-1} \dots y_1 \overset{*}{\Longrightarrow} x_1 x_2 \dots x_k \, z y_k y_{k-1} \dots y_1$ of G corresponds to a run $A_0 \vdash A_1 \vdash \dots \vdash A_k \vdash q_F$ of $\mathcal{A}^\Xi_G$, reading the word $(x_1, y_1)(x_2, y_2) \dots (x_k, y_k)z$, and vice versa.

---

[4] $\Xi := \{(x,y) \mid A \to xBy \in P\} \cup \{z \mid A \to z \in P\}$.

According to Definitions 10 and 12, if it is $x_1 x_2 \ldots x_k z y_k y_{k-1} \ldots y_1 = o u^n w v^n p$, for some strings o, u, w, v, p, then $o u^{n+1} w v^{n+1} p \in L(G)$, i.e., assuming that $x_i \ldots x_j = u$ and $y_j \ldots y_i = v$, $o u^{n+1} w v^{n+1} p = x_1 x_2 \ldots (x_i \ldots x_j)^2 x_{j+1} \ldots x_k z \ y_k y_{k-1} \ldots (y_j \ldots y_i)^2 y_{i-1} \ldots y_1$.
Hence, $(x_1, y_1)(x_2, y_2) \ldots (x_k, y_k) z = o' u'^m w'$, where $u' = (x_i, y_i) \ldots (x_j, y_j)$, and $(x_1, y_1) \ldots ((x_i, y_i) \ldots (x_j, y_j))^2 (x_{j+1}, y_{j+1}) \ldots (x_k, y_k) z = o' u'^{n+1} w' \in L(\mathcal{A}_G^\Xi)$.
The other direction is analogous. □

Theorem 27. *Let G be a linear NC OPG with OPM M, $L(G)$ is expressible in $FO_{(\Sigma, M)}$.*

Proof. From Lemma 26, we can build $\mathcal{A}_G^\Xi$, which defines a NC regular language. It is known from [28] that there exists an equivalent first-order formula $\varphi(\mathcal{A}_G^\Xi)$ on the alphabet Ξ.

We can build a $FO_{(\Sigma, M)}$ formula defining $L(G)$ in this way. First, for each $p \in \Xi$, where $p = (u, v)$, $u = u_1 u_2 \ldots u_m$, $v = v_1 v_2 \ldots v_n$, $m, n \geq 0$, $m + n > 0$, we introduce the following formula σ_p:

$$\sigma_p(x) := \begin{pmatrix} u_1(x) \wedge u_2(x+1) \wedge \\ \ldots \wedge u_n(x + m - 1) \end{pmatrix} \wedge \exists y \begin{pmatrix} x + m - 1 \curvearrowright y \wedge v_1(y) \wedge v_2(y+1) \wedge \\ \ldots \wedge v_n(y + n - 1) \end{pmatrix}$$

(the case $p \in \Sigma^+$ is trivial.) E.g. for $p = (\varepsilon, ab)$, $\sigma_p(x) = \exists y (x \curvearrowright y \wedge a(y) \wedge b(y+1))$.

It is easy to see that σ_p is a straightforward way to encode a stencil p into a $FO_{(\Sigma, M)}$ formula defining its structure.

Let us consider $\varphi(\mathcal{A}_G^\Xi)$, and obtain a trivially equivalent formula $\varphi'(\mathcal{A}_G^\Xi)$ by substituting each quantified subformula $\exists x(\rho)$ in it with $\exists x \left(\left(\bigvee_{p \in \Xi} p(x) \right) \wedge \rho \right)$.

Hence, we are stating that each quantified variable in $\varphi(\mathcal{A}_G^\Xi)$ correspond to a position in which there is a stencil.

To obtain a $FO_{(\Sigma, M)}$ formula ξ, such that $L(\xi) = L(G)$, we take $\varphi'(\mathcal{A}_G^\Xi)$, and substitute in it every subformula $p(x)$ with $\sigma_p(x)$, for each $p \in \Xi$, and variable x. □

6 Conclusion

To the best of our knowledge OPLs are the largest family among the many families of structured CFLs to enjoy closure w.r.t. most fundamental language operations and to be characterized in terms of a MSO logic that naturally extends the classic one for regular languages. In this paper we have introduced OPEs as an extension of Kleene's REs. We have shown that languages defined by OPEs coincide with OPLs and that FO-definable OPLs are those defined by SF OPEs and are NC, in sharp contrast with comparable results framed in the context of tree-languages [21,35]. Together with previous partial results [15,24] and the fact that linear NC OPLs are first-order definable (Sect. 5.1), they support our conjecture that OPLs jointly with our MSO and FO logics, perfectly extend the classic results of regular languages. Figure 4 summarizes past, present and "future" results on OPLs and their logics.

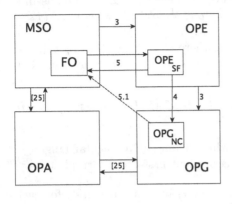

Fig. 4. The relations among the various characterizations of OPLs and their aperiodic subclass.

The figure immediately suggests a first further research step, i.e., making the internal triangle a square, as well as the external one: we conjecture that once the concept of NC OPLs has been put in the appropriate framework, a further characterization thereof in terms of a suitable subclass of OPAs should be possible but so far we did not pursue such an option.

The further goal that we wish to pursue is the complete reproduction of the historical path that, for regular languages, lead from the first characterization in terms of MSO logic to the restricted case of FO characterization of NC regular languages, to the temporal logic case which in turn is first-order complete, and, ultimately, to the success of model checking techniques.

Some proposals of temporal logic extension of the classical linear or branching time ones to cope with the typical nesting structure of CF languages have been already offered in the literature. E.g., [1,4,6] present different cases of temporal logics extended to deal with VPLs; they also prove FO-completeness of such logics but do not afford the relation between FO and MSO versions of their logics; see also [3]. A first example of temporal logic for OPLs and a related model checking algorithm have also been provided in [9].

Given that most, if not all, of the CF languages for practical applications are aperiodic, the final goal of building verification tools that cover a much wider application field than that of regular languages –and of VPLs too– does not seem unreachable.

Acknowledgments. We are grateful to the reviewers for their careful reading and suggestions.

References

1. Alur, R., Arenas, M., Barceló, P., Etessami, K., Immerman, N., Libkin, L.: First-order and temporal logics for nested words. In: Logical Methods in Computer Science, vol. 4, no. 4 (2008)
2. Alur, R., Madhusudan, P.: Adding nesting structure to words. J. ACM **56**(3), 1–43 (2009)
3. Alur, R., Bouajjani, A., Esparza, J.: Model checking procedural programs. Handbook of Model Checking, pp. 541–572. Springer, Cham (2018). https://doi.org/10.1007/978-3-319-10575-8_17
4. Alur, R., Chaudhuri, S., Madhusudan, P.: Software model checking using languages of nested trees. ACM Trans. Program. Lang. Syst. **33**(5), 15:1–15:45 (2011). https://doi.org/10.1145/2039346.2039347
5. Autebert, J.-M., Berstel, J., Boasson, L.: Context-free languages and pushdown automata. In: Rozenberg, G., Salomaa, A. (eds.) Handbook of Formal Languages, pp. 111–174. Springer, Heidelberg (1997). https://doi.org/10.1007/978-3-642-59136-5_3
6. Bozzelli, L., Sánchez, C.: Visibly linear temporal logic. In: Demri, S., Kapur, D., Weidenbach, C. (eds.) IJCAR 2014. LNCS (LNAI), vol. 8562, pp. 418–433. Springer, Cham (2014). https://doi.org/10.1007/978-3-319-08587-6_33
7. von Braunmühl, B., Verbeek, R.: Input-driven languages are recognized in log n space. In: Karpinski, M. (ed.) FCT 1983. LNCS, vol. 158, pp. 40–51. Springer, Heidelberg (1983). https://doi.org/10.1007/3-540-12689-9_92
8. Büchi, J.R.: Weak second-order arithmetic and finite automata. Math. Log. Q. **6**(1–6), 66–92 (1960)
9. Chiari, M., Mandrioli, D., Pradella, M.: Temporal logic and model checking for operator precedence languages. In: Orlandini, A., Zimmermann, M. (eds.) Proceedings Ninth International Symposium on Games, Automata, Logics, and Formal Verification, GandALF 2018, Saarbrücken, Germany, 26–28th September 2018. EPTCS, vol. 277, pp. 161–175 (2018). https://doi.org/10.4204/EPTCS.277.12
10. Crespi Reghizzi, S., Guida, G., Mandrioli, D.: Noncounting context-free languages. J. ACM **25**, 571–580 (1978)
11. Crespi Reghizzi, S., Guida, G., Mandrioli, D.: Operator precedence grammars and the noncounting property. SICOMP: SIAM J. Comput. **10**, 174–191 (1981)
12. Crespi Reghizzi, S., Mandrioli, D.: Operator precedence and the visibly pushdown property. J. Comput. Syst. Sci. **78**(6), 1837–1867 (2012)
13. Crespi Reghizzi, S., Mandrioli, D., Martin, D.F.: Algebraic properties of operator precedence languages. Inf. Control **37**(2), 115–133 (1978)
14. Crespi Reghizzi, S., Pradella, M.: Beyond operator-precedence grammars and languages. J. Comput. Syst. Sci. (2020). to appear
15. Crespi Reghizzi, S., Mandrioli, D.: A class of grammar generating non-counting languages. Inf. Process. Lett. **7**(1), 24–26 (1978). https://doi.org/10.1016/0020-0190(78)90033-9
16. Diekert, V., Gastin, P.: First-order definable languages. In: Logic and Automata: History and Perspectives, Texts in Logic and Games, pp. 261–306. Amsterdam University Press (2008)
17. Elgot, C.C.: Decision problems of finite automata design and related arithmetics. Trans. Am. Math. Soc. **98**(1), 21–52 (1961)
18. Ésik, Z., Iván, S.: Aperiodicity in tree automata. In: Bozapalidis, S., Rahonis, G. (eds.) CAI 2007. LNCS, vol. 4728, pp. 189–207. Springer, Heidelberg (2007). https://doi.org/10.1007/978-3-540-75414-5_12

19. Floyd, R.W.: Syntactic analysis and operator precedence. J. ACM **10**(3), 316–333 (1963)

20. Harrison, M.A.: Introduction to Formal Language Theory. Addison Wesley, Boston (1978)

21. Heuter, U.: First-order properties of trees, star-free expressions, and aperiodicity. ITA **25**, 125–145 (1991). https://doi.org/10.1051/ita/1991250201251

22. Langholm, T.: A descriptive characterisation of linear languages. J. Log. Lang. Inf. **15**(3), 233–250 (2006). https://doi.org/10.1007/s10849-006-9016-z

23. Lautemann, C., Schwentick, T., Thérien, D.: Logics for context-free languages. In: Pacholski, L., Tiuryn, J. (eds.) CSL 1994. LNCS, vol. 933, pp. 205–216. Springer, Heidelberg (1995). https://doi.org/10.1007/BFb0022257

24. Lonati, V., Mandrioli, D., Panella, F., Pradella, M.: First-order logic definability of free languages. In: Beklemishev, L.D., Musatov, D.V. (eds.) CSR 2015. LNCS, vol. 9139, pp. 310–324. Springer, Cham (2015). https://doi.org/10.1007/978-3-319-20297-6_20

25. Lonati, V., Mandrioli, D., Panella, F., Pradella, M.: Operator precedence languages: their automata-theoretic and logic characterization. SIAM J. Comput. **44**(4), 1026–1088 (2015)

26. Mandrioli, D., Pradella, M.: Generalizing input-driven languages: theoretical and practical benefits. Comput. Sci. Rev. **27**, 61–87 (2018). https://doi.org/10.1016/j.cosrev.2017.12.001

27. McNaughton, R.: Parenthesis grammars. J. ACM **14**(3), 490–500 (1967)

28. McNaughton, R., Papert, S.: Counter-Free Automata. MIT Press, Cambridge (1971)

29. Nowotka, D., Srba, J.: Height-deterministic pushdown automata. In: Kučera, L., Kučera, A. (eds.) MFCS 2007. LNCS, vol. 4708, pp. 125–134. Springer, Heidelberg (2007). https://doi.org/10.1007/978-3-540-74456-6_13

30. Pin, J.: Logic on words. In: Current Trends in Theoretical Computer Science, pp. 254–273 (2001)

31. Floyd, C.: Theory and practice of software development. In: Mosses, P.D., Nielsen, M., Schwartzbach, M.I. (eds.) CAAP 1995. LNCS, vol. 915, pp. 25–41. Springer, Heidelberg (1995). https://doi.org/10.1007/3-540-59293-8_185

32. Rabinovich, A.: A proof of Kamp's theorem. Log. Methods Comput. Sci. **10**(1), 1–16 (2014). https://doi.org/10.2168/LMCS-10(1:14)2014

33. Salomaa, A.K.: Formal Languages. Academic Press, New York (1973)

34. Thatcher, J.: Characterizing derivation trees of context-free grammars through a generalization of finite automata theory. J. Comput. Syst. Sci. **1**, 317–322 (1967)

35. Thomas, W.: Logical aspects in the study of tree languages. In: Courcelle, B. (ed.) 9th Colloquium on Trees in Algebra and Programming, CAAP 1984, Bordeaux, France, March 5–7, 1984, Proceedings, pp. 31–50. Cambridge University Press (1984)

36. Trakhtenbrot, B.A.: Finite automata and logic of monadic predicates. Doklady Akademii Nauk SSR **140**, 326–329 (1961). (in Russian)

Formal Verification of Parallel Stream Compaction and Summed-Area Table Algorithms

Mohsen Safari[✉] and Marieke Huisman

Formal Methods and Tools, University of Twente, Enschede, The Netherlands
{m.safari,m.huisman}@utwente.nl

Abstract. Dedicated many-core processors such as GPGPUs, enable programmers to design and implement parallel algorithms to optimize performance. The stream compaction and summed-area table algorithms are two examples where parallel versions have been proposed in the literature with substantial speed ups compared to sequential counterparts.

Since these two algorithms are widely used, their correctness is of the utmost importance, i.e., the algorithms must be functionally correct and their implementations must be memory safe. These algorithms use the parallel prefix sum algorithm internally. In our previous work, we verified two parallel prefix sum algorithms. In this paper, we show how we can reuse a verified sub-function (i.e., prefix sum) to prove more complicated algorithms (i.e., stream compaction and summed area table) in a modular way with less effort. Moreover, we demonstrate that it is feasible in practice to verify larger case studies by building the verification of the complicated algorithm on top of the basic one.

To show the correctness of the algorithms, we use deductive program verification based on permission-based separation logic, which is supported by the program verifier VerCors. To the best of our knowledge, we are the first to verify *functional correctness* of the *parallel* stream compaction and summed-area table algorithms for an arbitrary array size, using *tool support*.

Keywords: GPU verification · Deductive verification · Separation logic

1 Introduction

Many parallel algorithms have been proposed for optimizing performance by exploiting the new parallel architectures, and parallelizing sequential algorithms is an active area of research. General Purpose Graphics Processing Units (GPG-PUs) are one of the promising parallel architectures, where many threads execute the same instructions, but on different data (known as SIMD). Stream compaction and summed-area table [11] algorithms are two examples where the parallel (GPU-based) implementations [3,12–14,24] outperform the sequential (CPU-based) counterparts.

© Springer Nature Switzerland AG 2020
V. K. I. Pun et al. (Eds.): ICTAC 2020, LNCS 12545, pp. 181–199, 2020.
https://doi.org/10.1007/978-3-030-64276-1_10

Stream compaction reduces an input array to a smaller array by removing undesired elements. This is an important primitive operation on GPUs, because a variety of applications such as collision detection and sparse matrix compression rely on it. The reduction in size by eliminating undesired elements is useful because (1) the computation can be done more efficiently by not wasting the computation power on undesired elements and, (2) it greatly reduces the transfer costs between the CPU and GPU, especially for applications where data transfer between CPU and GPU is frequent.

A summed-area table is a two-dimensional (2D) table generated from a 2D input array where each entry in the table is the sum of all values in the square defined by the entry location and the upper-left corner in the input array. Generating such a table is useful in computer graphics and image processing [13].

Since these two algorithms are widely used in practice (also as a building block in other applications), their correctness is of the utmost importance. This means not only that the algorithms should be memory and thread safe (e.g., free of data races[1]), *but also* that they should be functionally correct, i.e., they should actually produce the result we expect. Concretely, functional correctness for stream compaction means that the result must be the compacted input array with exactly the desired elements. In case of the summed-area table, functional correctness means that the result must be a table, the same size as the input, where each entry contains the sum of all elements in the square defined by the entry location and the upper-left corner in the input.

The two algorithms exploit the prefix sum algorithm, which takes an array of integers and, for each element, computes the sum of the previous elements. In our previous work [23], we verified data race-freedom and functional correctness of two parallel prefix sum algorithms.

In this paper, we investigate (1) how we can profit from already verified sub-functions (i.e., prefix sum) to prove the stream compaction and summed-area table algorithms; i.e., how much effort is needed to adapt the specifications from [23] for the verification of these two algorithms; and (2) how much time is needed to verify them in comparison to the verification of our previous work on prefix sum. We believe such case studies are important to gain more insight in the effort that is needed to verify complex algorithms and how more automation can be added to the verification process. In general, proving functional correctness of parallel algorithms is a challenging task. In particular, proving functional correctness of these two algorithms is challenging because (1) in the stream compaction algorithm, the input of the prefix sum sub-function is an array of flag and the output is used as indices of elements in another array. Therefore, additional properties should be proved to reason about the prefix sum result to be safely used as indices; and (2) in the summed-area table algorithm, in addition to the prefix sum, the transposition operation is used intermittently. Due to these intermediate steps, we should store the manipulated values and

---

[1] A data race is a situation when two or more threads may access the same memory location simultaneously, and at least one of them is a write.

establish a formal relation between the values of each step in order to reason about the final result (i.e, output).

To prove memory safety and functional correctness of the stream compaction and summed-area table algorithms, we use VerCors [5], which is a deductive program verifier for concurrent programs. Deductive program verification is a static approach to verify program properties by augmenting the source code with pre- and postconditions. To guide verification, intermediate annotations are added to capture the intermediate properties of the program. Then, in our case, the annotated code is translated into proof obligations (via Viper [20]), which are discharged to an automated theorem prover; the SMT solver Z3 [19].

To the best of our knowledge, this is the only *tool-supported* verification of *data race-freedom* and *functional correctness* of the two parallel algorithms for any *arbitrary size of input*. None of the existing other approaches to analyze GPU applications is able to verify similar properties. Most approaches are dynamic [10,18,21,22,25], and only aim to find bugs. Other existing static verification techniques [2,9,15,17] either require a bound on the input size, or they do not fully model all aspects of GPU programming, such as the use of barriers. We show that the verification of larger case studies is feasible, by adding the verification of the more complex algorithm on top of the basic one, not only in theory, but also in practice using tool support. Moreover, our work enables the verification of other parallel algorithms that are built on top of the stream compaction and summed-area table algorithms, such as collision detection and box filtering.

Contributions. The main contributions of this paper are:

1. We provide a tool-supported proof of data race-freedom and functional correctness of the parallel stream compaction algorithm for any input size.
2. We show that the parallel summed-area table algorithm is data race-free and functionally correct for arbitrary input sizes using tool support.
3. We demonstrate how much effort and time needed in practice to verify complicated algorithms by reusing verified algorithms in a layered manner.

Organization. Section 2 discusses related work and Sect. 3 explains the necessary background. Sections 4 and 5 describe how to specify and verify the correctness of the stream compaction and summed-area table algorithms, respectively. Section 6 concludes the paper.

2   Related Work

GPGPU programming is becoming more popular because of its potential to increase the performance of programs. However, it is also highly error-prone due to its inherent parallization. Therefore, the demand for guaranteeing correctness of GPGPU programs is growing. There are only a few approaches to reason about GPGPU programs; most of them focus on finding data races.

In dynamic analysis, a program is instrumented to record memory accesses. Then, by running the instrumented program, data races might be identified (e.g., cuda-memcheck [21], Oclgrind [22] and GRace [25]). This technique depends on concrete inputs and cannot guarantee data race-freedom. Dynamic symbolic execution is a combination of static and dynamic analysis to combine concrete and symbolic inputs to find data races (e.g., GKLEE [18] and KLEE-CL [10]).

Static approaches analyse the complete state space of a program without running it. Deductive program verification as in VerCors, is a static approach, where a program is annotated with intermediate (invariant) properties. Tools such as PUG [17] and GPUVerify [2] use static analysis, but require less annotations. Except VerCors and VeriFast [15], none of these tools can reason about functional correctness of parallel programs. VeriFast aims at proving functional correctness of single-threaded and multi-threaded C and Java programs, but it is not specifically tailored to reason about GPGPU programs.

There is no previous work on formally verifying the parallel stream compaction and summed-area table algorithms on GPUs. To verify these two algorithms, the parallel prefix sum algorithms need to be verified, which has been done by Chong et al. [9] in addition to our previous work [23]. Chong et al. verify data race-freedom and propose a method to verify functional correctness of four different parallel prefix sum algorithms for a fixed input size. They show that if a parallel prefix sum algorithm is proven to be data race-free, then the correctness can be established by generating one test case. Then they use GPUVerify to prove data race-freedom of the parallel prefix sum algorithms for a fixed input size. In our previous work [23], we prove data-race freedom and functional correctness of two different parallel prefix sum algorithms using the VerCors verifier for any arbitrary size of input. We benefit from ghost variables to reason about in-place prefix sum algorithms. In our opinion, the advantages of our approach is that our verification approach for the prefix sum can be reused for these two new algorithms, while Chong would not be able to reuse his prefix sum approach to verify the parallel stream compaction and summed-area table algorithms.

3   Background

This section describes the program verifier VerCors and the logic behind it by illustrating an example. It then briefly discusses the parallel prefix sum algorithm which is used in both parallel stream compaction and summed-area table algorithms.

3.1   VerCors

VerCors[2] is a verifier to specify and verify (concurrent and parallel) programs written in a high-level language such as (subsets of) Java, C, OpenCL, OpenMP and PVL, where PVL is VerCors' internal language for prototyping new features. VerCors can be used to verify memory safety (e.g., data race-freedom) and

---

[2] The tool is available at: https://github.com/utwente-fmt/vercors.

List. 1. A simple annotated OpenCL program

```
1    /*@ context_everywhere array != NULL && array.length == size;
2         requires tid != size−1 ? Perm(array[tid+1], read) : Perm(array[0], read);
3         ensures Perm(array[tid], write);
4         ensures tid != size−1 ==> array[tid] == \old(array[tid+1]);
5         ensures tid == size−1 ==> array[tid] == \old(array[0]); @*/
6    __kernel void leftRotation(int array[], int size) {
7       int temp;
8       int tid = get_global_id(0);   // get the thread id
9       if (tid != size−1) { temp = array[tid+1]; } else { temp = array[0]; }
10
11      /*@ requires  tid != size−1 ? Perm(array[tid+1], read) : Perm(array[0], read);
12          ensures Perm(array[tid], write); @*/
13      barrier(CLK_GLOBAL_MEM_FENCE);
14      array[tid] = temp;
15   }
```

functional correctness of programs. The programs are annotated with pre- and postconditions in permission-based separation logic [1,7]. Permissions are used to capture which heap memory locations may be accessed by which threads, and are used to guarantee thread safety. Permissions are written as fractional values in the interval $(0, 1]$ (cf. Boyland [8]): any fraction in the interval $(0, 1)$ indicates a read permission, while 1 indicates a write permission.

Blom et al. [6] show how to use permission-based separation logic to reason about GPU kernels including barriers. We illustrate this logic by an example. Listing 1 shows a specification of a kernel that rotates the elements of an array to the left[3]. It is specified by a thread-level specification. To specify permissions, we use predicate $Perm(L, \pi)$ where L is a heap location and π a fractional value in the interval $(0, 1]$[4]. Pre- and postconditions, (denoted by keywords **requires** and **ensures**, respectively in lines 2–5), must hold at the beginning and the end of the function, respectively. The keyword `context_everywhere` is used to specify an invariant (line 1) that must hold throughout the function. As preconditions, each thread has read permission to its right neighbor (except thread "size-1" which has read permission to the first index) in line 2. The postconditions indicate (1) each thread has write permission to its location (line 3) and (2) the result of the function as a left rotation of all elements (lines 4–5). Each thread is responsible for one array location and it first reads its right location (line 9). Then it synchronizes in the barrier (line 13). When a thread reaches a barrier, it has to fulfill the barrier preconditions, and then it may assume the barrier postconditions. Thus barrier postconditions must follow from barrier preconditions. In this case, each thread gives up read permission on its right location and obtains write permission on its "own" location at index *tid* (lines 11–12). After that, each thread writes the value read before to its "own" location (line

---

[3] We assume there is one workgroup and "size" threads inside it.
[4] The keywords **read** and **write** can also be used instead of fractions in VerCors.

Input
3	6	1	7	2	4	0	9

Exclusive Prefix Sum

| 0 | 3 | 9 | 10 | 17 | 19 | 23 | 23 |

Inclusive Prefix Sum

| 3 | 9 | 10 | 17 | 19 | 23 | 23 | 32 |

Fig. 1. An example of exclusive and inclusive prefix sum of an input.

14). Note that the keyword \old is used for an expression to refer to the value of that expression before entering a function (lines 4–5). The OpenCL example (Listing 1) is translated into the PVL language of VerCors, using two parallel nested blocks. The outer block indicates the number of workgroups and the inner one shows the number of threads per workgroup (see [6] for more details). In this case study, we reason at the level of the PVL encoding directly, but it is straightforward to adapt this to the verification of the OpenCL kernel.

3.2   Prefix Sum

Figure 1 illustrates an example of the prefix sum operation. This operation is a basic block used in both stream compaction and summed-area table algorithms, defined as: given an array of integers, the prefix sum of the array is another array with the same size such that each element is the sum of all previous elements. An (inclusive) prefix sum algorithm has the following input and output:

– INPUT: an array *Input* of integers of size N.

– OUTPUT: an array *Output* of size N such that $Output[i] = \sum_{t=0}^{i} Input[t]$ for $0 \leq i < N$.

In the exclusive prefix sum algorithm, where the ith element is excluded from the summation, the output is as follows:

– OUTPUT: an array *Output* of size N such that $Output[i] = \sum_{t=0}^{i-1} Input[t]$ for $0 \leq i < N$.

Blelloch [4] introduced an exclusive parallel in-place prefix sum algorithm and Kogge-Stone [16] proposed an inclusive parallel in-place prefix sum algorithm. These two parallel versions are frequently used in practice (as a primitive operation in libraries AMD APP SDK[5], and NVIDIA CUDA SDK[6]).

4   Verification of Parallel Stream Compaction Algorithm

This section describes the stream compaction algorithm and how we verify it. First, we explain the algorithm and its encoding in VerCors. Then, we prove data

---

[5] http://developer.amd.com/tools/heterogeneous-computing/amd-accelerated-parallel-processing-app-sdk.

[6] https://developer.nvidia.com/gpu-computing-sdk.

Algorithm 1. Stream Compaction Algorithm

1: **function** STREAM_COMPACTION(**int**[] *Input*, **int**[] *Output*, **int**[] *Flag*, **int**[] *ExPre*, **int** *N*)
2:    **Par**(*tid* = 0.. *N*)
3:       EXCLUSIVE_PREFIXSUM(*Flag*, *ExPre*, *tid*, *N*);
4:       **Barrier**(*tid*);
5:       **if** *Flag*[*tid*] == *1* **then**
6:          *Output*[*ExPre*[*tid*]] = *Input*[*tid*];

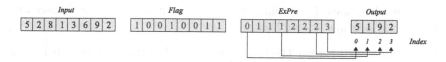

Fig. 2. An example of stream compaction of size 8.

race-freedom and we show how we prove functional correctness of the algorithm. Moreover, we show how we can reuse the verified prefix sum from our previous work [23] to reason about the stream compaction algorithm. We explain the main ideas mostly by using pictures instead of presenting the full specification[7].

4.1   Stream Compaction Algorithm

Given an array of integers as input and an array of booleans that flag which elements are desired, stream compaction returns an array that holds only those elements of the input whose flags are true. An algorithm is a stream compaction if it satisfies the following:

- INPUT: two arrays, *Input* of integers and *Flag* of booleans of size *N*.
- OUTPUT: an array *Output* of size *M* ($M \leq N$) such that
  - $\forall j. \, 0 \leq j < M: Output[j] = t \Rightarrow \exists i. \, 0 \leq i < N: Input[i] = t \wedge Flag[i].$
  - $\forall i. \, 0 \leq i < N: Input[i] = t \wedge Flag[i] \Rightarrow \exists j. \, 0 \leq j < M: Output[j] = t.$
  - $\forall i, j. \, 0 \leq i, j < N: (Flag[i] \wedge Flag[j] \wedge i < j \iff (\exists k, l. \, 0 \leq k, l < M:$
    $Output[k] = Input[i] \wedge Output[l] = Input[j] \wedge k < l)).$

Algorithm 1 shows the pseudocode of the parallel algorithm and Fig. 2 presents an example of stream compaction. Initially we have an input and a flag array (implemented as integers of zeros and ones). To keep the flagged elements and discard the rest, first we calculate the exclusive prefix sum (from [4]) of the flag array. Interestingly, for the elements whose flags are 1, the exclusive prefix sum indicates their location (index) in the output array. In the implementation, the input of the prefix sum function is *Flag* and the output is stored in *ExPre* (line 3). Then all threads are synchronized by the barrier in line 4, after which all the desired elements are stored in the output array (lines 5–6).

---

[7] The full specification is available at https://github.com/Safari1991/Prefixsum-Applications.

4.2 Data Race-Freedom

To prove data race-freedom, we specify how threads access shared resources by adding permission annotations to the code. In Algorithm 1, we have several arrays that are shared among threads. There are three locations in the algorithm where permissions can be redistributed: before Algorithm 1 as preconditions, in the exclusive prefix sum function as postconditions and in the barrier (redistribution of permissions). Figure 3 visualizes the permission pattern for those shared arrays, which reflects the permission annotations in the code according to these three locations. The explanation of the permission patterns in each array in these three locations is as follows:

- *Input*: since each thread (*tid*) only needs read permission (line 6 in Algorithm 1), we define each thread to have read permissions to its "own" location at index *tid* throughout the algorithm (Fig. 3). This also ensures that the values in *Input* cannot be changed.
- *Flag*: since *Flag* is the input of the exclusive prefix sum function, its permission pattern at the beginning of Algorithm 1 must match the permission preconditions of the exclusive prefix sum function. Thus, following the preconditions of this function (see [23]), we define the permissions such that each thread (*tid*) has read permissions to its "own" location (Fig. 3: left). The exclusive prefix sum function returns the same permissions for *Flag* in its postconditions (Fig. 3: middle). Since, each thread needs read permission in line 5 of Algorithm 1, we keep the same permission pattern in the barrier as well (Fig. 3: right).
- *ExPre*: since *ExPre* is the output of the exclusive prefix sum function, the permission pattern at the beginning of Algorithm 1 should match the permission preconditions of the exclusive prefix sum function (specified in [23]). Thus, each thread (*tid* < half *ExPre* size) has write permissions to locations $2 \times tid$ and $2 \times tid + 1$ (Fig. 3: left). As postcondition of the exclusive prefix sum function (specified in [23]), each thread has write permission to its "own" location in *ExPre* (Fig. 3: middle). Since each thread only needs read permission in line 6 of Algorithm 1, we change the permission pattern from write to read in the barrier (Fig. 3: right).
- *Output*: it is only used in line 6 of Algorithm 1 and its permissions are according to the values in *ExPre*. Thus, the initial permissions for *Output* can be arbitrary and in the barrier, we specify the permissions such that each thread (*tid*) has write permission in location *ExPre*[*tid*] if its flag is 1 (indicated by t_f in Fig. 3: right).

4.3 Functional Correctness

Proving functional correctness of the parallel stream compaction algorithm consists of two parts. First, we prove that the elements in the exclusive prefix sum function (*ExPre*) are in the range of the output, thus they can be used safely as indices in *Output* (i.e., line 6 in Algorithm 1). Second, we prove that *Output*

Locations / Arrays	At the beginning of the algorithm	After the exclusive prefix sum	After the barrier
Input	Rt_0 Rt_1 Rt Rt_3 Rt_4 Rt_5 Rt_6 Rt_7	Rt_0 Rt_1 Rt Rt_3 Rt_4 Rt_5 Rt_6 Rt_7	Rt_0 Rt_1 Rt Rt_3 Rt_4 Rt_5 Rt_6 Rt_7
Flag	Rt_0 Rt_1 Rt Rt_3 Rt_4 Rt_5 Rt_6 Rt_7	Rt_0 Rt_1 Rt Rt_3 Rt_4 Rt_5 Rt_6 Rt_7	Rt_0 Rt_1 Rt Rt_3 Rt_4 Rt_5 Rt_6 Rt_7
ExPre	Wt_0 Wt_0 Wt_1 Wt_3 Wt Wt Wt_3 Wt_3	Wt_0 Wt_1 Wt Wt_3 Wt_4 Wt_5 Wt_6 Wt_7	Rt_0 Rt_1 Rt Rt_3 Rt_4 Rt_5 Rt_6 Rt_7
Output	Wt_0 Wt_1 Wt Wt_3	Wt_0 Wt_1 Wt Wt_3	Wt_1 Wt_1 Wt_1 Wt_1
Index	0 1 3	0 1 3	0 1 3

Fig. 3. Permission pattern of arrays in stream compaction algorithm corresponding to Fig. 2; Rt_i / Wt_i means thread i has read/write permission. Green color indicates permission changes. (Color figure online)

contains all the elements whose flags are 1, and does not contain any elements whose flags are not 1. Moreover, the order of desired elements, the ones whose flags are 1, in *Input* must be the same as in *Output*.

To prove both parts, we use ghost variables[8], defined as sequences. There are some advantages of using ghost variables as sequences: (1) it is not required to define permissions over sequences; (2) we can define pure functions over sequences to mimic the actual computations over concrete variables; (3) we can easily prove desired properties (e.g., functional properties) over ghost sequences; and (4) ghost variables can act as histories for concrete variables whose values might change during the program. This gives us a global view (of program states) of how the concrete variables change to their final value. Concretely, we define two ghost variables, *inp_seq* and *flag_seq* as sequences of integers to capture all values in arrays *Input* and *Flag*, respectively. Since values in *Input* and *Flag* do not change during the algorithm[9], *inp_seq* and *flag_seq* are always the same as *Input* and *Flag*[10].

First, to reuse of the exclusive prefix sum specification (line 3 in Algorithm 1) from our previous work [23], we should consider two points: (1) the input to the exclusive prefix sum (*Flag*) in this paper is restricted to 0 and 1; and (2) the elements in the exclusive prefix sum function (*ExPre*) should be safely usable as indices in *Output* (i.e., line 6 in Algorithm 1). Therefore, we use VerCors to prove some suitable properties to reason about the values of the prefix sum of the flag. For space reasons, we show the properties without discussing the proofs here. The first property that we prove in VerCors is that the sum of a sequence of zeros and ones is non-negative[11]:

Property 4.1

$$(\forall i. 0 \leq i < |flag\_seq|: flag\_seq[i] = 0 \; vee \; flag\_seq[i] = 1) \Rightarrow$$
$$intsum(flag\_seq) \geq 0.$$

---

[8] Ghost variables are not part of the algorithm and are used only for verification purposes.

[9] Note that threads only have read permissions over *Input* and *Flag*.

[10] Thus, properties for *inp_seq* and *flag_seq* also hold for *Input* and *Flag*.

[11] The **intsum** operation sums up all elements in a sequence.

List. 2. The *filter* function

```
1   /*@ requires |inp_seq| == |flag_seq|;
2       requires (\forall int i; 0 ≤ i && i < |flag_seq|; flag_seq[i]==0 || flag_seq[i]==1);
3       ensures |\result| == intsum(flag_seq);
4       ensures 0 ≤ |\result| && |\result| ≤ |flag_seq|; @*/
5   static pure seq<int> filter(seq<int> inp_seq, seq<int> flag_seq) = |inp_seq|>0 ?
6       head(flag_seq)==1 ? seq<int>{head(inp_seq)} + filter(tail(inp_seq), tail(flag_seq))
7       : filter(tail(inp_seq), tail(flag_seq)) : seq<int>{};
```

We need Property 4.1 since the prefix sum for each element is the sum of all previous elements. We benefit from the first property to prove in VerCors that all the elements in the exclusive prefix sum of a sequence *flag_seq* (only zeros and ones) are greater than or equal to zero and less than or equal to the sum of elements in *flag_seq*[12]:

Property 4.2

$$(\forall i.0 \leq i < |flag\_seq|: flag\_seq[i] = 0 \ \lor \ flag\_seq[i] = 1) \Rightarrow$$
$$(\forall i.0 \leq i < |epsum(flag\_seq)|: epsum(flag\_seq)[i] \geq 0 \ \land$$
$$epsum(flag\_seq)[i] \leq intsum(flag\_seq)).$$

This gives the lower and upper bound of elements in the prefix sum, which are used as indices in *Output*. This property is not sufficient to prove that the elements are in the range of *Output* due to two reasons. First, an element in the prefix sum can be as large as the sum of ones in the flag. Hence, it might exceed *Output* size which is in the range 0 to $intsum(flag\_seq) - 1$. Second, we only use the elements in the prefix sum whose flags are 1. Property 4.2 does not specify those elements explicitly. Therefore, we prove another property in VerCors to explicitly specify the elements in the prefix sum whose flags are 1 as follows:

Property 4.3

$$(\forall i.0 \leq i < |flag\_seq|: flag\_seq[i] = 0 \ \lor \ flag\_seq[i] = 1) \Rightarrow$$
$$(\forall i.0 \leq i < |epsum(flag\_seq)| \ \land \ flag\_seq[i] = 1:$$
$$(epsum(flag\_seq)[i] \geq 0 \ \land \ epsum(flag\_seq)[i] < intsum(flag\_seq))).$$

Property 4.3 guarantees that the elements in the prefix sum whose flags are 1 are truly in the range of *Output*, and can be used safely as indices. Moreover, it has been proven in [23] that $epsum(flag\_seq)$ is equal to the result of the prefix sum function (i.e., *ExPre*).

Second, we reason about the final values in *Output*, using the following steps:

1. Define a ghost variable as a sequence.
2. Define a mathematical function that updates the ghost variable according to the actual computation of the algorithm.

---

[12] The **epsum** operation of a sequence returns an exclusive prefix sum of that sequence.

List. 3. The proof steps to relate *out_seq* to *Output* array

```
1   seq<int> out_seq = filter(inp_seq, flag_seq);
2   assert |out_seq| == intsum(flag_seq); // by line 4 in Listing 2
3   if(flag_seq[tid] == 1)
4       // applying Property 4.4
5       assert inp_seq[tid] == filter(inp_seq, flag_seq)[epsum(flag_seq)[tid]];
6       assert out_seq == filter(inp_seq, flag_seq); // by line 1
7       assert inp_seq[tid] == out_seq[epsum(flag_seq)[tid]]; // by lines 5-6
8       assert Output[ExPre[tid]] == Input[tid]; // by lines 5-6 in Algorithm 1
9       assert Output[ExPre[tid]] == out_seq[epsum(flag_seq)[tid]]; // by lines 7-8
```

3. Prove functional correctness over the ghost variables by defining a suitable property.
4. Relate the ghost variable to the concrete variable; i.e., prove that the elements in the ghost sequence are the same as in the actual array.

Following this approach, we define a ghost variable, *out_seq*, as a sequence of integers and a mathematical function, *filter*, as shown in Listing 2. This function computes the compacted list of an input sequence, *inp_seq*, by filtering it according to a flag sequence, *flag_seq* (where **head** returns the first element of a sequence and **tail** returns a new sequence by eliminating the first element). Thus, for each element in *inp_seq*, this function checks its flag to either add it to the result (line 6) or discard it (line 7). The function specification has two preconditions: (1) the length of both sequences is the same (line 1) and (2) each element in *flag_seq* is either 0 or 1 (lines 2). The postcondition states that the length of the compacted list (result) is the sum of all elements in *flag_seq* (line 3) which is at most the same length as *flag_seq* (line 4). We apply the *filter* function to *inp_seq* and *flag_seq* (as ghost statements) at the end of Algorithm 1 to update *out_seq*.

To reason about the values in *out_seq* and relate it to *inp_seq* and *flag_seq* we prove the following property in VerCors:

Property 4.4

$$(\forall i.0 \leq i < |flag\_seq|: flag\_seq[i] = 0 \ \vee \ flag\_seq[i] = 1) \Rightarrow$$
$$(\forall i.0 \leq i < |epsum(flag\_seq)| \ \wedge \ flag\_seq[i] = 1:$$
$$(inp\_seq[i] = filter(inp\_seq, flag\_seq)[epsum(flag\_seq)[i]])).$$

From Property 4.4, we can prove in VerCors that all elements in *inp_seq* (and *Input*) whose flags are 1 are in *out_seq* and the order is also preserved. Since we specify that the length of *out_seq* is the sum of all elements in the flag, which is the number of ones (line 4 in Listing 2), we also prove that there are no elements in *out_seq* whose flags are not 1.

The last step is to relate *out_seq* to *Output*. Listing 3 shows the proof steps which are located at the end of Algorithm 1. Through some smaller steps, and using Property 4.4 we prove in VerCors that *out_seq* and *Output* is the same

---

Algorithm 2. Summed-Area Table Algorithm

1: **function** SUMMED_AREA_TABLE(**int**[][] *Input*, **int**[][] *Temp*, **int**[][] *Output*, **int** N)
2: **for**(**int** $i = 0$; $i < N$; $i + +$)
3:   **Par**($tid = 0.. N$)   // First Prefix Sum
4:    INCLUSIVE_PREFIXSUM($Input[i]$, $Temp[i]$, $inp\_seq[i]$, $tmp1\_seq[i]$, tid, N);
5:   *Properties 1 and 2 (Table 1) hold here*
6: **Par**($tidX = 0.. N$, $tidY = 0.. N$)   // First Transposition
7:   int *temporary* = $Temp[tidX][tidY]$;
8:   **Barrier**($tidX$, $tidY$);
9:   $Temp[tidY][tidX]$ = *temporary*;
10: *tmp2_seq = transpose(tmp1_seq, 0, N)*;
11: *Properties 3 and 4 (Table 1) hold here*
12: **for**(**int** $i = 0$; $i < N$; $i + +$)
13: **Par**($tid = 0.. N$)   // Second Prefix Sum
14:   INCLUSIVE_PREFIXSUM($Temp[i]$, $Output[i]$, $tmp1\_seq[i]$, $tmp3\_seq[i]$, tid, N);
15: *Properties 5 and 6 (Table 1) hold here*
16: **Par**($tidX = 0.. N$, $tidY = 0.. N$)   // Second Transposition
17: int *temporary* = $Output[tidX][tidY]$;
18: **Barrier**($tidX$, $tidY$);
19: $Output[tidY][tidX]$ = *temporary*;
20: *out_seq = transpose(tmp3_seq, 0, N)*;
21: *Properties 7 and 8 (Table 1) hold here*

(line 9). Note that for each tid, $epsum(flag\_seq)[tid]$ is equal to $ExPre[tid]$ as proven in [23].

As we can see in this verification, we could reuse the specification of the verified prefix sum algorithm, by proving some more properties. We should note that the time we spent to verify the stream compaction algorithm is much less than the verification of the prefix sum algorithm.

5   Verification of Parallel Summed-Area Table Algorithm

This section discusses the summed-area table algorithm and its verification. As above, after describing the algorithm and its encoding in VerCors, we first prove data-race freedom and then explain how we prove functional correctness. We also show how we reuse the verified prefix sum from [23] in the verification of the summed-area table algorithm. Again, we only show the main ideas[13].

5.1   Summed-Area Table Algorithm

Given a 2D array of integers, the summed-area table is a 2D array with the same size where each entry in the output is the sum of all values in the square defined by the entry location and the upper-left corner in the input. The algorithm's input and output are specified in the following way:

---

[13] The verified specification is available at https://github.com/Safari1991/Prefixsum-Applications.

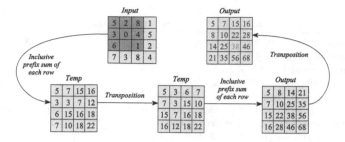

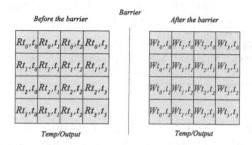

Fig. 4. An example of summed-area table of size 4×4.

Fig. 5. Permission pattern of matrix Temp/Output before and after the barrier in the transposition phase; $Rt_i, t_j / Wt_i, t_j$ means thread (i, j) has read/write permission.

– INPUT: a 2D array *Input* of integers of size $N \times M$.
– OUTPUT: a 2D array *Output* of size $N \times M$ such that

$$Output[i][j] = \sum_{t=0}^{i} \sum_{k=0}^{j} Input[t][k] \, for \, 0 \leq i < N \, and \, 0 \leq j < M.$$

Algorithm 2 shows the (annotated) pseudocode of the parallel algorithm and Fig. 4 shows an example for the summed-area table algorithm. For example, the red element 38 in *Output* is the sum of the elements in the red square in *Input*. We apply the inclusive prefix sum (from [16]) to each row of *Input* and store it in *Temp* (lines 2–4). Then, we transpose the *Temp* matrix (lines 6–9). Thereafter, we apply again the inclusive prefix sum to each row of *Temp* (lines 12–14). Finally, we transpose the matrix again, resulting in matrix *Output* (lines 16–19). The parallel transpositions after each prefix sum are determined by creating 2D thread blocks for each element of the matrix (lines 6–9 and 16–19) where each thread $(tidI, tidJ)$ stores its value into location $(tidJ, tidI)$ by first writing into a *temporary* variable (lines 7 and 17) and then synchronizing in the barrier (lines 8 and 18).

5.2 Data Race-Freedom

Since data race-freedom of the parallel inclusive prefix sum has been verified in our previous work [23], we only show data-race freedom of the transposition

List. 4. The *transpose* function

```
1    /*@ requires |xs| == N && (\forall int j; 0 ≤ j && j < N; |xs[j]| == N);
2        requires i ≥ 0 && i ≤ N;
3        ensures |\result| == N − i;
4        ensures (\forall int j; 0 ≤ j && j < N − i; |\result[j]| == N);
5        ensures (\forall int j; 0 ≤ j && j < N − i;
6            (\forall int k; 0 ≤ k && k < N; \result[j][k] == xs[k][i+j])); @*/
7    static pure seq<int> transpose(seq<seq<int>> xs, int i, int N) = i < N ?
8        seq<seq<int>> {transpose_helper(xs, 0, i, N)} + transpose(xs, i+1, N) :
9        seq<int> {};
10
11   /*@ requires |xs| == |N| && (\forall int j; 0 ≤ j && j < N; |xs[j]| == N);
12       requires k ≥ 0 && k ≤ N && i ≥ 0 && i < N;
13       ensures |\result| == N − k;
14       ensures (\forall int j; 0≤j && j<|\result|; \result[j] == xs[k + j][i]); @*/
15   static pure seq<int> transpose_helper(seq<seq<int>> xs, int k, int i, int N) =
16       k < N ? seq<int> {xs[k][i]} + transpose_helper(xs, k+1, i, N) : seq<int> {};
```

phases in Algorithm 2. As an example, Fig. 5 illustrates the permission pattern in a matrix *Temp* (and also *Output*) of size 4×4. Before the barrier (lines 7 and 14 in Algorithm 2) each thread (*tidI*, *tidJ*) has read permission in location (*tidI*, *tidJ*) in *Temp* (and also *Output*). In the barrier, the permission pattern changes such that each thread (*tidI*, *tidJ*) has write permission to location (*tidJ*, *tidI*). In this way, each thread (*tidI*, *tidJ*) can read its value from location (*tidI*, *tidJ*) (before the barrier) and write that value into location (*tidJ*, *tidI*) (after the barrier) safely.

5.3 Functional Correctness

Next, we discuss functional correctness of the parallel summed-area table algorithm. The approach to verify this algorithm is the same as before. First of all, we define two ghost variables: *inp_seq* is a sequence of sequences that captures the elements in *Input*, and *tmp1_seq* stores the inclusive prefix sum of elements in *Input* (see Fig. 6: step 1).

After applying the first prefix sum function, Properties 1 and 2 from Table 1 hold (line 5 in Algorithm 2). Property 1 specifies that *tmp1_seq* contains the inclusive prefix sum of the elements in *inp_seq*[14]. Property 2 shows the relation between *tmp1_seq*, and the actual array, *Temp*. We obtain these properties from the postconditions of the verified inclusive prefix sum (see [23]).

Now, we define a mathematical function *transpose*, as shown in Listing 4. This function computes the transposition of a sequence of sequences. The *transpose* function creates a sequence for each column i (starting from 0) as a new row i in the result, using a helper function (*transpose_helper*) to collect the *ith* elements of each row (in the input sequence)[15]. The preconditions of both functions

---

[14] The ipsum operation of a sequence returns an inclusive prefix sum of that sequence.
[15] Both functions are recursive and they are invoked with i and k equal to zero.

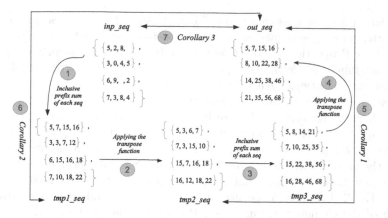

Fig. 6. An example of phases in the summed-area table algorithm over sequences as ghost variables. The sequences and functions capture the same arrays and computations as in Fig. 4.

specify the length of the input sequence and the range of the parameter's integer variables (lines 1–2 and 10–11). The postcondition of the *transpose_helper* function (lines 12–13) indicates that the result has the same size as each row and the return sequence contains the *ith* element of each row in the input sequence. The postcondition of the *transpose* function (lines 3–6) indicates that the result has the same size and indeed is the transposition of the input sequence.

Table 1. List of all properties in the summed-area table algorithm. Even numbers indicate the relation between the ghost and concrete variables. Odd numbers shows the relation between the ghost variables before and after each phase of the algorithm.

No.	Mathematical description of properties
1	$(\forall i.0 \leq i < |inp\_seq|: (\forall j.0 \leq j < |inp\_seq[i]|:$ $tmp1\_seq[i][j] = ipsum(inp\_seq[i])[j] = \sum_{t=0}^{j} inp\_seq[i][t]))$
2	$(\forall i.0 \leq i < |tmp1\_seq|: (\forall j.0 \leq j < |tmp1\_seq[i]|: tmp1\_seq[i][j] = Temp[i][j]))$
3	$(\forall i.0 \leq i < |tmp1\_seq|: (\forall j.0 \leq j < |tmp1\_seq[i]|: tmp2\_seq[i][j] = tmp1\_seq[j][i]))$
4	$(\forall i.0 \leq i < |tmp2\_seq|: (\forall j.0 \leq j < |tmp2\_seq[i]|: tmp2\_seq[i][j] = Temp[i][j]))$
5	$(\forall i.0 \leq i < |tmp2\_seq|:(\forall j.0 \leq j < |tmp2\_seq[i]|:$ $tmp3\_seq[i][j] = ipsum(tmp2\_seq[i])[j] = \sum_{t=0}^{j} tmp2\_seq[i][t]))$
6	$(\forall i.0 \leq i < |tmp3\_seq|: (\forall j.0 \leq j < |tmp3\_seq[i]|: tmp3\_seq[i][j] = Output[i][j]))$
7	$(\forall i.0 \leq i < |tmp3\_seq|: (\forall j.0 \leq j < |tmp3\_seq[i]|: out\_seq[i][j] = tmp3\_seq[j][i]))$
8	$(\forall i.0 \leq i < |out\_seq|: (\forall j.0 \leq j < |out\_seq[i]|: out\_seq[i][j] = Output[i][j]))$

We apply the *transpose* function to *tmp1_seq* right after the first transposition computation of the algorithm (line 10 in Algorithm 2). We store the result in a different sequence as $tmp2\_seq$. Figure 6: step 2, illustrates this phase of the algorithm over the sequences. From the postcondition of the $transpose$ function we have Properties 3 and 4 (Table 1) in line 11 of Algorithm 2. Property 3 shows that $tmp2\_seq$ is the transposition of $tmp1\_seq$ and Property 4 relates the ghost variable, $tmp2\_seq$ to the actual array $Temp$.

Then we have the second prefix sum function to compute the inclusive prefix sum of elements in $Temp$ and store it in $Output$. We define a ghost variable, $tmp3\_seq$, to store the inclusive prefix sum of elements in $tmp2\_seq$, which is the same as $Temp$ (lines 14 in Algorithm 2). Figure 6: step 3, shows this phase against the ghost variables. From the postcondition of the verified inclusive prefix sum (see [23]), it follows that Properties 5 and 6 (Table 1) hold in line 15 of Algorithm 2. Property 5 specifies that $tmp3\_seq$ contains the inclusive prefix sum of the elements in $tmp2\_seq$. Property 6 shows the relation between $tmp3\_seq$ and $Output$.

The last phase of the algorithm is the second transposition, but this time for $Output$. Therefore, we now apply the transposition function to the $tmp3\_seq$ ghost variable and store the result in another ghost variable, out_seq in line 20 of Algorithm 2 (see Fig. 6: step 4). At this point (line 21 in Algorithm 2) we have Properties 7 and 8 (Table 1). Property 7 indicates that out_seq is the transposition of $tmp3\_seq$ and Property 8 relates out_seq to $Output$.

As we can see in Property 8, we relate the final result between the ghost variable, out_seq and the actual array $Output$, but we still should reason about the values in out_seq (and correspondingly $Output$). To accomplish this, we prove several corollaries following from the properties in Table 1:

Corollary 1. *From Properties 7 and 5 we have:*

$$(\forall i.0 \leq i < |out\_seq| : (\forall j.0 \leq j < |out\_seq[i]|: out\_seq[i][j] = \sum_{t=0}^{i} tmp2\_seq[j][t])).$$

Corollary 2. *From Corollary 1 and Property 3 we have:*

$$(\forall i.0 \leq i < |out\_seq| : (\forall j.0 \leq j < |out\_seq[i]|: out\_seq[i][j] = \sum_{t=0}^{i} tmp1\_seq[t][j])).$$

Corollary 3. *From Corollary 2 and Property 1 we have:*

$$(\forall i.0 \leq i < |out\_seq| : (\forall j.0 \leq j < |out\_seq[i]|:$$

$$out\_seq[i][j] = \sum_{t_1=0}^{i} \sum_{t_2=0}^{j} inp\_seq[t_1][t_2])).$$

Corollary 1 relates out_seq to $tmp2\_seq$ (Fig. 6: step 5). Corollary 2 shows the relation between the ghost variables out_seq and $tmp1\_seq$ (Fig. 6: step 6). Corollary 3 proves the relation between inp_seq and out_seq (Fig. 6: step 7). As inp_seq and out_seq are the same as $Input$ and $Output$ (Property 8), respectively, we conclude functional correctness.

In this verification, we could easily reuse the specification of the verified prefix sum algorithm in a straightforward way without proving more properties. As a consequence, the verification of the summed-area table algorithm takes much less time than the verification of the prefix sum algorithm. Moreover, we verified the parallel transposition, which is also a primitive operation in GPGPUs, and thus its verification can be reused for the verification of other algorithms that use this operation.

6 Conclusion

In this paper, we have proven data race-freedom and functional correctness of the parallel stream compaction and summed-area table algorithms, for an arbitrary input size by encoding the algorithms into the VerCors verifier. The two algorithms are widely used as primitive operations in other algorithms (e.g., collision detection and sparse matrix compression). Proving functional correctness of both algorithms is challenging because both use other parallel algorithms as sub-routine (e.g., prefix sum and transposition). To overcome these challenges, we reuse previous work on the verification of parallel prefix sum algorithms. It is straightforward to reuse the verification of prefix sum in the summed-area table algorithm. However, the transposition operation is used intermittently in addition to the prefix sum sub-routine. We should establish a formal relation between each of these intermediate steps in order to reason about the final result. In the stream compaction algorithm, since the input to the prefix sum sub-routine is a flag array, we should prove more properties of the prefix sum. Moreover, we define ghost variables and suitable functions that mimic the actual computations in the algorithms.

The complete verification of both algorithms took 2 weeks, whereas in comparison the verification of prefix sum took a couple of months. This shows that less effort is needed to verify complicated algorithms by reusing verified subroutines in practice. Therefore, we believe that now it will be a minimal effort to verify even more complex algorithms that are built on top of the stream compaction and summed-area table algorithms. As future work, we would like to investigate how a substantial part of the required annotations, in particular those related to permissions, can be generated automatically. In addition, based on our verifications, we plan to develop a library of general properties for common GPGPU sub-routines in VerCors.

References

1. Amighi, A., Haack, C., Huisman, M., Hurlin, C.: Permission-based separation logic for multithreaded Java programs. LMCS **11**(1), 1–66 (2015)
2. Betts, A., Chong, N., Donaldson, A., Qadeer, S., Thomson, P.: GPUVerify: a verifier for GPU kernels. In: OOPSLA, pp. 113–132. ACM (2012)
3. Billeter, M., Olsson, O., Assarsson, U.: Efficient stream compaction on wide SIMD many-core architectures. In: Proceedings of the Conference on High Performance Graphics, vol. 2009, pp. 159–166 (2009)
4. Blelloch, G.E.: Prefix Sums and Their Applications. Synthesis of parallel algorithms. Morgan Kaufmann Publishers Inc., San Francisco (1993)

5. Blom, S., Darabi, S., Huisman, M., Oortwijn, W.: The VerCors tool set: verification of parallel and concurrent software. In: Polikarpova, N., Schneider, S. (eds.) IFM 2017. LNCS, vol. 10510, pp. 102–110. Springer, Cham (2017). https://doi.org/10.1007/978-3-319-66845-1_7
6. Blom, S., Huisman, M., Mihelčić, M.: Specification and verification of GPGPU programs. Sci. Comput. Program. **95**, 376–388 (2014)
7. Bornat, R., Calcagno, C., O'Hearn, P., Parkinson, M.: Permission accounting in separation logic. In: POPL, pp. 259–270 (2005)
8. Boyland, J.: Checking interference with fractional permissions. In: Cousot, R. (ed.) SAS 2003. LNCS, vol. 2694, pp. 55–72. Springer, Heidelberg (2003). https://doi.org/10.1007/3-540-44898-5_4
9. Chong, N., Donaldson, A.F., Ketema, J.: A sound and complete abstraction for reasoning about parallel prefix sums. In: ACM SIGPLAN Notices, vol. 49, pp. 397–409. ACM (2014)
10. Collingbourne, P., Cadar, C., Kelly, P.H.J.: Symbolic testing of OpenCL code. In: Eder, K., Lourenço, J., Shehory, O. (eds.) HVC 2011. LNCS, vol. 7261, pp. 203–218. Springer, Heidelberg (2012). https://doi.org/10.1007/978-3-642-34188-5_18
11. Crow, F.C.: Summed-area tables for texture mapping. In: Proceedings of the 11th annual conference on Computer graphics and interactive techniques, pp. 207–212 (1984)
12. Harris, M., Sengupta, S., Owens, J.D.: Parallel prefix sum (scan) with CUDA. GPU Gems **3**(39), 851–876 (2007)
13. Hensley, J., Scheuermann, T., Coombe, G., Singh, M., Lastra, A.: Fast summed-area table generation and its applications. In: Computer Graphics Forum, vol. 24, pp. 547–555. Wiley Online Library (2005)
14. Horn, D.: Stream reduction operations for GPGPU applications. GPU Gems **2**(36), 573–589 (2005)
15. Jacobs, B., Smans, J., Philippaerts, P., Vogels, F., Penninckx, W., Piessens, F.: VeriFast: a powerful, sound, predictable, fast verifier for C and Java. In: Bobaru, M., Havelund, K., Holzmann, G.J., Joshi, R. (eds.) NFM 2011. LNCS, vol. 6617, pp. 41–55. Springer, Heidelberg (2011). https://doi.org/10.1007/978-3-642-20398-5_4
16. Kogge, P.M., Stone, H.S.: A parallel algorithm for the efficient solution of a general class of recurrence equations. IEEE Trans. Comput. **100**(8), 786–793 (1973)
17. Li, G., Gopalakrishnan, G.: Scalable SMT-based verification of GPU kernel functions. In: SIGSOFT FSE 2010, Santa Fe, NM, USA, pp. 187–196. ACM (2010)
18. Li, G., Li, P., Sawaya, G., Gopalakrishnan, G., Ghosh, I., Rajan, S.P.: GKLEE: concolic verification and test generation for GPUs. In: ACM SIGPLAN Notices, vol. 47, pp. 215–224. ACM (2012)
19. de Moura, L., Bjørner, N.: Z3: an efficient SMT solver. In: Ramakrishnan, C.R., Rehof, J. (eds.) TACAS 2008. LNCS, vol. 4963, pp. 337–340. Springer, Heidelberg (2008). https://doi.org/10.1007/978-3-540-78800-3_24
20. Müller, P., Schwerhoff, M., Summers, A.J.: Viper: a verification infrastructure for permission-based reasoning. In: Jobstmann, B., Leino, K.R.M. (eds.) VMCAI 2016. LNCS, vol. 9583, pp. 41–62. Springer, Heidelberg (2016). https://doi.org/10.1007/978-3-662-49122-5_2
21. Nvidia: Cuda-memcheck: User manual (version 10) (2019). https://developer.nvidia.com/cuda-memcheck
22. Price, J., McIntosh-Smith, S.: Oclgrind: an extensible OpenCL device simulator. In: Proceedings of the 3rd International Workshop on OpenCL, p. 12. ACM (2015)

23. Safari, M., Oortwijn, W., Joosten, S., Huisman, M.: Formal verification of parallel prefix sum. In: Lee, R., Jha, S., Mavridou, A. (eds.) NFM 2020. LNCS, vol. 12229, pp. 170–186. Springer, Cham (2020). https://doi.org/10.1007/978-3-030-55754-6_10

24. Sengupta, S., Lefohn, A., Owens, J.: A work-efficient step-efficient prefix sum algorithm. In: Proceedings of the Workshop on Edge Computing Using New Commodity Architecture, May 2006

25. Zheng, M., Ravi, V.T., Qin, F., Agrawal, G.: GRace: a low-overhead mechanism for detecting data races in GPU programs. ACM SIGPLAN Not. **46**(8), 135–146 (2011)

Compositionality of Safe Communication in Systems of Team Automata

Maurice H. ter Beek[1]([⊠]) [iD], Rolf Hennicker[2], and Jetty Kleijn[3] [iD]

[1] ISTI–CNR, Pisa, Italy
maurice.terbeek@isti.cnr.it
[2] Ludwig-Maximilians-Universität München, Munich, Germany
[3] LIACS, Leiden University, Leiden, The Netherlands

Abstract. We study guarantees for safe communication in systems of systems composed of reactive components that communicate through synchronised execution of common actions. Systems are modelled as (extended) team automata, in which, in principle, any number of component automata can participate in the execution of a communicating action, either as a sender or as a receiver. We extend team automata with synchronisation type specifications, which determine specific synchronisation policies fine-tuned for particular application domains. On the other hand, synchronisation type specifications generate communication requirements for receptiveness and responsiveness. We propose a new, liberal version of requirement satisfaction which allows teams to execute arbitrary intermediate actions before being ready for the required communication, which is important in practice. Then we turn to the composition of systems and show that composition behaves well with respect to synchronisation type specifications. As a central result, we investigate criteria that ensure the preservation of local communication properties when (extended) team automata are composed. This is particularly challenging in the context of weak requirement satisfaction.

1 Introduction

We study guarantees for safe communication in systems of systems of interconnected, reactive components that communicate through synchronised execution of shared actions. We focus on the prevention of output actions from not being accepted (i.e. no message loss) and input actions from not being provided (i.e. no indefinite waiting). The lack of safe communication in modular system models may reveal design problems before implementation. To guarantee safe communication in such models, a characterisation for compatibility of two component interactions free from message loss and indefinite waiting was given in [15] and lifted to n-ary interactions in multi-component systems in [16]. Both approaches support compatibility for synchronous communication. A first exploration on how to generalise compatibility notions to arbitrary synchronisation policies was performed in [7] in the framework of team automata.

© Springer Nature Switzerland AG 2020
V. K. I. Pun et al. (Eds.): ICTAC 2020, LNCS 12545, pp. 200–220, 2020.
https://doi.org/10.1007/978-3-030-64276-1_11

Team automata [8,23] are a transition system model for systems of reactive components differentiating input (passive), output (active), and internal (privately active) actions, in the line of I/O automata [19,29], interface automata [20,21], component-interaction automata [14], modal I/O automata [27], and contract automata [3,4]. The distinguishing feature of team automata is their very loose nature of synchronisation according to which, in principle, any number of component automata can participate in the synchronised execution of a shared communicating action, either as a sender or as a receiver. Team automata can determine specific synchronisation policies defining when and which actions are executed and by how many components.

Conditions for safe communication in terms of receptiveness and responsiveness were considered in [2,12,18,22] for (web) services and in [6,7,10,16] for team automata. Output actions not accepted as input by some component are considered as message loss or as unspecified receptions [13,22]. If any (autonomously chosen) output action is accepted, we call this receptiveness [7]. Orthogonally, we recognise indefinite waiting for input to be received in the form of an appropriate output action provided by another component [15]. Since input relies on external choice, it is sufficient if only one of the enabled input actions is responded to (by other components), which we call responsiveness [6].

In [6], a representative set of synchronisation types was defined to classify synchronisation policies (e.g., binary communication, multi-cast communication, full synchronisation) realisable in team automata in terms of ranges for the number of sender and receiver components that can participate in a system communication. Moreover, a generic procedure was provided to derive requirements for receptiveness and responsiveness for each synchronisation type. Communication safety of team automata was expressed in terms of their compliance with receptiveness and responsiveness requirements. A team automaton is said to be compliant with a given set of communication requirements if in each reachable state of the team the desired communications can immediately occur; if the communication can eventually occur after some internal actions have been performed, it is said to be weakly compliant (à la weak compatibility [5,25]).

In the short paper contribution [10], we briefly reviewed our previous approach from [6] and we identified some limitations leading to issues for future research. A first issue was that the assignment of a single synchronisation type to a team, as in [6], is too restrictive and that we need to fine tune the number of synchronising sending and receiving components per action. For this purpose we introduce, in the current paper, synchronisation type specifications which assign a synchronisation type individually to each communicating action. Such specifications uniquely determine a team formalised by an extended notion of team automaton (ETA). On the other hand, any synchronisation type specification generates communication requirements to be satisfied by the team.

A second issue was that we realised that even the weak compliance notion proposed in [6] is too restrictive for practical applications. In the current paper, we overcome this problem by introducing a much more liberal compliance notion: if a group $\mathcal{J}$ of components has issued a communication request, then we allow the team to execute arbitrary other actions, not limited to internal ones, before being ready for the required communication (with the components in $\mathcal{J}$). This leads to a powerful compliance notion not studied before (as far as we know). This apparently simple generalisation has a significant consequence: among the 'arbitrary other actions' there may be output or input actions open to the environment. This is a potentially dangerous situation, since in this case local communication properties can be violated after composition with other teams.

This leads us to the third, perhaps most important, contribution of the current paper. We consider composition of systems and of teams. First, we show that composition behaves well with synchronisation types (Theorem 1). Then we investigate conditions under which communication properties are preserved by ETA composition. The principle idea is that for this it should be sufficient to consider interface actions and to check (global) compliance conditions for them. We formulate appropriate conditions, first for the case of (strong) receptiveness and responsiveness (Theorem 2) and then for the weak variant of the two, solving the problem sketched above (Theorem 3). An intuitive running example guides the reader through the paper.

Outline. After introducing extended team automata (ETA) in Sect. 2, we consider synchronisation type specifications and ETA determined by them in Sect. 3. (Weak) compliance of ETA with communication requirements and safe communication are treated in Sect. 4. In Sect. 5, we define the composition of systems and of teams, and we show that this works well with synchronisation type specifications. In Sect. 6, we provide our main compositionality results. Full proofs and some insightful counterexamples of the results presented in the latter two sections can be found in [9]. After discussing related work in Sect. 7, we conclude the paper in Sect. 8.

2   Background and Extended Team Automata

In this section, we summarise the basic notions concerning team automata and introduce extended team automata. In contrast to the 'classical' team automata from [8,23] and subsequent papers, extended team automata use system labels which, in addition to the executed action, specify the team members that participate in a synchronisation on an action. We start with some technical preliminaries concerning labelled transition systems which will be reused for the definitions of (local) component automata and (global) team automata.

A *labelled transition system* (LTS for short) is a quadruple $\mathcal{L} = (Q, \Sigma, \delta, I)$ consisting of a set Q of *states*, a set Σ of *actions* such that $Q \cap \Sigma = \varnothing$, a transition relation $\delta \subseteq Q \times \Sigma \times Q$ and a nonempty set $I \subseteq Q$ of *initial states*.

For an action $a \in \Sigma$, $\delta_a = \delta \cap (Q \times \{a\} \times Q)$ denotes the set of a-*transitions* of $\mathcal{L}$. Instead of $(p, a, p') \in \delta$ we may write $p \xrightarrow{a}_{\mathcal{L}} p'$. Action a is *enabled* in $\mathcal{L}$ at state $p \in Q$, denoted by $a \, en_{\mathcal{L}} \, p$, if there exists $p' \in Q$ such that $p \xrightarrow{a}_{\mathcal{L}} p'$. For $\Gamma \subseteq \Sigma$, we write $p \xrightarrow{\Gamma}^*_{\mathcal{L}} p'$ if there exist $p_0 \xrightarrow{a_1}_{\mathcal{L}} p_1, \ldots, p_{j-1} \xrightarrow{a_j}_{\mathcal{L}} p_j$ for some $j \geq 0$, with $p_0, \ldots, p_j \in Q$, $a_1, \ldots, a_j \in \Gamma$, $p = p_0$, and $p' = p_j$. A state $p \in Q$ is *reachable* if $p_0 \xrightarrow{\Sigma}{}^*_{\mathcal{L}} p$ for some $p_0 \in I$. The set of reachable states of $\mathcal{L}$ is denoted by $\mathcal{R}(\mathcal{L})$.

Component automata are LTSs with an additional distinction between input and output actions.[1] They form the basic building block of systems.

Definition 1 (Component automaton). *A* component automaton *(CA for short) is an LTS* $\mathcal{A} = (Q, \Sigma, \delta, I)$ *such that* Σ *is the union of two disjoint sets* Σ_{inp} *and* Σ_{out} *of* input *and* output *actions, respectively.* □

In figures, we emphasise the role of actions by adding suffix ? to input actions and ! to output actions.

Systems. A *system* is a pair $\mathcal{S} = (\mathcal{N}, (\mathcal{A}_i)_{i \in \mathcal{N}})$, where $\mathcal{N}$ is a finite, non-empty set of component names and $(\mathcal{A}_i)_{i \in \mathcal{N}}$ is an $\mathcal{N}$-indexed family of CA $\mathcal{A}_i = (Q_i, \Sigma_i, \delta_i, I_i)$ with actions $\Sigma_i = \Sigma_{i,inp} \cup \Sigma_{i,out}$. The *state space* of $\mathcal{S}$ is given by the Cartesian product $Q = \prod_{i \in \mathcal{N}} Q_i$. Hence a global *system state* is an $\mathcal{N}$-indexed family $q = (q_i)_{i \in \mathcal{N}}$ of local component states $q_i \in Q_i$. The *initial states* of $\mathcal{S}$ are given by the product $I = \prod_{i \in \mathcal{N}} I_i$. If $\varnothing \neq \mathcal{N}' \subseteq \mathcal{N}$ and $q = (q_i)_{i \in \mathcal{N}}$ is a system state, the *projection* of q to $\mathcal{N}'$ is defined by $\text{proj}_{\mathcal{N}'}(q) = (q_i)_{i \in \mathcal{N}'}$.

We refer to $\Sigma = \bigcup_{i \in \mathcal{N}} \Sigma_i$ as the set of *actions* of $\mathcal{S}$.[2] Within Σ, we identify $\Sigma_{com} = \bigcup_{i \in \mathcal{N}} \Sigma_{i,inp} \cap \bigcup_{i \in \mathcal{N}} \Sigma_{i,out}$ as the set of *communicating actions in $\mathcal{S}$*. Hence, an action of $\mathcal{S}$ is communicating in $\mathcal{S}$ if it occurs in (at least) one of its CA as an input action and in (at least) one of its CA as an output action.

For an action $a \in \Sigma$, we let $\text{dom}_{a,inp}(\mathcal{S}) = \{\, i \mid a \in \Sigma_{i,inp} \,\}$ be its *input domain* (in $\mathcal{S}$) and $\text{dom}_{a,out}(\mathcal{S}) = \{\, i \mid a \in \Sigma_{i,out} \,\}$ its *output domain* (in $\mathcal{S}$). Hence a communicating action of $\mathcal{S}$ is such that both its output and input domain in $\mathcal{S}$ are not empty.

Notation. *Up to and including Sect. 4, we fix $\mathcal{N}$ and $\mathcal{S}$ as above.* □

Example 1. Consider a distributed chat system, where buddies can interact once registered. For now, we consider two types of components: clients and servers, depicted in Fig. 1 (left and middle, respectively). The arbiter will join only later when we discuss system compositions. A server controls entries into the chat and exits from the chat, and coordinates the main activity: forwarding client messages to the chat. The communicating actions are partitioned into chat access actions (*join, leave, confirmJ, confirmL*) and chat messaging (*msg, fwdmsg*). The non-communicating actions are currently *ask*, *grant*, and *reject*. Let us assume a chat system $\mathcal{S}_{chat}$ consisting of two clients $\mathcal{A}_1$ and $\mathcal{A}_2$ and one server $\mathcal{A}_3$. Its state space consists of tuples (p, q, r) with client states p and q and server state r. □

---

[1] In general, and in the classical team automata approach, a component automaton can also have a distinguished set of internal actions. Since internal actions are not really relevant for the scope of this paper, we omit them for the sake of simplicity.

[2] If component automata were equipped with internal actions, then a syntactic composability constraint would have to be applied to $\mathcal{S}$ requiring that each internal action of a component automaton is unique to that component automaton.

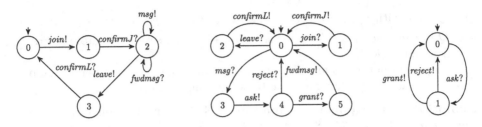

Fig. 1. [from left to right] CA for clients, servers, and arbiters [adapted from [10]]

We use extended labels as envisioned in [14] for multi component-interaction automata, to indicate explicitly which components are actively participating in system transitions. In the vector team automata of [11], vectors of component actions are used for this purpose, giving rise to a concurrent semantics.

Definition 2 (System labels). *Let $a \in \Sigma$. A system label for a (in S) is a triple (out, a, inp) where $out, inp \subseteq \mathcal{N}$ are subsets of $\mathcal{N}$ such that $out \cup inp \neq \varnothing$ and $a \in \Sigma_{i,out}$ for all $i \in out$ and $a \in \Sigma_{i,inp}$ for all $i \in inp$. The set of system labels for a in S is denoted by $\Lambda_a(S)$, while $\Lambda(S) = \bigcup_{a \in \Sigma} \Lambda_a(S)$ denotes the set of all system labels in S.* □

System labels provide an appropriate means to describe which components in a system execute together a computation step, i.e. a system transition.

Definition 3 (System transitions). *A triple $(q, \sigma, q') \in Q \times \Lambda(S) \times Q$ with system label $\sigma = (out, a, inp)$ is a system transition on a (in S) if $(q(i), a, q'(i)) \in \delta_i$ for all $i \in out \cup inp$ and $q(i) = q'(i)$ for all $i \in \mathcal{N} \setminus (out \cup inp)$.*
For $a \in \Sigma$, the set of all system transitions on a in S is denoted by $E_a(S)$, while $E(S) = \bigcup_{a \in \Sigma} E_a(S)$ denotes the set of all system transitions in S. □

If $t = (q, (out, a, inp), q') \in E(S)$ then any CA $\mathcal{A}_i$ for which $i \in out \cup inp$ is said to *participate in t*. If $i \in out$, then $\mathcal{A}_i$ is a *sender in t*, otherwise it is a *receiver*. Since, by definition of system labels, $out \cup inp \neq \varnothing$, at least one CA is participating in any system transition in S. Moreover, all system transitions in $E_a(S)$ are combinations of existing a-transitions from the CA in S and all possible combinations of a-transitions occur in $E_a(S)$. The elements of $E_a(S)$ are also referred to as *synchronisations on a*, even when only one CA participates. A synchronisation on a communicating action a in which a CA where a is an output action and a CA where a is an input action participate, is called a *communication*. Obviously, for a non-communicating action $a \in \Sigma$, either out or inp is empty in any system transition on a.

Example 2. The system transitions $E_{msg}(\mathcal{S}_{chat})$ of $\mathcal{S}_{chat}$ from Example 1 in which CA $\mathcal{A}_3$ participates are the following: $((2,2,0), (\varnothing, msg, \{\mathcal{A}_3\}), (2,2,3))$, $((2,2,0), (\{\mathcal{A}_1\}, msg, \{\mathcal{A}_3\}), (2,2,3))$, $((2,2,0), (\{\mathcal{A}_2\}, msg, \{\mathcal{A}_3\}), (2,2,3))$, and $((2,2,0), (\{\mathcal{A}_1, \mathcal{A}_2\}, msg, \{\mathcal{A}_3\}), (2,2,3))$. Using this notation, we thus express whether $\mathcal{A}_1$ or $\mathcal{A}_2$ participates or not in a synchronisation and hence whether or not a communication takes place. Note that not all system transitions are meaningful in applications. For instance, $((2, 2, 0), (\{\mathcal{A}_1, \mathcal{A}_2\}, msg, \{\mathcal{A}_3\}), (2, 2, 3))$ expresses that both clients join to send msg to the server. If we want to rule out undesired synchronisations we must declare a subset of admissible system transitions, which is the underlying idea of team automata.   □

Extended Team Automata. The CA combined in a system are meant to collaborate (form a team) through the simultaneous execution of shared actions. Such teams are formalised by our notion of extended team automaton. They are labelled transition systems with set of states Q and set of initial states I. Their transitions are always a subset ε of $E(\mathcal{S})$ containing the admissible system transitions. Such subset is called a *synchronisation policy*. From the software engineering perspective, it is the task of the team designer to determine an appropriate synchronisation policy for a given system of components. We use the system labels (out, a, inp) in $\Lambda(\mathcal{S})$ as the actions in team transitions. This is the main difference with the classical team automata from [8,23] and subsequent papers, where actions $a \in \Sigma$ would have been used in team transitions. However, to study communication properties and their compositionality, explicit rendering of the CA that actually participate in a transition of the team seems useful.

Definition 4 (Extended team automaton). *An extended team automaton (ETA for short) over $\mathcal{S}$ is an LTS $\mathcal{E} = (Q, \Lambda(\mathcal{S}), \varepsilon, I)$, where $\varepsilon \subseteq E(\mathcal{S})$ is a synchronisation policy over $\mathcal{S}$.*   □

3 Synchronisation Type Specifications

In [6], we proposed *synchronisation types* to specify in a convenient, syntactic way synchronisation policies. A synchronisation type (snd, rcv) determines ranges for the number of senders and the number of receivers that may take part in a communication. Both, the *sending multiplicity* snd and the *receiving multiplicity* rcv are given by intervals. If $snd = [o_1, o_2]$ (with $0 \le o_1 \le o_2$) and $rcv = [i_1, i_2]$ (with $0 \le i_1 \le i_2$) then at least o_1 and at most o_2 senders and at least i_1 and at most i_2 receivers are allowed. While o_1 and i_1 are always natural numbers, the upper delimiters o_2 and i_2 can also be given as $*$, which indicates that no upper limit is imposed. On the other hand, at most one of the lower delimiters o_1 or i_1 can be zero. In this case an output (respectively, input) of a communicating action can be performed by components without a participating receiver (respectively, sender).

Notable synchronisation types that can be defined include binary communication $([1, 1], [1, 1])$ and multicast communication $([1, 1], [0, *])$, in which exactly one CA outputs a communicating action while arbitrarily many CA input that action. We can also express full synchronisation on an action a by requiring as a synchronisation type for a (snd, rcv) with $snd = [\text{dom}_{a,out}, \text{dom}_{a,out}]$ and $rcv = [\text{dom}_{a,inp}, \text{dom}_{a,inp}]$.

For the following, recall that $\mathcal{S} = (\mathcal{N}, (\mathcal{A}_i)_{i \in \mathcal{N}})$ is a composable system with state space Q, actions Σ and communicating actions Σ_{com}. In [6], we considered the situation where all synchronisations in $\mathcal{S}$ follow a single synchronisation type used uniformly for all communicating actions of the system. In practice it is, however, necessary to relax this interpretation and define synchronisation types individually for each communicating action of the system. This leads to our new notion of synchronisation type specification.

Definition 5 (Synchronisation type specification). *A synchronisation type specification over $\mathcal{S}$ is a mapping st which assigns to all communicating actions $a \in \Sigma_{com}$ a synchronisation type $st(a) = (snd_{st(a)}, rcv_{st(a)})$.* □

For the non-communicating actions in $\mathcal{S}$ no synchronisation type is provided since this is only relevant when systems are composed; see Sects. 5 and 6. We will now discuss how a synchronisation policy, and hence an ETA, can be deduced from a synchronisation type specification.

Let (snd, rcv) be a synchronisation type with $snd = [o_1, o_2]$ and $rcv = [i_1, i_2]$. A system transition $(q, \sigma, q') \in Q \times \Lambda(\mathcal{S}) \times Q$ with $\sigma = (out, a, inp)$ is of type (snd, rcv) if $o_1 \leq \#out \leq o_2$ and $i_1 \leq \#inp \leq i_2$, assuming $n \leq *$ for any $n \in \mathbb{N}$.

Remark 1. Note that for typing system transitions we use in a crucial way the information provided by system labels. If we had mere actions as transition labels of communications, as in team automata, it would not be clear whether a CA with a 'self-loop' participates in a communication or not. Consider, for instance, the system labels and transition from Example 2. In a team automaton over $\mathcal{S}_{chat}$ there could be a transition $((2, 2, 0), msg, (2, 2, 3))$ in which it is not clear whether one, two, or none of the clients participate, i.e. whether or not $msg!$ is actually executed and by whom. In team automata, this is typically resolved by implicitly assuming that a loop of a CA in a transition implies its execution, a 'maximal' interpretation of ambiguous participation. □

Each synchronisation type specification determines a unique synchronisation policy and hence a unique ETA in the following way:

Definition 6 (Typed synchronisation policy). *Let st be a synchronisation type specification over $\mathcal{S}$.*

1. *The synchronisation policy determined by st, denoted by $\varepsilon(st)$, is defined by $\varepsilon(st)_a = \{ t \in E_a(\mathcal{S}) \mid t$ is of type $st(a) \}$ if $a \in \Sigma_{com}$; and $\varepsilon(st)_a = E_a(\mathcal{S})$ if $a \in \Sigma \setminus \Sigma_{com}$.*
2. *The ETA determined by st is $\mathcal{E}(st) = (Q, \Lambda(\mathcal{S}), \varepsilon(st), I)$.* □

Note that for non-communicating actions $a \in \Sigma \setminus \Sigma_{com}$ for which no synchronisation type is specified, $\varepsilon(st)$ is 'maximal' in the sense that we set $\varepsilon(st)_a = E_a(\mathcal{S})$. This means that we allow all possible synchronisations in $\mathcal{S}$. This is in contrast with [6], where we allowed arbitrary subsets of $E_a(\mathcal{S})$ rather than equality. It is, however, needed to get the compositionality results later on.

Example 3. Consider global state $(2, 0, 5)$ of the chat system $\mathcal{S}_{chat}$ from Examples 1–2, where client $\mathcal{A}_1$ can (autonomously) decide to execute either its output action *leave* or its output action *msg*. To enforce receptiveness, there must be at least one other CA ready to execute either action as an input action. Server $\mathcal{A}_3$ only has output action *fwdmsg* locally enabled. If we set $st_{chat}(fwdmsg) = ([1, 1], [0, *])$ as synchronisation type for *fwdmsg*, then the server is allowed to move to state 0 by executing its output action *fwdmsg* on its own (rather than in a communication) after which the server is ready to accept inputs as required. This synchronisation type is not suitable for the other actions, e.g. a client should be prohibited to *join* without acceptance by the server, thus $st_{chat}(join) = ([1, 1], [1, 1])$ would be appropriate. Therefore, we define a synchronisation type specification st_{chat} over $\mathcal{S}_{chat}$ such that $st_{chat}(fwdmsg) = ([1, 1], [0, *])$ and $st_{chat}(a) = ([1, 1], [1, 1])$ for all other communicating actions of $\mathcal{S}_{chat}$. The ETA determined by st_{chat} is $\mathcal{E}_{chat}(st_{chat})$. □

4 Communication Requirements and Compliance

The idea of communication-safety in team automata is as follows. At each reachable global state of a team, whenever a communicating action is enabled at the local states of some components $\mathcal{J}$ in accordance with the synchronisation type of that action, then all components in $\mathcal{J}$ can execute this action from their local states as a communication within the team.

Communication-Safety of ETA in a Nutshell. Before giving formal definitions, let us explain in a nutshell how our approach works. Consider an ETA $\mathcal{E}(st)$ and a communication action a with, for instance, synchronisation type $st(a) = ([1, 1], [1, *])$. Let $\mathcal{A}_i$ be a component of the system for which a is an output action and let q be a global state of $\mathcal{E}(st)$ such that a is enabled at the local state $q(i)$ of $\mathcal{A}_i$. Then we wish that a can be received by at least one other component in the team. We express this by a *receptiveness requirement* issued by component $\mathcal{A}_i$ and written as $\mathbf{rcp}(\{i\}, a)@q$. If the ETA $\mathcal{E}(st)$ is *compliant with* this requirement, it is guaranteed that in state q, component $\mathcal{A}_i$ can synchronise with other components in the team taking a as input.

Note that in case $\mathcal{A}_i$ could also execute another output action b with the same synchronisation type at state $q(i)$, subject to the corresponding receptiveness requirement, then the two requirements would be combined through a conjunction to $\mathbf{rcp}(\{i\}, a)@q \wedge \mathbf{rcp}(\{i\}, b)@q$. The reason for this is that components control their output actions and thus can internally decide which action to be sent. Hence, the choice of either of them should lead to a reception. The expression $\mathbf{rcp}(\{i\}, a)@q \wedge \mathbf{rcp}(\{i\}, b)@q$ is called a *receptiveness requirement generated by st*. Indeed, the information in the synchronisation type $([1, 1], [1, *])$ determines, due to the lower bound 1 of the output multiplicity $[1, 1]$, that already one component can induce a receptiveness requirement. On the other hand, the receive multiplicity $[1, *]$ tells us that a communication is really needed for the output of a. Indeed, if the receive multiplicity were $[0, *]$, then there would be no receptiveness requirement. If, however, the output multiplicity of a were $[2, *]$, then at least two components for which a is enabled in the current local states would be needed to issue a valid receptiveness requirement of the form $\mathtt{rcp}(\mathcal{J}, a)@q$ with $\mathcal{J}$ determining the set of output components.

For input actions one could require responsiveness with the intuition that enabled inputs should be served by appropriate outputs. Unlike output actions, however, input actions are controlled by the environment, i.e. input choice is external. Guaranteeing that for a choice of enabled inputs, *one of them* is supplied with an output of other components suffices for the progress of a component waiting for a signal. Hence, if component $\mathcal{A}_j$ enables input actions a and b in its local state $q(j)$, then the *responsiveness requirements*, denoted by $\mathtt{rsp}(\{j\}, a)@q$ and $\mathtt{rsp}(\{j\}, b)@q$ would be combined with a disjunction to $\mathtt{rsp}(\{j\}, a)@q \vee \mathtt{rsp}(\{j\}, b)@q$, which is called a *responsiveness requirement generated by st*. Of course, also responsiveness requirements can be issued by several components $\mathcal{J}$ instead of $\{j\}$.

In general, a team automaton $\mathcal{E}(st)$ over a system $\mathcal{S}$ is called *receptive* (respectively, *responsive*) if it is compliant with all receptiveness requirements (respectively, responsiveness requirements) generated by st at all reachable states of $\mathcal{E}(st)$. It is *communication-safe* if it is receptive and responsive.

Weak Compliance. In [6], we relaxed compliance to allow the team to execute some intermediate internal actions before being ready for the required communication. As anticipated in the introduction and in [10], in this paper we further relax the notion of *weak compliance* from [6]: if a group $\mathcal{J}$ of components has issued a communication request we allow the team to execute, without participation of $\mathcal{J}$, some arbitrary other actions before being ready for the required communication. This is a very flexible interpretation of interaction compatibility that, to the best of our knowledge, has not yet been studied in a similar way in the literature, likely because the permission of intermediate actions is dangerous for obtaining compositionality results. Its formal definition is given in Definition 9.

Formal Definitions and Examples. In the remainder of this section, we provide the formal definitions of the concepts explained above, partly illustrated by examples. The definitions of communication requirements and compliance are taken from [6], the definition of weak compliance in this general form is new and the proposal to derive communication requirements from synchronisation type specifications is inspired by [6], but simplified and at the same time generalised to fit with synchronisation types per action.

We still assume given a composable system $\mathcal{S} = (\mathcal{N}, (\mathcal{A}_i)_{i \in \mathcal{N}})$ with state space Q, actions Σ and communicating actions Σ_{com}.

Definition 7 (Communication requirements). *Let $a \in \Sigma_{com}$ and $q \in Q$.*

- *Let $\varnothing \neq \mathcal{J} \subseteq dom_{a,out}(\mathcal{S})$ be such that $a\, en_{\mathcal{A}_j}\, q(j)$ for all $j \in \mathcal{J}$. Then $\mathtt{rcp}(\mathcal{J}, a)@q$ is a receptiveness requirement for a at q.*

- Let $\varnothing \neq \mathcal{J} \subseteq dom_{a,inp}(\mathcal{S})$ be such that $a \, en_{\mathcal{A}_j} q(j)$ for all $j \in \mathcal{J}$. Then $rsp(\mathcal{J}, a)@q$ is a responsiveness requirement for a at q.
- A communication requirement at q is either the trivial requirement true or a receptiveness or responsiveness requirement at q or a conjunction or disjunction of communication requirements at q. □

When all non-trivial atomic requirements occurring in a communication requirement φ are receptiveness (respectively, responsiveness) requirements, we also refer to φ as a receptiveness (respectively, responsiveness) requirement.

Definition 8 (Compliance). *Let $\mathcal{E}$ be an ETA over $\mathcal{S}$ with synchronisation policy ε. Then $\mathcal{E}$ is compliant with a communication requirement φ at $q \in Q$ if either $q \notin \mathcal{R}(\mathcal{E})$ or $\varphi = true$, or one of the following holds:*

1. $\varphi = rcp(\mathcal{J}, a)@q$ *for some $\mathcal{J} \subseteq \mathcal{N}$ and $a \in \Sigma_{com}$, and there exists out $\supseteq \mathcal{J}$ and inp $\neq \varnothing$ such that $q \xrightarrow{(out,a,inp)}_{\varepsilon} q'$*
2. $\varphi = rsp(\mathcal{J}, a)@q$ *for some $\mathcal{J} \subseteq \mathcal{N}$ and $a \in \Sigma_{com}$, and there exists out $\neq \varnothing$ and inp $\supseteq \mathcal{J}$ such that $q \xrightarrow{(out,a,inp)}_{\varepsilon} q'$*
3. $\varphi = \psi_1 \wedge \psi_2$ *and $\mathcal{E}$ is compliant with ψ_1 at q and with ψ_2 at q*
4. $\varphi = \psi_1 \vee \psi_2$ *and $\mathcal{E}$ is compliant with ψ_1 at q or with ψ_2 at q* □

Note that when $\mathcal{E}$ is compliant with a requirement as in 1. and 2. above, then the components $\mathcal{J}$ can communicate through a synchronisation on a at q involving more CA from the output and input domains of a.

Recall that $\Lambda(\mathcal{S})$ denotes the labels of $\mathcal{E}$ and let $\Lambda_{\mathcal{J}}(\mathcal{S})$, with $\mathcal{J} \subseteq \mathcal{N}$, denote the set of labels in which CA from $\mathcal{J}$ participate, i.e. system labels (out, a, inp) such that $j \in out \cup inp$ for some $j \in \mathcal{J}$.

Definition 9 (Weak compliance). *Let $\mathcal{E}$ be an ETA over $\mathcal{S}$ with synchronisation policy ε. Weak compliance is defined analogously to Definition 8 but replacing 1. and 2. by the following items:*

1. $\varphi = rcp(\mathcal{J}, a)@q$ *for some $\mathcal{J} \subseteq \mathcal{N}$ and $a \in \Sigma_{com}$, and there exists $p \in Q$, out $\supseteq \mathcal{J}$ and inp $\neq \varnothing$ such that $q \xrightarrow{\Lambda(\mathcal{S}) \backslash \Lambda_{\mathcal{J}}(\mathcal{S})}_{\varepsilon}{}^{*} p \xrightarrow{(out,a,inp)}_{\varepsilon} q'$*
2. $\varphi = rsp(\mathcal{J}, a)@q$ *for some $\mathcal{J} \subseteq \mathcal{N}$ and $a \in \Sigma_{com}$, and there exists $p \in Q$, inp $\supseteq \mathcal{J}$ and out $\neq \varnothing$ such that $q \xrightarrow{\Lambda(\mathcal{S}) \backslash \Lambda_{\mathcal{J}}(\mathcal{S})}_{\varepsilon}{}^{*} p \xrightarrow{(out,a,inp)}_{\varepsilon} q'$* □

Compliance trivially implies weak compliance. Note that we require that the CA determined by $\mathcal{J}$ do not participate in the intermediate transitions. Moreover, it is possible that also CA not participating in the foreseen communication, do participate in the intermediate actions that are needed to reach the global team state where it can occur. This is a phenomenon known as 'state-sharing' (cf. [8,24]). It allows CA to influence potential synchronisations through their local states without participating in the actual transition.

Example 4. We continue Example 3. In global state $(2, 0, 5)$, $\mathcal{A}_2$ is locally enabled to execute its output action *join*. Recall that $st_{chat}(join) = ([1,1], [1,1])$.

Then the receptiveness requirement for *join* at state $(2, 0, 5)$ is $\mathtt{rcp}(\{\mathcal{A}_2\},$ *join*$)@(2,0,5)$, i.e. output action *join* of $\mathcal{A}_2$ must be received as input by at least one other CA. The only CA with *join* as an input action is the server $\mathcal{A}_3$, but *join* is not enabled at its local state 5. However, in an ETA $\mathcal{E}$ over $\mathcal{S}_{chat}$ where $\mathcal{A}_3$ can transit from state 5 to state 0 by a communication with $\mathcal{A}_1$ (or even alone) the CA $\mathcal{A}_3$ would subsequently be ready to execute *join* in a communication with $\mathcal{A}_2$. Since the intermediate move of the server to state 0 is allowed by our new notion of weak compliance, this $\mathcal{E}$ is weakly compliant with the given requirement.   □

As discussed above, the guidelines for when which choice of communication requirements is suitable, must consider the synchronisation types of actions. Let st be a synchronisation type specification over $\mathcal{S}$, $q \in Q$ and $a \in \Sigma_{com}$ such that $st(a) = ([o_1, o_2], [i_1, i_2])$.

A receptiveness requirement $\mathtt{rcp}(\mathcal{J}, a)@q$ is *valid for* $st(a)$ if $o_1 \leq |\mathcal{J}| \leq o_2$ and $i_1 \neq 0$. The *receptiveness requirement for q generated by st* is the conjunction[3]

$$\bigwedge \{\, \mathtt{rcp}(\mathcal{J}, a)@q \mid a \in \Sigma_{com}, \mathtt{rcp}(\mathcal{J}, a)@q \text{ is valid for } st(a) \,\}$$

A responsiveness requirement $\mathtt{rsp}(\mathcal{J}, a)@q$ is *valid for* $st(a)$ if $i_1 \leq |\mathcal{J}| \leq i_2$, $o_1 \neq 0$ and, for each $j \in \mathcal{J}$, $q(j)$ is a state at which only input actions are enabled.[4] The *responsiveness requirement for q generated by st* is the disjunction[5]

$$\bigvee \{\, \mathtt{rsp}(\mathcal{J}, a)@q \mid a \in \Sigma_{com}, \mathtt{rsp}(\mathcal{J}, a)@q \text{ is valid for } st(a) \,\}$$

In summary, each synchronisation type specification st for a system $\mathcal{S}$ of components determines a synchronisation policy, i.e. an ETA $\mathcal{E}(st)$, and generates at the same time communication requirements. Then $\mathcal{E}(st)$ is (weakly) communication-safe if it is (weakly) compliant with all requirements. This means that the components in $\mathcal{S}$ coordinated by the synchronisation policy determined by st work properly together.

Definition 10. *Let $\mathcal{E}(st)$ be an ETA determined by a synchronisation type specification st. $\mathcal{E}(st)$ is (weakly) receptive (respectively, (weakly) responsive) if it is (weakly) compliant at all $q \in \mathcal{R}(\mathcal{E}(st))$ with the receptiveness (respectively, responsiveness) requirement for q generated by st. $\mathcal{E}(st)$ is (weakly) communication-safe if it is receptive and responsive.*   □

Example 5. We continue Examples 1–4. Let st_{chat} be the chat system's synchronisation type specification as defined in Example 3. Let $\mathcal{E}_{chat}(st_{chat})$ be the ETA determined by st_{chat}. An example of a generated receptiveness requirement is $\mathtt{rcp}(\{\mathcal{A}_1\}, msg)@(2, 0, 5) \wedge \mathtt{rcp}(\{\mathcal{A}_1\}, leave)@(2, 0, 5) \wedge \mathtt{rcp}(\{\mathcal{A}_2\}, join)@(2, 0, 5)$.

---

[3] We use a conjunction here since outputs are autonomously decided by components.
[4] Otherwise the component has already a receptiveness requirement for an output.
[5] We use a disjunction here since inputs rely on external choice.

As explained in Example 4, $\mathcal{E}_{chat}(st_{chat})$ is weakly compliant with the second conjunct. It is also weakly compliant with the first conjunct as after moving on its own to state 0, the server can receive msg. Requirement $\mathrm{rcp}(\{\mathcal{A}_1\}, msg)@(2,0,3)$ is more tricky, since in state 3 the server already received a msg from client $\mathcal{A}_1$ who wants to send another msg. Due to the new weak compliance notion this is ok, since the server can execute its non-communicating external actions ask followed by, e.g., $reject$ to return to state 0 where it can receive msg. An example of a generated responsiveness requirement is $\mathrm{rsp}(\{\mathcal{A}_3\}, join)@(0,0,0) \vee \mathrm{rsp}(\{\mathcal{A}_3\}, leave)@(0,0,0) \vee \mathrm{rsp}(\{\mathcal{A}_3\}, msg)@(0,0,0)$. Clearly, $\mathcal{E}_{chat}(st_{chat})$ is only compliant with the first disjunct since either client can provide the required output action $join$. It is important to note that requirements generated from inputs rely on external choice of the environment and therefore it is sufficient if one of the offered inputs is served, which is expressed by the disjunction. We could only discuss here a few requirements, but a thorough analysis shows that indeed $\mathcal{E}_{chat}(st_{chat})$ is weakly receptive and weakly responsive.　　　□

5　Systems of Systems and ETA Compositions

In this section, we consider systems of systems and the composition of ETA given for each individual system. This yields ETA over the combined global systems. We also show how a global synchronisation type specification can be constructed from the local ones respecting the underlying local ETA composition.

Let $n \geq 1$ and let, for $k = 1,\ldots,n$, $\mathcal{S}_k = (\mathcal{N}_k, (\mathcal{A}_{k,i})_{i\in\mathcal{N}_k})$ be a system with $(\mathcal{A}_{k,i})_{i\in\mathcal{N}_k}$ an $\mathcal{N}_k$-indexed family of CA $\mathcal{A}_{k,i} = (Q_{k,i}, \Sigma_{k,i}, \delta_{k,i}, I_{k,i})$ where $\Sigma_{k,i} = \Sigma_{k,i,inp} \cup \Sigma_{k,i,out}$. Hence, $\Sigma_k = \bigcup_{i\in\mathcal{N}_k} \Sigma_{k,i}$ is the set of actions in $\mathcal{S}_k$ and $\Sigma_{k,com} = \bigcup_{i\in\mathcal{N}_k} \Sigma_{k,i,inp} \cap \bigcup_{i\in\mathcal{N}_k} \Sigma_{k,i,out}$ is its set of communicating actions.

To compose the single systems we assume that communicating actions within one system cannot be used to interact with other systems. So, we say that the family of systems $(\mathcal{S}_k)_{k\in[n]}$ is *composable* if for all $k \in [n]$ and for all $k \neq l \in [n]$, $\mathcal{N}_k \cap \mathcal{N}_l = \varnothing$ and $\Sigma_{k,com} \cap \Sigma_l = \varnothing$. Hence, in a composable family of systems, component names and communicating actions are unique to a system.

Definition 11 (System composition). *The composition of a composable family $(\mathcal{S}_k)_{k\in[n]}$ is the system $\bigotimes_{k\in[n]} \mathcal{S}_k = (\bigcup_{k\in[n]} \mathcal{N}_k, (\mathcal{A}_{k,i})_{(k,i)\in[n]\times\mathcal{N}_k})$.*　　□

Notation. *For the rest of the paper, we fix $n \in \mathbb{N}^{>0}$ and $\mathcal{S}_k$ for $k \in [n]$, as above. We moreover assume that $(\mathcal{S}_k)_{k\in[n]}$ is composable and that $\mathcal{S} = \bigotimes_{k\in[n]} \mathcal{S}_k$ with state space Q and initial states I.*　　□

The set of actions of $\mathcal{S}$ is $\Sigma = \bigcup_{(k,i)\in[n]\times\mathcal{N}_k} \Sigma_{k,i} = \bigcup_{k\in[n]} \Sigma_k$ and the set of communicating actions in $\mathcal{S}$ is

$$\Sigma_{com} = \bigcup_{(k,i)\in[n]\times\mathcal{N}_k} \Sigma_{k,i,inp} \cap \bigcup_{(k,i)\in[n]\times\mathcal{N}_k} \Sigma_{k,i,out}$$

Obviously, Σ_{com} contains the communicating actions $\Sigma_{k,com}$ of each subsystem $\mathcal{S}_k$ but also actions which occur as input action in a component of one sub-system and as output action in a component of another sub-system. The latter are called *interface actions* and defined by $\Sigma_{inf} = \Sigma_{com} \setminus \bigcup_{k \in [n]} \Sigma_{k,com}$.

Example 6. We now add an arbiter to the chat system $\mathcal{S}_{chat}$ from Examples 1–4 to regulate message forwarding by composing $\mathcal{S}_{chat}$ with the singleton system $\{\mathcal{A}_4\}$, depicted in Fig. 1 (right). The idea is that the server must *ask* the arbiter to *grant* or *reject* permission to forward a message. The two systems $\mathcal{S}_{chat}$ and $\{\mathcal{A}_4\}$ form a composable family of systems; *ask*, *grant*, and *reject* are the interface actions.   □

Given the composable family of systems $(\mathcal{S}_k)_{k \in [n]}$, we describe how to compose an extended team automaton over $\mathcal{S} = \bigotimes_{k \in [n]} \mathcal{S}_k$ from given ETA $\mathcal{E}_k = (Q_k, \Lambda(\mathcal{S}_k), \varepsilon_k, I_k)$ over $\mathcal{S}_k$, $k \in [n]$.

An ETA obtained as a composition of $(\mathcal{E}_k)_{k \in [n]}$ is an ETA over $\mathcal{S}$. So it has state space Q, set of initial states I, and set of actions Σ as defined above. The essential part concerns the choice of the synchronisation policy ε for the composed ETA. We proceed as follows to define the system transitions of ε for each $a \in \Sigma$:

1. For each non-communicating action $a \in \Sigma \setminus \Sigma_{com}$, we define

$$\varepsilon_a = \{ (q, (out, a, in), q') \in E_a(\mathcal{S}) \mid \text{for all } k \in [n], \text{s.t.} \, \mathcal{N}_k \cap (out \cup in) \neq \varnothing :$$
$$(proj_{\mathcal{N}_k}(q), (out \cap \mathcal{N}_k, a, in \cap \mathcal{N}_k), proj_{\mathcal{N}_k}(q')) \in \varepsilon_{k,a} \}$$

   Hence, ε_a is the set of all system transitions for a in $\mathcal{S}$ whose projections to sub-systems $\mathcal{S}_k$ having action a belong to $\varepsilon_{k,a}$.

2. If $a \in \Sigma_{com}$ (a communicating action in $\mathcal{S}$) we distinguish two cases:
   (a) $a \in \bigcup_{k \in [n]} \Sigma_{k,com}$: Then, by composability, there is exactly one $k \in \mathcal{K}$ such that $a \in \Sigma_{k,com}$ and a is unique to $\mathcal{S}_k$. Fix this k and define

$$\varepsilon_a = \{ (q, (out, a, in), q') \in E_a(\mathcal{S}) \mid$$
$$(proj_{\mathcal{N}_k}(q), (out, a, in), proj_{\mathcal{N}_k}(q')) \in \varepsilon_{k,a} \}$$

   Due to the uniqueness of a to $\mathcal{S}_k$, ε_a is the set of all extensions of system transitions in $\varepsilon_{k,a}$ to the state space of $\mathcal{S}$.

   (b) $a \in \Sigma_{inf}$: Now a is an action shared as input and output action of some components of $\mathcal{S}$ but not shared as an input and output action of components in any sub-system $\mathcal{S}_k$. Therefore it is the design choice of the overall system architect to determine a set of system transitions $\varepsilon_a \subseteq E_a(\mathcal{S})$.

This procedure leads to a unique ETA once a set of system transitions is provided for each interface action $a \in \Sigma_{inf}$.

Definition 12 (Composition of ETA). *Let for all $k \in [n]$, $\mathcal{E}_k$ be an ETA over $\mathcal{S}_k$ with ε_k its synchronisation policy. Let $\varepsilon_{inf} \subseteq \bigcup_{a \in \Sigma_{inf}} E_a(\mathcal{S})$ be a set of system transitions in $\mathcal{S}$ for the interface actions from Σ_{inf}.*

The extended team automata composition $\bigotimes_{k \in [n]}^{\varepsilon_{inf}} \mathcal{E}_k$ of $(\mathcal{E}_k)_{k \in [n]}$ w.r.t. ε_{inf} is the ETA over $\mathcal{S}$ with synchronisation policy ε such that:

1. For all $a \in \Sigma \setminus \Sigma_{com}$, ε_a is defined as in item 1. above.
2. For all $k \in [n]$ and $a \in \Sigma_{k,com}$, ε_a is defined as in item 2.(a) above.
3. For all $a \in \Sigma_{inf}$, $\varepsilon_a = (\varepsilon_{inf})_a$.

If $n = 2$ we write $\mathcal{E}_1 \otimes^{\varepsilon_{inf}} \mathcal{E}_2$ for $\bigotimes_{k \in [n]}^{\varepsilon_{inf}} \mathcal{E}_k$.   □

The next theorem shows the relationship between ETA composition and synchronisation types. If a family of ETAs is given, each one determined by a certain synchronisation type, then it is enough to specify synchronisation types for the interface actions in order to get the composition of the ETAs as an ETA generated by a single synchronisation type.

Theorem 1. Let for all $k \in [n]$, $\mathcal{E}_k(st_k)$ be an ETA determined by synchronisation type specification st_k and let $st_{inf}(a)$ be a synchronisation type for each interface action $a \in \Sigma_{inf}$. Then $\bigotimes_{k \in [n]}^{\varepsilon_{inf}} \mathcal{E}_k(st_k) = \mathcal{E}(st)$, where for all $a \in \Sigma_{inf}$, $(\varepsilon_{inf})_a = \{ t \in E_a(\mathcal{S}) \mid t \text{ is of type } st_{inf}(a) \}$ and st is the synchronisation type specification over $\mathcal{S}$, defined by:

1. $st(a) = st_k(a)$ for all $k \in [n]$ and $a \in \Sigma_{k,com}$ and
2. $st(a) = st_{inf}(a)$ for all $a \in \Sigma_{inf}$.

Proof. (sketch) The proof is straightforward using the (syntactic) composability assumption for systems and the definition of ETA composition.   □

6   Compositionality of Communication Properties

We now study compositionality of communication properties. The issue here is to investigate conditions under which communication properties are preserved by ETA composition. The principle idea is that for this it should be sufficient to consider interface actions and to check (global) compliance conditions for them. We start by considering receptiveness and responsiveness.

Theorem 2. Let $\mathcal{E}_k(st_k)$, $st_{inf}(a)$, and $\mathcal{E}(st)$ be as in Theorem 1 for all $k \in [n]$ and $a \in \Sigma_{inf}$.

1. Assume that $\mathcal{E}_k(st_k)$ is receptive for all $k \in [n]$. If, for all $q \in \mathcal{R}(\mathcal{E}(st))$ and $a \in \Sigma_{inf}$, $\mathcal{E}(st)$ is compliant with all receptiveness requirements $rcp(\mathcal{J}, a)@q$ that are valid for $st(a) = st_{inf}(a)$, then $\mathcal{E}(st)$ is receptive.
2. Assume that $\mathcal{E}_k(st_k)$ is responsive for all $k \in [n]$. If, for all $q \in \mathcal{R}(\mathcal{E}(st))$ for which the responsiveness requirement generated by st has the form[6]

$$\bigvee \{ rsp(\mathcal{J}, a)@q \mid a \in \Sigma_{inf}, rsp(\mathcal{J}, a)@q \text{ is valid for } st(a) = st_{inf}(a) \} \quad (1)$$

$\mathcal{E}(st)$ is compliant with (1), then $\mathcal{E}(st)$ is responsive.

---

[6] Thus, (1) involves only responsiveness requirements concerning interface actions.

Proof. (sketch) The proof relies on the fact that projections $proj_{N_k}(q)$ of globally reachable states $q \in \mathcal{R}(\mathcal{E}(st))$ to a sub-system $\mathcal{S}_k$ are reachable in $\mathcal{E}_k(st_k)$. Then one can propagate communication properties concerning communicating actions $a \in \Sigma_{k,com}$ from $\mathcal{E}_k(st_k)$ to $\mathcal{E}(st)$. For interface actions compliance of $\mathcal{E}(st)$ with communication requirements is anyway assumed as a proof obligation.   □

The following corollary reformulates the second case in Theorem 2 to make it symmetric to the first case. This yields, however, a strengthening of the condition in the second case of Theorem 2 disregarding the fact that for responsiveness requirements it is always sufficient if just one of the input alternatives is served.

Corollary 1. *Let $\mathcal{E}_k(st_k)$, $st_{inf}(a)$, and $\mathcal{E}(st)$ be as in Theorem 1 for all $k \in [n]$ and $a \in \Sigma_{inf}$. Assume that $\mathcal{E}_k(st_k)$ is responsive for all $k \in [n]$. If, for all $q \in \mathcal{R}(\mathcal{E}(st))$ and $a \in \Sigma_{inf}$, $\mathcal{E}(st)$ is compliant with all responsiveness requirements $rsp(\mathcal{J}, a)@q$ that are valid for $st(a) = st_{inf}(a)$, then $\mathcal{E}(st)$ is responsive.*   □

Next we consider compositionality of the weak notions of receptiveness and responsiveness. The idea is to require weak compliance of the global team with all communication requirements concerning interface actions and then to rely on weak receptiveness (respectively, weak responsiveness) of the sub-teams. How this works is demonstrated by the following example.

Example 7. Consider from Examples 1–6 the chat system $\mathcal{S}_{chat}$ and the singleton system $\{\mathcal{A}_4\}$ consisting of the arbiter. From Example 3 we take the synchronisation type specification st_{chat} for the chat system and the ETA $\mathcal{E}_{chat}(st_{chat})$ determined by st_{chat}. Since $\{\mathcal{A}_4\}$ has no communicating actions, there are no synchronisation types and the ETA determined by the empty synchronisation type specification $st_\varnothing$ is $\mathcal{E}_{arbiter}(st_\varnothing)$ which coincides with $\mathcal{A}_4$ but has system labels $(\varnothing, ask, \{\mathcal{A}_4\})$, $(\{\mathcal{A}_4\}, grant, \varnothing)$, and $(\{\mathcal{A}_4\}, reject, \varnothing)$ instead of ask, $grant$, and $reject$. The latter are the interface actions. For them we choose the synchronisation type $st_{inf}(ask) = st_{inf}(grant) = st_{inf}(reject) = ([1,1],[1,1])$.

Now consider the ETA composition $\mathcal{E}_{chat}(st_{chat}) \otimes \mathcal{E}_{arbiter}(st_\varnothing) = \mathcal{E}(st)$, where st is defined by st_{chat} and st_{inf} as described in Theorem 1. To show how weak receptiveness of $\mathcal{E}_{chat}(st_{chat})$ (cf. Example 5) can be propagated to $\mathcal{E}(st)$, we consider as an example the receptiveness requirement $rcp(\{\mathcal{A}_1\}, msg)@(2,0,3,0)$ concerning the communicating action msg of $\mathcal{E}_{chat}(st_{chat})$ at the global state $(2,0,3,0)$ of $\mathcal{E}(st)$. In state 3 the server already received a msg from client $\mathcal{A}_1$ who wants to send another msg. The weak compliance of the sub-team $\mathcal{E}_{chat}(st_{chat})$ with $rcp(\{\mathcal{A}_1\}, msg)@(2,0,3)$ has shown us (cf. Example 5) that in the scope of $\mathcal{E}_{chat}(st_{chat})$ the server can execute the interface action ask followed by, e.g., $reject$ to return to state 0 where it can receive msg. The crucial point is now that in the global scope of $\mathcal{E}(st)$ the server can communicate with the arbiter such that server and arbiter together perform ask followed by, e.g., $reject$ and thus the server returns to state 0 where it can receive msg. Hence the compliance of $\mathcal{E}_{chat}(st_{chat})$ with $rcp(\{\mathcal{A}_1\}, msg)@(2,0,3)$ is propagated to $\mathcal{E}(st)$.   □

The example shows that weak compliance of the overall ETA $\mathcal{E}(st)$ with communication requirements concerning interface actions (*ask* and *reject* in the example) is a crucial assumption needed for compositionality. But there is still a subtle point to be taken into account as illustrated in the next example.

Example 8. Let $\mathcal{A}_1$, $\mathcal{A}_2$, and $\mathcal{A}_3$ be the following three component automata:

$$\mathcal{A}_1 : p_0 \xrightarrow{a!} p_1, p_0 \xrightarrow{c?} p_2 \quad \mathcal{A}_2 : q_0 \xrightarrow{b!} q_1 \xrightarrow{a?} q_2 \quad \mathcal{A}_3 : r_0 \xrightarrow{c!} r_1 \xrightarrow{b?} r_2$$

Let system $\mathcal{S}_1$ consist of $\mathcal{A}_1$ and $\mathcal{A}_2$ and $\mathcal{S}_2$ be the system consisting only of $\mathcal{A}_3$. The only communicating action in $\mathcal{S}_1$ is a, since b and c are interface actions. Let $\mathcal{E}_1(st_1)$ be the ETA over $\mathcal{S}_1$ determined by $st_1(a) = ([1,1],[1,1])$. There are two receptiveness requirements generated by st_1 which are $\mathtt{rcp}(\{\mathcal{A}_1\}, a)@(p_0, q_0)$ and $\mathtt{rcp}(\{\mathcal{A}_1\}, a)@(p_0, q_1)$. Obviously, $\mathcal{E}_1(st_1)$ is weakly compliant with both. For instance the first one is satisfied by the system transitions

$$(p_0, q_0) \xrightarrow{(\{\mathcal{A}_2\}, b, \varnothing)}_{\mathcal{E}_1(st_1)} (p_0, q_1) \xrightarrow{(\{\mathcal{A}_1\}, a, \{\mathcal{A}_2\})}_{\mathcal{E}_1(st_1)} (p_1, q_2)$$

The intermediate transition before accepting a executes interface action b.

Since $\mathcal{S}_2$ has no communicating actions, there are no synchronisation types and the ETA determined by the empty synchronisation type specification $st_\varnothing$ is $\mathcal{E}_2(st_\varnothing)$ which coincides with $\mathcal{A}_3$ when actions are replaced by system labels. Now we set $st_{inf}(b) = st_{inf}(c) = ([1,1],[1,1])$ and consider the ETA composition $\mathcal{E}_1(st_1) \otimes \mathcal{E}_2(st_\varnothing) = \mathcal{E}(st)$. For interface action b we get receptiveness requirement $\mathtt{rcp}(\{\mathcal{A}_2\}, b)@(p_0, q_0, r_0)$ and for c we get $\mathtt{rcp}(\{\mathcal{A}_3\}, c)@(p_0, q_0, r_0)$. $\mathcal{E}(st)$ is weakly compliant with the first one and compliant with the second one. So all looks fine. In the first case the weak compliance holds because of the transitions

$$(p_0, q_0, r_0) \xrightarrow{(\{\mathcal{A}_3\}, c, \{\mathcal{A}_1\})}_{\mathcal{E}(st)} (p_2, q_0, r_1) \xrightarrow{(\{\mathcal{A}_2\}, b, \{\mathcal{A}_3\})}_{\mathcal{E}(st)} (p_2, q_1, r_2)$$

The subtle point is here that in the first transition $\mathcal{A}_3$ 'calls back' to a component in $\mathcal{S}_1$, namely $\mathcal{A}_1$, before satisfying the receptiveness requirement of $\mathcal{A}_2$. This creates a kind of cycle which makes the overall team $\mathcal{E}(st)$ not weakly compliant with $\mathtt{rcp}(\{\mathcal{A}_1\}, a)@(p_0, q_0, r_0)$. Indeed, if $\mathcal{A}_1$ wants to send a then $\mathcal{A}_2$ must first send b to $\mathcal{A}_3$ which must first send c to $\mathcal{A}_1$. Hence the requirement of $\mathcal{A}_1$ to send b is not satisfiable in the overall team. Therefore we must exclude the possibility of such 'call backs' when checking weak compliance for interface actions. This is taken into account in the conditions (a) and (b) of Theorem 3, where we consider weak compliance without participation of components of the sub-system where a requirement stems from. □

The necessary assumptions discussed so far for obtaining compositionality in the cases of weak receptiveness and weak responsiveness are summarised in the following theorem. It additionally requires determinism of the sub-teams in order to get a unique lifting of intermediate activities in sub-teams when weak compliance is considered.

Theorem 3. *Let $\mathcal{E}_k(st_k)$, $st_{inf}(a)$, and $\mathcal{E}(st)$ be as in Theorem 1 for all $k \in [n]$ such that $st_{inf}(a) = ([o_1, \#dom_{a,out}(\mathcal{S})], [i_1, \#dom_{a,inp}(\mathcal{S})])$ with $o_1, i_1 \in \{0, 1\}$*

for all $a \in \Sigma_{inf}$. Let each $\mathcal{E}_k(st_k)$ be deterministic and weakly receptive (respectively, weakly responsive).

Assume that $\mathcal{E}(st)$ is weakly compliant, for all $a \in \Sigma_{inf}$ and $q \in \mathcal{R}(\mathcal{E}(st))$, with all atomic communication requirements $rcp(\mathcal{J}, a)@q$ and $rsp(\mathcal{J}, a)@q$ that are valid for $st_{inf}(a)$. Moreover, assume that if $\varnothing \neq \mathcal{J} \subseteq \mathcal{N}_k$ for some $k \in [n]$, then the weak compliance holds 'without participation of components in $\mathcal{N}_k \setminus \mathcal{J}$', i.e. we assume that:

(a) *$rcp(\mathcal{J}, a)@q$ holds since there exist $p, q' \in Q$, out $\supseteq \mathcal{J}$ and $\varnothing \subseteq$ inp such*
   that out $\cap \mathcal{N}_k = \mathcal{J}$ and $q \xrightarrow{\Lambda(\mathcal{S}) \setminus \Lambda_{\mathcal{N}_k}(\mathcal{S})} {}^*_{\mathcal{E}(st)} p \xrightarrow{(out, a, inp)} \mathcal{E}(st) q'$, and

(b) *$rsp(\mathcal{J}, a)@q$ holds since there exist $p, q' \in Q$, $\varnothing \subseteq$ out and inp $\supseteq \mathcal{J}$ such*
   that inp $\cap \mathcal{N}_k = \mathcal{J}$ and $q \xrightarrow{\Lambda(\mathcal{S}) \setminus \Lambda_{\mathcal{N}_k}(\mathcal{S})} {}^*_{\mathcal{E}(st)} p \xrightarrow{(out, a, inp)} \mathcal{E}(st) q'$.

Then $\mathcal{E}(st)$ is weakly receptive (respectively, weakly responsive).

Proof. (sketch) For interface actions weak compliance of $\mathcal{E}(st)$ with communication requirements is anyway assumed as a proof obligation. For non-interface actions we have to propagate communication properties concerning communicating actions $a \in \Sigma_{k,com}$ from a sub-team $\mathcal{E}_k(st_k)$ to $\mathcal{E}(st)$. The tricky point is here that the notion of weak compliance in a sub-team is so flexible that it allows some intermediate actions before a desired output (respectively, input) is accepted by the sub-team $\mathcal{E}_k(st_k)$. In particular, the intermediate actions can be interface actions. Then it must be guaranteed that those interface actions can be executed as synchronisations in the overall team $\mathcal{E}(st)$ which is ensured by conditions (a) and (b). □

Example 9. Consider the ETA composition $\mathcal{E}_{chat}(st_{chat}) \otimes \mathcal{E}_{arbiter}(st_\varnothing) = \mathcal{E}(st)$ of Example 7. The ETA $\mathcal{E}_{chat}(st_{chat})$ is deterministic, weakly receptive, and weakly responsive (cf. Example 5) and so is, trivially, the ETA $\mathcal{E}_{arbiter}(st_\varnothing)$. Then for the interface actions *ask*, *grant*, and *reject* we obtain the receptiveness requirements $rcp(\{\mathcal{A}_3\}, ask)@(p, q, 3, 0)$, $rcp(\{\mathcal{A}_4\}, grant)@(p, q, 4, 1)$, and $rcp(\{\mathcal{A}_4\}, reject)@(p, q, 4, 1)$ for any states p and q of the two clients such that the given global state is reachable within $\mathcal{E}(st)$. Obviously, $\mathcal{E}(st)$ is (even) compliant with these requirements. Hence condition (a) of Theorem 3 holds.

Now on the other hand, for the interface actions we obtain the responsiveness requirements $rcp(\{\mathcal{A}_3\}, grant)@(p, q, 4, 1)$, $rcp(\{\mathcal{A}_3\}, reject)@(p, q, 4, 1)$, and $rcp(\{\mathcal{A}_4\}, ask)@(p, q, r, 0)$ for any local states p, q, r such that the given global state is reachable within $\mathcal{E}(st)$. Obviously, $\mathcal{E}(st)$ is (even) compliant with the first two requirements and with the third requirement if $r = 3$. In all other possible cases for r, $\mathcal{E}(st)$ is weakly compliant with $rcp(\{\mathcal{A}_4\}, ask)@(p, q, r, 0)$. For instance, in the initial state $(0, 0, 0, 0)$ there is a path in $\mathcal{E}(st)$ without participation of the arbiter reaching state $(2, 0, 3, 0)$ (where the server already received a *msg* from client $\mathcal{A}_1$). Then the input *ask* of the arbiter can be served by the server. Since this holds similarly in all other cases, condition (b) of Theorem 3 is satisfied. Hence, as a consequence of Theorem 3, $\mathcal{E}(st)$ is weakly receptive and weakly responsive. □

7   Related Work

In the literature, compatibility notions are typically restricted to receptiveness requirements in system models with binary, synchronous commmunication [4, 25–28]. Our approach is generic, generating notions of communication safety for various kinds of synchronisation types. Concerning receptiveness and synchronisation type $st(a) = ([1,1], [1,1])$ for all actions a, it subsumes, e.g., compatibility notions of [4, 15] and [20] (for closed systems), and, for a limited weak case, those of [22] and [5].

We are aware of just a few approaches that consider notions of compatibility with respect to responsiveness. Both [15] and [22] consider system models with synchronous composition. Notably, in [15] responsiveness is captured by deadlock-freeness, while in [22] responsiveness is expressed as part of the definition of bidirectional complementarity compatibility. The latter, however, does not support a choice of input actions like we do. Finally, [17] can express sending constraints on partners in an asynchronous environment. It supports two kinds of communication styles: client/server and peer-to-peer.

Synchronisation types constrain the number of components which can simultaneously execute a *shared* action. There are approaches which do not rely on shared actions but specify possible interactions by determining which actions may or must synchronise. This originates already in Winskel's synchronisation algebras [31] providing an abstract model to specify different synchronisation styles for parallel composition. For describing system architectures BIP [1] proposes interaction models using connectors for ports (actions) of components. Typical architecture styles can be graphically represented [30]. Also compositionality results are provided but the focus is not on the analysis of input and output compatibilities.

8   Conclusion

We considered ETA, their specification by synchronisation types, and their (weak) compliance with communication requirements generated from synchronisation type specifications. In this sense our approach is generic, generating notions of communication safety for various kinds of synchronisation types. An essential contribution concerns the composition of systems and of ETA, and the investigation of criteria ensuring preservation of communication properties by composition. Verification of communication requirements in concrete cases is still a tedious task, which should be supported by appropriate future tools. Moreover, the validation of our approach on the basis of larger case studies is a future goal. From a software engineering perspective we are also interested in hierarchical designs where sub-teams are first encapsulated into CA by hiding communicating actions to make analysis of larger systems feasible, e.g., by using techniques of minimisation with respect to observational equivalence. Moreover, to support reusability we could also add an explicit notion of system connector to match actions of different systems by renaming. A further desired extension concerns the introduction of designated states in CA where execution can stop but may also continue, in addition to states where progress is required. As sketched in [10], their addition has significant and useful consequences for the derivation of communication requirements and compliance.

Acknowledgments. We thank the anonymous reviewers for their useful comments. The first author is supported by MIUR PRIN 2017FTXR7S project IT MaTTerS (Methods and Tools for Trustworthy Smart Systems).

References

1. Attie, P., Baranov, E., Bliudze, S., Jaber, M., Sifakis, J.: A general framework for architecture composability. Formal Aspects Comput. **28**(2), 207–231 (2015). https://doi.org/10.1007/s00165-015-0349-8
2. Bartoletti, M., Cimoli, T., Zunino, R.: Compliance in behavioural contracts: a brief survey. In: Bodei, C., Ferrari, G.-L., Priami, C. (eds.) Programming Languages with Applications to Biology and Security. LNCS, vol. 9465, pp. 103–121. Springer, Cham (2015). https://doi.org/10.1007/978-3-319-25527-9_9
3. Basile, D., ter Beek, M.H., Legay, A.: Timed service contract automata. Innov. Syst. Softw. Eng. **16**(2), 199–214 (2019). https://doi.org/10.1007/s11334-019-00353-3
4. Basile, D., Degano, P., Ferrari, G.L.: Automata for specifying and orchestrating service contracts. Log. Methods Comput. Sci. **12**(4:6), 1–51 (2016). https://doi.org/10.2168/LMCS-12(4:6)2016
5. Bauer, S.S., Mayer, P., Schroeder, A., Hennicker, R.: On weak modal compatibility, refinement, and the MIO workbench. In: Esparza, J., Majumdar, R. (eds.) TACAS 2010. LNCS, vol. 6015, pp. 175–189. Springer, Heidelberg (2010). https://doi.org/10.1007/978-3-642-12002-2_15
6. ter Beek, M.H., Carmona, J., Hennicker, R., Kleijn, J.: Communication requirements for team automata. In: Jacquet, J.-M., Massink, M. (eds.) COORDINATION 2017. LNCS, vol. 10319, pp. 256–277. Springer, Cham (2017). https://doi.org/10.1007/978-3-319-59746-1_14
7. ter Beek, M.H., Carmona, J., Kleijn, J.: Conditions for compatibility of components: the case of masters and slaves. In: Margaria, T., Steffen, B. (eds.) ISoLA 2016. LNCS, vol. 9952, pp. 784–805. Springer, Cham (2016). https://doi.org/10.1007/978-3-319-47166-2_55
8. ter Beek, M.H., Ellis, C.A., Kleijn, J., Rozenberg, G.: Synchronizations in team automata for groupware systems. Comput. Supp. Coop. Work **12**(1), 21–69 (2003). https://doi.org/10.1023/A:1022407907596
9. ter Beek, M.H., Hennicker, R., Kleijn, J.: Compositionality of safe communication in systems of team automata. Technical report, Zenodo, September 2020. https://doi.org/10.5281/zenodo.4050293
10. ter Beek, M.H., Hennicker, R., Kleijn, J.: Team Automata@Work: on safe communication. In: Bliudze, S., Bocchi, L. (eds.) COORDINATION 2020. LNCS, vol. 12134, pp. 77–85. Springer, Cham (2020). https://doi.org/10.1007/978-3-030-50029-0_5
11. ter Beek, M.H., Kleijn, J.: Associativity of infinite synchronized shuffles and team automata. Fundam. Inform. **91**(3–4), 437–461 (2009). https://doi.org/10.3233/FI-2009-0051

12. Bordeaux, L., Salaün, G., Berardi, D., Mecella, M.: When are two web services compatible? In: Shan, M.-C., Dayal, U., Hsu, M. (eds.) TES 2004. LNCS, vol. 3324, pp. 15–28. Springer, Heidelberg (2005). https://doi.org/10.1007/978-3-540-31811-8_2

13. Brand, D., Zafiropulo, P.: On communicating finite-state machines. J. ACM **30**(2), 323–342 (1983). https://doi.org/10.1145/322374.322380

14. Brim, L., Cerná, I., Vareková, P., Zimmerova, B.: Component-interaction automata as a verification-oriented component-based system specification. ACM Softw. Eng. Notes **31**(2) (2006). https://doi.org/10.1145/1118537.1123063

15. Carmona, J., Cortadella, J.: Input/output compatibility of reactive systems. In: Aagaard, M.D., O'Leary, J.W. (eds.) FMCAD 2002. LNCS, vol. 2517, pp. 360–377. Springer, Heidelberg (2002). https://doi.org/10.1007/3-540-36126-X_22

16. Carmona, J., Kleijn, J.: Compatibility in a multi-component environment. Theor. Comput. Sci. **484**, 1–15 (2013). https://doi.org/10.1016/j.tcs.2013.03.006

17. Carrez, C., Fantechi, A., Najm, E.: Behavioural contracts for a sound assembly of components. In: König, H., Heiner, M., Wolisz, A. (eds.) FORTE 2003. LNCS, vol. 2767, pp. 111–126. Springer, Heidelberg (2003). https://doi.org/10.1007/978-3-540-39979-7_8

18. Castagna, G., Gesbert, N., Padovani, L.: A theory of contracts for web services. ACM Trans. Program. Lang. Syst. **31**(5), 19:1–19:61 (2009). https://doi.org/10.1145/1538917.1538920

19. David, A., Larsen, K.G., Legay, A., Nyman, U., Wąsowski, A.: Timed I/O automata: a complete specification theory for real-time systems. In: Proceedings of the 13th International Conference on Hybrid Systems: Computation and Control, HSCC 2010, pp. 91–100. ACM (2010). https://doi.org/10.1145/1755952.1755967

20. de Alfaro, L., Henzinger, T.A.: Interface automata. In: Proceedings of the 8th European Software Engineering Conference Held Jointly with 9th ACM SIGSOFT International Symposium on Foundations of Software Engineering, ESEC/FSE 2001, pp. 109–120. ACM (2001). https://doi.org/10.1145/503209.503226

21. de Alfaro, L., Henzinger, T.A.: Interface-based design. In: Broy, M., Grünbauer, J., Harel, D., Hoare, T. (eds.) Engineering Theories of Software Intensive Systems. NSS, vol. 195, pp. 83–104. Springer, Dordrecht (2005). https://doi.org/10.1007/1-4020-3532-2_3

22. Durán, F., Ouederni, M., Salaün, G.: A generic framework for n-protocol compatibility checking. Sci. Comput. Program. **77**(7–8), 870–886 (2012). https://doi.org/10.1016/j.scico.2011.03.009

23. Ellis, C.A.: Team automata for groupware systems. In: Proceedings of the 1st International ACM SIGGROUP Conference on Supporting Group Work: The Integration Challenge, GROUP 1997, pp. 415–424. ACM (1997). https://doi.org/10.1145/266838.267363

24. Engels, G., Groenewegen, L.: Towards team-automata-driven object-oriented collaborative work. In: Brauer, W., Ehrig, H., Karhumäki, J., Salomaa, A. (eds.) Formal and Natural Computing. LNCS, vol. 2300, pp. 257–276. Springer, Heidelberg (2002). https://doi.org/10.1007/3-540-45711-9_15

25. Hennicker, R., Bidoit, M.: Compatibility properties of synchronously and asynchronously communicating components. Log. Methods Comput. Sci. **14**(1), 1–31 (2018). https://doi.org/10.23638/LMCS-14(1:1)2018

26. Hennicker, R., Knapp, A.: Moving from interface theories to assembly theories. Acta Inf. **52**(2–3), 235–268 (2015). https://doi.org/10.1007/s00236-015-0220-7

27. Larsen, K.G., Nyman, U., Wąsowski, A.: Modal I/O automata for interface and product line theories. In: De Nicola, R. (ed.) ESOP 2007. LNCS, vol. 4421, pp. 64–79. Springer, Heidelberg (2007). https://doi.org/10.1007/978-3-540-71316-6_6

28. Lüttgen, G., Vogler, W., Fendrich, S.: Richer interface automata with optimistic and pessimistic compatibility. Acta Inf. **52**(4-5), 305–336 (2015). https://doi.org/10.1007/s00236-014-0211-0

29. Lynch, N.A., Tuttle, M.R.: An introduction to input/output automata. CWI Q. **2**(3), 219–246 (1989). https://ir.cwi.nl/pub/18164

30. Mavridou, A., Baranov, E., Bliudze, S., Sifakis, J.: Architecture diagrams: a graphical language for architecture style specification. EPTCS **223**, 83–97 (2016). https://doi.org/10.4204/eptcs.223.6

31. Winskel, G.: Synchronization trees. Theor. Comput. Sci. **34**(1), 33–82 (1984). https://doi.org/10.1016/0304-3975(84)90112-9

Analysis of Bayesian Networks
via Prob-Solvable Loops

Ezio Bartocci, Laura Kovács, and Miroslav Stankovič[(⊠)]

TU Wien, Vienna, Austria
{Ezio.Bartocci,Laura.Kovacs,Miroslav.Stankovic}@tuwien.ac.at

Abstract. Prob-solvable loops are probabilistic programs with polynomial assignments over random variables and parametrised distributions, for which the full automation of moment-based invariant generation is decidable. In this paper we extend Prob-solvable loops with new features essential for encoding Bayesian networks (BNs). We show that various BNs, such as discrete, Gaussian, conditional linear Gaussian and dynamic BNs, can be naturally encoded as Prob-solvable loops. Thanks to these encodings, we can automatically solve several BN related problems, including exact inference, sensitivity analysis, filtering and computing the expected number of rejecting samples in sampling-based procedures. We evaluate our work on a number of BN benchmarks, using automated invariant generation within Prob-solvable loop analysis.

1 Introduction

Bayesian networks (BNs) are well-established probabilistic models widely adopted to represent complex systems and to reason about their intrinsic uncertain knowledge. BNs are graphically depicted as directed acyclic graphs (DAGs) whose nodes represent random variables and edges capture conditional dependencies. Since the seminal work of [40], BNs have been extensively employed in several application domains including machine learning [22], speech recognition [44], sports betting [12], gene regulatory networks [20], diagnosis of diseases [24] and finance [39]. Part of their success is due to the inherited Bayesian inference framework enabling the prediction about the likelihood that one of several known causes is responsible for the evidence of an observed event.

Figure 1 illustrates a simple BN with two events that can cause the grass (G) to be wet: the rain (R) or an active sprinkler (S). When it rains the sprinkler is usually not active, so the rain has a direct effect on the use of the sprinkler. This dependency is provided by a *conditional probability table*, in short CPT, associated to the sprinkler random variable S. A CPT lists, for each possible combination of values of the parents' variables (one for each row of the table), the corresponding probability for the child's variable to have a certain discrete value (one for each column of the table). The random variables G, R, S of Fig. 1 are, for example, binary random variables with Bernoulli conditional distributions. However, in general BNs allow arbitrary types for their random variables and their conditional distributions.

This research was supported by the Vienna Science and Technology Fund (WWTF) under grant ICT19-018 (ProbInG), the ERC Starting Grant 2014 SYMCAR 639270 and the Austrian FWF project W1255-N23.

© Springer Nature Switzerland AG 2020
V. K. I. Pun et al. (Eds.): ICTAC 2020, LNCS 12545, pp. 221–241, 2020.
https://doi.org/10.1007/978-3-030-64276-1_12

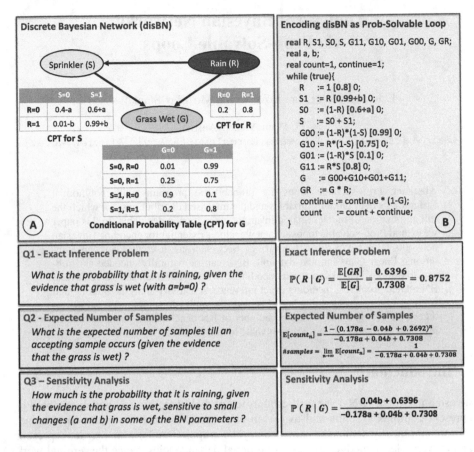

Fig. 1. Solving probabilistic inference, the expected number of samples and the sensitivity analysis for a discrete BN (disBN), by encoding the disBN as a Prob-solvable loop and computing automatically moment-based invariants (MBIs).

Probabilistic Inference. Given the BN in Fig. 1, the following can be asked:

Q1 - What is the probability that it is raining, given that the grass is wet?

The answer to this question can be obtained by solving a *probabilistic inference*, that is the problem to optimally estimate the probability of an event given an observed evidence. The works in [13,14] show that both *exact* and *approximated* (up to an arbitrary precision) methods to solve probabilistic inference are NP-hard.

How Many Samples? Approximating solutions for probabilistic inferences can be done using Monte Carlo sampling techniques [28,43]. For example, *rejection sampling* is one of the fundamental techniques for sampling from the joint (unconditional) distribution of the BN: a sample is accepted when it complies with the evidence, otherwise is rejected. Unfortunately, this method may require many samples before obtaining the

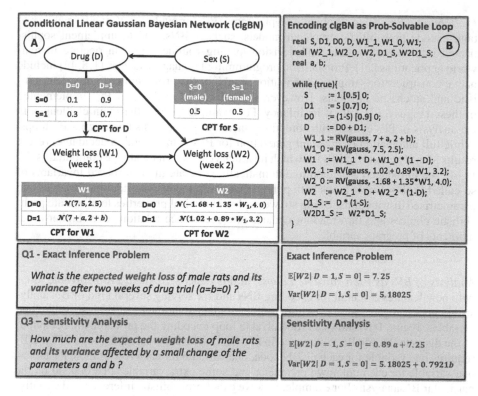

Fig. 2. Solving probabilistic inference and sensitivity analysis in a conditional linear Gaussian BN (clgBN), by encoding the clgBN as a Prob-solvable loop and computing MBIs.

first accepted samples, while most of the samples may be wasted simply because they do not satisfy the observations. Thus, an interesting question, investigated also in [7], is:

Q2 - What is the expected number of samples until an accepting sample occurs?

Sensitivity Analysis. As BN parameters are often provided manually or estimated from (incomplete) data, they are most likely to be imprecise or wrong. For example, in Fig. 1 the CPT of the random variable S contains imprecise symbolic parameters a and b. In this case, *sensitivity analysis* aims to answer the following question:

Q3 - How much does a small change in BN parameters affect probabilistic inference?

Probabilistic Programs. Probabilistic programs (PPs) provide a unifying framework to both encode probabilistic graphical models, such as BNs, and to implement sophisticated inference algorithms and decision making routines that can operate in real-world applications [21]. Probabilistic programming languages, such as [1, 8, 42] include native constructs for sampling distribution, enabling the programmer to mix deterministic and stochastic elements. However, the automated analysis of PPs implemented in these languages is still at its infancy. For example, one of the main challenges in the analysis of PPs comes with computing invariant properties summarizing PP loops. While full automation of invariant generation for PPs is in general undecidable, recent results identify classes of PPs for which invariants can automatically be computed [4, 7]. In [4], we introduced a method to automatically generate moment-based invariants of so-called Prob-solvable loops with polynomial assignments over random variables and parametrised distributions. Doing so, we exploit statistical properties to eliminate probabilistic choices and turn random updates into recurrence relations over higher-order moments of program variables.

Analysis of BNs as Prob-solvable Loops. In this paper we extend Prob-solvable loops with new features essential for encoding BNs and for solving several kind of BN analysis via invariant generation over higher-order statistical moments of Prob-solvable loop variables. Figure 1(B) shows a Prob-solvable loop encoding the probabilistic behaviour of the discrete BN (disBN) illustrated in Fig. 1(A). The Prob-solvable loop of Fig. 1(B) requires one variable for each disBN node, one variable for each row of the CPT tables, one variable for each unknown parameter and some extra variables that depend on the particular BN analysis. For example, to solve exact probabilistic inference and sensitivity analysis, we require an extra variable to store the product of the random variables G and R. On the other hand, to compute the expected number of samples until an accepting sample occurs, we would need other two auxiliary variables *count* and *continue*. Each row of each CPT is encoded as a probabilistic assignment in the Prob-solvable loop. Our approach generates moment-based invariants as quantitative invariants over higher-order moments to solve the three questions (Q1-Q3) of Fig. 1. The required Prob-solvable loop analysis requires however additional steps (e.g., calculating a limit) that are not yet supported in [4]. Moreover, while the Prob-solvable programming model of [4] can model the probabilistic behavior of disBNs, it cannot model other BN variants, such as BNs with Gaussian conditional dependencies as in Fig. 2(A). We therefore extend Prob-solvable loops with new features supporting Gaussian and uniform random variables depending on other random variables (Sect. 3) and show that these extensions allow us to solve BN problems via Prob-solvable loop reasoning (Sects. 4 and 5).

Our Contributions. (i) We prove that our extended model of Prob-solvable loops admits a decision procedure for computing moment-based invariants (Sect. 3). (ii) We provide a sound encoding of BNs as Prob-solvable loops, in particular addressing discrete BNs (disBNs), Gaussian BNs (gBNs), conditional linear Gaussian BNs (clgBNs) and dynamic BN (dynBNs) (Sect. 4). (iii) We formalize several BN problems as moment-based invariant generation tasks in Prob-solvable loops (Sect. 5). (iv) We implemented our approach in the MORA tool [6] and evaluated it on a number of examples, fully automating BN analysis via Prob-solvable loop reasoning (Sect. 5.4). Complete proofs for the theorems in this work as well as further details are available in the extended version [5].

2 Preliminaries

We first introduce basic notions from statistics in order to reason about probabilistic systems (Sect. 2.1), and refer to [35] for further details. We then adopt basic definitions and properties of Bayesian Networks (BNs) from [40] to our setting (Sect. 2.2). Throughout this paper, let $\mathbb{N}, \mathbb{R}$ denote the set of natural and real numbers, respectively.

2.1 Probability Space and Statistical Moments

We denote random variables by capital letters $X, Y, S, R, \ldots$ and program variables by small letters $x, y, \ldots$, all possibly with indices.

Definition 1 (Probability Space). *A probability space is a triple (Ω, F, P), where $\Omega \neq \emptyset$ is a sample space representing the set of outcomes, $F \subset 2^{\Omega}$ is a σ-algebra representing the set of events, and $P : F \to [0, 1]$ is a probability measure with $P(\Omega) = 1$.*

We now define random variables, together with their higher-order statistical moments, in order to reason about probabilistic properties.

Definition 2 (Random Variable). *A random variable $X : \Omega \to \mathbb{R}$ is a measurable function from a set Ω of possible outcomes to $\mathbb{R}$. If Ω is countable, the random variable X is called* discrete; *otherwise, X is* continuous.

In particular, in this paper we will be interested in the following random variables:

- Random variable X with Bernoulli distribution $Bern(p)$, given by probability p, where $\Omega = \{0, 1\}$ and $X(0) = 1 - p$ and $X(1) = p$;
- Random variable X with Gaussian distribution $\mathcal{G}(\mu, \sigma^2)$, given by mean μ and variance σ^2, where $\Omega = \mathbb{R}$ and probability density function $f(x) = \frac{1}{\sigma\sqrt{2\pi}} e^{-\frac{1}{2}\left(\frac{x-\mu}{\sigma}\right)^2}$.
- Random variable X with uniform distribution $\mathcal{U}(a, b)$, given by limits a, b where $\Omega = \mathbb{R}$ and probability density function $f(x) = \begin{cases} \frac{1}{b-a} & \text{for } z \in [a, b] \\ 0 & \text{for } z \notin [a, b] \end{cases}$.

Example 1. The variables R, S, G of the BN from Fig. 1(A) are Bernoulli random variables, with variable R given by probability 0.8. Figure 2(A) features two Bernoulli random variables S and D as well as two real-valued random variables $W1$ and $W2$ drawn from a Gaussian distribution. Note that the parameters of the Gaussian distribution of $W1$ depend on the values of D, whereas for $W2$ they depend on D and $W1$.

For a given random variable X we will denote by $\Omega(X)$ the sample space of X. When working with a random variable X, the most common statistical moment of X to consider is its first-order moment, called the expected value of X.

Definition 3 (Expected Value). *An* expected value of a random variable X *defined on a probability space* (Ω, F, P) *is the Lebesgue integral:* $\mathbb{E}[X] = \int_{\Omega} X \cdot dP$. *In the special case when* Ω *is discrete, that is the outcomes are* $x_1, \ldots, x_n$ *with corresponding probabilities* $p_1, \ldots, p_n$ *and* $n \in \mathbb{N}$, *we have* $\mathbb{E}[X] = \sum_{i=1}^{n} x_i \cdot p_i$. *The expected value of* X *is often also referred to as the* mean *or* μ *of* X.

The key ingredient in analyzing and deriving properties of a random variable X is the so-called characteristic function of X.

Definition 4 (Characteristic Function). *The* characteristic function *of a random variable* X, *denoted by* $\phi_X(t)$, *is the Fourier transform of its probability density function (pdf). That is,* $\phi_X(t) = \mathbb{E}[e^{itX}]$, *with a bijective relation between probability distributions and characteristic functions.*

The characteristic function $\phi_X(t)$ of a random variable X captures the value distribution induced by X. In particular, the characteristic function $\phi_X(t)$ of X enables inferring properties about distributions given by weighted sums of X and other random variables, and thus also about statistical higher-order moments of X.

Definition 5 (Higher-Order Moments). *Let* X *be a random variable,* $c \in \mathbb{R}$ *and* $k \in \mathbb{N}$. *We write* $Mom_k[X]$ *to denote the* kth *raw moment of* X, *which is defined as:*

$$Mom_k[X] = \mathbb{E}[X^k]. \tag{1}$$

Remark 1. For a Bernoulli random variable X with parameter probability p, all moments of X coincide with its probability. Thus, $Mom_k[X] = P(X = 1) = p$.

Example 2. Figure 1 lists the first-order moment $\mathbb{E}[G]$ of G, as well as the first-order moment $\mathbb{E}[GR]$ of the mixed random variable GR. The second-order moment of $W2$ is used to compute the variance $Var(W2)$ of $W2$ in Fig. 2.

2.2   Probabilistic Graphical Models as Bayesian Networks

Definition 6 (Bayesian Network (BN)). *A* Bayesian network (BN) *is a directed acyclic graph (DAG) in which each node is a discrete/continuous random variable. A set of directed links or arrows connects pairs of BN nodes. If there is an arrow from a BN node* Y *to a node* X, *then* Y *is said to be a* parent *of* X.

For a random variable/node X in a BN, we write $Par(X)$ to denote the set of parents of X in the BN. Each BN node X has a *conditional probability distribution* $P(X|Par(X))$ that quantifies the effect of the parents $Par(X)$ on the node X. Dependencies in a BN can be given in different forms and we overview the most common ones. For a discrete variable X, dependencies are often given by a conditional probability table, by listing all possible values of parent variables from $Par(X)$ and the corresponding values of X. In the case of a continuous variable X, dependencies can be specified using Gaussian distributions. Another common dependency in a BN is a deterministic one, where value of a node X is determined by values of its parents from $Par(X)$; that is, a binary variable can be true iff all its (binary) parents are true, or if one of its parents is true. We overview below BN variants, studied further in Sect. 4.

Definition 7 (Variants of Bayesian Networks).

- A discrete Bayesian Network (disBN) *is a BN whose variables are discrete.*
- A Gaussian Bayesian Network (gBN) *is a BN whose dependencies are given by Gaussian distributions in which, for any BN node X, we have* $P(X|Par(X)) = \mathcal{G}(\mu_X, \sigma_X^2)$, *with* $\mu_X = \alpha_X + \sum_{k=1}^{m_X} \beta_{X,k} Y_{X,k}$, $Par(X) = \{Y_1, \cdots, Y_{m_X}\}$ *and* σ_X^2 *is fixed.*
- A conditional linear Gaussian Bayesian Network (clgBN) *is a BN in which (i) continuous nodes X cannot be parents of discrete nodes Y; (ii) the local distribution of each discrete node Y is a conditional probability table (CPT); (iii) the local distribution of each continuous node X is a set of Gaussian distributions, one for each configuration of the discrete parents Y, with the continuous parents acting as regressors.*
- A dynamic Bayesian Network (dynBN) *is a structured BN consisting of a series of time slices that represent the state of all the BN nodes X at a certain time t. For each time-slice, a dependency structure between the variables X at that time is defined by intra-time-slice edges. Additionally, there are edges between variables from different slices—inter-time-slice edges, with their directions following the direction of time.*

Example 3. A disBN encoding the probabilistic model of the grass getting wet is shown in Fig. 1(A). Figure 2(A) lists a clgBN, describing a weight loss process in a drug trial performed on rats. The (Gaussian) random variables encoding weight loss for weeks 1 and 2 are respectively denoted with $W1$ and $W2$.

3   Programming Model: Extending Prob-solvable Loops

We introduce our programming model extending the class of *Prob-solvable loops* [4], allowing us to encode and analyze BN properties in Sect. 4. In particular, we extend [4] to support Prob-solvable loops with symbolic random variables encoding dependencies among other (random) variables, where Gaussian and uniform random variables can linearly depend on other program variables, encoding this way common BN dependencies. To this end, we consider probabilistic while-programs as introduced in [30,37] and restrict this class of programs to probabilistic programs with polynomial updates among random variables. We write $x := e_1[p]e_2$ to denote that the probability of the program variable x being updated with expression e_1 is $p \in [0,1]$, whereas the probability of x being updated with expression e_2 is $1 - p$. In the sequel, whenever we refer to a Prob-solvable loop/program, we mean a program as defined below.

Definition 8 (Prob-solvable Loop). *Let* $m \in \mathbb{N}$ *and* $x_1, \ldots, x_m$ *denote real-valued program variables. A Prob-solvable loop with variables* $x_1, \ldots, x_m$ *is a probabilistic program of the form*

$$I; while(true)\{U\}, \tag{2}$$

where:

- *(Initialization)* I *is a sequence of initial assignments over* $x_1, \ldots, x_m$. *That is, I is an assignments sequence* $x_1 := c_1; x_2 := c_2; \ldots; x_m := c_m$, *with* $c_i \in \mathbb{R}$ *representing a number drawn from a known distribution* [1] *- in particular, c_i can be a real constant.*

---

[1] A known distribution is a distribution with known and computable moments.

Algorithm 1. Moment-Based Invariants (MBIs) of Prob-solvable Loops

---

Input: Prob-solvable loop $\mathcal{P}$ with variables $\{x_1, \ldots, x_m\}$, and $k \geq 1$
Output: $MBIs$ of $\mathcal{P}$ of degree k
Assumptions: $n \in \mathbb{N}$ is an arbitrary loop iteration of $\mathcal{P}$

1: Extract moment-based recurrence relations of $\mathcal{P}$, for $i = 1, \ldots, m$:

$$\mathbb{E}[x_i(n+1)] = p_i \cdot \mathbb{E}[a_i x_i(n) + P_i(x_1(n), \ldots, x_{i-1}(n))]$$
$$+ (1 - p_i) \cdot \mathbb{E}[b_i x_i(n) + Q_i(x_1(n), \ldots, x_{i-1}(n))].$$

2: $MBRecs = \{\mathbb{E}[x_i(n+1)] \mid i = 1, \ldots, m\}$ ▷ initial set of moment-based recurrences
3: $S := \{x_1^k, \ldots, x_m^k\}$ ▷ initial set of monomials of $\mathbb{E}$-variables
4: **while** $S \neq \emptyset$ **do**
5:     $M := \prod_{i=1}^m x_i^{\alpha_i} \in S$, where $\alpha_i \in \mathbb{N}$
6:     $S := S \setminus \{M\}$
7:     $M' = M[x_i^{\alpha_i} \leftarrow upd_i]$, for each $i = m, \ldots, 1$ ▷ replace each $x_i^{\alpha_i}$ in M with upd_i

      where upd_i denotes:
$$p_i \cdot \left(a_i x_i + P_i(x_1, \ldots, x_{i-1})\right)^{\alpha_i} + (1 - p_i) \cdot \left(b_i x_i + Q_i(x_1, \ldots, x_{i-1})\right)^{\alpha_i}$$

8:     Rewrite M' as $M' = \sum N_j$ for monomials N_j over $x_1, \ldots, x_m$
9:     **Simplify moment-based recurrence** $\mathbb{E}[M(n+1)] = \mathbb{E}[\sum N_j]$ **using (5)-(6)**
                                  ▷ $M(n+1)$ denotes $\prod_{i=1}^m x_i(n+1)^{\alpha_i}$
10:    $MBRecs = MBRecs \cup \{\mathbb{E}[M(n+1)]\}$
                                 ▷ add $\mathbb{E}[M(n+1)]$ to the set of moment-based recurrences
11:    **for** each monomial N_j in M **do**
12:      **if** $\mathbb{E}[N_j] \notin MBRecs$ **then**   ▷ there is no moment-based recurrence for N_j
13:       $S = S \cup \{N_j\}$ ▷ add N_j to S
14: **end while**
15: $MBI = \{\mathbb{E}[x_i(n)^k] - f_{x_i,k}(n) = 0 \mid i = 1, \ldots, m\}$
                          ▷ $f_{x_i,k}(n)$ is the closed form solution of $\mathbb{E}[x_i^k]$
16: **return** $MBIs$ of $\mathcal{P}$ for the kth moments of $x_1, \ldots, x_m$

– *(Update) U denotes a sequence of m random updates, each update of the form:*

$$x_i := a_i x_i + P_i(x_1, \ldots, x_{i-1}) \; [p_i] \; b_i x_i + Q_i(x_1, \ldots, x_{i-1}), \quad\quad (3)$$

or, in case of a deterministic assignment,

$$x_i := a_i x_i + P_i(x_1, \ldots, x_{i-1}), \quad\quad (4)$$

where $a_i, b_i \in \mathbb{R}$ are constants and $P_i, Q_i \in \mathbb{R}[x_1, \ldots, x_{i-1}]$ are polynomials over program variables $x_1, \ldots, x_{i-1}$.
– *(Dependencies) The coefficients a_i, b_i and the coefficients of P_i and Q_i in the variable assignments (3)-(4) of x_i can be drawn from a random distribution as long as the moments of this distribution are known and either they are (i) Gaussian or uniform distributions linearly depending on x_i and other random variables x_j with $j \neq i$; or (ii) other known distributions independent from $x_1, \ldots, x_m$.*

Note that Prob-solvable loops support parametrised distributions, for example one may have the uniform distribution $\mathcal{U}(d_1, d_2)$ with arbitrary $d_1 < d_2 \in \mathbb{R}$ symbolic constants. Similarly, the probabilities p_i in the probabilistic updates (3) can be symbolic constants. The restriction on random variable dependencies from Definition 8 extends [4] by allowing parameters of Gaussian and uniform random variables x_i in Prob-solvable loop to be specified using previously updated program variables x_j and to depend on x_i linearly. In Theorem 1 we prove that this extension maintains the existence and computability of higher-order statistical moments of Prob-solvable loops, allowing us to derive all *moment-based invariants* of Prob-solvable loops of degree $k \geq 1$.

Definition 9 (Moment-Based Invariants (MBIs)). *Let $\mathcal{P}$ be a Prob-solvable loop and $n \in \mathbb{N}$ denote an arbitrary loop iteration of $\mathcal{P}$. Consider $k \in \mathbb{N}$ with $k \neq 0$. A moment-based invariant (MBI) of degree k over x_i of $\mathcal{P}$ is $\mathbb{E}[x_i(n)^k] = f_{x_i,k}(n)$, where $f_{x_i,k} : \mathbb{N} \to \mathbb{R}$ of n is a closed form expression for the kth (raw) higher-order moment of x_i, such that $f_{x_i,k}(b)$ depends only on n and the initial variable values of $\mathcal{P}$.*

In what follows, we consider an arbitrary Prob-solvable loop $\mathcal{P}$ and formalize our results relative to $\mathcal{P}$. Further, we reserve $n \in \mathbb{N}$ to denote an arbitrary loop iteration of $\mathcal{P}$. Note that MBIs of $\mathcal{P}$ yield functional representations of the kth higher-order moments of loop variables x_i at n. Hence, the MBIs $\mathbb{E}[x_i(n)^k] = f_{x_i,k}(n)$ are valid and invariant. In Algorithm 1 we show that MBIs of Prob-solvable loops can always be computed. As in [4], the main ingredient of Algorithm 1 are so-called $\mathbb{E}$-*variables* for capturing expected values and other higher-order moments of loop variables of $\mathcal{P}$.

Definition 10 ($\mathbb{E}$-variables of Prob-solvable Loops [4]). *An $\mathbb{E}$-variable of $\mathcal{P}$ is an expected value of a monomial over the random variables x_i of $\mathcal{P}$.*

Using Definition 10, in Algorithm 1 we compute $\mathbb{E}$-variables based on expected values $\mathbb{E}[x_i(n)]$ of loop variables x_i, as well as using higher-order and mixed moments of $\mathcal{P}$, such as $\mathbb{E}[x_i^k(n)]$ or $\mathbb{E}[x_ix_j(n)]$ (lines 3 and 9 of Algorithm 1). To this end, Algorithm 1 resembles the approach of [4] and extends it to handle Prob-solvable loops with dependencies among random variables drawn from Gaussian/uniform distributions (line 9 of Algorithm 1). More specifically, Algorithm 1 uses *moment-based recurrences over E-variables* from [4], describing the expected values $\mathbb{E}[x_i(n)]$ of x_i as functions of other E-variables (line 2 of Algorithm 1). To this end, note that Prob-solvable loop updates from (3)-(4) over x_i yield linear recurrences with constant coefficients over $\mathbb{E}[x_i(n)]$, by using the following simplification rules over $\mathbb{E}$-variables:

$$
\begin{aligned}
\mathbb{E}[expr_1 + expr_2] &\to \mathbb{E}[expr_1] + \mathbb{E}[expr_2] \\
\mathbb{E}[expr_1 \cdot expr_2] &\to \mathbb{E}[expr_1] \cdot \mathbb{E}[expr_2], \quad \text{if } expr_1, expr_2 \text{ are independent} \\
\mathbb{E}[c \cdot expr_1] &\to c \cdot \mathbb{E}[expr_1] \\
\mathbb{E}[c] &\to c \\
\mathbb{E}[\mathcal{D} \cdot expr_1] &\to \mathbb{E}[\mathcal{D}] \cdot \mathbb{E}[expr_1]
\end{aligned}
\tag{5}
$$

where $c \in \mathbb{R}$ is a constant, $\mathcal{D}$ is a known independent distribution, and $expr_1, expr_2$ are polynomial expressions over random variables. Yet, to address our Prob-solvable loop extensions compared to [4], in addition to (5) we need to ensure that dependencies among the random variables of $\mathcal{P}$ yield also moment-based recurrences. We achieve this by introducing the following two simplification rules over random variables with Gaussian/uniform distributions:

$$
\begin{aligned}
\mathcal{G}(expr_1, \sigma^2) &\to expr_1 + \mathcal{G}(0, \sigma^2), \\
\mathcal{U}(expr_1, expr_2) &\to expr_1 + (expr_2 - expr_1)\mathcal{U}(0, 1),
\end{aligned}
\tag{6}
$$

for arbitrary polynomial expressions $expr_1$, $expr_2$ over random variables. Using (6) in addition to (5), moment-based recurrences of Prob-solvable loops can always be computed as linear recurrences with constant coefficients over $\mathbb{E}$-variables (line 9 of Algorithm 1), implying thus the existence of closed form solutions of $\mathbb{E}$-variables and hence of MBIs of $\mathcal{P}$, as formalized below.

Theorem 1 (Moment-Based Invariants (MBIs) of Prob-solvable Loops). *Let $\mathcal{P}$ be a Prob-solvable loop with variables $\{x_1, \ldots, x_m\}$ and consider $k \in \mathbb{N}$ with $k \geq 1$. Algorithm 1 is sound and terminating, yielding MBIs of degree k of $\mathcal{P}$.*

Proof. We first prove correctness of the simplification rules (6), from which the soundness and termination of Algorithm 1 follows. Recall that there is a one-to-one correspondence between probability distributions and characteristic functions $\mathbb{E}[e^{itX}]$ of a random variable X. In particular, the characteristic function of a Gaussian distribution with parameters μ and σ^2 is $e^{i\mu t - \frac{1}{2}\sigma^2 t^2}$, and thus the characteristic function of $\mathcal{G}(expr_1, \sigma^2)$ is $\mathbb{E}[e^{it\mathcal{N}(expr_1, \sigma^2)}]$. Then,

$$
\mathbb{E}\left[e^{it\mathcal{N}(expr_1, \sigma^2)}\right] = \mathbb{E}\left[\int e^{it\mathcal{N}(y, \sigma^2)} f(y) dy\right] = \iint e^{itx} \frac{1}{\sqrt{2\pi\sigma^2}} e^{-\frac{(x-y)^2}{2\sigma^2}} f(y) dx dy
$$

$$
= \int e^{itx} \frac{1}{\sqrt{2\pi\sigma^2}} e^{-\frac{(x)^2}{2\sigma^2}} dx \int e^{ity} f(y) dy
$$

$$
= \mathbb{E}\left[e^{it\mathcal{N}(0, \sigma^2)}\right] \cdot \mathbb{E}\left[e^{it \cdot expr_1}\right] = \mathbb{E}\left[e^{it\left(\mathcal{N}(0, \sigma^2) + expr_1\right)}\right]
$$

by change of limits for $x \in \mathbb{R}$, where f is the probability density function of the random variable $expr_1$. Note that $\mathbb{E}\left[e^{it\left(\mathcal{N}(0, \sigma^2) + expr_1\right)}\right]$ corresponds to the characteristic function of $expr_1 + \mathcal{G}(0, \sigma^2)$, and hence the simplification rule $\mathcal{G}(expr_1, \sigma^2) \rightarrow expr_1 + \mathcal{G}(0, \sigma^2)$ of (6) is correct. The correctness of the simplification rule of (6) over uniform distributions can be established in a similar way.

Further, observe that polynomial expressions remain polynomial after applications of (6) (line 9 of Algorithm 1). Once Gaussian and uniform distributions depending on loop variables are replaced using (6), we are left with independent known distributions and polynomial expressions over random variables for which (5) can further be used, as in [4]. As Algorithm 1 extends [4] only with (6) (line 9 of Algorithm 1), using results of [4], we conclude that Algorithm 1 is both sound and terminating. □

Example 4. Consider the Prob-solvable loop in Fig. 2(B). An example of $\mathbb{E}$-variable would be $\mathbb{E}[W2^2]$, for which an MBI $\mathbb{E}[W2^2] = 4.01408a^2 + 53.83168a + 4.01408b + 250.3172$ is computed using Algorithm 1.

Remark 2. While Prob-solvable loops are non-deterministic, with trivial loop guards of *true*, we note that probabilistic loops bounded by a number of iterations (such as $n := 0; while(n < 1000)\{n := n + 1\}$) can be encoded as Prob-solvable loops.

4   Encoding BNs as Prob-solvable Loops

In this section we argue that Prob-solvable loops offer a natural way for encoding BNs, enabling further BN analysis via Prob-solvable loop reasoning in Sect. 5.

4.1 Modeling Local Probabilistic Models of BNs as Prob-solvable Loop Updates

A BN is fully specified by its local dependencies. We consider common local probabilistic models and encode these models as Prob-solvable loop instances, as follows.

Deterministic Dependency. We first explore local probabilistic models specifying
deterministic dependency, that is when the values of BN nodes X are determined by the
values of the parent variables from $Par(X)$. For example, when X is binary-valued,
such a deterministic dependency can be a Boolean expression. On the other hand, when
X is continuous, deterministic dependency can be a function over $Par(X)$.

For a continuous variable X whose value is given by a polynomial $Q(Par(X))$,
encoding deterministic dependencies as a Prob-solvable loop update is straightforward:
we simply set $X = Q(Par(X))$.

For a discrete random variable X, let $[X = x]$ be the expression such that $[X =
x] = 1$ if $X = x$ and 0 otherwise. Note that when X is binary-valued, we have $[X =
1] = X$ and $[X = 0] = 1 - X$. It follows that, in general, for a discrete variable X with
possible values $x = 0, 1, \cdots, k$, we have $[X = x] = \prod_{\substack{0 \le i < k \\ i \ne x}} \frac{X-i}{x-i}$. Furthermore, let

$[(X, Y) = (x, y)] = [X = x] \cdot [Y = y]$. Then, $[(X, Y) = (x, y)] = 1$ iff $X = x \wedge Y =
y$, and 0 otherwise. Finally, we write $[X \ne x]$ to denote $1 - [X = x]$. Observe that
$[X = x]$ and $[X \ne x]$ are polynomials in X, providing thus a natural way to specify
deterministic dependencies as updates (3)-(4) of Prob-solvable loops (see Algorithm 2).

Conditional Probability Tables – CPTs. As shown in Fig. 1(A), a common way to
specify BN dependencies among discrete variables is CPTs, with each CPT line representing a possible assignment of values of a BN node X to $Par(X)$. A CPT for X can
be turned into Prob-solvable loop updates, as follows.

We represent values of X with integers. For simplicity, assume that X is binary-
valued. Let $Par(X) = \{Y_1, \cdots, Y_k\}$ denote the parents of X. For each line L in the
CPT for X we introduce a new variable X_L. Each line L specifies values for $Par(X)$;
for example, $Y_1 = y_1, \cdots, Y_k = y_k$. Let $p_L := P(X = 1|L)$ and define

$$X_L = \prod_{0 < i \le k} [Y_i = y_i] \, [p_L] \, 0, \qquad (7)$$

encoding that the value of X_L is 0 if the values of Y_i are not specified in the respective
CPT line L; otherwise the value of X_L is 1 with probability p_L. We then set

$$X = \sum_{L \in CPT} X_L. \qquad (8)$$

Example 5. Using (7)-(8), the disBN of Fig. 1(A) is encoded as a Prob-solvable loop
in Fig. 1(B). While the parameters of S and G are not directly visible from the disBN,
these parameters are given by the expected values of S and G in the Prob-solvable
loop of Fig. 1(B). Note that Fig. 1(B) also features a GR variable corresponding to a
Bernoulli random variable depending on G and R, such that GR is 1 iff both G and R
are 1. The program variable *continue* samples a sequence of Bernoulli random variables (one for each iteration n), while the random variable *count* represents a geometric
distribution encoding the sum of *continue* values.

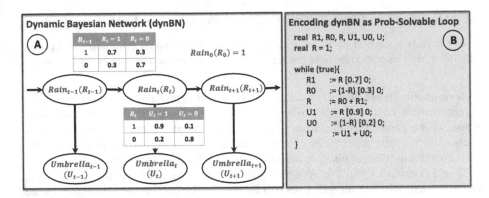

Fig. 3. In Fig. 3(B) we give the Prob-solvable loop encoding of the dynBN from Fig. 3(A).

Linear Dependency for Gaussian Variables. A local probabilistic model for a Gaussian random variable with continuous parents (as introduced in Definition 7) can be encoded as a Prob-solvable loops update, as follows:

$$X = RV(gauss, \alpha_X + \sum_{Y \in Par(X)} \beta_{X,Y} \cdot Y, \sigma_X^2),$$ (9)

where $\alpha_X, \beta_{X,Y}$ are constants, σ_X^2 is fixed and $RV(gauss, \mu, \sigma^2)$ denotes a Gaussian random variable drawn from a Gaussian distribution $\mathcal{G}(\mu, \sigma^2)$.

Conditional Linear Gaussian Dependency. By combining BN dependencies on discrete and continuous variables for a Gaussian random variable X, we can model conditional linear Gaussian dependencies for X. Let D be the joint distribution of the discrete parents of X and for each $d \in D$ let $\mathcal{G}_d$ be the Gaussian distribution associated with condition d (here $\mathcal{G}_d$ may depend on the values of continuous parents $Par(X)$ of X, as discussed in Sect. 3). The conditional linear Gaussian dependency for X can be modeled as the following Prob-solvable loop update:

$$\sum_{d \in \Omega(D)} [D = d] \cdot \mathcal{G}_d.$$ (10)

Example 6. Figure 2(B) shows the Prob-solvable loop encoding of the clgBN of Fig. 2(A). The random variables, W_1 and W_2 are given by conditional linear Gaussian dependency and encoded using (10). For simplicity, $W1$ and $W2$ are further split into variables $W1\_1$ and $W1\_2$, and $W2\_1$ and $W2\_2$, respectively, representing different values of $W1$ and $W2$ based on the value of D. Further, $D1\_S$ is a binary variable which is 1 iff D is 1 and S is 0, and $W2D1\_S$ represents the expected value of $W2 \cdot D1\_S$.

Temporal Dependencies in DynBNs. Dependencies in dynBNs are given by intra- and inter-time-slice edges. While the encoding of these dependencies is similar to the BN dependencies discussed above, there are two restrictions on the structure of the dynBNs ensuring that dynBNs can be encoded as Prob-solvable loops. First, dependency of a dynBN variable X on itself must be represented by a linear function. This restriction

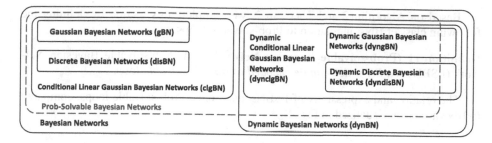

Fig. 4. BN hierarchy.

could be lifted for discrete variables, as discussed in Lemma 1. Second, a variable X can only depend on itself in previous time-slice and current time-slice variables.

Example 7. Figure 3(B) lists the Prob-solvable loop corresponding to Fig. 3(A). The Bernoulli random variables R and U are encoded using (7)-(8). The parameters of R and U change across iterations, corresponding to parameters in different time-slices of the dynBN; their concrete values are given by the expected values of R and U.

Algorithm 2. Encoding BN variants as Prob-solvable loops

    Input: BN
    Output: Prob-solvable program
    Notation: LPM denoting a local probabilistic model

1:   $Nodes :=$ topologically ordered set of BN nodes
2:   **for** X in $Nodes$ **do**
3:      **if** LPM of X is CPT **then**
4:         **for** each line L in the CPT **do** Set X_L as in (7)
5:         Set X as in (8)
6:      **if** LPM of X is a linear dependency for Gaussian variables **then** Set X as in (9)
7:      **if** LPM of X is a conditional linear Gaussian dependency **then** Set X as in (10)

4.2   Encoding BNs as Prob-solvable Loops

Section 4.1 encoded common local probabilistic models of BN dependencies as Prob-solvable loop updates. Since BNs are DAGs, BN nodes can be ordered in such a way that each BN node X depends only on previous BN variables— its parents $Par(X)$. Hence, BNs can be encoded as Prob-solvable loops, as shown in Algorithm 2 and stated below.

Theorem 2. *Every BN and dynBN[2] with local probabilistic models given by CPT or (conditional linear) Gaussian dependencies can be encoded as a Prob-solvable loop. In particular, disBNs, gBNs and clgBNs can be encoded as Prob-solvable loops.*

---

[2] subject to the restriction on structure of dynBN as discussed in Sect. 4.1.

Based on Algorithm 2 and Theorem 2, we complete this section by defining the following class of BNs, in relation to Prob-solvable loops.

Definition 11 (Prob-solvable Bayesian Networks). *A* Prob-solvable Bayesian Network (PSBN) *is a BN which can be encoded as a Prob-solvable loop.*

The relation and expressivity of PSBNs, and hence Prob-solvable loops, compared to BN variants is visualized in Fig. 4.

5   Automatic BN Analysis via Prob-solvable Loop Reasoning

We now show that several BN challenges can be automatically solved by generating moment-based invariants of Prob-solvable loops encoding the respective BNs. To this end, (i) we consider exact inference, sensitivity analysis, filtering and computing the expected number of rejecting samples in sampling-based BN procedures and (ii) formalize these BN problems as reasoning tasks within Prob-solvable loop analysis. We then (iii) encode BNs as Prob-solvable loop $\mathcal{P}$ using Algorithm 2 and (iv) generate moment-based invariants of $\mathcal{P}$ using Algorithm 1. We address steps (i)-(ii) in Sects. 5.1-5.3, and report on the automation of our work in Sect. 5.4.

5.1   Exact Inference in BNs

Common queries on BN properties address (i) the probability distributions of BN nodes X, for example by answering what is $P(X = x)$ or $P(X < c)$; (ii) the conditional probabilities of BN nodes X, Y, such as $P(X = x | Y = y)$; or (iii) the expected values and higher-order moments of BN nodes X, Y, for instance $\mathbb{E}[X], \mathbb{E}[X^2], \mathbb{E}[X | Y = y]$ and $\mathbb{E}[X^2 | Y = y]$. Here we focus on (iii) but show that, in some BN variants, queries related to (ii) can also be solved by our work.

Exact Inference in disBNs. In the case when a BN node X is binary-valued, we have $\mathbb{E}[X] = P(X = true)$. Furthermore, for any higher-order moment of X we also have $Mom_k[X] = P(X = true)$. For non-binary-valued but discrete BN node X, with values from $\{0, \ldots, m\}$, the higher-order moments of X are also computable. Moreover, the first $m-1$ moments are sufficient to fully specify probabilities $P(X = i)$, for $i \in \{0, \ldots, m - 1\}$, as proven below.

Lemma 1. *The probabilities, and hence the higher-order moments, of a discrete random variable X over $\{0, \ldots, m - 1\}$ are specified by the first $m - 1$ higher-order moments of X.*

Proof. Let $p_i := P(X = i)$, for $i \in \{0, \ldots, m - 1\}$. Then, $\sum_{0 \le i < m} i^k p_k = Mom_k(X)$, yielding $m-1$ linear equations over $p_0, \cdots, p_{m-1}$, with $k \in \{1, \cdots, m-1\}$. As we also have $\sum_{0 \le i < m} p_i = 1$, we have a linear system of m linearly independent equations, implying the existence of a unique solution which specifies the distribution of X. $\square$

For computing conditional expected values and higher-order moments, we show next that deriving $\mathbb{E}[X^k | D = i]$ is reduced to the problem of computing $\frac{\mathbb{E}[X^k \cdot [D=i]]}{\mathbb{E}[[D=i]]}$.

Lemma 2. *If* $D = i$ *with non-zero probability, we have* $\mathbb{E}[X^k|D = i] = \frac{\mathbb{E}[X^k \cdot [D=i]]}{\mathbb{E}[[D=i]]}$.

Proof. By partition properties for expected values, we have

$$\mathbb{E}[X^k[D = i]] = \mathbb{E}[X^k[D = i]|D = i]P(D = i) + \mathbb{E}[X^k[D = i]|D \neq i]P(D \neq i).$$

As $[D = i] = 1$ iff $D = i$, we derive $\mathbb{E}[X^k[D = i]|D = i] = \mathbb{E}[X^k|D = i]$ and $\mathbb{E}[X^k[D = i]|D \neq i] = 0$. Therefore, $\mathbb{E}[X^k|D = i] = \mathbb{E}[X^k|D = i]P(D = i)$. Since $P(D = i) \neq 0$, we conclude $\mathbb{E}[X^k|D = i] = \frac{\mathbb{E}[X^k \cdot [D=i]]}{\mathbb{E}[[D=i]]}$. □

Exact Inference in gBNs. Recall that a Gaussian distribution is specified by its first two moments, that is by its mean μ and variance σ^2. As all nodes in a gBN are Gaussian random variables, the first two moments of gBN nodes are sufficient to analyse gBN behaviour. Further, $\mathbb{E}[X]$ and $\mathbb{E}[X^2]$ of a gBN node X are computable using Algorithm 1.

Exact Inference in clgBNs. As continuous variables X in clgBNs are Gaussian random variables, the means and variance of X are also computable using Algorithm 1. However, clgBNs might also include discrete variables D, whose (conditional) higher-order moments can be computed as in Lemmas 1-2. Further, for a continuous variable X and a discrete variable D in a clgBN, we have

$$\mathbb{E}[X|D = i] = \frac{\mathbb{E}[X^k \cdot [D = i]]}{\mathbb{E}[[D = i]]},$$

allowing us, for example, to derive $\mathbb{E}[W2|D = 1] = 7.25 + 0.89a$ in Fig. 2.

Exact Inference in dynBNs. As dynBNs are infinite in nature, (infinite) Prob-solvable loops are suited to reason about dynBN inferences, such as (i) long-term behaviour or prediction and (ii) filtering and smoothing. A related problem is characterizing the dynBN behaviour after n iterations, and in particular for $n \to \infty$.

(i) Prediction and long-term behaviour in dynBNs By modeling dynBNs as Prob-solvable loops, we can compute/predict higher-order moments $\mathbb{E}[X_n^k]$ of dynBN nodes X using Algorithm 1, for an arbitrary n. Further, thanks to the existence of $\mathbb{E}[X_n^k]$ for Prob-solvable loops, we conclude that $\lim_{n \to \infty} \mathbb{E}[X_n^k]$ is also computable. Moreover, Algorithm 1 computes higher-order moments/MBIs in $O(1)$ time w.r.t. n, which is not the case of the $O(n)$ approach of the standard Forward algorithm.

(ii) Filtering and prediction in dynBNs Predicting next dynBNs states X_{t+1} given all observations $e_1, \ldots, e_{t+1}$ until time t can be expressed as $P(X_{t+1}|e_1, \ldots, e_{t+1})$, which in turn can be rewritten using Bayes' rule under the sensor Markov assumption (the evidence e_t depends only on program variables X_t from the same time-slice), as follows:

$$P(X_{t+1}|e_1, \ldots, e_{t+1}) = P(e_{t+1}|X_{t+1}) \cdot \sum_{x_t} P(X_{t+1}|x_t) \cdot P(x_t|e_1, \ldots, e_t),$$

where $P(e_{t+1}|X_{t+1})$ and $P(X_{t+1}|x_t)$ are specified by the BN, assuming discrete-valued observation variables. Filtering and prediction in dynBNs is thus computable using MBIs of Prob-solvable loops.

5.2   Number of BN Samples Until Positive BN Instance

As pointed out in [7], an interesting question about BNs is "Given a Bayesian network with observed evidence, how long does it take in expectation to obtain a single sample that satisfies the observations?". A related, though arguably simpler, question would require giving the expected number of positive instances (samples satisfying the observation) in N samples of BNs. Both of these questions can be answered using standard results from probability theory.

Lemma 3. *Given the probability p of a BN observation, the expected number of positive BN instances in N samples is pN. Further, the expected number of BN samples until the first positive BN instance is $\frac{1}{p}$.*

Although the lemma can be proven using standard techniques from probability, we note that the results can also be obtained using Prob-solvable loop reasoning, by relying on Algorithm 1, as illustrated next.

Example 8. For inferring the expected number of positive instances in N samples in Fig. 1, we first encode the observation in the BN as a new variable $GR = G \cdot R$, capturing the observation that the grass is wet and there was rain. We then transform the BN into a dynBN adding an inter-time-slice counter update $count = count + GR$. The expected number of positive instances is then the prediction $\mathbb{E}[count_n]$ for $n = N$.

For answering the question of [7], we again encode the observation first as above, e.g. $GR = G \cdot R$. We use a boolean variable to indicate whether there has been a positive instance $continue = continue \cdot [GR = 0]$, which is initiated as 1 (or *true*) and updated to 0 once $GR = 1$ and stays 0 thereafter. Finally, we update a loop counter as long as there was no positive instance observed with $count = count + continue$. The expected number of samples until the first positive instance is the long-term behaviour of $count$, i.e. $\lim_{n \to \infty} \mathbb{E}[count_n]$.

5.3   Sensitivity Analysis in BNs

As BNs rely on network parameters, a challenging task is to understand to what extent does a small change in a network parameter affect the outcome of particular BN query. This task is referred to as sensitivity analysis in BNs. More precisely, we would like to compute $P(X|e)$ and $\mathbb{E}[X|e]$ for a random variable X and evidence e as functions of a BN parameter(s) θ. For doing so, we note that Prob-solvable loops may use symbolic coefficients. Thus, replacing concrete BN probabilities with symbolic parameters and solving BN queries as discussed in Sect. 5.1, allow us to automate sensitivity analysis in BNs by computing MBIs of the respective Prob-solvable loops, using Algorithm 1.

Example 9. A sensitivity analysis in Fig. 2 could measure the effect of parameters of weight loss in week 1 on the conditional expectation $\mathbb{E}[W2|D = 1]$. That is, we compute $\mathbb{E}[W2|D = 1]$ as a function of parameters of $W1$. In this case, we introduce symbolic parameters a and b adjusting the parameters of weight loss in week 1 ($W1\_1$) when the drug was administered. Using Algorithm 1, we compute the MBIs $\mathbb{E}[W2^k \cdot D], \mathbb{E}[D]$, from which we have, for $k = 1$, $\mathbb{E}[W2|D = 1] = \frac{\mathbb{E}[W2 \cdot D]}{\mathbb{E}[D]} = 0.89a + 7.25$, answering the respective sensitivity analysis of Fig. 2.

Table 1. BN analysis via Prob-solvable loop reasoning within `Mora`.

BN	BN Problem	MBIs	BN Solutions
Grass – Fig. 1 (disBN) #nodes: 3, #edges: 3, #parameters: 7, #variables in Prob-solvable encoding: 9			
	Q1: $P(R\|G)$	$0.72s$	$P(R\|G) = 0.8752$
	Q2: Number of samples	$1.24s$	$\#samples = 1.37$
	Q3: Sensitivity analysis	$0.82s$	$\frac{0.04b+0.6396}{-0.178a+0.04b+0.7308}$
Alarm [41] (disBN) #nodes: 5, #edges: 4, #parameters: 10, #variables in Prob-solvable encoding: 13			
	Q1: $P(B\|A)$	$0.83s$	$P(B\|A) = 0.373551$
	Q1: $P(EQ\|M)$	$1.01s$	$P(EQ\|M) = 0.0358809$
	Q1: $P(\neg EQ \wedge \neg B\|A \wedge J)$	$1.53s$	$P(\neg EQ \wedge \neg B\|A \wedge J) = 0.396195$
	Q1: $P(EQ \wedge \neg B\|M \wedge J)$	$1.43s$	$P(EQ \wedge \neg B\|M \wedge J) = 0.175492$
	Q2: Number of samples (for $M \wedge J$)	$1.91s$	$\#samples = 19.978$
	Q3: Sensitivity analysis (all of above)	$3.36s$	$P(B\|A) = \frac{b(0.01g+0.94)}{-0.279bg+0.939b+0.289g+0.001}, \cdots$
Asia [34] (disBN) #nodes: 8, #edges: 8, #parameters: 18, #variables in Prob-solvable encoding: 24			
	Q1: $P(Asia, Lung\|Dysp)$	$2.25s$	$P(Asia, Lung\|Dysp) = 0.00045596785$
	Q2: Number of samples	$2.85s$	$\#samples = 1818.1818$
	Q3: Sensitivity analysis	$3.76s$	$P(Asia, Lung\|Dysp) = \frac{0.192a+0.29625b+0.0221625}{0.992a+0.62b+48.6054}$
Marks [36] (gBN) #nodes: 3, #edges: 3, #parameters: 6, #variables in Prob-solvable encoding: 5-6			
	Q1: Marks - expected values	$0.05s$	$\mathbb{E}[Stat] = 41.688, \cdots$
	Q3: Marks - sensitivity analysis EVs	$0.12s$	$\mathbb{E}[Stat] = 0.99\mu_{al}c + 1.0669\mu_{al} - 3.57c - 12.2967, \cdots$
	Q1: Marks - second moments	$0.11s$	$\mathbb{E}[Stat^2] = 2035.718, \cdots$
	Q3: Marks - sensitivity 2nd moments	$0.28s$	$\mathbb{E}[Stat^2] = 0.9801\mu_{al}^2 c^2 + \cdots + 0.0961\sigma_{an} + 438.4063, \cdots$
	Q1: Average - expected values	$0.08s$	$\mathbb{E}[AverageMark] = 46.271$
	Q3: Average - sensitivity EV	$0.18s$	$\mathbb{E}[AverageMark] = 0.33\mu_{al}c + 1.01897\mu_{al} - 1.19c - \cdots$
	Q1: Average - second moments	$0.13s$	$\mathbb{E}[AverageMark^2] = 2673.160$
	Q3: Average - sensitivity 2nd moment	$0.46s$	$\mathbb{E}[AverageMark^2] = 0.1089\mu_{al}^2 c^2 + \cdots + 0.190678\sigma_{an}$
Rats [17] – Fig. 2 (clgBN) #nodes: 4, #edges: 4, #parameters: 11, #variables in Prob-solvable encoding: 10			
	Q1: $\mathbb{E}[W2\|D]$	$0.49s$	$\mathbb{E}[W2\|D] = 15.02$
	Q3: $\mathbb{E}[W2\|D]$ sensitivity	$0.72s$	$\mathbb{E}[W2\|D] = 15.02 + 2.24a$
	Q1: $\mathbb{E}[W2^2\|D]$	$1.05s$	$\mathbb{E}[W2^2\|D] = 242.8356$
	Q3: $\mathbb{E}[W2^2\|D]$ sensitivity	$1.35s$	$\mathbb{E}[W2^2\|D] = 242.8356 + 5.0176b + 67.2896a + 5.0176a^2$
Umbrella [41] (dynBN) #nodes: 2, #edges: 2, #parameters: 3, #variables in Prob-solvable encoding: 6			
	Q1: Prediction	$0.56s$	$\mathbb{E}[R] = \frac{1}{2}((2/5)^n + 1)$
	Q1: Long-term behaviour		$\mathbb{E}[R] \to \frac{1}{2}$ as $n \to \infty$
	Q3: Prediction - sensitivity	$1.15s$	$\mathbb{E}[R] = \frac{(r-1)(r-0.3)^n - 0.3}{r-1.3}$
	Q3: Long-term - sensitivity		$\mathbb{E}[R] \to \frac{0.3}{1.3-r}$ as $n \to \infty$

5.4 Implementation and Experiments

We automated BN analysis via Prob-solvable loop reasoning by extending and using our tool `Mora` [6]. To this end, we first manually encoded BNs as Prob-solvable loops using Algorithm 2. We then extended `Mora` to support our extended programming model of Prob-solvable loops and integrated Algorithm 1 within `Mora`[3] to generate MBIs of Prob-solvable loops, solving thus the BN problems of Sects. 5.1–5.3. As benchmarks, we used 28 BN-related problems for 6 BNs taken from [17,29,34,36,41]. Table 1 summarizes our experiments. For each example of Table 1, we list the BN queries we considered, that is probabilistic inference (Q1), number of BN samples (Q2) and sensitivity analysis (Q3) as introduced in Sect. 1 and discussed in Sects. 5.1–5.3. Column 2 of Table 1 shows the time needed by `Mora` to compute moment-based invariants (MBIs) solving the respective BN problems. The last column of Table 1 gives our derived solutions for the considered BN queries. Our experiments were run on a MacBook Pro 2017 with 2.3 GHz Intel Core i5 and 8GB RAM.

6 Related Work

The classical approach to analyze probabilistic models is based on probabilistic model checking [2]. However, approaches [15,27,33] cannot yet handle unbounded and real variables that are required for example to encode Gaussian BNs, nor do they support invariant generation, which is a key step in our work.

In the context of probabilistic programs (PPs), a formal semantics for PPs was first introduced in [30], together with a deductive calculus to reason about expected running time of PPs [31]. This approach was further refined and extended in [37], by introducing weakest pre-expectations based on the weakest precondition calculus of [16]. While [37] infers quantitative invariants only over expected values of program variables, our moment-based invariants yield quantitative invariants over arbitrary higher-order moments, including expected values. Further, the setting of [37] considers PPs where the stochastic inputs are restricted to discrete distributions with finite support. To encode Gaussian BNs it is however necessary to handle also continuous distributions with infinite support, as described in our work.

The first semi-automatic and complete method synthesizing the linear quantitative invariants needed by [37] was introduced in [26]. To this end, PP loops are annotated with linear template invariants and constraint solving is used to find concrete values of the template parameters. Further extensions for template-based non-linear quantitative invariant generation have been proposed in [11,18]. A related line of research is given in [3], where martingales and user-provided hints are used to compute quantitative invariants of PPs. The recent work of [32] generalizes the use of martingales in conjunction with templates for computing higher-order moments of program variables, with the overall goal of approximating runtimes of randomized programs. Unlike these works, our approach extends Prob-solvable loops from [4] and provides a fully automated approach for deriving non-linear invariants over higher-order moments.

Several techniques infer runtimes and expected values of PPs, see e.g. [9,10,19,23,38]. To the best of our knowledge, however only [7] targets explicitly BNs on the source code level, by using a weakest precondition calculus similar to [25,37]. The PPs

---

[3] https://github.com/probing-lab/mora.

addressed in [7] are expressed in the *Bayesian Network Language* (BNL) fragment of the *probabilistic Guarded Command Language (pGCL)* of [37]. The main restriction of BNL is that loops prohibit undesired data flow across multiple loop iterations: it is not possible to assign to a variable the value of the same variable or another variable at the previous iteration. Furthermore, BNL does not natively allow to draw samples from Gaussian distribution, allowing thus only discrete BNs to be encoded in BNL. In contrast to [7], in our work we use Prob-solvable loops, as a subclass of PPs, to allow polynomial updates over random variables and parametric distributions. Variable updates of Prob-solvable loops can involve coefficients from Bernoulli, Gaussian, uniform and other distributions, whereas variable updates drawn from Gaussian and uniform distributions can depend on other program variables. Compared to [7], we thus support reasoning about (conditional linear) Gaussian BNs and our PPs also allow data flow across loop iterations which is necessary to encode dynamic BNs.

7 Conclusion

We extend the class of Prob-solvable loops with variable updates over Gaussian and uniform random variables depending on other program variables. We show that moment-based invariants (MBIs) in Prob-solvable loops can always be computed as quantitative invariants over higher-order moments of loop variables. We further encode BN variants as Prob-solvable loops, allowing us to turn several BN problems into the problem of computing MBIs of Prob-solvable loops. In particular, we automate the BN analysis of exact inference, sensitivity analysis, filtering and computing the expected number of rejecting samples in sampling-based procedures via Prob-solvable loop reasoning. As future work, we plan to further extend the class of Prob-solvable loops with more complex flow and arithmetic and address termination analysis of such loops.

References

1. Ai, J., et al: HackPPL: a universal probabilistic programming language. In: Proceeding of MAPL@PLDI, pp. 20–28 (2019)
2. Baier, C., Katoen, J.P.: Principles of Model Checking. The MIT Press, Cambridge (2008)
3. Barthe, G., Espitau, T., Ferrer Fioriti, L.M., Hsu, J.: Synthesizing probabilistic invariants via doob's decomposition. In: Chaudhuri, S., Farzan, A. (eds.) CAV 2016. LNCS, vol. 9779, pp. 43–61. Springer, Cham (2016). https://doi.org/10.1007/978-3-319-41528-4_3
4. Bartocci, E., Kovács, L., Stankovič, M.: Automatic generation of moment-based invariants for prob-solvable loops. In: Chen, Y.-F., Cheng, C.-H., Esparza, J. (eds.) ATVA 2019. LNCS, vol. 11781, pp. 255–276. Springer, Cham (2019). https://doi.org/10.1007/978-3-030-31784-3_15
5. Bartocci, E., Kovács, L., Stankovič, M.: Analysis of bayesian networks via prob-solvable loops. arXiv preprint arXiv:2007.09450 (2020)
6. Bartocci, E., Kovács, L., Stankovič, M.: MORA - automatic generation of moment-based invariants. TACAS 2020. LNCS, vol. 12078, pp. 492–498. Springer, Cham (2020). https://doi.org/10.1007/978-3-030-45190-5_28
7. Batz, K., Kaminski, B.L., Katoen, J.-P., Matheja, C.: How long, O Bayesian network, will I sample thee? In: Ahmed, A. (ed.) ESOP 2018. LNCS, vol. 10801, pp. 186–213. Springer, Cham (2018). https://doi.org/10.1007/978-3-319-89884-1_7
8. Bingham, E., et al.: Pyro: deep universal probabilistic programming. J. Mach. Learn. Res. **20**, 1–6 (2019)

9. Brázdil, T., Kiefer, S., Kucera, A., Vareková, I.H.: Runtime analysis of probabilistic programs with unbounded recursion. J. Comput. Syst. Sci. **81**(1), 288–310 (2015)

10. Celiku, O., McIver, A.: Compositional specification and analysis of cost-based properties in probabilistic programs. In: Fitzgerald, J., Hayes, I.J., Tarlecki, A. (eds.) FM 2005. LNCS, vol. 3582, pp. 107–122. Springer, Heidelberg (2005). https://doi.org/10.1007/11526841_9

11. Chen, Y.-F., Hong, C.-D., Wang, B.-Y., Zhang, L.: Counterexample-guided polynomial loop invariant generation by lagrange interpolation. In: Kroening, D., Păsăreanu, C.S. (eds.) CAV 2015. LNCS, vol. 9206, pp. 658–674. Springer, Cham (2015). https://doi.org/10.1007/978-3-319-21690-4_44

12. Constantinou, A.C., Fenton, N.E., Neil, M.: pi-Football: a Bayesian network model for forecasting association football match outcomes. Knowl. Based Syst. **36**, 322–339 (2012)

13. Cooper, G.F.: The computational complexity of probabilistic inference using bayesian belief networks. Artif. Intell. **42**(2–3), 393–405 (1990)

14. Dagum, P., Luby, M.: Approximating probabilistic inference in bayesian belief networks is NP-hard. Artif. Intell. **60**(1), 141–153 (1993)

15. Dehnert, C., Junges, S., Katoen, J.-P., Volk, M.: A storm is coming: a modern probabilistic model checker. In: Majumdar, R., Kunčak, V. (eds.) CAV 2017. LNCS, vol. 10427, pp. 592–600. Springer, Cham (2017). https://doi.org/10.1007/978-3-319-63390-9_31

16. Dijkstra, E.W.: Guarded commands, nondeterminacy and formal derivation of programs. Commun. ACM **18**(8), 453–457 (1975)

17. Edwards, D.: Introduction to Graphical Modelling. Springer Science & Business Media, New York (2012)

18. Feng, Y., Zhang, L., Jansen, D.N., Zhan, N., Xia, B.: Finding polynomial loop invariants for probabilistic programs. In: D'Souza, D., Narayan Kumar, K. (eds.) ATVA 2017. LNCS, vol. 10482, pp. 400–416. Springer, Cham (2017). https://doi.org/10.1007/978-3-319-68167-2_26

19. Fioriti, L.M.F., Hermanns, H.: Probabilistic termination: soundness, completeness, and compositionality. In: Proceedings of POPL, pp. 489–501 (2015)

20. Friedman, N., Linial, M., Nachman, I., Pe'er, D.: Using Bayesian networks to analyze expression data. J. Comput. Biol. **7**(3–4), 601–620 (2000)

21. Ghahramani, Z.: Probabilistic machine learning and artificial intelligence. Nature **521**, 452–459 (2015)

22. Heckerman, D.: A tutorial on learning wihtbayesian networks. In: Innovations in Bayesian Networks: Theory and Applications, Studies in Computational Intelligence, vol. 156, pp.33–82. Springer (2008). https://doi.org/10.1007/978-3-540-85066-3_3

23. Hehner, E.: A probability perspective. Formal Aspects Comput. **23**(4), 391–419 (2011). 10.1007/s00165-010-0157-0

24. Jiang, X., Cooper, G.: A Bayesian spatio-temporal method for disease outbreak detection. J. Am. Med. Inform. Assoc. **17**(4), 462–471 (2010)

25. Kaminski, B.L., Katoen, J.-P., Matheja, C., Olmedo, F.: Weakest precondition reasoning for expected run–times of probabilistic programs. In: Thiemann, P. (ed.) ESOP 2016. LNCS, vol. 9632, pp. 364–389. Springer, Heidelberg (2016). https://doi.org/10.1007/978-3-662-49498-1_15

26. Katoen, J.-P., McIver, A.K., Meinicke, L.A., Morgan, C.C.: Linear-invariant generation for probabilistic programs: automated support for proof-based methods. In: Cousot, R., Martel, M. (eds.) SAS 2010. LNCS, vol. 6337, pp. 390–406. Springer, Heidelberg (2010). https://doi.org/10.1007/978-3-642-15769-1_24

27. Katoen, J., Zapreev, I.S., Hahn, E.M., Hermanns, H., Jansen, D.N.: The ins and outs of the probabilistic model checker MRMC. Perform. Eval. **68**(2), 90–104 (2011)

28. Koller, D., Friedman, N.: Probabilistic Graphical Models - Principles and Techniques. MIT Press, Cambridge (2009)

29. Korb, K., Nicholson, A.: Bayesian Artificial Intelligence, 2nd edn. Chapman and Hall, Boca Raton (2010)

30. Kozen, D.: Semantics of probabilistic programs. J. Comput. Syst. Sci. **22**(3), 328–350 (1981)
31. Kozen, D.: A probabilistic PDL. J. Comput. Syst. Sci. **30**(2), 162–178 (1985)
32. Kura, S., Urabe, N., Hasuo, I.: Tail probabilities for randomized program runtimes via martingales for higher moments. In: Vojnar, T., Zhang, L. (eds.) TACAS 2019. LNCS, vol. 11428, pp. 135–153. Springer, Cham (2019). https://doi.org/10.1007/978-3-030-17465-1_8
33. Kwiatkowska, M., Norman, G., Parker, D.: PRISM 4.0: verification of probabilistic real-time systems. In: Gopalakrishnan, G., Qadeer, S. (eds.) CAV 2011. LNCS, vol. 6806, pp. 585–591. Springer, Heidelberg (2011). https://doi.org/10.1007/978-3-642-22110-1_47
34. Lauritzen, S.L., Spiegelhalter, D.J.: Local computation with probabilities on graphical structures and their application to expert systems (with discussion). Roy. Stat. Soc. B (Stat. Methodol.) **50**(2), 157–224 (1988)
35. Lin, G.L.: Characterizations of Distributions via Moments. Indian Statistical Institute, Kolkata (1992)
36. Mardia, K.V., Kent, J.T., Bibby, J.M.: Multivariate Analysis. Academic Press, Cambridge (1979)
37. McIver, A., Morgan, C.: Abstraction Refinement and Proof for Probabilistic Systems. Monographs in Computer Science. Springer, New York (2005)
38. Monniaux, D.: An abstract analysis of the probabilistic termination of programs. In: Cousot, P. (ed.) SAS 2001. LNCS, vol. 2126, pp. 111–126. Springer, Heidelberg (2001). https://doi.org/10.1007/3-540-47764-0_7
39. Neapolitan, R., Jiang, X.: Probabilistic Methods for Financial and Marketing Informatics. Morgan Kaufmann, San Francisco (2010)
40. Pearl, J.: Bayesian Networks: A model of self-activated memory for evidential reasoning. In: Proceedings of Cognitive Science Society, pp. 329–334 (1985)
41. Russell, S.J., Norvig, P.: Artificial Intelligence - A Modern Approach. Pearson Education, London (2010)
42. Tran, D., Hoffman, M.D., Saurous, R.A., Brevdo, E., Murphy, K., Blei, D.M.: Deep Probabilistic Programming. CoRR abs/1701.03757 (2017)
43. Yuan, C., Druzdzel, M.J.: Importance sampling algorithms for bayesian networks: principles and performance. Math. Comput. Model. **43**(9), 1189–1207 (2006)
44. Zweig, G., Russell, S.J.: Speech recognition with dynamic bayesian networks. In: Proceedings of AAAI, pp. 173–180 (1998)

Semantics of a Relational λ-Calculus

Pablo Barenbaum[1]([✉]), Federico Lochbaum[2], and Mariana Milicich[3]

[1] Universidad de Buenos Aires and Universidad Nacional de Quilmes, Bernal,
Argentina
pbarenbaum@dc.uba.ar
[2] Universidad Nacional de Quilmes, Bernal, Argentina
federico.lochbaum@gmail.com
[3] Universidad de Buenos Aires, Buenos Aires, Argentina
milicichmariana@gmail.com

Abstract. We extend the λ-calculus with constructs suitable for relational and functional–logic programming: non-deterministic choice, fresh
variable introduction, and unification of expressions. In order to be able
to unify λ-expressions and still obtain a confluent theory, we depart from
related approaches, such as λProlog, in that we do not attempt to solve
higher-order unification. Instead, abstractions are decorated with a *location*, which intuitively may be understood as its memory address, and we
impose a simple *coherence* invariant: abstractions in the same location
must be equal. This allows us to formulate a *confluent* small-step operational semantics which only performs first-order unification and does
not require *strong* evaluation (below lambdas). We study a simply typed
version of the system. Moreover, a denotational semantics for the calculus is proposed and reduction is shown to be sound with respect to the
denotational semantics.

Keywords: Lambda calculus · Semantics · Relational programming ·
Functional programming · Logic programming · Confluence

1 Introduction

Declarative programming is defined by the ideal that programs should resemble
abstract specifications rather than concrete implementations. One of the most
significant declarative paradigms is *functional programming*, represented by languages such as Haskell. Some of its salient features are the presence of first-class
functions and inductive datatypes manipulated through pattern matching. The
fact that the underlying model of computation—the λ-calculus—is *confluent*
allows one to reason equationally about the behavior of functional programs.

Another declarative paradigm is *logic programming*, represented by languages
such as Prolog. Some of its salient features are the ability to define relations

Work partially supported by project grants ECOS Sud A17C01, PUNQ 1346/17, and
UBACyT 20020170100086BA.

V. K. I. Pun et al. (Eds.): ICTAC 2020, LNCS 12545, pp. 242–261, 2020.
https://doi.org/10.1007/978-3-030-64276-1_13

rather than functions, and the presence of existentially quantified *symbolic variables* that become instantiated upon querying. This sometimes allows to use *n*-ary relations with various patterns of instantiation, *e.g.* add(3, 2, X) computes X := 3 + 2 whereas add(X, 2, 5) computes X := 5 - 2. The underlying model of computation is based on *unification* and refutation search with *backtracking*.

The idea to marry functional and logic programming has been around for a long time, and there have been many attempts to combine their features gracefully. For example, λProlog (Miller and Nadathur [20,22]) takes Prolog as a starting point, generalizing first-order terms to λ-*terms* and the mechanism of first-order unification to that of *higher-order unification*. Another example is Curry (Hanus et al. [10,11]) in which programs are defined by equations, quite like in functional languages, but evaluation is non-deterministic and evaluation is based on *narrowing*, *i.e.* variables become instantiated in such a way as to fulfill the constraints imposed by equations.

One of the interests of combining functional and logic programming is the fact that the increased expressivity aids declarative programming. For instance, if one writes a parser as a function parser : String ⟶ AST, it should be possible, under the right conditions, to *invert* this function to obtain a pretty-printer pprint : AST ⟶ String:

$$\text{pprint ast} = \nu \text{ source } . \ ((\text{ast} \overset{\bullet}{=} \text{parse source}) \ ; \ \text{source})$$

In this hypothetical functional–logic language, intuitively speaking, the expression $(\nu x.\, t)$ creates a fresh symbolic variable x and proceeds to evaluate t; the expression $(t \overset{\bullet}{=} s)$ unifies t with s; and the expression $(t; s)$ returns the result of evaluating s whenever the evaluation of t succeeds.

Given that unification is a generalization of pattern matching, a functional language with explicit unification should in some sense generalize λ-*calculi with patterns*, such as the Pure Pattern Calculus [14]. For example, by relying on unification one may build *dynamic* or *functional patterns*, *i.e.* patterns that include operations other than constructors. A typical instance is the following function last : [a] ⟶ a, which returns the last element of a non-empty cons-list:

$$\text{last (xs ++ [x])} = x$$

Note that ++ is not a constructor. This definition may be desugared similarly as for the pprint example above:

$$\text{last lst} = \nu \text{ xs } . \ \nu \text{ x. } (\text{lst} \overset{\bullet}{=} (\text{xs ++ [x]})); \ x$$

Still another interest comes from the point of view of the *proposition-as-types correspondence*. Terms of a λ-calculus with types can be understood as encoding proofs, so for instance the identity function $(\lambda x : A.\, x)$ may be understood as a proof of the implication $A \to A$. From this point of view, a functional–logic program may be understood as a *tactic*, as can be found in proof assistants such as Isabelle or Coq (see *e.g.* [29]). A term of type A should then be understood as a non-deterministic procedure which attempts to find a proof of A and it may leave holes in the proof or even fail. For instance if P is a property on natural numbers, p is a proof of $P(0)$ and q is a proof of $P(1)$, then $\lambda n.\, ((n \stackrel{\bullet}{=} 0); p) \oplus ((n \stackrel{\bullet}{=} 1); q)$ is a tactic that given a natural number n produces a proof of $P(n)$ whenever $n \in \{0, 1\}$, and otherwise it fails. Here $(t \oplus s)$ denotes the *non-deterministic alternative* between t and s.

The goal of this paper is to **provide a foundation for functional–logic programming** by **extending the λ-calculus with relational constructs**. Recall that the syntactic elements of the λ-calculus are λ-terms $(t, s, \ldots)$, which inductively may be *variables* $(x, y, \ldots)$, *abstractions* $(\lambda x.\, t)$, and *applications* $(t\, s)$. Relational programming may be understood as the purest form of logic programming, chiefly represented by the family of miniKanren languages (Byrd et al. [5,8]). The core syntactic elements of miniKanren, following for instance Rozplokhas et al. [25] are goals $(G, G', \ldots)$ which are inductively given by: *relation symbol invocations*, of the form $R(T_1, \ldots, T_n)$, where R is a relation symbol and $T_1, \ldots, T_n$ are terms of a first-order language, *unification* of first-order terms $(T_1 \stackrel{\bullet}{=} T_2)$, *conjunction* of goals $(G; G')$, *disjunction* of goals $(G \oplus G')$, and *fresh variable introduction* $(\nu x.\, G)$.

Our starting point is a "chimeric creature"—a functional–logic language resulting from cross breeding the λ-calculus and miniKanren, given by the following abstract syntax:

$t, s ::=$	x	variable		$\mathbf{c}$	constructor
	$\lambda x.\, t$	abstraction		$t\, s$	application
	$\nu x.\, t$	fresh variable introduction		$t \oplus s$	non-deterministic choice
	$t; s$	guarded expression		$t \stackrel{\bullet}{=} s$	unification

Its informal semantics has been described above. Variables $(x, y, \ldots)$ may be instantiated by unification, while constructors $(\mathbf{c}, \mathbf{d}, \ldots)$ are constants. For example, if $\mathtt{coin} \stackrel{\mathrm{def}}{=} (\mathbf{true} \oplus \mathbf{false})$ is a non-deterministic boolean with two possible values and $\mathtt{not} \stackrel{\mathrm{def}}{=} \lambda x.\, ((x \stackrel{\bullet}{=} \mathbf{true}); \mathbf{false}) \oplus ((x \stackrel{\bullet}{=} \mathbf{false}); \mathbf{true})$ is the usual boolean negation, the following non-deterministic computation:

$$(\lambda x.\, \lambda y.\, (x \stackrel{\bullet}{=} \mathtt{not}\, y); \mathbf{pair}\, x\, y)\, \mathtt{coin}\, \mathtt{coin}$$

should have two results, namely **pair true false** and **pair false true**.

Structure of This Paper. In Sect. 2, we discuss some technical difficulties that arise as one intends to provide a formal operational semantics for the informal functional–logic calculus sketched above. In Sect. 3, we refine this rough proposal into a calculus we call the λ^{U}-*calculus*, with a formal small-step operational semantics (Definition 3.1). To do so, we distinguish *terms*, which represent a single choice, from *programs*, which represent a non-deterministic alternative between zero or more terms. Moreover, we adapt the standard first-order unification algorithm to our setting by imposing a *coherence* invariant on programs. In Sect. 4, we study the operational properties of the λ^U-calculus: we provide an inductive characterization of the set of normal forms (Proposition 4.1), and we prove that it is confluent (Theorem 4.4) (up to a notion of structural equivalence). In Sect. 5, we propose a straightforward system of simple types and we show that it enjoys subject reduction (Proposition 5.2). In Sect. 6, we define a (naive) denotational semantics, and we show that the operational semantics is sound (although it is not complete) with respect to this denotational semantics (Theorem 6.2). In Sect. 7, we conclude and we lay out avenues of further research.

Note. Most proofs have been ommited from this paper. For details, see the extended version[1].

2   Technical Challenges

This section is devoted to discussing technical stumbling blocks that we encountered as we attempted to define an operational semantics for the functional–logic calculus incorporating all the constructs mentioned in the introduction. These technical issues motivate the design decisions behind the actual λ^U-calculus defined in Sect. 3. The discussion in this section is thus **informal**. Examples are carried out with their hypothetical or intended semantics.

Locality of Symbolic Variables. The following program introduces a fresh variable x and then there are two alternatives: either x unifies with $\mathbf{c}$ and the result is x, or x unifies with $\mathbf{d}$ and the result is x. The expected reduction semantics is the following. The constant $\mathbf{ok}$ is the result obtained after a successful unification:

$$\nu x. \left(((x \overset{\bullet}{=} \mathbf{c}); x) \oplus ((x \overset{\bullet}{=} \mathbf{d}); x) \right) \rightarrow ((x \overset{\bullet}{=} \mathbf{c}); x) \oplus ((x \overset{\bullet}{=} \mathbf{d}); x) \text{ with } x \text{ fresh}$$
$$\rightarrow (\mathbf{ok}; \mathbf{c}) \oplus ((x \overset{\bullet}{=} \mathbf{d}); x) \qquad (\bigstar)$$
$$\rightarrow (\mathbf{ok}; \mathbf{c}) \oplus (\mathbf{ok}; \mathbf{d})$$
$$\twoheadrightarrow \mathbf{c} \oplus \mathbf{d}$$

Note that in the step marked with ($\bigstar$), the variable x becomes instantiated to $\mathbf{c}$, but *only to the left of the choice operator* ($\oplus$). This suggests that programs should consist of different *threads* fenced by choice operators. Symbolic variables should be local to each thread.

Need of Commutative Conversions. Redexes may be *blocked* by the choice operator—for example in the application $((t \oplus \lambda x.\, s)\, u)$, there is a potential β-redex $((\lambda x.\, s)\, u)$ which is blocked. This suggests that *commutative conversions* that distribute the choice operator should be incorporated, allowing for instance a reduction step $(t \oplus \lambda x.\, s)\, u \rightarrow t\, u \oplus (\lambda x.\, s)\, u$. In our proposal, we force in the

---

[1] https://arxiv.org/abs/2009.10929.

syntax that a program is always written, canonically, in the form $t_1 \oplus \ldots \oplus t_n$, where each t_i is a deterministic program (*i.e.* choice operators may only appear inside lambdas). This avoids the need to introduce commutative rules.

Confluence Only Holds Up to Associativity and Commutativity. There are two ways to distribute the choice operators in the following example:

$$t_1(s_1 \oplus s_2) \oplus t_2(s_1 \oplus s_2) \longleftarrow (t_1 \oplus t_2)(s_1 \oplus s_2) \longrightarrow (t_1 \oplus t_2)s_1 \oplus (t_1 \oplus t_2)s_2$$

$$\downarrow \qquad\qquad\qquad\qquad\qquad\qquad\qquad\qquad\qquad \downarrow$$

$$(t_1 s_1 \oplus t_1 s_2) \oplus (t_2 s_1 \oplus t_2 s_2) \quad\cdots\cdots\cdots\cdots\quad \equiv \quad\cdots\cdots\cdots\cdots\quad (t_1 s_1 \oplus t_2 s_1) \oplus (t_1 s_2 \oplus t_2 s_2)$$

The resulting programs cannot be equated unless one works up to an equivalence relation that takes into account the associativity and commutativity of the choice operator. As we mentioned, the $\lambda^{\mho}$-calculus works with programs in canonical form $t_1 \oplus \ldots \oplus t_n$, so there is no need to work modulo associativity. However, we do need commutativity. As a matter of fact, we shall define a notion of *structural equivalence* ($\equiv$) between programs, allowing the arbitrary reordering of threads. This relation will be shown to be well-behaved, namely, a *strong bisimulation* with respect to the reduction relation, *cf.* Lemma 3.3.

Non-deterministic Choice is an Effect. Consider the program $(\lambda x.\, x\, x)(\mathbf{c} \oplus \mathbf{d})$, which chooses between $\mathbf{c}$ and $\mathbf{d}$ and then it produces two copies of the chosen value. Its expected reduction semantics is:

$$(\lambda x.\, x\, x)(\mathbf{c} \oplus \mathbf{d}) \rightarrow (\lambda x.\, x\, x)\mathbf{c} \oplus (\lambda x.\, x\, x)\mathbf{d} \twoheadrightarrow \mathbf{c}\,\mathbf{c} \oplus \mathbf{d}\,\mathbf{d}$$

This means that the first step in the following reduction, which produces two copies of $(\mathbf{c} \oplus \mathbf{d})$ cannot be allowed, as it would break confluence:

$$(\lambda x.\, x\, x)(\mathbf{c} \oplus \mathbf{d}) \not\rightarrow (\mathbf{c} \oplus \mathbf{d})(\mathbf{c} \oplus \mathbf{d}) \twoheadrightarrow \mathbf{c}\,\mathbf{c} \oplus \mathbf{c}\,\mathbf{d} \oplus \mathbf{d}\,\mathbf{c} \oplus \mathbf{d}\,\mathbf{d}$$

The deeper reason is that non-deterministic choice is a side-effect rather than a value. Our design decision, consistent with this remark, is to follow a **call-by-value** discipline. Another consequence of this remark is that the choice operator should not commute with abstraction, given that $\lambda x.\, (t \oplus s)$ and $(\lambda x.\, t) \oplus (\lambda x.\, s)$ are not observationally equivalent. In particular, $\lambda x.\, (t \oplus s)$ is a value, which may be *copied*, while $(\lambda x.\, t) \oplus (\lambda x.\, s)$ is not a value. On the other hand, if W is any *weak* context, *i.e.* a term with a hole which does *not* lie below a binder, and we write $\mathsf{W}\langle t \rangle$ for the result of plugging a term t into the hole of W, then $\mathsf{W}\langle t \oplus s \rangle = \mathsf{W}\langle t \rangle \oplus \mathsf{W}\langle s \rangle$ should hold.

Evaluation Should Be Weak. Consider the term $F \stackrel{\text{def}}{=} \lambda y.\, ((y \stackrel{\bullet}{=} x); x)$. Intuitively, it unifies its argument with a (global) symbolic variable x and then returns x. This poses two problems. First, when x becomes instantiated to y, it may be outside the scope of the abstraction binding y, for instance, the step

$F x = (\lambda y. ((y \overset{\bullet}{=} x); x)) x \rightarrow (\lambda y. (\mathbf{ok}; y)) y$ produces a meaningless free occurrence of y. Second, consider the following example in which two copies of F are used with different arguments. If we do **not** allow evaluation under lambdas, this example fails due to a unification clash, *i.e.* it produces no outputs:

$$(\lambda f. (f \mathbf{c}) (f \mathbf{d})) F \rightarrow (F \mathbf{c}) (F \mathbf{d})$$
$$\rightarrow ((\mathbf{c} \overset{\bullet}{=} x); x) ((\mathbf{d} \overset{\bullet}{=} x); x)$$
$$\rightarrow (\mathbf{ok}; \mathbf{c}) ((\mathbf{d} \overset{\bullet}{=} \mathbf{c}); \mathbf{c}) \qquad (\bigstar)$$
$$\rightarrow \texttt{fail}$$

Note that in the step marked with ($\bigstar$), the symbolic variable x has become instantiated to $\mathbf{c}$, leaving us with the unification goal $\mathbf{d} \overset{\bullet}{=} \mathbf{c}$ which fails. On the other hand, if we were to allow reduction under lambdas, given that there are no other occurrences of x anywhere in the term, in one step F becomes $\lambda y. (\mathbf{ok}; y)$, which then behaves as the identity:

$$(\lambda f. (f \mathbf{c}) (f \mathbf{d})) F \not\rightarrow (\lambda f. (f \mathbf{c}) (f \mathbf{d})) (\lambda y. \mathbf{ok}; y)$$
$$\rightarrow ((\lambda y. \mathbf{ok}; y) \mathbf{c}) ((\lambda y. \mathbf{ok}; y) \mathbf{d})$$
$$\twoheadrightarrow \mathbf{c} \mathbf{d}$$

Thus allowing reduction below abstractions in this example would break confluence. This suggests that evaluation should be **weak**, *i.e.* it should not proceed below binders.

Avoiding Higher-order Unification. The calculus proposed in this paper rests on the design choice to *avoid* attempting to solve higher-order unification problems. Higher-order unification problems can be expressed in the syntax: for example in $(f \mathbf{c} \overset{\bullet}{=} \mathbf{c})$ the variable f represents an unknown value which should fulfill the given constraint. From our point of view, however, this program is stuck and its evaluation cannot proceed—it is a normal form. However, note that we **do** want to allow *pattern matching* against functions; for example the following should succeed, instantiating f to the identity:

$$(\mathbf{c} f \overset{\bullet}{=} \mathbf{c}(\lambda x. x)); (f \overset{\bullet}{=} f) \rightarrow (\lambda x. x) \overset{\bullet}{=} (\lambda x. x) \rightarrow \mathbf{ok}$$

The decision to sidestep higher-order unification is a debatable one, as it severely restricts the expressivity of the language. But there are various reasons to explore alternatives. First, higher-order unification is undecidable [12], and even second order unification is known to be undecidable [16]. Huet's semi-decision procedure [13] does find a solution should it exist, but even then higher-order unification problems do not necessarily possess *most general unifiers* [9], which turns confluence hopeless[2]. Second, there are decidable restrictions of higher-order unification which do have most general unifiers, such as *higher-order pattern unification* [19] used in λProlog, and *nominal unification* [30] used in αProlog. But

---

[2] Key in our proof of confluence is the fact that if σ and σ' are most general unifiers for unification problems G and G' respectively, then the most general unifier for $(\mathsf{G} \cup \mathsf{G}')$ is an instance of both σ and σ'. See Example 4.5.

these mechanisms require *strong* evaluation, *i.e.* evaluation below abstractions, departing from the traditional execution model of eager applicative languages such as in the Lisp and ML families, in which closures are opaque values whose bodies cannot be examined. Moreover, they are formulated in a necessarily typed setting.

The calculus studied in this paper relies on a standard first-order unification algorithm, with the only exception that abstractions are deemed to be equal if and only if they have the same "identity". Intuitively speaking, this means that they are stored in the same memory location, *i.e.* they are represented by the same pointer. This is compatible with the usual implementation techniques of eager applicative languages, so it should allow to use standard compilation techniques for λ-abstractions. Also note that the operational semantics does not require to work with typed terms—in fact the system presented in Sect. 3 is untyped, even though we study a typed system in Sect. 5.

3   The λ^U-Calculus—Operational Semantics

In this section we describe the operational semantics of our proposed calculus, including its syntax, reduction rules (Definition 3.1), an invariant (*coherence*) which is preserved by reduction (Lemma 3.2), and a notion of structural equivalence which is a *strong bisimulation* with respect to reduction (Lemma 3.3).

Syntax of Terms and Programs. Suppose given denumerably infinite sets of *variables* $\mathsf{Var} = \{x, y, z, \ldots\}$, *constructors* $\mathsf{Con} = \{\mathbf{c}, \mathbf{d}, \mathbf{e}, \ldots\}$, and *locations* $\mathsf{Loc} = \{\ell, \ell', \ell'', \ldots\}$. We assume that there is a distinguished constructor $\mathbf{ok}$. The sets of *terms* $t, s, \ldots$ and *programs* $P, Q, \ldots$ are defined mutually inductively as follows:

$t ::= x$	variable		$\mid \mathbf{c}$	constructor	
$\mid \lambda x.\, P$	abstraction		$\mid \lambda^\ell x.\, P$	allocated abstraction	
$\mid t\, t$	application		$\mid \nu x.\, t$	fresh variable introduction	
$\mid t; t$	guarded expression		$\mid t \overset{\bullet}{=} t$	unification	

$P ::= \mathbf{fail}$	empty program
$\mid t \oplus P$	non-deterministic choice

The set of *values* $\mathsf{Val} = \{\mathsf{v}, \mathsf{w}, \ldots\}$ is a subset of the set of terms, given by the grammar $\mathsf{v} ::= x \mid \lambda^\ell x.\, P \mid \mathbf{c}\, \mathsf{v}_1 \ldots \mathsf{v}_n$. Values of the form $\mathbf{c}\, \mathsf{v}_1 \ldots \mathsf{v}_n$ are called *structures*.

Intuitively, an (unallocated) abstraction $\lambda x.\, P$ represents the static code to create a closure, while $\lambda^\ell x.\, P$ represents the closure created in runtime, stored in the memory cell ℓ. When the abstraction is evaluated, it becomes decorated with a location (*allocated*). We will have a rewriting rule like $\lambda x.\, P \to \lambda^\ell x.\, P$ where ℓ is fresh.

Notational Conventions. We write $\mathsf{C}, \mathsf{C}', \ldots$ for *arbitrary contexts*, *i.e.* terms with a single free occurrence of a hole $\square$. We write $\mathsf{W}, \mathsf{W}', \ldots$ for *weak contexts*, which do not enter below abstractions nor fresh variable declarations, *i.e.* $\mathsf{W} ::= \square \mid \mathsf{W}\,t \mid t\,\mathsf{W} \mid \mathsf{W}; t \mid t; \mathsf{W} \mid \mathsf{W} \overset{\bullet}{=} t \mid t \overset{\bullet}{=} \mathsf{W}$. We write $\oplus_{i=1}^{n} t_i$ or also $t_1 \oplus t_2 \ldots \oplus t_n$ to stand for the program $t_1 \oplus (t_2 \oplus \ldots (t_n \oplus \mathtt{fail}))$. In particular, if t is a term, sometimes we write t for the *singleton* program $t \oplus \mathtt{fail}$. The set of free variables $\mathsf{fv}(t)$ (resp. $\mathsf{fv}(P)$) of a term (resp. program) is defined as expected, noting that fresh variable declarations $\nu x.\,t$ and both kinds of abstractions $\lambda x.\,P$ and $\lambda^{\ell} x.\,P$ bind the free occurrences of x in the body. Expressions are considered up to α-equivalence, *i.e.* renaming of all bound variables. Given a context or weak context C and a term t, we write $\mathsf{C}\langle t \rangle$ for the (capturing) substitution of $\square$ by t in C. The set of locations $\mathsf{locs}(t)$ (resp. $\mathsf{fv}(P)$) of a term (resp. program) is defined as the set of all locations ℓ decorating any abstraction on t. We write $t\{\ell := \ell'\}$ for the term that results from replacing all occurrences of the location ℓ in t by ℓ'. The program being evaluated is called the *toplevel program*. The toplevel program is always of the form $t_1 \oplus t_2 \ldots \oplus t_n$, and each of the t_i is called a *thread*.

Operations with Programs. We define the operations $P \oplus Q$ and $\mathsf{W}\langle P \rangle$ by induction on the structure of P as follows; note that the notation "$\oplus$" is overloaded both for consing a term onto a program and for concatenating programs:

$$\mathtt{fail} \oplus Q \overset{\text{def}}{=} Q \qquad\qquad \mathsf{W}\langle \mathtt{fail} \rangle \overset{\text{def}}{=} \mathtt{fail}$$

$$(t \oplus P) \oplus Q \overset{\text{def}}{=} t \oplus (P \oplus Q) \qquad\qquad \mathsf{W}\langle t \oplus P \rangle \overset{\text{def}}{=} \mathsf{W}\langle t \rangle \oplus \mathsf{W}\langle P \rangle$$

Substitutions. A *substitution* is a function $\sigma : \mathsf{Var} \to \mathsf{Val}$ with *finite support*, *i.e.* such that the set $\mathsf{supp}(\sigma) \overset{\text{def}}{=} \{x \mid \sigma(x) \neq x\}$ is finite. We write $\{x_1 \mapsto \mathsf{v}_1, \ldots, x_n \mapsto \mathsf{v}_n\}$ for the substitution σ such that $\mathsf{supp}(\sigma) = \{x_1, \ldots, x_n\}$ and $\sigma(x_i) = \mathsf{v}_i$ for all $i \in 1..n$. A *renaming* is a substitution mapping each variable to a variable, *i.e.* a substitution of the form $\{x_1 \mapsto y_1, \ldots, x_n \mapsto y_n\}$.

If $\sigma : \mathsf{Var} \to \mathsf{Val}$ is a substitution and t is a term, t^{σ} denotes the capture-avoiding substitution of each occurrence of a free variable x in t by $\sigma(x)$. Capture-avoiding substitution of a single variable x by a value v in a term t is written $t\{x := \mathsf{v}\}$ and defined by $t^{\{x \mapsto \mathsf{v}\}}$. Subsitutions ρ, σ may be *composed* as follows: $(\rho \cdot \sigma)(x) \overset{\text{def}}{=} \rho(x)^{\sigma}$. Substitutions can also be applied to weak contexts, taking $\square^{\sigma} \overset{\text{def}}{=} \square$. A substitution σ is *idempotent* if $\sigma \cdot \sigma = \sigma$. A substitution σ is *more general* than a substitution ρ, written $\sigma \lesssim \rho$ if there is a substitution τ such that $\rho = \sigma \cdot \tau$.

Unification. We describe how to adapt the standard first-order unification algorithm to our setting, in order to deal with unification of λ-abstractions. As mentioned before, our aim is to solve only first-order unification problems. This means that the unification algorithm should only deal with equations involving terms which are already *values*. Note that unallocated abstractions $(\lambda x.\,P)$ are *not* considered values; abstractions are only values when they are allocated $(\lambda^{\ell} x.\,P)$. Allocated abstractions are to be considered equal if and only if they are decorated with the same location. Note that terms of the form $x\,t_1 \ldots t_n$

are *not* considered values if $n > 0$, as this would pose a higher-order unification problem, possibly requiring to instantiate x as a function of its arguments.

We expand briefly on why a naive approach to first-order unification would not work. Suppose that we did not have locations and we declared that two abstractions $\lambda x. P$ and $\lambda y. Q$ are equal whenever their bodies are equal, up to α-renaming (*i.e.* $P\{x := y\} = Q$). The problem is that this notion of equality is not preserved by substitution, for example, the unification problem given by the equation $\lambda x. y \overset{\bullet}{=} \lambda x. z$ would *fail*, as $y \neq z$. However, the variable y may become instantiated into z, and the equation would become $\lambda x. z \overset{\bullet}{=} \lambda x. z$, which succeeds. This corresponds to the following critical pair in the calculus, which cannot be closed:

$$\mathtt{fail} \leftarrow (\lambda x. y \overset{\bullet}{=} \lambda x. z); (y \overset{\bullet}{=} z) \rightarrow (\lambda x. z \overset{\bullet}{=} \lambda x. z); \mathsf{ok} \rightarrow \mathsf{ok}; \mathsf{ok}$$

This is where the notion of *allocated abstraction* plays an important role. We will work with the invariant that if $\lambda^\ell x. P$ and $\lambda^{\ell'} y. Q$ are two allocated abstractions in the same location ($\ell = \ell'$) then their bodies will be equal, up to α-renaming. This ensures that different allocated abstractions are still different after substitution, as they must be decorated with different locations.

Unification Goals and Unifiers. A *goal* is a term of the form $\mathsf{v} \overset{\bullet}{=} \mathsf{w}$. A *unification problem* is a finite set of goals $\mathsf{G} = \{\mathsf{v}_1 \overset{\bullet}{=} \mathsf{w}_1, \ldots, \mathsf{v}_n \overset{\bullet}{=} \mathsf{w}_n\}$. If σ is a substitution we write G^σ for $\{\mathsf{v}_1{}^\sigma \overset{\bullet}{=} \mathsf{w}_1{}^\sigma, \ldots, \mathsf{v}_n{}^\sigma \overset{\bullet}{=} \mathsf{w}_n{}^\sigma\}$. A *unifier* for $\mathsf{G} = \{\mathsf{v}_1 \overset{\bullet}{=} \mathsf{w}_1, \ldots, \mathsf{v}_n \overset{\bullet}{=} \mathsf{w}_n\}$ is a substitution σ such that $\mathsf{v}_i{}^\sigma = \mathsf{w}_i{}^\sigma$ for all $1 \leq i \leq n$. A unifier σ for G is *most general* if for any other unifier ρ one has $\sigma \lesssim \rho$.

Coherence Invariant. As mentioned before, we impose an invariant on programs forcing that allocated abstractions decorated with the same location must be syntactically equal. Moreover, we require that allocated abstractions do not refer to variables bound outside of their scope, *i.e.* that they are in fact closures. Note that the source program trivially satisfies this invariant, as it is expected that allocated abstractions are not written by the user but generated at runtime.

More precisely, a set X of terms is **coherent** if the two following conditions hold. **(1)** Consider any allocated abstraction under a context C, *i.e.* let $t \in X$ such that $t = \mathsf{C}\langle \lambda^\ell x. P \rangle$. Then the context C does not bind any of the free variables of $\lambda^\ell x. P$. **(2)** Consider any two allocated abstractions in t and s with the same location, *i.e.* let $t, s \in X$ be such that $t = \mathsf{C}\langle \lambda^\ell x. P \rangle$ and $s = \mathsf{C}'\langle \lambda^\ell y. Q \rangle$, Then $P\{x := y\} = Q$.

We extend the notion of coherence to other syntactic categories as follows. A term t is coherent if $\{t\}$ is coherent. A program $P = t_1 \oplus \ldots \oplus t_n$ is *coherent* if each thread t_i is coherent. A unification problem G is *coherent* if it is coherent seen as a set. Note that a program may be coherent even if different abstractions in different threads have the same location. For example, $(\lambda^\ell x. x\, x \overset{\bullet}{=} \lambda^\ell y. \mathbf{c}) \oplus (\lambda^{\ell'} y. y)$ is not coherent, whereas $(\lambda^\ell x. x\, x \overset{\bullet}{=} \lambda^\ell y. y\, y) \oplus (\lambda^\ell y. \mathbf{c})$ is coherent.

Unification Algorithm. The standard Martelli–Montanari [17] unification algorithm can be adapted to our setting. In particular, there is a computable function $\mathsf{mgu}(-)$ such that if G is a coherent unification problem then either $\mathsf{mgu}(\mathsf{G}) = \sigma$, *i.e.* $\mathsf{mgu}(\mathsf{G})$ returns a substitution σ which is an idempotent most general unifier for G, or $\mathsf{mgu}(\mathsf{G}) = \perp$, *i.e.* $\mathsf{mgu}(\mathsf{G})$ fails and G has no unifier. Moreover, it can be shown that if the algorithm succeeds, the set $\mathsf{G}^\sigma \cup \{\sigma(x) \mid x \in \mathsf{Var}\}$ is coherent. The algorithm, formal statement and proofs are detailed in the appendix .

Operational Semantics. The λ^{U}-**calculus** is the rewriting system whose objects are programs, and whose reduction relation is given by the union of the following six rules:

Definition 3.1 (Reduction rules).

$$P_1 \oplus \mathsf{W}\langle \lambda x.\, P \rangle \oplus P_2 \xrightarrow{\text{alloc}} P_1 \oplus \mathsf{W}\langle \lambda^\ell x.\, P \rangle \oplus P_2 \qquad \text{if } \ell \notin \mathsf{locs}(\mathsf{W}\langle \lambda x.\, P \rangle)$$
$$P_1 \oplus \mathsf{W}\langle (\lambda^\ell x.\, P)\, \mathsf{v} \rangle \oplus P_2 \xrightarrow{\text{beta}} P_1 \oplus \mathsf{W}\langle P\{x := \mathsf{v}\} \rangle \oplus P_2$$
$$P_1 \oplus \mathsf{W}\langle \mathsf{v}; t \rangle \oplus P_2 \xrightarrow{\text{guard}} P_1 \oplus \mathsf{W}\langle t \rangle \oplus P_2$$
$$P_1 \oplus \mathsf{W}\langle \nu x.\, t \rangle \oplus P_2 \xrightarrow{\text{fresh}} P_1 \oplus \mathsf{W}\langle t\{x := y\} \rangle \oplus P_2 \qquad \text{if } y \notin \mathsf{fv}(\mathsf{W})$$
$$P_1 \oplus \mathsf{W}\langle \mathsf{v} \stackrel{\bullet}{=} \mathsf{w} \rangle \oplus P_2 \xrightarrow{\text{unif}} P_1 \oplus \mathsf{W}\langle \mathsf{ok} \rangle^\sigma \oplus P_2 \qquad \text{if } \mathsf{mgu}(\{\mathsf{v} \stackrel{\bullet}{=} \mathsf{w}\}) = \sigma$$
$$P_1 \oplus \mathsf{W}\langle \mathsf{v} \stackrel{\bullet}{=} \mathsf{w} \rangle \oplus P_2 \xrightarrow{\text{fail}} P_1 \oplus P_2 \qquad \text{if } \mathsf{mgu}(\{\mathsf{v} \stackrel{\bullet}{=} \mathsf{w}\}) \textit{ fails}$$

Note that all rules operate on a single thread and they are **not** closed under any kind of evaluation contexts. The `alloc` rule allocates a closure, *i.e.* whenever a λ-abstraction is found below an evaluation context, it may be assigned a fresh location ℓ. The `beta` rule applies a function to a value. The `guard` rule proceeds with the evaluation of the right part of a guarded expression when the left part is already a value. The `fresh` rule introduces a fresh symbolic variable. The `unif` and `fail` rules solve a unification problem, corresponding to the success and failure cases respectively. If there is a unifier, the substitution is applied to the affected thread. For example:

$$
\begin{aligned}
(\lambda x.\, x \oplus (\nu y.\, ((x \stackrel{\bullet}{=} \mathsf{c}\, y); y)))\, (\mathsf{c}\, \mathsf{d}) &\xrightarrow{\text{alloc}} (\lambda^\ell x.\, x \oplus (\nu y.\, ((x \stackrel{\bullet}{=} \mathsf{c}\, y); y)))\, (\mathsf{c}\, \mathsf{d}) \\
&\xrightarrow{\text{beta}} \mathsf{c}\, \mathsf{d} \oplus \nu y.\, ((\mathsf{c}\, \mathsf{d} \stackrel{\bullet}{=} \mathsf{c}\, y); y) \\
&\xrightarrow{\text{fresh}} \mathsf{c}\, \mathsf{d} \oplus ((\mathsf{c}\, \mathsf{d} \stackrel{\bullet}{=} \mathsf{c}\, z); z) \\
&\xrightarrow{\text{unif}} \mathsf{c}\, \mathsf{d} \oplus (\mathsf{ok}; \mathsf{d}) \\
&\xrightarrow{\text{guard}} \mathsf{c}\, \mathsf{d} \oplus \mathsf{d}
\end{aligned}
$$

Structural Equivalence. As already remarked in Sect. 2, we will not be able to prove that confluence holds strictly speaking, but only *up to reordering of threads* in the toplevel program. Moreover the `alloc` and `fresh` rules introduce fresh names, and, as usual the most general unifier is unique only *up to renaming*. These conditions are expressed formally by means of the following relation of structural equivalence.

Formally, **structural equivalence** between programs is written $P \equiv Q$ and defined as the reflexive, symmetric, and transitive closure of the three following axioms:

1. $\equiv$-swap: $P \oplus t \oplus s \oplus Q \equiv P \oplus s \oplus t \oplus Q$.
2. $\equiv$-var: If $y \notin \mathsf{fv}(t)$ then $P \oplus t \oplus Q \equiv P \oplus t\{x := y\} \oplus Q$.
3. $\equiv$-loc: If $\ell' \notin \mathsf{locs}(t)$, then $P \oplus t \oplus Q \equiv P \oplus t\{\ell := \ell'\} \oplus Q$.

In short, $\equiv$-swap means that threads may be reordered arbitrarily, $\equiv$-var means that symbolic variables are local to each thread, and $\equiv$-loc means that locations are local to each thread.

The following lemma establishes that the coherence invariant is closed by reduction and structural equivalence, which means that the λ^{U}-calculus is well-defined if restricted to coherent programs. In the rest of this paper, we always assume that **all programs enjoy the coherence invariant**.

Lemma 3.2. *Let P be a coherent program. If $P \equiv Q$ or $P \to Q$, then Q is also coherent.*

The following lemma establishes that reduction is well-defined modulo structural equivalence (*i.e.* it lifts to $\equiv$-equivalence classes):

Lemma 3.3. *Structural equivalence is a strong bisimulation with respect to $\to$. Precisely, let $P \equiv P' \xrightarrow{\mathsf{x}} Q$ with $\mathsf{x} \in \{\mathtt{alloc}, \mathtt{beta}, \mathtt{guard}, \mathtt{fresh}, \mathtt{unif}, \mathtt{fail}\}$. Then there exists a program Q' such that $P \xrightarrow{\mathsf{x}} Q' \equiv Q$.*

Example 3.4 (Type inference algorithm). As an illustrative example, the following translation $\mathbb{W}[-]$ converts an untyped λ-term t into a λ^{U}-term that calculates the principal type of t according to the usual Hindley–Miller [21] type inference algorithm, or fails if it has no type. Note that an arrow type $(A \to B)$ is encoded as $(\mathbf{f}\, A\, B)$:

$$\mathbb{W}[x] \overset{\text{def}}{=} a_x \qquad \mathbb{W}[\lambda x.\, t] \overset{\text{def}}{=} \nu a_x.\, \mathbf{f}\, a_x\, \mathbb{W}[t] \qquad \mathbb{W}[t\, s] \overset{\text{def}}{=} \nu a.\, ((\mathbb{W}[t] \overset{\bullet}{=} \mathbf{f}\, \mathbb{W}[s]\, a); a)$$

For instance, $\mathbb{W}[\lambda x.\, \lambda y.\, y\, x] = \nu a.\, \mathbf{f}\, a\, (\nu b.\, \mathbf{f}\, b\, (\nu c.\, (b \overset{\bullet}{=} \mathbf{f}\, a\, c); c)) \twoheadrightarrow \mathbf{f}\, a\, (\mathbf{f}\, (\mathbf{f}\, a\, c)\, c)$.

4   Operational Properties

In this section we study some properties of the operational semantics. First, we characterize the set of *normal forms* of the λ^{U}-calculus syntactically, by means of an inductive definition (Proposition 4.1). Then we turn to the main result of this section, proving that it enjoys confluence up to structural equivalence (Theorem 4.4).

Characterization of Normal Forms. The set of **normal terms** $t^\star, s^\star, \ldots$ and **stuck terms** $S, S', \ldots$ are defined mutually inductively as follows. A normal term is either a value or a stuck term, *i.e.* $t^\star ::= \mathbf{v} \mid S$. A term is stuck if the judgment $t\triangledown$ is derivable with the following rules:

$$\frac{n > 0}{x\, t_1^\star \ldots t_n^\star \triangledown}\ \text{stuck-var} \qquad \frac{t_i^\star \triangledown \ \text{for some}\ i \in \{1, 2, \ldots, n\}}{\mathbf{c}\, t_1^\star \ldots t_n^\star \triangledown}\ \text{stuck-cons}$$

$$\frac{t_1^\star \bigtriangledown \quad n \geq 0}{(t_1^\star; t_2^\star)\, s_1^\star \dots s_n^\star \bigtriangledown} \text{ stuck-guard} \qquad \frac{t_i^\star \bigtriangledown \text{ for some } i \in \{1,2\} \quad n \geq 0}{(t_1^\star \overset{\bullet}{=} t_2^\star)\, s_1^\star \dots s_n^\star \bigtriangledown} \text{ stuck-unif}$$

$$\frac{t^\star \bigtriangledown \quad n \geq 0}{(\lambda^\ell x.\, P)\, t^\star\, s_1^\star \dots s_n^\star \bigtriangledown} \text{ stuck-lam}$$

The set of **normal programs** $P^\star, Q^\star, \dots$ is given by the following grammar: $P^\star ::= \mathtt{fail} \mid t^\star \oplus P^\star$. For example, the program $(\lambda^\ell x.\, x \overset{\bullet}{=} x) \oplus ((y\,\mathbf{c} \overset{\bullet}{=} \mathbf{d}); \mathbf{e}) \oplus z\,(z\,\mathbf{c})$ is normal, being the non-deterministic alternative of a value and two stuck terms. Normal programs capture the notion of normal form:

Proposition 4.1. *The set of normal programs is exactly the set of $\rightarrow$-normal forms.*

Confluence. In order to prove that the λ^U-calculus has the Church–Rosser property, we adapt the method due to Tait and Martin-Löf [4, Sect. 3.2] by defining a *simultaneous reduction relation* $\Rightarrow$, and showing that it verifies the diamond property (*i.e.* $\Leftarrow\Rightarrow\; \subseteq\; \Rightarrow\Leftarrow$) and the inclusions $\rightarrow\; \subseteq\; \Rightarrow\; \subseteq\; \twoheadrightarrow$, where $\twoheadrightarrow$ denotes the reflexive–transitive closure of $\rightarrow$. Actually, these properties only hold up to structural equivalence, so our confluence result, rather than the usual inclusion $\twoheadleftarrow\twoheadrightarrow\; \subseteq\; \twoheadrightarrow\twoheadleftarrow$, expresses the weakened inclusion $\twoheadleftarrow\twoheadrightarrow\; \subseteq\; \twoheadrightarrow\equiv\twoheadleftarrow$.

To define the relation of simultaneous reduction, we use the following notation, to lift the binary operations of unification $(t \overset{\bullet}{=} s)$, guarded expression $(t; s)$, and application $(t\,s)$ from the sort of terms to the sort of programs. Let $\star$ denote a binary term constructor (*e.g.* unification, guarded expression, or application). Then we write $(\bigoplus_{i=1}^n t_i) \star (\bigoplus_{j=1}^m s_j) \overset{\text{def}}{=} \bigoplus_{i=1}^n \bigoplus_{j=1}^m (t_i \star s_j)$.

First, we define a judgment $t \overset{\mathsf{G}}{\Rightarrow} P$ of simultaneous reduction, relating a term and a program, parameterized by a set G of unification goals representing pending constraints:

$$\frac{}{x \overset{\varnothing}{\Rightarrow} x} \text{ Var} \qquad \frac{}{\mathbf{c} \overset{\varnothing}{\Rightarrow} \mathbf{c}} \text{ Cons} \qquad \frac{}{\nu x.\, t \overset{\varnothing}{\Rightarrow} \nu x.\, t} \text{ Fresh}_1 \qquad \frac{t \overset{\mathsf{G}}{\Rightarrow} P \quad x \text{ fresh}}{\nu x.\, t \overset{\mathsf{G}}{\Rightarrow} P} \text{ Fresh}_2$$

$$\frac{}{\lambda x.\, P \overset{\varnothing}{\Rightarrow} \lambda x.\, P} \text{ Abs}_1^\mathsf{C} \qquad \frac{\ell \text{ fresh}}{\lambda x.\, P \overset{\varnothing}{\Rightarrow} \lambda^\ell x.\, P} \text{ Abs}_2^\mathsf{C} \qquad \frac{}{\lambda^\ell x.\, P \overset{\varnothing}{\Rightarrow} \lambda^\ell x.\, P} \text{ Abs}^\mathsf{A}$$

$$\frac{t \overset{\mathsf{G}}{\Rightarrow} P \quad s \overset{\mathsf{H}}{\Rightarrow} Q}{t\,s \overset{\mathsf{G \uplus H}}{\Longrightarrow} P\,Q} \text{ App}_1 \qquad \frac{}{(\lambda^\ell x.\, P)\,\mathsf{v} \overset{\varnothing}{\Rightarrow} P\{x := \mathsf{v}\}} \text{ App}_2 \qquad \frac{t \overset{\mathsf{G}}{\Rightarrow} P \quad s \overset{\mathsf{H}}{\Rightarrow} Q}{t; s \overset{\mathsf{G \uplus H}}{\Longrightarrow} P; Q} \text{ Guard}_1$$

$$\frac{t \overset{\mathsf{G}}{\Rightarrow} P}{\mathsf{v}; t \overset{\mathsf{G}}{\Rightarrow} P} \text{ Guard}_2 \qquad \frac{t \overset{\mathsf{G}}{\Rightarrow} P \quad s \overset{\mathsf{H}}{\Rightarrow} Q}{t \overset{\bullet}{=} s \overset{\mathsf{G \uplus H}}{\Longrightarrow} P \overset{\bullet}{=} Q} \text{ Unif}_1 \qquad \frac{}{\mathsf{v} \overset{\bullet}{=} \mathsf{w} \overset{\{\mathsf{v} \overset{\bullet}{=} \mathsf{w}\}}{\Longrightarrow} \mathbf{ok}} \text{ Unif}_2$$

As usual, most term constructors have two rules, the rule decorated with "1" is a congruence rule which chooses not to perform any evaluation on the root of the term, while the rule decorated with "2" requires that there is a redex at the root of the term, and contracts it. Note that rule $\mathtt{Unif}_2$ does *not* perform the unification of $\mathtt{v}$ and $\mathtt{w}$ immediately; it merely has the effect of propagating the unification constraint.

Using the relation defined above, we are now able to define the relation of **simultaneous reduction** between programs:

$$\frac{}{\mathtt{fail} \Rightarrow \mathtt{fail}}\ \text{Fail} \qquad \frac{t \overset{\mathsf{G}}{\Rightarrow} P \quad Q \Rightarrow Q' \quad P' = \begin{cases} P^\sigma & \text{if } \sigma = \mathsf{mgu}(\mathsf{G}) \\ \mathtt{fail} & \text{if } \mathsf{mgu}(\mathsf{G}) \text{ fails} \end{cases}}{t \oplus Q \Rightarrow P' \oplus Q'}\ \text{Alt}$$

The following lemma summarizes some of the key properties of simultaneous reduction. Most are straightforward proofs by induction, except for item 3.:

Lemma 4.2 (Properties of simultaneous reduction).

1. **Reflexivity.** $t \overset{\varnothing}{\Rightarrow} t$ and $P \Rightarrow P$.
2. **Context closure.** If $t \overset{\mathsf{G}}{\Rightarrow} P$ then $\mathsf{W}\langle t \rangle \overset{\mathsf{G}}{\Rightarrow} \mathsf{W}\langle P \rangle$.
3. **Strong bisimulation.** *Structural equivalence is a strong bisimulation with respect to* $\Rightarrow$, *i.e. if* $P \equiv P' \Rightarrow Q$ *then there is a program* Q' *such that* $P \Rightarrow Q' \equiv Q$.
4. **Substitution.** If $t \overset{\mathsf{G}}{\Rightarrow} P$ then $t^\sigma \overset{\mathsf{G}^\sigma}{\Longrightarrow} P^\sigma$.

The core argument is the following adaptation of Tait–Martin-Löf's technique, from which confluence comes out as an easy corollary. See in the appendix for details.

Proposition 4.3 (Tait–Martin-Löf's technique, up to $\equiv$).

1. $\to\ \subseteq\ \Rightarrow\equiv$
2. $\Rightarrow\ \subseteq\ \twoheadrightarrow\equiv$
3. $\Rightarrow$ *has the diamond property, up to* $\equiv$, *that is:*
   If $P_1 \Rightarrow P_2$ *and* $P_1 \Rightarrow P_3$ *then* $P_2 \Rightarrow\equiv P_4$ *and* $P_3 \Rightarrow\equiv P_4$ *for some* P_4.

Theorem 4.4 (Confluence). *The reduction relation* $\to$ *is confluent, up to* $\equiv$. *More precisely, if* $P_1 \twoheadrightarrow P_2$ *and* $P_1 \twoheadrightarrow P_3$ *then there is a program* P_4 *such that* $P_2 \twoheadrightarrow\equiv P_4$ *and* $P_3 \twoheadrightarrow\equiv P_4$.

Example 4.5. Suppose that $\sigma = \mathsf{mgu}(\mathtt{v}_1 \overset{\bullet}{=} \mathtt{v}_2)$ and $\tau = \mathsf{mgu}(\mathtt{w}_1 \overset{\bullet}{=} \mathtt{w}_2)$. Consider:

$$(\mathtt{v}_1^\tau \overset{\bullet}{=} \mathtt{v}_2^\tau)\,\mathbf{ok}\,t^\tau \leftarrow (\mathtt{v}_1 \overset{\bullet}{=} \mathtt{v}_2)\,(\mathtt{w}_1 \overset{\bullet}{=} \mathtt{w}_2)\,t \to \mathbf{ok}\,(\mathtt{w}_1^\sigma \overset{\bullet}{=} \mathtt{w}_2^\sigma)\,t^\sigma$$

Then both $\sigma' = \mathsf{mgu}(\mathtt{v}_1^\tau \overset{\bullet}{=} \mathtt{v}_2^\tau)$ and $\tau' = \mathsf{mgu}(\mathtt{w}_1^\sigma \overset{\bullet}{=} \mathtt{w}_2^\sigma)$ must exist, and the peak may be closed as follows:

$$(\mathtt{v}_1^\tau \overset{\bullet}{=} \mathtt{v}_2^\tau)\,\mathbf{ok}\,t^\tau \to \mathbf{ok}\,\mathbf{ok}\,(t^\tau)^{\sigma'} \equiv \mathbf{ok}\,\mathbf{ok}\,(t^\sigma)^{\tau'} \leftarrow \mathbf{ok}\,(\mathtt{w}_1^\sigma \overset{\bullet}{=} \mathtt{w}_2^\sigma)\,t^\sigma$$

the equivalence relies on the fact that $\tau' \circ \sigma$ and $\sigma' \circ \tau$ are both most general unifiers of $\{\mathtt{v}_1 \overset{\bullet}{=} \mathtt{v}_2, \mathtt{w}_1 \overset{\bullet}{=} \mathtt{w}_2\}$, hence $(t^\tau)^{\sigma'} \equiv (t^\sigma)^{\tau'}$, up to renaming.

5   Simple Types for λ^{U}

In this section we discuss a simply typed system for the λ^{U}-calculus. The system does not present any essential difficulty, but it is a necessary prerequisite to be able to define the denotational semantics of Sect. 6. The main result in this section is subject reduction (Proposition 5.2).

Note that, unlike in the simply typed λ-calculus, reduction may create free variables, due to fresh variable introduction. For instance, in the reduction step $\mathbf{c}(\nu x.\, x) \rightarrow \mathbf{c}\, x$, a new variable x appears free on the right-hand side. Therefore the subject reduction lemma has to *extend* the typing context in order to account for freshly created variables. This may be understood only as a matter of notation, *e.g.* in a different presentation of the λ^{U}-calculus the step above could be written as $\mathbf{c}(\nu x.\, x) \rightarrow \nu x.\,(\mathbf{c}\, x)$, using a *scope extrusion* rule reminiscent of the rule to create new channels in process calculi (*e.g.* π-calculus), avoiding the creation of free variables.

Types and Typing Contexts. Suppose given a denumerable set of *base types* $\alpha, \beta, \gamma, \ldots$. The sets of *types* $\mathsf{Type} = \{A, B, \ldots\}$ and *typing contexts* $\Gamma, \Delta, \ldots$ are given by:

$$A, B, \ldots ::= \alpha \mid A \rightarrow B \qquad \Gamma ::= \varnothing \mid \Gamma, x : A$$

we assume that no variable occurs twice in a typing context. Typing contexts are to be regarded as finite sets of assumptions of the form $(x : A)$, *i.e.* we work implicitly modulo contraction and exchange. We assume that each constructor $\mathbf{c}$ has an associated type $\mathcal{T}_{\mathbf{c}}$.

Typing Rules. Judgments are of the form. "$\Gamma \vdash X : A$" where X may be a term or a program, meaning that X has type A under Γ. The typing rules are the following:

$$\frac{(x : A) \in \Gamma}{\Gamma \vdash x : A}\ \text{t-var} \qquad \frac{}{\Gamma \vdash \mathbf{c} : \mathcal{T}_{\mathbf{c}}}\ \text{t-cons} \qquad \frac{\Gamma, x : A \vdash P : B}{\Gamma \vdash \lambda^{(\ell)}x.\, P : A \rightarrow B}\ \text{t-lam(1)}$$

$$\frac{\Gamma \vdash t : A \quad \Gamma \vdash s : A}{\Gamma \vdash t \overset{\bullet}{=} s : \mathcal{T}_{\mathsf{ok}}}\ \text{t-unif} \qquad \frac{\Gamma \vdash t : \mathcal{T}_{\mathsf{ok}} \quad \Gamma \vdash s : A}{\Gamma \vdash t; s : A}\ \text{t-guard}$$

$$\frac{\Gamma, x : A \vdash t : B}{\Gamma \vdash \nu x.\, t : B}\ \text{t-fresh} \qquad \frac{}{\Gamma \vdash \mathtt{fail} : A}\ \text{t-fail} \qquad \frac{\Gamma \vdash t : A \quad \Gamma \vdash P : A}{\Gamma \vdash t \oplus P : A}\ \text{t-alt}$$

Note that all abstractions are typed in the same way, regardless of whether they are allocated or not. A unification has the same type as the constructor $\mathbf{ok}$, as does t in the guarded expression $(t; s)$. A freshly introduced variable of type A represents, from the logical point of view, an unjustified assumption of A. The empty program $\mathtt{fail}$ can also be given any type. All the threads in a program must have the same type. The following properties of the type system are routine:

Lemma 5.1. *Let X stand for either a term or a program. Then:*

1. **Weakening.** *If $\Gamma \vdash X : A$ then $\Gamma, x : B \vdash X : A$.*
2. **Strengthening.** *If $\Gamma, x : A \vdash X : B$ and $x \notin \mathsf{fv}(X)$, then $\Gamma \vdash X : B$.*
3. **Substitution.** *If $\Gamma, x : A \vdash X : B$ and $\Gamma \vdash s : A$ then $\Gamma \vdash X\{x := s\} : B$.*
4. **Contextual substitution.** *$\Gamma \vdash \mathsf{W}\langle t \rangle : A$ holds if and only if there is a type B such that $\Gamma, \square : B \vdash \mathsf{W} : A$ and $\Gamma \vdash t : B$ hold.*
5. **Program composition/decomposition.** *$\Gamma \vdash P \oplus Q : A$ holds if and only if $\Gamma \vdash P : A$ and $\Gamma \vdash Q : A$ hold.*

Proposition 5.2 (Subject reduction). *Let $\Gamma \vdash P : A$ and $P \to Q$. Then $\Gamma' \vdash Q : A$, where $\Gamma' = \Gamma$ if the step is derived using any reduction rule other than* fresh, *and $\Gamma' = (\Gamma, x : B)$ if the step introduces a fresh variable $(x : B)$.*

Proof. By case analysis on the transition $P \to Q$, using Lemma 5.1. The interesting case is the unif case, which requires proving that the substitution σ returned by mgu(G) preserves the types of the instantiated variables.

6   Denotational Semantics

In this section we propose a *naive* denotational semantics for the λ^{U}-calculus. The semantics is naive in at least three senses: first, types are interpreted merely as sets, rather than as richer structures (*e.g.* complete partial orders) or in a more abstract (*e.g.* categorical) framework. Second, since types are interpreted as sets, the *multiplicities* of results are not taken into account, so for example $[\![x \oplus x]\!] = [\![x]\!] \cup [\![x]\!] = [\![x]\!]$. Third, and most importantly, the denotation of abstractions $(\lambda x. P)$ is conflated with the denotation of allocated abstractions $(\lambda^{\ell} x. P)$. This means that the operational semantics cannot be complete with respect to the denotational one, given that for example $\lambda^{\ell} x. x$ and $\lambda^{\ell'} x. x$ have the same denotation but they are not observationally equivalent[3]. Nevertheless, studying this simple denotational semantics already presents some technical challenges, and we regard it as a first necessary step towards formulating a better behaved semantics[4].

Roughly speaking, the idea is that a type A shall be interpreted as a set $[\![A]\!]$, while a program P of type A shall be interpreted as a subset $[\![P]\!] \subseteq [\![A]\!]$. For example, if $[\![\mathtt{Nat}]\!] = \mathbb{N}$, then given constructors $\mathbf{1} : \mathtt{Nat}$, $\mathbf{2} : \mathtt{Nat}$ with their obvious interpretations, and if $add : \mathtt{Nat} \to \mathtt{Nat} \to \mathtt{Nat}$ denotes addition, we expect that:

$$[\![(\lambda f : \mathtt{Nat} \to \mathtt{Nat}. \, \nu y. \, ((y \overset{\bullet}{=} \mathbf{1}); add \, y \, (f \, y)))(\lambda x. x \oplus \mathbf{2})]\!] = \{1 + 1, 1 + 2\} = \{2, 3\}$$

---

[3] *E.g.* $\lambda^{\ell} x. x \overset{\bullet}{=} \lambda^{\ell} x. x$ succeeds but $\lambda^{\ell} x. x \overset{\bullet}{=} \lambda^{\ell'} x. x$ fails.

[4] We expect that a less naive semantics should be stateful, involving a *memory*, in such a way that abstractions $(\lambda x. P)$ allocate a memory cell and store a closure, whereas allocated abstractions $(\lambda^{\ell} x. P)$ denote a memory location in which a closure is already stored.

The soundness result that we shall prove states that if $P \twoheadrightarrow Q$ then $[\![P]\!] \supseteq [\![Q]\!]$. Intuitively, the possible behaviors of Q are among the possible behaviors of P.

To formulate the denotational semantics, for ease of notation, we work with an *à la Church* variant of the type system. That is, we suppose that the set of variables is partitioned in such a way that each variable has an intrinsic type. More precisely, for each type A there is a denumerably infinite set of variables $x^A, y^A, z^A, \ldots$ of that type. We also decorate each occurrence of `fail` with its type, *i.e.* we write $\mathtt{fail}^A$ for the empty program of type A. Sometimes we omit the type decoration if it is clear from the context. Under this assumption, it is easy to show that the system enjoys a strong form of *unique typing*, *i.e.* that if X is a typable term or program then there is a unique derivation $\Gamma \vdash X : A$, up to weakening of Γ with variables not in $\mathsf{fv}(X)$. This justifies that we may write $\vdash X : A$ omitting the context.

Domain of Interpretation. We suppose given a **non-empty** set S_α for each base type α. The *interpretation* of a type A is a set written $[\![A]\!]$ and defined recursively as follows, where $\mathcal{P}(X)$ is the usual set-theoretic power set, and Y^X is the set of functions with domain X and codomain Y:

$$[\![\alpha]\!] \overset{\text{def}}{=} \mathsf{S}_\alpha \qquad [\![A \to B]\!] \overset{\text{def}}{=} \mathcal{P}([\![B]\!])^{[\![A]\!]}$$

Note that, for every type A, the set $[\![A]\!]$ is non-empty, given that we require that S_α be non-empty. This decision is not arbitrary; rather it is necessary for soundness to hold. For instance, operationally we have that $x^A; y^B \xrightarrow{\text{guard}} y^B$, so denotationally we would expect $[\![x^A; y^B]\!] \supseteq [\![y^B]\!]$. This would not hold if $[\![A]\!] = \varnothing$ and $[\![B]\!] \neq \varnothing$, as then $[\![x^A; y^B]\!] = \varnothing$ whereas $[\![y^B]\!]$ would be a non-empty set.

Another technical constraint that we must impose is that *the interpretation of a value should always be a singleton*. For example, operationally we have that $(\lambda x : \mathtt{Nat}.\, x + x)\, \mathtt{v} \twoheadrightarrow \mathtt{v} + \mathtt{v}$, so denotationally, by soundness, we would expect that $[\![(\lambda x : \mathtt{Nat}.\, x + x)\, \mathtt{v}]\!] \supseteq [\![\mathtt{v} + \mathtt{v}]\!]$. If we had that $[\![\mathtt{v}]\!] = \{1, 2\}$ is not a singleton, then we would have that $[\![(\lambda x.\, x + x)\, \mathtt{v}]\!] = \{1 + 1, 2 + 2\}$ whereas $[\![\mathtt{v} + \mathtt{v}]\!] = \{1 + 1, 1 + 2, 2 + 1, 2 + 2\}$.

Following this principle, given that terms of the form $\mathbf{c}\, \mathtt{v}_1 \ldots \mathtt{v}_n$ are values, their denotation $[\![\mathbf{c}\, \mathtt{v}_1 \ldots \mathtt{v}_n]\!]$ must always be a singleton. This means that constructors must be interpreted as singletons, and constructors of function type should always return singletons (which in turn should return singletons if they are functions, and so on, recursively). Formally, any element $a \in [\![\alpha]\!]$ is declared to be α-**unitary**, and a function $f \in [\![A \to B]\!]$ is $(A \to B)$-**unitary** if for each $a \in [\![A]\!]$ the set $f(a) = \{b\} \subseteq [\![B]\!]$ is a singleton and b is B-unitary. Sometimes we say that an element a is *unitary* if the type is clear from the context. If f is $(A \to B)$-unitary, and $a \in [\![A]\!]$ sometimes, by abuse of notation, we may write $f(a)$ for the unique element $b \in f(a)$.

Interpretation of Terms. For each constructor $\mathbf{c}$, we suppose given a $\mathcal{T}_\mathbf{c}$-unitary element $\underline{\mathbf{c}} \in [\![\mathcal{T}_\mathbf{c}]\!]$. Moreover, we suppose that the interpretation of constructors is *injective*, *i.e.* that $\underline{\mathbf{c}}(a_1) \ldots (a_n) = \underline{\mathbf{c}}(b_1) \ldots (b_n)$ implies $a_i = b_i$ for all $i = 1..n$.

An *environment* is a function $\rho : \mathsf{Var} \to \bigcup_{A \in \mathsf{Type}} \llbracket A \rrbracket$ such that $\rho(x^A) \in \llbracket A \rrbracket$ for each variable x^A of each type A. If ρ is an environment and $a \in \llbracket A \rrbracket$, we write $\rho[x^A \mapsto a]$ for the environment that maps x^A to a and agrees with ρ on every other variable. We write Env for the set of all environments.

Let $\vdash t : A$ (resp. $\vdash P : A$) be a typable term (resp. program) and let ρ be an environment. If $\vdash X : A$ is a typable term or program, we define its *denotation under the environment* ρ, written $\llbracket X \rrbracket_\rho$ as a subset of $\llbracket A \rrbracket$ as follows:

$$\llbracket x^A \rrbracket_\rho \stackrel{\text{def}}{=} \{\rho(x^A)\}$$

$$\llbracket \mathbf{c} \rrbracket_\rho \stackrel{\text{def}}{=} \{\underline{\mathbf{c}}\}$$

$$\llbracket \lambda x^A . P \rrbracket_\rho \stackrel{\text{def}}{=} \{f\} \quad \text{where } f : \llbracket A \rrbracket \to \mathcal{P}(\llbracket B \rrbracket) \text{ is given by } f(a) = \llbracket P \rrbracket_{\rho[x^A \mapsto a]}$$

$$\llbracket \lambda^\ell x^A . P \rrbracket_\rho \stackrel{\text{def}}{=} \{f\} \quad \text{where } f : \llbracket A \rrbracket \to \mathcal{P}(\llbracket B \rrbracket) \text{ is given by } f(a) = \llbracket P \rrbracket_{\rho[x^A \mapsto a]}$$

$$\llbracket t \, s \rrbracket_\rho \stackrel{\text{def}}{=} \{b \mid \exists f \in \llbracket t \rrbracket_\rho, \ \exists a \in \llbracket s \rrbracket_\rho, \ b \in f(a)\}$$

$$\llbracket t \stackrel{\bullet}{=} s \rrbracket_\rho \stackrel{\text{def}}{=} \{\underline{\mathbf{ok}} \mid \exists a \in \llbracket t \rrbracket_\rho, \ \exists b \in \llbracket s \rrbracket_\rho, \ a = b\}$$

$$\llbracket t ; s \rrbracket_\rho \stackrel{\text{def}}{=} \{a \mid \exists b \in \llbracket t \rrbracket_\rho, \ a \in \llbracket s \rrbracket_\rho\}$$

$$\llbracket \nu x^A . t \rrbracket_\rho \stackrel{\text{def}}{=} \{b \mid \exists a \in \llbracket A \rrbracket, \ b \in \llbracket t \rrbracket_{\rho[x^A \mapsto a]}\}$$

$$\llbracket \mathtt{fail}^A \rrbracket_\rho \stackrel{\text{def}}{=} \varnothing$$

$$\llbracket t \oplus P \rrbracket_\rho \stackrel{\text{def}}{=} \llbracket t \rrbracket_\rho \cup \llbracket P \rrbracket_\rho$$

The denotation of a toplevel program is written $\llbracket P \rrbracket$ and defined as the union of its denotations under all possible environments, *i.e.* $\llbracket P \rrbracket \stackrel{\text{def}}{=} \bigcup_{\rho \in \mathsf{Env}} \llbracket P \rrbracket_\rho$.

Proposition 6.1 (Properties of the denotational semantics).

1. **Irrelevance.** *If ρ and ρ' agree on $\mathsf{fv}(X)$, then $\llbracket X \rrbracket_\rho = \llbracket X \rrbracket_{\rho'}$. Here X stands for either a program or a term.*
2. **Compositionality.**
   2.1 $\llbracket P \oplus Q \rrbracket_\rho = \llbracket P \rrbracket_\rho \cup \llbracket Q \rrbracket_\rho$.
   2.2 *If W is a context whose hole is of type A, then $\llbracket \mathsf{W}\langle t \rangle \rrbracket_\rho = \{b \mid a \in \llbracket t \rrbracket_\rho, b \in \llbracket \mathsf{W} \rrbracket_{\rho[\square^A \mapsto a]}\}$.*
3. **Interpretation of values.** *If v is a value then $\llbracket v \rrbracket_\rho$ is a singleton.*
4. **Interpretation of substitution.**
   Let $\sigma = \{x_1^{A_1} \mapsto v_1, \ldots, x_n^{A_n} \mapsto v_n\}$ be a substitution such that $x_i \notin \mathsf{fv}(v_j)$ for all i, j. Let $\llbracket v_i \rrbracket_\rho = \{a_i\}$ for each $i = 1..n$ (noting that values are singletons, by the previous item of this lemma). Then for any program or term X we have that $\llbracket X^\sigma \rrbracket_\rho = \llbracket X \rrbracket_{\rho[x_1 \mapsto a_1]...[x_n \mapsto a_n]}$.

To conclude this section, the following theorem shows that the operational semantics is sound with respect to the denotational semantics.

Theorem 6.2 (Soundness). *Let $\Gamma \vdash P : A$ and $P \to Q$. Then $\llbracket P \rrbracket \supseteq \llbracket Q \rrbracket$. The inclusion is an equality for all reduction rules other than the $\mathtt{fail}$ rule.*

Example 6.3. Consider the reduction $\nu x. \left((\lambda z. \nu y. ((z \stackrel{\bullet}{=} \mathbf{t}\, 1\, y); (\mathbf{t}\, y\, x))) (\mathbf{t}\, x\, 2) \right)$
$\twoheadrightarrow \mathbf{t}\, 2\, 1$. If $\llbracket \mathtt{Tuple} \rrbracket = \llbracket \mathtt{Nat} \rrbracket \times \llbracket \mathtt{Nat} \rrbracket = \mathbb{N} \times \mathbb{N}$, the constructors $1 : \mathtt{Nat}$, $2 : \mathtt{Nat}$ are

given their obvious interpretations and $t : \mathtt{Nat} \to \mathtt{Nat} \to \mathtt{Tuple}$ is the pairing function[5], then for any environment ρ, if we abbreviate $\rho' := \rho[x \mapsto n][z \mapsto p][y \mapsto m]$, we have:

$$\llbracket \nu x.\, \big((\lambda z.\, \nu y.\, ((z \overset{\bullet}{=} t\,1\,y); (t\,y\,x)))\,(t\,x\,2)\big) \rrbracket_\rho$$

$$= \{\llbracket (\lambda z.\, \nu y.\, ((z \overset{\bullet}{=} t\,1\,y); (t\,y\,x)))\,(t\,x\,2) \rrbracket_{\rho[x \mapsto n]} \mid n \in \mathbb{N}\}$$

$$= \{r \mid n \in \mathbb{N}, f \in \llbracket \lambda z.\, \nu y.\, ((z \overset{\bullet}{=} t\,1\,y); (t\,y\,x)) \rrbracket_{\rho[x \mapsto n]}, p \in \llbracket t\,x\,2 \rrbracket_{\rho[x \mapsto n]}, r \in f(p)\}$$

$$= \{r \mid n, m \in \mathbb{N}, p \in \llbracket t\,x\,2 \rrbracket_{\rho[x \mapsto n]}, r \in \llbracket (z \overset{\bullet}{=} t\,1\,y); (t\,y\,x) \rrbracket_{\rho'}\}$$

$$= \{r \mid n, m \in \mathbb{N}, p \in \{(n, 2)\}, r \in \llbracket (z \overset{\bullet}{=} t\,1\,y); (t\,y\,x) \rrbracket_{\rho'}\}$$

$$= \{r \mid n, m \in \mathbb{N}, p \in \{(n, 2)\}, b \in \llbracket z \overset{\bullet}{=} t\,1\,y \rrbracket_{\rho'}, r \in \llbracket t\,y\,x \rrbracket_{\rho'}\}$$

$$= \{r \mid n, m \in \mathbb{N}, p \in \{(n, 2)\}, p = (1, m), r \in \llbracket t\,y\,x \rrbracket_{\rho'}\}$$

$$= \{r \mid n \in \{1\}, m \in \{2\}, p \in \{(1, 2)\}, r \in \llbracket t\,y\,x \rrbracket_{\rho'}\}$$

$$= \{(2, 1)\}$$

$$= \llbracket t\,2\,1 \rrbracket_\rho$$

An example in which the inclusion is proper is the reduction step $\lambda^\ell x.\, x \overset{\bullet}{=} \lambda^{\ell'} x.\, x \xrightarrow{\text{fail}} \mathtt{fail}$. Note that $\llbracket \lambda^\ell x.\, x \overset{\bullet}{=} \lambda^{\ell'} x.\, x \rrbracket = \{\underline{\mathbf{ok}}\} \supsetneq \varnothing = \llbracket \mathtt{fail} \rrbracket$, given that our naive semantics equates the denotations of the abstractions, i.e. $\llbracket \lambda^\ell x.\, x \rrbracket = \llbracket \lambda^{\ell'} x.\, x \rrbracket$, in spite of the fact that their locations differ.

7   Conclusion

In this work, we have proposed the λ^U-calculus (Definition 3.1) an extension of the λ-calculus with relational features, including non-deterministic choice and first-order unification. We have studied some of its operational properties, providing an inductive **characterization of normal forms** (Proposition 4.1), and proving that it is **confluent** (Theorem 4.4) up to structural equivalence, by adapting the technique by Tait and Martin-Löf. We have proposed a system of simple types enjoying **subject reduction** (Proposition 5.2). We have also proposed a naive denotational semantics, in which a program of type A is interpreted as a set of elements of a set $\llbracket A \rrbracket$, for which we have proven **soundness** (Theorem 6.2). The denotational semantics is not complete.

As of the writing of this paper, we are attempting to formulate a refined denotational semantics involving a notion of *memory*, following the ideas mentioned in footnote (See Footnote 4). One difficulty is that in a term like $((x \overset{\bullet}{=} \lambda z.\, z); y)((y \overset{\bullet}{=} \lambda z.\, z); x)$, there seems to be a cyclic dependency between the denotation of the subterm on the left and denotation of the subterm on the right, so it is not clear how to formulate the semantics compositionally.

We have attempted to prove normalization results for the simply typed system, until now unsuccessfully. Given a constructor $c : (A \to A) \to A$, a self-looping term $\omega(c\,\omega)$ with $\omega \overset{\text{def}}{=} \lambda x^A.\, \nu y^{A \to A}.\, ((c\,y \overset{\bullet}{=} x); y\,x)$ can be built, so some form of *positivity condition* should be imposed. Other possible lines for future work include studying the relationship between calculi with patterns and λ^U by means of translations, and formulating richer type systems. For instance,

---

[5] Precisely, $\underline{t}(n) = \{f_n\}$ with $f_n(m) = \{(n, m)\}$.

one would like to be able to express *instantiation restrictions*, in such a way that a fresh variable representing a natural number is of type $\mathtt{Nat}^-$ while a term of type $\mathtt{Nat}^+$ represents a fully instantiated natural number.

Related Work. On **functional–logic** programming, we have mentioned λProlog [20,22] and Curry [10,11]. Other languages combining functional and logic features are Mercury [28] and Mozart/Oz [31]. There is a vast amount of literature on functional–logic programming. We mention a few works which most resemble our own. Miller [18] proposes a language with lambda-abstraction and a decidable extension of first-order unification which admits most general unifiers. Chakravarty et al. [6] and Smolka [27] propose languages in which the functional–logic paradigm is modeled as a concurrent process with communication. Albert et al. [1] formulate a *big-step* semantics for a functional–logic calculus with narrowing. On pure **relational** programming (without λ-abstractions), recently Rozhplokas et al. [25] have studied the operational and denotational semantics of miniKanren. On **λ-calculi with patterns** (without full unification), there have been many different approaches to their formulation [2,3,14,15,23]. On **λ-calculi with non-deterministic choice** (without unification), we should mention works on the λ-calculus extended with *erratic* [26] as well as with *probabilistic* choice [7,24].

Acknowledgements. To Alejandro Díaz-Caro for supporting our interactions. To Eduardo Bonelli, Delia Kesner, and the anonymous reviewers for their feedback and suggestions.

References

1. Albert, E., Hanus, M., Huch, F., Oliver, J., Vidal, G.: Operational semantics for functional logic languages. Electronic Notes Theor. Comput. Sci. **76**, 1–19 (2002)
2. Arbiser, A., Miquel, A., Ríos, A.: A lambda-calculus with constructors. In: Pfenning, F. (ed.) RTA 2006. LNCS, vol. 4098, pp. 181–196. Springer, Heidelberg (2006). https://doi.org/10.1007/11805618_14
3. Ayala-Rincón, M., Bonelli, E., Edi, J., Viso, A.: Typed path polymorphism. Theoretical Comput. Sci. **781**, 111–130 (2019)
4. Barendregt, H.: The Lambda Calculus: Its Syntax and Semantics, vol. 103. Elsevier (1984)
5. Byrd, W.E.: Relational programming in miniKanren: techniques, applications, and implementations. [Bloomington, Ind.]: Indiana University (2010)
6. Chakravarty, M.M., Guo, Y., Köhler, M., Lock, H.C.: Goffin: higher-order functions meet concurrent constraints. Sci. Comput. Program. **30**(1–2), 157–199 (1998)
7. Faggian, C., Rocca, S.R.D.: Lambda calculus and probabilistic computation. In: 34th Annual ACM/IEEE Symposium on Logic in Computer Science, LICS 2019, Vancouver, BC, Canada, June 24–27, 2019. pp. 1–13. IEEE (2019)
8. Friedman, D.P., Byrd, W.E., Kiselyov, O.: The Reasoned Schemer. The MIT Press, Cambridge (2005)
9. Gould, W.E.: A Matching Procedure for Omega-Order Logic. Ph.D. thesis, Princeton University (1966)
10. Hanus, M.: Functional logic programming: from theory to curry. In: Voronkov, A., Weidenbach, C. (eds.) Programming Logics. LNCS, vol. 7797, pp. 123–168. Springer, Heidelberg (2013). https://doi.org/10.1007/978-3-642-37651-1_6

11. Hanus, M.: A unified computation model for functional and logic programming. In: Lee, P., Henglein, F., Jones, N.D. (eds.) Conference Record of POPL 1997: The 24th ACM SIGPLAN-SIGACT Symposium on Principles of Programming Languages, Papers Presented at the Symposium, Paris, France, 15–17 January 1997. pp. 80–93. ACM Press (1997)

12. Huet, G.P.: The undecidability of unification in third order logic. Inf. Control **22**(3), 257–267 (1973)

13. Huet, G.P.: A unification algorithm for typed λ-calculus. Theoretical Comput. Science **1**(1), 27–57 (1975)

14. Jay, B., Kesner, D.: Pure Pattern Calculus. In: Sestoft, P. (ed.) ESOP 2006. LNCS, vol. 3924, pp. 100–114. Springer, Heidelberg (2006). https://doi.org/10.1007/11693024_8

15. Klop, J.W., Van Oostrom, V., De Vrijer, R.: Lambda calculus with patterns. Theoretical Comput. Sci. **398**(1–3), 16–31 (2008)

16. Levy, J., Veanes, M.: On the undecidability of second-order unification. Inf. Comput. **159**(1–2), 125–150 (2000)

17. Martelli, A., Montanari, U.: An efficient unification algorithm. ACM Trans. Program. Lang. Syst. (TOPLAS) **4**(2), 258–282 (1982)

18. Miller, D.: A logic programming language with lambda-abstraction, function variables, and simple unification. J. Logic Comput. **1**(4), 497–536 (1991)

19. Miller, D.: Unification of simply typed lambda-terms as logic programming. Technical Report MS-CIS-91-24, University of Pennsylvania (1991)

20. Miller, D., Nadathur, G.: Programming with Higher-Order Logic. Cambridge University Press, Cambridge (2012)

21. Milner, R.: A theory of type polymorphism in programming. J. Comput. Syst. Sci. **17**(3), 348–375 (1978)

22. Nadathur, G., Miller, D.: Higher-order logic programming. In: Proceedings of the Third International Logic Programming Conference, pp. 448–462 (1984)

23. Petit, B.: Semantics of typed lambda-calculus with constructors. Log. Methods Comput. Sci. **7**(1), 536 (2011)

24. Ramsey, N., Pfeffer, A.: Stochastic lambda calculus and monads of probability distributions. In: Proceedings of the 29th ACM SIGPLAN-SIGACT Symposium on Principles of Programming Languages, pp. 154–165 (2002)

25. Rozplokhas, D., Vyatkin, A., Boulytchev, D.: Certified semantics for minikanren. In: Proceedings of the 2019 MiniKanren and Relational Programming Workshop, pp. 80–98 (2019)

26. Schmidt-Schauß, M., Huber, M.: A lambda-calculus with letrec, case, constructors and non-determinism. arXiv preprint cs/0011008 (2000)

27. Smolka, G.: A foundation for higher-order concurrent constraint programming. In: Mathematical Methods in Program Development, pp. 433–458. Springer, Heidelberg (1997). https://doi.org/10.1007/978-3-642-60858-2_24

28. Somogyi, Z., Henderson, F., Conway, T.: The execution algorithm of mercury, an efficient purely declarative logic programming language. J. Logic Program. **29**(1–3), 17–64 (1996)

29. The Coq Development Team: The Coq proof assistant reference manual. LogiCal Project (2004). http://coq.inria.fr, version 8.0

30. Urban, C., Pitts, A.M., Gabbay, M.J.: Nominal unification. Theor. Comput. Sci. **323**(1–3), 473–497 (2004)

31. Van Roy, P. (ed.): MOZ 2004. LNCS, vol. 3389. Springer, Heidelberg (2005). https://doi.org/10.1007/b106627

Implementing Hybrid Semantics: From Functional to Imperative

Sergey Goncharov[1], Renato Neves[2]([⊠]), and José Proença[3]

[1] Department of Computer Science, FAU Erlangen-Nürnberg, Erlangen, Germany
sergey.goncharov@fau.de
[2] University of Minho and INESC-TEC, Braga, Portugal
nevrenato@gmail.com
[3] CISTER/ISEP, Porto, Portugal
pro@isep.ipp.pt

Abstract. Hybrid programs combine digital control with differential equations, and naturally appear in a wide range of application domains, from biology and control theory to real-time software engineering. The entanglement of discrete and continuous behaviour inherent to such programs goes beyond the established computer science foundations, producing challenges related to e.g. infinite iteration and combination of hybrid behaviour with other effects. A systematic treatment of *hybridness* as a dedicated computational effect has emerged recently. In particular, a generic idealized functional language HYBCORE with a sound and adequate operational semantics has been proposed. The latter semantics however did not provide hints to implementing HYBCORE as a runnable language, suitable for hybrid system simulation (e.g. the semantics features rules with uncountably many premises). We introduce an imperative counterpart of HYBCORE, whose semantics is simpler and runnable, and yet intimately related with the semantics of HYBCORE at the level of *hybrid monads*. We then establish a corresponding soundness and adequacy theorem. To attest that the resulting semantics can serve as a firm basis for the implementation of typical tools of programming oriented to the hybrid domain, we present a web-based prototype implementation to evaluate and inspect hybrid programs, in the spirit of GHCI for HASKELL and UTOP for OCAML. The major asset of our implementation is that it formally follows the operational semantic rules.

1 Introduction

The Core Idea of Hybrid Programming. Hybrid programming is a rapidly emerging computational paradigm [26,29] that aims at using principles and techniques from programming theory (e.g. compositionality [12,26], Hoare calculi [29,34], theory of iteration [2,8]) to provide formal foundations for developing computational systems that interact with physical processes. Cruise controllers are a typical example of this pattern; a very simple case is given by the hybrid program below.

```
while true do {
    if v ⩽ 10 then (v′ = 1 for 1) else (v′ = −1 for 1)    (cruise controller)
}
```

In a nutshell, the program specifies a digital controller that periodically measures and regulates a vehicle's velocity (v): if the latter is less or equal than 10 the controller accelerates during 1 time unit, as dictated by the program statement $v' = 1$ for 1 ($v' = 1$ is a differential equation representing the velocity's rate of change over time. The value 1 on the right-hand side of for is the duration during which the program statement runs). Otherwise, it decelerates during the same amount of time ($v' = -1$ for 1). Figure 1 shows the output respective to this hybrid program for an initial velocity of 5.

Note that in contrast to standard programming, the cruise controller involves not only classical constructs (while-loops and conditional statements) but also differential ones (which are used for describing physical processes). This cross-disciplinary combination is the core feature of hybrid programming and has a notably wide range of application domains (see [29, 30]). However, it also hinders the

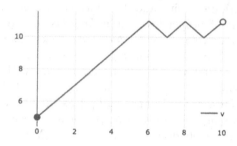

Fig. 1. Vehicle's velocity

use of classical techniques of programming, and thus calls for a principled extension of programming theory to the hybrid setting.

As is already apparent from the (cruise controller) example, we stick to an *imperative* programming style, in particular, in order to keep in touch with the established denotational models of physical time and computation. A popular alternative to this for modelling real-time and hybrid systems is to use a *declarative* programming style, which is done e.g. in real-time Maude [27] or Modelica [10]. A well-known benefit of declarative programming is that programs are very easy to write, however on the flip side, it is considerably more difficult to define what they exactly mean.

Motivation and Related Work. Most of the previous research on formal hybrid system modelling has been inspired by automata theory and Kleene algebra (as the corresponding algebraic counterpart). These approaches led to the well-known notion of hybrid automaton [17] and Kleene algebra based languages for hybrid systems [18,19,28]. From the purely semantic perspective, these formalizations are rather close and share such characteristic features as *nondeterminism* and what can be called *non-refined divergence*. The former is standardly justified by the focus on formal verification of safety-critical systems: in such contexts overabstraction is usually desirable and useful. However, coalescing *purely* *hybrid* behaviour with nondeterminism detaches semantic models from their prototypes as they exist in the wild. This brings up several issues. Most obviously, a nondeterministic semantics, especially not given in an operational form, cannot directly serve as a basis for languages and tools for hybrid system testing and simulation. Moreover, models with nondeterminism baked in do not provide a clear indication of how to combine hybrid behaviour with effects other than nondeterminism (e.g. probability), or to combine it with nondeterminism in a different way (*van Glabbeek's spectrum* [36] gives an idea about the diversity of potentially arising options). Finally, the Kleene algebra paradigm strongly suggests a relational semantics for programs, with the underlying relations connecting a state on which the program is run with the states that the program can reach. As previously indicated by Höfner and Möller [18], this view is too coarse-grained and contrasts to the trajectory-based one where a program is associated with a trajectory of states (recall Fig. 1). The trajectory-based approach provides an appropriate abstraction for such aspects as notions of convergence, periodic orbits, and duration-based predicates [5]. This potentially enables analysis of properties such as *how fast* our (cruise controller) example reaches the target velocity or for *how long* it exceeds it.

The issue of *non-refined divergence* mentioned earlier arises from the Kleene algebra law $p; 0 = 0$ in conjunction with Fischer-Ladner's encoding of while-loops while b do { p } as $(b;p)^*; \neg b$. This creates a havoc with all divergent programs while true do { p } as they become identified with divergence 0, thus making the above example of a (cruise controller) meaningless. This issue is extensively discussed in Höfner and Möller's work [18] on a *nondeterministic* algebra of trajectories, which tackles the problem by disabling the law $p; 0 = 0$ and by introducing a special operator for infinite iteration that inherently relies on nondeterminism. This iteration operator inflates trajectories at so-called 'Zeno points' with arbitrary values, which in our case would entail e.g. the program

$$x := 1; \texttt{while true do } \{ \texttt{ wait } x; x := x/2 \} \qquad \text{(zeno)}$$

to output at time instant 2 all possible values in the valuation space (the expression wait t represents a wait call of t time units). More details about Zeno points can be consulted in [14,18].

In previous work [12,14], we pursued a *purely hybrid* semantics via a simple *deterministic functional* language HYBCORE, with while-loops for which we used Elgot's notion of iteration [8] as the underlying semantic structure. That resulted in a semantics of finite and infinite iteration, corresponding to a refined view of divergence. Specifically, we developed an operational semantics and also a denotational counterpart for HYBCORE. An important problem of that semantics, however, is that it involves infinitely many premises and requires calculating total duration of programs, which precludes using such semantics directly in implementations. Both the above examples (cruise controller) and (zeno) are affected by this issue. In the present paper we propose an *imperative* language with a denotational semantics similar to HYBCORE's one, but now provide a clear recipe for executing the semantics in a constructive manner.

Overview and Contributions. Building on our previous work [14], we devise operational and denotational semantics suitable for implementation purposes, and provide a soundness and adequacy theorem relating both these styles of semantics. Results of this kind are well-established yardsticks in the programming language theory [37], and beneficial from a practical perspective. For example, small-step operational semantics naturally guides the implementation of compilers for programming languages, whilst denotational semantics is more abstract, syntax-independent, and guides the study of program equivalence, of the underlying computational paradigm, and its combination with other computational effects.

As mentioned before, in our previous work [14] we introduced a simple functional hybrid language HYBCORE with operational and denotational monad-based semantics. Here, we work with a similar imperative while-language, whose semantics is given in terms of a global state space of trajectories over $\mathbb{R}^n$, which is a commonly used carrier when working with solutions of systems of differential equations. A key principle we have taken as a basis for our new semantics is the capacity to determine behaviours of a program p by being able to examine only some subterms of it. In order to illustrate this aspect, first note that our semantics does not reduce program terms p and initial states σ (corresponding to valuation functions $\sigma : \mathcal{X} \to \mathbb{R}$ on program variables $\mathcal{X}$) to states σ', as usual in classical programming. Instead it reduces *triples* p,σ,t of programs p, initial states σ and time instants t to a state σ'; such a reduction can be read as "given σ as the initial state, program p produces a state σ' at time instant t". Then, the reduction process of p,σ,t to a state only examines fragments of p or unfolds it when strictly necessary, depending of the time instant t. For example, the reduction of the (cruise controller) unfolds the underlying loop only twice for the time instant $1 + 1/2$ (the time instant $1 + 1/2$ occurred in the second iteration of the loop). This is directly reflected in our prototype implementation of an interactive evaluator of hybrid programs LINCE. It is available online and comes with a series of examples for the reader to explore (http://arcatools.org/lince). The plot in Fig. 1 was automatically obtained from LINCE, by calling on the previously described reduction process for a predetermined sequence of time instants t.

For the denotational model, we build on our previous work [12,14] where hybrid programs are interpreted via a suitable monad $\mathbf{H}$, called the *hybrid monad* and capturing the computational effect of *hybridness*, following the seminal approach of Moggi [24,25]. Our present semantics is more lightweight and is naturally couched in terms of another monad $\mathbf{H}_S$, parametrized by a set S. In our case, as mentioned above, S is the set of trajectories over $\mathbb{R}^n$ where n is the number of available program variables $\mathcal{X}$. The latter monad is in fact parametrized in a formal sense [35] and comes out as an instance of a recently emerged generic construction [7]. A remarkable salient feature of that construction is that it can be instantiated in a constructive setting (without using any choice principles) – although we do not touch upon this aspect here, in our view this reinforces the fundamental nature of our semantics. Among various benefits of $\mathbf{H}_S$ over $\mathbf{H}$, the former monad enjoys a construction of an iteration operator (in the sense of Elgot [8]) as a *least fixpoint*, calculated as a limit of an ω-chain of approximations, while for **H** the construction of the iteration operator is rather intricate and no similar characterization is available. A natural question that arises is: how are **H** and $\mathbf{H}_S$ related? We do answer it by providing an instructive connection, which sheds light on the construction of **H**, by explicitly identifying semantic ingredients which have to be added to $\mathbf{H}_S$ to obtain **H**. Additionally, this results in "backward compatibility" with our previous work.

Document Structure. After short preliminaries (Sect. 2), in Sect. 3 we introduce our while-language and its operational semantics. In Sects. 4 and 5, we develop the denotational model for our language and connect it formally to the existing hybrid monad [12,14]. In Sect. 6, we prove a soundness and adequacy result for our operational semantics w.r.t. the developed model. Section 7 describes LINCE's architecture. Finally, Sect. 8 concludes and briefly discusses future work. Omitted proofs and examples are found in the extended version of the current paper [15].

2   Preliminaries

We assume familiarity with category theory [1]. By $\mathbb{R}$, $\mathbb{R}_+$ and $\bar{\mathbb{R}}_+$ we respectively denote the sets of reals, non-negative reals, and extended non-negative reals (i.e. $\mathbb{R}_+$ extended with the infinity value ∞). Let $[0, \bar{\mathbb{R}}_+)$ denote the set of downsets of $\bar{\mathbb{R}}_+$ having the form $[0, d]$ ($d \in \mathbb{R}_+$) or the form $[0, d)$ ($d \in \bar{\mathbb{R}}_+$). We call the elements of the dependent sum $\sum_{I \in [0, \bar{\mathbb{R}}_+)} X^I$ *trajectories* (over X). By $[0, \mathbb{R}_+]$, $[0, \mathbb{R}_+)$ and $[0, \bar{\mathbb{R}}_+)$ we denote the following corresponding subsets of $[0, \bar{\mathbb{R}}_+)$: $\{[0, d] \mid d \in \mathbb{R}_+\}$, $\{[0, d) \mid d \in \mathbb{R}_+\}$ and $\{[0, d) \mid d \in \bar{\mathbb{R}}_+\}$. By $X \uplus Y$ we denote the *disjoint union*, which is the categorical coproduct in the category of sets with the corresponding left and right injections $\mathsf{inl} : X \to X \uplus Y$, $\mathsf{inr} : Y \to X \uplus Y$. To reduce clutter, we often use plain union $X \cup Y$ in place of $X \uplus Y$ if X and Y are disjoint by construction.

By $a \lhd b \rhd c$ we denote the case distinction construct: a if b is true and c otherwise. By $!$ we denote the *empty function*, i.e. a function with the empty domain. For the sake of succinctness, we use the notation e^t for the function application $e(t)$ with real-value t.

3   An Imperative Hybrid While-Language and Its Semantics

This section introduces the syntax and operational semantics of our language. We first fix a stock of n-variables $\mathcal{X} = \{x_1, \ldots, x_n\}$ over which we build atomic programs, according to the grammar

$$\mathrm{At}(\mathcal{X}) \ni x := t \mid x_1' = t_1, \ldots, x_n' = t_n \text{ for } t$$

$$\mathrm{LTerm}(\mathcal{X}) \ni r \mid r \cdot x \mid t + s$$

where $x \in \mathcal{X}$, $r \in \mathbb{R}$, $t_i, t, s \in \text{LTerm}(\mathcal{X})$. An atomic program is thus either a classical assignment $x := t$ or a differential statement $x'_1 = t_1, \ldots, x'_n = t_n$ for t. The latter reads as *"run the system of differential equations $x'_1 = t_1, \ldots, x'_n = t_n$ for t time units"*. We then define the while-language via the grammar

$$\text{Prog}(\mathcal{X}) \ni a \mid p; q \mid \text{if } b \text{ then } p \text{ else } q \mid \text{while } b \text{ do } \{ p \}$$

where $p, q \in \text{Prog}(\mathcal{X})$, $a \in \text{At}(\mathcal{X})$ and b is an element of the free Boolean algebra generated by the terms $t \leqslant s$ and $t \geqslant s$. The expression wait t (from the previous section) is encoded as the differential statement $x'_1 = 0, \ldots, x'_n = 0$ for t.

Remark 1. The systems of differential equations that our language allows are always linear. This is not to say that we could not consider more expressive systems; in fact we could straightfowardly extend the language in this direction, for its semantics (presented below) is not impacted by specific choices of solvable systems of differential equations. But here we do not focus on such choices regarding the expressivity of continuous dynamics and concentrate on a core hybrid semantics instead on which to study the fundamentals of hybrid programming.

In the sequel we abbreviate differential statements $x'_1 = t_1, \ldots, x'_n = t_n$ for t to the expression $\bar{x}' = \bar{t}$ for t, where $\bar{x}'$ and $\bar{t}$ abbreviate the corresponding vectors of variables $x'_1 \ldots x'_n$ and linear-combination terms $t_1 \ldots t_n$. We call functions of type $\sigma : \mathcal{X} \to \mathbb{R}$ *environments*; they map variables to the respective valuations. We use the notation $\sigma \triangledown [\bar{v}/\bar{x}]$ to denote the environment that maps each x_i in $\bar{x}$ to v_i in $\bar{v}$ and the rest of variables in the same way as σ. Finally, we denote by $\phi_\sigma^{\bar{x}' = \bar{t}} : [0, \infty) \to \mathbb{R}^n$ the solution of a system of differential equations $\bar{x}' = \bar{t}$ with σ determining the initial condition. When clear from context, we omit the superscript in $\phi_\sigma^{\bar{x} = \bar{t}}$. For a linear-combination term t the expression $t\sigma$ denotes the corresponding interpretation according to σ and analogously for $b\sigma$ where b is a Boolean expression.

We now introduce a small-step operational semantics for our language. Intuitively, the semantics establishes a set of rules for reducing a triple $\langle$program statement, environment, time instant$\rangle$ to an environment, via a *finite* sequence of reduction steps. The rules are presented in Fig. 2. The terminal configuration $\langle skip, \sigma, t \rangle$ represents a successful end of a computation, which can then be fed into another computation (via rule (**seq-skip**$^\rightarrow$)). Contrastingly, $\langle stop, \sigma, t \rangle$ is a terminating configuration that inhibits the execution of subsequent computations. The latter is reflected in rules (**diff-stop**$^\rightarrow$) and (**seq-stop**$^\rightarrow$) which entail that, depending on the chosen time instant, we do not need to evaluate the whole program, but merely a part of it – consequently, infinite while-loops need not yield infinite reduction sequences (as explained in Remark 2). Note that time t is consumed when applying the rules (**diff-stop**$^\rightarrow$) and (**diff-seq**$^\rightarrow$) in correspondence to the duration of the differential statement at hand. The rules (**seq**) and (**seq-skip**$^\rightarrow$) correspond to the standard rules of operational semantics for while languages over an imperative store [37].

(asg→)	$x := t, \sigma, t \rightarrow skip, \sigma \nabla [t\sigma/x], t$	
(diff-stop→)	$\bar{x}' = \bar{u} \text{ for } t, \sigma, t \rightarrow stop, \sigma \nabla [\phi_\sigma(t)/\bar{x}], 0$	*(if $t < t\sigma$)*
(diff-skip→)	$\bar{x}' = \bar{u} \text{ for } t, \sigma, t \rightarrow skip, \sigma \nabla [\phi_\sigma(t\sigma)/\bar{x}], t - (t\sigma)$	*(if $t \geqslant t\sigma$)*
(if-true→)	$\text{if } b \text{ then } p \text{ else } q, \sigma, t \rightarrow p, \sigma, t$	*(if $b\sigma = \top$)*
(if-false→)	$\text{if } b \text{ then } p \text{ else } q, \sigma, t \rightarrow q, \sigma, t$	*(if $b\sigma = \bot$)*
(wh-true→)	$\text{while } b \text{ do } \{ p \}, \sigma, t \rightarrow p \text{; while } b \text{ do } \{ p \}, \sigma, t$	*(if $b\sigma = \top$)*
(wh-false→)	$\text{while } b \text{ do } \{ p \}, \sigma, t \rightarrow skip, \sigma, t$	*(if $b\sigma = \bot$)*

$$\textbf{(seq-stop}\rightarrow\textbf{)} \quad \frac{p, \sigma, t \rightarrow stop, \sigma', t'}{p\,;q, \sigma, t \rightarrow stop, \sigma', t'} \qquad \textbf{(seq-skip}\rightarrow\textbf{)} \quad \frac{p, \sigma, t \rightarrow skip, \sigma', t'}{p\,;q, \sigma, t \rightarrow q, \sigma', t'}$$

$$\textbf{(seq}\rightarrow\textbf{)} \quad \frac{p, \sigma, t \rightarrow p', \sigma', t'}{p\,;q, \sigma, t \rightarrow p'\,;q, \sigma', t'} \qquad \textit{(if } p' \neq stop \textit{ and } p' \neq skip \textit{)}$$

Fig. 2. Small-step Operational Semantics

Remark 2. Putatively infinite while-loops do not necessarily yield infinite reduction steps. Take for example the while-loop below whose iterations have always duration 1.

$$x := 0 \,; \text{while true do } \{ x := x + 1 \,; \text{wait } 1 \} \tag{1}$$

It yields a finite reduction sequence for the time instant $1/2$, as shown below:

$x := 0 \,; \text{while true do } \{ x := x + 1 \,; \text{wait } 1 \}, \sigma, 1/2 \rightarrow$
    $\{ \text{by the rules } (\textbf{asg}\rightarrow) \text{ and } (\textbf{seq-skip}\rightarrow) \}$
$\text{while true do } \{ x := x + 1 \,; \text{wait } 1 \}, \sigma \nabla [0/x], 1/2 \rightarrow$
    $\{ \text{by the rule } (\textbf{wh-true}\rightarrow) \}$
$x := x + 1 \,; \text{wait } 1 \,; \text{while true do } \{ x := x + 1 \,; \text{wait } 1 \}, \sigma \nabla [0/x], 1/2 \rightarrow$
    $\{ \text{by the rules } (\textbf{asg}\rightarrow) \text{ and } (\textbf{seq-skip}\rightarrow) \}$
$\text{wait } 1 \,; \text{while true do } \{ x := x + 1 \,; \text{wait } 1 \}, \sigma \nabla [0 + 1/x], 1/2 \rightarrow$
    $\{ \text{by the rules } (\textbf{diff-stop}\rightarrow) \text{ and } (\textbf{seq-stop}\rightarrow) \}$
$stop, \sigma \nabla [0 + 1/x], 0$

The gist is that to evaluate program (1) at time instant $1/2$, one only needs to unfold the underlying loop until surpassing $1/2$ in terms of execution time. Note that if the wait statement is removed from the program then the reduction sequence would not terminate, intuitively because all iterations would be instantaneous and thus the total execution time of the program would never reach $1/2$.

The following theorem entails that our semantics is deterministic, which is instrumental for our implementation.

Theorem 1. *For every program* p, *environment* σ, *and time instant* t *there is at most one* applicable reduction rule.

Let $\to^\star$ be the transitive closure of the reduction relation $\to$ that was previously presented.

Corollary 1. *For every program term* p, *environments* σ, σ', σ'', *time instants* t, t', t'', *and termination flags* s, s' $\in$ {*skip*, *stop*}, *if* p,σ,t $\to^\star$ s,σ',t' *and* p,σ,t $\to^\star$ s',σ'',t'', *then the equations* s = s', $\sigma' = \sigma''$ *and* t' = t'' *must hold.*

Proof. Follows by induction on the number of reduction steps and Theorem 1.□

As alluded above, the operational semantics treats time as a resource. This is formalised below.

Proposition 1. *For all program terms* p *and* q, *environments* σ *and* σ', *and time instants* t, t' *and* s, *if* p,σ,t $\to$ q,σ',t' *then* p,σ,t + s $\to$ q,σ',t' + s; *and if* p,σ,t $\to$ *skip*,σ',t' *then* p,σ,t + s $\to$ *skip*,σ',t' + s.

4   Towards Denotational Semantics: The Hybrid Monad

A mainstream subsuming paradigm in denotational semantics is due to Moggi [24,25], who proposed to identify a *computational effect* of interest as a monad, around which the denotational semantics is built using standard generic mechanisms, prominently provided by category theory. In this section we recall necessary notions and results, motivated by this approach, to prepare ground for our main constructions in the next section.

Definition 1 (Monad). *A monad* **T** *(on the category of sets and functions) is given by a triple* $(T, \eta, (-)^\star)$, *consisting of an endomap* T *over the class of all sets, together with a set-indexed class of maps* $\eta_X : X \to TX$ *and a so-called* Kleisli lifting *sending each* $f : X \to TY$ *to* $f^\star : TX \to TY$ *and obeying* monad laws: $\eta^\star = \mathsf{id}$, $f^\star \cdot \eta = f$, $(f^\star \cdot g)^\star = f^\star \cdot g^\star$ *(it follows from this definition that* T *extends to a functor and* η *to a natural transformation).*

A monad morphism $\theta : \mathbf{T} \to \mathbf{S}$ *from* $(T, \eta^{\mathbf{T}}, (-)^{\star\mathbf{T}})$ *to* $(S, \eta^{\mathbf{S}}, (-)^{\star\mathbf{S}})$ *is a natural transformation* $\theta : T \to S$ *such that* $\theta \cdot \eta^{\mathbf{T}} = \eta^{\mathbf{S}}$ *and* $\theta \cdot f^{\star\mathbf{T}} = (\theta \cdot f)^{\star\mathbf{S}} \cdot \theta$.

We will continue to use bold capitals (e.g. **T**) for monads over the corresponding endofunctors written as capital Romans (e.g. T).

In order to interpret while-loops one needs additional structure on the monad.

Definition 2 (Elgot Monad). *A monad* **T** *is called* Elgot *if it is equipped with an* iteration *operator* $(-)^\dagger$ *that sends each* $f : X \to T(Y \uplus X)$ *to* $f^\dagger : X \to TY$ *in such a way that certain established axioms of iteration are satisfied [2, 16].*

Monad morphisms between Elgot monads are additionally required to preserve iteration: $\theta \cdot f^{\dagger\mathbf{T}} = (\theta \cdot f)^{\dagger\mathbf{S}}$ *for* $\theta : \mathbf{T} \to \mathbf{S}$, $f : X \to T(Y \uplus X)$.

For a monad $\mathbf{T}$, a map $f : X \to TY$, called a *Kleisli map*, is roughly to be regarded as a semantics of a program p, with X as the semantics of the input, and Y as the semantics of the output. For example, with T being the *maybe monad* $(-) \uplus \{\bot\}$, we obtain semantics of programs as partial functions. Let us record this example in more detail for further reference.

Example 1. (Maybe Monad $\mathbf{M}$). The maybe monad is determined by the following data: $MX = X \uplus \{\bot\}$, the unit is the left injection $\mathsf{inl} : X \to X \uplus \{\bot\}$ and given $f : X \to Y \uplus \{\bot\}$, $f^\star$ is equal to the copairing $[f, \mathsf{inr}] : X \uplus \{\bot\} \to Y \uplus \{\bot\}$.

It follows by general considerations (enrichment of the category of Kleisli maps over complete partial orders) that $\mathbf{M}$ is an Elgot monad with the following iteration operator $(-)^\natural$: given $f : X \to (Y \uplus X) \uplus \{\bot\}$, and $x_0 \in X$, let $x_0, x_1, \ldots$ be the longest (finite or infinite) sequence over X constructed inductively in such a way that $f(x_i) = \mathsf{inl}\,\mathsf{inr}\,x_{i+1}$. Now, $f^\natural(x_0) = \mathsf{inr}\,\bot$ if the sequence is infinite or $f(x_i) = \mathsf{inr}\,\bot$ for some i, and $f^\natural(x_0) = \mathsf{inl}\,y$ if for the last element of the sequence x_n, which must exist, $f(x_n) = \mathsf{inl}\,\mathsf{inl}\,y$.

Other examples of Elgot monad can be consulted e.g. in [16].

The computational effect of *hybridness* can also be captured by a monad, called *hybrid monad* [12,14], which we recall next (in a slightly different but equivalent form). To that end, we also need to recall *Minkowski addition* for subsets of the set $\bar{\mathbb{R}}_+$ of extended non-negative reals (see Sect. 2): $A + B = \{a + b \mid a \in A, b \in B\}$, e.g. $[a, b] + [c, d] = [a + c, b + d]$ and $[a, b] + [c, d) = [a + c, b + d)$.

Definition 3. (Hybrid Monad H). *The* hybrid monad $\mathbf{H}$ *is defined as follows.*

- $HX = \sum_{I \in [0, \mathbb{R}_+]} X^I \uplus \sum_{I \in [0, \bar{\mathbb{R}}_+)} X^I$, *i.e. it is a set of trajectories valued on X and with the domain downclosed. For any $p = \mathsf{inj}\langle I, e \rangle \in HX$ with $\mathsf{inj} \in \{\mathsf{inl}, \mathsf{inr}\}$, let us use the notation $p_\mathsf{d} = I$, $p_\mathsf{e} = e$, the former being the duration of the trajectory and the latter the trajectory itself. Let also $\varepsilon = \langle \emptyset, ! \rangle$.*
- $\eta(x) = \mathsf{inl}\langle [0, 0], \lambda t.\, x \rangle$, *i.e. $\eta(x)$ is a trajectory of duration 0 that returns x.*
- *given $f : X \to HY$, we define $f^\star : HX \to HY$ via the following clauses:*

$$f^\star(\mathsf{inl}\langle I, e \rangle) = \mathsf{inj}\langle I + J, \lambda t.\, (f(e^t))_\mathsf{e}^0 \triangleleft t < d \triangleright (f(e^d))_\mathsf{e}^{t-d} \rangle$$
$$\text{if } I' = I = [0, d] \text{ for some } d, f(e^d) = \mathsf{inj}\langle J, e' \rangle$$

$$f^\star(\mathsf{inl}\langle I, e \rangle) = \mathsf{inr}\langle I', \lambda t.\, (f(e^t))_\mathsf{e}^0 \rangle \qquad\qquad\qquad\qquad \text{if } I' \neq I$$
$$f^\star(\mathsf{inr}\langle I, e \rangle) = \mathsf{inr}\langle I', \lambda t.\, (f(e^t))_\mathsf{e}^0 \rangle$$

where $I' = \bigcup \{[0, t] \subseteq I \mid \forall s \in [0, t].\, f(e^s) \neq \mathsf{inr}\varepsilon\}$ and $\mathsf{inj} \in \{\mathsf{inl}, \mathsf{inr}\}$.

The definition of the hybrid monad $\mathbf{H}$ is somewhat intricate, so let us complement it with some explanations (details and further intuitions about the hybrid monad can also be consulted in [12]). The domain HX constitutes three types of trajectories representing different kinds of hybrid computation:

- *(closed) convergent:* $\mathsf{inl}\langle [0, d], e \rangle \in HX$ (e.g. instant termination $\eta(x)$);

- *open divergent*: $\mathsf{inr}\langle[0,d),e\rangle \in HX$ (e.g. instant divergence $\mathsf{inr}\varepsilon$ or a trajectory $[0,\infty) \to X$ which represents a computation that runs *ad infinitum*);
- *closed divergent*: $\mathsf{inr}\langle[0,d],e\rangle \in HX$ (representing computations that start to diverge *precisely* after the time instant d).

The Kleisli lifting $f^\star$ works as follows: for a given trajectory $\mathsf{inj}\langle I,e\rangle$, we first calculate the largest interval $I' \subseteq I$ on which the trajectory $\lambda t \in I'.f(e^t)$ does not instantly diverge (i.e. $f(e^t) \neq \mathsf{inr}\varepsilon$) throughout, hence I' is either $[0,d']$ or $[0,d')$ for some d'. Now, the first clause in the definition of $f^\star$ corresponds to the successful composition scenario: the argument trajectory $\langle I,e\rangle$ is convergent, and composing f with e as described in the definition of I' does not yield divergence all over I. In that case, we essentially concatenate $\langle I,e\rangle$ with $f(e^d)$, the latter being the trajectory computed by f at the last point of e. The remaining two clauses correspond to various flavours of divergence, including divergence of the input ($\mathsf{inr}\langle I,e\rangle$) and divergences occurring along $f \cdot e$. Incidentally, this explains how closed divergent trajectories may arise: if $I' = [0,d']$ and d' is properly smaller than d, then we diverge precisely *after* d', which is possible e.g. if the program behind f continuously checks a condition which did not fail up until d'.

5   Deconstructing the Hybrid Monad

As mentioned in the introduction, in [14] we used $\mathbf{H}$ for giving semantics to a *functional* language HYBCORE whose programs are interpreted as morphisms of type $X \to HY$. Here, we are dealing with an *imperative* language, which from a semantic point of view amounts to fixing a type of *states* S, shared between all programs; the semantics of a program is thus restricted to morphisms of type $S \to HS$. As explained next, this allows us to make do with a simpler monad $\mathbf{H}_S$, globally parametrized by S. The new monad $\mathbf{H}_S$ has the property that $H_S S$ is naturally isomorphic to HS. Apart from (relative to $\mathbf{H}$) simplicity, the new monad enjoys further benefits, specifically $\mathbf{H}_S$ is mathematically a better behaved structure, e.g. in contrast to $\mathbf{H}$, Elgot iteration on $\mathbf{H}_S$ is constructed as a least fixed point. Factoring the denotational semantics through $\mathbf{H}_S$ thus allows us to bridge the gap to the operational semantics given in Sect. 3, and facilitates the soundness and adequacy proof in the forthcoming Sect. 6.

In order to define $\mathbf{H}_S$, it is convenient to take a slightly broader perspective. We will also need to make a detour through the topic of ordered monoid modules with certain completeness properties so that we can characterise iteration on $\mathbf{H}_S$ as a least fixed point.

Definition 4. (Monoid Module, Generalized Writer Monad [14]). *Given a (not necessarily commutative) monoid* $(\mathbb{M},+,0)$, *a monoid module is a set* $\mathbb{E}$ *equipped with a map* $\triangleright : \mathbb{M} \times \mathbb{E} \to \mathbb{E}$ *(monoid action), subject to the laws* $0 \triangleright e = e$, $(m+n) \triangleright e = m \triangleright (n \triangleright e)$.

Every monoid-module pair $(\mathbb{M}, \mathbb{E})$ *induces a* generalized writer monad $\mathbf{T} = (T, \eta, (-)^*)$ *with* $T = \mathbb{M} \times (-) \cup \mathbb{E}$, $\eta_X(x) = \langle 0, x \rangle$, *and*

$$f^*(m, x) = (m + n, y) \quad where \quad m \in \mathbb{M}, x \in X, f(x) = \langle n, y \rangle \in \mathbb{M} \times Y$$
$$f^*(m, x) = m \triangleright e \quad where \quad m \in \mathbb{M}, x \in X, f(x) = e \in \mathbb{E}$$
$$f^*(e) = e \quad where \quad e \in \mathbb{E}$$

This generalizes the writer monad $(\mathbb{E} = \emptyset)$ *and the exception monad* $(\mathbb{M} = 1)$.

Example 2. A simple motivating example of a monoid-module pair $(\mathbb{M}, \mathbb{E})$ is the pair $(\mathbb{R}_+, \bar{\mathbb{R}}_+)$ where the monoid operation is addition with 0 as the unit and the monoid action is also addition.

More specifically, we are interested in *ordered monoids* and *(conservatively) complete monoid modules*. These are defined as follows.

Definition 5 (Ordered Monoids, (Conservatively) Complete Monoid Modules [7]). *We call a monoid* $(\mathbb{M}, 0, +)$ *an ordered monoid if it is equipped with a partial order* $\leqslant$, *such that 0 is the least element of this order and* $+$ *is right-monotone (but not necessarily left-monotone).*

An ordered $\mathbb{M}$-module *w.r.t. an ordered monoid* $(\mathbb{M}, +, 0, \leq)$, *is an* $\mathbb{M}$-module $(\mathbb{E}, \triangleright)$ *together with a partial order* $\sqsubseteq$ *and a least element* $\perp$, *such that* $\triangleright$ *is monotone on the right and* $(-\triangleright \perp)$ *is monotone, i.e.*

$$\frac{}{\perp \sqsubseteq x} \qquad \frac{x \sqsubseteq y}{a \triangleright x \sqsubseteq a \triangleright y} \qquad \frac{a \leq b}{a \triangleright \perp \sqsubseteq b \triangleright \perp}$$

We call the last property restricted left monotonicity.

An ordered $\mathbb{M}$-module is $(\omega\text{-})$complete *if for every* ω-chain $s_1 \sqsubseteq s_2 \sqsubseteq \ldots$ *on* $\mathbb{E}$ *there is a least upper bound* $\bigsqcup_i s_i$ *and* $\triangleright$ *is continuous on the right, i.e.*

$$\frac{}{\forall i.\, s_i \sqsubseteq \bigsqcup_i s_i} \qquad \frac{\cdot \, \forall i.\, s_i \sqsubseteq x}{\bigsqcup_i s_i \sqsubseteq x} \qquad \frac{}{a \triangleright \bigsqcup_i s_i \sqsubseteq \bigsqcup_i a \triangleright s_i}$$

(the law $\bigsqcup_i a \triangleright s_i \sqsubseteq a \triangleright \bigsqcup_i s_i$ *is derivable). Such an* $\mathbb{M}$-module *is* conservatively complete *if additionally for every* ω-chain $a_1 \sqsubseteq a_2 \sqsubseteq \ldots$ *in* $\mathbb{M}$, *such that the least upper bound* $\bigvee_i a_i$ *exists,* $(\bigvee_i a_i) \triangleright \perp = \bigsqcup_i a_i \triangleright \perp$.

A homomorphism $h : \mathbb{E} \to \mathbb{F}$ *of (conservatively) complete monoid* $\mathbb{M}$-modules *is required to be monotone and structure-preserving in the following sense:* $h(\perp) = \perp$, $h(a \triangleright x) = a \triangleright h(x)$, $h(\bigsqcup_i x_i) = \bigsqcup_i h(x_i)$.

The completeness requirement for $\mathbb{M}$-modules has a standard motivation coming from domain theory, where $\sqsubseteq$ is regarded as an *information order* and completeness is needed to ensure that the relevant semantic domain can accommodate infinite behaviours. The conservativity requirement additionally ensures that the least upper bounds, which exist in $\mathbb{M}$ agree with those in $\mathbb{E}$. Our main example is as follows (we will use it for building $\mathbf{H}_S$ and its iteration operator).

Definition 6 (Monoid Module of Trajectories). *The ordered monoid of finite open trajectories* $\left(\mathsf{Trj}_S, \frown, \langle \emptyset, !\rangle, \leq\right)$ *over a given set S, is defined as follows:* $\mathsf{Trj}_S = \sum_{I \in [0, \mathbb{R}_+)} S^I$, *the unit is the empty trajectory* $\varepsilon = \langle \emptyset, !\rangle$; *summation is concatenation of trajectories* $\frown$, *defined as follows:*

$$\langle [0, d_1), e_1\rangle \frown \langle [0, d_2), e_2\rangle = \langle [0, d_1 + d_2), \lambda t.\ e_1^t \lhd t < d_1 \rhd e_2^{t-d_1}\rangle.$$

The relation $\leq$ is defined as follows: $\langle [0, d_1), e_1\rangle \leq \langle [0, d_2), e_2\rangle$ *if $d_1 \leq d_2$ and $e_1^t = e_2^t$ for every $t \in [0, d_1)$. We can additionally consider both sets $\sum_{I \in [0, \bar{\mathbb{R}}_+)} S^I$ and $\sum_{I \in [0, \bar{\mathbb{R}}_+]} S^I$ as Trj_S-modules, by defining the monoid action $\rhd$ also as concatenation of trajectories and by equipping these sets with the order $\sqsubseteq$:* $\langle I_1, e_1\rangle \sqsubseteq \langle I_2, e_2\rangle$ *if $I_1 \subseteq I_2$ and $e_1^t = e_2^t$ for all $t \in I_1$.*

Consider the following functors:

$$H'_S X = \sum_{I \in [0, \mathbb{R}_+)} S^I \times X \cup \sum_{I \in [0, \bar{\mathbb{R}}_+)} S^I \tag{2}$$

$$H_S X = \sum_{I \in [0, \mathbb{R}_+)} S^I \times X \cup \sum_{I \in [0, \bar{\mathbb{R}}_+]} S^I \tag{3}$$

Both of them extend to monads $\mathbf{H}'_S$ and $\mathbf{H}_S$ as they are instances of Definition 4. Moreover, it is laborious but straightforward to prove that both $H'_S X$ and $H_S X$ are conservatively complete Trj_S-modules on X [7], i.e. conservatively complete Trj_S-modules, equipped with distinguished maps $\eta : X \to H'_S X$, $\eta : X \to H_S X$. In each case η sends $x \in X$ to $\langle \varepsilon, x\rangle$. The partial order on $H'_S X$ (which we will use for obtaining the least upper bound of a certain sequence of approximations) is given by the clauses below and relies on the previous order $\leqslant$ on trajectories:

$$\frac{}{\langle\langle I, e\rangle, x\rangle \sqsubseteq \langle\langle I, e\rangle, x\rangle} \qquad \frac{\langle I, e\rangle \leqslant \langle I', e'\rangle}{\langle I, e\rangle \sqsubseteq \langle\langle I', e'\rangle, x\rangle} \qquad \frac{\langle I, e\rangle \leqslant \langle I', e'\rangle}{\langle I, e\rangle \sqsubseteq \langle I', e'\rangle}$$

The monad given by (2) admits a sharp characterization, which is an instance of a general result [7]. In more detail,

Proposition 2. *The pair $(H'_S X, \eta)$ is a free conservatively complete Trj_S-module on X, i.e. for every conservatively complete Trj_S-module $\mathbb{E}$ and a map $f : X \to \mathbb{E}$, there is unique homomorphism $\hat{f} : H'_S X \to \mathbb{E}$ such that $\hat{f} \cdot \eta = f$.*

Intuitively, Proposition 2 ensures that $H'_S X$ is a *least* conservatively complete Trj_S-module generated by X. This characterization entails a construction of an iteration operator on $\mathbf{H}'_S$ as a least fixpoint. This, in fact, also transfers to $\mathbf{H}_S$ (as detailed in the proof of the following theorem).

Theorem 2. *Both $\mathbf{H}'_S$ and $\mathbf{H}_S$ are Elgot monads, for which $f^\dagger$ is computed as a least fixpoint of ω-continuous endomaps $g \mapsto [\eta, g]^* \cdot f$ over the function spaces $X \to H'_S Y$ and $X \to H_S Y$ correspondingly.*

In this section's remainder, we formally connect the monad $\mathbf{H}_S$ with the monad $\mathbf{H}$, the latter introduced in our previous work and used for providing a semantics to the functional language HYBCORE. In the following section we provide a semantics for the current imperative language via the monad $\mathbf{H}_S$. Specifically, in this section we will show how to build $\mathbf{H}$ from $\mathbf{H}_S$ by considering additional semantic ingredients on top of the latter.

Let us subsequently write η^S, $(-)_S^\star$ and $(-)_S^\dagger$ for the unit, the Kleisli lifting and the Elgot iteration of $\mathbf{H}_S$. Note that $S, X \mapsto \mathbf{H}_S X$ is a *parametrized monad* in the sense of Uustalu [35], in particular $\mathbf{H}_S$ is functorial in S and for every $f : S \to S'$, $H_f : H_S \to H_{S'}$ is a monad morphism.

Then we introduce the following technical natural transformations $\iota :$ $H_S X \to X \uplus (S \uplus \{\bot\})$ and $\tau : H_{S \uplus Y} X \to H_S X$. First, let us define ι:

$$\iota(I, e, x) = \begin{cases} \text{inr inl } e^0, & \text{if } I \neq \emptyset \\ \text{inl } x, & \text{otherwise} \end{cases} \qquad \iota(I, e) = \begin{cases} \text{inr inl } e^0, & \text{if } I \neq \emptyset \\ \text{inr inr } \bot, & \text{otherwise} \end{cases}$$

In words: ι returns the initial point for non-zero length trajectories, and otherwise returns either an accompanying value from X or $\bot$ depending on that if the given trajectory is convergent or divergent. The functor $(-) \uplus E$ for every E extends to a monad, called the *exception monad*. The following is easy to show for ι.

Lemma 1. *For every S, $\iota : H_S \to (-) \uplus (S \uplus \{\bot\})$ is a monad morphism.*

Next we define $\tau : H_{S \uplus Y} X \to H_S X$:

$$\tau(I, e, x) = \begin{cases} \langle I, e, x \rangle, & \text{if } I = I' \\ \langle I', e' \rangle, & \text{otherwise} \end{cases} \qquad \tau(I, e) = \langle I', e' \rangle$$

where $\langle I', e' \rangle$ is the largest such trajectory that for all $t \in I'$, $e^t = \text{inl} e'^t$.

$$[\![\mathbf{x} := \mathbf{t}]\!](\sigma) = \eta(\sigma \nabla [\mathbf{t}\sigma/\mathbf{x}])$$

$$[\![\bar{\mathbf{x}}' = \bar{\mathbf{u}} \,\text{for}\, \mathbf{t}]\!](\sigma) = \langle [0, \mathbf{t}\sigma), \lambda t.\, \sigma \nabla [\phi_\sigma(t)/\bar{\mathbf{x}}], \sigma \nabla [\phi_\sigma(\mathbf{t}\sigma)/\bar{\mathbf{x}}] \rangle$$

$$[\![\mathbf{p} \,;\, \mathbf{q}]\!](\sigma) = [\![\mathbf{q}]\!]^\star([\![\mathbf{p}]\!](\sigma))$$

$$[\![\text{if}\, \mathbf{b}\, \text{then}\, \mathbf{p}\, \text{else}\, \mathbf{q}]\!](\sigma) = [\![\mathbf{p}]\!](\sigma) \triangleleft \mathbf{b}\sigma \triangleright [\![\mathbf{q}]\!](\sigma)$$

$$[\![\text{while}\, \mathbf{b}\, \text{do}\, \{\, \mathbf{p}\, \}]\!](\sigma) = (\lambda \sigma.\, (\hat{H} \,\text{inr})([\![\mathbf{p}]\!](\sigma)) \triangleleft \mathbf{b}\sigma \triangleright \eta(\text{inl}\, \sigma))^\dagger(\sigma)$$

Fig. 3. Denotational semantics.

Lemma 2. *For all S and Y, $\tau : H_{S \uplus Y} \to H_S$ is a monad morphism.*

We now arrive at the main result of this section.

Theorem 3. *The correspondence $S \mapsto H_S S$ extends to an Elgot monad as follows:*

$$\eta(x \in S) = \eta^S(x),$$

$$(f : X \to H_S S)^* = H_X X \xrightarrow{H_{\iota'} \cdot f^{\mathrm{id}}} H_{S \uplus \{\bot\}} X \xrightarrow{\tau} H_S X \xrightarrow{f_S^*} H_S S \ ,$$

$$(f : X \to H_{S \uplus X}(S \uplus X))^\dagger = X \xrightarrow{f_{S \uplus X}^\dagger} H_{S \uplus X} S \xrightarrow{H_{[\mathrm{inl}, (\iota' \cdot f)^{\natural}]} \mathrm{id}} H_{S \uplus \{\bot\}} S \xrightarrow{\tau} H_S S \ .$$

where $\iota' = [\mathrm{inl}, \mathrm{id}] \cdot \iota : H_S S \to S \uplus \{\bot\}$ and $(-)^{\natural} : (X \to (S \uplus X) \uplus \{\bot\}) \to (X \to S \uplus \{\bot\})$ is the iteration operator of the maybe-monad $(-) \uplus \{\bot\}$ (as in Example 1). Moreover, thus defined monad is isomorphic to **H**.

Proof (Proof Sketch). It is first verified that the monad axioms are satisfied using abstract properties of ι and τ, mainly provided by Lemmas 1 and 2. Then the isomorphism $\theta : H_S S \cong HS$ is defined as expected: $\theta([0, d), e, x) = \mathrm{inl}\langle [0, d], \hat{e} \rangle$ where $e^t = \hat{e}^t$ for $t \in [0, d)$, $\hat{e}^d = x$; and $\theta(I, e) = \mathrm{inr}\langle I, e \rangle$. It is easy to see that θ respects the unit. The fact that θ respects Kleisli lifting amounts to a (tedious) verification by case distinction. Checking the formula for $(-)^\dagger$ amounts to transferring the definition of $(-)^\dagger$, as defined in previous work [13], along θ. See the full proof in [15]. □

6   Soundness and Adequacy

Let us start this section by providing a denotational semantics to our language using the results of the previous section. We will then provide a soundness and adequacy result that formally connects the thus established denotational semantics with the operational semantics presented in Sect. 3.

First, consider the monad in (3) and fix $S = \mathbb{R}^{\mathcal{X}}$. We denote the obtained instance of H_S as $\hat{H}$. Intuitively, we interpret a program p as a map $[\![\mathrm{p}]\!] : S \to \hat{H}S$ which given an environment (a map from variables to values) returns a trajectory over S. The definition of $[\![\mathrm{p}]\!]$ is inductive over the structure of p and is given in Fig. 3.

In order to establish soundness and adequacy between the small-step operational semantics and the denotational semantics, we will use an auxiliary device. Namely, we will introduce a *big-step* operational semantics that will serve as midpoint between the two previously introduced semantics. We will show that the small-step semantics is equivalent to the big-step one and then establish soundness and adequacy between the big-step semantics and the denotational one. The desired result then follows by transitivity. The big-step rules are presented in Fig. 4 and follow the same reasoning than the small-step ones. The expression $\mathrm{p}, \sigma, \mathrm{t} \Downarrow \mathrm{r}, \sigma'$ means that p paired with σ evaluates to r, σ' at time instant t.

$$(\textbf{diff-stop}\Downarrow) \quad \frac{t < s\sigma}{\overline{x}' = \overline{t} \text{ for } s, \sigma, t \ \Downarrow \ stop, \sigma\nabla[\phi_\sigma(t)/\overline{x}]}$$

$$(\textbf{diff-skip}\Downarrow) \quad \frac{}{\overline{x}' = \overline{t} \text{ for } t, \sigma, t\sigma \ \Downarrow \ skip, \sigma\nabla[\phi_\sigma(t\sigma)/\overline{x}]}$$

$$(\textbf{asg}\Downarrow) \quad \frac{}{x := t, \sigma, 0 \ \Downarrow \ skip, \sigma\nabla[t\sigma/x]} \qquad (\textbf{seq-stop}\Downarrow) \quad \frac{p, \sigma, t \ \Downarrow \ stop, \sigma'}{p;q, \sigma, t \ \Downarrow \ stop, \sigma'}$$

$$(\textbf{seq-skip}\Downarrow) \quad \frac{p, \sigma, t \ \Downarrow \ skip, \sigma' \quad q, \sigma', t' \ \Downarrow \ r, \sigma''}{p;q, \sigma, t + t' \ \Downarrow \ r, \sigma''} \qquad (r \in \{stop, skip\})$$

$$(\textbf{if-true}\Downarrow) \quad \frac{b\sigma = \top \quad p, \sigma, t \ \Downarrow \ r, \sigma'}{\text{if } b \text{ then } p \text{ else } q, \sigma, t \ \Downarrow \ r, \sigma'} \qquad (r \in \{stop, skip\})$$

$$(\textbf{if-false}\Downarrow) \quad \frac{b\sigma = \bot \quad q, \sigma, t \ \Downarrow \ r, \sigma'}{\text{if } b \text{ then } p \text{ else } q, \sigma, t \ \Downarrow \ r, \sigma'} \qquad (r \in \{stop, skip\})$$

$$(\textbf{wh-true}\Downarrow) \quad \frac{b\sigma = \top \quad p; \text{while } b \text{ do } \{p\}, \sigma, t \ \Downarrow \ r, \sigma'}{\text{while } b \text{ do } \{p\}, \sigma, t \ \Downarrow \ r, \sigma'} \qquad (r \in \{stop, skip\})$$

$$(\textbf{wh-false}\Downarrow) \quad \frac{b\sigma = \bot}{\text{while } b \text{ do } \{p\}, \sigma, 0 \ \Downarrow \ skip, \sigma}$$

Fig. 4. Big-step Operational Semantics

Next, we need the following result to formally connect both styles of operational semantics.

Lemma 3. *Given a program* p, *an environment* σ *and a time instant* t

1. *if* $p, \sigma, t \ \rightarrow \ p', \sigma', t'$ *and* $p', \sigma', t' \ \Downarrow \ skip, \sigma''$ *then* $p, \sigma, t \ \Downarrow \ skip, \sigma''$;
2. *if* $p, \sigma, t \ \rightarrow \ p', \sigma', t'$ *and* $p', \sigma', t' \ \Downarrow \ stop, \sigma''$ *then* $p, \sigma, t \ \Downarrow \ stop, \sigma''$.

Proof. The proof follows by induction over the derivation of the small step relation. □

Theorem 4. *The small-step semantics and the big-step semantics are related as follows. Given a program* p, *an environment* σ *and a time instant* t

1. $p, \sigma, t \ \Downarrow \ skip, \sigma'$ *iff* $p, \sigma, t \ \rightarrow^* \ skip, \sigma', 0$;
2. $p, \sigma, t \ \Downarrow \ stop, \sigma'$ *iff* $p, \sigma, t \ \rightarrow^* \ stop, \sigma', 0$.

Proof. The right-to-left direction is obtained by induction over the length of the small-step reduction sequence using Lemma 3. The left-to-right direction follows by induction over the proof of the big-step judgement using Proposition 1. □

Finally, we can connect the operational and the denotational semantics in the expected way.

Theorem 5 (Soundness and Adequacy). *Given a program* p, *an environment* σ *and a time instant* t

1. $\mathbf{p},\sigma,\mathbf{t} \to^* skip,\sigma',0$ *iff* $\llbracket \mathbf{p} \rrbracket (\sigma) = (\mathbf{h} : [0,\mathbf{t}) \to \mathbb{R}^{\mathcal{X}}, \sigma')$;
2. $\mathbf{p},\sigma,\mathbf{t} \to^* stop,\sigma',0$ *iff either* $\llbracket \mathbf{p} \rrbracket (\sigma) = (\mathbf{h} : [0,\mathbf{t}') \to \mathbb{R}^{\mathcal{X}}, \sigma'')$ *or* $\llbracket \mathbf{p} \rrbracket (\sigma) =$ $\mathbf{h} : [0,\mathbf{t}') \to \mathbb{R}^{\mathcal{X}}$, *and in either case with* $\mathbf{t}' > \mathbf{t}$ *and* $h(\mathbf{t}) = \sigma'$.

Here, "soundness" corresponds to the left-to-right directions of the equivalences and "adequacy" to the right-to-left ones.

Proof. By Theorem 4, we equivalently replace the goal as follows:

1. $\mathbf{p},\sigma,\mathbf{t} \Downarrow skip,\sigma'$ iff $\llbracket \mathbf{p} \rrbracket (\sigma) = (\mathbf{h} : [0,\mathbf{t}) \to \mathbb{R}^{\mathcal{X}}, \sigma')$;
2. $\mathbf{p},\sigma,\mathbf{t} \Downarrow stop,\sigma'$ iff either $\llbracket \mathbf{p} \rrbracket (\sigma) = (\mathbf{h} : [0,\mathbf{t}') \to \mathbb{R}^{\mathcal{X}}, \sigma'')$ or $\llbracket \mathbf{p} \rrbracket (\sigma) = \mathbf{h} :$ $[0,\mathbf{t}') \to \mathbb{R}^{\mathcal{X}}$, and in either case with $\mathbf{t}' > \mathbf{t}$ and $h(\mathbf{t}) = \sigma'$.

Then the "soundness" direction is obtained by induction over the derivation of the rules in Fig. 4. The "adequacy" direction follows by structural induction over p; for while-loops, we call the fixpoint law $[\eta, f^{\dagger}]^* \cdot f = f^{\dagger}$ of Elgot monads.   □

7   Implementation

This section presents our prototype implementation – LINCE – which is available online both to run in our servers and to be compiled and executed locally (http://arcatools.org/lince). Its architecture is depicted in Fig. 5. The dashed rectangles correspond to its main components. The one on the left (**Core engine**) provides the parser respective to the while-language and the engine to evaluate hybrid programs using the small-step operational semantics of Sect. 3. The one on the right (**Inspector**) depicts trajectories produced by hybrid programs according to parameters specified by the user and provides an interface to evaluate hybrid programs at specific time instants (the initial environment $\sigma : \mathcal{X} \to \mathbb{R}$ is assumed to be the function constant on zero). As already mentioned, plots are generated by automatically evaluating at different time instants the program given as input. Incoming arrows in the figure denote an input relation and outgoing arrows denote an output relation. The two main components are further explained below.

Core Engine. Our implementation extensively uses the computer algebra tool SAGEMATH [31]. This serves two purposes: (1) to solve systems of differential equations (present in hybrid programs); and (2) to correctly evaluate if-then-else

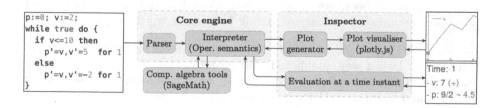

Fig. 5. Depiction of LINCE's architecture

statements. Regarding the latter, note that we do not merely use predicate functions in programming languages for evaluating Boolean conditions, essentially because such functions tend to give wrong results in the presence of real numbers (due to the finite precision problem). Instead of this, LINCE uses SAGEMATH and its ability to perform advanced symbolic manipulation to check whether a Boolean condition is true or not. However, note that this will not always give an output, fundamentally because solutions of linear differential equations involve transcendental numbers and real-number arithmetic with such numbers is undecidable [20]. We leave as future work the development of more sophisticated techniques for avoiding errors in the computational evaluation of hybrid programs.

Inspector. The user interacts with LINCE at two different stages: (a) when inputting a hybrid program and (b) when inspecting trajectories using LINCE's output interfaces. The latter case consists of adjusting different parameters for observing the generated plots in an optimal way.

Event-Triggered Programs. Observe that the differential statements $x_1' = t, \ldots, x_n' = t$ for t are *time-triggered*: they terminate precisely when the instant of time t is achieved. In the area of hybrid systems it is also usual to consider *event-triggered* programs: those that terminate *as soon as* a specified condition ψ becomes true [6,11,38]. So we next consider atomic programs of the type $x_1' = t, \ldots, x_n' = t$ until ψ where ψ is an element of the free Boolean algebra generated by $t \leqslant s$ and $t \geqslant s$ where $t, s \in \text{LTerm}(\mathcal{X})$, signalling the termination of the program. In general, it is impossible to determine with *exact* precision when such programs terminate (again due to the undecidability of real-number arithmetic with transcendental numbers). A natural option is to tackle this problem by checking the condition ψ periodically, which essentially reduces event-triggered programs into time-triggered ones. The cost is that the evaluation of a program might greatly diverge from the nominal behaviour, as discussed for instance in documents [4,6] where an analogous approach is discussed for the well-established simulation tools SIMULINK and MODELICA. In our case, we allow programs of the form $x_1' = t, \ldots, x_n' = t$ until$_\epsilon$ ψ in the tool and define them as the abbreviation of while $\neg\psi$ do $\{ x_1' = t, \ldots, x_n' = t$ for $\epsilon \}$. This sort of abbreviation has the advantage of avoiding spurious evaluations of hybrid programs w.r.t. the established semantics. We could indeed easily allow such event-triggered programs natively in our language (i.e. without recurring to abbreviations) and extend the semantics accordingly. But we prefer not to do this at the moment, because we wish first to fully understand the ways of limiting spurious computational evaluations arising from event-triggered programs.

Remark 3. SIMULINK and MODELICA are powerful tools for simulating hybrid systems, but lack a well-established, formal semantics. This is discussed for example in [3,9], where the authors aim to provide semantics to subsets of SIMULINK and MODELICA. Getting inspiration from control theory, the language of SIMULINK is circuit-like, block-based; the language of MODELICA is *acausal*

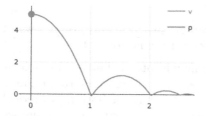 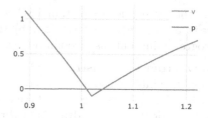

Fig. 6. Position of the bouncing ball over time (plot on the left); zoomed in position of the bouncing ball at the first bounce (plot on the right).

and thus particularly useful for modelling electric circuits and the like which are traditionally modelled by systems of equations.

Example 3 (Bouncing Ball). As an illustration of the approach described above for event-triggered programs, take a bouncing ball dropped at a positive height p and with no initial velocity v. Due to the gravitational acceleration g, it falls to the ground and bounces back up, losing part of its kinetic energy in the process. This can be approximated by the following hybrid program

$$(p' = v, v' = g \, \mathtt{until}_{0.01} \, p \leqslant 0 \wedge v \leqslant 0) \, ; (v := v \times -0.5)$$

where 0.5 is the dampening factor of the ball. We now want to drop the ball from a specific height (e.g. 5 m) and let it bounce until it stops. Abbreviating the previous program into b, this behaviour can be approximated by $p := 5; v := 0; \mathtt{while} \ \mathbf{true} \ \mathtt{do} \ \{ \ b \ \}$. Figure 6 presents the trajectory generated by the ball (calculated by LINCE). Note that since $\epsilon = 0.01$ the ball reaches below ground, as shown in Fig. 6 on the right. Other examples of event- and time-triggered programs can be seen in LINCE's website.

8 Conclusions and Future Work

We introduced small-step and big-step operational semantics for hybrid programs suitable for implementation purposes and provided a denotational counterpart via the notion of Elgot monad. These semantics were then linked by a soundness and adequacy theorem [37]. We regard these results as a stepping stone for developing computational tools and techniques for hybrid programming; which we attested with the development of LINCE. With this work as basis, we plan to explore the following research lines in the near future.

Program Equivalence. Our denotational semantics entails a natural notion of program equivalence (denotational equality) which inherently includes classical laws of iteration and a powerful *uniformity* principle [33], thanks to the use of Elgot monads. We intend to further explore the equational theory of our language so that we can safely refactor/simplify hybrid programs. Note that the theory includes equational schema like $(x := a; x := b) = x := b$ and $(\text{wait } a; \text{wait } b) = \text{wait } (a + b)$ thus encompassing not only usual laws of programming but also axiomatic principles behind the notion of time.

New Program Constructs. Our while-language is intended to be as simple as possible whilst harbouring the core, uncontroversial features of hybrid programming. This was decided so that we could use the language as both a theoretical and practical basis for advancing hybrid programming. A particular case that we wish to explore next is the introduction of new program constructs, including e.g. non-deterministic or probabilistic choice and exception operations $\text{raise}(\text{exc})$. Denotationally, the fact that we used monadic constructions readily provides a palette of techniques for this process, e.g. tensoring and distributive laws [22, 23].

Robustness. A core aspect of hybrid programming is that programs should be *robust*: small variations in their input should *not* result in big changes in their output [21, 32]. We wish to extend LINCE with features for detecting non-robust programs. A main source of non-robustness are conditional statements $\text{if } b \text{ then } p \text{ else } q$: very small changes in their input may change the validity of b and consequently cause a switch between (possibly very different) execution branches. Currently, we are working on the systematic detection of non-robust conditional statements in hybrid programs, by taking advantage of the notion of δ-perturbation [20].

Acknowledgements. The first author would like to acknowledge support of German Research Council (DFG) under the project *A High Level Language for Monad-based Processes (GO 2161/1–2)*. The second author was financed by the ERDF – European Regional Development Fund through the Operational Programme for Competitiveness and Internationalisation – COMPETE 2020 Programme and by National Funds through the Portuguese funding agency, FCT – Fundação para a Ciência e a Tecnologia, within project POCI-01-0145-FEDER-030947. The third author was partially supported by National Funds through FCT/MCTES, within the CISTER Research Unit (UIDB/04234/2020); by COMPETE 2020 under the PT2020 Partnership Agreement, through ERDF, and by national funds through the FCT, within project POCI-01-0145-FEDER-029946; by the Norte Portugal Regional Operational Programme (NORTE 2020) under the Portugal 2020 Partnership Agreement, through ERDF and also by national funds through the FCT, within project NORTE-01-0145-FEDER-028550; and by the FCT within project ECSEL/0016/2019 and the ECSEL Joint Undertaking (JU) under grant agreement No 876852. The JU receives support from the European Union's Horizon 2020 research and innovation programme and Austria, Czech Republic, Germany, Ireland, Italy, Portugal, Spain, Sweden, Turkey.

References

1. Adámek, J., Herrlich, H., Strecker, G.: Abstract and Concrete Categories. Wiley, New York (1990)
2. Adámek, J., Milius, S., Velebil, J.: Elgot theories: a new perspective on the equational properties of iteration. Math. Structures Comput. Sci. **21**(2), 417–480 (2011)
3. Bouissou, O., Chapoutot, A.: An operational semantics for Simulink's simulation engine. In: ACM SIGPLAN Notices, vol. 47, pp. 129–138. ACM (2012)

4. Broman, D.: Hybrid simulation safety: limbos and zero crossings. In: Lohstroh, M., Derler, P., Sirjani, M. (eds.) Principles of Modeling. LNCS, vol. 10760, pp. 106–121. Springer, Cham (2018). https://doi.org/10.1007/978-3-319-95246-8_7

5. Chaochen, Z., Hoare, C.A.R., Ravn, A.P.: A calculus of durations. Inf. Process. Lett. **40**(5), 269–276 (1991)

6. Copp, D.A., Sanfelice, R.G.: A zero-crossing detection algorithm for robust simulation of hybrid systems jumping on surfaces. Simulation Modell. Pract. Theory **68**, 1–17 (2016)

7. Diezel, T.L., Goncharov, S.: Towards constructive hybrid semantics. In: Ariola, Z.M. (ed.) 5th International Conference on Formal Structures for Computation and Deduction (FSCD 2020), vol. 167 of LIPIcs, pp. 24:1–24:19, Dagstuhl, Germany, 2020. Schloss Dagstuhl-Leibniz-Zentrum für Informatik

8. Elgot, C.: Monadic computation and iterative algebraic theories. In: Studies in Logic and the Foundations of Mathematics, vol. 80, pp. 175–230. Elsevier (1975)

9. Foster, S., Thiele, B., Cavalcanti, A., Woodcock, J.: Towards a UTP semantics for modelica. In: Bowen, J.P., Zhu, H. (eds.) UTP 2016. LNCS, vol. 10134, pp. 44–64. Springer, Cham (2017). https://doi.org/10.1007/978-3-319-52228-9_3

10. Fritzson, P.: Principles of object-oriented modeling and simulation with Modelica 3.3: a cyber-physical approach. Wiley, New York (2014)

11. Goebel, R., Sanfelice, R.G., Teel, A.R.: Hybrid dynamical systems. IEEE Control Syst. **29**(2), 28–93 (2009)

12. Goncharov, S., Jakob, J., Neves, R.: A semantics for hybrid iteration. In: 29th International Conference on Concurrency Theory, CONCUR 2018. Schloss Dagstuhl - Leibniz-Zentrum fuer Informatik (2018)

13. Goncharov, S., Jakob, J., Neves, R.: A semantics for hybrid iteration. CoRR, abs/1807.01053 (2018)

14. Goncharov, S., Neves, R.: An adequate while-language for hybrid computation. In: Proceedings of the 21st International Symposium on Principles and Practice of Programming Languages 2019, PPDP 2019, pp. 11:1–11:15, New York, NY, USA, ACM (2019)

15. Goncharov, S., Neves, R., Proença, J.: Implementing hybrid semantics: From functional to imperative. CoRR, abs/2009.14322 (2020)

16. Goncharov, S., Schröder, L., Rauch, C., Piróg, M.: Unifying guarded and unguarded iteration. In: Esparza, J., Murawski, A.S. (eds.) FoSSaCS 2017. LNCS, vol. 10203, pp. 517–533. Springer, Heidelberg (2017). https://doi.org/10.1007/978-3-662-54458-7_30

17. Henzinger, T.A.: The theory of hybrid automata. In: LICS 1996: Logic in Computer Science, 11th Annual Symposium, New Jersey, USA, July 27–30, 1996, pp. 278–292. IEEE (1996)

18. Höfner, P., Möller, B.: An algebra of hybrid systems. J. Logic Algebraic Programm. **78**(2), 74–97 (2009)

19. Huerta, J.J., Munive, Y., Struth, G.: Verifying hybrid systems with modal kleene algebra. In: Desharnais, J., Guttmann, W., Joosten, S. (eds.) Relational and Algebraic Methods in Computer Science, pp. 225–243. Springer, Cham (2018)

20. Kong, S., Gao, S., Chen, W., Clarke, E.: dReach: reachability analysis for hybrid systems. In: Baier, C., Tinelli, C. (eds.) TACAS 2015. LNCS, vol. 9035, pp. 200–205. Springer, Heidelberg (2015). https://doi.org/10.1007/978-3-662-46681-0_15

21. Liberzon, D., Morse, A.S.: Basic problems in stability and design of switched systems. IEEE Control Syst. **19**(5), 59–70 (1999)

22. Lüth, C., Ghani, N.: Composing monads using coproducts. In: Wand, M., Jones, S.L.P. (eds.) 7th ACM SIGPLAN International Conference ICFP 2002: Functional Programming, Pittsburgh, USA, October 04–06, 2002, pp. 133–144. ACM (2002)

23. Manes, E., Mulry, P.: Monad compositions I: general constructions and recursive distributive laws. Theory Appl. Categories **18**(7), 172–208 (2007)

24. Moggi, E.: Computational lambda-calculus and monads. In: Proceedings of the Fourth Annual Symposium on Logic in Computer Science (LICS 1989), Pacific Grove, California, USA, June 5–8, 1989, pp. 14–23. IEEE Computer Society (1989)

25. Moggi, E.: Notions of computation and monads. Inf. Comput. **93**(1), 55–92 (1991)

26. Neves, R.: Hybrid programs. Ph.D. thesis, Minho University (2018)

27. Ölveczky, P.C., Meseguer, J.: Semantics and pragmatics of real-time maude. Higher-order Symbolic Comput. **20**(1–2), 161–196 (2007)

28. Platzer, A.: Differential dynamic logic for hybrid systems. J. Automated Reason. **41**(2), 143–189 (2008)

29. Platzer, A.: Logical Analysis of Hybrid Systems: Proving Theorems for Complex Dynamics. Springer, Heidelberg (2010)

30. Rajkumar, R.R., Lee, I., Sha, L., Stankovic, J.: Cyber-physical systems: the next computing revolution. In: DAC 2010: Design Automation Conference, 47th ACM/IEEE Conference, Anaheim, USA, June 13–18, 2010, pp. 731–736. IEEE (2010)

31. Stein, W., et al.: Sage Mathematics Software (Version 6.4.1). The Sage Development Team (2015). http://www.sagemath.org

32. Shorten, R., Wirth, F., Mason, O., Wulff, K., King, C.: Stability criteria for switched and hybrid systems. Soc. Ind. Appl. Math. (review) **49**(4), 545–592 (2007)

33. Simpson, A., Plotkin, G.: Complete axioms for categorical fixed-point operators. Logic in Comput. Sci. LICS **2000**, 30–41 (2000)

34. Suenaga, K., Hasuo, I.: Programming with infinitesimals: a WHILE-language for hybrid system modeling. In: Aceto, L., Henzinger, M., Sgall, J. (eds.) ICALP 2011. LNCS, vol. 6756, pp. 392–403. Springer, Heidelberg (2011). https://doi.org/10.1007/978-3-642-22012-8_31

35. Uustalu, T.: Generalizing substitution. RAIRO-Theor. Inf. Appl. **37**(4), 315–336 (2003)

36. van Glabbeek, R.: The linear time-branching time spectrum (extended abstract). In: Theories of Concurrency, CONCUR 1990, vol. 458, pp. 278–297 (1990)

37. Winskel, G.: The Formal Semantics of Programming Languages: An Introduction. MIT Press, Cambridge (1993)

38. Witsenhausen, H.: A class of hybrid-state continuous-time dynamic systems. IEEE Trans. Automatic Control **11**(2), 161–167 (1966)

Implementation Correctness
for Replicated Data Types, Categorically

Fabio Gadducci[1]([✉]), Hernán Melgratti[2], Christian Roldán[3],
and Matteo Sammartino[4]

[1] Dipartimento di Informatica, Università di Pisa, Pisa, Italy
fabio.gadducci@unipi.it
[2] ICC – Universidad de Buenos Aires – CONICET, Buenos Aires, Argentina
[3] IMDEA Software Institute, Madrid, Spain
[4] Royal Holloway University of London, University College London, London, UK

Abstract. Replicated Data Types (RDTs) have been introduced as an abstraction for dealing with weakly consistent data stores, which may (temporarily) expose multiple, inconsistent views of their state. In the literature, RDTs are usually presented in set-theoretical terms: Only recently different specification flavours have been proposed, among them a denotational formalism that inter alia captures specification refinement. So far, however, no abstract model has been proposed for the implementations and their correctness with respect to specifications. This paper fills the gap: We first give categorical constructions for distilling an operational model from a specification, as well as its implementations, and then we define a notion of implementation correctness via simulation.

Keywords: Replicated data types · Specification · Operational semantics · Functorial characterisation · Implementation correctness

1 Introduction

Replicated data types (RDTs) are abstractions for building distributed systems on top of weak-consistent stores, i.e., systems that tolerate temporary data inconsistencies to favour availability. Different specification approaches for RDTs have been proposed in the literature [2–5,7,8,10,11,14,16]. Despite stylistic differences, they abstractly represent the state of a system in terms of two relations defined on executed operations: *visibility*, which explains the partial view of the state over which each operation is executed, and *arbitration*, which totally orders operations and is used for resolving conflicting effects of concurrent operations.

Research partially supported by the MIUR PRIN 2017FTXR7S "IT-MaTTerS", by the EU H2020 RISE programme under the Marie Skłodowska-Curie grant agreement 778233, by the UBACyT projects 20020170100544BA and 20020170100086BA, by the PIP project 11220130100148CO and by the EPSRC Standard Grant EP/S028641/1.

© Springer Nature Switzerland AG 2020
V. K. I. Pun et al. (Eds.): ICTAC 2020, LNCS 12545, pp. 283–303, 2020.
https://doi.org/10.1007/978-3-030-64276-1_15

$$
\mathcal{S}_{Ctr}\left(\begin{array}{cc} \langle\texttt{inc},ok\rangle & \langle\texttt{inc},ok\rangle \\ \downarrow & \swarrow \quad \downarrow \\ \langle\texttt{rd},2\rangle & \langle\texttt{rd},1\rangle \end{array}\right) = \left\{\begin{array}{cc} \langle\texttt{inc},ok\rangle & \langle\texttt{rd},1\rangle \quad \cdots \\ | & | \\ \langle\texttt{rd},1\rangle & \langle\texttt{inc},ok\rangle \\ | & | \\ \langle\texttt{inc},ok\rangle & \langle\texttt{inc},ok\rangle \\ | & | \\ \langle\texttt{rd},2\rangle & \langle\texttt{rd},2\rangle \end{array}\right\} \quad \mathcal{S}_{Ctr}\left(\begin{array}{c} \langle\texttt{inc},ok\rangle \\ \downarrow \\ \langle\texttt{rd},0\rangle \end{array}\right) = \emptyset
$$

Fig. 1. *Counter* specification.

Consider an RDT *Counter*, which has 0 as initial value and the operations inc to increment it and rd to read its value. By following the functional approach proposed in [7,8], the RDT *Counter* is specified as a function $\mathcal{S}_{Ctr}$ that maps visibilities into sets of arbitrations, both of them represented as directed graphs labelled by pairs $\langle operation, result\rangle$. Figure 1 illustrates two cases for the definition of $\mathcal{S}_{Ctr}$. The left-most equation considers the case in which the state consists of four operations: two incs that return *ok* and two rds that respectively returns 1 and 2. The arrows in the visibility (i.e., the graph on the left-hand side of the equation) denotes the fact that the execution of one rd sees the effects of the execution of the two incs while the other sees just one of them. Intuitively, the arrows justify the values returned by each rd. In this case, $\mathcal{S}_{Ctr}$ maps that visibility graph into a non-empty set of arbitrations, i.e., a set of total orders of executed operations. While the leftmost arbitration is immediate, the rightmost one shows that arbitrations do not necessarily preserve the order of the visibility graph: While this may seem counterintuitive, it is a design choice that allows more flexibility and is adopted by most of the current proposals for RDTs. The situation illustrated by the equation on the right is different, because the result of rd is defined as 0, which is deemed inconsistent with the fact that the execution of that rd sees one inc. For this reason, $\mathcal{S}_{Ctr}$ maps such visibility into an empty set of arbitrations (i.e., the visibility describes an unreachable state).

As shown in [9], a large class of functional specifications, dubbed *coherent*, can be characterised as functors between the categories **PIDag**$(\mathcal{L})$ of visibilities and **SPath**$(\mathcal{L})$ of sets of arbitrations, where $\mathcal{L}$ is a fixed set of operations labels. In this paper, we take advantage of the functorial characterisation of specifications to develop a notion of implementation and implementation correctness for RDTs. We first provide a systematic way for recovering an operational semantics out of a specification. This is achieved by constructing the *category of elements* $\mathbf{E}(\mathbb{F})$ of the functor $\mathbb{F}$ associated with a specification. Objects in $\mathbf{E}(\mathbb{F})$ are pairs $\langle G, P\rangle$ describing the states of the RDT in terms of a visibility G and an arbitration P. Arrows of $\mathbf{E}(\mathbb{F})$ stand for computations. Then, by following the approach in [12], we recover an LTS from $\mathbf{E}(\mathbb{F})$ by assigning labels to the computations (arrows) of $\mathbf{E}(\mathbb{F})$: The labels provide the contextual information that explains the way in which a local computation is embedded into a global context. The obtained semantics is then an operational specification for the implementation of the RDT. Usually, RDTs are implemented by several replicas that keep their own local state and propagate changes asynchronously. Such behaviour can be understood in terms of two labelled transition systems (LTSs): One that describes the behaviour of a single replica, and another one, obtained by composition, that accounts for the concurrent execution of several interacting replicas. Our first observation is that usual implementations of well-known RDTs exhibit a preordered monoidal structure on states, where the order accounts for the evolution of the system and the monoidal operator for state composition. Consequently, the computation space of a replica can be defined in terms of the power-domain construction over the corresponding monoid. Then, the behaviour of a replica can be represented by a functor that maps sequences of operations into computations. The category of elements associated with the implementation functor is used again to recover a contextual LTS, in this case, for an implementation. Consequently, implementation correctness can be straightforwardly stated in terms of contextual simulation between the recovered LTSs. In this way, we reframe previous ad-hoc formulations of implementation correctness by applying well-known notions in concurrency theory, thus paving the way for the application of more standard techniques in the analysis of RDTs.

The paper is structured as follows. Section 2 recalls the functorial presentation of RDTs specifications [9]. Section 3 presents the basics of state-based implementation of RDTs and the running examples. Section 4 recasts the set-theoretical presentation [7] of the operational semantics of RDTs in terms of categories of elements and introduces contextual LTSs. Section 5 illustrates a categorical model for implementations and characterises their correctness via simulation relations.

2   Background

Notation. Given a finite set E, a (binary) *relation* ρ over E, written $\langle E, \rho \rangle$, is a subset $\rho \subseteq E \times E$. We write $\emptyset$ for the empty relation and $e \, \rho \, e'$ to mean $(e, e') \in \rho$. A subset $E' \subseteq E$ is *downward closed* with respect to ρ if $e \, \rho \, e'$ implies $e \in E'$, for all $e' \in E'$. We write $\lfloor e \rfloor_\rho$ for the smallest downward closed set with respect to ρ including $e \in E$, omitting the subscript ρ if clear from the context.

Let $\mathcal{L}$ be a finite set of *labels*. A *labelled graph* is a triple $\langle \mathcal{E}, \prec, \lambda \rangle$, where $\mathcal{E}$ is the set of vertices (they actually stand for "events", hence the notation), $\prec \subseteq \mathcal{E} \times \mathcal{E}$ is the (directed) connectivity relation, i.e., $e \prec e'$ means that there is an edge from e to e', and $\lambda \colon \mathcal{E} \to \mathcal{L}$ is a labelling function, assigning a label to each vertex. A graph is *acyclic* if the transitive closure of $\prec$ is a strict partial order. We write $\mathcal{E}_G$, $\prec_G$ and λ_G for the corresponding component of a specific graph G. A *path* $\langle \mathcal{E}, \leq, \lambda \rangle$ is a graph where $\leq$ is a total order. Given a graph $G = \langle \mathcal{E}, \prec, \lambda \rangle$ and a subset $\mathcal{E}' \subseteq \mathcal{E}$, we denote by $G|_{\mathcal{E}'}$ the obvious restriction (and the same applies to a path P).

We denote with $\mathbb{G}(\mathcal{L})$ and $\mathbb{P}(\mathcal{L})$ the collections of (finite) graphs and (finite) paths, respectively, labelled on $\mathcal{L}$ and with ϵ the empty graph. Also, when the set

$$
\mathcal{S}_{mvR}\left(\begin{array}{c} \langle\mathtt{wr}(1),ok\rangle \quad \langle\mathtt{wr}(3),ok\rangle \\ \langle\mathtt{wr}(2),ok\rangle \\ \langle\mathtt{rd},\{2\}\rangle \longrightarrow \langle\mathtt{rd},\{2,3\}\rangle \end{array}\right) = \left\{\begin{array}{cccc} \langle\mathtt{wr}(1),ok\rangle & \langle\mathtt{wr}(1),ok\rangle & \langle\mathtt{rd},\{2,3\}\rangle & \cdots \\ | & | & | \\ \langle\mathtt{wr}(2),ok\rangle & \langle\mathtt{wr}(2),ok\rangle & \langle\mathtt{wr}(3),ok\rangle & \cdots \\ | & | & | \\ \langle\mathtt{rd},\{2\}\rangle & \langle\mathtt{rd},\{2\}\rangle & \langle\mathtt{wr}(1),ok\rangle & \cdots \\ | & | & | \\ \langle\mathtt{wr}(3),ok\rangle & \langle\mathtt{rd},\{2,3\}\rangle & \langle\mathtt{wr}(2),ok\rangle & \cdots \\ | & | & | \\ \langle\mathtt{rd},\{2,3\}\rangle & \langle\mathtt{wr}(3),ok\rangle & \langle\mathtt{rd},\{2\}\rangle & \cdots \end{array}\right\}
$$

Fig. 2. Specification of a multi-value Register

of labels $\mathcal{L}$ is chosen, we let $\mathbb{G}(\mathcal{E},\lambda)$ and $\mathbb{P}(\mathcal{E},\lambda)$ be the collections of graphs and paths, respectively, whose vertices are those in $\mathcal{E}$ and are labelled by $\lambda : \mathcal{E} \to \mathcal{L}$.

2.1 Replicated Data Types

We briefly recall the functional model of RDTs introduced in [7].

Definition 1 (Specifications). *A specification $\mathcal{S}$ is a function $\mathcal{S} : \mathbb{G}(\mathcal{L}) \to 2^{\mathbb{P}(\mathcal{L})}$ such that $\mathcal{S}(\epsilon) = \{\epsilon\}$ and $\forall\mathtt{G}.\ \mathcal{S}(\mathtt{G}) \in 2^{\mathbb{P}(\mathcal{E}_\mathtt{G},\lambda_\mathtt{G})}$.*

A specification $\mathcal{S}$ maps a graph (interpreted as the visibility relation of a RDT) to a set of paths (that is, the admissible arbitrations of the events). Indeed, each $\mathrm{P} \in \mathcal{S}(\mathtt{G})$ is a path over $\mathcal{E}_\mathtt{G}$, hence a total order of the events in $\mathtt{G}$.

Example 1 (Multi-value Register). A common abstraction of a memory cell in a replicated system is given by a *multi-value Register*. Differently from a traditional register, a multi-value one may contain several values when it is updated concurrently. Hence, we can fix the following set of labels

$$
\mathcal{L}_{mvR} = \{\langle\mathtt{wr}(k),ok\rangle \mid k \in \mathbb{N}\} \cup (\{\mathtt{rd}\} \times 2^{\mathbb{N}})
$$

where $\langle\mathtt{wr}(k),ok\rangle$ stands for an operation that writes the integer k and $\langle\mathtt{rd},S\rangle$ for a read that retrieves the (possibly empty) set of values S stored in the register. The return value of every write operation is ok since they always succeed.

The specification is given by $\mathcal{S}_{mvR} : \mathbb{G}(\mathcal{L}_{mvR}) \to 2^{\mathbb{P}(\mathcal{L}_{mvR})}$ defined as follows

$$
\mathrm{P} \in \mathcal{S}_{mvR}(\mathtt{G}) \text{ iff } \left\{\begin{array}{l} \forall e \in \mathcal{E}_\mathtt{G}. \\ \lambda(e) = \langle\mathtt{rd},S\rangle \Rightarrow S = \{k \mid \exists e' \prec_\mathtt{G} e.\ \lambda(e') = \langle\mathtt{wr}(k),ok\rangle \wedge \\ \quad (\forall e'' \prec_\mathtt{G} e, k'.\ e' \prec_\mathtt{G} e'' \Rightarrow \lambda(e'') \neq \langle\mathtt{wr}(k'),ok\rangle)\} \end{array}\right.
$$

The condition on the right requires that any event e in $\mathtt{G}$ associated with a read (i.e., labelled by $\langle\mathtt{rd},S\rangle$) returns a set S that contains all values written by maximal (according to $\prec_\mathsf{G}$) concurrent updates seen by it. If this is the case, all arbitrations are admissible, i.e., $\mathsf{P} \in \mathcal{S}_{mvR}(\mathsf{G})$ for all P, otherwise $\mathcal{S}_{mvR}(\mathsf{G}) = \emptyset$.

An instance of $\mathcal{S}_{mvR}$ is shown in Fig. 2, where G consists of three writes: $\mathtt{wr}(2)$ overwrites $\mathtt{wr}(1)$, and both are concurrent with $\mathtt{wr}(3)$. Additionally, there are two reads: One observes all writes (right-most at the bottom), the other does not see $\mathtt{wr}(3)$ (left-most one). Both reads return the set of values written by the maximal observed events: None of them returns 1 because it has been overwritten by 2. A graph is mapped by $\mathcal{S}_{mvR}$ to $\emptyset$ if it describes an inconsistent configuration, e.g., if the return value of one read in Fig. 2 were changed to $\{1\}$.

According to $\mathcal{S}_{mvR}$, events can be arbitrated in any order, allowing read events to happen before observed writes (as in the second and third path in Fig. 2). This a common approach in the specification of RDTs [4] because it allows permissive strategies for implementation (we refer to [7] for details). If needed, a specification can explicitly exclude arbitrations (as illustrated in Example 2).

Example 2 (Last-write wins Register). An alternative to the *multi-value Register* is the *last-write wins Register*, in which every read returns the last written value according to arbitration. We take the following set of labels

$$\mathcal{L}_{\mathcal{S}_{lwwR}} = \{\langle \mathtt{wr}(k), ok\rangle, \langle \mathtt{rd}, k\rangle \mid k \in \mathbb{N}\} \cup \{\langle \mathtt{rd}, \bot\rangle\}$$

where $\bot$ is the initial value of a register. Its specification $\mathcal{S}_{lwwR}$ is given by

$$\mathsf{P} \in \mathcal{S}_{lwwR}(\mathsf{G}) \text{ iff } \begin{cases} \forall \mathsf{e} \in \mathcal{E}_\mathsf{G}. \\ \lambda(\mathsf{e}) = \langle \mathtt{rd}, \bot\rangle \Rightarrow \forall \mathsf{e}' \prec_\mathsf{G} \mathsf{e}, k'. \lambda(\mathsf{e}') \neq \langle \mathtt{wr}(k'), ok\rangle \wedge \\ \lambda(\mathsf{e}) = \langle \mathtt{rd}, k\rangle \Rightarrow \exists \mathsf{e}' \prec_\mathsf{G} \mathsf{e}. \lambda(\mathsf{e}') = \langle \mathtt{wr}(k), ok\rangle \wedge \\ \quad (\forall \mathsf{e}'' \prec_\mathsf{G} \mathsf{e}, k'. \mathsf{e}' <_\mathsf{P} \mathsf{e}'' \Rightarrow \lambda(\mathsf{e}'') \neq \langle \mathtt{wr}(k'), ok\rangle) \end{cases}$$

According to $\mathcal{S}_{lwwR}$, a read returns $\bot$ when it does not observe any write. On the contrary, a read e returns a natural number k when it observes some event e' that writes k. In such case, the arbitration P must order e' as the maximal event (accordingly to $<_\mathsf{P}$) among all write operations seen by e. In this way, the specification constrains the allowed arbitrations of a graph.

We now restrict our attention to *coherent* specifications, which suffice for the standard specification of RDTs [7] and are amenable to categorical characterisation, as illustrated in the next section. Coherence expresses that admissible arbitrations of a visibility graph are obtained by composing the admissible arbitrations corresponding to smaller visibilities. Its formal definition relies on an auxiliary operation for composing sets of paths. We say that the paths of a set $\mathcal{X} = \{\mathsf{P}_i\}_{i \in I}$ are *compatible* if we have $\lambda_j(\mathsf{e}) = \lambda_k(\mathsf{e})$ for all $\mathsf{e} \in \mathcal{E}_j \cap \mathcal{E}_k$.

Definition 2 (Product). *The product of a set $\mathcal{X}$ of compatible paths is*

$$\bigotimes \mathcal{X} = \{\mathsf{P} \mid \mathsf{P} \text{ is a path over } \bigcup_i \mathcal{E}_i \text{ and } \mathsf{P}|_{\mathcal{E}_i} \in \mathcal{X} \}$$

The product of paths is analogous to the synchronous product of transition systems: Common elements are identified and the remaining ones can be freely interleaved, as long as the original orders are respected. A set of sets of paths $\mathcal{X}_1, \mathcal{X}_2, \ldots$ is compatible if $\bigcup_i \mathcal{X}_i$ is so, and we can define $\bigotimes_i \mathcal{X}_i$ as $\bigotimes \bigcup_i \mathcal{X}_i$.

Definition 3 ((Past-)Coherent Specification). *Let $\mathcal{S}$ be a specification. We say that $\mathcal{S}$ is past-coherent (briefly, coherent) if $\forall G \neq \epsilon.\ \mathcal{S}(G) = \bigotimes_{e \in \mathcal{E}_G} \mathcal{S}(G|_{\lfloor e \rfloor})$.*

In a coherent specification $\mathcal{S}$ the arbitrations of a configuration G (i.e., the set of paths $\mathcal{S}(G)$) are the composition of the arbitrations of its sub-graphs $G|_{\lfloor e \rfloor}$. It can be shown that the specifications in Example 1 and 2 are coherent.

2.2 Categorical Model of Specifications

We now recall important definitions and results from [9]. We start off by introducing the category of binary relations.

Definition 4 ((Binary Relation) Morphisms). *A (binary relation) morphism $f : \langle E, \rho \rangle \to \langle T, \gamma \rangle$ is a function $f : E \to T$ such that $e\ \rho\ e'$ implies $f(e)\ \gamma\ f(e)'$ for all $e, e' \in E$. A morphism $f : \langle E, \rho \rangle \to \langle T, \gamma \rangle$ is past-reflecting (shortly, pr-morphism) if $t\ \gamma\ f(e)$ implies that there is $e' \in E$ such that $e'\ \rho\ e$ and $t = f(e')$ for all $e \in E$ and $t \in T$.*

Past-reflecting morphisms are known under various names in different contexts, e.g. as bounded morphisms in modal logic. The intuition is that morphisms add no dependencies in the past of an event, hence the chosen name.

Both classes of morphisms are closed under composition: **Bin** denotes the category of relations and their morphisms and **PBin** the sub-category of pr-morphisms. The category **Bin** has both finite limits and finite colimits, which are computed point-wise as in **Set**. The structure is largely lifted to **PBin**: Finite colimits and binary pullbacks in **PBin** are computed as in **Bin**. Yet there is no terminal object, as morphisms into the singleton are clearly not past-reflecting.

Given a set of labels $\mathcal{L}$, the category of labelled relations is $\mathbf{Bin}(\mathcal{L})$.

Definition 5 (Category of labelled relations). *The category $\mathbf{Bin}(\mathcal{L})$ is defined as the comma category $U_r \downarrow \mathcal{L}$, where $U_r : \mathbf{Bin} \to \mathbf{Set}$ is the inclusion into $\mathbf{Set}$. Explicitly, an object in $\mathbf{Bin}(\mathcal{L})$ is a triple (E, ρ, λ) for a labeling function $\lambda : E \to \mathcal{L}$. A label-preserving morphism $(E, \rho, \lambda) \to (E', \rho', \lambda')$ is a morphism $f : (E, \rho) \to (E', \rho')$ such that $\lambda(s) = \lambda'(f(s))$ for all $s \in E$.*

The category $\mathbf{PBin}(\mathcal{L})$ is defined analogously, with the requirement that the morphisms are also past-reflecting. In both categories, finite colimits and binary pullbacks always exist and are essentially computed as in **Bin**. Two subcategories are used for both the syntax and the semantics of specifications.

Definition 6 (PDag/Path). **PDag** *is the full sub-category of* **PBin** *whose objects are acyclic graphs, and the same for* **Path** *with respect to* **Bin** *and paths.*

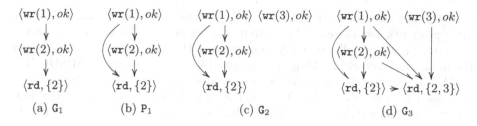

Fig. 3. Some labelled graphs

As for relations, suitable comma categories capture labelled paths and graphs, which are respectively called **PDag**($\mathcal{L}$) and **Path**($\mathcal{L}$). Once more, finite colimits and binary pullbacks always exist and are essentially computed as in **Bin**.

Example 3. We illustrate some labelled graphs in Fig. 3 and remark that P_1 is the only path in the figure. Note that G_1 is not a path because the relation is not transitive. There is an obvious label-preserving morphism $f_1 : G_1 \to P_1$, but this is not a pr-morphism because the edge from $\langle \mathtt{wr}(1), ok \rangle$ to $\langle \mathtt{rd}, \{2\} \rangle$ in P_1 is not matched in G_1. On the contrary, there is no morphism from P_1 to G_1. Note that the label-preserving morphisms $f_2 : P_1 \to G_2$ and $f_3 : G_2 \to G_3$ are pr-morphisms (and consequently, $f_2; f_3 : P_1 \to G_3$ is so).

Model of Specifications. Specifications are modelled as functors from graphs to sets of paths. *Saturation* is used to define morphisms between sets of paths.

Definition 7 (Path saturation). *Let* P *be a path and* $f : (\mathcal{E}_P, \lambda_P) \to (\mathcal{E}, \lambda)$ *a label-preserving function. The saturation of* P *along* f *is defined as*

$$\mathtt{sat}(P, f) = \{Q \mid Q \in \mathbb{P}(\mathcal{E}, \lambda) \text{ and } f \text{ induces a morphism } f : P \to Q \text{ in } \mathbf{Path}(\mathcal{L})\}$$

Saturation is generalised to sets of paths $\mathcal{X} \subseteq \mathbb{P}(\mathcal{E}, \lambda)$ *as* $\bigcup_{P \in \mathcal{X}} \mathtt{sat}(P, f)$.

Definition 8 (ps-morphism). *Let* $\mathcal{X}_1 \subseteq \mathbb{P}(\mathcal{E}_1, \lambda_1)$ *and* $\mathcal{X}_2 \subseteq \mathbb{P}(\mathcal{E}_2, \lambda_2)$ *be sets of paths. A path-set morphism (shortly, ps-morphism)* $f : \mathcal{X}_1 \to \mathcal{X}_2$ *is a label-preserving function* $f : (\mathcal{E}_1, \lambda_1) \to (\mathcal{E}_2, \lambda_2)$ *such that* $\mathcal{X}_2 \subseteq \mathtt{sat}(\mathcal{X}_1, f)$.

There is a ps-morphism from set of paths $\mathcal{X}_1$ to set of paths $\mathcal{X}_2$ if any path in $\mathcal{X}_2$ can be obtained by adding events to a path in $\mathcal{X}_1$. This notion captures the idea that arbitrations of larger visibilities are extensions of smaller visibilities.

Example 4. Consider the label-preserving function $f_2 : (\mathcal{E}_{P_1}, \lambda_{P_1}) \to (\mathcal{E}_{G_2}, \lambda_{G_2})$ in Example 3. Then $\mathtt{sat}(P_1, f_2)$ contains four paths, all of them an extension of P_1 obtained by inserting a new event labelled by $\langle \mathtt{wr}(3), ok \rangle$ at any arbitrary position. Moreover, there exists a ps-morphism $f : \{P_1\} \to \mathcal{X}$ for any $\mathcal{X} \subseteq \mathtt{sat}(P_1, f_2)$.

Definition 9 (Sets of Paths Category). $\mathbf{SPath}(\mathcal{L})$ *is the category whose objects are sets of paths labelled over* $\mathcal{L}$ *and arrows are ps-morphisms.*

PIDag($\mathcal{L}$) is the sub-category of acyclic graphs and monic pr-morphisms: It lacks pushouts, but these can be computed in **PDag**($\mathcal{L}$). We say that a functor $\mathbb{F}$ *weakly* preserves colimits if any diagram in **PIDag**($\mathcal{L}$) that is a colimit (via the inclusion functor) in **PDag**($\mathcal{L}$) is mapped by $\mathbb{F}$ to a colimit in **SPath**($\mathcal{L}$).

We now summarise the completeness results presented in [9], albeit slightly rephrased for the sake of simplicity and technical convenience in our developments. We characterise pr-morphisms that add a single event $\top$ to a graph.

Definition 10 (Extension). *Let* $f : \langle \mathcal{E}_1, \prec_1, \lambda_1 \rangle \to \langle \mathcal{E}_2, \prec_2, \lambda_2 \rangle$ *be a mono pr-morphism. It is an* extension *along* ℓ *(shortly, ℓ-extension) if* $\mathcal{E}_2 = \mathcal{E}_1 + \{\top\}$, $f : \mathcal{E}_1 \to \mathcal{E}_1 + \{\top\}$ *is the associated injection, and* $\lambda_2(\top) = \ell$.

A graph G is *rooted* if there is an event $e \in \mathcal{E}_G$ such that $G = G|_{\lfloor e \rfloor}$. An extension $f : G_1 \to G_2$ is a root extension if G_2 is rooted. It is analogously defined when a mono ps-morphism $f : \mathcal{X}_1 \to \mathcal{X}_2$ is a *ps-extension* (along ℓ).

Example 5. Assuming f_2 and f_3 in Example 3 are mono, then the former is an extension along $\langle wr(3), ok \rangle$ and the latter is an extension along $\langle rd, \{2,3\} \rangle$. Since G_3 is rooted, f_3 is a rooted extension; however, f_2 is not rooted because G_2 is not. Note that $f_2 ; f_3$ is a pr-morphism but not an extension because the target G_3 adds two new events to the source P_1. Moreover, the ps-morphisms in Example 4 induced by f_2 are ps-extensions (along $\langle wr(3), ok \rangle$).

Definition 11. *A functor* $\mathbb{F} : \mathbf{PIDag}(\mathcal{L}) \to \mathbf{SPath}(\mathcal{L})$ *is* coherent *if it maps root ℓ-extensions to ℓ-extensions and weakly preserves finite colimits.*

Coherent functors thus preserve monos. Combined with the simpler definition of extension, now easily applied to paths, it allows for a more general presentation of a key result in previous work [9, Theorem 33] (and an immediate instantiation to Propositions 34 and 35 therein), as stated below.

Theorem 1. *Coherent functors induce coherent specifications, and vice versa.*

The core of the result above can be immediately derived from the lemma below, which will have an interest of its own in the following pages. Intuitively, it says that, for each graph G, a coherent functor gives a set of paths which is the product of paths for sub-graphs of G, as required by coherence (Definition 3).

Lemma 1. *Let* $\mathbb{F}$ *be a coherent functor and* $f_i : G \hookrightarrow G_i$ *($i = 1, 2$) mono pr-morphisms such that* $\mathcal{E}_G = \mathcal{E}_{G_1} \cap \mathcal{E}_{G_2}$. *Then there exists a pushout in* **SPath**($\mathcal{L}$)

$$
\begin{array}{ccc}
\mathbb{F}(G) & \xrightarrow{\;\mathbb{F}(f_1)\;} & \mathbb{F}(G_1) \\
{\scriptstyle \mathbb{F}(f_2)}\downarrow & & \uparrow \\
\mathbb{F}(G_2) & \longrightarrow & \mathbb{F}(G_1) \otimes \mathbb{F}(G_2)
\end{array}
$$

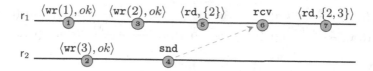

Fig. 4. Execution

$$(\text{READ}) \; \langle r, S \rangle \xrightarrow{\text{rd}, \pi_1 S} \langle r, S \rangle \qquad\qquad (\text{WRITE}) \; \langle r, S \rangle \xrightarrow{\text{wr}(a), ok} \langle r, \{(a, \pi_2 S \rhd r)\} \rangle$$

$$(\text{SEND}) \; \langle r, S \rangle \xrightarrow{\text{snd}, \langle r, S \rangle} \langle r, S \rangle \qquad\qquad (\text{RCV}) \; \langle r, S \rangle \xrightarrow{\text{rcv}, \langle r', S' \rangle} \langle r, S \oplus S' \rangle$$

Fig. 5. Implementation of data type *multi-value Register*

3   State-Based Implementations of Replicated Data Types

An RDT is implemented on top of a set of replicas, which serve requests from clients according to their local state and communicate asynchronously their local changes. Figure 4 illustrates a scenario involving two replicas, namely r_1 and r_2, that implement a *multi-value Register* (as specified in Example 1). A horizontal line corresponds to a replica and shows the relative order (from left to right) in which events occur in that replica. The depicted scenario shows a concrete execution that generates the visibility graph in Fig. 2. The two writes on r_1 are totally ordered (events **1** and **3**); consequently, 2 overwrites 1. The remaining write takes place on r_2 (event **2**) and is unknown to r_1 until r_2 propagates its changes. Hence, the first read on r_1 (event **5**) returns 2, which is the last written value in r_1.note Replicas communicate their local changes by using primitives **snd** and **rcv**. Event **6** in r_1 denotes the synchronisation of its local state with the state of r_2, i.e., r_1 becomes aware of the written value 3 (depicted by the dashed line between events **4** and **6**). Since writes in r_1 and r_2 are concurrent, the last read on r_1 returns the set of maximal concurrent updates, i.e., $\{2, 3\}$.

A crucial aspect in the implementation of RDTs concerns the information exchanged through **snd** and **rcv**. Under the *state-based* approach, replicas communicate their own local states [4] while they only communicate operations (or their effects) under the *operation-based* approach [14]. Hereafter, we will focus on state-based implementations. We write Σ for the set of possible states $\sigma, \sigma_0, \ldots$ of a replica, and define the behaviour of a replica implementing a specification $\mathcal{S} : \mathbb{G}(\mathcal{L}) \to 2^{\mathbb{P}(\mathcal{L})}$ with a labelled transition system $(\Sigma, \mathcal{A}_\mathcal{S}, \to)$, where

$$\mathcal{A}_\mathcal{S} = \mathcal{L} \cup (\{\text{rcv, snd}\} \times \Sigma)$$

is the set of labels that, in addition to the RDT operations, includes $\langle \text{snd}, \sigma \rangle$ and $\langle \text{rcv}, \sigma \rangle$ for replica synchronisation.

Example 6. We present an implementation for a *multi-value Register* based on version vectors in [6,15], in which each replica maintains a set with all maximal

(READ) $\langle r,(t,a)\rangle \xrightarrow{\text{rd},a} \langle r,(t,a)\rangle$ (WRITE) $\langle r,(t,a)\rangle \xrightarrow{\text{wr}(b),\text{ok}} \langle r,\max\{(t,a),(t',b)\}\rangle$

(SEND) $\langle r,(t,a)\rangle \xrightarrow{\text{snd},\langle r,(t,a)\rangle} \langle r,(t,a)\rangle$ (RCV) $\langle r,(t,a)\rangle \xrightarrow{\text{rcv},\langle r',(t',b)\rangle} \langle r,\max\{(t,a),(t',b)\}\rangle$

Fig. 6. Implementation of data type *last-write wins Register*.

concurrent written values. The implementation associates a *version vector* to each written value to determine if two writes are concurrent or causally ordered. A version vector is just a mapping from replicas to natural numbers. Given a set of replicas $\mathcal{R}$, $(\mathbb{N}^{\mathcal{R}}, \leq)$ is the poset of version vectors, where $\leq$ is the standard partial order of a function space, i.e., $\forall v, v' \in \mathbb{N}^{\mathcal{R}}$. $v \leq v$ iff $\forall r \in \mathcal{R}$. $v(r) \leq v(r)$. We equip version vectors with an operation $\triangleright : 2^{\mathbb{N}^{\mathcal{R}}} \times \mathcal{R} \to \mathbb{N}^{\mathcal{R}}$ that takes a set of version vectors V and a replica r and generates a new version vector that dominates all elements in V, defined as

$$(V \triangleright r)(r') = \begin{cases} 1 + \max_0\{v(r') \mid v \in V\} & \text{if } r' = r \\ \max_0\{v(r') \mid v \in V\} & \text{if } r' \neq r \end{cases}$$

where $\max_0$ denotes the maximum of a set with the provision that $\max_0 \emptyset = 0$.

Each replica maintains a set $S \in 2^{\mathbb{N} \times \mathbb{N}^{\mathcal{R}}}$ of pairs (n, v), where n is a written value and v is a version vector. We write π_i for the i-th projection of a product (and also for its obvious extension to sets of tuples), and consider $\mathbb{N} \times \mathbb{N}^{\mathcal{R}}$ ordered by $\leq$, where $e \leq e'$ iff $\pi_2 e \leq \pi_2 e'$. Consequently, the maximal concurrent written values in a set $S \in 2^{\mathbb{N} \times \mathbb{N}^{\mathcal{R}}}$ are the *maximal elements* $\|S\|$ defined as $\{u \in S \mid \nexists v \in S, u \leq v\}$. The combination $S_1 \oplus S_2$ of two sets S_1 and S_2 is $\|S_1 \cup S_2\|$.

The behaviour of a replica implementing a *multi-value Register* is defined by the LTS $\langle \Sigma, \mathcal{A}_{\mathcal{S}_{mvR}}, \to \rangle$ where

- $\Sigma = \mathcal{R} \times \{\|S\| \mid S \in 2^{\mathbb{N} \times \mathbb{N}^{\mathcal{R}}}\}$, i.e., each state consists of the identifier of the replica and a set of maximal concurrent written values;
- $\mathcal{A}_{\mathcal{S}_{mvR}} = \mathcal{L}_{\mathcal{S}_{mvR}} \cup (\{\text{snd}, \text{rcv}\} \times \Sigma)$, i.e., the set of labels accounts for the operations of the RDT;
- $\to$ is given by the inference rules in Fig. 5. A read returns the set of locally-stored values (π_1 discards all version vectors), while a write updates the local state with a singleton containing the written value and a version vector that dominates all known values. Rule (SEND) propagates the local state while (RCV) combines the local state with the one received from another replica.

Example 7. We now describe the implementation based on timestamps proposed in [15] for the *last-write wins Register* in Example 2. Let $(\mathbb{T}, <)$ be the totally-ordered set of timestamps. Then, the implementation is the LTS $\langle \Sigma, \mathcal{A}_{\mathcal{S}_{lwwR}}, \to \rangle$ where

- $\Sigma = \mathcal{R} \times (\mathbb{T} \times (\mathbb{N} \cup \{\bot\}))$, i.e., the state $\langle r,(t,a)\rangle$ of a replica r contains the current value a of the register and its associated timestamp. We establish that

$\perp < n$ for all $n \in \mathbb{N}$ and consider $\mathbb{T} \times (\mathbb{N} \cup \{\perp\})$ lexicographically ordered, i.e., $(t, \mathsf{a}) \leq (t', \mathsf{a}')$ when either $t < t'$ or $t = t'$ and $\mathsf{a} \leq \mathsf{a}'$.

- $\mathcal{A}_{\mathcal{S}_{lwwR}} = \mathcal{L}_{\mathcal{S}_{lwwR}} \cup (\{\mathtt{snd}, \mathtt{rcv}\} \times \Sigma)$ is the set of the data type operations;
- $\rightarrow$ is given by the inference rules in Fig. 6. As for the *multi-value Register*, a read just retrieves the value stored in the replica but does not alter its state. A write may change the state of the replica by picking the maximum pair according to lexicographic order. The timestamp t' on the right-hand-side of the rule (WRITE) should be understood as any $t' \in \mathbb{T}$. Rules (SEND) and (RCV) are analogous to the previous example.

4 From Specifications to LTS

We can exploit the structure of coherent functors to recover an operational interpretation of specifications. In the following, we consider a coherent functor $\mathbb{F} : \mathbf{PIDag}(\mathcal{L}) \rightarrow \mathbf{SPath}(\mathcal{L})$. We construct its *category of elements*, which is reminiscent of the category of elements for a presheaf (see e.g. [13, Chapter 5]). Following this analogy, given a pr-morphism $\mathtt{f} : \mathtt{G} \rightarrow \mathtt{G}_1$ and $\mathtt{P} \in \mathbb{F}(\mathtt{G})$, we denote $\mathbb{F}(\mathtt{f})(\mathtt{P})$ the set of paths in $\mathbb{F}(\mathtt{G}_1)$ that are in the "image" of $\mathtt{P}$ via $\mathbb{F}(\mathtt{f})$, formally specified as $\mathbb{F}(\mathtt{G}_1) \cap \mathtt{sat}(\mathtt{P}, \mathtt{f})$.

Definition 12 (Category of elements). *The category of elements* $\mathbf{E}(\mathbb{F})$ *of* $\mathbb{F}$ *is obtained as follows*

- *objects are pairs* $\langle \mathtt{G}, \mathtt{P} \rangle$, *such that* $\mathtt{G} \in \mathbf{PIDag}(\mathcal{L})$ *and* $\mathtt{P} \in \mathbb{F}(\mathtt{G})$;
- *arrows* $\mathtt{f} : \langle \mathtt{G}, \mathtt{P} \rangle \rightarrow \langle \mathtt{G}_1, \mathtt{P}_1 \rangle$ *are pr-morphisms* $\mathtt{f} : \mathtt{G} \rightarrow \mathtt{G}_1$ *such that* $\mathtt{P}_1 \in \mathbb{F}(\mathtt{f})(\mathtt{P})$.

Intuitively, arrows in $\mathbf{E}(\mathbb{F})$ stand for the possible ways a path in $\mathbb{F}(\mathtt{G})$ can evolve according to $\mathbb{F}(\mathtt{f})$. The category $\mathbf{E}(\mathbb{F})$ is clearly an LTS, since each category is so. We note that our way of distilling an LTS is similar to how one obtains an LTS from a relation presheaf [17, Definition 4.1].

Example 8. Consider the functor $\mathbb{M}(\mathcal{S}_{mvR})$ induced by the coherent specification $\mathcal{S}_{mvR}$ in Example 1. An object $\langle \mathtt{G}, \mathtt{P} \rangle$ of the category of elements $\mathbf{E}(\mathbb{M}(\mathcal{S}_{mvR}))$ represents a state of the RDT where the events in the visibility graph $\mathtt{G}$ are arbitrated according to $\mathtt{P} \in \mathcal{S}_{mvR}(\mathtt{G})$. An arrow $\mathtt{f} : \langle \mathtt{G}, \mathtt{P} \rangle \rightarrow \langle \mathtt{G}_1, \mathtt{P}_1 \rangle$ in $\mathbf{E}(\mathbb{M}(\mathcal{S}_{mvR}))$ describes a computation where the visibility $\mathtt{G}$ is extended to $\mathtt{G}_1$ and the arbitration $\mathtt{P}$ to $\mathtt{P}_1$. For instance, take the graphs $\mathtt{G}_2$ and $\mathtt{G}_3$ in Fig. 3c and Fig. 3d, and the unique pr-morphism $\mathtt{f} : \mathtt{G}_2 \rightarrow \mathtt{G}_3$. If $\mathtt{P}_2$ is a total order of the events in $\mathtt{G}_2$, then there is a ps-morphism $\mathtt{f} : \{\mathtt{P}_2\} \rightarrow \mathtt{sat}(\mathtt{P}_2, \mathtt{f})$. Moreover, $\mathcal{S}_{mvR}(\mathtt{G}_3) \cap \mathtt{sat}(\mathtt{P}_2, \mathtt{f}) = \mathtt{sat}(\mathtt{P}_2, \mathtt{f})$ because $\mathcal{S}_{mvR}$ imposes no constraint on the admissible arbitrations of a consistent visibility. Therefore, there is a morphism $\mathtt{f} : \langle \mathtt{G}_2, \mathtt{P}_2 \rangle \rightarrow \langle \mathtt{G}_3, \mathtt{P}_3 \rangle$ for any $\mathtt{P}_3 \in \mathtt{sat}(\mathtt{f}, \mathtt{P}_2)$ in $\mathbf{E}(\mathbb{M}(\mathcal{S}_{mvR}))$.

A pr-morphism may not induce an arrow in the category of elements, as $\mathtt{f} : \mathtt{G}_2 \rightarrow \mathtt{G}_4$ with $\mathtt{G}_2$ from Fig. 3c and $\mathtt{G}_4$ its root extension along $\langle \mathtt{rd}, \{1\} \rangle$. Indeed, $\mathcal{S}_{mvR}(\mathtt{G}_4) = \emptyset$, and hence $\mathbb{M}(\mathcal{S}_{mvR})(\mathtt{f})(\mathtt{P}) = \emptyset$ for any $\mathtt{P} \in \mathcal{S}_{mvR}(\mathtt{G}_2)$.

An analogous situation occurs when the specification restricts the allowed arbitrations, as $\mathcal{S}_{lwwR}$ in Example 2. Consider the root extension $\mathtt{f} \colon \mathtt{G} \to \mathtt{G}_1$ along $\langle \mathtt{rd}, \{2\} \rangle$, with $\mathtt{G}_1$ as in Fig. 3a and $\mathtt{G}$ is $\mathtt{G}_1$ without the event $\langle \mathtt{rd}, \{2\} \rangle$. Then we have $\mathcal{S}_{lwwR}(\mathtt{G}_1) = \{\mathtt{P}_1\}$, and $\mathcal{S}_{lwwR}(\mathtt{G})$ contains two paths: $\mathtt{P}$, which keeps the order of writes as in $\mathtt{P}_1$, and $\mathtt{P}'$, which inverts it. The latter cannot be extended to any path in $\mathcal{S}_{lwwR}(\mathtt{G}_1)$, as writes are in the wrong order. In fact, there is no $\mathtt{f} \colon \langle \mathtt{G}, \mathtt{P}' \rangle \to \langle \mathtt{G}_1, \mathtt{P}_1 \rangle$ in $\mathbf{E}(\mathbb{M}(\mathcal{S}_{lwwR}))$. Contrastingly, we have that $\mathtt{f} \colon \langle \mathtt{G}, \mathtt{P}' \rangle \to \langle \mathtt{G}_1, \mathtt{P}'' \rangle$ is an arrow of $\mathbf{E}(\mathbb{M}(\mathcal{S}_{mvR}))$ for any $\mathtt{P}'' \in \mathtt{sat}(\mathtt{f}, \mathtt{P}')$, as the order of writes is irrelevant for $\mathcal{S}_{mvR}$.

4.1   One- and Multi-replica LTSs

In [7, Definition 16] an LTS modelling the operational behaviour of a single replica – *one-replica* in short – is derived from a specification as follows

$$\langle \mathtt{G}, \mathtt{P} \rangle \xrightarrow{\ell} \langle \mathtt{G}_1, \mathtt{P}_1 \rangle \quad \Longleftrightarrow \quad \mathtt{G}_1 = \mathtt{G}^\ell, \ \mathtt{P}_1|_{\mathcal{E}_\mathtt{G}} = \mathtt{P}$$

where $\mathtt{G}^\ell$ is the root extension along ℓ of $\mathtt{G}$. That is, a pair evolves to one where the visibility relation is augmented with a top event labelled ℓ and the path is obtained by adding the new event to $\mathtt{P}$. This way of augmenting the visibility can be formalised as a root ℓ-extension. In fact, the one-replica LTS precisely corresponds to a sub-category of $\mathbf{E}(\mathbb{F})$ consisting only of such extensions.

Lemma 2. *Let $\mathbf{E}_\mathtt{o}(\mathbb{F})$ be $\mathbf{E}(\mathbb{F})$ restricted to root ℓ-extensions, for all $\ell \in \mathcal{L}$. Then the one-replica LTS coincides with the LTS for $\mathbf{E}_\mathtt{o}(\mathbb{F})$.*

This is easily seen: Each root ℓ-extension corresponds uniquely to a ℓ-labelled one-replica transition, and between any two graphs there is at most one root extension, so that also the label is implicitly recovered.

The next step is to characterise *multi-replica* LTS as in [7, Definition 20], which model multiple replica evolving concurrently. We recall the main concepts. Suppose we have two replica, and the current state for each is $\langle \mathtt{G}_i, \mathtt{P}_i \rangle$. Let us further assume that $\mathtt{G}_1$ and $\mathtt{G}_2$ are compatible [7, Definition 19], i.e., there is a span $\mathtt{f}_i : \mathtt{G} \to \mathtt{G}_i$ of mono pr-morphisms such that $\mathcal{E}_\mathtt{G} = \mathcal{E}_{\mathtt{G}_1} \cap \mathcal{E}_{\mathtt{G}_2}$ (thus, shared nodes have the same labels). Finally, let $\mathtt{G}_1 \sqcup \mathtt{G}_2$ (which is just set-theoretical union) and the obvious morphisms be the pushout. Then a *replicated state* is of the form $\langle \mathtt{G}_1 \sqcup \mathtt{G}_2, \mathtt{P} \rangle$, where $\mathtt{P} \in \mathtt{P}_1 \otimes \mathtt{P}_2$, i.e., $\mathtt{P}$ is obtained by "synchronising" the individual arbitrations. The multi-replica LTS is derived from the one-replica LTS by adding the following inference rule

$$(\text{COMP}) \ \frac{\langle \mathtt{G}_1, \mathtt{P}|_{\mathcal{E}_{\mathtt{G}_1}} \rangle \xrightarrow{\ell} \langle \mathtt{G}_1', \mathtt{P}_1' \rangle \qquad \mathtt{P}' \in \mathtt{P} \otimes \mathtt{P}_1'}{\langle \mathtt{G}_1 \sqcup \mathtt{G}_2, \mathtt{P} \rangle \xrightarrow{\ell} \langle \mathtt{G}_1' \sqcup \mathtt{G}_2, \mathtt{P}' \rangle}$$

Intuitively, global computations are derived from computations of single replica.

We can recover the multi-replica LTS by exploiting the structure of coherent functors. We need two technical lemmata. The first says that certain pushouts in $\mathbf{SPath}(\mathcal{L})$ can be decomposed as pushouts over singleton path sets. The second says that every extension is determined by a root extension along the same label.

Lemma 3 (Decomposition). *Consider the following diagrams in* $\mathbf{SPath}(\mathcal{L})$

$$
\begin{array}{ccc}
\mathcal{X} \xrightarrow{\;f_2\;} \mathcal{X}_2 & \qquad & \{P\} \xrightarrow{\;\overline{f}_2\;} \{P_2\} \\
{\scriptstyle f_1}\downarrow \qquad \downarrow {\scriptstyle f_3} & & {\scriptstyle \overline{f}_1}\downarrow \qquad \downarrow {\scriptstyle \overline{f}_3} \\
\mathcal{X}_1 \xrightarrow{\;f_4\;} \mathcal{X}_1 \otimes \mathcal{X}_2 & & \{P_1\} \xrightarrow{\;\overline{f}_4\;} P_1 \otimes P_2
\end{array}
$$

If the diagram on the left is a pushout, then for all $P_1 \in \mathcal{X}_1$ *and* $P_2 \in \mathcal{X}_2$ *there are pushouts as shown on the right such that* f_i *and* $\overline{f}_i$ *have the same underlying function on events.*

Lemma 4. *Let* $f : G \to G_1$ *be a pr-morphism in* $\mathbf{PIDag}(\mathcal{L})$. *Then it is an* ℓ-*extension if and only if there exists a pushout in* $\mathbf{PDag}(\mathcal{L})$

$$
\begin{array}{ccc}
\overline{G} \xrightarrow{\;\overline{f}\;} \overline{G}_1 \\
\downarrow \qquad \downarrow \\
G \xrightarrow{\;f\;} G_1
\end{array}
$$

such that $\overline{f}$ *is a root* ℓ-*extension.*

We now show that transitions of the multi-replica LTS are precisely those corresponding to ℓ-extensions. Intuitively, an ℓ-extension describes a "local" augmentation of a graph, corresponding to a step of computation of a single replica.

Proposition 1. *Let* $\mathbf{E}_\mathbf{m}(\mathbb{F})$ *be* $\mathbf{E}(\mathbb{F})$ *restricted to* ℓ-*extensions, for all* $\ell \in \mathcal{L}$. *Then the multi-replica LTS coincides with the LTS for* $\mathbf{E}_\mathbf{m}(\mathbb{F})$.

Example 9. Consider once more the category $\mathbb{M}(\mathcal{S}_{mvR})$ discussed in Example 8. By Lemma 2, the behaviour of a single replica is characterised by morphisms associated with root extensions. The morphism $f: \langle G_2, P_2 \rangle \to \langle G_3, P_3 \rangle$ described in Example 8 corresponds to a one-replica transition with label $\langle \mathbf{rd}, \{2,3\} \rangle$. In fact, its underlying pr-morphism $f: G_2 \to G_3$ is a root extension, accounting for the occurrence of the event $\langle \mathbf{rd}, \{2,3\} \rangle$ that sees any other event in the configuration; this may happen locally if all events in other replicas have been already propagated. Contrastingly, the extension $f': P_1 \to G_2$ accounts for a new event $\langle \mathbf{wr}(3), ok \rangle$ that is unaware of any other event, and hence, executed in a completely different replica. This corresponds to multi-replica transitions $f': \langle P_1, P \rangle \to \langle G_2, P' \rangle$, where P' arbitrates the additional event $\langle \mathbf{wr}(3), ok \rangle$ anywhere in P. The local one-replica execution originating this transition is obtained via Lemma 4: It is $f: \langle \emptyset, \emptyset \rangle \to \langle \langle \mathbf{wr}(3), ok \rangle, \langle \mathbf{wr}(3), ok \rangle \rangle$ (here we write $\langle \mathbf{wr}(3), ok \rangle$ for the one-node graph/path), with the underlying pr-morphism $\emptyset \to \langle \mathbf{wr}(3), ok \rangle$ a root morphism.

4.2   Contextual LTS

So far, the category of elements allowed to recast the set-theoretical presentation of one- and multi-replica LTSs. However, its strength is in allowing to obtain a new LTS that is reminiscent of the category of contexts à la Leifer-Milner [12], where arrows represent contexts enabling a transition from the source to the target of the arrow. Here, observations are pairs of an event plus an embedding that records how the resulting local visibility embeds into the global one. These additional observations will be needed for defining a correct notion of simulation.

Definition 13. *The context LTS is obtained by taking elements $\langle G, P \rangle$ of $\mathbf{E}(\mathbb{F})$ as states, and by labelled transitions triples*

$$\langle G, P \rangle \xrightarrow{\langle f, \overline{f} \rangle} \langle G_1, P_1 \rangle$$

such that $f : \langle G, P \rangle \to \langle G_1, P_1 \rangle$ *and* $\overline{f} : \langle \overline{G}_1, \overline{P}_1 \rangle \to \langle G_1, P_1 \rangle$ *are arrows of* $\mathbf{E}(\mathbb{F})$ *and there exists a pushout in* $\mathbf{PDag}(\mathcal{L})$

$$
\begin{array}{ccc}
\overline{G} & \longrightarrow & \overline{G}_1 \\
\downarrow & & \downarrow{\scriptstyle \overline{f}} \\
G & \xrightarrow{\ f\ } & G_1
\end{array}
$$

Note that each arrow $f : \langle G, P \rangle \to \langle G_1, P_1 \rangle$ of $\mathbf{E}(\mathbb{F})$ induces at least one labelled transition (it suffices to consider for $\overline{f}$ the identity of G_1), but they could actually be more. In fact, all labels can be constructively obtained, since in $\mathbf{PDag}(\mathcal{L})$ pushouts along monos are also pullbacks, and the arrow $[f, \overline{f}] : G + \overline{G}_1 \to G_1$ uniquely induced by the coproduct must be epi.

Also note that if we restrict to consider only injections, the pair $\langle f, \overline{f} \rangle$ is uniquely characterized by $\langle \overline{G}_1, \overline{P}_1 \rangle$. In order to simplify some definitions, in the following we abuse notation and denote as $\langle \overline{G}_1, \overline{P}_1 \rangle$ such a label $\langle f, \overline{f} \rangle$.

Finally, it is noteworthy that the context LTS includes also the one- and multi-replica, as stated by the result below.

Lemma 5. *The LTS for* $\mathbf{E}_o(\mathbb{F})$ *($\mathbf{E}_m(\mathbb{F})$) coincides with the restriction of the contextual LTS to transitions whose labels are pairs* $\langle f, \mathrm{id} \rangle$*, where* f *is a root extension (an extension, respectively).*

For the former, note that if f is a root extension, then a mono pr-morphism forming a pushout square has to be an isomorphism. Instead, should f be an extension, a few alternatives for the second component of the label are available, such as taking for $\overline{G}_1$ the smallest graph such that $G \sqcup \overline{G}_1 = G_1$. However, the choice is immaterial for our later results on simulation, and further abusing notation we simply denote as ℓ a label $\langle f, \mathrm{id} \rangle$ such that f is an ℓ-extension.

Example 10. Consider the multi-replica transition arrow $\mathtt{f}' \colon \langle P_1, P \rangle \to \langle G_2, P' \rangle$ of Example 9. Since we have the arrow $\mathtt{f} \colon \langle \emptyset, \emptyset \rangle \to \langle \langle \mathtt{wr}(3), ok \rangle, \langle \mathtt{wr}(3), ok \rangle \rangle$ in the category of elements, $\mathtt{f}'$ yields the following context LTS transition

$$\langle P_1, P \rangle \xrightarrow{\langle \mathtt{f}', \overline{\mathtt{f}}' \rangle} \langle G_2, P' \rangle$$

where $\overline{\mathtt{f}}'$ is the embedding of the one-node graph $\langle \mathtt{wr}(3), ok \rangle$ into G_2. As mentioned, we can just use $\langle \langle \mathtt{wr}(3), ok \rangle, \langle \mathtt{wr}(3), ok \rangle \rangle$ as label, since this is uniquely determined. This label conveys the information about the resulting visibility and arbitration pair for the acting replica.

5   Implementation Model

In this section we present our model for implementations. Similarly to what we have done for specifications, the aim is to obtain implementation LTSs as the category of elements of suitable functors. Our models are based on a power-domain construction, modelling non-determinism. We will show that we can capture several RDTs, and characterise implementation correctness via simulation.

5.1   Implementations as Functors over Power-Domains

Our model for implementations is inspired by [17], where LTSs are modelled as functors from the free monoid over labels, represented as a one-object category, to a suitable category of non-deterministic computations. This allows modelling sequences of transitions as compositions of computations. In our setting, we introduce a *one-replica* category representing the free monoid of labels of a replica.

Definition 14 (One-replica category). *The* one-replica category **IR** *is the category with one object, and where morphisms are words over* $\mathcal{L} \cup \{\mathtt{rcv}\}$.

In order to capture the behaviour of a set of replicas $\mathcal{R}$, we need to account for the fact that single replicas must show the "same" behaviour. For instance, in the *multi-value Register* implementation LTS (see Example 6), the (WRITE) operation on two replicas r and s have to return exactly the same set of version vectors $\mathbb{N}^{\mathcal{R}}$, up to a swapping of r and s in their domain.

We formalise this constraint by introducing the category $\mathbf{IR}(\mathcal{R})$, containing $\#\mathcal{R}$ isomorphic copies of **IR**. That is, that category comes equipped with isomorphisms $\iota_{r,s} \colon r \to s$ for each $r, s \in \mathcal{R}$ such that $\iota_{r,r} = id_r = \iota_{r,s}; \iota_{s,r}$. Furthermore, we require a *naturality* condition, namely, for all words w over $\mathcal{L} \cup \{\mathtt{rcv}\}$ we have $\iota_{r,s}; w = w; \iota_{r,s}$. This constraint precisely enforces the requirement on the behaviour of the single replicas, which are now the same up to naturality. For the sake of clarity, we usually suffix arrows associated to elements of $\mathcal{L} \cup \{\mathtt{rcv}\}$ with the replica they belong to, e.g. $\ell \colon r \to r$ is denoted as ℓ_r.

We now move to define a category where the arrows of $\mathbf{IR}(\mathcal{R})$ are interpreted as non-deterministic computations. Here we assume a category $\mathbf{M}$ where objects are states and arrows stand for sets of *deterministic* computations. We shall see later how to instantiate $\mathbf{M}$ for RDTs.

Definition 15 (Power-domain category). *Let $\mathbf{M}$ be a small category. Then, its* power-domain $\mathbf{P}(\mathbf{M})$ *is the category whose objects are sets of objects of $\mathbf{M}$ and arrows are pairs $(R, \{f_i\}_{i \in R}) : X \to Y$ such that $R \subseteq X \times Y$ is a relation and $\{f_i\}_{i \in R}$ is a family (indexed by pairs $\langle x, y \rangle$ in R) of non-empty sets of arrows in $\mathbf{M}$ such that $f_{\langle x, y \rangle} \subseteq Hom_{\mathbf{M}}[x, y]$. If $\mathbf{M}$ is (symmetric) monoidal, so is $\mathbf{P}(\mathbf{M})$.*

An element of $f_{\langle x, y \rangle}$ is thus an arrow in $\mathbf{M}$ from x to y. For simplicity, we often denote $\{f_i\}_{i \in R}$ as f_R. Also, given element $x \in X$ and morphism $(R, f_R) : X \to Y$, we denote as $(R, f_R)(x)$ the set $\{y \mid \langle x, y \rangle \in R\}$.

Definition 16 (Implementation). *Let $\mathbf{M}$ be a category. An* implementation *of $\mathcal{R}$ in $\mathbf{M}$ is a functor $\mathbb{I} : \mathbf{IR}(\mathcal{R}) \to \mathbf{P}(\mathbf{M})$ such that $\mathbb{I}(r) = \mathbb{I}(s)$ for all $r, s \in \mathcal{R}$.*

An implementation functor thus maps each replica into the same set of possible states S, and the arrows of a replica are (morally) mapped to relations over $S \times S$. More precisely, $\mathbb{I}(g)(x)$ is the set of states that are reachable from x after observing g; this will be used later on to synthesise the corresponding LTS. The naturality of the isomorphisms $\iota_{r,s}$ guarantees that the replicas exhibit the "same" behaviour, yet only up to isomorphism, which takes care of the possible permutations among replicas.

5.2   From Implementations to Replica LTSs

We now define the category of elements $\mathbf{E}(\mathbb{I})$ for an implementation $\mathbb{I}$ as in Definition 12. It is rewritten here for the sake of clarity.

Definition 17 (Category of elements, II). *The category of elements $\mathbf{E}(\mathbb{I})$ of $\mathbb{I}$ is obtained as*

- *states are pairs $\langle r, x \rangle$, such that $r \in \mathcal{R}$ and $x \in \mathbb{I}(r)$;*
- *arrows $g : \langle r, x \rangle \to \langle s, y \rangle$ are arrows $g : r \to s$ such that $y \in \mathbb{I}(g)(x)$.*

It now suffices to apply the machinery used for obtaining context LTSs.

Definition 18 (Implementation LTS). *The implementation LTS is obtained by taking elements $\langle r, m \rangle$ of $\mathbf{E}(\mathbb{I})$ as states, and by labelled transitions triples*

$$\langle r, m \rangle \xrightarrow{\langle g, \bar{g} \rangle} \langle r, n \rangle$$

such that $g : \langle r, m \rangle \to \langle r, n \rangle$ and $\bar{g} : \langle s, o \rangle \to \langle r, n \rangle$ are arrows of $\mathbf{E}(\mathbb{I})$.

We restricted to transitions over the same replica, but of course this is just for convenience, since all our examples fit into this pattern. Also, note that each arrow $g : \langle r, m \rangle \to \langle r, n \rangle$ of $\mathbf{E}(\mathbb{I})$ induces at least one labelled transition.

5.3 Deterministic Computations

Given a state, what we need is the possibility for it to a) evolve towards a different state and b) be combined with other states. We formalise these ideas via *pre-ordered monoids*, i.e., structures $\mathcal{M} = \langle M, \leq, \otimes, 1 \rangle$ consisting of a set M, a pre-order $\leq \subseteq M \times M$, and an associative binary operation $\otimes : M \times M \to M$ with an identity element $1 \in M$ such that $1 \leq x$ and $x \leq y$ implies $x \otimes w \leq y \otimes w$[1].

Remark 1. In order to take into account the isomorphic behaviour of distinct replicas, the pre-ordered monoid $\mathcal{M}$ should come equipped with a group action that preserves both the order and the monoidal structure of $\mathcal{M}$. However, all our cases will fit the bill. First of all note that given a set N, the cartesian product $\mathcal{M} \times \mathcal{M}$ and the function space $\mathcal{M}^N$ are pre-ordered monoids, with $\mathcal{M}$ a sub-monoid of $\mathcal{M}^N$ and $\mathcal{M}^N \times \mathcal{M}^N$ equal to $(\mathcal{M} \times \mathcal{M})^N$. Also, $\mathcal{M}^N$ is equipped with a group action $\Pi(N) \times \mathcal{M}^N \to \mathcal{M}^N$ given by the permutation group $\Pi(N)$ on N, and if X, Y are sub-monoids of $\mathcal{M}^N$ that are closed under the group action, then also the sub-monoid $X \times Y$ of $(\mathcal{M} \times \mathcal{M})^N$ is closed. Thus, all of our examples fit into the shape $\mathcal{M}^{\mathcal{R}}$, for $\mathcal{R}$ the set of replicas at hand.

Example 11. Let us consider the *multi-value Register* from Example 1. Recall that states of a replica r consist of a sets of pairs $(n, v) \in \mathbb{N} \times \mathbb{N}^{\mathcal{R}}$, where n is a written value and v is a version vector. In the implementation (Fig. 5) these sets can evolve to: a) themselves (rules (READ) and (SEND)); b) to a set containing a pair dominating the source state (rule (WRITE)) and to a set obtained as the combination of the source state and the received one (rule (RCV)).

These evolutions can be modeled as a pre-ordered monoid structure over $2^{\mathbb{N} \times \mathbb{N}^{\mathcal{R}}}$, namely $\mathcal{M} = \langle 2^{\mathbb{N} \times \mathbb{N}^{\mathcal{R}}}, \leq, \oplus, \emptyset \rangle$, where $\leq$ and $\oplus$ are defined as in Example 6.

Example 12. Consider the implementation of *last-write wins Register* in Example 7. The current state of replica r consists of a timestamp $t \in \mathbb{T}$ and the value in the register $\mathsf{a} \in \mathbb{N} \cup \{\bot\}$. The evolution of pairs $\langle t, \mathsf{a} \rangle$ in the implementation is captured via the pre-ordered monoid $\langle \mathbb{T} \times \mathbb{N}_\bot, \leq, \max, \langle \bot, \bot \rangle \rangle$, where $\leq$ stands for lexicographic order and $\max\{p, q\} = q$ if and only if $p \leq q$. This max operation is precisely what is used to define the rules (WRITE) and (RCV) in Fig. 6.

Given a pre-ordered monoid $\mathcal{M}$ modelling the deterministic behaviour of replicas, we can easily derive a category of deterministic computations. This is intended to be used as base category for the power domain construction of Sect. 5.1.

Definition 19 (Category of deterministic computations). *The category* $\mathcal{C}(\mathcal{M})$ *has objects the elements of $\mathcal{M}$ and arrows are defined for all m, n elements of $\mathcal{M}$ as follows: $f_{m,n} : m \to n$ if $m \leq n$, with $f_{m,m} = id_m$ and $f_{n,m}; f_{m,o} = f_{n,o}$.*

---

[1] Note that this is more general than the lattice of states proposed in [14]. First of all, we consider a pre-order instead of a partial order, and furthermore we do not require $\otimes$ to be induced by $\leq$. This weakening results in an algebraic structure that allows for modelling a large family of RDTs.

Note that $\mathcal{C}(\mathcal{M})$ is a strict monoidal category, inheriting its structure from $\mathcal{M}$. It is a thin category (for each pair of objects there is at most one arrow) and it is strictly symmetric if $\otimes$ is commutative, yet it is not skeletal, since isomorphisms are not identities. All arrows are mono as well as epi, and 1 is the initial object, while pushouts and pullbacks do not necessarily exist.

Example 13. The corresponding category of computations $\mathcal{C}(\mathcal{M})$ for the implementation of a *multi-value Register* (Example 11) has sets $S \in 2^{\mathbb{N} \times \mathbb{N}^{\mathcal{R}}}$ as objects and arrows $f_{S,S'} : S \to S'$ with $S \leq S'$. We may attempt to interpret labels as arrows of $\mathcal{C}(\mathcal{M})$, which would work for the operations of the data type, i.e., wr and rd, even if the latter might be partial. For rcv, however, the target of each arrow would depend on the received state. We avoid considering different receive operations, and we describe them non-deterministically via the power-domain construction. In fact, the objects of $\mathbf{P}(\mathcal{C}(\mathcal{M}))$ are sets of sets of pairs, i.e., $X \subseteq 2^{\mathbb{N} \times \mathbb{N}^{\mathcal{R}}}$. Each arrow $(R, f_R) : X \to Y$ represents a computation in which a replica starting on some state $S \in X$ will end up in some state $S' \in (R, f_R)(S)$.

With the monoidal structure in place, we instantiate our development of the previous section and obtain an implementation LTS better suited for our notion of simulation. Implementation functors are of the form $\mathbb{I} : \mathbf{IR}(\mathcal{R}) \to \mathbf{P}(\mathcal{C}(\mathcal{M}))$, with $\mathcal{M}$ a pre-ordered monoid, and the derived replica LTS has transitions

$$\langle r, m \rangle \xrightarrow{\langle g, \overline{g} \rangle} \langle r, n \rangle$$

where m and n are elements of the monoid. We impose the further requirement that rcv must accept any possible state that it receives, so that $\mathbb{I}(r)$ is a sub-monoid of $\mathcal{M}$ and $\mathbb{I}(\mathrm{rcv}_r)(m) = m \otimes \mathbb{I}(r)$ for all $r \in \mathcal{R}$ and $m \in \mathbb{I}(r)$. This implies that $\mathbb{I}(\mathrm{rcv}_r) = \mathbb{I}(\mathrm{rcv}_s)$ for all $r, s \in \mathcal{R}$ and that the operation behaves symmetrically, i.e. $m \otimes o \in \mathbb{I}(\mathrm{rcv}_r)(m) \cap \mathbb{I}(\mathrm{rcv}_r)(o)$ for all $r \in \mathcal{R}$ and $m, o \in \mathbb{I}(r)$.

Finally, with an abuse of notation, we denote as ℓ the label $\langle \ell, id_r \rangle$ and as $\langle s, o \rangle$ the label $\langle \mathrm{rcv}, \overline{g} \rangle$ such that $\overline{g} : \langle s, \mathbb{I}(\iota_{r,s})(o) \rangle \to \langle r, m \otimes o \rangle$ is obtained by composing the arrows $\iota_{s,r} : \langle s, \mathbb{I}(\iota_{r,s})(o) \rangle \to \langle r, o \rangle$ and $\mathrm{rcv}_r : \langle r, o \rangle \to \langle r, m \otimes o \rangle$ (noting that there is no ambiguity since $\mathbb{I}(\iota_{r,s})(o)$ is a singleton).

Example 14. We now consider the implementation functor $\mathbb{I}$ for the *multi-value Register*. We have $\mathbb{I}(r) = \{\|S\| \mid S \in 2^{\mathbb{N} \times \mathbb{N}^{\mathcal{R}}}\}$, i.e., a set containing all sets of maximal pairs. An arrow in $\mathbf{IR}(\mathcal{R})$ (i.e., a sequence of operations) is mapped by $\mathbb{I}$ to an arrow $\mathbb{I}(r) \to \mathbb{I}(r)$. For instance, $\mathbb{I}(\langle \mathrm{wr}(\mathsf{a}), ok \rangle_r)$ is defined such that $\mathbb{I}(\langle \mathrm{wr}(\mathsf{a}), ok \rangle_r)(S) = \{\{(\mathsf{a}, \pi_2 S \triangleright r)\}\}$ for all $S \in \mathbb{I}(r)$, i.e., wr(a) can be performed over any state S, and this operation (deterministically) changes the state by a set containing just a pair with the written value and a dominating version vector. Analogously, $\mathbb{I}(\langle \mathrm{rd}, V \rangle_r)$ is defined such that $\mathbb{I}(\langle \mathrm{rd}, V \rangle_r)(S) = \{S\}$ if $\pi_1 S = V$ and $\mathbb{I}(\langle \mathrm{rd}, V \rangle_r)(S) = \emptyset$ otherwise, i.e., a read operation that returns V can be performed only over a state S that contains exactly the values V, otherwise such an operation cannot occur. Finally, $\mathbb{I}(\mathrm{rcv}_r)(S) = \{S \oplus S' \mid S' \in \mathbb{I}(r)\}$, i.e., a receive can augment the state S with any received state S'.

Now, the category of elements for the functor $\mathbb{I}$ introduced above generates the transition system in Fig. 5, if we disregard labels. Labels are actually recovered by the corresponding implementation LTS; in particular the label $\langle \mathrm{rcv}, \overline{g} \rangle$ makes the connection between the received state and the target of the arrow, which is analogous to rule (Rcv).

5.4   Implementation Correctness via Simulation

We are now ready to characterise implementation correctness as a simulation relation between the context LTS and the implementation LTS for a given RDT. The starting point is what usually occurs in higher-order calculi: Since the label of a transition may be a process, the notion of simulation has to take also labels into account. Thus, our proposal is the following.

Definition 20 (Implementation correctness). *Let S be a specification, C_S the context LTS, and $\mathcal{I}_S$ the implementation LTS. An* implementation relation *$\mathcal{R}_S$ is a relation between states in $\mathcal{I}_S$ and C_S such that if $(\sigma, \langle \mathsf{G}, \mathsf{P} \rangle) \in \mathcal{R}_S$ then*

1. *if $\sigma \xrightarrow{\ell} \sigma'$ then $\exists \mathsf{G}', \mathsf{P}'$ such that $\langle \mathsf{G}, \mathsf{P} \rangle \xrightarrow{\ell} \langle \mathsf{G}', \mathsf{P}' \rangle$ and $(\sigma', \langle \mathsf{G}', \mathsf{P}' \rangle) \in \mathcal{R}_S$;*
2. *if $\sigma \xrightarrow{\sigma'} \sigma''$ then $\exists \mathsf{G}', \mathsf{G}'', \mathsf{P}', \mathsf{P}''$ such that $\langle \mathsf{G}, \mathsf{P} \rangle \xrightarrow{\langle \mathsf{G}', \mathsf{P}' \rangle} \langle \mathsf{G}'', \mathsf{P}'' \rangle$, $(\sigma', \langle \mathsf{G}', \mathsf{P}' \rangle) \in \mathcal{R}_S$, and $(\sigma'', \langle \mathsf{G}'', \mathsf{P}'' \rangle) \in \mathcal{R}_S$.*

We write $\sim_S$ for the largest implementation relation.

Given the way we distilled labels, the definition above does coincide with the notion of implementation correctness as given in [7, Definition 21]. A distinction between one- and multi-replica simulation can be recovered just by suitably restricting the context LTS, that is, item 1 above, by requiring ℓ to be arising from either a root extension or an extension, respectively.

6   Conclusions and Further Works

In our paper we considered RDTs, and we laid out the basis for an algebraic characterisation of their operational semantics as well as of their implementation correctness in terms of (higher-order) simulation. The core of our contribution lies precisely in the formalism behind such characterisations. Our proposal builds on [9] and improves [7] and similar set-theoretical characterisations, which are now made precise and recast into standard notions from the literature, thus allowing for the use of a large body of methods and techniques in the analysis of RDTs. We offered a few examples for showing the adequateness of our proposal, even if its strength needs to be further checked by a larger number of case studies.

In order to stress the methodological points, we adopted some simplifications. The most notable is the removal of the snd label from our transition systems. Indeed, in our examples, and, in in fact, in most case studies we are aware of, a replica always spawns a full copy of itself, thus from the point of view of simulation it is irrelevant, and it would be in any case captured by the identity arrow on the category of replicas. The modelling of replica communication [7], where the action of sending will play a larger role, is the subject of ongoing work.

Our construction of transition systems out of a category of elements follows an already established pattern for pre-sheaves and simulation, most notably in [17]. The distilling of labels is clearly reminiscent of the *contexts as labels* paradigm advanced by Leifer and Milner [12], and it would fit in its less constrained version proposed in [1]. Since this was not the main methodological issue of the paper, we adopted a presentation requiring some ingenuity.

References

1. Bonchi, F., Gadducci, F., Monreale, G.V.: A general theory of barbs, contexts, and labels. ACM Trans. Comput. Logic **15**(4), 35:1–35:27 (2014)
2. Bouajjani, A., Enea, C., Hamza, J.: Verifying eventual consistency of optimistic replication systems. In: Jagannathan, S., Sewell, P. (eds.) POPL 2014, pp. 285–296. ACM (2014)
3. Burckhardt, S., Gotsman, A., Yang, H.: Understanding eventual consistency. Technical Report, MSR-TR-2013-39, Microsoft Research (2013)
4. Burckhardt, S., Gotsman, A., Yang, H., Zawirski, M.: Replicated data types: specification, verification, optimality. In: Jagannathan, S., Sewell, P. (eds.) POPL 2014, pp. 271–284. ACM (2014)
5. Cerone, A., Bernardi, G., Gotsman, A.: A framework for transactional consistency models with atomic visibility. In: Aceto, L., de Frutos-Escrig, D. (eds.) CONCUR 2015. LIPIcs, vol. 42, pp. 58–71. Schloss Dagstuhl - Leibniz-Zentrum für Informatik (2015)
6. DeCandia, G., et al.: Dynamo: Amazon's highly available key-value store. In: Bressoud, T.C., Kaashoek, M.F. (eds.) SOSP 2007, pp. 205–220. ACM (2007)
7. Gadducci, F., Melgratti, H., Roldán, C.: On the semantics and implementation of replicated data types. Sci. Comput. Program. **167**, 91–113 (2018)
8. Gadducci, F., Melgratti, H., Roldán, C.: A denotational view of replicated data types. In: Jacquet, J.-M., Massink, M. (eds.) COORDINATION 2017. LNCS, vol. 10319, pp. 138–156. Springer, Cham (2017). https://doi.org/10.1007/978-3-319-59746-1_8
9. Gadducci, F., Melgratti, H.C., Roldán, C., Sammartino, M.: A categorical account of replicated data types. In: Chattopadhyay, A., Gastin, P. (eds.) FSTTCS 2019. LIPIcs, vol. 150, pp. 42:1–42:15. Schloss Dagstuhl - Leibniz-Zentrum für Informatik (2019)
10. Gotsman, A., Burckhardt, S.: Consistency models with global operation sequencing and their composition. In: Richa, A.W. (ed.) DISC 2017. LIPIcs, vol. 91, pp. 23:1–23:16. Schloss Dagstuhl - Leibniz-Zentrum für Informatik (2017)
11. Kaki, G., Earanky, K., Sivaramakrishnan, K.C., Jagannathan, S.: Safe replication through bounded concurrency verification. In: OOPSLA 2018. PACMPL, vol. 2, pp. 164:1–164:27. ACM (2018)
12. Leifer, J.J., Milner, R.: Deriving bisimulation congruences for reactive systems. In: Palamidessi, C. (ed.) CONCUR 2000. LNCS, vol. 1877, pp. 243–258. Springer, Heidelberg (2000). https://doi.org/10.1007/3-540-44618-4_19
13. Mac Lane, S., Moerdijk, I.: Sheaves in Geometry and Logic. U. Springer, New York (1992). https://doi.org/10.1007/978-1-4612-0927-0

14. Shapiro, M., Preguiça, N., Baquero, C., Zawirski, M.: Conflict-free replicated data types. In: Défago, X., Petit, F., Villain, V. (eds.) SSS 2011. LNCS, vol. 6976, pp. 386–400. Springer, Heidelberg (2011). https://doi.org/10.1007/978-3-642-24550-3_29
15. Shapiro, M., Preguiça, N., Baquero, C., Zawirski, M.: A comprehensive study of convergent and commutative replicated data types. Technical Report RR-7506, Inria-Centre Paris-Rocquencourt (2011)
16. Sivaramakrishnan, K.C., Kaki, G., Jagannathan, S.: Declarative programming over eventually consistent data stores. In: Grove, D., Blackburn, S. (eds.) PLDI 2015, pp. 413–424. ACM (2015)
17. Sobociński, P.: Relational presheaves, change of base and weak simulation. J. Comput. Syst. Sci. **81**(5), 901–910 (2015)

Tool Paper

Qsimulation V2.0: An Optimized Quantum Simulator

Hua Wu[1], Yuxin Deng[1(✉)], Ming Xu[1], and Wenjie Du[2]

[1] Shanghai Key Laboratory of Trustworthy Computing, MOE International Joint
Lab of Trustworthy Software, International Research Center of Trustworthy Software,
East China Normal University, Shanghai, China
coconuteva@qq.com,yxdeng@sei.ecnu.edu.cn,mxu@cs.ecnu.edu.cn
[2] Shanghai Normal University, Shanghai, China
wenjiedu@shnu.edu.cn

Abstract. Qsimulation is a tool for simulating quantum computation
on classical computers, which allows a user to write quantum programs
in a simple quantum programming language, draw quantum circuits, and
view the results of executing them. Similar to many other quantum simulation tools, the performance of Qsimulation largely depends on its capacity of dealing with matrix operations. In this paper we present Qsimulation V2.0, an optimized quantum simulator that implements a new
algorithm for accelerating matrix-vector multiplications. The algorithm
is based on matrix decomposition using tensor products and suitable for
simulating the execution of quantum circuits. Experimental results show
that Qsimulation V2.0 outperforms the open source frameworks Qiskit
and ProjectQ.

Keywords: Quantum computation · Quantum simulator ·
Optimization

1 Introduction

Quantum computation has been a topic of great interest for the last two decades
[10]. Benefiting from the superposition of quantum states, quantum computers
can accelerate computation remarkably compared with classical computers [7,9,
12]. While a lot of experimental physicists and computer scientists are currently
trying to build scalable quantum computers, e.g. [1], it appears that simulation of
quantum computation will be at least as critical as circuit simulation in classical
VLSI design [16].

As early as in 1980s Richard Feynman observed that simulating quantum
processes on classical hardware seems to require super-polynomial (in the number
of qubits) memory and time [16]. With the rapid development of hardware, the

Supported by the National Natural Science Foundation of China (61672229, 61832015,
62072176, 1187122), the Inria-CAS joint project Quasar, and the Fundamental
Research Funds for the Central Universities.

V. K. I. Pun et al. (Eds.): ICTAC 2020, LNCS 12545, pp. 307–316, 2020.
https://doi.org/10.1007/978-3-030-64276-1_16

simulation of more and more qubits becomes gradually possible. Using quantum circuits to simulate quantum computation has become the mainstream. Up to now, a large number of quantum languages are springing up to simulate quantum computing, such as Quipper [6], Q# [15], Qiskit [3], and ProjectQ [14].

State-of-the-art algorithms for simulating quantum computation on classical computers can be mainly divided into two categories: (i) the state-vector approach stores a quantum state as a vector and lets it evolve during quantum computation; (ii) the tensor-based approach represents quantum states as tensors and specifies the input and output states as rank-1 Kronecker projectors [8]. The first approach is limited by the number of qubits due to the exponential growth of the Hilbert space, and the second one is less sensitive to the number of qubits and has been pursued more actively. However, if a quantum state is entangled, it is impossible to decompose the state into the form of a product of states of individual subsystems. Therefore, an entangled state still needs to be represented by a vector. When the number of qubits in an entangled state is very large, the consumption of space and time grows exponentially. For example, in the cases of major interest – Shor's and Grover's algorithms – quantum simulation is still performed with straightforward linear-algebraic tools and requires astronomic resources [16].

Qsimulation [4] is a quantum simulator designed with the first approach. The bottleneck of its performance lies in manipulating large matrices. We observe that a quantum circuit consists of many steps, and in each step the common pattern is to apply some quantum gates in parallel to a number of qubits. Very often, a relatively small number of qubits are involved in the computation of each step while many other qubits remain idle, though the whole circuit could be large in both width and depth. Since the computation in each step can be viewed as the multiplication of a unitary matrix with a state vector, the above observation inspires us to decompose the unitary matrix as a tensor product of smaller matrices representing the parallel gates applied to some qubits together with identity matrices representing the idleness of other qubits. To some extent, we combine the state-vector and the tensor-based approaches. We implement this idea in an optimized algorithm for matrix-vector multiplication, exploit multithreaded programming, and incorporate the new algorithm in Qsimulation V2.0. We have conducted experiments on various quantum algorithms, such as Grover's algorithm [7,10], Simon's algorithm [13], Bernstein-Vazirani algorithm [2]. It turns out that Qsimulation V2.0 has almost doubled the number of qubits that can be handled by Qsimulation V1.0. It outperforms Qiskit in most cases by taking almost one-third the time, and it is nearly 30 times faster than ProjectQ when the number of qubits is large.

The rest of the paper is organized as follows. In Sect. 2, we give the necessary notations about quantum bits and gates. A brief introduction to Qsimulation is given in Sect. 3. In Sect. 4 we explain the main idea for our new algorithm of computing matrix-vector multiplication. The algorithm itself is presented in Sect. 5. In Sect. 6 we use several typical quantum algorithms to show the performance of Qsimulation before and after the optimization, and we compare Qsimulation

V2.0 with Qiskit and ProjectQ. In Sect. 7, we discuss further optimization with multithreaded programming. Finally, we conclude in Sect. 8.

All the Java code and supplementary materials are available at the link https://github.com/coconutoe/quantum.

2 Notations About Quantum Bits and Gates

Bit is a fundamental concept of classical computation and classical information. Quantum computation and quantum information are built upon an analogous concept, the quantum bit, or qubit for short [10]. For a qubit, there are two possible states, which correspond to the states 0 and 1 for a classical bit. The qubit states are expressed as $|0\rangle$ and $|1\rangle$, in which notation like '$| \rangle$' is called the Dirac notation and it is the standard notation for states in quantum mechanics. The difference between bits and qubits is that a qubit can be in a state other than $|0\rangle$ or $|1\rangle$. The state of a qubit can be linear combinations of other states, often called superpositions: $|\psi\rangle = \alpha |0\rangle + \beta |1\rangle$, where α and β are complex numbers and the normalization condition $|\alpha|^2 + |\beta|^2 = 1$ must be satisfied. Put another way, the state of a qubit is a unit vector in a two-dimensional complex vector space. The special states $|0\rangle$ and $|1\rangle$ form an orthonormal basis for this vector space. Multiple qubits can be similarly denoted. For example, we write $\frac{|00\rangle + |11\rangle}{\sqrt{2}}$ for the state of a two-qubit system such that both qubits are in the same states $|0\rangle$ and $|1\rangle$ with equal chance. More detailed account can be found in [10].

Quantum gates are also analogous to gates in classical circuits, in which logic gates are used to process classical bits. The function of a quantum gate in quantum circuits is to convert the states of qubits. For example, quantum gate NOT can change quantum state $|0\rangle$ to $|1\rangle$. In fact, a quantum gate is essentially a unitary matrix. For example, the *Hadamard* gate is defined as $H \equiv \frac{1}{\sqrt{2}} \begin{pmatrix} 1 & 1 \\ 1 & -1 \end{pmatrix}$, and the *NOT* gate mentioned earlier is $X \equiv \begin{pmatrix} 0 & 1 \\ 1 & 0 \end{pmatrix}$.

3 A Brief Introduction to Qsimulation

Qsimulation [4] is a lightweight quantum simulator intended to be used by instructors and novices to design and test simple quantum programs and circuits. It contains three main ingredients:

- an imperative language for writing simple quantum programs;
- an interpreter that can translate a quantum program into a quantum circuit;
- an interactive user interface that allows a user to simulate the execution of a quantum program or a circuit.

As a domain-specific high-level language, the imperative language of Qsimulation follows Selinger's slogan of "quantum data, classical control" [11]. Besides assignments, sequential composition, and conditionals, it has quantum initialization, unitary operations, and measurements to deal with quantum data. It also has auxiliary assemblies, including quantum types and a series of reentrant encapsulated functions to simplify programming.

The interpreter accepts a quantum program and translates it into a quantum circuit. Furthermore, the interpreter is also designed as an execution engine. It conforms to the rules of quantum mechanics [10], represents a quantum state as a complex vector and a quantum gate as a complex matrix. In the current work, we propose an algorithm about decomposing matrices into blocks so to accelerate matrix-vector multiplication and an engineering method to optimize the linear algebra calculation inside the simulator.

The graphic user interface facilitates a user to design quantum programs and circuits. In Fig. 1, we show the interface with a quantum circuit whose input quantum state is |110⟩. By making use of the buttons in the left part of the panel, we can easily drag and drop built-in gates to the quantum circuit in the middle of the panel. A user can also write a quantum program in the coding editor and then run it. The results are displayed in the lower part of the middle panel. By clicking the icons above the panel, we can perform some general operations such as importing and saving files. The graphic user interface is convenient and intuitive for a user to better understand the circuit model of a quantum algorithm. It is a useful assistant for an instructor to teach simple quantum algorithms. With the help of Qsimulation, students can have a more intuitive understanding of quantum circuits.

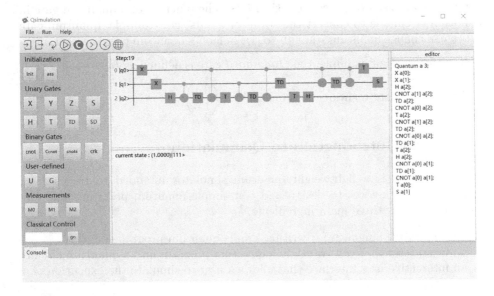

Fig. 1. Interface of Qsimulation V2.0

4 Main Idea of the Optimization Algorithm

The evolution process of a quantum state can be described by a quantum circuit. A unitary gate in the circuit corresponds to a unitary matrix, say U, and a quantum state to a unit vector, say $|\psi\rangle$. After applying the unitary matrix to the state, we obtain a new state given by the vector $U|\psi\rangle$. For example, consider a quantum circuit made up of n qubits. The size of the unitary matrix U is $N \times N$, where $N = 2^n$. The size of the unit vector $|\psi\rangle$ is N, so is the size of the resulting vector $U|\psi\rangle$. It is easy to see that the time complexity of the matrix-vector multiplication is $\mathcal{O}(N^2)$, when addition and multiplication are considered as basic operations of cost $\mathcal{O}(1)$. In practice, however, a quantum algorithm consists of a series of quantum gates, most of which are *Pauli* gates or $CNOT$ gates in typical quantum algorithms such as Deutsch-Jozsa algorithm [5,10], Grover's algorithm [7,10], Simon's algorithm [13], and Bernstein-Vazirani algorithm [2]. Fortunately, the dimension of the matrix corresponding to each gate is usually no more than four. That is, most quantum operations may just be applied to a few qubits, resulting in a large number of zero entries in the unitary matrix U. We will decompose matrix U into some blocks, and then perform matrix multiplication for blocks. We aim to reduce the time complexity to nearly $\mathcal{O}(N)$ in the optimized approach of matrix multiplication. The discussion will be carried out in three cases: (1) $U = I \otimes U_e$, (2) $U = U_e \otimes I$, (3) $U = I \otimes U_e \otimes I$, where each I represents an identity matrix and $\otimes$ stands for the tensor product operation of matrices, according to different positions of the quantum operation represented by the matrix U_e. The first two cases are special forms of the last case. We separate them out for the convenience of presentation.

Let us start with a general discussion of the mathematical tools needed in the above three cases, regardless of concrete quantum circuits. In the following discussion, we assume that the matrix U_e has dimension M and is expressed as $U_e = (u_{i,j})_{M \times M}$ with $0 \leq i, j \leq M - 1$. Analogously, the dimension of U is assumed to be N, and the vector $|\psi\rangle$ is $(c_0, c_1, \ldots, c_{N-1})^\mathrm{T}$.

4.1 Case $U = I \otimes U_e$

The dimension of I is $L = N/M$ in this case. Then, we have

$$U|\psi\rangle = \begin{pmatrix} U_e & & & \\ & U_e & & \\ & & \ddots & \\ & & & U_e \end{pmatrix} \begin{pmatrix} c_0 \\ c_1 \\ \vdots \\ c_{N-1} \end{pmatrix} = \begin{pmatrix} U_e|\psi_0\rangle \\ U_e|\psi_1\rangle \\ \vdots \\ U_e|\psi_{L-1}\rangle \end{pmatrix} \tag{1}$$

where $|\psi_i\rangle = \left(c_{M \cdot i}, c_{M \cdot i+1}, \ldots, c_{M \cdot (i+1)-1}\right)^\mathrm{T}$ is a segment of $|\psi\rangle$, for $i = 0, \ldots, L - 1$. We can see that the multiplication of the $N \times N$ matrix by the N-dimensional vector is decomposed into L multiplications of $M \times M$ matrices by M-dimensional vectors. The overall time complexity becomes $\mathcal{O}(M^2 \cdot L) = \mathcal{O}(M \cdot N)$. In many applications, the dimension of U_e is far smaller than that of U so that M can be regarded as a fairly small constant. Thus the final time complexity is nearly $\mathcal{O}(N)$.

4.2   Case $U = U_e \otimes I$

The dimension of I is also $L = N/M$ in this case. Then, we have

$$U \left| \psi \right> = \begin{pmatrix} u_{0,0}I & u_{0,1}I & \cdots & u_{0,M-1}I \\ u_{1,0}I & u_{1,1}I & \cdots & u_{1,M-1}I \\ \vdots & \vdots & \ddots & \vdots \\ u_{M-1,0}I & u_{M-1,1}I & \cdots & u_{M-1,M-1}I \end{pmatrix} \begin{pmatrix} c_0 \\ c_1 \\ \vdots \\ c_{N-1} \end{pmatrix}. \tag{2}$$

For any $0 \le i, j \le M - 1$, the $(i \cdot L + j)$-th element of the resulting $U \left| \psi \right>$ is $\sum_{k=0}^{M-1} u_{i,k} \cdot c_{j+k \cdot L}$. As in the first case, we regard M as a fairly small constant. Thus the time complexity of the matrix multiplication becomes $\mathcal{O}(N)$, which is far less than the original $\mathcal{O}(N^2)$.

4.3   Case $U = I \otimes U_e \otimes I$

Let L_l be the dimension of I on the left of U_e, and L_r the dimension of I on the right. Again, the dimension of U_e is M. That is, the dimension of U is $N = L_l \cdot M \cdot L_r$. Then, we have

$$U \left| \psi \right> = \begin{pmatrix} U_e \otimes I & & & \\ & U_e \otimes I & & \\ & & \ddots & \\ & & & U_e \otimes I \end{pmatrix} \begin{pmatrix} c_0 \\ c_1 \\ \vdots \\ c_{N-1} \end{pmatrix} = \begin{pmatrix} (U_e \otimes I) \left| \psi_0 \right> \\ (U_e \otimes I) \left| \psi_1 \right> \\ \vdots \\ (U_e \otimes I) \left| \psi_{L_l-1} \right> \end{pmatrix} \tag{3}$$

where $\left| \psi_i \right> = \left(c_{M \cdot L_r \cdot i}, c_{M \cdot L_r \cdot i+1}, \ldots, c_{M \cdot L_r \cdot (i+1)-1} \right)^{\mathrm{T}}$ is a segment of $\left| \psi \right>$, for $i = 0, \ldots, L_l - 1$. Here $(U_l \otimes I) \left| \psi_i \right>$ can be obtained through the method in the second case. As in the previous cases, M is usually a small constant. So the time complexity is $\mathcal{O}(N)$ in total, far less than the original $\mathcal{O}(N^2)$.

5   The Optimization Algorithm

We introduce the sub-procedure **UTensorI** given in Algorithm 1 that will be called in the main procedure **ITensorUTensorI** given in Algorithm 2.

The essence of **UTensorI** is actually the decomposition of matrices according to the formula (2) in Sect. 4.2. Regard the whole matrix I as a block. Then $U = U_e \otimes I$ becomes a matrix of M^2 unit matrices with different coefficients. In order to calculate $U \left| \psi \right>$, we divide $\left| \psi \right>$ into M blocks, each of which has the same dimension as matrix I and is multiplied by a coefficient. In this way, the calculation of a large complex matrix multiplied by a vector becomes the calculation of many smaller unit matrices multiplied by vectors.

The pseudo code in Algorithm 1 describes the details of the procedure. The outermost for loop traverses the block matrix of $U = U_e \otimes I$ by block lines. The middle for loop traverses each row of the decomposed matrix and records the final result. The innermost for loop accumulates the values of the entries in

---

Algorithm 1: Procedure **UTensorI**

Input: (1) $IDimension$: the dimension of matrix I;
(2) $uGate$: the matrix U_e;
(3) $qsIn$: a vector representing the quantum state before the evolution.
Output: $qsOut$: a vector representing the quantum state after the evolution.

1 **for** $i = 0 \rightarrow (uGate.dimension - 1)$ **do**
2   **for** $j = 0 \rightarrow (IDimension - 1)$ **do**
3        $temp \leftarrow Complex.ZERO$;
4   **for** $k = 0 \rightarrow (uGate.dimension - 1)$ **do**
5           $temp \leftarrow temp + uGate[i][k] * qsIn[j + k * IDimension]$;
6   **end**
7        $qsOut[i * IDimension + j] \leftarrow temp$;
8   **end**
9 **end**

Algorithm 2: Procedure **ITensorUTensorI**

Input: (1) $IlDimension$: the dimension of the left matrix I;
(2) $IrDimension$: the dimension of the right matrix I;
(3) $uGate$: the matrix U_e;
(4) $qsIn$: a vector representing the quantum state before the evolution.
Output: $qsOut$: a vector representing the quantum state after the evolution.

1 $i \leftarrow 0$;
2 $m \leftarrow IrDimension * uGate.dimension$;
3 **while** $i < IlDimension$ **do**
4     $vectorTemp[0 : m] \leftarrow qsIn[i * m : (i + 1) * m]$;
5     $qsOut[i * m : (i + 1) * m] \leftarrow$ **UTensorI**$(IrDimension, uGate, vectorTemp)$;
6     $i \leftarrow (i + 1)$;
7 **end**
8 **Notation:** $v_2[i_2 : i_2 + j_1 - i_1] \leftarrow v_1[i_1 : j_1]$ denotes the assignment of the i_2-th to the $(i_2 + j_1 - i_1)$-th elements of v_2 by the i_1-th to the j_1-th elements of v_1.

---

the result vector. We regard $uGate.dimension$ as a small constant, so the time complexity of Algorithm 1 is $\mathcal{O}(IDimension)$.

The main procedure **ITensorUTensorI** is described by the pseudo code in Algorithm 2. Since $U_e \otimes I$ has already been solved by Algorithm 1, we can treat $U_e \otimes I$ as a larger unitary matrix with a calculation cost of $\mathcal{O}(IrDimension)$ without caring about its internal details. The following discussion will only focus on $I \otimes U_e$. Note that $I \otimes U_e$ can be partitioned into diagonally identical matrices U_e, and other elements are all zero as discussed in Sect. 4.1. Then the calculation is simplified to the form of $IlDimension$ U_e's right multiplied by vectors. The procedure **ITensorUTensorI** has only one layer of while loop, which is used to control the number of times that U_e is multiplied by a vector on the right, and puts the corresponding results into the final position of the result vector. The total time complexity of Algorithm 2 is $\mathcal{O}(IlDimension \cdot IrDimension)$.

6   Experimental Results

We have carried out experiments in Qsimulation on various quantum algorithms such as Deutsch-Jozsa algorithm, Bernstein-Vazirani algorithm, Grover's algorithm, and compared the running time of those algorithms before and after the optimization. As we can see from Table 1, the efficiency in Qsimulation V2.0 has been greatly improved. For example, the running time of Deutsch-Jozsa algorithm (11 qubits) is about 59 times less after the optimization. Since Qsimulation V1.0 can simulate quantum circuits up to 11 qubits in a laptop, our experimental settings are all within 11 qubits. In fact, Qsimulation V2.0 allows us to simulate quantum circuits up to 22 qubits in the same laptop. In addition, we run the same algorithms with two other software tools: Qiskit and ProjectQ, where Qiskit is an open source quantum programming library developed by IBM and ProjectQ was developed by ETH Zurich and has been open-sourced since 2006. When the running time exceeds 30000 ms, we force the termination of the programs. It can be seen that Qsimulation V2.0 outperforms Qiskit by taking almost one-third the time, and it performs bettern than ProjectQ in most cases. As a matter of fact, ProjectQ merely performs well when the number of qubits is small. Its performance decreases drastically when the number of qubits increases.

Table 1. The running time of various algorithms

Algorithms	Qubits	Time(ms)			
		Qsimulation V1.0	Qsimulation V2.0	Qiskit	ProjectQ
Deutsch-Jozsa [5, 10]	11	8277	138	8811	≥30000
Simon [13]	10	635	7.5	15.1	9
Bernstein-Vazirani [2]	10	1148	9	15.5	9.3
Superdense Coding [10]	2	1.25	1.125	5.5	1
Teleportation [10]	3	3.5	1.625	5.875	1.125
Grover [7, 10]	9	5978	172	669	≥30000

We then compare Qsimulation V2.0 with Qiskit and ProjectQ on quantum circuits with more qubits. We first prepare an entangled state with 18 qubits: $\frac{1}{\sqrt{2}}(|00\ldots0\rangle + |11\ldots1\rangle)$. More specifically, we apply the *Hadamard* gate H on the first qubit, and then use that qubit to control the *NOT* gate X acted on each of the other 17 qubits. Then in different cases we apply different gates on the 18 qubits. For example, in the case $18H$, the gate H is applied on each qubit; in the case $9H\_9Y$, we apply the H gate on 9 qubits and the *Pauli-Y* gate on 9 other qubits. We record the running time on Qsimulation V2.0, Qiskit and ProjectQ, respectively.

It can be seen from Table 2 that the running time of Qsimulation V2.0 is close to one-third of that of Qiskit in most cases, and the efficiency of ProjectQ is the worst, with the running time being about 10 times of Qiskit.

Table 2. Quantum gates acted on entangled states (ms)

Gates	18H	18X	18Y	18Z	9H_9X	9H_9Y	9H_9Z	6X_6Y_6Z
Qsimulation V2.0	830	782	824	790	786	831	812	823
Qiskit [3]	2229	2221	2198	2217	2298	2193	2201	2254
ProjectQ [14]	21198	20565	19725	27286	21016	22145	21803	18220

7 Further Optimization by Multithreading

The mathematical description of a quantum evolution is essentially a matrix-vector multiplication. In the first stage of optimization, we divided the matrix into blocks for calculation. On this basis, we will introduce multi-threaded parallel computation. The reason why parallel computation is feasible is that calculating each element of the resulting matrix is independent. For example, for any matrices A and B, with the sizes $r \times s$ and $s \times t$, respectively, we can calculate the product of A and B like $C = AB = (c_{ij})$, where $c_{ij} = \sum_{k=1}^{s} a_{ik} \cdot b_{kj}$ ($1 \leq i \leq r$, $1 \leq j \leq t$). It can be seen that calculating each c_{ij} is mutually independent. That is, no matter which element is calculated first, the calculation of other elements will not be affected. So we can use multithreading to calculate each element in parallel. Theoretically, the time complexity will decrease from $\mathcal{O}(r \cdot s \cdot t)$ to $\mathcal{O}(s)$. If $r = s$ and $t = 1$, the matrices operation will be reduced to a matrix-vector multiplication, and the time complexity will drop from $\mathcal{O}(s^2)$ to $\mathcal{O}(s)$ by the multithreading optimization.

Since our tool is developed in Java, our multithreaded parallel computation is implemented by the fork/join framework. In the actual experiments, parallel computation with three threads and quantum circuits with 21 qubits are used. When the number of qubits is less than 20, almost no optimization can be observed in that it takes time to start multithreading and the greater the amount of computation, the greater the advantage of multithreading. We just use a simple quantum circuit to verify the idea. We first initialize 21 qubits, and then apply quantum operations on the 21 qubits respectively. We record the running time of single-thread version and 3-thread version in Table 3. It can be seen that the running time of multithreaded programming indeed decreases.

Table 3. The running time of single-thread and multi-threads (ms)

Gates	21H	21X	21Y	21Z	7X_7Y_7Z
Single-th	22778	22499	21997	22179	22573
3-ths	13439	13329	13886	13919	13323

8   Conclusion

We have presented Qsimulation V2.0 that uses a new algorithm to compute matrix-vector multiplication. We have conducted experiments and found that it has almost doubled the number of qubits that can be handled by Qsimulation, and it outperforms Qiskit in most cases by taking almost one-third the time, let alone ProjectQ, which turns out to be 10 times slower than Qiskit when the number of qubits is large. From the engineering point of view, we have used multithreading to further optimize our algorithm and shown its effectiveness by experiments. Note that the space complexity is also reduced, which is reflected from the fact that more qubits can be simulated.

References

1. Arute, F., et al.: Quantum supremacy using a programmable superconducting processor. Nature **574**, 505–510 (2019)
2. Bernstein, E., Vazirani, U.: Quantum complexity theory. SIAM J. Comput. **26**(5), 1411–1473 (1997)
3. Cross, A.: The IBM Q experience and QISKit open-source quantum computing software. APS March Meet. **63**(1), 2018 (2018)
4. Deng, X., Deng, Y.: Qsimulation: a tool for simulating quantum computation (in Chinese). Comput. Eng. Sci. **041**, 843–850 (2019)
5. Deutsch, D., Jozsa, R.: Rapid solution of problems by quantum computation. Proc. Royal Soc. London Series A **439**(1907), 553–558 (1992)
6. Green, A.S., Lumsdaine, P.L., Ross, N.J., Selinger, P., Valiron, B.: Quipper: a scalable quantum programming language. ACM SIGPLAN Notices **48**(6), 333–342 (2013)
7. Grover, L.K.: A fast quantum mechanical algorithm for database search. In: Proceedings of the 28th Annual ACM Symposium on the Theory of Computing, pp. 212–219 (1996)
8. Guo, C., et al.: General-purpose quantum circuit simulator with projected entangled-pair states and the quantum supremacy frontier. Phys. Rev. Lett. **123**(19), 321 (2019)
9. Harrow, A.W., Hassidim, A., Lloyd, S.: Quantum algorithm for solving linear systems of equations. Physics **103**(10), (2008)
10. Nielsen, M., Chuang, I.: Quantum Computation and Quantum Information. Cambridge University Press, Cambridge (2011)
11. Selinger, P.: Towards a quantum programming language. Math. Structures Comput. Sci. **14**(4), 527–586 (2004)
12. Shor, P.W.: Algorithms for quantum computation: Discrete logarithms and factoring. In: IEEE Computer Society, pp. 124–134 (1994)
13. Simon, D.R.: On the power of quantum computation. SIAM J. Comput. **26**(5), 1474–1483 (1997)
14. Steiger, D., Häner, T., Troyer, M.: ProjectQ: An open source software framework for quantum computing. Quantum, **2** (2016)
15. Tolba, A.S., Rashad, M.Z., El-Dosuky, M.A.: Q#, a quantum computation package for the.net platform. ArXiv abs/1302.5133 (2007)
16. Viamontes, G.F., Rajagopalan, M., Markov, I., Hayes, J.: Gate-level simulation of quantum circuits. In: Proceedings of the ASP-DAC Asia and South Pacific Design Automation Conference, pp. 295–301 (2003)

Author Index

Barenbaum, Pablo 242
Bartocci, Ezio 221

Crespi Reghizzi, Stefano 161

Damiani, Ferruccio 103
Deng, Yuxin 307
Du, Wenjie 307

Erofeev, Evgeny 123, 143

Gadducci, Fabio 283
Gengelbach, Arve 23
Genitrini, Antoine 83
Goncharov, Sergey 262

Havelund, Klaus 3
Hennicker, Rolf 200
Huisman, Marieke 181

Kleijn, Jetty 200
Kovács, Laura 221
Kurklu, Elif 3

Lienhardt, Michael 103
Lochbaum, Federico 242

Mandrioli, Dino 161
Melgratti, Hernán 283

Midya, Abhisek 43
Milicich, Mariana 242

Neves, Renato 262

Ogata, Kazuhiro 64

Paolini, Luca 103
Pépin, Martin 83
Peschanski, Frédéric 83
Pradella, Matteo 161
Proença, José 262

Riesco, Adrián 64
Roldán, Christian 283

Safari, Mohsen 181
Sammartino, Matteo 283
Stankovič, Miroslav 221

ter Beek, Maurice H. 200
Tredup, Ronny 123, 143

Vaandrager, Frits 43

Weber, Tjark 23
Wu, Hua 307

Xu, Ming 307

Printed in the United States
By Bookmasters